The Origins

and Development

of the

English Language

SECOND EDITION

THOMAS PYLES

NORTHWESTERN UNIVERSITY

The Origins

and Development

of the

English Language

SECOND EDITION

HARCOURT BRACE JOVANOVICH, INC.

New York   Chicago

San Francisco   Atlanta

Library of Congress Catalog Card Number: 78-151063

ISBN: 0-15-567603-2

PRINTED IN THE UNITED STATES OF AMERICA

Preface

This Second Edition of *Origins*—to use the more familiar short title instead of the more accurately descriptive longer one—has been to some extent rewritten, considerably augmented, and brought up to date. There is some reorganization of the earlier material as well: the chapter on the phonology of current English, in addition to being extensively revised, has been placed before that on the history of writing, where I now believe it should have been in the first place; and the chapter dealing with loan-words is now in what seems a more appropriate position, immediately following that on coinages and adaptations. The discussion of recent theoretical linguistic studies in the opening chapter has been somewhat expanded, and several maps and other graphic materials from the accompanying workbook *Problems in the Origins and Development of the English Language* and elsewhere have been incorporated into the text. Finally, errors of omission and commission have been corrected wherever perceived by me or pointed out by learned friends.

The method of treatment remains descriptive—unabashedly so, for it seems likely that this will continue to be the most effective method of setting forth historical data for a good many years to come. To deal thus traditionally with such materials is not by implication to belittle or even to question the significance of the theoretical studies that have multiplied at such a mind-boggling rate since about 1960. Some of these, which a few commentators thought should have provided the groundwork for the first edition of this book (1964), are even now outmoded and others are under fire. There can be no doubt, however, that they have made a lasting impression upon our thinking about language.

But this is not a book about current linguistic theories, and it employs no polemics. Its primary concern, as is implicit in its title, is the internal history of our language, presented in a chronological treatment of its phonological and grammatical development from prehistoric times to the present. Purely external history, so admirably treated in other books, is thus purposely kept to a minimum — a few paragraphs here and there in the chapters dealing with Old English and Middle English. Though hundreds of words are cited throughout, vocabulary accretions as such, along with the cultural and political forces leading to their adoption, have been dealt with in a single penultimate chapter.

The treatment of writing is somewhat fuller than is usual in works of comparable scope. Its relationship to speech is explored in some detail, with the hope of dissipating a good many popular misconceptions which plague the professional student of language.

A good deal of attention has been given to British and American differences, certainly more than is customary in books of American provenience. Interesting and sometimes significant as such differences are, they are nevertheless viewed in what I hope is a proper perspective and without the least trace of nationalistic bias. For it is the *English* language, wherever spoken by those whose mother tongue it is, which is our chief concern. Neither British nor American linguistic provincialism has much place in a world as cozy as science and technology have made ours, whether we like it or not.

Early Modern English — the language of Shakespeare and the King James version of the Bible, so like our own that we are sometimes unaware of subtle and important differences — has been treated in more detail than is usual in books attempting to cover developments in our language in the millennium and a half stretching from the first English settlement of Britain in the mid-fifth century to our own day. Perhaps because of its very familiarity, the speech of this early yet modern period has been considered somehow less important, or at least more expendable, than that of earlier periods. The similarities between it and current speech can be quite deceptive, as anyone who has had to listen to the exegetical flights and fancies of badly informed commentators knows perfectly well.

I remain indebted to Kenneth G. Wilson, of the University of Connecticut, who read the manuscript of the first edition and made some very wise and helpful suggestions. More immediately, as far as this Second Edition is concerned, I am indebted to John Algeo, of the University of Florida, who read the entire manuscript with keen critical eye, and to I. Willis Russell, of the University of Alabama, who ever since the first edition was published has given me the benefit of his learning and his long experience as a teacher. With both these men I have been in fairly constant communication. Virginia Glenn McDavid and William Card, both of Chicago State College, and Michael J. Capek, of Princeton University, have furnished me with detailed critiques of the first edition. I have taken full advantage of the scholarly and pedagogical acumen of all these. Over the years since its publication, I have received altogether amiable letters and notes discussing various details of the first edition from Paul G. Chapin, Robert G. Flick, Robert C. Olson, James Ivan Miller, Jr., and Robert C. Rudolph; some of these may by now have forgotten that they ever wrote, but I have remembered and have profited by their kindness and interest. Finally, I am indebted to the authors of reviews of the first edition, who noted a few genuine slips and some merely apparent ones attributable to the difficulty of writing a simple and completely unambiguous statement of fact about so complex a thing as language. Whatever shortcomings remain are my own unhappy responsibility.

T. P.

Table of Contents

Preface v

I Facts, Assumptions, 1
and Misconceptions About Language

II The Sounds and Spelling 29
of Current English

III Letters and Sounds: 50
A Brief History of Writing

IV The Backgrounds of English 78

V The Old English Period 113
(449–1100)

VI The Middle English Period 152
(1100–1500)

VII The Modern English Period 181
to 1800: Sounds and Spellings

VIII *The Modern English Period*   195
      to 1800: Forms and Syntax

  IX *Recent British*   229
      and American English

   X *New Words from Old:*   275
      Coinages and Adaptations

  XI *Foreign Elements in*   313
      the English Word Stock

 XII *Words and Meanings*   342

      Selected Bibliography   364

      Index of Modern English   377
      Words, Affixes, and Phrases

      Subject Index   399

The Origins

and Development

of the

English Language

SECOND EDITION

I

Facts, Assumptions, and Misconceptions About Language

Language, man's greatest intellectual tool, is immensely old, precisely as old as our remotest human ancestors; for it is language that makes our species human, strikingly differentiating us from all other species. We may be fairly sure that our ancestors were making use of the complicated and highly systematized set of vocal sounds that go to make up language when the woolly-haired rhinoceros and the mammoth roamed the earth. According to archaeological evidence, man was using tools approximately a million years ago, a fact that presupposes his ability to hand down knowledge concerning their construction and use to his descendants. How long it took that group of hominids of which man—*Homo sapiens*—is the sole survivor to develop this ability we have no way of knowing.[1]

THEORIES OF THE ORIGIN OF LANGUAGE

We shall not here speculate overmuch on the ultimate origins of language, since we have no real information on the subject. The earliest languages of which we have any records are already in a high stage of

[1] For the bearing of language on man's place in nature, see Charles F. Hockett, *A Course in Modern Linguistics* (New York, 1958), pp. 569–86, and Hockett and Robert Ascher, "The Human Revolution," *Current Anthropology*, 5 (1964), 135–68. The latter is conveniently available in the Bobbs-Merrill Reprint Series in the Social Sciences (No. A-306). See also Louis Carini, "On the Origins of Language," *Current Anthropology*, 11 (1970), 165–66.

development. The same is true of languages spoken by primitive peoples. The problem of how language began has naturally tantalized philosophical minds, and many theories have been advanced, to which waggish scholars have given such fancifully descriptive names as the pooh-pooh theory, the bow-wow theory, the ding-dong theory, and the yo-he-ho theory. The nicknames indicate how seriously the theories need be taken: they are based respectively on the notions that language was in the beginning ejaculatory, echoic (onomatopoeic), characterized by a mystic appropriateness of sound to sense in contrast to being merely imitative, or made up of grunts and groans emitted in the course of group actions and coming in time to be associated with those actions.[2]

We cannot know, then, how language began; we can be sure only of its immense antiquity. However man started to talk, he did so a breathtakingly long time ago, and it was not until much later that he devised a system of making marks in or on wood, stone, and the like to represent what he said when he talked. Compared with language, writing is a newfangled invention, although certainly none the less brilliant for being so. But it is merely symbolization of the sounds man makes in speaking or, as with ideographic writing, to be discussed in Chapter III, the objects he perceives and the ideas he has, and thus not really language at all, though for convenience' sake and by long tradition we speak of written language in contrast to spoken language. The earliest writings (in Sumerian) go back only about five thousand years, but man had been talking, as we have seen, for hundreds of thousands of years before these first documents.

WRITING AND SPEECH

No system of writing that would be comprehensible to more than a few people can hope to accomplish all that we accomplish when we speak. Such phenomena as intonation, stress, and the transition from one sound to another (sometimes confusingly called juncture) are symbolized in writing with varying degrees of satisfactoriness.

[2] For a good, readable discussion of these theories, see Otto Jespersen, *Language: Its Nature, Development and Origin* (New York, 1922), Chapter 21, "The Origin of Speech." Jespersen makes some additional speculations. For other plausible speculations, see G[eorge] L. T[rager] and J[oshua] Wh[atmough], "Language," *Encyclopædia Britannica* (Chicago, 1969), and the materials by Hockett and by Hockett and Ascher cited in the preceding footnote. For a brief exposition of the reconstructions by Hockett and Ascher, see Harry Hoijer, "The Origin of Language," *Linguistics Today*, ed., Archibald A. Hill (New York and London, 1969), pp. 50–58.

We can, in fact, indicate certain types of transitions—the pauses or halts that we make in speech—more clearly by the spaces that we leave between words when we write than we ordinarily are able to do when we speak. *Grade A* may well be heard as *gray day,* but there is no mistaking the one phrase for the other in writing, as is indicated by our writing of them here. Much has been made by structural linguists of the difference between, say, *night rate* and *nitrate* (a pet example), the first with "open" transition signaled by a slight pause between the *t* and the *r,* the second with what is called "close" transition (no pause) between the two sounds. It is certain that, if we pronounce *night rate* and *nitrate* in isolation, the contrast will be evident. In actual running speech, however, the exact kind of transition—whether open or close—may not be clearly discernible to a listener.[3] It is likely that this point of transition is more clearly fixed in the speaker's psyche than in his actual performance. If this were not so, earlier *a nadder* would never have become *an adder,* nor would *an ewt* have become *a newt.*

Similarly, the comma distinguishes "a pretty, hot day" from "a pretty hot day" more clearly than these are often distinguished in actual speech. But the question mark does not distinguish between "Why did you do it?" (I didn't hear you the first time you told me), with rising pitch at the end, and "Why did you do it?" (You didn't tell me), with falling terminal pitch. Nor can we show in writing the very apparent difference between *sound quality* 'tone' and *sound quality* 'good grade' (as in "The sound quality of the recording was excellent" and "The materials were of sound quality")—a difference which we show very easily in speech by strongly stressing *sound* in the first sentence and the first syllable of *quality* in the second. *Incense* 'enrage' and *incense* 'aromatic substance for burning' are likewise sharply differentiated in speech by the position of the stress, as *sewer* 'conduit' and *sewer* 'one who sews' are differentiated by vowel quality. But in writing we can distinguish these words only in context, as we must do with words both written and pronounced identically, like *bear* 'carry' and *bear* 'animal.' On the other hand, some words pronounced alike are distinguished from each other in writing; *bare* is thus distinguished from the words cited in the preceding sentence, as *weak* is distinguished from *week.* Here the written forms rule out the slight possibility of ambiguity inherent in such phrases as "a bear behind" and "a week back" when

---

[3] Fortunately there is here little possibility of ambiguity, for context would determine whether night rates or nitrates were being discussed.

these are spoken. Homonyms[4] make up the very stuff and substance of much nursery humor, as in the examples just cited, but Shakespeare was by no means averse to this sort of thing: puns involving *tale* and *tail, whole* and *hole, hoar* and *whore,* and a good many other homonyms (some, like *stale* and *steal,* are homonyms no longer) are of rather frequent occurrence in the writings of our greatest poet.

Everyone who writes is aware of the fact that to compose a completely foolproof sentence about anything beyond the bread-and-butter matters of everyday life is one of the most difficult tasks in the world; and professional writers know this better than others. Many a man who has tried to carry on a courtship or preserve a marriage by post has been made painfully conscious of the dangers of ambiguity residing in written communication, transcending immeasurably such easily resolved ambiguities as have been heretofore discussed. For one thing, in our very striving for clarity in our writing we frequently condense what we might have spoken and what, having been spoken, might have been further clarified by repetition or by paraphrasing and accompanied by such manifestations as gestures, various modifications of voice, and facial expressions, all of which may play an important part in communication, though they are not language.

Such specialized gestures as the indifferent shrug of the shoulders, the admonitory shaking of the finger, the lifting up of the hand in greeting and the waving of it in parting, the widening of the eyes in astonishment, the scornful lifting of the brows, the approving nod, and the disapproving sideways shaking of the head—all these need not accompany speech at all; they may of themselves be communicative. Accompanying speech, they may be more or less unconscious, like such postures as may be assumed by persons talking together, indicating their sympathy (or lack of it) with each other's ideas. The study of such communicative body movements is known as kinesics.

The different tones of voice that we employ optionally in speaking— the drawl, the sneer, the shout, the whimper, the simper, and the like— also play a part in communication ("I didn't mind what he said, I just didn't like his tone of voice"). But, like the gestures that accompany

[4] Such words as have been discussed here are usually called homonyms. The overlapping terms *homograph* 'a word written like another word of different meaning that may or may not be pronounced like it' and *homophone* 'a word pronounced like another word of different meaning that may or may not be written like it' may also be used, depending upon one's concern with one or the other, writing or pronunciation.

speech, they are not language, but rather paralanguage.[5] Other vocalizations that are communicative, like laughing, crying, groaning, and yelping, usually do not accompany speech at all.

The conventions of writing differ somewhat, but not really very much, from those of ordinary speech. For instance, we ordinarily write *was not, do not, would not,* although we usually say *wasn't, don't, wouldn't.* Furthermore, our choice of words is likely to differ occasionally and to be made with somewhat more care in writing than in ordinary, everyday speech. But these are stylistic rather than linguistic matters, as is also the fact that writing tends to be somewhat more conservative than speech.

A DEFINITION OF LANGUAGE

For our purposes language will be defined as systematized combinations of sounds which have meaning for all persons in a given cultural community. For those languages which have been recorded (and there are some which have never been written down), writing is the graphic representation of these combinations of sounds. This definition of language does not include such gestures, facial expressions, and other body movements as have been mentioned, which, though they play a part in communication, will not be considered further in this book.

Perhaps the most important word in our definition is *systematized.* We speak in certain patterns, or according to a certain system. Thus, according to the sound-system of Modern English, the consonant combination *mb* never occurs at the beginning or at the end of any word. As a matter of fact, it did occur in final position in earlier stages of our language, which is why it was necessary in the preceding statement to specify "Modern English." Despite its complete absence in this position in the sound-system of English for at least six hundred years, we still insist — such is the conservatism of writing habits — that the *b* be written in *lamb, climb, tomb, dumb,* and a number of other words. But this same combination, which now occurs only medially in English (as in *tremble*), may well occur in final or even in initial position in the sound-systems of other languages. Initial *mb* is indeed a part of the systems of certain African languages, as in Efik and Ibibio *mbakara* 'white man,' which in the speech of the Gullahs — black Americans living along the coastal region of Georgia and South Carolina who have

---

[5] For a full discussion of paralanguage, see George L. Trager, "Paralanguage: A First Approximation," *Studies in Linguistics,* 13 (1958), 1–12. See also Henry Lee Smith, Jr., "Language and the Total System of Communication," *Linguistics Today,* pp. 89–102.

preserved a number of words and structural features which their ancestors brought from Africa—has become *buckra*. It is notable that the Gullahs have simplified the initial consonant combination of this African word to conform to the pattern of their native English speech.

The sounds of a language recur again and again according to a well-defined system, not haphazardly; for without system communication would be impossible. The same is true of all linguistic features, not sound alone. Thus, according to the grammatical system of English, a very large number of words take a suffix written -*s* to indicate plurality or possession (in which case it is a comparatively recent convention of writing to add an apostrophe). This suffix is variously pronounced. *Duck,* for instance, adds the sound which is usually indicated by *s; dog* adds the sound which is usually indicated by *z;* and *horse* adds a syllable consisting of a vowel sound plus the *z* sound.

Words which can be thus modified in form for the purposes specified are traditionally called nouns. They fit into certain definite patterns in English utterances. *Alcoholic,* for instance, fits into the system of English in the same way as *duck, dog,* and *horse:* "Alcoholics need understanding" (compare "Ducks need water"), "An alcoholic's perceptions are faulty" (compare "A dog's perceptions are keen"), and the like. But it may also modify a noun and be modified by an adverb: *an alcoholic drink, a somewhat alcoholic taste,* and the like; and words that operate in this way are called adjectives. *Alcoholic* is thus both adjective and noun, depending upon the way it functions in the system of English. Such an utterance as "Alcoholic worries" is ambiguous because our system, like all linguistic systems, is not completely foolproof. But the headline "President-Threatening Alcoholic Worries U.S. Agents," while certainly no model of English style, is not really ambiguous, but only momentarily irritating. We know at second glance that *Alcoholic* is here a noun, the subject of a verb *Worries* (rather than the modifier of a plural noun *Worries*) because of what follows in the pattern: *U.S. Agents,* the object of *Worries*. What we have here is the most frequently occurring of all English sentence patterns: subject-verb-complement.

FOR DIFFERENT LANGUAGES, DIFFERENT SYSTEMS

It is obvious that every language must have its own system, though it may share certain features with other languages. What has been said of the capacity of the typical English noun to add a sibilant suffix for pluralizing or indicating possession is, for instance, not at all true of the typical Modern French noun, which has no possessive form and which in isolation remains unchanged in the plural. The fact that singular *ami* and plural *amis* are written differently is merely a historical feature of the French writing system. The two forms are actually identical in speech except when *amis* is "in liaison," that is, followed by a word beginning with a vowel sound, in which case the normally "silent" -*s* is pronounced. The French noun, then, would require a definition different in some of its details from that of the English noun.

Pidgin English and other languages spoken by primitive peoples are just as systematic as English, or as Classical Latin for that matter. Since system in languages *is* grammar in its widest sense, it is obviously impossible for there to be a grammarless language. When Dr. Johnson remarked that English had no grammar, he was thinking of the complicated system of word-endings of Latin as constituting grammar. It would have been remarkable if anyone had thought otherwise in his day. But the fact is that English "The fire cooks the meat," Melanesian Pidgin "Fire i-cookim abus,"[6] and Latin "Ignis carnem coquet" all have grammar. The systems are of course different, but no one system can be said to be superior to another. In the sentence from Pidgin, for instance, the ending -*im* of the verb indicates that a direct object follows; in "The meat cooks," no such ending would be used: "Abus i-cook." This ending is a systematic grammatical device indicating the same grammatical relationship as the accusative ending -*em* (with which it of course has no connection) of the Latin noun. In the system of English, the position of *meat* in the sentence indicates the same grammatical relationship. Position is, however, relatively unimportant in Latin: "Carnem ignis coquet" means the same thing as "Ignis carnem coquet," inasmuch as the direct object is clearly labeled by the ending. To reverse the meaning (with nonsensical effect) one would have to change only the *form* of the words, as follows: "Caro ignem coquet." The order of the words makes no difference. In English (as also in Pidgin), the same reversal in meaning is accomplished without change of form, but of word order only: "The meat cooks the fire."

The acquisition of language — that is, the mastery of one of the complicated linguistic systems by which man, and man alone, communicates — would seem to be an arduous task. But it is a task that normal children all over the world seem not to mind in the least. Even children

---

[6] This sentence, with spelling slightly modified, is taken from *Hands Off Pidgin English!* (Sydney, Australia, 1955), by Robert A. Hall, Jr., to whom I am also indebted for the other grammatical statements about Melanesian Pidgin English in this text.

in daily contact with a language other than their "home" language – the native language of their parents – readily acquire that second language, even to the extent of speaking it with a native "accent." Noam Chomsky has pointed out what should be apparent to all, that "a young child of immigrant parents may learn a second language in the streets, from other children, with amazing rapidity . . . while the subtleties that become second nature to the child may elude his parents despite high motivation and continued practice."[7] After childhood, most minds undergo some sort of "hardening" in this respect, perhaps in the late teens. But children seem to be genetically equipped with some sort of built-in "device" that makes the acquisition of languages possible. It is not of course claimed that a child of five or so has acquired all of the words he will need to know as he grows up. What is true is that he has rather fully mastered the system by means of which he will speak of many things for the rest of his life. The immensity of his accomplishment can be appreciated by anyone who has learned a second language as an adult.

DO BIRDS AND BEASTS REALLY TALK?

Language, it has been pointed out, is an exclusively human phenomenon. Many of the lower animals are physically just about as well equipped as man to produce speech sounds, and some – certain birds, for instance – have in fact been taught to do so. What we call our speech organs are actually organs with primary functions quite different from the production of speech sounds, functions such as the ingestion and mastication of food. But no other species makes use of a system of sounds which even remotely resembles human language, despite the fondly held belief, as yet unsubstantiated by any truly scientific evidence, that porpoises thus "talk" to one another. The fetching Sarah, a seven-year-old chimpanzee, as reported under "Behavior" in *Time* (September 21, 1970), is able to "converse" after a fashion with the psychologist whose protégé she is, not by means of speech sounds but with metal-based nonalphabetic symbols which she places on a magnetized board. She could at the time of the article comprehend the meaning of about 120 different symbols and had evinced an elementary grasp of syntax.

There is, however, ample evidence that certain animals communi-

---

[7] Review of *Verbal Behavior* by B. F. Skinner, *Language*, 35 (1959), 42.

cate with others of their kind in an elementary and nonlinguistic fashion. Leaving sexual posturings and similar kinesic phenomena out of the question, it has in fact been established that gibbons do so in a very limited way by a system of differentiated vocal noises – warning calls, calls having to do with the search for food, and the like. This is the nearest we get to human language among the lower animals, but still, if one may be allowed to say so, a far cry from it. As Hockett and Ascher suggest (see footnote 1), language may well have developed out of blendings of such calls, whereby in the course of heaven only knows how many scores of millennia a closed and nonproductive system of nine or ten calls became an open and productive system making possible the production of an infinite number of different sentences. Or it may be that a sudden mutation endowed the human species with the genetic ability to acquire a language system that bears little similarity to the vocalizations of the apes. However it came about, it would seem that only man has developed such a system; man alone can talk about the manifold things that concern him, ranging all the way from food, shelter, and sex – the most drastic concerns of his remotest ancestors – to transubstantiation, relativity, and transformational-generative grammar.

LANGUAGE SYSTEMS
ARE CONVENTIONS

No one would deny, of course, that there are features shared by all languages – features that must be regarded as natural, inherent, or universal. Thus the human vocal apparatus (lips, teeth, tongue, and so forth) makes it inevitable that human languages will have only a limited range of sounds. Likewise, since all men live in the same universe and perceive it through the same senses with more or less the same basic mental equipment, it is hardly surprising that they should find it necessary to talk about more or less the same things in more or less similar ways.

Nevertheless, the systems that operate in the world's many languages are, it is important to remember, arbitrary and conventional; that is to say, there is usually no connection between the sounds we make and the phenomena of life. This is to some extent true even of the comparatively small number of echoic words, like *bow-wow,* which seems to those of us who speak English as our native language to be a fairly accurate imitation of the sounds made by a dog, though it is highly doubtful that a dog would agree, particularly a French dog, which says *gnaf-gnaf,* or a German one, which says *wau-wau,* or a Japanese one, which says *wung-wung.*[8]

The common man thinks unquestioningly that his language is the best — and so it is for him, inasmuch as he mastered it well enough for his own purposes so long ago that he cannot remember when. It seems to him more logical, more sensible, more right — in short, more *natural* — than the way foreigners talk. But, as we have seen, there is nothing really natural about any language, since all these highly systematized and conventionalized methods of human communication must be acquired. There is, for instance, nothing natural in our use of *is* in such a sentence as "The woman is busy." The utterance can be made just as effectively without the meaningless verb form which is conventional in English, and some languages do get along perfectly well without it. This use of *is* (and other forms of the verb *to be*) was, as a matter of fact, late in developing and has never developed in Russian and the other languages of the Balto-Slavic group.

To the speaker of Russian it is thus more "natural" to say "Zhenshchina zanyata" — literally "Woman busy" — which sounds to our ears so much like baby talk that the unsophisticated speaker of English might well conclude (and how wrong he would be!) that Russian is strictly a childish tongue. It will be noted also that the system of Russian manages to struggle along without the definite article, which in most other Indo-European languages has developed out of the demonstrative pronoun. As a matter of fact, the speaker of Russian never misses the definite article — nor should we if its use had not become conventional with us.

To our hypothetical common man, calling the organ of sight *eye* will seem to be perfectly natural and right, and those who call it anything else — like the Germans, who call it *Auge,* the Russians, who call it *glaz,* or the Japanese, who call it *me* — he is likely to regard as either perverse or simply unfortunate because they do not speak languages in which things are properly designated. The fact is, however, that *eye,* which we pronounce exactly like the nominative form of the first person singular pronoun (a fact which might be cited against it by a foreign

---

[8] The reader interested in the sounds made by foreign animals will do well to look into Noel Perrin's instructive and highly amusing "Old Macberlitz Had a Farm" (*New Yorker*, January 27, 1962, pp. 28–29), and the erudite comments by the ambassador from Norway, Paul Koht (in a letter to the editor of the *New Yorker*, February 24, 1962, p. 125), from which he may acquire from a native speaker valuable information about the sounds uttered by Norwegian cows (*mmmøøø*), sheep (*mæ*), pigs (*nøff-nøff*), and other creatures. Norwegian hens very sensibly say *klukk-klukk,* though doubtless with a heavy Norwegian accent.

hypothetical common man), is the name of the organ in question only in our present English linguistic system. It has not always been so. Londoners at the time of the accession of King Edward III in 1327 pronounced the word with two syllables, the vowel of the first syllable being that which we pronounce nowadays in *see*. In the course of the fourteenth century the final unstressed vowel sound (pronounced like the -*a* in *Ida*) was lost, though we continue to this day to write it, calling it "silent *e*." And, if we chose to go back to King Alfred's day, we should find yet another pronunciation and, in addition, a different way of writing the word from which Modern English *eye* has developed. When a Scottish plowboy says "ee" for *eye,*[9] he is not being quaint, or whimsical, or perverse, or stupid. He is merely using that development of a variant form of the word (one which had approximately the vowel sound of *date*) current in his own linguistic system—a perfectly "legitimate" pronunciation which happens not to occur in that type of English spoken in the southern part of England and, for reasons which have nothing to do with "good" or "bad," by educated speakers of English all over the English-speaking world. Knowledge of such changes within a single language should be sufficient to dissipate the notion that any one word or any one form of a word is more appropriate except in a purely chronological and social sense than any other word or form.

WRITING IS NOT LANGUAGE

Misconceptions about language are very widespread and by no means confined to hypothetical common men. Very often these false notions grow out of a confusion of writing with language. It is, for example, quite generally supposed by English-speaking people that their language is a "difficult" language, or at least more difficult than, say, Spanish. But the fact seems to be that every normal child in the world has acquired a mastery of the grammar of his native language—it makes no difference whether it be English, Chinese, Russian, or Hottentot—by the time he is about five years old. He does not need to go to school to learn how to produce grammatical sentences; however acquired, the grammatical system of his native tongue is a part of him before the school bus—apparently no child walks to school nowadays—arrives to pick him up for the first time. He may of course make so-

---

[9] As in Robert Burns's "To a Mouse":

> Still thou art blest, compared wi' me!
> The present only toucheth thee:
> But och! I backward cast my e'e,
> On prospects drear!

cial errors like saying *throwed, mans,* and *stang* for the prescribed *threw, men,* and *stung.* These can hardly be regarded as errors in English, but merely as very sensible forms that analogically conform to the patterns of *rowed, pans,* and *rang.* He does not say "The bit man dog the," nor would any native speaker, no matter how "disadvantaged"; he would say "The dog bit the man," unless he really meant to say "The man bit the dog"—in which case he would say just that, though he might use *bited* instead of *bit* in both sentences. Practically all that he learns subsequently are words and, depending upon the intellectual and social backgrounds of his life, certain stylistic variations—elegancies like the nominative absolute or the counterfactual subjunctive, and a more sophisticated use of relative clauses and other forms of subordination. He may also have to perfect the articulation of some sounds or combinations of sounds. But what he has yet to learn about his language is trivial in comparison with what the child has already easily and unconsciously acquired.

For adults learning a second language, one language may certainly be more difficult than another, but this is an altogether different matter from what we have been discussing. The grown-up native speaker of English may well find French easier than German, or vice versa, and either of these easier than Russian, Chinese, or Arabic. But there is no evidence whatever that little children in Paris, Berlin, Moscow, Peking, and Cairo complain about the difficulty of learning their native languages; they take the process—if it can indeed be called a process— well in their stride. It is true, however, that some languages have writing systems which are in one way or another less efficient than those of other languages. This fact has nothing to do with language itself, for, as we have observed, writing is but a symbolization of language.

Nevertheless, such words as *through, though, bough, rough,* and *cough* are time and again cited as evidence of the devilishness of the English language, inasmuch as, though all are spelled with *-ough,* all have different vowel sounds, with a final consonant occurring in the last two which is nonexistent in the first three. "How can the poor foreigner ever learn such a language?" it is asked.

All that is really proved by such examples is that English has a highly conservative spelling system: our spellings frequently indicate pronunciations which have not been current since Middle English times. But as *language,* English would be no easier if we wrote *thru, tho, bow, ruf,* and *cawf.* Immigrants forced to learn the language "by ear," as we all learned it as children, would not confuse these words in their speech any more than we do—though of course they would have some difficulty in reading and writing.

Out of this confusion of writing and language emerge such notions as that of the late Senator Robert L. Owen of Oklahoma, who believed that a new international alphabet would remove all language barriers and hence bring about universal brotherhood and understanding—the underlying assumption being that understanding inevitably brings about agreement. With the best will in the world, Owen invented such an alphabet—a "global alphabet," he called it—and conducted a long crusade to have it taught in the Oklahoma school system. He claimed that "through it I can teach any reasonably intelligent man Chinese in two months. . . . It is a means by which we can teach the English language to all the world at high speed and negligible cost."[10] The first of these claims is true only in the sense that, if both parties knew Chinese to begin with, the senator could have taught his pupil to *write* that language in his "global alphabet"—quite a different thing from teaching him the Chinese language. As a matter of fact, Chinese could be written in any alphabet and frequently is written in the Roman alphabet.

How far this sort of misconception can go is illustrated by the editorial pronouncement of a metropolitan daily newspaper,[11] commenting upon the various spellings of the name of a now happily forgotten Iranian premier as *Mossadegh, Mossadeq, Moussadek,* and *Musaddiq.* The editorial writer concludes that "if no agreement can be reached on the spelling of one man's name, consider how much greater is the problem of translating accurately the fine shades of meaning in an address by a statesman of Pakistan, Turkey, or Ethiopia."

Now, no one would deny the difficulties of accurate translation, but these have nothing whatever to do with the way a word (in this instance a proper name) is transliterated from one alphabet into another. The name of a great Russian writer whom English-speaking people know as *Chekhov* is written in other spelling systems according to the various ways of transliterating Russian, which uses the Cyrillic rather than the Roman alphabet: the French write *Tchékhov;* the Italians, *Čechov;* the Germans, *Tschechow;* the Swedes, *Tjechov;* and the Spanish, *Tchejoff, Tchekov,* or *Chejov.* The fact that these variant writings give a fairly close approximation of the Russian pronunciation to one familiar with the phonetic and orthographic systems of the languages cited is all that is really important. The writer himself wrote his name Чехов, which, despite its strangeness to our eyes, does not indicate that Russian is an uncommonly difficult language or that, in the interests of international

[10] Cited by Leonard Bloomfield in "Secondary and Tertiary Responses to Language," *Language,* 20 (1944), 49.

[11] The Jacksonville *Florida Times-Union,* October 28, 1951, p. 8.

"understanding," the Russians ought to adopt our way of writing — or, for that matter, that we ought to adopt theirs. Names, like all other words, were in existence long before anybody ever wrote them, and the way one writes them is purely and simply a matter of tradition. Had the Russians long ago settled upon Chinese ideograms as the basis of their writing system, their language would have had precisely the same development which it has had, and the great writer would have had the same name as that under which he is known to us. When, in 1928, Mustafa Kemal Pasha (later Kemal Atatürk) as president of Turkey substituted the Roman alphabet for the Arabic in writing Turkish, the Turkish language changed no more than time changed when he introduced the Gregorian calendar in his country.

THE NOTION OF LINGUISTIC CORRUPTION

Another widely held notion is that there are ideal forms of languages, these being thought of as "pure," and that existing languages represent corruptions of these. Thus, the Greek spoken today is supposed to be a degraded form of Classical Greek rather than what it really is, a development therefrom. Since the Romance languages are developments of Latin, it would follow from this point of view that these also are corrupt, although this assumption is not usually made. Those who admire or profess to admire Latin literature sometimes suppose that a stage of perfection had been reached in Classical Latin and that every divergent development in Latin was indicative of steady and irreparable deterioration. From this point of view the late development of Latin spoken in the early Middle Ages (sometimes called Vulgar, or popular, Latin) is "bad" Latin, which, strange as it may seem, was ultimately to become "good" Italian, French, Spanish, and so on.

It is obvious that such notions, despite their tenacity, are completely invalid. They are based to some extent upon yet another notion — that languages which make use of complicated systems of endings for case, tense, mood, gender, and the like are superior ("more expressive of fine shades of meaning" is a frequent description) to those which, like English and French, do not. This notion is particularly dear to the hearts of those who have a smattering of classical learning and who in support of the supposed superiority of the classical languages point to the fact that Greece and Rome produced great literature. But literary excellence has little or nothing to do with language *as* language. Speakers of English have also produced some rather great literature at various stages in its development, as all the world agrees: *Beowulf* in Old English, *Troilus and Criseyde* and *Sir Gawain and the*

Green Knight in Middle English, and *Hamlet* and *Paradise Lost* in Modern English. Literature of high quality may be written in any language provided some of its speakers are interested in, and capable of, writing such literature.

Instead of retaining a complicated system of inflections (variations in the form of words, usually by means of endings) such as we find in Latin, Greek, and Sanskrit, many modern languages make use of other devices to indicate grammatical relationships—word order, for instance, and what Charles Carpenter Fries in *The Structure of English* (New York, 1952) and elsewhere has called "function words," which include words traditionally called prepositions, auxiliaries, conjunctions, articles and words which may be substituted for them (such as possessive and demonstrative pronouns), and adverbs of negation and degree. Latin *pater Caroli* 'Charles's father,' for instance, came to be expressed in French, Spanish, and Italian respectively by *le père de Charles, el padre de Carlos,* and *il padre di Carlo* 'the father of Charles.'[12] The Latin genitive has been completely lost in the languages derived from Latin, its function being performed by a preposition meaning 'of.'

This loss of the genitive in the Romance languages ought to be — and doubtless is — considered degenerative by those who believe in linguistic corruption. Inflectional complexity is dearly beloved by those who fancy that they know their way about, even if somewhat gropingly, in the classical languages. Such persons are likely to regard English, which, though it has retained its genitive, has lost most of its other inflectional devices in the course of its development, as crude and barbarous. If this were the sole criterion for their judgment, they would of course be logically committed to a similar low opinion of the Romance languages.

Indo-European, the origin of practically all the languages of Europe as well as some Asiatic ones, was even more complex than the classical languages. In addition to the case forms found in most Latin nouns, for instance, the Indo-European noun had also an instrumental, a locative, and a vocative form, the last two of which survive only very rarely in Latin. Now, carrying to its logical conclusion the point of view of such linguistic commentators as have been cited, we really ought to speak reconstructed Indo-European. Think of the "fine shades of meaning" which might be expressed by the locative, the vocative, and the instrumental cases!

---

[12] Note that English, which has never lost the genitive inflection, can use either construction.

As a matter of fact, however, most of us get along very well without these shades. We do not in the least miss the various uses of the almost lost subjunctive mood in English, and are impatient when we must use the subjunctive in speaking languages which have preserved it, such as German, French, and Spanish.

Because we hear so much of "pure" English, it is perhaps well that we examine this particular notion in some detail before passing on to more important matters. When Captain Frederick Marryat, an English novelist, visited the United States in 1837–38, he thought it "remarkable how very debased the language has become in a short period in America," adding that "if their lower classes are more intelligible than ours, it is equally true that the higher classes do not speak the language so purely or so classically as it is spoken among the well-educated English." Both statements are nonsense. The first is based upon the captain's apparent notion that the English language had reached a stage of perfection at the time America was first settled by English-speaking people, after which, presumably because of the innate depravity of those Englishmen who brought their language to the New World, it had taken a steadily downward course, whatever that may mean. One wonders, also, precisely how Marryat knew what constituted "classical" or "pure" English. It is probable that he was merely attributing certain superior qualities to that type of English which he was accustomed to hear from persons of good social standing in the land of his birth and which he himself spoke. Any divergence therefrom was "debased": "My speech is pure; thine, wherein it differs from mine, is corrupt."

In our own day these concepts of linguistic purity and corruption survive, so that even so highly sophisticated a fictional character as Dr. Peter Alden in George Santayana's *The Last Puritan* (New York, 1936) is made to say of his son's speech, "I should like his English to be fundamentally pure; then all the abominable speech he will have to hear will seem to him absurd and amusing. . . ." (p. 80). If instead of "fundamentally pure" Dr. Alden had said "aesthetically pleasing to persons in our station of life" or "highly cultivated" (in contrast to ordinary "abominable" speech), no one could quarrel with such a statement of his personal preferences. To claim that these preferences are for what is "fundamentally pure" is quite another matter.

That the equally sophisticated author himself had the same notion of educated speech as pure and of common speech—actually more conservative in many details than educated speech—as debased is indicated by a good many pseudolinguistic pronouncements of his own throughout the novel, as in his description of the speech of Fräulein

Irma, a German governess, as "British — musical, colloquial, and pure" (p. 91).[13] Santayana, who spent much of his life in the United States, seems here to be implying that the development of the English language in America has been somehow inferior to that which has occurred in England. Somewhat different these developments have certainly been, but it would be impossible to determine by any objective standards that one has been good and the other bad, though one type of English may be more pleasing than another to a given person or group. It is indeed likely that most of us, for reasons which have nothing to do with language as such, would prefer Sir John Gielgud's reading of Shakespeare to that of, say, Marlon Brando. It is ironical that in a number of details Brando's native speech resembles that heard in the Globe Theatre of Shakespeare's day more closely than does Gielgud's — for instance, in its retention of *r* before consonants and in final position and of the so-called "flat *a*" in words like *path, staff, master,* and perhaps in its intonation as well.

THE QUESTION OF USAGE

The concept of an absolute and unwavering, presumably God-given standard of linguistic correctness (sometimes confused with "purity") is so widespread, even among the educated, as to merit some attention here. Those who subscribe to this notion become greatly exercised over such matters as the split infinitive, the "incorrect" position of *only,* and the preposition ending a sentence. All these supposed "errors" have been committed time and again by eminent writers and speakers, so that one wonders how those who condemn them know that they are bad. Robert Lowth, who wrote one of the most influential English grammars of the eighteenth century (*A Short Introduction to English Grammar,* 1762), was praised by one of his admirers for showing "the grammatic inaccuracies that have escaped the pens of our most distinguished writers."

One would suppose that the usage of "our most distinguished

---

[13] Santayana, as might be expected of one with his cultivated use of English, uses *colloquial* in the sense 'familiar, easy-going, informal,' the meaning which it still has among the highly educated. It is notable that in common usage the word has come to mean 'regional' or 'local' (doubtless because of the phonetic similarity of *colloquialism* and *localism*). Hence a word which for many denotes a quality altogether attractive and desirable (and in fact usually unavoidable) has come frequently to denote what is supposed to be bad, as in the statement of one described in an Associated Press news item of September 6, 1953, as a voice coach for various eminent actors and actresses: "If you speak with a nasal twang or a colloquial accent . . . you are handicapping yourself, no matter what your business."

writers" would be good usage. But Lowth and his followers knew, or thought they knew, better; and their attitude survives to this day. This is not, of course, to deny that there are standards of usage, but only to suggest that even in the reputedly democratic society in which we live any set of standards which are to have validity must be based on the usage of speakers and writers of generally acknowledged excellence. These would nowadays almost inevitably be persons of education, though it has not always been so; other ages have not placed so high a premium on mere literacy as our own. Distressing as it may be to all idealists, what we think of as "good" English has grown out of the usage of generations of well-born and well-bred persons many of whom could neither read nor write. In the late fifteenth century, William Caxton, obviously a highly literate man, used to submit his work to the Duchess of Burgundy (an English lady despite her French title), who "oversawe and corrected" it. We have no information as to the speed and ease with which the Duchess read, but it is highly likely that she was considerably less literate than was Caxton himself. Yet to Caxton the "correctness" of the usage of a lady of the court was unassailable, whereas he would seem to have had little faith in what came naturally to him, a brilliant son of the bourgeoisie. His standard of excellence was the usage of persons of good position—quite a different thing from our own servile obedience to the mandates of badly informed "authorities" who, when not guided by their own prejudices, attempt to settle questions of usage by the same methods as those which were employed by Lowth and his followers in the eighteenth century.

LANGUAGE AND NATION

Another fondly held belief is that a language somehow expresses the collective "soul" of its speakers. Certainly no one would deny that the external history of a nation may be reflected in its word stock; this the history of the English language demonstrates eloquently. But this is not the same thing as supposing that the attitudes toward life and the habits of mind of a people are reflected in the grammatical structure of their language. Such a thesis as Otto Jespersen's "As the language is, so also is the nation"[14] is quite indefensible, though still believed so tenaciously that to gainsay it is likely to bring down coals of fire on one's head. If it were merely a notion held by a lunatic fringe of society, there would be little point in mentioning it here. But the fact is that it is as widely believed by otherwise educated people as the equally untenable notion that climate affects language, which, if true, would mean

---

[14] *Growth and Structure of the English Language*, 9th ed. (Oxford, 1954), p. 16.

among other things that we ought to talk faster and louder in winter than in summer.[15]

Because it has vitiated much of our thinking about language, one more popular misconception must be mentioned—the notion that certain languages are more "expressive" than others. Now the fact is that all languages are about equally expressive, if by the term we mean 'efficient for purposes of communication.' It is obvious that members of one linguistic community will not need or want to express all that the members of another community might consider important. In short, the Eskimo feels no need to discuss Zen Buddhism, the quantum theory, or campus unrest. But he can talk about what is important to his own culture, and doubtless with greater efficiency in some instances than can the anthropologist who must describe that culture in, say, English—a language which might well impress the Eskimo as being quite "primitive" because it has only one widely used word for the frozen vapor which falls in white flakes (*snow*), whereas his language has many words for many different kinds of snow. Furthermore, he can make a good many grammatical distinctions in his language that we are not in the least concerned with making in ours. These also doubtless seem so essential to him that, if he ever gave the matter a thought, he might well regard English as sadly deficient in its grammar as well as in its word stock.

One of the most important tenets of the layman's linguistic creed is that any thoughtful, well-educated person, no matter what his special training may have been, is competent to make authoritative pronouncements about the language which he speaks or, for that matter, about any language with which he has a passing acquaintance. The late Leonard Bloomfield, an authority on American Indian languages, tells of being informed by a physician that Chippewa has only a few hundred words—a patently fantastic statement to make concerning any language. Says Bloomfield, "When I tried to state the diagnostic setting, the physician, our host, briefly and with signs of displeasure repeated his statement, and then turned his back to me."[16] This was a more or

[15] Witness the following statement from Miriam Chapin's *How People Talk* (New York, 1947): "It is true that the south seems to soften sounds; witness Louisiana's slurred r's and drawled vowels . . . ." (p. 18). Presumably the heat is held responsible for these phenomena, though it should be pointed out that the loss of *r* under certain circumstances is paralleled in eastern New England and in England. As for the drawl, whatever the term means, Noah Webster reprobated his fellow New Englanders for their "drawling, whining cant" in his *Dissertations on the English Language* (1789), though the drawl is now supposed to be characteristic of Southern American speech.

[16] "Secondary and Tertiary Responses to Language," p. 49.

less typical (to adopt Bloomfield's term) "tertiary response to language" — a response that seems to be practically inevitable when one has tried to enlighten someone else who has made a statement about language (a "secondary response") that is open to question. As we proceed, we hope it will become increasingly obvious that the study of language, like language itself, has order, discipline, and system, and that consequently the layman's opinions about language are no more reliable than his opinions about medicine, physics, or engineering.

The linguistic commentator with a heavily authoritative air about matters of usage is usually to be distrusted when his pronouncements deny social acceptability to locutions that we have read in reputable books and heard from the lips of reputable speakers. Thus, when the writer of a syndicated newspaper column solemnly informs his linguistically insecure readers that it is incorrect to say "There were 400 people present" because one should never use *people* after a number, but only *persons,* we are quite justified in asking how he knows this. And, inasmuch as there could not possibly be any way of knowing other than by divine inspiration, we are equally justified in assuming that the current preference of a large majority of educated speakers for *people* in such a construction is sufficient to establish it as "correct," that is, in good usage. Likewise, when we come upon lists of words which practically everyone is supposed to mispronounce, we are surely justified in asking ourselves how the compilers of such lists know how the words ought to be pronounced, unless they too are divinely inspired by a linguistic Jehovah who watches over the destiny of the English language.

The plain fact is that there has been an appalling lag between attitudes toward language and the brilliant research which the present century has seen. In no way has this fact been more strikingly illustrated than by the furor of indignation which met the publication of *Webster's Third New International Dictionary* in 1961. Newspaper and magazine editors, as well as critics who should have known better, exposed the fact that they did not know what a dictionary is supposed to be, namely, a record of the words of a language, though no really complete record could ever be made. It was apparent that otherwise educated people believed that it should be only a record of what they thought of as "good" words, though it would be very difficult to arrive at any complete agreement among the critics themselves as to which words are "good," and therefore worthy of recording, and which ones "bad," and by the same token unworthy. Magazines that pride themselves on their modernity in the arts and sciences took a stand on language that was little in advance of the prescriptivism which has flourished among linguistically naive and insecure people since the eighteenth century. The whole sorry business has been chronicled in *Dictionaries and* That *Dictionary* (subtitled *A Casebook on the Aims of Lexicographers and the Targets of Reviewers*), edited by James Sledd and Wilma R. Ebbitt (Chicago, 1962) — a work which should, but will not, make a good many popular pundits hang their heads in shame.

THE SCHOLARLY STUDY OF LANGUAGE

The nineteenth century concerned itself largely with establishing the relationships of the various Indo-European languages, of which a résumé will be given in Chapter IV. Once this had been accomplished, scholars were provided with a vast and fascinating body of data to describe, analyze, and classify yet further. They were for the most part not much given to philosophizing or to theorizing, with the exception of the Dane Otto Jespersen, who had imagination and daring that enabled him to anticipate later theories, even though he may not always have perceived the full implications of his keen perceptions.

Before the end of that century the first three volumes and a large part of the fourth volume (it was originally published in sections) of that great monument of English scholarship, *A New English Dictionary on Historical Principles,*[17] had been published, Henry Sweet had laid the groundwork for the study of English phonology, and the American Dialect Society had been formed. The first quarter of the present century witnessed the appearance of most of the great descriptive, analytical, and historical work of Jespersen, the German Karl Luick, the Dutchmen E. Kruisinga and H. Poutsma, and the Englishman H. C. Wyld, among others. In 1921 appeared the American Edward Sapir's *Language: An Introduction to the Study of Speech,* a learned and highly readable book addressed to the general public as well as to students of linguistics, and in 1933 the American Leonard Bloomfield's great *Language,* a revised and enlarged version of his *Introduction to the Study of Language* (1914). Bloomfield's book has been of tremendous influence; it has with good reason been called the Bible of American structural linguistics.[18]

---

[17] Now usually called the *Oxford English Dictionary* (see p. 75, n. 38). It lists a great many words that must have been considered "bad" at the time.

[18] Bloomfield and Sapir were both, it should be noted, students of exotic, specifically American Indian, languages. They perceived the tremendous importance of linguistic structure far more clearly than could those whose studies had been confined to the Indo-European languages, which are structured similarly to one another.

Structural grammar is essentially nonmentalistic, obviously influenced in this respect by the behaviorist psychology in vogue in Bloomfield's day. Most of his followers, however, did not stress this influence. In Bloomfield's words, the mentalistic theory regarding human conduct, including speech, "supposes that the variability of human conduct is due to the interference of some non-physical factor, a *spirit* or *will* or *mind* . . . that is present in every human being," and that, moreover, "is entirely different from material things and accordingly follows some other kind of causation or perhaps none at all."[19] His own view, which he prefers to call mechanistic rather than materialistic, holds that "the variability of human conduct, including speech, is due only to the fact that the human body is a very complex system" and hence that "human actions . . . are part of cause-and-effect sequences exactly like those which we observe, say in the study of physics or chemistry" (p. 33).

In order to understand how language works, say the structuralists, we must rigorously analyze its symbolizing devices. Distinctive sounds, or phonemes, concerning which we shall have more to say in the following chapter, are the smallest units of symbolization. They are isolable, that is, capable of being segmented; and they go to make up morphemes, the smallest meaningful units in speech.[20] (A few morphemes, like *a, ay* 'ever,' *owe,* and *awe,* are single phonemes, but ordinarily phonemes by themselves are meaningless.) Structural grammar thus starts with the smallest units, the segmentable sounds, determining which of these are distinctive, proceeds to the smallest meaningful forms of speech — words and affixes — and thence to syntax, the arrangement of words to make sentences. But syntax had to wait a long time. When the structuralists finally got around to it, the same technique of smaller to larger prevailed in what was called immediate-constituent analysis; the sentence was conceived of as a sequence of segmentable and classifiable elements.[21]

In 1951 appeared *An Outline of English Structure* (Norman, Okla.), by George L. Trager and Henry Lee Smith, Jr., and, in 1952, Charles Carpenter Fries's *The Structure of English.* Trager and Smith concern themselves primarily with a description of the phonology of English, though they also treat morphology (the inflectional system) and syntax.

---

[19] *Language* (New York, 1933), p. 32.

[20] For instance, *hat, bang, pre-, -ed,* and *-ing. Hats, banged, banging,* and *preview* are made up of two morphemes each, and *previewed* of three.

[21] For an excellent brief discussion of structural principles, see Dwight Bolinger, *Aspects of Language* (New York, 1968), pp. 193–99.

Fries concerns himself almost wholly with English sentence structure. These proved to be highly germinative works. Books exemplifying the structural principles laid down in them include Archibald A. Hill's *Introduction to Linguistic Structures* (New York, 1958), Charles F. Hockett's aforementioned *A Course in Modern Linguistics,* H. A. Gleason, Jr.'s *An Introduction to Descriptive Linguistics,* rev. ed. (New York, 1961), and W. Nelson Francis' *The Structure of American English* (New York, 1958).

From the descriptivist-structural framework has arisen a new and thriving specialty, sociolinguistics. The word itself is so new that it is not listed in any general dictionary current up to 1971. Sociolinguistics is concerned with the relationship between language and society and thus with the social stratification of languages, that is, with social dialects. It has grown out of what are conceived to be the special needs and problems of recent times, particularly as these have come to light in urban areas — specifically in the "inner cities," the so-called ghettos, which used to be designated as slum areas.[22]

The transformational-generative analysis of Noam Chomsky, developed out of the important work of Zellig S. Harris exemplified in his *Methods in Structural Linguistics* (Chicago, 1951), is a more recent approach to the study of syntax, quite different from that of the structural linguists, who, as we have seen, conceive of the sentence as a combination of classifiable elements in sequence. Chomsky's *Syntactic*

[22] For a representative selection of linguistically oriented writings on the available theory, design, research, and pedagogical applications in the area of social dialects, see Roger Shuy, "A Selective Bibliography on Social Dialects," *The Linguistic Reporter: Newsletter of the Center for Applied Linguistics,* 10 (June, 1968), 1–5. Model full-length studies of social dialects are William Labov's seminal *The Social Stratification of English in New York City* (Washington, D.C., 1966), a publication of the Center for Applied Linguistics, Lee A. Pederson's *The Pronunciation of English in Metropolitan Chicago, Publication of the American Dialect Society,* No. 44 (University, Ala., 1965), and Juanita Virginia Williamson, *A Phonological and Morphological Study of the Speech of the Negro of Memphis, Tennessee, Publication of the American Dialect Society,* No. 50 (University, Ala., 1968). For important comments on the study of urban speech, see Hans Kurath, "The Investigation of Urban Speech and Some Other Problems Confronting the Student of American English," *Publication of the American Dialect Society,* No. 49 (University, Ala., April, 1968), pp. 1–7. For a severe and witty critique of the pedagogical applications of social dialect studies, see James Sledd, "Bi-Dialectalism: The Linguistics of White Supremacy," *English Journal,* 58 (1969), 1307–15. Sledd has little sympathy with the "basic assumption of bi-dialectalism . . . that the prejudices of middle-class whites cannot be changed but must be accepted and indeed enforced" and regrets that "in a school system run like ours by white businessmen, instruction in the mother tongue includes formal initiation into the linguistic prejudices of the middle class."

Structures (The Hague, 1962), a brief but formidable work[23] full of abstract symbols and mathematical phraseology, has for its purpose the formulation of principles which will, in his own words, "generate all of the grammatical sequences of L [a given language] and none of the ungrammatical ones." Chomsky attempts a "rigorous account of the process by which a grammar generates sentences,"[24] by means of "transforms," or syntactic structures which closely parallel other syntactic structures: thus "John's avoidance of publicity" is a "transform" of "John avoids publicity," as the passive construction "Publicity is avoided by John" is a transform of "John avoids publicity." In arriving at the "phrase-structure rules" which, it is hoped, will ultimately account for the generation of "all and only" the grammatical sentences of a language, the transformational-generativist makes use of something very like the immediate-constituent analysis of structural grammar; but, whereas the structuralist starts with these constituents, the transformational-generativist starts with the "well-formed" (grammatical) sentence and proceeds to its parts. Its diagrams are like upside-down trees, and its formulas are algebraically expressed.

If the structuralists are indeed aware of a unique linguistic creativity of the human mind — later theorists have assumed that they are not and are "mere taxonomists" — they certainly had little to say for it and, as we have seen, Bloomfield set himself firmly against any such notion. The transformational-generative theory is, on the contrary, based on nothing so mechanistic and spiritually arid as stimulus-response psychology, but on precisely this peculiar capacity shared by all normal human beings by virtue of their possession of a built-in language-learning device, the precise nature of which cannot of course be perfectly understood.

This device — in Chomsky's words the "innate mental structure that makes acquisition of language possible"[25] — enables a native speaker to comprehend as grammatical "all and only" those sentences that are "well formed";[26] moreover, it enables him to utter a theoretically infi-

---

[23] Considerably more readable is his *Aspects of the Theory of Syntax* (Cambridge, Mass., 1965), in which the exegesis is not so highly condensed as in *Syntactic Structures*.

[24] "A Transformational Approach to Syntax," *Studies in American English* (Third Texas Conference on Problems of Linguistic Analysis in English [Austin, Tex., 1962]), p. 126.

[25] *Language and Mind* (New York, 1968), p. 69.

[26] Thus, to use a justly famous example of Chomsky's, "Colorless green ideas sleep furiously," though nonsensical, would be immediately recognized by any native speaker of English as grammatical. The same recognition would not be forthcoming for "Furiously sleep ideas green colorless" (*Syntactic Structures*, p. 15).

nite number of sentences that have not been uttered before and will not be uttered again. He thus *knows* the grammar of his language, and this knowledge constitutes his *competence;* his *performance* may fall far short of this, but, according to the transformationalists, performance is not the main concern of the philosophical linguist.[27]

As one of the chief fuglemen of transformational theory puts it, "the taxonomic [descriptive and structural] linguist confines linguistic investigation to stating those facts about the structure of a natural language which can be found within the framework of a classificational system, while the mentalist goes far beyond this in seeking a full answer" to the three questions (1) "What is known by a speaker who is fluent in a natural language?" (2) "How is such linguistic knowledge put into operation to achieve communication?" and (3) "How do speakers come to acquire this ability?" He goes on to say, "Taxonomic linguistics can only describe the utterances of a language; mentalistic linguistics not only can do this but can also explain how speakers communicate by using the utterances, and how the ability to communicate is acquired."[28]

Essential to transformational theory is the distinction of *surface* (grammatical) structure and *deep* (conceptual) structure, stemming from the recognition in the rationalist Cartesian Port-Royal *Grammar* (1660)—in Chomsky's words, "the work that initiated the tradition of philosophical grammar"[29]—of the importance of the phrase as a grammatical unit: earlier grammar, he says, "had been largely a grammar of word classes and inflections." Chomsky cites an illustrative sentence of the Port-Royal grammarians, "Invisible God created the visible world." This, he points out, contains three propositions: that God is invisible, that He created the world, and that the world is visible. The deep structure of a sentence consists in such an intuitive mental analysis of its surface structure into such interrelating propositions, which are "present to the mind, though rarely articulated in the signal [that is, the sound], when the sentence is uttered" (p. 15).

Deep structures are "by certain mental operations" related to the surface structures, these operations being known as transformations.

---

[27] Chomsky is reported on one occasion to have taken dialectologists to task because they dealt with what people actually said (their performance) rather than what they intended to say (their competence). (Raven I. McDavid, Jr., "A Theory of Dialect," Georgetown University Monograph Series on Languages and Linguistics, No. 22 [1969], pp. 45–46.)

[28] Jerrold J. Katz, "Mentalism in Linguistics," *Language,* 40 (1964), 136–37.

[29] *Language and Mind,* p. 14.

The generative grammar of a language, then, to quote Chomsky once more, "must contain a system of rules that characterizes deep and surface structures and the transformational relation between them, and — if it is to accommodate the creative aspect of language use — that does so over an infinite domain of paired deep and surface structures" (p. 15).

It is not difficult to see how this recognition of deep structures underlying surface structures should have led to a revival of the old concept of a universal language, that is, to a general theory of language that underlies all particular languages. A fundamental assumption of this conception is that, though the surface structures of different languages show wide variation, the deep structures — what is present in the mind though not necessarily spoken — vary little.

The fullest critique of transformational-generative grammar is that of Charles F. Hockett in *The State of the Art* (The Hague, 1968). Hockett, while believing that Chomsky's views are "largely in error," nevertheless admits that "his particular pattern of error tells us some things about language that were formerly unknown or obscure." Syntactic transformations, however, "are helping us to discover subtle facts about various languages, and are surely here to stay."[30]

The first chapter of *The State of the Art* is an excellent survey of the development of American linguistic theory up to about 1950. The book is, unfortunately, not written for the general reader; it is difficult to see how it could have been. Chomsky's "The Current Scene in Linguistics,"[31] however, is a readable, brief, and, naturally, somewhat biased exposition of the development of linguistic theory from the late seventeenth century (a period which has influenced him greatly) to the present.

More recently the transformationalists have moved on from syntax to a more detailed study of phonology (the starting point of the structuralists), as exemplified in *The Sound Pattern of English* (New York, 1968), by Chomsky and Morris Halle, a work which shows some concern for recent linguistic history. It is not milk for babes and was never intended to be. The book was preceded by a number of articles dealing with transformationalist phonology.[32]

Transformational-generative grammar has been widely publicized (at least, in the scholarly world) since the appearance of *Syntactic*

---

[30] All quoted matter in this paragraph is from Hockett's Preface.

[31] *College English*, 27 (1966), 587–95.

[32] Notably by Chomsky's "Some General Properties of Phonological Rules," *Language*, 43 (1967) 102–28.

Structures and has made a tremendous impact upon our thinking about language. But there are other ways of looking at the subject than those already discussed, some of them even more recent than the Chomskyan way.[33] Perhaps the most prominent of these is the stratificational theory as it is being developed by Sydney Lamb and H. A. Gleason, Jr. It holds that the two levels of deep structure and surface structure are insufficient to explain the facts of language, which involve not two but several levels, or strata, arranged in groups of two under the three headings semology (meaning), grammar (syntax), and phonology (sound). It thus views language not as a simple system but as a number of subsystems.

Perception of the existence of such strata is of course no new thing for grammarians. As John Algeo has put it, "The question is . . . not whether a grammar is stratified, but whether it is explicitly stratified." He goes on to say, "If the stratification is explicit, the following questions become relevant: How many strata does the grammar recognize? What is the internal structure of each stratum? How are the strata related to one another?"[34] The answers to these questions are the concern of the stratificationalists, who make use of highly elaborate "circuitry diagrams" with various kinds of lines and nodes.

It is obvious that the scholarly study of language has been as lively and productive in recent years as it was in its beginnings. Grammatical theories have multiplied at such a dizzying rate that it has become practically impossible for older scholars, with their own colorful gardens to cultivate, to keep up with them. These theories have been formulated by remarkably keen-minded men, whose prose styles sometimes leave something to be desired and who are on occasion intransigent and even vituperative in their attitudes regarding rival theories. And no single theory is one hundred percent foolproof, nor is it really to be expected that any should be.

What should emerge from the foregoing brief sketch of recent developments in the study of grammar is that there is indeed no such thing as *the* grammar of English, or for that matter of any other natural language, any more than there is *a* grammar that as yet adequately ex-

---

[33] For a brief résumé by John Algeo of Kenneth Pike's tagmemic theory — a tagmeme is the smallest unit of grammatical form, as the phoneme is of phonological form and the morpheme of vocabulary — and of M. A. K. Halliday's systemic theory, which has in some degree grown out of the theories of J. R. Firth of the University of London, see Thomas Pyles and John Algeo, *English: An Introduction to Language* (New York, 1970), pp. 181–82.

[34] "Stratificational Grammar," *Journal of English Linguistics*, 3 (1969), 2. See also his "On Defining a Stratum," *Emory University Quarterly*, 23 (1967), 263–94.

plains anything so complex as a natural language. There are, rather, *grammars,* all of them embodying much that is true and good.

But public attitudes have remained comparatively unaffected by all this scholarly activity, to some extent perhaps because the materials and methods are difficult and popularizers have been lacking. The fact seems to be, indeed, that in the opinion of the public the linguist is, or at least ought to be, concerned wholly with matters of usage and, since he is at least held to be an expert on language, if a pretty poor booby in other respects, he ought to make up his mind about such matters as the incorrectness of *it's me,* split infinitives, *ain't, finalize, to contact,* and other similar trivialities. It is apparent from the badly informed pseudolinguistic pontifications of people who are otherwise well informed—the "Usage Panel" of the *American Heritage Dictionary* (Boston, 1969), composed of more than a hundred of "America's most famous writers, editors, and speakers," is a case in point—that Otto Jespersen and the scholarly editors of *A New English Dictionary on Historical Principles* would still be looked upon as wild-eyed and linguistically subversive radicals if the enlightened principles underlying their work were in the least comprehended.

Thus, in a period which has witnessed the most exciting linguistic research since the days of Rask, Grimm, and Bopp, whom we shall encounter in a later chapter, otherwise educated people—people who would scorn to believe in a Ptolemaic cosmology and who pride themselves on knowing a lot about environmental contamination and outer space—have remained practically unaffected by it all. It must of course be admitted that such research is not spectacular except when it utilizes machines of one sort or another, as in machine translation.

We shall later examine in somewhat more detail the beginnings of some of the more preposterous notions about English usage, notions which are responsible for still-current linguistic attitudes. For the time being it is sufficient that we be warned that we shall learn little about language unless we reject such erroneous attitudes as have been the subject of much of this chapter.

II

The Sounds and Spelling of Current English

The Roman alphabet has always been inadequate for the phonetic representation of the English language, most strikingly so for Modern English. We have, for example, only five vowel symbols, *a, e, i, o,* and *u;* that this number is wholly inadequate is indicated by the fact that the first of these alone may have as many as six different sound values, as in *cat, cate, calm, any, call,* and *was* (riming with *fuzz*). In our treatment of English sounds we shall have recourse to a way of writing in which the same symbols are used consistently for the same sounds, rather than using the awkward expedient of riming words or of referring to the initial consonant of, say, *thy* in order to distinguish this sound from the phonetically different though identically written consonant of *thigh*.

We have just mentioned "same sounds," and it thus becomes necessary to point out that what are commonly regarded as the same sounds may vary from language to language. In English, for instance, the vowel sound of *sit* and the vowel sound of *seat* are distinctive. There are many pairs of words, contrastive pairs as they are called, the difference in which resides solely in a distinctive quality which these sounds have for us: *bit–beat, mill–meal, fist–feast, lick–leak,* to cite only a few such pairs. But in Spanish this difference, so important in English, is of no significance at all; there are no such contrastive pairs, and hence the two vowels in question are felt, not as distinctive sounds, but as one and the same. The native speaker of Spanish, when he learns English, is as likely as not to say "I seat in the sit" for "I sit in the seat" — a mistake which would be impossible, except as a slip of the tongue, for the native speaker of English.

THE PHONEME

What in any language is regarded as the "same sound" is actually a group of similar sounds which make up what is known as a phoneme. A phoneme is thus the smallest *distinctive* unit of speech; it consists of a number of allophones, that is, of similar sounds which are not distinctive. Thus, speakers of English regard as the "same sound" the sound spelled *t* in *tone* and *stone,* though actually a different sound is symbolized by the letter *t* in each of these words: in *tone* the initial consonant is aspirated, that is, followed by a breath-puff, which may be clearly felt if one holds one's hand before one's lips when pronouncing the word; in *stone,* this aspiration is lacking. Nevertheless, both sounds belong to, or are allophones of, the English *t* phoneme, which differs according to the phonetic environment in which it occurs. To put it in another way, the allophones occur in what is called complementary distribution: that is to say, each occurs in a specific environment—in this instance, the unaspirated *t* occurring only after *s,* a position never occupied by the aspirated sound, so that there is no overlapping of these two allophones.[1] To put it in yet another way, there are in English no pairs of words the members of which are distinguished solely by the presence or absence of the aspiration; hence, from a phonemic point of view, the two *t*-like sounds in English are the same because they are nondistinctive. They merely occur in different environments, one initially, the other after *s.* But the two sounds might well be phonemic in other languages, and in fact are: in Chinese, for instance, the difference between aspirated and unaspirated *t* is quite significant, the aspiration or the lack of it distinguishing between words otherwise identical, just as *t* and *p* in English *tone* and *pone* do. Classical Greek had different symbols for these sounds, Θ and T, and carefully differentiated them, whereas the Romans had only the unaspirated sound represented by Greek T—that which is preceded in English by *s.* It was not until the classical period that they transliterated Θ by TH and presumably tried to pronounce *theta* in loan-words as an aspirate, that is, as *t* plus *h.*

It is usual to write phonemes within slanting lines, or virgules (also called slashes), thus /t/. In this book we shall ordinarily use rather "broad" phonetic transcriptions enclosed in square brackets, showing

---

[1] There are other allophones of the phoneme written *t;* for instance, as it occurs in American English medially in *item, little,* and *matter,* in which it is very like [d], and in a certain type of New York City speech in the same position as a glottal stop, that is, a "catch" in the throat, notably in *battle* and *bottle.*

only the gross characteristics of speech and for the most part ignoring allophonic features such as the allophones of /t/ that have just been described, the so-called clear *l* of *silly* as contrasted with the dark *l* of *sill* (both allophones of the phoneme /l/), and the like. Although broad transcriptions of speech are not in principle the same as phonemic transcriptions, in actual practice most of them do not differ in the least from phonemic transcriptions. In other words, nonsignificant features will not as a rule concern us any more than if the transcriptions were labeled as phonemic by putting them within slanting lines. But, since we shall have occasion to use some symbols for sounds that are not really distinctive, we shall, to avoid confusion, hereafter use only square brackets for transcriptions, thereby avoiding at the same time the shadier areas of phonemic theory.[2]

THE ORGANS OF SPEECH

The diagrammatic cross section of a head reproduced on p. 32 shows the principal organs by which speech is produced. As has been pointed out in Chapter I, none of these originally had any such function; all have been adapted to the articulation of speech sounds. Reference to the chart will clarify such terms as *labial, alveolar,* and *velar* used in describing the place of articulation of English consonants. After the symbols for the consonants have been listed, they will be discussed according to the manner of their articulation, as indicated by such terms as *stop, fricative,* and *affricate.*

THE CONSONANTS OF ENGLISH

Consonants are classified according to their place of articulation (that is, as labial, alveolar, and so on), their manner of articulation, and whether or not vibration of the so-called vocal cords is a component of their articulation. The chart on p. 33 exemplifies such a classification for the consonants of Modern English, with [w] appearing twice because both the lips and the tongue are involved in its production; illustrative words are supplied only for symbols not occurring in conventional writing and for [j], the value of which is not self-evident:

---

[2] On this point, see Dwight Bolinger, *Aspects of Language* (New York, 1968), pp. 43–46.

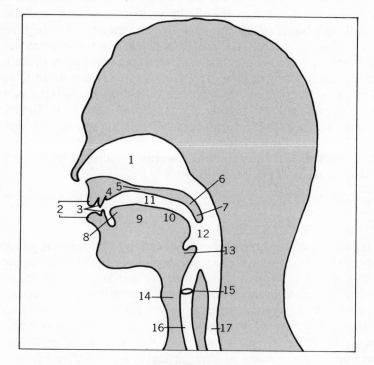

THE ORGANS OF SPEECH

1. Nasal cavity
2. Lips
3. Teeth
4. Alveolar ridge
5. Hard palate
6. Velum
7. Uvula
8. Tip of tongue
9. Front of tongue
10. Back of tongue
11. Oral cavity
12. Pharynx
13. Epiglottis
14. Larynx
15. Vocal cords
16. Trachea
17. Esophagus

PLACE OF ARTICULATION

		LABIAL		DENTAL			PALATOVELAR		GLOTTAL
		Bilabial	Labiodental	Interdental	Alveolar	Alveolo-palatal	Palatal	Velar	
Stops:	voiced	b			d			g	
	voiceless	p			t			k	
Fricatives:	voiced		v	ð(*thy*)	z	ž(*vision*)			
	voiceless		f	θ(*thigh*)	s	š(*shun*)			h
Affricates:	voiced					ǰ(*gem*)			
	voiceless					č(*chum*)			
Nasals:		m			n			ŋ(*sing*)	
Liquids:	lateral				l				
	retroflex				r				
Semivowels:		w					j(*yet*)	(w)	

MANNER OF ARTICULATION

THE CONSONANTS

Referring to the chart, we see that [p], [t], and [k] are voiceless stops (also called plosives and explosives), so designated because in their production an actual stoppage is made at a given point in the mouth and is then broken down by an explosion of breath with no accompanying vibrancy. But, if vibrancy is added to the articulations necessary to make these sounds, the resulting sounds are what are usually called voiced stops, [b], [d], and [g]. With stoppage at the lips, the result is [p] or [b]; hence these are called respectively the voiceless and voiced labial stops. With stoppage made by tongue against teeth (more accurately, at the point where the gums meet the teeth), the result is [t] or [d]; hence these sounds are called respectively the voiceless and voiced alveolar stops. With stoppage made against the velum, or soft palate, which may be discerned by running the tongue back along the roof of the mouth until it reaches that part which is soft and spongy, the result is [k] or [g]; hence these sounds are called respectively the voiceless and voiced velar stops. Both [k] and [g] have palatal (more forward) varieties, depending upon contiguous vowels, as in *kin* contrasted with *calm* and *give* contrasted with *gone,* but these subphonemic differences will be ignored where we are dealing with Modern English: one symbol for each is sufficient.

For those sounds called fricatives (or spirants), incomplete stoppage is made at corresponding positions, so that the air must "rub" (Lat. *fricāre*) its way through instead of breaking down a complete obstruction as with the stops. Velar fricatives were current in Old and Middle English, as they still are in German, for example German *Nacht* 'night.'[3] These had palatal allophones, occurring when the contiguous vowel was front (see the vowel chart below, p. 40), as, again in German, *nicht* 'not.' The voiceless fricative [h] can probably be best described, as it traditionally is, as a breathing. Although for the sake of convenience it is classified in the chart above as glottal, it has, as Hans Kurath points out, "as many positional allophones as the number of vowels and semivowels that can follow it."[4]

The voiced and voiceless affricates begin with articulation as if, respectively, for the stops [d] and [t], followed by, respectively, the fricatives [ž] and [š]. Some analysts in fact write them [dž] and [tš], but it is now more usual to regard them as unitary phonemes and write the first [ǰ] and the second [č].

---

[3] For the phonetic symbols used for representing the velar and palatal fricatives, see below, p. 106 n. 43.

[4] *A Phonology and Prosody of Modern English* (Ann Arbor, Mich., 1964), p. 66.

Those consonants articulated by obstructing the oral passage and letting the breath and voice flow through the nose are called nasals, namely the bilabial [m], with lips completely closed; the alveolar [n], with stoppage made at tooth-and-gum line; and the velar [ŋ], with stoppage made at velum. The nasals may by themselves form syllables, as in *open* [-pm] (where the labial [m] is the result of assimilation to the preceding labial [p]), *rotten* [-tn], and *bacon* [-kŋ] (where the velar [ŋ] is the result of assimilation to the preceding velar [k]). Since such words may be, and sometimes are, pronounced with an unstressed [ə] (for which see below, p. 45), we may regard the syllabic quality of the consonants as allophonic and write the final syllables as [-pən], [-tən], and [-kən]. (The assimilatory [m] and [ŋ] would not of course occur with an intervening vowel.) But it should be remembered that the intervening [ə] is often, and in some instances usually, nonexistent.

In the articulation of [l] and [r], breath and voice flow out at the sides of the tongue; the sounds are hence called liquids, and, like the nasals, may be syllabic, as in *ripple* [-pl] and *matter* [-tr]. For the reasons stated in regard to the syllabic nasals, we shall henceforth write such syllabic liquids [-əl] and [-ər]. The similarity in the articulation of [l] and [r] is indicated by their historical alternation, as in *Sarah-Sally, Katherine-Kathleen,* and in the related words *stella* (Latin), *astēr* (Greek), and *steorra* (Old English) 'star.' The principal allophones of *l* have been mentioned on page 31, above. Among the allophones of *r* are the fricative sound heard after [t], [d], and [θ], as in *true, drew,* and *threw,* and the tongue-flap occurring between vowels in Standard British English, as in *America, worry,* and *very.*[5] The usual description of the sound symbolized by *r* as retroflex ('bent back') refers to the position assumed by the tongue in its articulation.

Standard British English has no [r] before a consonant sound (as in *farm, far distances*) and in final position in an utterance (as in "The distance is far"); to put it in another way, in this type of speech [r] is pronounced only when a vowel follows in the same word (as in *daring*) or in one immediately following (the "linking *r*" as in *there is* and *far away*). This loss of [r], stemming from the folk speech of the eastern counties north of the Thames, occurs also in the speech of eastern New England, New York City, and much of the American coastal South. The speech of the last-named region frequently lacks linking *r* as well. Most American speech, however, preserves the sound under all conditions, as does the folk speech of the South and the West of Eng-

---

[5] Sometimes spelled "veddy" in caricatures of British speech.

land (see p. 263). An intrusive [r] occurs in the usage of a goodly percentage of the speakers of Standard British English,[6] as in *law*[r] *enforcement*. Essentially analogical with the etymological [r] which is retained before a word beginning with a vowel (linking *r*), this intrusive [r] is also common in eastern New England and New York City, but not in the South, where linking *r* is rare. An intrusive preconsonantal [r] occurs in western Pennsylvania and adjacent regions in *wash* and *Washington*.

Failure to understand that [r] is lacking before a consonant or in final position in Standard British English has led to American misunderstanding of such British spellings as *aren't I*, *'arf* (for Cockney *half*), and *Eeyore,* Christopher Robin's donkey companion,[7] and consequently of the instruction given by the London *Observer* that the Italian surname of Sir Harold Caccia, former British ambassador to the United States, should be "pronounced Catcher" (June 22, 1956, p. 7). Equally puzzling for one whose speech was not *r*-less would be the complaint of the *Evening Standard* that some people pronounce the latter part of Sophia Loren's first name in the English fashion, "to sound like fire" (September 15, 1956, p. 5).

Because of their vocalic quality, [w] and [j] are called semivowels. Many phonemicists write the symbols *w* and *y* (for the *j* usual with historical and comparative linguists) to indicate the transitional sounds in *plow, high,* and *boy*: thus, /plaw/, /hay/, /bɔy/. We shall here use [ʊ] and [ɪ] to indicate these off-glides — the vowel symbols used to indicate respectively the *u* of *put* and the *i* of *pit*.

THE SPELLING OF ENGLISH CONSONANT SOUNDS

Most of the spelling symbols for consonants are used in phonetic or phonemic writing with the values that these usually or exclusively have in ordinary writing. The illustrative words supplied below will

---

[6] G. B. Shaw, whose speech lacked this characteristic, deplores the intrusion, incorrectly associating it solely with the usage of the man in the street (in a singularly ill-informed preface which he wrote for R. A. Wilson's *The Miraculous Birth of Language* [London, 1941], p. 19). Shaw's example, equating *Maria Ann* with *Maria ran*, would be about as likely to occur in aristocratic as in common speech.

[7] In Standard British English, *an't*, a variant of *ain't*, is a homophone of *aren't* (and also of *aunt*). The *r* in *aren't I* is thus merely a spelling serving to indicate the quality of the vowel; the same quality is indicated by the *r* in *'arf*. *Eeyore,* which A. A. Milne could just as well have spelled *Eeyaw*, is what Cockney donkeys presumably say instead of *hee-haw*.

give some idea of the variety of ways in which our conventional spelling symbolizes the sounds of speech. What we think of as the normal or usual spellings are given first, in the various positions in which they occur (initially, medially, finally), followed by a semicolon. After the semicolon come spellings that are relatively rare, a few of them unique. The words cited to illustrate unusual spellings have been assembled not for the purpose of stocking an Old Curiosity Shop of English orthography or to encourage in any way the popular notion that our spelling is chaotic—which it is not—but to show the diversity of English spelling, a diversity for which, as we shall see in subsequent chapters, there are invariably historical reasons, including the errors of the learned. A few British pronunciations that are, or ought to be, of interest to educated Americans are included; these are labeled BE, for British English. Characteristically American pronunciations are labeled AE, for American English.

The Stops
[b] *bib, ruby, rabble, ebb, tribe; cupboard, bheesty*

[p] *pup, stupid, apple, ripe; Lapp, grippe, Clapham, hiccough*

[d] *dud, body, muddle, add, bride, seethed; bdellium, dhoti, Gandhi*

[t] *toot, booty, matter, butt, rate, hopped; cigarette, Thomas, ptomaine, receipt, debt, subtle, phthisic, indict, victuals, veldt*

[g] *gag, lager, laggard, egg; guess, vague, ghost, aghast, Haigh, mortgage, blackguard*

[k] *kit, naked, take, pick, mackerel, car, bacon, music; queer, piquet, queue, physique, trek* (*k* by itself in final position being rare), *chukker, chasm, machination, school, stomach, sacque, khaki*

The Fricatives
[v] *valve, over; Slav, Stephen, Ifor,* (sometimes) *schwa*

[f] *fife, if, raffle, off; soften, rough, toughen, phantom, sphinx, elephant, Ralph, Chekhov,* BE *lieutenant*

[ð] *then, either, eth, bathe; eisteddfod, ye*[8]

---

[8] See below, p. 60, for *ye*, more properly written *y^e* or with the *e* directly over the *y*.

[θ][9] *thin, ether, froth; phthalein, chthonian*

[z] *zoos, fizzle, fuzz, ooze, visage, phase; fez, possess, Quincy* (Mass.), *clothes,*[10] *xylophone, raspberry, czar*[11]

[s] *sis, pervasive, vise, passive, mass, cereal, acid, vice; sword, answer, scion, descent, evanesce, schism, psychology, Tucson, façade, isthmus*[12]

[ž][13] medially: *leisure, azure, delusion, equation;* initially and finally in a few recent borrowings from French: *genre* and *rouge;* the sound, not native to English, seems to be gaining ground, perhaps to some extent because of a smattering of school French, though the words in which it is new in English are not of French provenience, for instance, *adagio, rajah, Taj (Mahal),* and *cashmere*[14]

[š][15] *shush, marshal; chamois, machine, cache, martial, precious, tension, passion, fashion, sure, ocean, luscious, nausea, crescendo, fuchsia*[16]

[h] *ha, Mohawk; who,* school-Spanish *Don Quixote* (as "Donkey Hoty"), recent *junta* (though the word had since the seventeenth century been regarded as English and therefore pronounced with the beginning consonant and vowel of *junk*), *Mojave, gila*

---

[9] It would really be more appropriate to use þ to indicate this sound in a historical survey of the English language, in which the runic symbol is a traditional writing. It is in fact the symbol employed in the *Oxford English Dictionary,* in H. C. Wyld's *The Universal Dictionary of the English Language* (London, 1932), in Jespersen's *A Modern English Grammar on Historical Principles* (7 vols., Copenhagen, 1909–49), and in a good many other important works as well. But because of the general familiarity nowadays with θ for this value — a value which it never had in Classical Greek — I have chosen to use it here rather than be accused of a rage for singularity.

[10] As naturally pronounced by many, who thus distinguish it from the verb *clothes.* Speakers on the auditory mass media and other spelling-pronouncers pronounce noun and verb alike. Note the rime in Ophelia's song: "Then up he rose, & don'd his clothes" (*Hamlet* IV.v.52).

[11] The sequence [gz] is written *x* in *exalt* and *exist,* and *xh* in *exhaust* and *exhilarate.*

[12] The sequence [ks] is written *x* in *fix* and *exit, xe* in British English *axe.* The sequence [ts] is written *z* in *schizophrenia* and *Mozart, zz* in *mezzo* (also pronounced with [dz]).

[13] The International Phonetic Alphabet symbol is [ʒ].

[14] The sequence [gž] is written *x* in *luxurious.*

[15] IPA [ʃ].

[16] The sequence [kš] is written *x* in *luxury, xi* in *anxious,* and *cti* in *action.*

The Affricates

[ǰ]¹⁷ *judge, major, gem, regiment, George, surgeon, region, budget; exaggerate, raj, educate, grandeur, soldier, spinach, congratulate* (common on the networks, but regarded by many as nonstandard)

[č]¹⁸ *church, lecher, butcher, itch; Christian, niche, nature, cello, Czech,* BE *Marjoribanks* (a variant of *Marchbanks* and pronounced identically)

The Nasals

[m] *mum, clamor, summer, time; comb, plumber, solemn, government, paradigm,* BE *programme*

[n] *nun, honor, dine, inn, dinner; know, gnaw, sign, mnemonic, pneumonia*

[ŋ] *sing, wringer, finger, sink; tongue, handkerchief,* BE *charabanc,* BE *Altrincham,* BE *restaurant, Pago Pago*

The Liquids

[l] *lapel, felon, fellow, fell, hole; Lloyd, kiln, Miln(e)*¹⁹

[r] *rear, baron, barren, err, bare; write, rhetoric, bizarre, hemorrhage, catarrh*

The Semivowels

[w] *won, which;*²⁰ *languish, question, ouija, Oaxaca, huarache,* AE *Juan*²¹

[j]²² *yet, bullion; canyon, (La) Jolla,* BE *capercailzie* 'wood grouse,' BE *bouillon, jaeger, hallelujah,* [nj] *chignon,* [nj] *cañon*²³

THE VOWELS OF ENGLISH

Vowels, the principal sounds of syllables, occur either alone, as in *open* (in which the *o* makes the first syllable) or combined with con-

---

¹⁷ IPA [dʒ].

¹⁸ IPA [tʃ].

¹⁹ The *n* of *kiln* and *Miln(e)* ceased to be pronounced in Middle English times, but pronunciation with *n* is common nowadays because of the spelling.

²⁰ A fairly large, if decreasing, number of Americans have in *wh*-words not [w] but a voiceless sound written [w̥] or [ʍ] by phoneticians. Phonemicists write it /hw/.

²¹ In *one*, the initial [w] is not symbolized.

²² Because *y* was used exclusively as a vowel symbol in Old English, it is best to use here another symbol — that conventional in the the alphabet of the International Phonetic Association — for what is usually thought of as the "*y*-sound" in Modern English.

²³ For [ju], see [u], below, p. 46.

sonants (sounds which go with vowels, or sonants, to make syllables), as in *potent* (in which *o* is preceded by a consonant), or as in *portent* (in which the vowel symbolized by *o* is both preceded and followed by a consonant). In the vowel chart which follows, the vowels are shown according to the position of the tongue relative to the roof of the mouth (high, mid, low) and to the position of the highest part of the tongue (front, central, back). The chart may be taken to represent a cross section of the oral cavity, facing left.

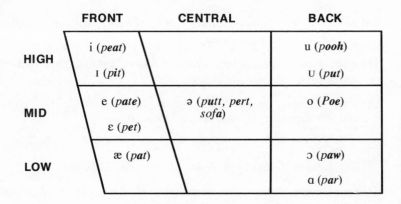

	FRONT	CENTRAL	BACK
HIGH	i (*peat*) ɪ (*pit*)		u (*pooh*) ʊ (*put*)
MID	e (*pate*) ɛ (*pet*)	ə (*putt, pert, sofa*)	o (*Poe*)
LOW	æ (*pat*)		ɔ (*paw*) ɑ (*par*)

It should be borne in mind that some of the tongue positions cited for vowels are only approximate, and that there may be a range between back and central for some of the nonfront vowels. And it is well to have in mind also the words of the great English phonetician Daniel Jones:

> It is difficult, though not impossible to describe a vowel-sound in writing in such a manner as to give the reader an idea of what it sounds like. The only way of doing this is to relate the unknown vowels to vowels already known to him. . . . People's vowels vary greatly, and a description based on the vowels presumed to be used in particular words may be correct for one reader, but is sure to be misleading for many others.[24]

For the reader not familiar with phonetic or phonemic transcription, it will be helpful to remember that some of the vowel symbols, specifically *a, e,* and *i,* do not represent the various sounds that they usually have in current English spelling, but rather, approximately those sounds that they represent in languages other than English using the Roman alphabet, for instance, French, Italian, and German. That is to

[24] *The Pronunciation of English,* 4th ed. (London, 1958), p. 18.

say, in transcribing Modern English words we must use [i] for that sound that is written *i* in other languages, but which, except for words recently borrowed by English from these other languages (for example *police*), is most frequently written *e, ee, ea, ie,* and *ei* in Modern English; and we shall use [e] for that sound which is usually written *a* (followed by a consonant plus "silent *e*") or *ai* in Modern English (as in *bate, bait*). English *o* and *u* frequently correspond to the *o* and *u* of other languages, in which case they are transcribed [o] and [u], as in *roll* [rol] and *rule* [rul]. *A* with its "Italian" value in the spelling of English words occurs before *r* and *lm;* in *father, mama, papa* and sometimes in *rather* (always in Standard British English); in certain types of American English after *w* (as in *watch*); and in post-eighteenth-century Standard British English in about 150 other common words in which an older vowel sound, preserved in American English, acquired this value when followed by a voiceless fricative other than [š] (by [s] in *grass, ask, last,* by [f] in *staff, half, laugh,* by [θ] in *bath*) or by [m] or [n] plus another consonant (*example, command, aunt, dance*). All these examples were pronounced in Standard British English during the seventeenth and eighteenth centuries precisely as in the speech of most Americans today. The forms *mammy* and *pappy* indicate older pronunciations of *mama* and *papa*.

Of the vowels listed above [i], [ɪ], [e], [ɛ], and [æ], because of the positions assumed by the tongue in their articulation, are classified as front vowels, and [u], [ʊ], [o], [ɔ], and [ɑ] as back vowels. Both series have been given in descending order, that is, in relation to the height of the tongue as indicated by the downward movement of the lower jaw in their articulation: thus [i] is the highest front vowel and [æ] the lowest, as [u] is the highest back vowel and [ɑ] the lowest. All the back vowels save [ɑ] and one front vowel, [y], which no longer occurs in English (see pp. 122–23), are pronounced with some degree of rounding of the lips and hence are called rounded vowels.[25] As regards the position of the body of the tongue, [ə] is central. The symbol is here used to represent the stressed central vowel of *putt* and *pert* as well as the unstressed central vowel of *sofa,* though it should be noted that some styles of transcription use [ə] only for the unstressed central vowel, representing the stressed central vowel by [ʌ] when no *r* follows (as in *putt*) and by [ɜ] before *r* (as in *pert*). In the writer's speech, un-

---

[25] Thus we may speak of *putt* (a variant of *put* used in the game of golf) as showing "unrounding" of the earlier vowel sound which survives in its variant. Compare, however, *put, full, bush,* all having rounded vowels, with *cut, gull, blush,* with later unrounding.

stressed [ə] is somewhat more front than the stressed vowel of *putt* and somewhat more back than that of *pert;* but such slight differences are for present purposes perhaps better ignored.

Not charted is [a], the vowel sound sometimes heard in eastern New England speech in *ask, half, laugh, path,* and the like; it is intermediate between [ɑ] and [æ], and is usually the first element of the so-called diphthongs in *right* and *rout,* which we shall write respectively as [aɪ] and [aʊ]. We shall have occasion to refer to it later as a phoneme of late Middle English.

In what is probably still the most familiar type of phonemic transcription for current English, as set forth by George L. Trager and Henry Lee Smith, Jr., in their *Outline of English Structure* (Norman, Okla., 1951), all tense vowels of current English are analyzed as diphthongs, or sequences of vowels and semivowels functioning as off-glides. In this system, for instance, /iy/, /ey/, /ow/, and /uw/ correspond to our [i], [e], [o], and [u] respectively. The nineteenth-century phoneticians, notably Henry Sweet, recorded the off-glides which they heard in such words as *beet, bait,* and *boat,* and Leonard Bloomfield in his ground-breaking *Language* (New York, 1933) also analyzed the long vowels as diphthongal. Kemp Malone in "The Phonemes of Current English," published in his *Studies in Heroic Legend and in Current Speech* (Copenhagen, 1959), points out, however, that "the distinctive feature is not the off-glide but the quality of the vowel and in fact we distinguish the vowels of *beat* and *bit* with ease by their difference in quality whether an off-glided allophone of the former vowel is used or not" (p. 239). It is no part of our present purpose to resolve the matter, even if it were possible to do so. Single symbols will serve that purpose best, except for those sounds traditionally called diphthongs — [aɪ] and [aʊ], referred to in the preceding paragraph, and [ɔɪ] (below, p. 48).

Some analysts, mostly British, write [i:] for our [i], the colon signifying length, and [i] for our [ɪ]; similarly [e:] for our [e] and [e] for our [ɛ], [u:] for our [u] and [u] for our [ʊ]. To do so has the advantage of reducing the number of vowel symbols in phonetic writing, but seems to imply, albeit unintentionally, that the vowels in question are distinguished primarily by length or lack of it rather than by their quality.

In most types of current English vowel length is hardly ever a distinguishing factor. We distinguish, for example, *bad* from *bat, bag* from *back,* and *lab* from *lap* not by the longer vowel in the first of each pair, but by the final consonants. Some speakers do indeed distinguish *can* 'to preserve in tins' from *can* 'to be able,' *halve* from *have, balm* from *bomb,* and *vary* from *very* by length in the vowel of the first of each pair.²⁶ Such distinctions need not concern us except for Old, Middle, and early Modern English, when vowel quantity was of considerably more importance.

THE SPELLING OF ENGLISH VOWEL SOUNDS

As with the consonants, words are supplied below to illustrate the various spellings of each vowel. There is nothing prescriptive implied in the illustrative words, all of which occur in Standard English with the vowel sound indicated, though some may have widespread alternative pronunciations. As with the consonant sounds, what may be thought of as ordinary, usual, or common spellings are cited first and set off from rare or unique spellings by a semicolon. It will be necessary to treat stressed [ɪ] and [ə] separately from the same sounds when unstressed.

The Front Vowels

[i] *evil, cede, meter, accretion, eel, lee, eat, sea; ceiling, lief, trio, police, people,* BE *geyser* 'gas water-heater,' *key, quay, Beauchamp, Aesop, Oedipus, Leigh,* BE *retch, camellia,*²⁷ BE (for the Cambridge college) *Caius* [kiz]

[ɪ] stressed: *it; English, sieve, renege, been, symbol, build, busy, women,* old-fashioned *teat*

before [r]: *mere, near, peer; pier, mirror, weird, lyric*

unstressed in initial syllables: *illume, elude; Aeneas, hysteria*

unstressed in medial syllables: *aerial, area; Israel, Ephraim, Nausicaa*²⁸

unstressed followed by a consonant in final syllables: *topic,*

²⁶ In the Southeastern American English described by James Sledd in his *A Short Introduction to English Grammar* (Chicago, 1959), *bulb* (with no [l]) is thus distinguished from *bub,* and similarly *burred* (no [r]) from *bud, stirred* (no [r]) from *stud.* (p. 51). In *r*-less speech, when [ɑ] occurs before etymological *r,* length may likewise be a distinguishing factor, for instance, *part* [pɑ̄t] and *pot* [pɑt].

²⁷ The last two cited words are exceptional in that the spelling *e* represents [i] rather than the expected [ɛ] before *tch* and before a double consonant symbol. Pronunciation of *retch* as [rɛč] based on the spelling – the only pronunciation current in America – is becoming increasingly common in England.

²⁸ Followed by another vowel, unstressed medial [ɪ] may alternate with [i] in different dialects. When no other vowel follows, [-ɪ-] and [-ə-] alternate in such words as *terrify, maximum, ceremony, telephone.* In American English [-ə-] is practically invariable in these and similar words.

bucket, college; mischief, forfeit, biscuit, minute (n.), *marriage, portrait, palace, lettuce, tortoise,* old-fashioned *Calais* [-ɪs],[29] *dactyl, Tyrwhitt,* some of which occur with [ə]

unstressed standing alone in final syllables: *body, honey; Macaulay, specie, Burleigh, Ralegh,* BE *Calais* [kǽlɪ], BE *café* [kǽfɪ], *recipe, guinea, coffee,* BE *ballet* [bǽlɪ]. *taxi,* BE *Beaulieu* [bjúlɪ], BE *Carew, challis, chamois*[30]

[e] *ape, basin, faint, gray; great, emir, fey, eh, Baal, rein, reign, maelstrom,* BE *gaol, gauge, weigh,* BE *Ralph,* BE *halfpenny, mesa, fete, chef (d'oeuvre), champagne, Montaigne;* alone in final syllables: AE *café, Iowa* (locally), *cachet, foyer, melee, Castlereagh*

[ɛ] *bet, threat;* BE *ate, again, says, many,* BE *Pall Mall, catch* (alternating with [æ]), *friend, heifer, Reynolds, leopard, eh, phlegm, aesthetic;* alternating with [æ] before [r] in American English: *bare, air, prayer, their; aeronaut*

[æ] *at; plaid, baa, ma'am, Spokane,* BE *The Mall* (London), *salmon, Cædmon,* AE *draught, meringue*

The Central Vowel

[ə] (schwa) stressed: *but; other, blood, does* (v.), *young, was* (alternating with [ɑ]), *pandit, uh, ugh, twopence;* before preconsonantal or final *r*[31]: *urge, erg, bird, earn; word, journal, masseur, myrrh*[32]

---

[29] As in the name of the town in Maine. Compare Browning's rime of *malice* with *Calais* in "De Gustibus."

[30] Many Americans use [i] in the final syllable of such words; others use a high central vowel that phoneticians write with a barred small capital *i* — thus, ɨ. In final position the unstressed vowel may in fact range from [ɪ] through various gradations to [i]; if followed by a consonant, as we have seen, it might be pronounced [ə]. Readers who feel that they have [i] in the final syllables of words like *Betty* and *taxi* should of course use that symbol in their transcriptions. Their pronunciation is widespread and is probably gaining ground.

[31] In "*r*-less" speech there would of course be no [r]; hence the use of the spelling symbol here and elsewhere when appropriate. In such speech the vowel may be transcribed [ə].

[32] In words that had earlier [ʊr] followed by a vowel, like *courage, worry, hurry, thorough,* Standard British English has a syllabic division different from that of most American English, as in [kə́-rij] in contrast to AE [kə́r-ij]. The Standard British English pronunciation is also current in Metropolitan New York and to a lesser extent in other parts of the Atlantic seaboard; the noncoastal American pronunciation is also current in British folk speech. See Hans Kurath and Raven I. McDavid, Jr., *The Pronunciation of English in the Atlantic States* (Ann Arbor, Mich., 1961), p. 127.

unstressed in initial syllables: *alone, elope* (alternating with [ɪ] and [i]), *molasses, sustain, authority; blancmange*

unstressed in medial syllables: *malady, remedy, ruminate, melody, syrupy, Aeschylus, Renaissance, limousine*[33]

unstressed standing alone in final syllables: *Cuba; Noah, Goethe, piano, borough, window, bureau, Edinburgh* [-brə],[34] and alternating with [ɪ] or [i] in *Cincinnati, Miami, Missouri*

unstressed in final syllables followed by a consonant other than *r: bias, lien, martin, melon, bonus, famous; Durham, foreign, Lincoln, Chisholm*

unstressed in initial syllables with *r* plus another consonant: *pervade, pursue*[35]

unstressed in medial syllables with *r* plus another consonant: *gabardine, haberdasher, importunity, bifurcate; avoirdupois*

unstressed in final syllables ending in *r: bursar, butter, actor; nadir, femur, glamour, Tourneur*

unstressed in final syllables with *r* plus another consonant: *coward, shepherd, Cranford, Rayburn; cupboard, Osbourne*

The final and preconsonantal [r] of most Americans is replaced by [ə] in *r*-less speech after [ɪ] as in *ear, beard;* after [ɛ] or [æ] as in *their, cairn;* after [ɔ] as in *for, form;* after [o] (for those who have this vowel in some words before [r]) as in *four, force;* after [ʊ] as in *tour, bourse* and [jʊ] as in *pure, cured;* after [aɪ] as in *ire, tired;* after [aʊ] as in *our, scoured;* and sometimes after [ɑ] as in *far, farm.*

An intrusive [ə] sometimes occurs between consonants in certain words, for instance between [l] and [m] in *elm, film,* [n] and [r] in *Henry,* [r] and [m] in *alarum* (an archaic variant of *alarm*), [s] and [m] in *Smyrna* (in the usual local pronunciation of New Smyrna Beach, Florida), [θ] and [r] in *arthritis,* and [θ] and [l] in *athlete.* The name of this phenomenon is *svarabhakti* (from Sanskrit), and such a vowel is called a svarabhakti vowel. If, however, one does not care to use so

---

[33] For the alternation of medial [ə], [ɪ], and [i] in some words, see above, p. 43, n. 28.
[34] In the last five words cited, [-ə] alternates with a rounded vowel resembling [ʊ], and in *piano, window, borough, bureau, widow, arrow, narrow,* and the like — particularly in younger-generation speech — with [o].
[35] In these words and those cited in the following sections, *r*-less speech has [ə] alone, in contrast to the [ər] of *r*-ish speech.

flamboyant a word, one can always fall back on *epenthesis (epenthetic)* or *anaptyxis (anaptyctic).* Perhaps it is just as well to say "intrusive schwa."

The Back Vowels

[u] *ooze, too, to, tomb, you, rude, rue, new; pooh, shoe, Cowper, boulevard, through, brougham, Bohun, fruit, Buhl,* nautical *leeward, Sioux, rheumatic, Devereux, lieutenant,*[36] *Leveson* [lúsən], *bouillon, rendezvous, ragout,* and alternating with [ʊ] in *room, roof,* and other words written with *oo*

Spellings other than with *o, oo,* and *ou* usually represent, or have represented, the sequence [ju], occurring after [b] (*bureau, beauty*), [p] (*pew, pure*), [g] (*gules, gewgaw*), [k] (*cue, queue, Kew*), [v] (*view*), [f] (*few, fuel, feud*), and [m] (*music, mew*). After other consonants there is considerable variation between [u] and [ju] — after [n] as in *nuclear, news,* and *neutral;* after [t] as in *tune* and *Teuton;* after [d] as in *dew* and *duty;* after [θ] as in *thew;* after [s] as in *sue* and *sewer;* and after [z] as in *resume.* After [č] and [ǰ], older [ju] is now quite rare. Many older-generation speakers have [ju] after [l] as in *lewd, lute.* Initially and after [h], the [j] is always present in the *o*-less words, as in *use, Europe, ewe, hue, hew, human,* and BE *Hulme* [hjum]. In its spelling the Scottish surname *Home* [hjum] must be regarded as exceptional.

[ʊ] *good, pull; wolf, could, Boer, Wodehouse, worsted* 'fabric'

[o] *go, rode, road, toe, tow, owe, oh; soul, brooch, folk, beau, chauffeur,* AE *cantaloupe, picot, though, yeoman, cologne, sew, cocoa, Pharaoh,* (military) *provost*[37]

[ɔ] *all, war, law, awe, cause, gone, or, oar, ore;*[38] *four, broad, talk,*

---

[36] British English has [lefténənt] for the army subaltern, but the naval officer is usually a [leténənt].

[37] Many persons in New England and the South, Canada, the English Midland, northern England, and Scotland have [o] before [r] in such words as *four, oar, ore,* and *door.* Such speakers distinguish *oar* and *ore* [or] from *or* [ɔr], *four* and *fore* from *for, hoarse* from *horse, mourn* from *morn, boarder* from *border,* and use [or] in words written *-oor* (though it is of course not implied that the writing has anything to do with the matter), for instance *door* and *floor.* The distinction of [or] and [ɔr] is a historical one, but is not maintained in Standard British English and in many types of American English, which have [ɔr] in all these words.

[38] But see the preceding footnote for *oar, ore, four,* and *door.*

ought, aught, door, Omaha, Utah, Arkansas, Mackinac, BE *Marlborough,* BE (for the Oxford college) *Magdalen* [módlɪn],[39] *Gloucester, Faulkner, Maugham, Strachan,* AE *reservoir,* (for many speakers) *sure*

[ɑ] *father, art, stop;*[40] *heart, sergeant, solder, ah, calm,*[41] *bureaucracy, baccarat, ennui, aunt,*[42] *kraal, soiree* ([wɑ], as also in other recent French loans written with *oi*)

Most of the words in which Standard British English has [ɑ] in contrast to American English [æ], a contrast alluded to above (p. 41), are listed in John S. Kenyon's *American Pronunciation,* 10th ed. (Ann Arbor, Mich., 1961), pp. 179–80.

American English shows considerable variation between [ɑ] and [ɔ]; in certain regions there may be no distinction between *naughty* and *knotty, auto* and *Otto, caller* and *collar.* All may have [ɑ], or all may have [ɔ]. Most types of American speech, however, have [ɔ] in the first of each pair, [ɑ] in the second. In some Southwestern American speech, such as that of Lyndon B. Johnson, [ɑ] occurs before [r] in *form* as well as in *farm,* in *or* as well as in *are.* Before [g], before [r] followed by a vowel, and after [w], [ɑ] and [ɔ] vary, as Hans Kurath says, "not only regionally, but from word to word."[43] A particular speaker may, for instance, have [ɔ] in *log, dog, fog,* but [ɑ] in *bog, cog, clog;* [ɔ] in *oral, sorority, florid, Cloris,* but [ɑ] in *moral, Dorothy, Florida, Doris;* and a similarly erratic distribution in words like *swan, watch, swamp,* and *wash.* Another speaker might have quite another distribution of the sounds in question.

[39] The name of the Cambridge college is written *Magdalene,* but is pronounced exactly the same.

[40] The [ɑ] is so-called short-*o* words like *got, stop, clock,* and *collar* prevails in American English. It would seem to be gaining ground in Standard British English, where the vowel in such words used to be exclusively a slightly rounded one similar to [ɔ] (the symbol used by many British phoneticians for it). My own observations regarding this change agree with those of C. K. Thomas, who notes the British use of the unrounded vowel in such words in his *An Introduction to the Phonetics of American English,* 2nd ed. (New York, 1958), p. 205.

[41] Because of the spelling, many Americans, mostly younger-generation ones, insert [l] in this word and others spelled *al,* for instance, *palm, psalm, balm,* and *alms.*

[42] Pronunciation of this word with [ɑ], though regarded by many as a mere affectation, is by no means uncommon in American English. It is of course usual in British English.

[43] *A Phonology and Prosody of Modern English* (Ann Arbor, Mich., 1961), p. 112.

The Diphthongs

[aɪ] *ride, hie, my, style, stile, dye; buy, I, eye, ay, aye, pi, night, height, isle, aisle, Geiger, Van Eyck, Van Dyck, kaiser, guile, maestro, choir*

[aʊ] *how, house; bough, Macleod, sauerkraut*

[ɔɪ] *oil, boy; buoy* (sometimes as [búɪ] in AE), *Reuters* (English news agency), *Boulogne, poi*

FURTHER COMMENTS ON TRANSCRIPTION

In the chapters on Old, Middle and early Modern English, where we shall have to deal specifically with vowel quantity, macrons will be placed over phonetic symbols as also for conventional spelling symbols to indicate vowel length. Where, in dealing with current English, we have no particular concern with vowel quantity, length will not be indicated:[44] the difference in quality between [u] and [ʊ] is usually all that need be noted; similarly with the qualitative difference between [e] and [ɛ], [i] and [ɪ], where the first member of each pair is pronounced with tongue tense, the second with tongue relatively lax, or slack.

In the occasional transcriptions of words in the following chapters, primary stress will be indicated (as it has already been indicated in a few instances) by the familiar rightward slanting accent marks over the appropriate vowel symbols; the same marks will be used for conventionally spelled words when stress is involved: thus, [sófə] or *sófa*, [əbáʊt] or *abóut*. For syllables bearing what is traditionally called secondary stress, but tertiary stress in the analysis of George L. Trager and Henry Lee Smith, Jr.,[45] the likewise familiar leftward slanting marks will be used: thus, [ɛ̀mənèt] or *émanàte*. What is in effect the reduced primary stress occurring in word groups and called secondary stress in Trager-Smith terminology may be indicated — though we shall have little need to do so — by a circumflex accent mark: thus, [əlɚ̂t pətról] or *alêrt patról,* [əndəmînɪšt vígər] or *ùndimînished vígor.* Such stress is relative; the cited words having it would in isolation be *alért* and *ùndimínished.* What we shall call unstressed syllables (those with "weak stress" in the Trager-Smith analysis) will not be marked in any way.

[44] On the matter of vowel length in current English, see above, pp. 42–43.
[45] *An Outline of English Structure* (Norman, Okla., 1951).

SOME CONCLUDING REMARKS
ON ENGLISH SPELLING

Old English used the symbols *a, e, i, o, u,* and the double symbol *æ* with approximately the values these had in the Latin alphabet at the time the English learned to write with that alphabet. The same holds roughly true for Middle English, which discontinued the use of *æ* and ascribed additional values to *e(e)* and *o(o),* to be treated below, pp. 160–62. It is not really until we come to Modern English times that we find such diversity of spellings for single sounds as has been illustrated by the many examples cited above. Some of the reasons for the present state of English spelling practices will be discussed in the next chapter.

III

Letters and Sounds
A Brief History of Writing

Writing, as we have seen, is a product of comparatively recent times. With it, history begins; without it, we must depend upon the archaeologist. The entire period during which men have been making conventionalized markings on stone, wood, clay, metal, parchment, paper, or any other surface to symbolize their speech is really no more than a moment in the vast period during which they have been combining vocal noises systematically for the purpose of communicating with each other.

IDEOGRAPHIC AND SYLLABIC WRITING

There can be no doubt that writing grew out of drawing, the wordless comic-strip type of drawing done by savage peoples. The American Indians made many such drawings. It is not surprising that certain conventions should have developed in them, such as horizontal and vertical lines on a chief's gravestone to indicate respectively the number of his campaigns and the number of wounds he received in the course of those campaigns,[1] or the lines rising from an eagle's head to indicate that the figure represents the chief of the eagle totem, in a "letter" from this chief to the president of the United States (represented as a white-faced man in a white house).[2] But such drawings,

[1] Cited in Holger Pedersen, *Linguistic Science in the Nineteenth Century,* trans. John Webster Spargo (Cambridge, Mass., 1931), p. 143.

[2] Reproduced in E. H. Sturtevant, *An Introduction to Linguistic Science* (New Haven, Conn., 1947), p. 20, from Henry R. Schoolcraft, *Historical and Statistical Information Respecting the Indian Tribes of the United States.* There are many excellent reproductions of such drawings in Chapter 2 ("Forerunners of Writing") of I. J. Gelb's *A Study of Writing,* 2nd ed. (Chicago, 1963), also available in paperback (Phoenix).

communicative as they may be in a narrow sense once one understands their conventions, give no idea of actual words. Any identity of wording in their interpretation would be purely coincidental. No line, no element, even remotely suggests speech sounds, and hence such drawings tell us nothing of the language of those who made them. When such use of symbols standing for ideas which can be pictured — rather than for the sounds which go to make up words — reaches a more or less wholly conventional stage, it becomes ideographic, like Chinese writing, in which every word has a symbol based not upon the phonetic structure of the word but upon its meaning.

Another method, fundamentally different, probably grew out of ideographic "writing": the use of the phonogram, which is concerned with sound rather than with meaning. Ultimately, by a sort of punning process, pictures came to be used as in a rebus — that is, as if we were to draw a picture of a tie to represent the first syllable of the word *tycoon* and of a coon to represent the second. In such a method we may see the beginnings of a syllabary, in which symbols, in time becoming so conventionalized as to be unrecognizable as actual pictures, are used to represent syllables.

FROM SEMITIC SYLLABARY
TO GREEK ALPHABET

Semitic writing, the basis of our own and indeed of all alphabetic writing, was not itself alphabetic; rather, it was a syllabary, using symbols for syllables consisting of a specific consonant plus any vowel. There were ways of indicating specific long vowels, but such devices were used sparingly and were actually syllabic symbols that ordinarily stood for syllables beginning with certain consonants. These symbols so used are called by scholars *matres lectionis* 'mothers of reading,' apparently a loan-translation from a Hebrew term. Since Semitic had certain consonantal sounds not found in other languages, the symbols for syllables beginning with these sounds were readily available for use as specific vowel symbols by the Greeks when they adopted for their own use the Semitic writing system, which they called Phoenician,[3] using even the Semitic names of the symbols, which they adapted to Greek phonetic patterns: thus *aleph* 'ox' and *beth* 'house' became *alpha* and *beta* because words ending in consonants (other than *n, r,* and *s*) are not in accord with Greek patterns. The fact that the Greeks used the Semitic names, which had no other meaning for them, is

---

[3] To the Greeks, all eastern non-Greeks were *Phoenices,* just as to the Anglo-Saxons all Scandinavians were *Dene* 'Danes.'

powerful evidence—if such were needed for what nobody doubts anyway—that the Greeks did indeed acquire their writing from the Semites, as they freely acknowledged having done. The order of the letters
and their highly similar forms are additional evidence of this fact.

The symbol A, which from our modern point of view the Semites
and the early Greeks drew lying on its side, indicated in Semitic a
syllable beginning with a glottal consonant which did not exist in Greek,
or for that matter in any other Indo-European language. Its Semitic
name was *'aleph,* the initial apostrophe here indicating the consonant
in question; and, because the name means 'ox,' it has been thought to
represent an ox's head, though interpreting many of the Semitic signs
as pictorial characters presents as yet insuperable difficulties.[4] By ignoring the initial Semitic consonant, the Greeks adapted this symbol as
a vowel, which, as we have seen, they called *alpha. Beth* was ultimately somewhat modified in form to B by the Greeks, who wrote it
and other reversible letters facing in either direction; in the early days
of writing they wrote from right to left as the Semitic peoples usually
did, and as Hebrew is still written.[5] From the Greek modifications of
the Semitic names of the first two letters, the word *alphabet,* as everyone knows, is ultimately derived.

THE GREEK VOWEL SYMBOLS

The brilliant Greek notion of using as vowel symbols those Semitic
syllabic symbols which began with non-Greek sounds gave them an
alphabet in the modern sense of the word.[6] Thus, Semitic *yod* became
iota (I) and was used for the Greek vowel *i;* at the time the symbol was
taken over, Greek had no need for the corresponding semivowel [j]
with which the Semitic word *yod* began. Just as they had changed *aleph*
into a vowel symbol by dropping the initial Semitic consonant, so also
the Greeks dropped the consonant of Semitic *he* and called it *epsilon*
(E), that is, *e psilon 'e* simple, or *e* without the aspirate.' Semitic *ayin,*

---

[4] See Gelb, pp. 140–41.

[5] Sometimes the early Greeks would change direction in alternate lines, starting, for
instance, at the right, then changing direction at the end of the line and going from left to
right, and continuing this change of direction throughout. Solon's laws were so written.
The Greeks had a word for the fashion—*boustrophedon* 'as the ox turns in plowing,' a
wondrous word indeed, which may even be used in English if one is skillful enough to
steer conversation in such a way as to make occasion for its use. Those who are fortunate
enough to find such occasion stress the first and third syllables (respectively [bu] or [baʊ]
and [fi]).

[6] The earliest writing in the Greek alphabet to come down to us is at least as old as the
eighth century B.C., perhaps somewhat older.

symbolizing a syllable beginning with a voiced pharyngeal fricative nonexistent in Greek, became for the Greeks *omicron* (O), that is, *o mikron* 'o little.' Semitic *heth* was at first used as a consonant and called *heta,* but the "rough breathing" sound which it symbolized was lost in several Greek dialects, notably the Ionic of Asia Minor, where the symbol was called *eta* (H) and used for long [e]. The vowel symbol *omega* (Ω), that is, *o mega* 'o big,' was a Greek innovation, as was also *upsilon* (Υ), that is, *u psilon* 'u simple.' *Upsilon* was born of the need for a symbol for a vowel sound corresponding to Semitic *waw,* which was used for the semivowel [w]. This sound was lost in Ionic, as also in other dialects, and *waw,* which came to be called *digamma* because it looked like one gamma on top of another (F), ceased to be used except as a numeral—but not before the Romans had taken it over and assigned a different value to it.

THE GREEK CONSONANT SYMBOLS

Practically all of the remaining Semitic symbols were used for the Greek consonants, the Semitic values of their first elements remaining for the most part unchanged; the same was true of their graphic forms.[7] *Gimel* became *gamma* (Γ), *daleth* became *delta* (Δ), and so on. The early Greek alphabet ended with *tau* (T). The consonant symbols *phi* (Φ), *chi* (X), and *psi* (Ψ) were later Greek additions.

THE ROMANS ADOPT THE GREEK ALPHABET

The Ionic alphabet, adopted at Athens, became the standard for the writing of Greek, but it was the somewhat different Western form of the alphabet which the Romans, perhaps by way of the Etruscans, were to adopt for their own use. The Romans used a curved form of *gamma* (C), the third letter, which at first had for them the same value [g] as for the Greeks but in time came to be used for [k]. Another symbol was thus needed for the [g] sound. This need was remedied in time by a simple modification in the shape of C, resulting in G: thus C and G are both derived from Greek Γ. The C was, however, sometimes used for both [g] and [k], a custom which survived in later times in such abbreviations as *C.* for *Gaius* and *Cn.* for *Gnaeus.*

Rounded forms of *delta* (D), *pi* (P), and *sigma* (S), as well as of

---

[7] A good idea of the shapes of the letters and the very slight modifications made by the early Greeks may be obtained from the charts in Gelb, p. 177, and Pedersen, p. 179. Gelb also gives the Latin forms, and Pedersen the highly similar Indian ones, Indian writings from the third century B.C. onward being inscribed in an alphabet adapted from the Semitic.

gamma, were used by the Romans. These were not Roman innovations; all of them occur in Greek also, though the more familiar Greek literary forms are angular (Δ, Π, and Σ). The occurrence of such rounded forms was doubtless due in early times to the use of pen and ink; the angular forms reflect the use of cutting tool on stone.

Epsilon (E) was adopted without change. The sixth position was filled by F, the Greek *digamma* (earlier *waw*). The Romans gave this symbol the value [f]. Following it came the modified *gamma,* G. H was used as a consonant, as in Semitic and also in Western Greek at the time the Romans adopted it.

The Roman gain in having a symbol for [h] was slight, for the aspirate was almost as unstable a sound in Latin as it is in Cockney English; ultimately, as in Greek, it was lost completely. Among the Romance languages—those derived from Latin, such as Italian, French, Spanish, and Portuguese—there is no need for the symbol, since there is no trace of the sound, though it may be retained in spelling because of conservatism, as in some French and Spanish words, for example French *heure* and Spanish *hora* 'hour' (but compare Fr. *avoir* with Sp. *haber* 'to have').

Iota (I) was for the Romans both semivowel and vowel, as illustrated respectively by the two *i*'s in *iudices*[8] 'judges,' the first syllable of which is like English *you;* the lengthened form of this letter, that is, *j,* did not appear until medieval times, when the minuscule form of writing developed.[9] The majuscule form of this newly shaped *i,* that is, J (for whose uses see pp. 61–62), is a product of modern times. *Kappa* (K) was used in only a few words by the Romans, who, as we have seen, had already ascribed to C the Greek value of this symbol. Next came the Western Greek form of *lambda,* L, corresponding to Ionic Λ. M and N, from *mu* and *nu,* require no comment. *Xi* (Ξ), with the value [ks], following Greek *nu,* was not taken over into Latin; thus in the Roman alphabet O immediately followed N. *Pi* (Π) having been adopted in its rounded form P, it was necessary for the Romans to use a tailed form of *rho* (P), as the early Greeks also had sometimes done, thus R. The symbol Q (*koppa*) stood for a sound which had dropped out of Greek, though the symbol continued to be used as a numeral in that language. The Romans used it as a variant of C in one position only, preceding V; thus, the sequence [kw] was written QV—the *qu* of printed texts. *Sigma* in its rounded form S was adopted unchanged. *Tau* (T) was like-

[8] Because of our primary concern with writing in this chapter, the familiar editorial macrons (as for the long *u* in this word) will not be used in any cited words.
[9] In ancient writing only majuscules (capital letters) were used.

wise unchanged. *Upsilon* was adopted in the form V and used for both consonant ([w], later [v]) and vowel ([u], [ʊ]).

The symbol Z (Greek *zeta*), which had occupied seventh place in the early Roman alphabet but had become quite useless in Latin because of rhotacism (see p. 108, n. 46), was reintroduced and placed at the end of the alphabet in the time of Cicero, when a number of Greek words were coming to be used in Latin. Another form of *upsilon*, Y, was used in such words to indicate the Greek vowel sound, which was like French *u* and German *ü*. *Chi* (X) was used with the Western Greek value [ks], the sound of Ionic X being represented in Classical Latin by CH, just as TH and PH were used to represent Greek *theta* (Θ) and *phi* (Φ) respectively. Actually these were accurate enough representations of the Classical Greek sounds, which most scholars agree were similar to the aspirated initial sounds of English *kin, tin,* and *pin.* The Romans in their transcriptions very sensibly symbolized the aspiration, or breath-puff, by H. The sounds symbolized in Latin by C, T, and P apparently lacked such aspiration, as *k, t,* and *p* do in English when preceded by *s,* for example, *skin, sting,* and *spin.*

LATER DEVELOPMENTS OF THE ROMAN AND GREEK ALPHABETS

Even though it lacked a good many symbols for sounds in the modern languages of Europe, the Roman alphabet was taken over by the various European peoples, though not by those Slavic peoples who in the ninth century got their alphabet, called Cyrillic from the Greek missionary leader Cyril, direct from the Greek. The Greek missionaries, sent out from Byzantium, added a number of symbols for sounds which were not in Greek, for example Ш for [š]. B was used for [v], which sound the symbol also symbolized in some positions in Greek; a modification, Б, was used for [b]. *Sigma* was written C in later Greek, and C has thus the value [s] in the writing of those Slavic peoples — the Russians, the Bulgarians, and the Serbs — who use this alphabet. Those Slavs whose Christianity stems from Rome — the Poles, the Czechs, the Slovaks, the Croats, and the Slovenians — use the Roman alphabet, adapted by diacritical markings (for example Polish *ć* and Czech *č*) and by combinations of letters (for example Polish *cz, sz*) to symbolize sounds for which the Roman alphabet naturally made no provision.

THE USE OF DIACRITICAL MARKINGS

In various ways the Roman alphabet has been eked out by those who have adopted it. Such un-Latin sounds as the *o*-umlaut and the *u*-umlaut of German are written *ö* and *ü;* as we have seen, Y had been borrowed by the Romans from the Greeks for the sound indicated by the latter. The *ä* as now pronounced does not differ from the sound indicated in German by *e;* for instance, *Bäder* 'baths' and *geben* 'to give,' which have the same long vowel; and *Hände* 'hands' and *senden* 'to send,' which have the corresponding short one. Other languages also use the dieresis — the superposed dots — to indicate vowel quality: Danish, Icelandic, Norwegian, Swedish, Slovak, Albanian (*ë* only), and, among the non-Indo-European languages, Estonian, Finnish, Hungarian, and Turkish. Its occasional use in old-fashioned English spellings like *preëminent* and French words like *Noël* is for quite a different purpose — to indicate that two adjacent vowel symbols represent separate sounds.

Other expedients are the acute accent marks of French *é*, of Czech and Icelandic *á, é, í, ó, ú,* and *ý,* of Hungarian *á, é, í, ó,* and *ú* (with double acute accent marks for *ő* and *ű* also), and of Polish *ó, ć, ń, ś,* and *ź;*[10] the grave accent marks of French *à* and *è;* the circumflex accent marks in French *â, ê, î, ô,* and *û* and Rumanian *â* and *î;* the wedge (*hacek*) of *ě; č; ň, ř, š,* and *ž* in Czech; the tilde of Portuguese *ã* and *õ*[11] and of Spanish *ñ;* the cedilla of French, Portuguese, and Turkish *ç* (in Turkish it symbolizes [č]); the bar of Polish *ł;* and the circle of Swedish and Norwegian *å* and Czech *ů.* There are still other, less familiar diacritical markings. Lithuanian makes very free use of such devices.

THE USE OF DIGRAPHS

Digraphs (pairs of letters to represent single sounds), or even longer sequences like German *sch,* have also been made use of to indicate un-Latin sounds, such as those which we spell *sh, ch, th,* and *dg.* In *gu,* as in *guest* and *guilt,* the *u* has the sole function of indicating that the *g* stands for [g] of *go* rather than the [j] that we might expect it to represent before *e* or *i,* as in *gesture* and *gibe.* The *h* of *gh* performs a similar useful function in *Ghent,* but not in *ghost* and *ghastly.* English makes no use of diacritical marks save for the rare dieresis, preferring other devices such as the aforementioned use of digraphs and of entirely different symbols for mutated (umlauted) vowels: for example

[10] Acute accent marks are also used in Spanish, but only to indicate stress where it might otherwise be in question; they do not indicate either the quality or the quantity (relative length) of the vowels which they are placed above.

[11] To indicate nasal vowels. For the same purpose Polish uses a hook under the vowel symbol (ą, ę); so does Lithuanian, for purely historical reasons, inasmuch as the nasalization has been lost in that language. French uses no special marking for this purpose.

English writes *man, men;* compare the German method of indicating the same vowel change in *Mann, Männer.*

ADDITIONAL SYMBOLS

Furthermore, as has been noted in the case of the Cyrillic alphabet, other symbols have been used, such as the runic þ (called *thorn*) and ƿ (called *wynn*) used by the English, along with their modification of *d* as ð (called *eth*), all now abandoned as far as English writing is concerned. The þ and the ð were adopted by the Scandinavians, who got the alphabet from the English. They used the former symbol at the beginning of a word, where it indicated the voiceless fricative [θ], and the latter in all other positions, where it indicated the voiced fricative [ð]. Subsequently the first of these sounds became [t] (or [d] in words regularly lacking stress such as pronouns and definite articles) except in Icelandic, which alone uses þ. In modern times ð came to be written *d* by the Scandinavians, but Icelandic reintroduced ð in the nineteenth century.

The ligature *œ,* which indicated a single vowel sound in post-Classical Latin, was used in early Old English for the *o*-umlaut sound (as in German *schön*). When this sound was later unrounded, there was no further need for *œ* in English. It was, however, taken over by the Scandinavians, who have long since given up the symbol, the Danes having devised ø and the Swedes using ö. It has been used in English in a few classical loan-words, for instance, *amœba* and *cœnobite,* more recently written with unligatured *oe* in British English. (American usage has simple *e* in these words, but retains unligatured *oe* as a transliteration of Greek *oi* in *coelom, coelacanth* and for Latin *oe* in *coelostat.*)

For the vowel sound of *cat,* the English used the digraph *ae,* later written prevailingly as a ligature — that is, as *æ,* the symbol used for the same sound in the alphabet of the International Phonetic Association. This digraph they also got from Latin, in which the classical value (as in German *Kaiser,* from *Caesar*) had long before shifted to a vowel sound roughly similar in value to that which the English ascribed to it. The *æ* was called *æsc* 'ash,' the name of the runic symbol which represented the same sound, though it in no way resembled the Latin-English digraph. In Middle English times, beginning around 1100, the symbol went out of use. Today *æ* is used in Danish, Norwegian, and Icelandic. It occurs occasionally, with a quite different value, in loan-words of classical origin, like *encyclopædia* and *anæmia,* spelled *encyclopedia* and *anemia* in current American usage. (British English now usually has unligatured *ae* in such words.)[12]

THE GERMANIC RUNES

In the early Middle Ages various script styles — the "national hands" — developed in those lands which had been provinces of the Roman Empire. But Latin writing, as well as the Latin tongue, all but disappeared in the Roman colony of Britannia, which the Romans had perforce practically abandoned even before the arrival of the English. These Germanic invaders of a land whose population was predominantly Celtic had available to them when they wished to write, which was certainly not very often, the twenty-four runes, to which they added six. These runes, in the beginning associated with pagan mysteries — the word *rune* means 'secret' — were angular letters intended originally to be cut or scratched in wood[13] and, though perhaps ill adapted to any sustained composition, served well enough for inscriptions, charms, and the like. Their close similarities to both Greek and Latin symbols make it obvious that, though the order of the symbols is quite different,[14] they are derived from the Roman alphabet, with which the Germanic peoples could easily have acquired familiarity, or from some early Italic alphabet akin to the Roman alphabet.

THE EARLIEST ENGLISH WRITING

Although St. Augustine and his Roman missionaries must have written the sixth-century Italian script, this hand never established itself in England. The script used in the Old English manuscripts is based upon the Irish modification of the Roman alphabet. This so-called Insular hand was used for English writings until the Norman Conquest. It is generally accepted that the Irish, whose conversion to Christianity antedated that of the English, taught the English how to write. The Insular hand is still used in the writing of Irish Gaelic.

To read Old English in the Insular hand of the manuscripts requires little adjustment for the modern student, once he becomes accustomed

[12] The ligature still occurs, for understandably traditional reasons, on the spine and title page of the *Encyclopædia Britannica,* though unligatured *ae* is used in the article "Encyclopaedia."

[13] The word *write* is akin to the German word *reissen* 'to tear.' *Book* is generally thought to be related to *beech.* It has been plausibly suggested that the runes were originally scratched, cut, or torn in strips of beechwood or in the bark of beech trees.

[14] As modified by the English, the first group of letters consists of characters corresponding to *f, u, þ, o, r, c, g,* and *w.* The English runic "alphabet" is sometimes called *futhorc* from the first six of these.

to the aforementioned *æsc*, the peculiar forms of *f*, *g*, and *r*, the *eth*, the runes called *thorn* and *wynn*, and the three forms of *s*, one of which, called "long *s*," looks very much like an *f* in modern typography except that the horizontal stroke does not go through the top of the letter. This particular variant of *s* (ſ) was used until the end of the eighteenth century save in final position, printers following what was the general practice of the manuscripts. It is illustrated in this book only in the chapter "Rosemary" quoted from Banckes's *Herball* and the passage from *1 Henry IV* (taken from the First Folio) in Chapter VII. Elsewhere, in briefer quotations and citations of words, *s* has been substituted for it.

THE LATER FATE OF THORN, ETH, AND WYNN

The earliest English texts—those written before 900—used the digraph *th* instead of *þ*. Toward the end of the Middle English period, around 1400, the same digraph—the Roman transliteration of *theta*—was gradually reintroduced, and English printers regularized its use instead of the single symbol which for centuries had supplanted it. Similarly, *u* and *uu*, used for [w] in early manuscripts, were supplanted by *ƿ*, which continued in use for a long time, though not quite so long as *þ*. The earlier English symbol, *uu*, had in the meantime been adopted on the Continent, whence it was brought back to England by Norman scribes in a ligatured form as *w*. The origin of this symbol is accurately indicated by its name, *double-u*.

The *þ* was used in Old English for both the initial sound of *thin* and that of *thine*. Even before the introduction of *þ*, the English had crossed the Irish *d*, presumably to represent the second of these sounds, though actually they used the symbol to represent precisely the same two sounds for which they used first *th*, then *þ*. From a phonetic point of view, it would have made excellent sense to use *þ* exclusively for the first of these sounds and to write the *ð* within words to indicate the second, which never occurred initially or finally in Old English;[15] but to do so would hardly have occurred to our ancestors, to whom the two sounds were merely positional variants of a single sound. Even so, the situation was not really so bad—again from a phonetic point of view—as the modern use of the single digraph *th* for no fewer than three different sounds, as in *thin*, *thine*, and *thyme* (traditionally pronounced

---

[15] It occurs initially in current English only in *the, this, that, these, those, they, their(s), them, then, there, though, than, thus,* the more or less archaic *thou, thee, thy, thine,* and the more or less literary *thence* and *thither. Thither* is also very frequently pronounced— usually in reading aloud, for the word can hardly be regarded as current in spoken English—with the initial sound of *thin.*

[taɪm], though a new pronunciation based on the spelling is occasionally heard, mainly from younger-generation speakers). The *ð* gradually disappeared during the Middle English period, but *þ,* as we have seen, continued in use until the very end of the Middle Ages.

In a few words *y* (which *þ* in its later form had come to resemble) was used as a representation of *þ;* for example *y*ᵗ or *ẏ* was used as an abbreviation for *that*[16] and *y*ᵉ or *ẏ* for *the.* The latter abbreviation survives to our own day in such pseudoantique absurdities as "Ye Olde Choppe Suey Shoppe," in which it is usually pronounced as if it were the same word as the old nominative second person plural pronoun *ye.* Needless to say at this point, there is no justification whatever for such a pronunciation. The two words were carefully distinguished, and would have been even had they been printed identically. The fact is, however, that they were also carefully distinguished in printing, as in writing, by the superior *e,* either following the *y* or directly over it, for the definite article. Though *y*ᵗ or *ẏ* could hardly be read as any other word, it too was always written with the superior *t.*

YOGH

The Old English symbol *ʒ* was an Irish form; *g* entered the English alphabet later from the Continent. In late Old English *ʒ* had three values, as we shall see (pp. 124–25). In Middle English times it acquired a somewhat different form, *ʒ* (called *yogh*),[17] and was used for two sounds that came to be spelled *y* and *gh* later in the period. Old English, for instance, wrote *ʒeldan* 'to yield,' *cniht* 'knight,' and *þurh* 'through'; early Middle English wrote the same words *ʒelde(n), cniʒt,* and *þurʒ;* later Middle English (as in Chaucer) wrote them *yelde(n), knyght,* and *thurgh.*[18] The characteristic conservatism of Modern English spelling is reflected in our retention of the *gh* in writing, though the earlier phonetic symbolism of this digraph (the same as that of *ch* in German) has been lost in all types of English save Scots for so long that the modern speaker of English must laboriously learn how to articulate

---

[16] Old English used a crossed *thorn* as an abbreviation of the same word.

[17] This symbol, which continued to be written in Scotland long after the English had given it up, has been mistaken for *z* — the symbol which printers, having no *ʒ* in their fonts, used for it — as in the pronunciation of the names *Kenzie* (compare *Kenny,* with revised spelling to indicate a pronunciation somewhat closer to the historical one) and *Menzies.* For other examples of this erroneous interpretation of *ʒ* as *z,* see Otto Jespersen, *A Modern English Grammar on Historical Principles* (Copenhagen, 1909–49), I, 22–23.

[18] Note that one of the two sounds written in early Middle English with *yogh* was in Old English written not with the earlier form of that letter, but with *h.* Later these different sounds were differentiated in writing, as they had been in Old English.

the sound in question when he studies German. Nevertheless, we go on writing words which once contained the sound just as if it had survived, and such sensible spellings as *tho, thru,* and *nite* meet with widespread disapproval.

After the Norman Conquest, the French form *g* supplanted Old English ȝ to indicate [g] in English words; and, with the introduction of French words into English, the newer symbol was used also with the value which it had in Old French before *e* and *i,* for instance *gem* and *age* — the same value that it has in Modern English. Modern English thus preserves in loan-words what was formerly the French value of *g* when followed by *e* or *i;* in Modern French the older sound has become that of the final consonant of *rouge,* or the medial sound of English *measure.* No native English words, incidentally, begin with this older sound. It occurs initially only in loan-words, for example *gentle* and *juggle* (Old French), *generate*[19] and *judicial* (Latin). In Latin, as we have seen (p. 54), the letter *i* was used both as vowel and as semivowel. It was only as the Romance languages developed from Latin, however, that there came to be a really sharp differentiation in the pronunciation of these two sounds, the semivowel coming to acquire the sound preserved initially in such loan-words as *judge* (from OF *iuge,* ultimately Lat. *iudex*) — that is, a sound identical with that of the final consonant [j] of the same word. Hence the identity of sound indicated by *j* (which, as we have seen, was merely another way of writing *i*) and *g* before *e* and *i.*

THE USE OF J
When the prolonged and curved *i* — that is, the *j* — came into being, it was used merely as a variant of *i* in final position, especially when preceded by another *i,* as in Latin *filii.* The dot, incidentally, was not originally part of minuscule *i,* but is a development of the faint sloping line which came to be put above this insignificant letter to distinguish it from the strokes of contiguous letters such as *m, n,* and *u,* as well as to distinguish double *i* from *u.* It was later extended by analogy to the *j,* where, because of the different shape of the letter, it performed no useful purpose. Since English scribes used *y* for *i* in final position,[20] the use of *j* in English was long more or less confined to the representation of numerals, for instance *iij* for *three* and *vij* for *seven.*

---

[19] Note that we pronounce the *g* before *e* and *i* in Latin loan-words (and before *y* in those which are ultimately Greek, like *gymnasium*) in the Old French way, as we also pronounce the name of the letter itself. The Romans pronounced the name of the letter *gay,* the initial sound of which indicates its only value in Classical Latin.

[20] Compare *marry* with *marries* and *married; holy day* with *holiday.*

The present use of *i* for vowel and *j* for consonant was not established until the seventeenth century. In the King James Bible (1611) and the First Folio (1623) of Shakespeare, for instance, *i* is used for both values; see, for instance, the passage from the First Folio at the end of Chapter VII, in which Falstaff's first name occurs as *Iack*.[21] For a long time after the distinction in writing was made, however, the feeling persisted that *i* and *j* were one and the same letter: Dr. Johnson's *Dictionary* (1755) puts them together, and this practice continued well into the nineteenth century.

THE USES OF U AND V

It was similar with the curved and angular forms of *u* — that is, *u* and *v*. Although consonantal and vocalic *u* came in Latin to be sharply differentiated in sound early in the Christian Era, when consonantal *u*, hitherto pronounced [w], became [v], the two symbols *u* and *v* continued to be used more or less indiscriminately for either vowel or consonant. When *v* came to be used in English in Middle English times, the scribes followed the Continental practice of using either symbol for either value; as a general thing, though, *v* was used initially and *u* elsewhere, regardless of the sound indicated, as in *very, vsury* (*usury*), and *euer* (*ever*), except in the neighborhood of *m* and *n,* where for the sake of legibility *v* was frequently used in other than initial position for the vowel. Continental printers in time came to use *v* and *u* for consonant and vowel respectively, and before the middle of the seventeenth century English printers were generally making the same distinction. As with *i* and *j,* catalogues, indexes, and the like put *u* and *v* together well into the nineteenth century; in dictionaries *vizier* was followed by *ulcer, unzoned* by *vocable,* and *iambic* was set between *jamb* and *jangle.* Many editions of old texts, particularly those used in schools, substitute *j* and *v* for *i* and *u* when these indicate consonants, and *u* for initial *v* when this indicates a vowel, representing, for example, *iaspre, liue,* and *vnder* as *jaspre* 'jasper,' *live,* and *under.* Except for the two extended passages reproduced in Chapter VII, this practice will here be followed when older writers are cited, as also for citations of individual words from older periods. The matter is purely graphic; no question of linguistic evidence is involved.

The consonant sound [v] did not occur initially in Old English, or,

---

[21] Everywhere else the use of *i* and *j,* like that of *u* and *v* to be discussed immediately below, will be made to conform to present practice.

for that matter, in any other Germanic language in its oldest form.[22] Old English used *f* for the [v] which developed internally, as in *drifen* 'driven,' *hæfde* 'had,' and *scofl* 'shovel.' Except for a very few words which have entered Standard English from Southern English dialects, in which initial [f] became [v] — for instance *vixen,* the feminine of *vox* 'fox' — no Standard English words of native origin begin with [v]. Practically all our words with initial *v* have been taken from Latin or French. No matter how familiar such words as *vulgar* (Latin), *vocal* (Latin), *very* (French), and *voice* (French) may be to us now, they were once regarded as foreign words — as indeed they are, despite their long naturalization. The introduction of the letter *v* (that is, *u*) to indicate the prehistoric Old English development of [f] to [v] was an innovation of Anglo-Norman scribes in Middle English times: thus the Middle English form of Old English *drifen* was written *driven* (that is, *driuen*).

OTHER ROMAN CONSONANT SYMBOLS
IN ENGLISH

B, d, h, k, l, m, n, p, r, s, t, and *x* ([ks]) have been used throughout the history of the Roman alphabet to represent the same (or in some instances approximately the same) sounds which they symbolize in English today, though it should be remembered that the breathing originally indicated by Latin *h* was lost in Latin (see p. 54) and that hence the symbol has no phonetic significance in those Latin-derived languages which retain it here and there in their spelling.[23] Its use to indicate the aspirate in English (and the other Germanic languages as well) is due to scholarly tradition, for the aspirate had been lost in Latin long before the Germanic peoples learned to write.

The later influence of Classical Latin caused French scribes to restore the *h* in many words, for instance *habit, herbage,* and *homme,* though it was of course never pronounced. It was also sometimes inserted in English words of French origin where it was not etymological, for instance *habundance* (mistakenly regarded as coming from *habere* 'to have') and *abhominable* (supposed to be from Lat. *ab* plus *homine,*

---

[22] In Modern German the letter *v* regularly occurs in initial position as a writing for [f], for instance *Vater* 'father.' German [v] in initial position is a late medieval development from [w], as the retention of *w* in the spelling indicates, for instance *Weg* 'way.'

[23] Portuguese uses *h* purely as a diacritic in the combinations *lh* and *nh,* symbolizing the sounds which Spanish has chosen to indicate by *ll* and *ñ* and Italian by *gl* and *gn* respectively, for example Latin *filius* 'son,' Portuguese *filho,* Italian *figlio.* Spanish, French, Italian, and Portuguese all use *ch,* with differing values.

explained as 'away from man, hence bestial'). When Shakespeare's pedant Holofernes by implication recommended this latter misspelling and consequent mispronunciation with [h] in *Love's Labour's Lost* V.i.26 ("This is abhominable, which he would call abbominable"),[24] he was in very good company, at least as far as the writing of the word is concerned, for the error had been current since Middle English times. Writers of Medieval Latin and Old French were similarly misled by a false notion of the etymology of the word. Because of the influence of writing, *h* has gradually come to be pronounced in all English loanwords from French except *honor, honest, hour,* and *heir.* Pronunciation of *herb* without [h] is, however, still usual in American English; less usual, though by no means uncommon in American usage, is omission of [h] in *humble* — a pronunciation regarded by Dickens as old-fashioned, not to say vulgar, in the British speech of his day, otherwise there would have been no point in his indicating Uriah Heep's pronunciation of the word as *'umble.* In *humor,* present usage wavers; pronunciation of this word without [h] is certainly commoner in educated American speech than in Standard British English.

Names in *H-* from the classical languages were somewhat more familiar in Middle English times in their French than in their classical forms; Chaucer, for instance, has *Omer, Ector, Ercules,* and *Eleyne,* along with such inverted spellings as *Habradate* (for *Abradates*) and *Helie* (*Eli*) — the last of Hebrew origin — indicating equally well that [h] was not pronounced in such words. The classical forms, with *H* written and pronounced wherever called for by the classical etymology, became much more usual after the Renaissance, though *Ector* and *Omer,* which looks deceptively Mohammedan when spelled *Omar* (as in the name of General Omar Bradley, born in Missouri), survive in the southern American hill country and the areas settled therefrom. It is not surprising that those lowland Scotsmen who colonized the "King's plantation" in Ulster and whose descendants crossed the Atlantic and settled the Blue Ridge, the Appalachians, and the Ozarks should have been little affected by the classical culture of the Renaissance. *Ellen* survives in all parts of the English-speaking world; it is thought of not as a variant of *Helen,* but as a separate name.

---

[24] This (with correction of an obvious printer's error) and all other quotations from Shakespeare's plays are from the First Folio (facsimile ed., London, 1910) with the line numbering of the *Globe* edition (1891) as given in Bartlett's *Concordance.* Roman type will be substituted for the annoying italic used for proper names occurring in speeches in the Folio, except for one instance in the passage cited on pp. 193–94.

UNETYMOLOGICAL H AFTER T

During the Renaissance *h* was inserted after *t* in a number of foreign words, for instance *throne*, from Old French *trone*. The French word is from Latin *thronus*, borrowed from Greek, the *th* being, as we have seen (p. 55), the normal Roman transliteration of Greek θ. The English respelling ultimately gave rise to a change in the initial sound, as also in *theater* and *thesis*, which earlier had initial [t]; similarly with the internal consonant sound spelled *th* in *anthem, apothecary, Catherine* (the pet forms *Kate* and *Kit* preserve the older sound), and *Anthony* (compare *Tony*), which to a large extent has retained its historically correct pronunciation in British, but not in American, English. The only American pronunciation of *Anthony* is precisely parallel with the universal English pronunciation of *anthem* and the other words cited. It is sometimes heard even in reference to Mark Antony, where the spelling does not encourage it. The *h* of *author*, from Old French *autor* (modern *auteur*), going back to Latin *auctor*, was first inserted by French scribes, to whom an *h* after *t* indicated no difference in pronunciation. When in the sixteenth century this fancy spelling began to be used in the English loan-word, the way was paved for the modern pronunciation, historically a mispronunciation. It was almost inevitable, in the light of the slavish subservience which even partially literate people show toward writing, that the *th* should be given a value which it has in native words which were written with *þ* in Old and Middle English. *Elizabeth, Arthur,* and *Dorothy* were formerly pronounced with [t], as the pet names *Betty, Art,* and *Dot* indicate. *Thomas* and *Theresa* have remained unaffected by their spellings; a spelling pronunciation of *Esther* is occasionally heard from the half-educated, but not from either cultured or illiterate speakers. *Thames* as the name of an estuary in Connecticut is frequently pronounced as the spelling seems to indicate it should be. Such is the effect of literacy divorced from tradition. But, as we have seen, the same thing has happened many times in the history of English, and is in no wise indicative of a particularly American form of linguistic depravity. In *Waltham,* for instance, the *t* and the *h* are in different syllables from a historical point of view, the *-ham* being from Old English *ham* 'home, village.' The two symbols have, however, been mistakenly regarded by people familiar with spelling — not by illiterates, we may be sure — as equivalent to the digraph *th;* hence, on both sides of the Atlantic, frequent pronunciation of this word with medial [θ] — just as if one were to pronounce *courthouse* as [kɔ́rθàʊs]. *Gotham*, when used as a nickname for New York City, is invariably pronounced with the same medial consonant, though in British English, as the name of a town in Nottinghamshire, it continues to be pronounced [gótəm]. *Chatham,* which is parallel in structure, usually has medial [t], though there is an overcareful American pronunciation as *chat-ham* doubtless regarded as an educated improvement upon [čǽtəm].[25]

THE DIGRAPH PH

H after *p,* according to Latin custom (see p. 55), was used in a good many English words of Greek origin to indicate the post-Classical value of φ in Greek, as well as replacing *f* in a few words not from Greek, for instance the proper name *Ralph,* previously and still to a large extent in England pronounced to rime with *waif*.[26] (The *l* is also mere window-dressing from a historical point of view.) Ordinarily, however, *ph* indicates genuine Greek origin.

THE DIGRAPH CH

H after *c* was used by French scribes, or by English ones under French influence, to indicate the initial sound of *child* (OE *cild*) in all words regardless of their origin; following a short vowel the trigraph *cch* (supplanting earlier *chch*) was commonly used in Middle English times—*catch* appears as *cache, cacche,* and *cachche*—but *tch* had come to be usual under the same circumstances by the sixteenth century. *Ch* was also, as we have seen, a transliteration of Greek *chi* (X), pronounced [k] in *chorus, machination,* and the like, and was sometimes inserted under classical influence in words where it did not belong, for example *schedule* (from OF *cedule*), for which Noah Webster recommended the American spelling pronunciation with initial [sk],[27] as if this were a Greek loan. *Schism,* though ultimately Greek, was taken from Old French *cisme,* the spelling of which was in the sixteenth century made to conform to the Greek original. The word is,

---

[25] A precisely similar misinterpretation of *s* and *h* as constituting a digraph occurs in *Lewisham* and *Evesham,* in which pronunciation with medial [š] has become practically universal, though in the beginning such pronunciation was parallel with the childish misreading of *mishap* to rime with *bishop.*

[26] As in Act II of W. S. Gilbert's *H.M.S. Pinafore:*

> In time each little waif
> Forsook his foster-mother,
> The well-born babe was Ralph—
> Your captain was the other!!!

[27] The British English pronunciation with the first syllable as [šɛd] is also erroneously based upon the misspelling. The historically correct pronunciation would begin with [s].

however, still pronounced with initial [s] by cultured speakers, but pronunciation with [sk] is frequently heard nowadays.

THE DIGRAPH GH

H after *g* has been discussed in another connection (pp. 60–61); *gh* also came to be used — or rather misused from a purely rational point of view — after 1400 to indicate [g] in some English words, the practice surviving in *ghost* (OE *gast* – ME *go(o)st*), *aghast,* and *ghastly.* It also occurs in words of exotic origin as a transliteration of non-Roman symbols indicating non-Roman sounds, for instance *ghazi* and *ghoul,* and in *gherkin* and *Ghent,* where it performs the genuinely useful purpose of indicating that these words are not to be pronounced like *jerkin* and *gent.*

THE DIGRAPHS SC AND SH

In early Old English times *sc* symbolized [sk], but during the course of the Old English period the graphic sequence continued to indicate the later development of [sk] into the sound symbolized from Middle English times to the present by *sh.* The *sh* was an innovation of Anglo-Norman scribes (OE *sceal* – ME and ModE *shall*), who earlier had used *s, ss,* and *sch* for the same purpose. The digraph *sc* thus occurs after the Old English period only in borrowed words. In those ultimately Latin or Greek, regardless of their immediate source as far as English is concerned, *sc* may indicate either [s] or [sk], depending upon the following sound, for example (with [s]) *scion, science, scene,* (with [sk]) *scandal, scorpion, sculpture, scripture.* English words of Scandinavian origin use *sc* for [sk] before *a, o, u,* and *r,* as in *scant, scowl, scurf,* and *scrape,* though *sk* may also occur before the cited vowels, as in *skald, skoal,* and *skull.* In *scent* and *scythe* the *c* is a late and an etymologically altogether unjustifiable insertion; in the latter word, as well as in *scissors* (OF *cisoires*), there has been confusion with Latin *scindere* 'to cut' (past participle *scissum*).

THE SEQUENCE WH

Middle English scribes preferred the writing *wh* for the phonetically more accurate *hw* used in Old English times, for example Old English *hwæt*–Middle and Modern English *what.* For a large part of the English-speaking world the *h* in the graphic sequence *wh,* save for the exceptions noted in the last sentence of this paragraph, has no phonetic significance; it is, however, significant as far as the speech of northern England, Scotland, Ireland, and parts of the United States is concerned. Spoken differentiation of such pairs as *whale–wail, when–*

wen, and *which–witch* in American English is doubtless attributable largely to the influence of those Ulster Scots, or Scotch-Irish as they are sometimes misleadingly called, who began arriving in America in large numbers around the end of the first quarter of the eighteenth century and who settled first the Pennsylvania back country and subsequently a large part of the country away from the Atlantic Coast.[28] In *whole* (OE *hal*) and *whore* (OE *hore*), the *w* indicates what was a dialectal pronunciation which seems to have become fairly common in the sixteenth century; the unwritten [w] of *one* and *once* is of the same dialectal origin. In *who, whom, whose* there has been loss of earlier [w].

C AND K

Under French influence, scribes in Middle English times used *c* before *e* and *i (y)* in French loan-words, for example *citee* 'city' and *grace,* with an earlier French value of this symbol [ts], later becoming [s]. In Old English writing *c* never indicated [s], but only [k] and [č]. Thus, with the introduction of the newer French value, *c* remained an ambiguous symbol, though in a different way: it came to represent [k] before *a, o,* and *u* and before consonants, and [s] before *e* and *i (y)*. *K,* used occasionally in Old English writing, thus came to be increasingly used before *e* and *i (y)* in Middle English times (OE *cyn(n)* 'race' – ME *kin, kyn*) to indicate the stop sound, so that *c* might be reserved for the sibilant, as in *certain* (compare *curtain,* with *c* indicating [k] before *u*). *Ck* is usual for [k] after short vowels, but the ending *-ick* has been simplified to *-ic* in *music, critic, physic,* and the like. In recent loans, with final stress, the French spelling is used, as in *critique* and *physique,* which are regarded as different words from *critic* and *physic.*

Z AND S

Z was sometimes used in Old English times in loan-words, in which it had the value [ts] – as such alternate spellings as *dracontse–draconze* 'dragon-wort' indicate – the same value which the symbol has to some extent in Italian (for example in *grazie* 'thanks') and always in German (for example *Zeit* 'time'). The French also wrote *z* for the consonant sequence [ts], and the Modern English value of the letter reflects the

[28] For the geographical distribution of [hw] and [w] in the eastern United States, see Raven I. McDavid, Jr., and Virginia Glenn McDavid, "*h* Before Semivowels in the Eastern United States," *Language,* 28 (1952), 41–62, and Raven I. McDavid, Jr., "Our Initial Consonant 'H'," *College English,* 11 (1950), 458–59.

Old French loss of [t] in this sequence. When this occurred, words which had been spelled with *z* could be spelled with *s*. The French change in sound and spelling thus made *z* available for the sound which it represents in both French and English today. Although occurring in English mainly in loan-words, *z* came to replace *s* in a number of native words, for example *freeze* (ME *fresen*), but with little consistency (compare *cheese*, from ME *chese*). Neither the symbol nor the sound which it came to symbolize occurs initially in native English words, save dialectally in the southwestern counties of England. Confusion of *ʒ* with *z*, leading to miswritings and ultimately to mispronunciations, has been discussed in another connection (see n. 17).

THE SEQUENCE QU AND THE DIGRAPHS GU *AND* DG

French scribal practices are responsible for the Middle English spelling *qu*, which French inherited from Latin, replacing Old English *cw* (that is, *cp*), as in *quellen* 'to kill,' *queen*, and *quethen* 'to say,' which despite their French look are all native English words, in Old English respectively *cwellan, cwen,* and *cweðan.* Also French is the writing *gu* (see p. 56), in which the *u,* earlier pronounced in Central French, was used in some words as a mere diacritic to indicate [g] before *e* and *i (y).* This usage did not become really common, however, until well into the Modern English period, around 1650. The *u* has also been inserted before *a* in *guard,* where there is no real excuse for it. Also French in origin is the digraph *gg,* supplanting in medial and final positions Old English *cg* (OE *ecg*–ME *egge*), later written *dg(e),* as in Modern English *edge.*

THE VALUES OF VOWEL SYMBOLS

Our knowledge of the scholarly pronunciation of Latin in the early Middle Ages is obviously an important basis for our reconstruction of the pronunciation of English in its earlier periods. The vowel symbols were used in our earliest writing with the values which these symbols had in the Latin alphabet as acquired by the English from the Irish missionaries—for instance, *a, e,* and *i* were approximately as in the later English loan-words *mirage* (never as in *rage*), *fete* (never as in *mete*),[29] and *machine* (never as in *mine*). *O* and *u* when they symbolize

---

[29] In natural English speech pronounced the same as *fate,* though a desire to be "correct" on the part of those who have had a smattering of French in school has given rise to an affected pronunciation with [ɛ].

long vowels have had approximately[30] the same values in earlier periods which they now have in *rode* and *rude,* though both letters have symbolized other sounds as well. The other three vowel symbols, however, approximate their Latin values much more closely in other writing systems than they do in Modern English. Because of a radical change in English long vowels which occurred in the course of the fifteenth century (to be discussed in Chapter VII), the long sounds indicated by these symbols acquired qualities quite different from their former ones. As a consequence of the retention of earlier spellings for shifted sounds, the vowel symbols *a, e,* and *i* have acquired for us values ([e], [i], [aɪ]) quite different from those ([ɑ], [e], [i]) which they have in all other languages using the Greek or Roman alphabets. This fact is undoubtedly one of the reasons why foreigners are so often confused by English spelling.

DOUBLE LETTERS

To indicate vowel length, Middle English writing frequently employed double letters, particularly *ee* and *oo,* the practice becoming general in the East Midland dialect late in the period. These particular doublings have survived into our own day, though of course they do not indicate the same sounds as in Middle English. As a matter of fact, both *ee* and *oo* were ambiguous in the Middle English period, as every student of Chaucer must learn. One of the vowel sounds indicated by Middle English *ee* came generally to be written *ea* in the course of the sixteenth century; for the other sound *ee* was retained, alongside *ie* and, less frequently, *ei* — spellings which were also used to some extent in Middle English. An earlier value of the writing *ea* is preserved in *yea, break, great,* and *steak,* and an even earlier value survives in the vowels of *death, head, deaf,* and a number of other words.

Double *o* came to be commonly used in later Middle English times for the long low-back rounded vowel [ɔ], the vowel which developed out of Old English long *a.* Unfortunately for the beginning student, the same double *o* was used for the continuation of Old English long *o.* As a result of this duplication, *rood* 'rode' (OE *rad*) and *rood* 'rood' (OE *rod*) were written with identical vowel symbols, though they were no

---

[30] In comparatively recent times the long vowel symbolized by *o* acquired a so-called off-glide which the native English-speaking student of foreign languages must learn to leave off if his pronunciation is to be acceptable. He must not, for instance, pronounce French *rose,* Italian and Spanish *rosa,* and German *Rose* with the *u*-glide which many of us have in English *rose.*

more nearly alike in pronunciation than are their modern forms. Final unstressed *e* following a single consonant also indicated vowel length in Middle English, as in *fode* 'food' and *fede* 'to feed'; this corresponds to the "silent *e*" of Modern English, as in *case, mete, bite, rote,* and *rule.* Doubled consonants, which indicated consonant length in earlier periods, began in Middle English times to indicate also that a preceding vowel was short. Surviving examples are *dinner* and *bitter,* as contrasted with *diner* and *biter.* In the north of England *i* was frequently used after a vowel to indicate that it was long, a practice responsible for such spellings as *raid* (literally a 'riding,' from OE *rad,* noun), *Reid* (a long-voweled variant of *red,* surviving only as a proper name), and Scots *guid,*[31] as in Robert Burns's "Address to the Unco Guid, or the Rigidly Righteous." In the Modern English period, though there are instances as early as the thirteenth century, *a* has also been widely used after *o* for the same purpose of indicating length of the preceding vowel, as in *road, boat,* and the like. After *e,* as we have seen in the preceding paragraph, *a* had a qualitative as well as a quantitative function.

O AND OU FOR U

Short *u* was commonly written *o* during the latter part of the Middle English period if *m, n, u* (*v, w*) were contiguous. The Middle English writings *sone* 'son' and *sonne* 'sun' thus indicate the same vowel sound [U] that these words had in Old English, when they were written respectively *sunu* and *sunne. O* for *u* survives in a number of Modern English words besides *son,* for example *come* (OE *cuman*), *wonder* (OE *wundor*), *monk* (OE *munuc*),[32] *honey* (OE *hunig*), *tongue* (OE *tunge*), and *love* (OE *lufu*), which last, if it had not used the *o* spelling, would have been written *luue* (as indeed it was for a time) until the seventeenth-century distinction of *u* and *v.* The French spelling *ou* came to be used generally in the fourteenth century to represent English long *u,* for example *hous* (OE *hus*), and sometimes represented the short *u* as well. Before a vowel the *u* of the digraph *ou* might well be mistaken as representing [v], for which the same symbol was used. To avoid confusion (as in *douer,* which was a possible writing for both *dower* and *Dover*),[33] *u* was doubled in this position — that is, writ-

---

[31] The original long vowel, as in *food,* has undergone shortening in Standard English *good.*

[32] But Middle English *nonne* 'nun' (OE *nunne*) has returned to the earlier way of indicating its vowel sound.

[33] To use an apt example supplied by Jespersen, *Modern English Grammar,* I, 89.

ten *uu,* later *w.* This use of *w* would of course have been unnecessary if *u* and *v* had been differentiated as they are now. *W* also came to be used instead of *u* in final position. *U* occurs in this position in *you* and *thou,* but both words were frequently written with *-ow* in former times.

Y *IN OLD AND MIDDLE ENGLISH*

As will be pointed out in Chapter V, the letter *y* in Old English writing symbolized a rounded front vowel. Later pronunciation of the Old English vowel without lip-rounding caused it to fall together with *i,* so that *y* might be used for both vowel and consonant. In other words, Middle English scribes used *y* for one of the values of *ȝ* (see p. 60) and also, for the sake of legibility, as a variant of *i* in the vicinity of stroke letters, for example *myn homcomynge* 'my home-coming.' Late in the Middle English period there was a tendency to write *y* for long *i* generally. *Y,* as we have seen (p. 61), was regularly used in final position.

RENAISSANCE RESPELLINGS

Certain Renaissance respellings, for instance *throne* (p. 65) and *schedule* (p. 66), which have ultimately effected changes in traditional pronunciations, have already been mentioned. *Debt* and *doubt* are likewise fancy respellings of *det* (Middle English, from Old French) and *dout* (ME *doute,* also from Old French), the *b* having been inserted because it was perceived that these words were ultimately derivatives of Latin *debitum* and *dubitare* respectively; similarly with the *c* in *indict* and the *b* in *subtle.* If those learned men responsible for such respellings thought to effect a change in pronunciation like that which Shakespeare's schoolmaster Holofernes recommended,[34] they have not been successful so far as these words are concerned.

Comptroller is a pseudolearned respelling of *controller,* taken by English from Old French. The fancy spelling is doubtless due to an erroneous association with French *compte* 'count.' The word has fairly recently acquired a new pronunciation based on the misspelling. *Receipt* and *indict,* both taken from Anglo-French, and *victual,* from Old French, have been similarly remodeled to give them a Latin look; their

---

[34] In the passage referred to on p. 64, he speaks of those "rackers of ortagriphie [orthography]" (for to him, as to many after him, spelling set the standard for pronunciation) who say *dout* and *det* when they should say *doubt* and *debt.* "D, e, b, t, not d, e, t," he says, unaware that the word was indeed written *d, e, t* before schoolmasters like himself began tinkering with spelling.

traditional pronunciations have not as yet been affected. *Parliament,* a respelling of the English loan-word *parlement* (a derivative of Fr. *parler* 'to speak'), has also quite recently acquired a pronunciation such as the later spelling seems to indicate to literate, if unsophisticated, speakers — a pronunciation occasionally heard from such high-powered speakers as television and radio news commentators, who have tremendous prestige in modern life.[35] It is not unlikely that many who have previously used the traditional trisyllabic pronunciation will in time mend their ways and adopt the four-syllabled one based on the contemporary spelling. This may well seem to them more "correct" for the very reason that it is so based. It is thus obvious that in a period of widespread (if perhaps only thinly spread) literacy, misunderstanding of the true relationship of writing to speech can bring about changes in language.

Another such change of long standing has resulted from the insertion of *l* in *fault* (ME *faute,* from Old French), a spelling suggested by Latin *fallita* and strengthened by the analogy of *false,* which has come to us direct from Latin *falsus.* For a while the word continued to be pronounced without the *l,* riming with *ought* and *thought* in seventeenth-century poetry. In Dr. Johnson's day there was wavering, as Johnson himself testifies in the *Dictionary,* between the older *l*-less and the newer pronunciation with *l.* The eighteenth-century orthoepists indicate the same wavering. These were men who conceived of themselves as exercising a directive function; they recommended and condemned, usually on quite irrelevant grounds. Seldom were they content merely to record variant pronunciations. Thomas Sheridan, the distinguished father of a more distinguished son named Richard Brinsley, in his *General Dictionary of the English Language* (1780) decides in favor of the *l*-less pronunciation of *fault,* as does James Elphinston in his *Propriety Ascertained* (1787). Robert Nares in his *Elements of Orthoëpy* (1784) records both pronunciations and makes no attempt to make a choice between them. John Walker in his *Critical Pronouncing Dictionary* (1791) declared that to omit the *l* made a "disgraceful exception," for the word would thus "desert its relation to the Latin *falsitas.*" The history of the *l* of *vault* is quite similar.

---

[35] The spelling pronunciation is not exclusively American, as one might expect it to be. In the English Angel recording of *H.M.S. Pinafore,* George Baker, who sings the role of Admiral Sir Joseph Porter and is described in the accompanying booklet as "perhaps the greatest patter singer who has ever lived," manages to pronounce the *i* (in the lines "I grew so rich that I was sent/ By a pocket borough into Parliament"). It is highly improbable that the pronunciation is intended to characterize Sir Joseph as a self-made man.

SPELLING PRONUNCIATIONS

Regardless of the method by which they have been taught, or have taught themselves, to read, it is likely that most literate people attribute sounds to the letters of the alphabet. This is to put the cart before the horse, for, as should be perfectly clear by now, letters do not "have" sounds, but merely symbolize them. Nevertheless, the literate person is likely to feel that he does not really know a word — say, a name that he has not heard clearly — until the question "How do you spell it?" — much more frequently asked under such circumstances than "How do you speak it?" — has been answered.[36]

A knowledge of spelling has been responsible for changing the pronunciation of certain words whose written forms for one reason or another do not indicate pronunciations which had become traditional. For instance, simply because it occurs in writing, the *t* of *often* has come to be pronounced once again, as it was in earlier days and up until well into the seventeenth century,[37] though the pronunciation with *t* is not yet recorded by all current dictionaries. It is sufficiently widespread, however, that it is probably safe to predict that in another generation or so only philologists will get the point of the *orphan–often* dialogue in Gilbert and Sullivan's *The Pirates of Penzance,* culminating in Major-General Stanley's question to the Pirate King, "When you said 'orphan,' did you mean 'orphan' — a person who has lost his parents, or 'often' — frequently?" This will of course make no sense with

---

[36] This is amusingly illustrated in the 1960 motion picture version of H. G. Wells's *The Time Machine,* when the Time Traveler, projected hundreds of thousands of years into the future, asks a beautiful blonde Eloi girl what her name is. Inasmuch as the English language has by an unexplained miracle not changed in the least during this vast space of time, the girl understands him perfectly and replies "Weena." "How do you spell it?" immediately asks the Time Traveler. This is too much for Weena, who has no notion of spelling. Wrinkling his brow and taking careful thought, the Traveler proceeds to trace the letters *W, E, E, N, A* in the earth, thus making the name somehow more "real" than it had previously been for him, and presumably for the illiterate girl as well. In justice to H. G. Wells, it should be stated that the incident does not occur in the story as he wrote it.

[37] Jespersen, *Modern English Grammar,* I, 275, is probably overstating somewhat when he says that the *t* seems to have been "always" mute in the eighteenth and nineteenth centuries, for Walker, though he records only [ɔ́fən], states in the introduction to his *Dictionary* that in this word "the *t* begins to be pronounced." Though within the memory of the present writer such pronunciation has been considered affected — *nouveau riche,* as it were, and hence lacking "status" — it must now be considered both "Queen's English" and "President's English." I have not heard Elizabeth II pronounce the word, it is true, but both her father and her uncle, the duke of Windsor as Prince of Wales, used the form with *t* in public addresses. The usage of two kings should be sufficient to establish a pronunciation as Standard English.

the restoration of the *t* in *often;* the words will no longer be homophones, or even near-homophones as they are in American English with the *r* of *orphan* pronounced. *The Oxford English Dictionary,*[38] whose *O* installments were published in the early years of the present century, records only the pronunciation without *t,* but adds the comment that pronouncing the *t* is "now frequent in the south of England, and is often used in singing."

Reanalysis of the compound *forehead,* with restressing of the second element and the *h* pronounced, was also in the beginning due to a mistaken notion of the relationship between writing and speech. This pronunciation is, as far as I can tell, universal among younger-generation speakers, and is, it must be admitted, perfectly natural with them, since they learned so to pronounce the word long before they knew how to spell it, the analytical pronunciation having originated, though at first frowned upon, at least a generation ago. Reanalysis of *breakfast* as *break* plus *fast* would be quite parallel to what has happened in the case of *forehead.*

Such is the misunderstanding of writing as it is related to speech that many people suppose that the "best" speech is that which conforms most closely to the notions which they have acquired about the writing system, though this supposition has not as yet been extended to such words as *through* and *night.* Because of mass education, what is essentially a secondary factor—writing—has begun to affect pronunciation more than it ever did before. This tendency is, as we have seen, quite the reverse of what happened in earlier times, before English spelling became fixed, when writing was made to conform to speech. To put it in different terms: whereas in previous periods the purpose of writing was conceived to be the visual representation of speech, nowadays many conceive speech—ideally, at any rate—as the oral representation of writing.

Words which we have never heard spoken we must necessarily pronounce as their spellings seem to indicate, assuming that there is no dictionary handy. There are no grounds for reproach if a child reads *misled* as if it were the preterit of a hypothetical verb *to misle.* The

---

[38] The title of this work, one of the monuments of English scholarship, will be hereafter abbreviated *OED.* It is still frequently called the *NED* from its older title *A New English Dictionary on Historical Principles.* Its first installment (*A* to *Ant*) was published in 1884; its last—*Wise* to *Wyzen* (*X* to *Zyxt* had already appeared in 1921), in 1928. It was reissued in 1933 with a new title page and a supplement of additions and corrections made necessary by the fact that publication of the work had extended over a period of nearly half a century. It is, as the newer title indicates, published by the Oxford University Press.

great scholar W. W. Skeat of Cambridge once declared that "I hold firmly to the belief . . . that no one can tell how to pronounce an English word unless he has at some time or other *heard* it," and refused to hazard an opinion on the pronunciation of a number of very rare words — among them *aam, abrus, abactinal,* and *acaulose* — going on to say, "It would be extremely dishonest in me to pretend to have any opinion at all as to such words as these."[39] A number of common, everyday words which for one reason or another have become less used than they formerly were have acquired pronunciations based upon their written forms, for instance *clapboard,* pronounced like *clabbered* until fairly recently, but now usually analyzed as *clap* plus *board;* the same sort of analysis might occur also in *cupboard* if houses of the future should be built without cupboards or if builders should think up some fancy name for them, like "food preparation equipment storage areas."[40] A number of generations ago, when a grindstone was much more a part of daily life than it is now, the word rimed with *Winston.*

It is similar with proper names which we have not heard spoken. Our only guide is spelling, and no one, particularly no American, is to be much blamed for pronouncing *Daventry, Shrewsbury,* and *Cirencester* as their spellings seem to indicate they "should" be pronounced; as a matter of fact, many English people treat in exactly the same way these words, whose traditional pronunciations as [déntrɪ], [šrózbərɪ], and [sísɪtə] (or [sízɪtər], with British dialectal final [r], an even older pronunciation) have become somewhat old-fashioned.[41] Although, as all educated Americans are perfectly well aware, the colleges at Oxford and Cambridge whose names are written respectively *Magdalen* and *Magdalene* are still called *maudlin,*[42] a London bus conductor would

[39] Quoted in *Funk and Wagnalls New Standard Dictionary of the English Language* (New York, 1925), p. 2762.

[40] This is not outside the realm of possibility. In luxury advertisements a kitchen is sometimes referred to as a "food preparation area."

[41] According to Daniel Jones, *English Pronouncing Dictionary,* 13th ed., rev. A. C. Gimson (London, 1967), "members of county families," that is, landed gentry, generally pronounce [sísɪtə], but the townspeople pronounce the name in what they presumably suppose to be a more "correct" fashion — as spelled. Also according to Jones, [šrózbərɪ] is "the pronunciation used by those connected with Shrewsbury School" — a famous grammar school founded in 1551 — "and by many residents in the neighbourhood, especially members of county families," but the usual pronunciation of the townspeople and of outsiders is that suggested by the spelling, with [šrú-].

[42] The pronunciation is based on Old French *Madelaine,* whereas the written forms are Latin. Compare Caius College, Cambridge, named for an English doctor named Keys who adopted a Latin written form for his name.

be baffled at the request to be put down at "Tibbald's" Road; it would be necessary to pronounce *Theobald* as spelled, for the pronunciation indicated by Pope's spelling "Tibbald" (in reference to the Shakespearean commentator Lewis Theobald) is now quite old-fashioned.

IV

The Backgrounds
of English

Language tends to change for a variety of reasons. Moreover, this manifold tendency is operating all the time in all languages, though its operations are not perceptible save to a few persons who for one reason or another concern themselves with such matters and who may note changes in word usage and in the pronunciation of individual words (like *ration,* which used to rime with *passion,* but has comparatively recently acquired a pronunciation riming with *nation*) in the course of a lifetime. But such changes as these are really quite minor in relation to the changes in sounds and grammar which take place in the course of centuries—changes which would make the English of Geoffrey Chaucer, if we were happily able to resurrect him, seem very different from our own speech. That of Alfred the Great, who lived about as long before Chaucer as we live after him, would seem quite like a foreign language to all who had not made a special study of Old English.

Passage of time and geographical separation are but contributory factors and not direct causes of linguistic change. Thus, the English language as Americans speak it today has become differentiated from present Standard British English in certain respects in the relatively short time that has elapsed since its speakers became separated, though never really isolated, from the mother country. The English language of the seventeenth century suffered no sea changes when it was brought across the Atlantic: the first Englishmen to settle in America spoke exactly as they had spoken at home. Nevertheless, changes have certainly come to pass. Those which have occurred in British English are, as a matter of fact, considerably more far-reaching and more fundamental than anything which has happened independently in American English — the treatment of *a* in words of the *staff, glass,* and *path* type, the treatment of *r* preceding a consonant or in final position, and the treatment of the penultimate syllables of polysyllabic words in *-ary, -ery,* and *-ory,* for instance. American English preserves the older British treatment; Standard British English has changed in all these respects since the seventeenth century.

We can say precisely what has happened in any sort of linguistic change, and we can also as a rule say where a particular change occurred and assign to it an approximate chronology. But we can supply a precise reason only for those changes due to analogy, which is a mental process, even though it need not be conscious. We can describe what happened as "rounding" when Old English *ā* (in *stān, hām, bān,* and so forth) came invariably to be pronounced [ɔ] south of the Humber, and we can say, if we take spellings with *o* as indicating a rounded vowel different from that written *a* in the Old English words, approximately when this began to happen (late eleventh century). But *why* it happened, or, for that matter, why this later sound was subsequently raised to [ō], as in Modern English *stone, home, bone,* and so forth, we cannot really explain. We can only declare that certain tendencies toward changes of various sorts have prevailed at certain times and in certain places, and that these changes have accomplished themselves, not haphazardly, but with the greatest regularity. We can usually map the exact course of such changes, and we can describe them accurately in phonological terms.

There is considerable disagreement over whether sound change occurs gradually, over several generations of speakers, or suddenly. The traditional view is that it is gradual. Transformational-generativists argue hotly that it occurs suddenly,[1] as when a child says [wɑps] for *wasp,* though of course it is denied by no one that such changes *spread* gradually.[2]

A phonological phenomenon of fairly recent times is the increasing loss of [l] in the medial sequence [lj], as in *William, million, volume,* and *value.* A consistently *l*-less pronunciation of such words — a pronunciation previously regarded as substandard — occurs frequently in the usage of speakers over the auditory mass media. Whether or not this particular feature will become general in Eng-

---

[1] The arguments are summarized, from a generativist point of view, by Robert D. King, *Historical Linguistics and Generative Grammar* (Englewood Cliffs, N. J., 1969), pp. 106–19.

[2] This particular one is not likely to spread at all, but it is interesting to note that the childish slip by sheer coincidence shows the regular development of Old English *wæps.*

lish is impossible to say. A parallel loss of palatal *l* occurred a long time ago in French, as in *bouillon,* and in some varieties of Spanish, as in *caballo.* A further spread in English will not, it is safe to say, be due entirely to the prestige of mass-media speakers, despite the conviction of many that, all authority to the contrary, George I of England, a native speaker of German, introduced the pronunciation [áɪðər] for *either* and that the [θ] heard in most of Spain (but not in Spanish America) for *c* (before *e* or *i*) and *z* is attributable to the fact that a certain Spanish king (I have never been able to pin down his identity) had a lisp.

LANGUAGE FAMILIES

In the discussion of so-called linguistic families which follows, we must bear in mind that a language is not born, nor does it put out branches like a tree—nor, for that matter, does it die except when every single one of its speakers dies, as has happened to Etruscan, Gothic, Cornish, and a good many other languages. When we speak of Latin as a dead language, we are referring to a highly artificial literary language; but spoken Latin still lives in various developments in Italian, French, Spanish, and the other Romance languages.

Hence the terms *family, ancestor, parent,* and other genealogical expressions when applied to languages must be regarded as no more than metaphors. Languages are developments of older languages rather than descendants in the sense in which people are descendants of their forefathers. Thus, Italian and Spanish are different developments of an earlier, more unified language, Latin. Latin in turn is one of a number of developments, which include Oscan and Umbrian, of a still earlier language called Italic. Italic in its turn is a development of Indo-European. Whether or not Indo-European has affinities with other languages spoken in prehistoric times and is hence a development of an even earlier language, no one is prepared to say with certainty; for, as we have seen, we are quite in the dark about how it all began.

Older scholars—and they were to some extent theorists—classified languages as monosyllabic, agglutinative, incorporative, and inflective, these being exemplified respectively by Chinese, Turkish, Eskimo, and Latin. The monosyllabic languages were supposed to represent the most primitive type—a notion which doubtless grew out of investigations into languages of our own Indo-European group, with their large number of monosyllabic roots. But even the earliest (middle of second millennium B.C.) records of Chinese, a monosyllabic language in its modern form, represent not a primitive but actually a late stage in linguistic development. It obviously cannot be inferred from such evidence as this that our prehistoric ancestors prattled in words of one syllable each.

The older scholars also observed, quite correctly, that in certain languages, such as Turkish and Hungarian, words were made up of parts "stuck together," as it were; hence the term *agglutinative*. In such languages the suffixal elements are usually whole syllables having very definite meanings. The inflectional suffixes of the Indo-European languages were supposed likewise once to have been independent words; hence, some believed that the inflective languages had grown out of the agglutinative. Little was known of what were called incorporative languages, in which all sentence elements are combined into a single word; the elements have no independent existence, but can appear only as infixes.

The trouble with such a classification was that, though apparently objective, it was not really so, but was instead based on the out-of-date theory that early man spoke in monosyllables. Furthermore, the difference between agglutinative and inflective was not well defined, and there was considerable overlapping. Nevertheless, the terms are useful and widely used in the description of specific languages or even groups of languages. Modern objective and well-informed typological classifications have been especially useful in showing language similarities and differences from a particular point of view.

From our point of view, however, a much more satisfactory classification of languages is the so-called genetic one, made on the basis of such correspondences of sound and structure as indicate relationship through common origin. Perhaps the greatest contribution of nineteenth-century linguistic scholars was the painstaking investigation of these correspondences, many of which had been noted long before.

Such investigation indicated unmistakably that practically all of the languages of Europe (and hence of the Americas and other parts of the world colonized by Europeans) and some of Asia have in common certain characteristics of sound and structure and to some extent a stock of words which make it perfectly obvious that they have all developed out of a single language spoken in prehistoric times. This earlier language is usually called Indo-European.[3] What it was called

---

[3] *Indo-Germanic* is not now much used except by German scholars. Its coinage was not due to German patriotism; it was intended to do no more than indicate what were thought to be the easternmost and westernmost limits of the geographical distribution of

by those who spoke it we have no way of knowing, nor do we know what they called themselves. We shall here follow the usual practice of referring to them as the Indo-Europeans, but it must always be borne in mind that the term has no racial connotations; it refers only to a group of people who lived in a relatively small area in early times and who spoke a more or less unified language out of which many languages have developed in the course of thousands of years. These languages are spoken today by approximately half of the world's population.

THE NON-INDO-EUROPEAN LANGUAGES

Before proceeding to a more detailed discussion of the Indo-European group, we may perhaps best delimit it by briefly noting those languages and groups of languages which are *not* Indo-European. Two important groups have names which reflect the Biblical attempt to derive all the races of men from the three sons of Noah: the Semitic (from the Latin form of the name of the eldest son, more correctly called Shem in English) and the Hamitic. The term *Japhetic,* once used for Indo-European, has happily long been obsolete. On the basis of many phonological and morphological features which they share, Semitic and Hamitic are thought by many scholars to be related through a hypothetical common ancestor, Hamito-Semitic; there are also those who believe in an ultimate relationship, impossible to prove, between Semitic and Indo-European.

The Semitic group includes the following languages: (Eastern) Akkadian, called Assyrian in the periods of the oldest texts, and later Babylonian; (Western) Hebrew, Aramaic[4] (the native speech of Jesus Christ), Phoenician, and Moabitic; (Southern) Arabic and Ethiopic. Of these, only Arabic is spoken by large numbers of people over a widespread area. Hebrew has comparatively recently been revived in

---

the languages recognized as belonging to the group. Another term, *Aryan,* has been used synonymously. Originally this term referred only to the Asiatic languages of the group. This is still the reference which it has in learned use, where its occurrence is now somewhat rare, *Indo-Iranian* and *Indo-Persian* being the preferred terms.

[4] Formerly—and incorrectly—called Chaldean, Chaldaic, or Chaldee. Though he should have known better, the foundations of modern linguistic science having already been laid in his day. Noah Webster thought that "Chaldee," which he believed to be the language of pre-polyglot Babel, was the ancestor of all languages. In his *American Dictionary of the English Language* (1828) he proposed a good many "Chaldee" etymologies which later and better-informed editors have quietly consigned to the wastepaper basket.

Israel, to some extent for nationalistic reasons.[5] Ethiopic survives mainly in Geez, a Christian liturgical and learned language of Ethiopia, and in Amharic, which is used in state documents in that country. It is interesting to note that two of the world's most important religious documents are written in Semitic languages – the Old Testament in Hebrew (with large portions of the books of Ezra and Daniel in Aramaic) and the Koran in Arabic.

To the Hamitic group belong Egyptian (called Coptic after the close of the third century of the Christian Era), the Berber dialects of North Africa, and various Cushitic[6] dialects spoken along the upper Nile. Coptic is used in the liturgy of the Coptic Christian Church in Egypt, much as Geez is used in the Ethiopian Church and Latin in the Roman Catholic Church, but is not spoken elsewhere. Arabic became the national language of Egypt in the course of the sixteenth century.

Semitic is thus essentially Asiatic, and Hamitic North African. Hamitic is in no way related to any of the languages spoken by blacks in central and southern Africa, the vast region south of the Sahara. These languages are usually classified into three main groups: Sudanese, extending to the equator, a large and highly diversified group of languages whose relationships to one another are difficult and in some cases impossible to establish; Bantu, extending from the equator to the extreme south, a large and well-defined group of related languages; and Hottentot and Bushman, remotely related languages spoken by small groups of people in the extreme southwestern part of Africa. Hottentot and Bushman have no relationship to the other black groups, nor is it demonstrable that the Sudanese and the Bantu groups are in any way connected with each other.

Languages belonging to the Dravidian group were once spoken throughout India, where the earlier linguistic situation was radically affected by the Aryan invasion. These are the aboriginal languages of India. They are now spoken mainly in southern India.

The Indo-Chinese group includes Chinese proper and the languages of Tibet and Indochina. Japanese is totally unrelated, though it has borrowed the Chinese written characters and many Chinese words. Attempts to relate Korean to either Chinese or Japanese have not been successful. Ainu, the language of the aborigines of Japan, is totally

---

[5] Hebrew is not of course to be confused with Yiddish (that is, Jüdisch), a German dialect to be further defined later. It has become a sort of international language of the Jews, with a literature of high quality. American newspapers printed in Yiddish use Hebrew characters.

[6] Cush was a son of Ham.

unrelated to any other language of which we have any knowledge; it is now spoken by no more than a handful of people.

A striking characteristic of the Malay-Polynesian languages is their wide geographical distribution in the islands of the Indian and the Pacific oceans, stretching from Madagascar to Easter Island. The more or less moribund Australian native languages, spoken by only a few Australian aborigines nowadays, have no connection at all with Malay-Polynesian, nor have the more than a hundred Papuan languages spoken in New Guinea and neighboring islands.

The American Indian languages constitute a geographic rather than a linguistic grouping, comprising many languages showing very little relationship, if any, to one another. It has been estimated[7] that at the time of Columbus' discovery only about a million and a half Indians occupied the huge area north of Mexico, with about forty million more in Mexico and Central America, the Antilles, and South America. A very important and widespread group of American Indian languages is known as the Uto-Aztecan, which includes Nahuatl, the language spoken by the Aztecs, and various closely related dialects. Aleut and Eskimo, which are very similar to each other, are spoken in the Aleutians and all along the extreme northern coast of America and north to Greenland. The isolation of the various groups, small in number to begin with and spread over so large a territory, may to some extent account for the great diversity of American Indian tongues.

Basque, spoken in many dialects by no more than half a million people living in the region of the Pyrenees, has always been something of a popular linguistic mystery. It now seems fairly certain, on the basis of coins and scanty inscriptions of the ancient Iberians, that Basque is related to the almost completely lost language of those people who once inhabited the Iberian peninsula and in Neolithic times were spread over an even larger part of Europe. Efforts to relate it to Etruscan, a language of which we know very little, to the non-Indo-European languages spoken in the Caucasus Mountains (not mentioned elsewhere here), and to the Hamitic languages have not been successful.

An important group of non-Indo-European languages spoken in Europe, as well as in parts of Asia, is the Ural-Altaic, which falls into two subgroups: the Ural, or Finno-Ugric, which includes Finnish, Estonian, Livonian, Lappish, and Hungarian, among others of less importance; and the very remotely related Altaic — though there are those who deny any such connection. Altaic includes several varieties

---

[7] By P. Rivet, cited by Willem L. Graff, *Language and Languages* (New York, 1932), p. 427.

of Turkish, such as Ottoman Turkish (Osmanli) and that spoken in Turkestan and in the Azerbaijan Soviet Socialist Republic, as well as Mongolian and Manchu.

The foregoing is by no means a complete survey of non-Indo-European languages. We have merely mentioned some of the most important groups and individual languages, along with some which are of little significance as far as the numbers or the present importance of their speakers are concerned, but which are nevertheless interesting for one reason or another. Louis H. Gray lists twenty-six linguistic groups and two isolated languages (spoken respectively in China and India by small groups of people), and comes up with a total of 2796 languages, of which 132 are Indo-European.[8] His figure coincides with that arrived at by the French Academy. But Gray rightly had no faith in such a count, for, as he points out, it is often impossible to reach agreement as to what constitutes a language: the line demarcating dialect and language is difficult to draw, and linguists do not always agree on where it should be drawn. Furthermore, depending largely upon one's point of view, Old English, Middle English, and Modern English might be regarded as one, two (on the basis that the transition from Middle English to Modern English is somewhat less well defined than that from Old English to Middle English), or three. And there are yet further difficulties pointed out by Gray, who concludes that between 2500 and 3500 might be given as an estimate, but admits that such an estimate is "so rough as to be practically worthless."

EARLY STUDIES
OF THE INDO-EUROPEAN GROUP

The concept of an Indo-European group of languages—and subsequently of other groups as well, for the work of the early Indo-Europeanists gave impetus to the study of non-Indo-European languages also—may be said to have grown out of British rule in India. It was this which was responsible for a wider knowledge of Sanskrit in Europe—to all intents and purposes a third ancient language with which to compare Latin and Greek. Latin had previously been supposed to be a degenerate form of Greek. Such an explanation of the correspondences between Sanskrit and the two hitherto-known ancient languages would obviously not do, for India was completely outside the sphere of Greco-Latin civilization.

For this new concept a remarkably versatile man, a veritable eighteenth-century "admirable Crichton," was largely responsible. A

---

[8] *Foundations of Language* (New York, 1939), p. 418.

former member of Dr. Johnson's brilliant circle, Sir William Jones was at the age of thirty-seven judge of the supreme court of judicature at Fort William (Calcutta) in Bengal after a brilliant career as Orientalist, student of many languages, poet, classicist, jurisconsult, and public official in England, where he had withdrawn as a parliamentary candidate for Oxford University just before election day because of his sympathetic view of the American cause in the War of Independence and his opposition to the slave trade.

Shortly after his arrival in India, Jones founded the Bengal Asiatic Society. In a paper read before that group in 1786, he declared that Sanskrit bore to Greek and Latin "a stronger affinity . . . than could possibly have been produced by accident; so strong, indeed, that no philologer could examine them all three without believing them to have sprung from some common source, which, perhaps, no longer exists," going on to say that "there is a similar reason for supposing that both the Gothick [that is, the Germanic] and the Celtick . . . had the same origin with the Sanscrit."

Before Jones's time a good deal was known of many languages other than the classical ones, and some attempts at classification had been made. A few Europeans, mostly missionaries, had even learned something of Sanskrit, and some of them had noted "affinities," or correspondences, with European languages. As early as the sixteenth century an Italian merchant in India pointed out in a letter the striking similarity of Sanskrit *deva-* 'God' to Italian *dio;* of *sarpa* 'snake' to his *serpe;* and of the numerals *sapta* 'seven,' *aštau* 'eight,' and *nava* 'nine' to his native *sette, otto,* and *nove.*[9] Had he been able to hear more of the ancient language known to and used by Hindu scholars of his day, he would have noted other such striking correspondences: in the numerical system alone, for example, *dvau/due* 'two,' *trayas/tre* 'three,' *čatvār-/quattro* 'four,' and *daśa/dieci* 'ten.'[10]

But Jones's clear statement, showing full realization of the relationship of Sanskrit to the principal European languages through a common ancestor, came just when the time was ripe for it, and may thus be said to have been the starting point for modern comparative linguistics. It only remained for more able, if less versatile, men to work out the details necessary to establish beyond any doubt the essential unity of

---

[9] Cited by Paul Thieme in "The Indo-European Language," *Scientific American,* October, 1958, pp. 63–74 — a fascinating article intended for the general educated reader.

[10] The medial consonant of *daśa* was a palatal fricative approximating [ç], the final sound of German *ich.*

that great group of related languages which we call the Indo-European family.

The first man to present a systematic comparison of a number of these languages was a German scholar with the unforgettable name of Franz Bopp. In 1816 Bopp published a brilliant study of the verbal endings of Sanskrit, Persian, Greek, Latin, and Germanic, and, in installments at intervals from 1833 to 1852, a huge comparative grammar in which he added Old Slavic and Lithuanian to the languages just named. He was later to add Armenian, Albanian, and Celtic. It was Bopp's work which got comparative Indo-European grammar on its feet.

But even before the publication of Bopp's first work the young Danish scholar Rasmus Rask had written a prize-winning essay on the origin of Old Norse in which he recognized the relationship of the Germanic, Hellenic, Italic, and Baltic groups and expressed the belief that Indo-Iranian might also be related. By the time his essay was published, in 1818, he had perceived that Armenian was Indo-European. It was not until somewhat later that he admitted Albanian to the family.

Rask clearly perceived that sound shifts were regular, not sporadic, and recognized the Germanic sound shift later to be more expertly codified by Jacob Grimm in the second edition of his *Deutsche Grammatik* (1822).[11] This sound shift, to be discussed in some detail later, was in time to be associated with Grimm's name as Grimm's Law.[12] There is, however, some justice in the statement of Otto Jespersen that "if any man is to give his name to this law, a better name would be 'Rask's Law,' for all these transitions . . . are enumerated in Rask's *Undersøgelse* [the essay of 1818] . . . which Grimm knew before he wrote a single word about the sound shift."[13] In any case, the relationship of the Germanic languages, including English, to the other members of the group was now made perfectly clear.

Comparative and historical linguistics thus began with the study of the Indo-European family. Similar study of other languages and groups of languages was to come later, and as a result of the principles educed

[11] By *deutsch* Grimm meant 'Germanic,' not merely 'German.'

[12] It is an amusing irony that this great scholar, who never married, should be best known as the "author," with his brother Wilhelm, of a beloved nursery classic — the famous *Grimm's Fairy Tales*. The brothers Grimm, both of them fascinated by folklore, in the scientific study of which they were pioneers, were the collectors of the stories which have delighted generations of children despite the disapproval of modern child psychologists.

[13] *Language: Its Nature, Development and Origin* (New York, 1922), p. 43.

by the nineteenth-century Indo-Europeanists. Bopp, Rask, and Grimm had laid solid foundations for such studies, among them identifying the Germanic, Balto-Slavic, Celtic, Italic, Hellenic, and Indo-Iranian groups of languages as subgroups of Indo-European, along with the individual languages Armenian and Albanian. There followed in the course of the nineteenth century a series of brilliant and exciting studies, mostly by German scholars, which are still the basis of modern linguistic study. The story is best told by Holger Pedersen in his *Linguistic Science in the Nineteenth Century.*[14] The discovery and deciphering of writings in Tocharian and Hittite, found respectively in East Turkestan and Asia Minor, and the identification of the first of these languages as Indo-European in origin and the second as either Indo-European in origin or a language of common origin with Indo-European[15] are achievements of the twentieth century. They are also discussed by Pedersen in the work cited.

INFLECTION
IN THE INDO-EUROPEAN LANGUAGES

All the Indo-European languages are inflective — that is, all are characterized by a grammatical system based on modifications in the form of words, by means of endings and vowel changes,[16] to indicate such grammatical functions as case, number, tense, person, mood, and the like. The older inflectional system is very imperfectly represented in most modern languages: English, French, and Spanish, for instance, have lost much of the inflectional complexity which was once characteristic of these languages; German retains considerably more, with its various forms of the noun and the article and its so-called strong adjective declension. Sanskrit is notable for the remarkably clear picture it gives us of the older Indo-European inflectional system; it retains much that has been lost or changed in the other Indo-European languages, so that its forms show us, even better than Greek or Latin can do, what the system of Indo-European must have been.

Traces of this inflectional system which survive in varying degrees in other related languages led the early Indo-Europeanists to the discovery of the relationship of languages as widely separated geographi-

---

[14] Translated from the Danish by John Webster Spargo (Cambridge, Mass., 1931). For a briefer treatment, see John T. Waterman, *Perspectives in Linguistics* (Chicago, 1963).

[15] Those who hold to the second of these alternatives, notably the late American Hittitologist, E. H. Sturtevant, hypothesize a parent language called Indo-Hittite, from which both Indo-European and Hittite stem.

[16] As in Modern English *boy–boys; who–whom–whose; walk–walks–walked–walking; man–man's–men–men's; sing–sings–sang–singing.*

cally as Icelandic and Sanskrit. Once one understands and makes allowances for the regularly occurring sound changes, the relationship of the personal endings of the verb in the various Indo-European languages becomes perfectly clear. For example, the present indicative of the Sanskrit verb corresponding to English *to bear* runs as follows:

SINGULAR	PLURAL
1. bharā-mi 'I bear'	1. bharā-mas 'we bear'
2. bhara-si 'thou bearest'	2. bhara-tha 'you bear'
3. bhara-ti 'he beareth'	3. bhara-nti 'they bear'

The only irregularity here is the occurrence of *-mi* in the first person singular, as against *-ō* in the Greek and Latin forms to be cited immediately below. It was a peculiarity of Sanskrit to extend *-mi,* the regular first-person ending of verbs which had no vowel affixed to their roots, to those which did have such a vowel.[17]

Leaving out of consideration for the moment differences in vowels and in initial consonants, compare now the present indicative forms as they have developed from Indo-European into Greek and Latin, with special regard to the personal endings:

GREEK	LATIN
pherō[18]	ferō[18]
pherei-s	fer-s[20]
pherei[19]	fer-t
phero-mes (Doric)	feri-mus
phere-te	fer-tis
phero-nti (Doric)	feru-nt

[17] This vowel (for example the *-a* suffixed to the root *bhar-* of the Sanskrit word cited) is called the thematic vowel. The root of a word plus such a suffix is called the stem. To these stems are added endings. The comparatively few verbs lacking such a vowel in Indo-European are called athematic. The *m* in English *am* is a remnant of the Indo-European ending of such athematic verbs.

[18] In Indo-European thematic verbs the first person present indicative had no ending at all, but only a lengthening of the thematic vowel.

[19] The expected form would be *phere-ti.* The ending *-ti,* however, does occur elsewhere in the third person singular, for instance in Doric *didōti* 'he gives.'

[20] In this verb the loss of the thematic vowel is exceptional. The expected forms would be *feri-s, feri-t, feri-tis* in the second and third persons singular and the second person plural, respectively. Compare *legō, mittō, scrībō,* and other verbs of the third conjugation, all of which have the thematic vowel throughout, for example *legis, legit, legitis,* and so forth.

Comparison of the personal endings of the verbs in these and other languages leads inevitably to the conclusion that the Indo-European endings had to be as follows (the Indo-European reconstruction of the entire word is given in parentheses):

-ō, -mi	(*bherō)[21]
-si	(*bheresi)
-ti	(*bhereti)
-mes, -mos	(*bheromes)
-te	(*bherete)
-nti	(*bheronti)

Note now in Gothic and Old English the Germanic development of these personal endings:

GOTHIC	EARLY OLD ENGLISH
bair-a	ber-u, -o
bairi-s	biri-s
bairi-þ	biri-þ
bairi-m	bera-þ[22]
bairi-þ	bera-þ
baira-nd	bera-þ

Germanic *þ* corresponds as a rule to Indo-European *t* (see p. 107). Leaving out of consideration such details as the *-nd* (instead of expected *-nþ*) in the Gothic third person plural form, for which there is a soundly based explanation, it is perfectly clear that the Germanic personal endings correspond to those of the non-Germanic Indo-

[21] An asterisk before a form indicates that it is a reconstruction of what can be assumed to have existed on the basis of comparative study. Since Indo-European was spoken only in prehistoric times, all forms cited as existing in that language are necessarily reconstructions; the same is true of cited forms of any language in a prehistoric stage, for instance Germanic and very early Old English. The asterisk is also placed before a form assumed to have been current during the historical period though not actually recorded. Some of the forms from Greek and Latin in the two preceding footnotes might also have been preceded by asterisks, though labeling them "expected forms" in contrast to the forms which are actually attested gives sufficient notice that they are hypothetical and thus satisfies the claims of scholarly integrity. Square brackets are unnecessary in the discussion of prehistoric sound changes, since it is obvious that the letters under these circumstances are used exclusively as phonetic symbols.

[22] From the oldest period of Old English the form of the third person plural was used throughout the plural. This form, *beraþ,* from earlier *beranþ,* shows Anglo-Frisian loss of *n* before *þ*.

European languages. A complete comparison of the Germanic languages makes possible a reconstruction of the proto-Germanic endings in the same way that the Indo-European forms have been reconstructed. As has been seen, no guesswork is involved in such reconstruction.

COGNATE WORDS
IN THE INDO-EUROPEAN LANGUAGES

Words of similar structure and similar, related, and in many instances identical meanings in the various languages of the Indo-European group may be recognized, once one knows what to expect in the way of sound-shifting, as cognate — that is, of common origin (Lat. *co* plus *gnātus* 'born together'). Thus all the roots just cited (*bhar-, pher-, fer-, bair-, ber-*) are of common origin, all being developments of Indo-European **bher-;* so, for that matter, are the thematic vowels and the personal endings, though the untrained observer may sometimes find it difficult to recognize the relationship. For cognates, as we have seen, do not necessarily look much alike: sound shifts have occurred in the various languages of the Indo-European group (these languages may also be referred to as cognate) which may make related words as unlike in sound as *father,* Sanskrit *pitā,* and Irish Gaelic *athir*[23] — all developments of Indo-European **pətēr.* Sometimes, however, there is sufficient similarity — for example between *maharaja,* ultimately Sanskrit, and Latin *māius rēx* 'great king' — to be apparent even to the untrained observer.

The most frequently cited cognate words are those which have been preserved in a large number of Indo-European languages; some have in fact been preserved in all. These common related words include the numerals from one to ten; the word meaning the sum of ten tens (*cent-, sat-, hund-*) in various quite dissimilar-looking but nonetheless quite regular developments; words for certain bodily parts (related, for example, to *heart, lung, head, foot*); words for certain natural phenomena (related, for example, to *air, night, star, snow, sun, moon, wind*); certain plant and animal names (related, for example, to *beech, corn, wolf, bear*); and certain cultural terms (related, for example, to *yoke, mead, weave, sew*). It is interesting to note in passing that cognates of practically all of our taboo words — those monosyllables that pertain to sex and excretion and which seem to cause great pain to many people — are to be found in other Indo-European languages. Historically, if not socially, these ancient words are just as legitimate as any other words.

---

[23] Indo-European *p,* which corresponds to Germanic *f,* was lost completely in Celtic.

One needs no special training to perceive that our *one, two, three* are akin to Latin *ūnus, duo, trēs;* to Greek *oinē* 'one-spot on a die,' *dyo, treis;* to Welsh *un, dau, tri;* to Gothic *ains, twai, *þreis;* and to Dutch *een, twee, drie.* Comparison of the forms designating the second digit indicates that non-Germanic (as in the Latin, Welsh, and Greek forms) *d* corresponds to Germanic (English, Gothic, Dutch) *t.* A similar comparison of the forms for the third digit indicates that non-Germanic *t* corresponds to Germanic *þ,* the initial sound of *three* and *þrír* in English and Icelandic. Allowing for later changes, as in the case of *þ,* which became *d* in German (*drei* 'three'),[24] as also in Dutch, and *t* in Danish, Norwegian, and Swedish (*tre*), these same correspondences come to light perfectly regularly in other cognates in which the consonants in question appear. We may safely assume, for reasons unnecessary to go into here, that the non-Germanic consonants are older than the Germanic ones. Hence we may accept with the greatest confidence (assuming a similar comparison of the vowel systems) the reconstructions **oinos, *dwo, *treies* as accurately representing the Indo-European forms from which the existing forms have developed. The comparative linguists have of course used all the Indo-European languages as a basis for their conclusions regarding correspondences, not just a few such as are cited here.

INDO-EUROPEAN CULTURE

On the basis of these cognates, which must not be confused with loan-words, we can infer a good deal about the state of culture attained by the Indo-Europeans before the various migrations began, probably during the third millennium B.C. or even somewhat earlier.[25] This culture was not contemptible; it was in fact considerably more advanced than that of some groups of people living today. As we have seen, they had a clear sense of family relationship and hence of the family organization, and they could count. They made use of gold and perhaps silver as well; copper and iron were not to come until later. They drank a honey-flavored alcoholic beverage whose name has come down to us as *mead.* Words corresponding to *wheel, axle,* and *yoke* make it perfectly clear that they used wheeled vehicles. They were small farmers, not nomads, who worked their fields with plows, and they had domesti-

---

[24] German has *t* from earlier *þ* in a very few words, for instance, *tausend* 'thousand.'

[25] See Calvert Watkins, "Indo-European and the Indo-Europeans," particularly the subsection "Lexicon and Culture," in the Appendix to *The American Heritage Dictionary* (Boston, 1969). In an appendix to this Appendix ("Guide to the Appendix"), Watkins lists the Indo-European stems that occur in items listed in the dictionary proper. It all makes for fascinating, and at the same time rewarding, browsing.

cated animals and fowls. They had religious feeling of a sort, with a conception, not of God, but of gods. This much we can say on the basis of forms which were not actually recorded until long after Indo-European had ceased to be a more or less unified language.

THE INDO-EUROPEAN HOMELAND

Conjectures differ as to the original Indo-European homeland—or at least the earliest for which we have any evidence. Plant and animal names are the principal clues, and the flora and fauna which these denote are northern European. The existence of cognates denoting trees which grow in northern Europe (*oak, birch, willow*), though they may grow elsewhere as well, coupled with the absence of such related words for Mediterranean or Asiatic trees (*olive, cypress, palm*); the similar occurrence of cognates of *wolf, bear, lax*[26] (Old English *leax* 'salmon'), and of a word signifying 'turtle,' but none for creatures indigenous to Asia—all this points to northern Europe as the predispersion home, just as the absence of a common word for *ocean* indicates, though it does not in itself prove, that this homeland was inland. Paul Thieme in his cogently reasoned *Die Heimat der indogermanischen Gemeinsprache* (Wiesbaden, 1954) and in the article cited above (n. 9) localizes the Indo-European homeland in the northern part of Central Europe, between the Vistula and the Elbe, on the basis of evidence adduced from the prehistoric geographical distribution of the beech, the turtle, and the salmon. Other Indo-Europeanists have argued from similar evidence for southern Russia, the Carpathians, Scandinavia, and southwestern Asia. The preponderance of scholarly opinion nowadays is in favor of a European center of dispersion—an opinion which implies that the earliest migrations were in a southeasterly direction.

THE MAIN DIVISIONS
OF THE INDO-EUROPEAN GROUP

Of some Indo-European languages—for example Phrygian, Scythian, Macedonian, and Illyrian—we possess only the scantiest remains. We may be certain that others have disappeared without leaving a trace. Members of the following subgroups survive as living tongues: Indo-Iranian, Balto-Slavic, Hellenic, Italic, Celtic, and Germanic.

[26] This word seems to have gone out of general use in English a long time ago. Its Yiddish cognate (written *lox,* in German *Lachs*) has recently entered English as a loanword. There are cognates in Lithuanian, Old Prussian, Russian, Tocharian, and other languages.

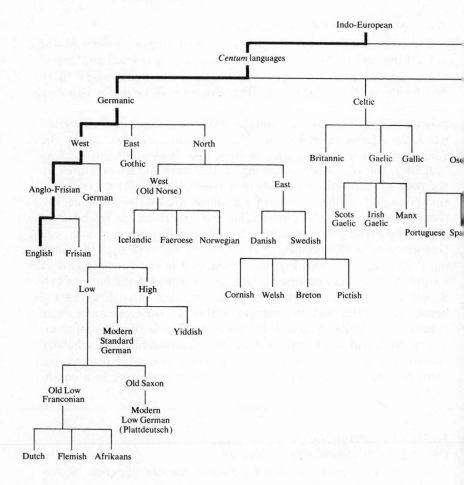

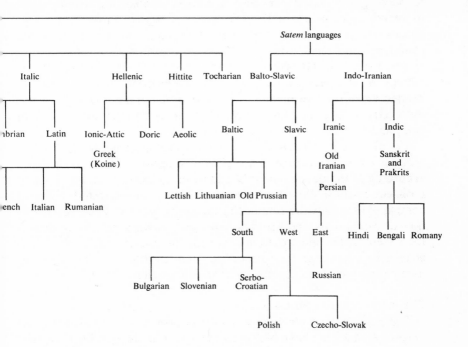

Satem languages

Italic   Hellenic   Hittite   Tocharian   Balto-Slavic   Indo-Iranian

ıbrian   Latin   Ionic-Attic   Doric   Aeolic   Baltic   Slavic   Iranic   Indic

Greek
(Koine)

Old
Iranian

Sanskrit
and
Prakrits

ench   Italian   Rumanian   Lettish   Lithuanian   Old Prussian   Persian

South   West   East   Hindi   Bengali   Romany

Bulgarian   Slovenian   Serbo-
Croatian   Russian

Polish   Czecho-Slovak

INDO-EUROPEAN
AND THE
MORE IMPORTANT LANGUAGES
DEVELOPED FROM IT

Albanian and Armenian are also Indo-European, but do not fit into any of these subgroups.

The Indo-European languages have been conveniently classified into *satem* languages and *centum* languages, *satem* and *centum* being respectively the Avestan (a form of Old Persian) and Latin words corresponding to *hundred*. The classification is based on the development, in very ancient times, of Indo-European palatal *k*. In the *satem* languages — Indo-Iranian, Balto-Slavic, Armenian, and Albanian — this *k* sound became some sort of sibilant: for example Sanskrit (Indic) *śatam*, Lithuanian (Baltic) *šiṁtas*, Old Slavic *sŭto*.[27] In the other Indo-European languages the earlier *k* of Indo-European **kmtóm* either remained or, in the Germanic group, shifted to *h* in the First Consonant Shift (Grimm's Law), as in Greek (Hellenic) *(he)katon*, Welsh (Celtic) *cant*, and Old English (Germanic) *hund*.[28]

The discovery of Tocharian, a *centum* language, early in our century was somewhat disturbing to the general supposition that this division according to the development of Indo-European palatal *k* represented a dialectal split in Indo-European, with those who migrated eastward coming to assibilate the sound. But the assumption of an earlier migration of Tocharians and Hittites, who also spoke a *centum* language, from Central Europe would account for the presence of *centum* languages in what was thought of as *satem* territory. It must be remembered, however, that this is only an inference.

The Indo-Iranian Languages

The Indo-Iranian (*Iranian* is another form of *Aryan*) group is the oldest for which we have historical records. It is the usual opinion that the Vedic hymns, written in an early form of Sanskrit, date from about the middle of the second millennium B.C. Classical Sanskrit appears more than a thousand years later. It is much more systematized than Vedic Sanskrit, for it had been seized upon by a tribe of grammarians who formulated rules for writing it; even so, this was probably not until

---

[27] Linguistic history often repeats itself: the prehistoric treatment of palatal *k* in the *satem* languages resulting ultimately in its becoming a sibilant was precisely the same thing which took place much later — perhaps about the third century of the Christian Era — in Latin *centum* (and in all other words in which the sound [k], spelled with *c* in Latin, occurred before the palatal, or front, vowels *e* and *i*). This change is responsible for the occurrence of a sibilant in all the languages derived from Latin; for example the [č] in Italian *cento* and the [s] in French *cent,* Portuguese *cento,* and non-Castilian Spanish *ciento.*

[28] Modern English *hundred* is a compound, first occurring late in the Old English period. The *-red* is a development of what was once an independent word meaning 'number.'

Sanskrit was ceasing to be widely spoken. The most remarkable of the Indian grammarians was Panini, who, at about the same time (fourth century B.C.) that the Greeks were indulging in more or less reckless speculations about language and in fantastic etymologizing,[29] wrote a grammar of Sanskrit which to this day holds the admiration of linguistic scholars. But there were yet others whose work, motivated as was Panini's by the importance of preserving unchanged the language of the old sacred literature, puts much of the grammatical writing of the Greeks and Romans to shame.

The written language was fixed by these grammarians, and Sanskrit is still written by Indian scholars according to their rules. It is in no sense dead as a written language; its status is roughly comparable to that of Latin in medieval and Renaissance Europe.

Indic dialects had developed, as we might expect, long before Sanskrit became an inflexible and learned language. These are known as Prakrits, and some of them—notably Pali, the religious language of Buddhism—achieved high literary status. From these Prakrits are indirectly derived the various non-Dravidian languages of India, the most widely known of which are Bengali, Hindi, Hindustani (a variety of Hindi, with mixed word stock), and Urdu, derived from Hindustani. Gypsy, or Romany,[30] is also an Indic dialect, with many loan-words from other languages acquired in the course of the Gypsies' wanderings. When they first appeared in Europe in the late Middle Ages, many people supposed them to be Egyptians—whence the name given them in English and some other languages. A long time passed before the study of their language was to indicate unmistakably that they had come originally from northwestern India.

Those Indo-Europeans who settled permanently in the Iranian Plateau developed a sacred language, Avestan, sometimes incorrectly called Zend,[31] preserved in the religious book the Avesta, after which the language is named. There are no modern descendants of Avestan, which is by some believed to be the language of the Medes, whose name is frequently coupled with that of the Persians, most notably in

---

[29] The Romans later did no better, even deriving names of things from what they were *not*. Thus they fancied *bellum* 'war' was so named because it was not *bellus* 'beautiful.' The Middle Ages and the Renaissance failed to improve much on the Romans.

[30] *Romany* has nothing to do with *Rome, Romance, Romaic* (Modern Greek), or *Rumanian*, but is derived from Gypsy *rom* 'man,' ultimately Sanskrit. The *rye* of *Romany rye* (that is, 'Gypsy gentlemen') likewise has nothing to do with the cereal crop, but is a Gypsy word akin to Sanskrit *rājan* 'king,' as well as to Latin *rēx* and German *Reich*.

[31] Actually the Middle Persian language of later commentaries on the Avesta.

the phrase "the law of the Medes and Persians, which altereth not" (Daniel vi.8). Avestan was the language of the sage Zarathustra— Zoroaster to the Greeks—many of whose followers fled to India at the time of the Mohammedan conquest of their country in the eighth century. These are the ancestors of the modern Parsees (that is, Persians) of Bombay. Persian is a different dialect from Avestan; it is the dialect of the district known to the Greeks as Persis, whose inhabitants under the leadership of the great Cyrus in the sixth century B.C. became the predominant tribe.

Armenian and Albanian

Armenian and Albanian, as we have seen, do not fit into any subgroups. The first has in its word stock so many Persian loan-words that it was once supposed to belong to the Indo-Iranian group; there are also many borrowings from Greek and from Arabic and Syrian. Albanian also has a mixed vocabulary, with words from Italian, Slavic, Turkish, and Greek.

The Balto-Slavic Languages

The relationship between the Baltic and the Slavic languages is quite remote, yet so unmistakable that we must assume a common ancestor closer than Indo-European, called Balto-Slavic. The chief Baltic language is Lithuanian; the closely related Lettish is spoken in Latvia, to the north of Lithuania and like it now a part of the Soviet Union. Lithuanian is a notable example of a language which has changed little for thousands of years and hence, like Sanskrit and Greek, has preserved old forms lost in related languages. Still another Baltic language, Prussian, was spoken as late as the seventeenth century in what is now called East Prussia, which was considered outside of Germany until the early years of the nineteenth century. Prussia in time became the predominant state of the new German Empire. The Prussians, like the Lithuanians and the Letts, were heathens until the end of the Middle Ages, when they were converted at the point of the sword by the Knights of the Teutonic Order—a military order which was an outcome of the Crusades. The aristocracy of the region (their descendants are the Prussian *Junkers*) came to be made up of members of this order, who, having saved the souls of the heathen Balts, proceeded to take over their lands.

Slavic falls into three main subdivisions: East Slavic includes Great Russian (or just Russian), the common and literary language of Russia; Ukrainian (or Ruthenian), sometimes called Little Russian; and White Russian (or Byelorussian), spoken in the region directly to the north of the Ukraine. West Slavic includes Polish, Czech, the highly similar Slovak, and Sorbian (or Wendish), a language spoken by a small group of people in East Germany; these languages have lost many of the early forms preserved in East Slavic. The South Slavic languages are Bulgarian, Serbo-Croatian, and Slovenian. The oldest Slavic writing which we know is in Old Bulgarian, sometimes called Old Church Slavic (or Old Church Slavonic), which remained a liturgical language long after it ceased to be generally spoken.

Modern Greek and the Hellenic Dialects

In ancient times there were many Hellenic dialects, among them Aeolic, Doric, and Ionic, which included Attic. As in the course of history Athens came to assume tremendous prestige, its dialect, Attic — that of all the giants of the Age of Pericles — became the basis of a standard for the entire Greek world, a koine (that is, *koinē* [*dialektos*] 'common [dialect]') which was ultimately to drive out the other Hellenic dialects. The various local dialects spoken in Greece today, as well as the standard language, are thus all derived from Attic. With all their glorious ancient literature, the Greeks have not had a modern literary language until comparatively recently. This "purified" literary language makes considerable use of words revived from ancient Greek, as well as a number of ancient inflectional forms; it has become the ordinary language of the upper classes. A more natural development of the Attic koine is spoken by the masses and hence called *demotike*.

The Italic Languages

As in the ancient Hellenic world, so also in ancient Italia there were a number of dialects, among them Oscan, Umbrian, and Latin, the speech of Latium, whose chief city was Rome. As Rome came to dominate the Italic world, spreading its influence into Gaul, Spain, and the Illyrian and Danubian countries (and even into Britain, where it failed to displace Celtic), it became a koine as the dialect of Athens had done.

Spoken Latin, as has been noted, survives in the Romance languages. It was quite a different thing from the more or less artificial literary language of Cicero. All the Romance languages — such as Italian, Spanish, Catalan, Galician, Portuguese, French, Provençal, and Rumanian — are developments of the Vulgar Latin (so called because it was the speech of the *vulgus* 'common people') spoken in various parts of the Roman Empire in the early Middle Ages. Rhaeto-Romanic comprises a number of dialects spoken in the most easterly Swiss canton called the Grisons (German *Graubünden*) and in the Tyrol. In southern Belgium a dialect of French, called Walloon, is spoken. Other French dialects have included Norman — the source of the Anglo-Norman dialect spoken in England after the Norman Conquest — Picard, and the dialect of Paris and the surrounding regions (the Île-de-France), which for obvious reasons became Standard French.[32] For similar reasons the speech of the old kingdom of Castile, the largest and most important part of Spain, became Standard Spanish.[33] Because of the cultural preeminence of Tuscany during the Italian Renaissance, the speech of that region — and specifically of the city of Florence — became the standard of Italian speech. Both Dante and Petrarch wrote in this form of Italian.

The Celtic Languages

Celtic shows such striking correspondences with Italic in certain parts of its verbal system and in inflectional endings as to indicate a relationship between them which is rather close, though not so close as that between Indic and Iranian or Baltic and Slavic. Some scholars therefore group them together as developments of a language which they call Celto-Italic.

The Celts were spread over a huge territory in Europe long before the emergence in history of the Germanic peoples. Before the beginning of the Christian Era Celtic languages were spoken over the greater part of central and western Europe, and by the latter part of the third century B.C. even in Asia Minor, in the region called for them Galatia, to whose inhabitants Paul later addressed a famous letter. As the fortunes and the warlike vigor of the Celts declined, their languages were supplanted by those of their conquerors. Thus, the Celtic language spoken in Gaul (called Gallic or Gaulish) gave way completely to the Latin spoken by the Roman conquerors, which was to develop into French.

Roman rule seems to have had comparatively little effect on the continued use of their language by the British Celts. But they were ultimately to give it up after the Angles, Saxons, and Jutes arrived — though not altogether, for British (Brythonic, Britannic) Celtic still

---

[32] The highly similar varieties of French spoken in Quebec, Nova Scotia, New Brunswick, and Louisiana are developments of the dialects of northern France and are no more to be regarded as "corruptions" of modern Standard French than American English is to be regarded as a corruption of the present British Standard. The "Cajuns" (that is, Acadians) of Louisiana are descendants of exiles from Nova Scotia, which was earlier a French colony called Acadia.

[33] The fact that Spanish America was settled in large part from Andalusia rather than from Castile accounts for the most important differences in pronunciation between Latin-American Spanish and the standard language of Spain.

lives, if somewhat feebly, in Welsh (Cymric) and in Breton. Breton is the language of the descendants of those Britons who, around the time of the Anglo-Saxon invasion of their island and even somewhat before that time, crossed the Channel and settled in the Gaulish province of Armorica, naming their new home for their old one – Brittany. Breton is thus more closely related to Welsh than to long-extinct Gallic. There have been no native speakers of Cornish, another British language, since the early nineteenth century. Still another British language, Pictish, preserved in a few glosses and place-name elements, was spoken by the Picts in the northwestern part of Britain, in which many Gaelic Celts also settled. These Irishmen, or Scots (*Scotti*) as they were then called, named their new home Scotia, or Scotland.

The Celtic language which spread from Ireland, called Gaelic or Goidelic, was of a type somewhat different from that of the Britons. It was ultimately adopted by the Picts and survives in Scots Gaelic, sometimes called Erse, a word which is simply a variant of *Irish*. Scots Gaelic is spoken in the remoter parts of the Scottish highlands and in a somewhat different development on the Isle of Man (where it is called Manx). In Ireland, which was little affected by either the Roman or the later Anglo-Saxon invasions, Irish Gaelic survived until well into the nineteenth century, but ultimately gave way to English. It has fairly recently been revived for nationalistic reasons in Eire, but this resuscitation, roughly comparable to the official use of Hebrew in modern Israel, cannot be regarded as in any sense a natural development. It is taught, probably somewhat perfunctorily, in the schools.

The Germanic Languages

The Germanic group merits a somewhat fuller treatment than has been given to any of the other groups because English belongs to it. In the course of many centuries certain radical developments occurred in the more or less unified language spoken by those Indo-European peoples living in Denmark and the regions thereabout – developments which differentiate it from all the other Indo-European languages more markedly than these are differentiated from Proto-Indo-European and hence from one another. The period during which these developments were occurring we may refer to as Pre-Germanic. *Germanic*[34] is the usual term for the relatively unified language – distinctive in many of its

---

[34] This term seems preferable to *Teutonic* or *Gothonic*. When the Romans referred to the Germanic nations (or to Germania), they included in the term Goths, Germans, Angles, Saxons, Frisians, and Scandinavians. Unfortunately *Germanic* has acquired a more limited meaning in English, with nationalistic connotations, but there are equally important objections to the other terms used.

sounds, its inflections, its accentual system, and its word stock — which resulted from these developments.

Unfortunately for us, those who spoke this particular development of Indo-European did not write. Germanic is to German, Dutch, the Scandinavian languages, and English as Latin is to Italian, French, and Spanish. But Germanic, which was probably being spoken shortly before the beginning of the Christian Era, must be reconstructed just like Indo-European. Latin, on the other hand, is amply recorded.

Spread over a large area as Germanic in time came to be, it was inevitable that more and more marked dialectal differences should have occurred, leading to a division into East Germanic, West Germanic, and North Germanic. The only East Germanic language of which we have any detailed knowledge is Gothic. The North Germanic languages are Danish, Swedish, Norwegian, Icelandic, and Faeroese, the last named highly similar to Icelandic and spoken in the Faeroe Islands, located in the North Atlantic about midway between Iceland and Great Britain. The West Germanic languages are High German,[35] Low German (*Plattdeutsch*), Dutch[36] and the practically identical Flemish, Frisian, and English. Some scholars prefer to group Gothic with the North Germanic languages because of certain parallels which indicate that it was closer to Old Norse than to West Germanic. But, as E. Prokosch has pointed out, "these are hardly more important than the parallels between Gothic and West Germanic on the one hand, and Norse and West Germanic on the other," concluding that "none of these three groups of parallels is important enough to have any influence on the classification of the Germanic languages, and it seems best to consider the three groups independent branches."[37]

THE MAJOR CHANGES
FROM INDO-EUROPEAN TO GERMANIC

Germanic became differentiated from Indo-European principally in the following respects:

    1. All Indo-European distinctions of tense and aspect[38] were lost in

---

[35] Yiddish (Judeo-German) is a development of a number of medieval High German dialects, with many words from Hebrew and Slavic.

[36] Afrikaans is a development of seventeenth-century Dutch spoken in South Africa.

[37] *A Comparative Germanic Grammar* (Philadelphia, 1939), p. 30.

[38] A modification of the form of verbs to indicate whether an action or state is viewed with regard to its beginning, duration, incompletion, completion, or repetition. Languages which lack inflectional forms to indicate such stages in action or being must employ phrases to express them, for instance *he is walking, he is being* (incompleted action or state), *he has walked, he has been* (completed action or state), and the like.

the verb save for the present and the preterit[39] tenses. This simplification of a more complex Indo-European verbal system (though it was not so complex as what developed in Latin, Greek, and Sanskrit) is reflected in all the languages which have developed out of Germanic — in English *bind–bound,* as well as in German *binden–band,* Old Norse *binda–band,* and all the rest. There is in no Germanic language anything comparable to such forms as those of the Latin future, perfect, pluperfect, and future perfect forms (for instance *laudābō, laudāvī, laudāveram, laudāverō*), which must be rendered in the Germanic languages by verb phrases (for instance English *I shall praise, I have praised, I had praised, I shall have praised*).

2. Germanic developed a preterit tense form with a dental suffix, that is, one containing *d* or *t.* All languages derived from Germanic thus have two types of verbs. Those which are distinctly Germanic — that is, those which employ the dental suffix — were called "weak" by Jacob Grimm because, being incapable of the type of internal change of *rise–rose* and *sing–sang* (which he called "strong"), they had to make do with suffixes (*"mit äusseren Mitteln"*), like *step-stepped* and *talk–talked.* Although Grimm's terminology is not very satisfactory, it has become traditional and is at least as realistic as "regular" and "irregular." An overwhelming majority of our verbs add the dental suffix in the preterit — it is indeed the only living method of inflection for tense in English as in all the other Germanic languages[40] — and this method has thus been thought of as "regular." Historically speaking, however, the vowel gradation of the strong verbs is quite regular, and some of the weak verbs would probably seem quite irregular to the untrained observer. *Bring, think,* and *buy,* for instance, are weak verbs, as the dental suffix of *brought, thought,* and *bought* indicates; the vowel changes here are due not to Indo-European vowel gradation, but to special factors. The suffix is the real test. No attempt at explaining the origin of this suffix has been wholly satisfactory. Many have thought that it was originally an independent word meaning, and cognate with, *do;* but there are grave objections to this theory.

---

[39] From a historical and comparative point of view, *preterit* is a better term than *past,* which is good enough if our concern is only with the present state of the Germanic languages. *Preterit* designates the absolute past (*walked, was*) without reference to such aspects of past action or state as are expressed in *was walking, was being* (imperfect, or incompleted, action or state), *had eaten, had been* (perfect, or completed, action or state), or to any other stages of past action or state.

[40] For example, new verbs form their preterit so: *elbow–elbowed, televise–televised, rev–revved,* and so forth. Furthermore, as we shall see later, many verbs which were once strong have become weak.

3. For adjectives, Germanic had a so-called weak declension, to be used chiefly when preceded by a pronoun (that is, a pronominal adjective, including the demonstrative pronoun which developed into the definite article). Thus in Old English, *þā geongan ceorlas* 'the young fellows (churls),' with the weak form of *geong*, but *geonge ceorlas* 'young fellows,' with the strong form; likewise in German, *die jungen Kerle*, but *junge Kerle*. This particular Germanic characteristic cannot be illustrated in Modern English, inasmuch as in the course of its development English has lost all such declension of the adjective.

4. The "free" accentual system of Indo-European, in which any syllable of a word might be accented, gave way to another type of accentuation in which the first syllable was regularly stressed in all words except compound verbs like modern *believe* and *forget*—that is, verbs in which the initial syllable was a prefix. None of the Germanic languages has anything comparable to the shifting accentuation of Latin *vírī* 'men,' *virórum* 'of the men' or of *hábeō*, 'I have,' *habémus* 'we have.' Compare the paradigms of the Greek and Old English developments of Indo-European **pətér* 'father.'

GREEK

Singular nominative	patér
Singular genitive	patrós
Singular dative	patrí
Singular accusative	patéra
Singular vocative	páter
Plural nominative	patéres (same for vocative)
Plural genitive	patérōn
Plural dative	patrási
Plural accusative	patéras

OLD ENGLISH

Singular nom., dat., acc.	fǽder
Singular genitive	fǽder(es)
Plural nom., acc.	fǽderas
Plural genitive	fǽdera
Plural dative	fǽderum

In these paradigms it will be noted that in the Greek forms the accent may occur on the suffix, the ending, or the root, unlike the Old English forms, which are representative of the Germanic accentual system in having their accent fixed on the root. Germanic accent is predominantly a matter of stress (loudness) rather than pitch (tone); Indo-European would seem to have had both types of accent at different stages of its development.

5. Indo-European vowels underwent Germanic modification. Indo-European *o*, retained in Latin, became *a* (compare Lat. *octo* 'eight,' Gothic *ahtau*); Indo-European *ā* became *ō* (Lat. *māter* 'mother,' OE *mōdor*); and there were other changes as well, which we shall not go into here.

6. The Indo-European stops *bh, dh, gh, p, t, k, b, d,* and *g* – that is, the *sounds* later symbolized by these letters – all underwent modification in what is called the First Sound Shift or, less happily, Grimm's Law. These modifications were gradual, extending over rather long periods of time. Rather than use reconstructed forms preceded by asterisks, we may illustrate this shift – really a series of shifts – by showing correspondences between a non-Germanic language, usually Latin, and English.[41]

a. Indo-European *bh, dh, gh* became respectively Germanic *ƀ, ð, ʒ,*[42] and later, in initial position at least, *b, d, g*. Stated in phonetic terms, aspirated voiced stops became voiced fricatives and then unaspirated voiced stops. *Bh* appears in Latin initially as *f* (medially as *b*), in Greek as *φ* (an aspirated *p*, later becoming [f]), written *ph* in Latin transcriptions of Greek, as we have seen in the preceding chapter. *Dh* also became *f* in Latin initially, but *d* medially; in Greek the Indo-European sound appears as *θ* (an aspirated *t*), the *th* of Latin transcriptions. *Gh* appears in Latin as *h*, but medially as *g;* in Greek as *χ* (an aspirated *k*), the *ch* of Latin transcriptions. Unless these non-Germanic changes are borne in mind, the examples to be cited below will not make sense. Except for initial *b*, the other stops are preserved in

---

[41] Derivatives of many of the Latin and Greek cognates to be cited below occur in English as loan-words, some having entered by way of French. Compare, for instance, such pairs as *fraternity–brotherhood, fragile–breakable, fundament–bottom, horticulture–gardening, paternal–fatherly, pyrotechnics–fireworks, pedal–foot, tenuous–thin, cornet–horn, cordial–hearty, canine–hound, gelid–cold,* and so forth.

[42] The *ƀ* symbolizes a voiced bilabial fricative (IPA [β]), the sound symbolized in Spanish by *b* or *v*. The *ð* stands for precisely the sound which it symbolizes in the alphabet of the International Phonetic Association, the initial consonant of *them.* The *ʒ* indicates the velar fricative plus voice, or resonance (IPA [ɣ]). Authorities identify it with the medial consonant of North German *sagen;* but, unless one has a North German handy, this is of little help. The symbol was used in the course of the Old English period with this value, as well as for [g] and [j].

Latin and Greek. Correspondences may be noted in the following pairs of related words, in which the first member of each pair is Latin unless otherwise labeled:

INDO-EUROPEAN *bh* (LATIN *f*, GREEK *ph*) / GERMANIC *b*

---

frāter / brother   fundus (for **fudnus*) / bottom
fiber / beaver   fāgus / beech
flāre / blow   (Gr.) phōgein 'to roast' / bake
fra(n)go / break

INDO-EUROPEAN *dh* (LATIN *f*, GREEK *th*) / GERMANIC *d*

---

fi(n)gere 'to mold' / dough   (Gr.) thē- 'to place' / do
foris / door   (Gr.) thygatēr / daughter

INDO-EUROPEAN *gh* (LATIN *h*, GREEK *ch*) / GERMANIC *g*

---

hortus / OE geard 'yard'   (Gr.) cholē (whence *cholera*) / gall
hostis / guest   (pre)he(n)dere 'to take' / get
homo / gome (obsolete)   haedus 'kid' / goat

b. Except when preceded by *s*, the Indo-European voiceless stops *p, t, k* became respectively the voiceless fricatives *f, þ, x*[43] (later *h* in initial position):

INDO-EUROPEAN *p* / GERMANIC *f*

---

pater / father   portus / ford
piscis / fish   pullus / foal
pellis / fell 'animal hide'   ped- / foot
(Gr.) pyr / fire   pecu 'cattle' / fee
                                       (cf. Ger. *Vieh* 'cattle')

---

[43] That is, the velar fricative and doubtless also its palatal allophone. The *x* is thus used here without brackets and similarly throughout this chapter with the value which it has in the alphabet of the International Phonetic Association. (IPA uses [ç] for the more forward variety.) It should not be confused with the letter *x* as used since Old English times to spell [ks].

INDO-EUROPEAN *t* / GERMANIC *þ*

trēs / three	tenuis / thin
torrēre 'to dry' / thirst	tumēre 'to swell' / thumb
	(that is, fat finger)
tu / thou	tonāre / thunder

INDO-EUROPEAN *k* / GERMANIC *h*

cornū / horn	cent- / hund(red)
cord- / heart	celāre 'to hide' / hele
	(obsolete), hall, hell
quod / what (OE *hwæt*)	capere 'to take' / heave, have
cervus / hart	canis / hound

c. The Indo-European voiced stops *b, d, g* became respectively the voiceless stops *p, t, k.* Initial *b* was very infrequent in Indo-European. Rasmus Rask cites Greek *kannabis* and Old Norse *hampr* (English *hemp*) as showing the correspondence of *b* and *p.* Latin *turba* 'crowd' and English *thorp* 'town' (as in *Halethorp* and, with metathesis,[44] *Winthrop*) have also been cited. Other certain examples are hard to come by. The shifting of *d* and *g* is illustrated by the following cognates:

INDO-EUROPEAN *d* / GERMANIC *t*

duo / two	(Gr.) drys 'oak' / tree
dentis / tooth	decem / ten (Gothic *taíhun*)
domāre / tame	edere / eat

INDO-EUROPEAN *g* / GERMANIC *k*

genu / knee (loss of	(Gr.) gynē 'woman' / queen, quean
[k-] is modern)	
ager 'field' / acre	grānum / corn
genus / kin	(g)noscere / know, can

Although we cannot be sure of the chronology of these consonant

---

[44] A change in the position of sounds or syllables in a word, in this instance of [r].

changes,[45] it is certain that they stretched over centuries — perhaps as much as a millennium. Each set of shifts was completed before the next began; the First Sound Shift was no circular process. It is obvious, for instance, that the shift of Indo-European *b, d,* and *g* to Germanic *p, t,* and *k* must have occurred long after Indo-European *p, t,* and *k* had become Germanic *f, þ,* and *x;* otherwise, the Germanic *p, t,* and *k* from Indo-European *b, d,* and *g* would have gone on to become *f, þ,* and *x* also, and we should have no native words with *p, t,* and *k.*

FIRST SOUND SHIFT (GRIMM'S LAW)

IE bh, dh, gh ———→ (respectively) Gmc ƀ, ð, ȝ ———————→ b, d, g

IE p, t, k ———————→ (respectively) Gmc f, þ, x (→ h initially)

IE b, d, g ———————→ (respectively) Gmc p, t, k

The First Sound Shift antedated the Stress Shift described above, for, at a time when the stress had not yet settled on the first syllables of all Germanic words, the voiceless fricatives *f, þ,* and *x* underwent a further modification in those words in which they were not immediately preceded by the stressed syllable: they were voiced, becoming respectively ƀ, ð, and ȝ. Under the same circumstances, the voiceless fricative *s,* hitherto unchanged from Indo-European, became *z.* The new ƀ, ð, and ȝ underwent the same later developments as the ƀ, ð, and ȝ which had resulted from the shifting of Indo-European *bh, dh,* and *gh.* In Old English, for instance, the ð appears as *d* (as in all other old West Germanic languages) and the ȝ as *g* (under certain circumstances as *w*). The *z* appears as *r*[46] in all recorded Germanic languages save Gothic.

These occurrences of voiced fricatives where according to Grimm's Law we should expect to find voiceless ones were explained by a Danish scholar named Karl Verner in 1875 as being due to the fact that the stress did not immediately precede the consonant in question before the Germanic shift to the first syllable. The same phenomenon

[45] But see the excellently reasoned article by W. F. Twaddell, "The Inner Chronology of the Germanic Consonant Shift," *Journal of English and Germanic Philogy,* 38 (1939), 337–59.

[46] This shift of *z* to *r,* known as *rhotacism* (that is, *r*-ing, from Gr. *rho,* the name of the letter), is by no means peculiar to Germanic: compare Latin *flōs* 'flower,' which has *r* in all forms other than the nominative singular — for instance the genitive singular *flōris,* from earlier **flōz-,* the original *s* being here voiced because of its position between vowels.

may be observed in Modern English words of foreign origin such as *exert* [ɪgzɔ́rt] and *exist* [ɪgzíst] (compare *exercise* [ɛ́ksərsàɪz] and *exigent* [ɛ́ksɪjənt]). For the Germanic languages, such voicing, occurring in prehistoric times, is said to be according to Verner's Law. Grimm, who recognized but failed to comprehend the reason for the voicing, called it "grammatical change" (*grammatischer Wechsel*). The phenomenon is most obvious in the preterit plural and the past participial forms of some Germanic strong verbs — forms in which the stress did not originally fall on the root: thus, in Old English, *sēaþ* '(I, he, she, it) seethed,' but *sudon* '(we, you, they) seethed' and *soden* (past participle). The *d* of the last two forms has developed from Germanic *ð;* in pre-Stress-Shift Germanic these forms did not have initial stress. It is similar with Old English *lēas* '(I, he, she, it) lost' contrasted with *luron* '(we, you, they) lost' and *loren* (past participle), in which the *s,* after being voiced to become z in those forms lacking initial stress, has been subsequently rhotacized.

One further illustration must suffice. Germanic developments of the Indo-European word meaning 'male parent' are evidenced in Gothic *faðar,* written *fadar* (but the *d* in this position most likely indicated the voiced fricative), Icelandic *faðir,* and Old English *fæder* (in which the *d* is, as we have seen, a West Germanic development of earlier *ð*).[47] In all these forms we should ordinarily expect to find *þ* medially, since the Indo-European medial consonant was *t*. But examination of early cognate forms in non-Germanic languages reveals that the stressed syllable in this word followed rather than immediately preceded the *t,* as in Greek *patḗr,* Sanskrit *pitā́.* When the Germanic stress shifted to the first syllable, the reason for the voicing of the consonant was completely obscured. It required comparative linguistics (or comparative philology, as it was then called) to solve the puzzle presented by such apparent exceptions to the workings of the First Sound Shift — to demonstrate that they were *only* apparent, and not real exceptions.

7. Germanic has a large number of words which have no known cognates in other Indo-European languages. These could of course have existed in Indo-European and have been lost; it is also possible that they were taken from non-Indo-European languages originally spoken in the area occupied by the Germanic peoples. A few words which are apparently distinctively Germanic, given in their Modern

---

[47] The fact that Modern English *father* has the same medial consonant as Proto-Germanic is sheer coincidence. The [ð] in this word, like that in *mother,* is comparatively recent — perhaps no older than the sixteenth century. Earlier [d] was "sometimes heard" in northern England and the lowlands of Scotland at the time of the publication of the relevant section of the *OED* (1895), and may still be.

VERNER'S LAW

Later developments in the various Germanic languages which have obscured the workings of the shift are not indicated in the table below, where each of the consonants in question plus *A* stands for a syllable headed by that consonant, *O* standing for any preceding syllable; thus, *OtÁ* represents Indo-European *pǝtér* 'father,' *kmtóm* 'hundred,' and so forth:

IE OpÁ————→Gmc OfÁ →ObÁ→ÓbA
IE OtÁ ————→Gmc OþÁ→OðÁ→ÓðA (→WGmc ÓdA)
IE OkÁ————→Gmc OxÁ→OʒÁ→ÓʒA
IE OsÁ (remains) Gmc OsÁ→OzÁ→ÓzA→ÓrA (except in Gothic)

English forms, are *rain, drink, drive, broad, hold,*[48] *wife, meat,* and *fowl.*

The earliest records in any Germanic language, aside from a few proper names recorded by classical authors, a few loan-words in Finnish, and some runic inscriptions found in Scandinavia, are those of Gothic.[49] For almost all our knowledge of Gothic we are indebted to a translation of parts of the New Testament made in the fourth century by Wulfila (*Ulfilas* to the Greeks), bishop of the Visigoths, those Goths who lived north of the Danube. There are also small fragments of two other books of the Bible and of a commentary on the Gospel of John. Late as they are in comparison with the literary records of Sanskrit, Iranian, Greek, and Latin, these remains of Gothic provide us with a clear picture of a Germanic language in an early stage of development and hence are of tremendous importance to the student of Germanic languages. Etymological dictionaries of English cite Gothic cognates of English words (for instance *light–leihts, find–finþan*) when the related Gothic form occurs in the literature cited above. Gothic as a spoken tongue disappeared a long time ago without leaving a trace. No modern

[48] These are all cited in their modern High German forms (*Regen, trinken, treiben, breit, halten*) by Robert Priebsch and W. E. Collinson, *The German Language*, 4th ed., rev. (London, 1958), pp. 281–82.

[49] *Gothic* was in the seventeenth and eighteenth centuries extended to mean 'Germanic,' even in the linguistic sense, but this meaning is now happily obsolete. It also came to mean 'romantically medieval' – a meaning which survives in the name of a fictional genre (*Gothic novel*) and of a style of architecture.

Germanic languages are derived from it, nor are there any Gothic loan-words in any of the Germanic languages. Vandalic and Burgundian were apparently also East Germanic in structure, but we know little more of them at first hand than a few proper names. Certain differences between modern Standard German and the other West Germanic languages are due to a second sound shift — the so-called High German Shift — which occurred comparatively recently as linguistic history goes. It was nearing its completion by the end of the eighth century of our era. This shift began in the southern, mountainous part of Germany and spread northward, stopping short of the low-lying northern section of the country. The *high* in High German (*Hochdeutsch*) and the *low* in Low German (*Plattdeutsch*) refer only to relative distances above sea level. High German became in time Standard German, relegating Low German to the status of a peasant patois in Germany.

FROM GERMANIC TO ENGLISH

The Continental home of the English was north of the area in which the High German Shift occurred. But even if this had not been so, the English language would have been unaffected by changes which had not begun to occur at the time of the Anglo-Saxon migrations to Britain, which began as early as the mid-fifth century. Consequently English has the earlier consonantal characteristics of Germanic, which among the West Germanic languages it shares with Low German, Dutch, Flemish, and Frisian. We may illustrate the High German shift in part by contrasting English and High German forms, as follows: earlier Germanic *p* appears in High German as *pf* or, after vowels, as *ff* (*pepper–Pfeffer*); earlier *t* appears as *ts* (spelled *z*) or, after vowels, as *ss* (*tongue–Zunge; water–Wasser*); earlier *k* appears after vowels as *ch* (*break–brechen*); earlier *d* appears as *t* (*dance–tanzen*).

The German spoken by more or less simple folk in northern Germany is a development of Old Saxon, and it alone now bears the proper name Low German, though as we have seen it is only one type of low German. Dutch and the practically identical Flemish are the modern forms of Low Franconian, spoken respectively in Holland and, side by side with French, in Belgium. Formerly spoken in a much larger area, including the west coast of Schleswig, Frisian has survived principally in the northern Dutch province of Friesland and in some of the islands off the coast. English and Frisian share certain features not found elsewhere in the Germanic group to such an extent that scholars regard them as developments of a relatively unified prehistoric language called Anglo-Frisian, a subgroup of West Germanic. Old English, Old

Frisian, and Old Saxon, sometimes grouped together as Ingvaeonic,[50] share alike the older consonantal characteristics and are likewise distinguished from Old High German in other rather striking ways. One of these is the loss of nasal consonants before the fricatives *f, s,* and *þ,* with lengthening of the preceding vowel: compare (Old) High German *gans* with Old English *gōs* 'goose,' Old High German *fimf* (Modern German *fünf*) with Old English *fīf* 'five,' (Old) High German *mund* (Germanic *munþ-*) with Old English *mūd* 'mouth.' But Old English and Old Frisian are distinguished in equally striking ways from Old Saxon;[51] hence the postulated Anglo-Frisian as the most immediate common source of English and Frisian.[52]

English, then, began its separate existence as a form of Germanic brought by pagan warrior-adventurers from the Continent to the then relatively obscure island which the Romans called Britannia and which had up until a short time before been part of their mighty empire. There, in the next five centuries or so, it was to develop into an independent language quite distinct from any Germanic language spoken on the Continent. Moreover, it had become a language sufficiently rich in its word stock, thanks largely to the impetus given to learning by the introduction of Christianity, that, as Kemp Malone puts it, "by the year 1000, this newcomer could measure swords with Latin in every department of expression, and was incomparably superior to the French speech that came in with William of Normandy."[53]

---

[50] From the term used by Tacitus in *Germania* ii (in the form *Ingaevones*) for that group of the Germanic peoples who lived "near to the ocean" (*proximi Oceano*). The name is ultimately Germanic, appearing in Old English as *Ingwine* 'Ing's friends,' Ing having supposedly been a Germanic wonder-worker. The *Beowulf* poet somehow connects the term with the Danes. It should be noted that Tacitus' division of the people of Germania into Ingaevones, Herminones, and Istaevones is very ancient and that Tacitus actually knew little about such divisions.

[51] For discussion and exemplification of these, see A. Campbell, *Old English Grammar* (Oxford, 1959), pp. 2–3, 50–54, 173–79.

[52] It is the belief of some scholars that the Old Saxon which we know mainly from two ninth-century poems (the *Heliand* and the *Genesis*) might have been influenced by Old High German, and that in an earlier period it might well have exhibited all those features usually regarded as peculiarly Old English and Old Frisian.

[53] *A Literary History of England,* ed. Albert C. Baugh (New York, 1948), p. 10.

V

The Old English
Period (449–1100)

A Celtic people had been in Britain for many centuries before Julius Caesar's invasion of that island in 55 B.C. The subsequent occupation, not really begun in earnest until the time of the Emperor Claudius almost a century later, was to make Britain – that is, Britannia – a part of the Roman Empire for a period somewhat longer than that intervening between the first permanent English settlement in America and our own day. It is not therefore surprising that there are so many Roman remains in modern England, some of them discovered quite recently in the very heart of London in the course of clearing away the rubble of World War II bombings. Despite the long occupation, the British Celts continued to speak their own language, though many of them, particularly those in the towns and cities who wanted to "get on," learned to speak and write the language of their Roman rulers. It was not until Britain became England that the survival of British Celtic was seriously threatened.

After the Roman legionaries were withdrawn from Britain in the early years of the fifth century, Picts from the north and Scots from the west savagely attacked the unprotected British Celts, who after generations of foreign domination had neither the heart nor the skill in weapons to put up much resistance. This was Celt eat Celt, for it should be remembered that the Picts were themselves British Celts, and the Scots – that is, Irishmen – were Gaelic Celts (see p. 101). These same Picts and Scots, as well as ferocious Germanic sea raiders whom the Romans called Saxons, had earlier been a very considerable nuisance to the Roman soldiers and their commanders during the latter half of the fourth century.

113

THE COMING OF THE ENGLISH

According to the Venerable Bede's account in his *Ecclesiastical History of the English Nation,* written in Latin and completed around 730, almost three centuries after the event, the Britons appealed to Rome for help. What relief they got, a single legion, was only temporarily effectual. When Rome could or would help no more, the wretched Britons — still according to Bede — ironically enough called the "Saxons" to their aid "from the parts beyond the sea." As a result of this appeal, shiploads of Germanic warrior-adventurers began to arrive. The date which Bede gives for the first landing — 449 — cannot be far out of the way, if at all. With it the Old English period begins. With it, too, we may in a sense begin thinking of Britain as England — the land of the Angles — for, even though the long ships carried Jutes,[1] Saxons, Frisians, and, doubtless, members of other tribes as well, their descendants a century and a half later were already beginning to think of themselves as Englishmen and of their speech as English. (They naturally had no suspicion that it was "Old" English.) The name of a single tribe was thus to be adopted as a national name (prehistoric Old English **Angli,* becoming *Engle*), for what specific reasons we have no way of knowing.

These Germanic sea raiders, ancestors of the English, in short order gave the Pictish and Scottish aggressors what was coming to them. Then, with eyes ever on the main chance, a complete lack of any sense of international morality, and no fear whatever of being prosecuted as war criminals, they very unidealistically, though as it turned out sensibly, proceeded to subjugate and ultimately to dispossess the Britons whom they had come ostensibly to help. Word reached Continental kinsmen and friends of the cowardice of the Britons and the fertility of the island, and in the course of the next hundred years or so more and more of those whom Bede, our primary source for this period, calls Saxons, Angles, and Jutes arrived "from the three most powerful nations of Germania" to seek their fortunes in a new land.

About all that we can be certain of about the events of these exciting times is that the invading newcomers belonged to various Germanic tribes speaking a number of closely related and hence very similar regional types of Germanic, that they came from the great North German plain, including the southern part of the Jutland peninsula (the modern Schleswig-Holstein), and that by the time St. Augustine arrived to convert them to Christianity at the end of the sixth century

[1] More properly *Iuts* or *Euts*. The *I* of Bede's *Iuti* and *Iutae* was confused with *J* so long ago that the error has become traditional.

they held in their possession practically all of what is now known as England. As for the ill-advised Britons, their plight was hopeless; many fled to Wales and Cornwall, some crossed the Channel to Brittany, others were ultimately assimilated to the English by marriage or otherwise; many, we may be sure, lost their lives in the long-drawnout fighting.

The Germanic tribesmen who came first — Bede's *Iutae, Iuti,* or "Jutes," led by the synonymously named brothers Hengest[2] and Horsa (both names mean 'horse') — settled principally in the southeastern part of the island, still called by its Celtic name of Kent. Subsequently Continental Saxons were to occupy the rest of the region south of the Thames, and Angles, stemming presumably from the hook-shaped peninsula in Schleswig known as Angeln, settled the large area stretching from the Thames northward to the Scottish highlands, except for the extreme southwestern portion (Wales).

The Germanic settlement comprised seven kingdoms, the Anglo-Saxon Heptarchy: Kent, Essex, Sussex, Wessex, East Anglia, Mercia, and Northumbria — the last, the land north of the Humber, being an amalgamation of two earlier kingdoms, Bernicia and Deira (see map on next page). Kent early became the chief center of culture and wealth, and by the end of the sixth century its King Ethelbert (Æðelberht) could lay claim to the hegemony over all the other kingdoms south of the Humber. Later, in the seventh and eighth centuries, this supremacy was to pass to Northumbria, with its great centers of learning at Lindisfarne, at Wearmouth, and at Jarrow, Bede's own monastery; then to Mercia; and finally to Wessex, with its brilliant line of kings beginning with Egbert (Ecgberht), who overthrew the Mercian king in 825, and culminating in his grandson, the superlatively great

---

[2] He has been identified with the Hengest who plays a prominent role in the story of the fight at Finn's Borough, recounted in *Beowulf,* lines 1063–1159, and independently in a fragment of another Old English poem. This Hengest of Old English heroic poetry is the retainer of the Danish king Hnæf and, after Hnæf's fall in the treacherous sortie at Finn's Borough, makes peace of a sort with the victorious Finn, king of Frisia, whose subjects also included the Eote (the Old English equivalent of Bede's *Iuti*). The *Beowulf* poet tells us nothing of Hengest's subsequent career, but leaves him brooding vengeance for the death of his lord; he is mentioned only as a prominent Danish warrior in the fragment. Vengeance is later executed upon Finn by a Danish fleet, but what part, if any, Hengest took in it we are not told. The identification of this Hengest with the man mentioned by Bede presupposes that somehow after the death of Finn he, presumably a Dane, became king of the Jutes, at the same time acquiring an ancestry befitting an Anglo-Saxon monarch, for Bede tells us that Hengest and Horsa were the great-grandsons of Woden, the chief Germanic god. That the two Hengests were one and the same man seems on the whole unlikely, yet the possibility tantalizes.

Alfred, whose successors after his death in 899 took for themselves the title *Rex Anglorum* 'King of the English.'

The most important event in the history of Anglo-Saxon culture (which in its broadest sense includes American) occurred in 597, when Gregory I dispatched a band of missionaries to the Angles (*Angli,* as he called them, thereby departing from the usual Continental designation of them as *Saxones*), in accordance with a resolve he had made some years before. The leader of this band was, as everyone knows, St. Augustine — not to be confused with the African-born bishop of Hippo of the same name who wrote *The City of God* more than a century earlier. The apostle to the English and his fellow bringers of the Word, who landed on the Isle of Thanet in Kent, were received by King Ethelbert courteously, if at the beginning a trifle warily. Already somewhat ripe for conversion through his marriage to a Christian Frankish princess, Ethelbert was himself baptized in a matter of months. Four years later, in 601, Augustine was consecrated first Archbishop of Canterbury, and there was a church in England. Later, Irish missionaries who had come from Iona to found a monastery at Lindisfarne made many converts in Northumbria and Mercia. In the course of the seventh century the new faith spread rapidly,[3] and by the end of that century England had become a most important part of Christendom.

THE VIKING CONQUESTS

The Christian descendants of Germanic raiders who had looted, pillaged, and finally taken the land of Britain by force of arms were themselves to undergo harassment from other Germanic invaders, beginning in the latter years of the eighth century, in the course of which pagan Viking raiders sacked various churches and monasteries, including Lindisfarne and Bede's own beloved Jarrow. In the course of the first half of the following century there were other more or less disorganized but disastrous raids in the South. Then, in 865 a great and expertly organized army landed in East Anglia, led by the unforgettably named Ivar the Boneless and his brother Halfdan, sons of Ragnar Lothbrok (*Loðbrók* 'Shaggy-pants'),[4] and during the course of the next fifteen years gained possession of practically the whole eastern part of England.[5]

In 870 began the attack upon Wessex, ruled by Ethelred (Æðelræd) with the able assistance of his brother Alfred, who was to succeed him in the year following. After years of discouragement, very few victories, and many crushing defeats, Alfred in 878 won a signal victory at Edington over Guthrum, the Danish king of East Anglia, who promised not only to depart from Wessex but also to be baptized. Alfred was godfather for him when the sacrament was later administered.

The troubles with the Danes, as they were called by the English,

---

[3] But not without some scandalous backsliding on the part of Ethelbert's own son Eadbald, who later fully repented. There was also a serious reversion to heathenism in Essex.

[4] According to the legend, Ivar was born with gristle instead of bone because his father had refused his bewitched bride's plea for a deferment of the consummation of their marriage for three nights. Ragnar is said to have been put to death in a snake pit in York. On this occasion his wife, the lovely Kraka, who felt no resentment toward him, had furnished him with a magical snake-proof coat; but it was of no avail, for his executioners made him remove his outer garment. Ivar Ragnarsson's unique physique seems to have been no handicap to a brilliant if rascally career as warrior.

[5] The story of these bloodstained times is well and succinctly related in Chapter 2 of Peter Hunter Blair's *An Introduction to Anglo-Saxon England* (Cambridge, Eng., 1956).

though there were Norwegians and later Swedes among them, were by no means over. There were further attacks, but these were so successfully repulsed by the English that ultimately, in the tenth century, Alfred's son and grandsons (three of whom became kings) were able to carry out his plans for the consolidation of England, which by this time had a sizable and peaceful Scandinavian population.

Then, in the latter years of the tenth century, trouble started again with the arrival of a fleet of warriors led by Olaf Tryggvason, later king of Norway, who was in a few years to be joined by the Danish king Svein Forkbeard. For more than twenty years there were repeated attacks, most of them crushing defeats for the English, beginning with the glorious if unsuccessful stand made by the men of Essex under the valiant Byrhtnoth in 991, celebrated in the fine Old English poem *The Battle of Maldon*. As a rule, however, the onslaughts of the later Northmen were not met with such vigorous resistance, for these were the bad days of the second Ethelred, known as *Unræd,* that is, 'unadvised,' but frequently misunderstood as 'unready.' After the deaths in 1016 of Ethelred and his son Edmund Ironside, who survived his father by little more than half a year, Cnut, son of Svein Forkbeard, who himself was for a short time recognized as king of England, came to the throne. The line of Alfred was not to be restored until 1042, with the accession of Edward the Confessor, though Cnut in a sense allied himself with that line by marrying Ethelred's widow Emma of Normandy (the English preferred to call her Ælgifu),[6] who thus became the mother of two English kings by different fathers: by Ethelred, of Edward the Confessor, and by Cnut, of Harthacnut. (She was not the mother of Ethelred's son Edmund Ironside.)

As has been pointed out, those whom the English called Danes (*Dene*) were not all from Denmark. Linguistically, however, this fact is of little significance, for the various Scandinavian tongues were in those days little differentiated from one another. Furthermore, they were sufficiently like Old English as to make possible communication of a sort without great difficulty between the English and the Scandinavians. The English were perfectly aware of their racial as well as their linguistic kinship with the Scandinavians, many of whom had become their neighbors: the Old English poem *Beowulf* is exclusively concerned with events of Scandinavian legend and history, and approximately a century and a half after the composition of this great

---

[6] As if to compound the confusion of these early times, Cnut's first wife or mistress, whom he set aside, was also named Ælgifu. She was the mother of King Harold Harefoot.

literary masterpiece, Alfred, who certainly had no reason to love the Danes, interpolated in his translation of the history of Orosius the first geographical account of the countries of the North, in the famous story of the voyages of Ohthere and Wulfstan.

THE SCANDINAVIANS BECOME ENGLISH

Despite the enmity and the bloodshed, then, there was a feeling among the English that when all was said and done the Northmen belonged to the same "family" as themselves — a feeling which their ancestors could never have experienced regarding the British Celts. Whereas the earlier raids had been dictated largely by the desire to pillage and to loot — even though a good deal of Scandinavian settlement resulted — the tenth-century and early eleventh-century invaders from the North seem to have been much more interested in colonization than their predecessors had been. This was successfully accomplished in East Anglia (Norfolk and Suffolk), Lincolnshire, Yorkshire, Westmorland, Cumberland, and Northumberland. The Danes settled down peaceably enough in time, living side by side with Englishmen; Scandinavians were good colonizers, willing to assimilate themselves to their new homes. As John Richard Green eloquently sums it up, "England still remained England; the conquerors sank quietly into the mass of those around them; and Woden yielded without a struggle to Christ."[7]

And what of the impact of this assimilation upon the English language, which is our main concern here? Old English and Old Norse had a whole host of frequently used words in common. Jespersen cites, among others, *man, wife, mother, folk, house, thing, winter, summer, will, can, come, hear, see, think, ride, over, under, mine,* and *thine.*[8] In some instances where related words differed noticeably in form, the Scandinavian form has won out, for example *sister* (ON *systir;* OE *sweostor*). Scandinavian contributions to the English word stock will be discussed in more detail in a later chapter.

It has been supposed that other fundamental characteristics of English may be due to Scandinavian influence. Jespersen, in the previously cited work, thought it "probable" that the English use of relative clauses without pronouns (as in "The man the committee chose was unavailable") or without conjunctive *that* (as in "He thought the

---

[7] *A Short History of England* (1874), cited in Otto Jespersen, *Growth and Structure of the English Language,* 9th ed. (Oxford, 1954), p. 58.

[8] *Growth and Structure,* p. 60. Jespersen is of course referring to older forms of these words.

window was broken"), the use of *shall* and *will* as future auxiliaries, and the placing of the genitive before instead of after the noun may have been due to such influence (p. 70). But the fact is that all these constructions either occurred in Old English before the beginning of the Viking period or do not occur in Old Norse as we know it from runic inscriptions made before the beginning of that period.[9] There is thus no good reason to attribute these syntactical characteristics of English to Scandinavian influence.

THE OLD ENGLISH DIALECTS

Four principal dialects were spoken in Anglo-Saxon England: Kentish, the speech of the Jutes who settled in Kent; West Saxon, spoken in the region south of the Thames exclusive of Kent; Mercian, spoken from the Thames to the Humber exclusive of Wales; and Northumbrian, whose localization (north of the Humber) is adequately indicated by its name. Mercian and Northumbrian have certain characteristics in common which distinguish them from West Saxon and Kentish, and are sometimes grouped together as Anglian, since those who spoke these north-of-the-Thames dialects were predominantly Angles. There were presumably other dialects, but we possess no written remains of them. The records of Anglian and Kentish are scant, but much West Saxon writing has come down to us, though probably only a fraction of what once existed. It should be stressed that Old English dialectal differences were slight as compared with those which were later to develop and nowadays sharply differentiate the speech of the lowland Scottish shepherd from that of his South-of-England counterpart.

Hence, although Modern Standard English is in large part a descendant of the Mercian speech of the eastern section of the Midland area, the dialect of Old English which will be described in this chapter is West Saxon. During the time of Alfred and for a long time thereafter, Winchester, the capital of Wessex and therefore in a sense of all England, was a center of English culture, thanks to the encouragement given by Alfred himself to learning. Though London was at the same time an important and thriving commercial city, it did not acquire its cultural or even its political importance until later.

It is thus in West Saxon that most of the extant Old English manuscripts — all in fact which may be regarded as literature — are available to us. Fortunately, however, we are at no great disadvantage when we

---

[9] This has been pointed out by Max S. Kirch, "Scandinavian Influence on English Syntax," *PMLA,* 74 (1959), 503-10.

study the West Saxon dialect in relation to Modern English: because dialectal differences were not great, the Old English forms cited in what follows may usually be regarded without reference to the fact that they occur in West Saxon rather than in Mercian writings. Occasionally a distinctive Mercian form (labeled Anglian if it happens to be identical with the Northumbrian form) has been cited as more obviously similar to the standard modern form than is the West Saxon form, for instance Anglian *ald,* which regularly develops into Modern English *old.* The West Saxon form was *eald.*

The Old English to be described here is of about the year 1000 — roughly that of the period during which Ælfric, the most representative writer of the late tenth and early eleventh centuries, was flourishing.[10] This development of English, which became the literary standard, is sometimes called classical Old English; that of the Age of Alfred, who reigned in the latter years of the ninth century, is usually included in what is called early West Saxon, though it is actually rather late early West Saxon. It is, however, about all that we know of the early West Saxon dialect from manuscript evidence.

The Old English period spans somewhat more than six centuries, the dates ascribed to it being more or less arbitrary. In a period of more than six hundred years many changes are bound to occur in sounds, in grammar, and in vocabulary. Some of these are evident from a comparison of the earliest writings with the later ones. (Written records of English are, incidentally, older than those of any other West Germanic language.) By a comparative study of all the Germanic languages and dialects, linguists are able to reconstruct prehistoric Old English and to infer changes which took place in that stage in the development of our language. With such early changes we shall be concerned here only incidentally.

THE PRONUNCIATION OF OLD ENGLISH

For the pronunciation of the Old English words cited in the following discussion, the reader will do well to review the treatment of Old English scribal practices in Chapter III, and to remember that our knowledge of the phonology of an older form of any language can be only approximate. The precise quality of any speech sound at any given period in the vast pretape-recording era stretching behind us in time

---

[10] It is the language of this period which is concisely treated by Kemp Malone in the opening chapter of *A Literary History of England,* ed. Albert C. Baugh (New York, 1948) and in detail by Randolph Quirk and C. L. Wrenn in *An Old English Grammar* (London, 1955).

cannot ever be determined with absolute certainty. It should further be borne in mind that in Old English times as today there were regional and individual differences, and doubtless social differences as well. A period in which all members of a given linguistic community speak exactly alike, let alone an entire nation, is inconceivable.

As regards stress in Old English, we are on rather certain ground. We have already seen in another connection (pp. 104–105) that Old English words of more than one syllable, like those in all other Germanic languages, were regularly stressed on their first syllables. Exceptions to this rule are verbs with prefixes, which were generally stressed on the first syllable of their second element: *wiðféohtan* 'to fight against,' *onbíndan* 'to unbind,' *ofdrǽdan*[11] 'to dread.' *Be-, for-,* and *ge-* were not stressed, regardless of whether or not they were used with verbs: *bebód* 'commandment,' *forsóð* 'forsooth,' *gehǽp* 'convenient.' Other compounds had the customary Germanic stress on the first syllable; those consisting of two nouns or a noun and an adjective had secondary stress in their second elements: *lárhùs* 'school,' *híldedèor* 'fierce in battle.' This heavy stressing of the first syllable of practically all words has had a far-reaching effect upon the development of English. Because of it, the vowels of final syllables began to be reduced to a uniform sound as early as the tenth century, as not infrequent interchanges of one letter for another in the texts indicate, though most scribes continued to spell according to tradition. In general the stress system of Old English was simple as compared to that of Modern English, with its many loan-words of non-Germanic origin, like *matérnal, philósophy, sublíme,* and *tabóo.*

As we have seen in Chapter II, the vowel symbols used in writing Old English, except for *æ*, symbolized what are sometimes referred to as "Continental" values – approximately those of Italian, Spanish, German, and to some extent of French as well. In other words, the *a* of the Old English texts indicates a vowel of the quality of [ɑ] short or long; likewise, to long *e, i, o,* and *u* may be assigned the same values which these symbols have when written in square brackets in the system of phonetic transcription set forth on pp. 40–43. When short, they were approximately [ɛ], [ɪ], [ɔ], and [ʊ] respectively. Short *æ* was as in *mat;* long *æ* was approximately the same sound prolonged, but somewhat tenser. *Y,* used exclusively as a vowel symbol in Old English, indicated a rounded front vowel, long as in German *Bühne,* short as in

---

[11] The macron in Old English forms is editorial. Vowel quantity was not customarily indicated in Old English writing, for readers needed no such indication of what they unconsciously did in speaking their native language.

fünf. Later losing its rounded quality, long and short *y* fell together with long and short *i.*

In the examples which follow, the Modern English form in parentheses, when its vowel differs in sound from that of the Old English form, illustrates a typical Modern English development of the Old English sound:

a as in *habban* (have)	*ī* as in *rīdan* (ride)
ā as in *hām* (home)	*o* as in *moððe* (moth)
æ as in *þæt* (that)	*ō* as in *fōda* (food)
ǣ as in *dǣl* (deal)	*u* as in *sundor* (sunder)
e as in *settan* (set)	*ū* as in *mūs* (mouse)
ē as in *fēdan* (feed)	*y* as in *fyllan* (fill)
i as in *sittan* (sit)	*ȳ* as in *mȳs* (mice)

Late West Saxon had two long diphthongs, *ēa* and *ēo*, to the first elements of which may be assigned respectively the values [ǣ] and [ē]. The second elements of both, once differentiated, had been reduced to unstressed [ə], which in the course of the eleventh century was lost; to put it in another way, these long diphthongs became monophthongs that continued to be differentiated, at least in the standard pronunciation, until well into the Modern English period but ultimately fell together as [ī], as in *beat* from Old English *bēatan, creep* from *crēopan.* According to the traditional view, *ea* and *eo* in such words as *seah*[12] 'saw,' *eoh* 'horse,' *eall* 'all,' *heard* 'hard,' *meolc* 'milk,' *weorc* 'work,' and *geard* 'yard' resulted from certain prehistoric Old English sound changes known as "breaking" and "palatal diphthongization" and indicated short diphthongs of the same quality as the identically written long ones, approximately [æə] and [ɛə]. A more recent view holds that Old English actually had no such short diphthongs but that the writings *ea* and *eo* in such words were nothing more than scribal indications of the velar or palatal nature of contiguous consonants.[13]

[12] Old English verbs had the same form in the first and third persons of the preterit singular. This is the form here and hereafter cited as the preterit singular.
[13] See especially Marjorie Daunt, "Old English Sound-Changes Reconsidered in Relation to Scribal Tradition and Practice," *Transactions of the Philological Society 1939*, pp. 108–37, and R. P. Stockwell and C. W. Barritt, "Some Old English Graphemic-Phonemic Correspondences — *æ, ea,* and *a*," *Studies in Linguistics: Occasional Papers No. 4* (Washington, D. C., 1951). These views have been criticized by, among others, Sherman M. Kuhn and Randolph Quirk, "Some Recent Interpretations of Old English Digraph Spellings," *Language,* 29 (1953), 143–56. There is further discussion by Stockwell, Barritt, Kuhn, and Quirk in *Language,* 31 (1955), 372–401.

124   *The Old English Period*

The consonant symbols *b, d, l, m, n, k* (rarely used), *p, t, w* (that is, *p*), and *x* had in all positions the same values which these letters represent in Modern English. The doubling of consonant symbols between vowels indicated length; thus the *t*'s of *sittan* indicated the medial single consonant sound frequently heard in *hot tamale,* which is of longer duration than the medial consonant of Modern English *sitting;* similarly *ll* in *fyllan* indicated the lengthened medial *l* of *full-length,* in contrast to the short *l* of *holy; cc* as in *racca* 'part of a ship's rigging' was a long [k] as in *bookkeeper,* in contrast to *beekeeper,* and hence *racca* was distinguished from *raca* 'rake'; and so on.

The sound represented by *c* depended upon contiguous sounds. If these were back vowels, the letter indicated the velar stop [k] (*camp* 'battle,' *corn* 'corn,' *cūð* 'known,' *lūcan* 'to lock,' *acan* 'to ache,' *bōc* 'book'); if they were front (or had been in early Old English), the sound indicated was the affricate [č] (*cild* 'child,' *cēosan* 'to choose,' *ic* 'I,' *lǣce* 'physician,' *rīce* 'kingdom,' *mēce* 'sword'). In *cēpan* 'to keep,' *cynn* 'race, kin,' and a number of other words, the root vowels are mutated back vowels (Germanic **kōpjan, *kunjō*); hence the palatalization of [k] resulting in Old English [č] did not occur.[14] In *bēc* 'books' from prehistoric Old English **bōci* and *sēcan*[15] 'to seek' from prehistoric Old English **sōcjan,* the immediately following *i* and *j* effected both palatalization of the original [k] (written *c* in the Old English reconstructions) and mutation of the original vowel. In *swylc* 'such,' *ǣlc* 'each,' and *hwylc* 'which,' an earlier *ī* before the *c* has been lost; but even without this information, we have a guide in the modern forms cited as definitions; similarly we may know from modern *keep* and *kin* that the Old English initial sound was [k].[16] Preconsonantal *c* was always [k], as in *cnāwan* 'to know,' *cræt* 'cart,' and *cwellan* 'to kill.' The digraphs *cg* and *sc* were in post-Old English times replaced by *dg* and *sh* respectively—spellings which indicate to the modern reader exactly the sounds the older spellings represented, for example *ecg* 'edge,' *scīr* 'shire,' *scacan* 'to shake,' and *fisc* 'fish.'

The pronunciation of *g* (that is, *ȝ*) also depended upon neighboring

[14] Mutation is a change in a vowel sound brought about by a sound in the following syllable. The mutation of a vowel by a following *i* or *j* (as in the examples) is called *i*-mutation. See also below, pp. 129–30.

[15] For this word, Old English scribes frequently wrote *secan,* the extra *e* functioning merely as a diacritic to indicate that the preceding *c* symbolized [č] rather than [k]. Compare the Italian use of *i* after *c* preceding *a, o,* or *u* to indicate precisely the same thing, as in *ciarlare* 'to prate,' *cioccolata* 'chocolate,' and *ciuffo* 'toupee.'

[16] Unfortunately for easy tests, *seek* does not show palatalization (though *beseech* does) and the mutated plural of *book* has not survived.

sounds. The symbol indicated in late Old English the velar voiced stop [g] before consonants (*gnēað* 'niggardly,' *glæd* 'glad, gracious'), initially before back vowels (*galan* 'to sing,' *gōs* 'goose,' *gūð* 'war'), and initially before front vowels which had resulted from the mutation of back vowels (*gēs* 'geese' from prehistoric Old English **gōsi*, *gǣst* 'goest' from **gāis*). Medially or finally in the combination *ng* the letter indicated the same sound—that of Modern English *linger* as contrasted with *ringer* (*bringan* 'to bring,' *hring* 'ring').[17] The same symbol indicated [j] initially before *e, i,* and the *y* which was usual in late West Saxon for earlier *ie* (*gecoren* 'chosen,' *gēar* 'year,' *giftian* 'to give a woman in marriage,' *gydd* 'song'), medially between front vowels (*slægen* 'slain,' *twēgen* 'twain'), and finally when it followed a front vowel in either a word or a syllable (*dæg* 'day,' *mægden* 'maiden,' *legde* 'laid,' *stigrāp* 'stirrup,' *manig* 'many'). In practically all other circumstances *g* indicated the voiced velar fricative referred to above (p. 105, n. 42) as the earliest Germanic development of Indo-European *gh*—a sound difficult to describe for English-speaking people nowadays, nor is much gained by attempting to pronounce it except for professional purposes (*dragan* 'to draw,' *lagu* 'law,' *hogu* 'care,' *folgian* 'to follow,' *sorgian* 'to sorrow,' *swelgan* 'to swallow'). It later became [w], as in Middle English *drawen, lawe, howe,* and so on.

In Old English, [v], [z], and [ð] were not phonemes; they occurred only medially. There were thus no contrastive pairs like *feel/veal, leaf/leave, thigh/thy, mouth* (n.)*/mouth* (v.), *seal/zeal, face/phase,* and hence there were no distinctive symbols for the voiceless and voiced sounds. The symbols *f, s,* and *þ* (or *ð,* used more or less interchangeably with it)[18] thus indicated both the voiceless fricatives [f], [s], [θ] (as in *fōda* 'food,' *lof* 'praise'; *sunu* 'son,' *mūs* 'mouse'; *þorn* 'thorn,' *pæð* 'path') and, between voiced sounds, the corresponding voiced fricatives [v], [z], [ð] (as in *cnafa* 'boy,' *hæfde* 'had'; *lēosan* 'to lose,' *hūsl* 'Holy Communion'; *brōðor* 'brother,' *fæðm* 'fathom'). In a very few Latin loan-words which began with [v],[19] Old English sometimes used *f*

[17] Thus [ŋ] was not an Old English phoneme, but merely an allophone of *n*. There were no contrastive pairs like *sin/sing* and *thin/thing,* nor were there to be any such in English until the Modern English loss of [g] in what had previously been a consonant sequence.

[18] In words cited hereafter, *þ* will be used only initially; elsewhere *ð* will be used, in accordance with the preferred practice of many scribes in late Old English times. When Old English texts are cited, as on pp. 146 and 147–50, the usage of the manuscripts will be exactly followed. Note that, though ambiguous in Old English, *ð* is used in phonetic and phonemic script for the voiced sound only.

[19] Late Latin [v] is a development of Classical Latin [w], the sound usually taught nowadays in the schools.

(which indeed indicated [v], as we have seen, under certain circumstances), for example *fers* (Lat. *versus*) and *Firgilius* (*Virgilius*). It is possible that the English actually pronounced [f] in these words, in the Irish fashion. Occasionally *v* (written *u,* of course) also occurs in such borrowings.

Initially, *r* may have been a trill, but preconsonantally and finally it was in West Saxon probably the so-called retroflex *r* general in American English except for eastern New England and the tidewater South. Initial *h* was about as in Modern English, but elsewhere it stood for the fricatives [x] or [ç], the velar or palatal quality depending as always upon the neighboring vowel, for example (with [x]) *seah* 'saw,' *þurh* 'through,' *þōhte* 'thought' (verb); (with [ç]) *syhð* 'sees,' *miht* 'might,' *fēhð* 'takes.' Of the sequences *hl* (as in *hlāf* 'loaf'), *hn* (as in *hnitu* 'nit'), *hr* (as in *hræfn* 'raven'), and *hw* (as in *hwæl* 'whale'), only the last[20] survives. The rare use of *z* with the value [ts] has been previously referred to (pp. 68–69).

OTHER DIFFERENCES
BETWEEN OLD ENGLISH AND MODERN ENGLISH

Aside from its pronunciation and its word stock, Old English differs markedly from Modern English in having grammatical gender in contrast to the Modern English system of gender based on sex or sexlessness and in the degree of inflection of the noun, the adjective, and the demonstrative and interrogative pronouns. The personal pronouns have preserved much of their ancient complexity in Modern English. The verb in Old English, except for the more extensive use of the subjunctive, is only slightly more complex than in Modern English, as we shall see, but Old English had a considerably larger number of strong verbs than has Modern English.

The three genders of Indo-European were preserved in Germanic and survived in English well into the Middle English period; they survive in German and Icelandic to this day. Doubtless the gender of a noun originally had nothing to do with sex, nor does it necessarily have sexual connotations in those languages which have retained grammatical (as opposed to "natural") gender. Old English *wīf* 'wife, woman' is neuter, as is its German cognate *Weib;* so is *mægden* 'maiden,' like German *Mädchen. Bridd* 'young bird' is masculine; *bearn* 'son, bairn' is neuter. *Brēost* 'breast' and *hēafod* 'head' are neuter, but *brū* 'eye-

[20] Later, and less accurately, spelled *wh-.*

brow,' *wamb* 'belly,' and *eaxl* 'shoulder' are feminine. *Strengðu* 'strength' is feminine, *broc* 'affliction' is neuter, and *drēam* 'joy' is masculine.

Where sex was patently involved, however, this complicated and to us illogical system was beginning to break down even in Old English times. It must have come to be difficult, for instance, to refer to one who was obviously a woman — that is, a *wīf* — with the pronoun *hit* 'it,' or to a *wīfmann* — a compound from which our word *woman* is derived — with *hē* 'he,' the compound being masculine because of its second element; and there are in fact a number of instances in Old English of the conflict of grammatical gender with the developing concept of natural gender.

Old English word order is somewhat less fixed than that of Modern English, but in general is about the same. Old English declarative sentences tend to fall into the subject-verb-complement order which is usual in Modern English, for example "Hē wæs swīðe spēdig man" ('He was a very successful man') and "Eadwine eorl cōm mid landfyrde and drāf hine ūt" ('Earl Edwin came with a land army and drove him out'). Declarative sentences which do not conform to this pattern sometimes occur when the object of the verb is a pronoun ("Se hālga Andreas him andswarode," that is, 'The holy Andrew him answered') and usually when the sentence begins with *þā* 'then, when' or *ne* 'not' ("Þā sealde se cyning him sweord," that is, 'Then gave the king him a sword'; "Ne can ic nōht singan," that is, 'Cannot I nought sing [I cannot sing anything]'); in sentences of the first type the object may precede the verb, and in those of the second type the verb may precede the subject. In dependent clauses the verb usually comes last, as always in German ("God geseah þā þæt hit gōd wæs" — 'God saw then that it good was'; "Sē micla here, þe wē gefyrn ymbe sprǣcon . . ." — 'The great army, which we before about spoke . . .'). Interrogative sentences follow in Old English the same verb-subject-complement pattern as in Modern English ("Hæfst þū ǣnigne gefēran?" 'Hast thou any companion?').

Old English will inevitably seem to the modern reader a crabbed and difficult language full of needless complexities. Actually the inflection of the noun was somewhat less complex in Old English than it was in Germanic, Latin, and Greek and, naturally, considerably less so than in Indo-European, with its eight cases (nominative, accusative, genitive, dative, ablative, instrumental, locative, and vocative). No Old English noun had more than six forms; but even this number will seem exorbitant to the speaker of Modern English, who uses only two forms for all but a few nouns: a general form without ending and a form ending in -s.[21]

NOUNS

Almost half of the nouns frequently encountered in Old English are masculine,[22] and most of these are a-stems — the a being the sound with which the stem ended in Germanic. These correspond to the o-stems of Indo-European, as exemplified by nouns of the second declension (the numbering of declensions is traditional and purely arbitrary) in Latin and Greek: Greek *philos* 'friend,' Latin *servos* (later *servus*) 'slave.' The terminology is of significance only in a historical sense as far as Old English is concerned. For example Germanic *wulfaz* (nominative singular) and *wulfan* (accusative singular) appear in Old English simply as *wulf* 'wolf,' with both suffix and ending completely lost.

Such nouns (in which, because of change and loss of sounds in final syllables, the older distinctive nominative and accusative forms, as well as those for the dative and instrumental, had fallen together) show six different forms, for example *hund* 'dog':

SINGULAR		PLURAL	
Nom., acc.	hund	Nom., acc.	hundas
Gen.	hundes	Gen.	hunda
Dat., ins.[23]	hunde	Dat.	hundum

More than a third of all commonly used nouns were inflected according to this pattern, which was in time to be extended to practically all nouns. The Modern English possessive singular and general plural form in -s comes directly from the Old English genitive singular and nominative-accusative plural forms — two different forms until very late Old English times, when they fell together because of the reduc-

---

[21] The fact that the forms ending in -s are written differently is quite irrelevant; the apostrophe for the genitive is a fairly recent convention. As far as speech is concerned, *boys, boy's,* and *boys'* are the same.

[22] This and some subsequent statistical statements have been derived from Quirk and Wrenn, *An Old English Grammar,* p. 20.

[23] Hereafter the term *instrumental* will ordinarily be used only for distinctive forms, occurring in the masculine and neuter singular of the "strong" adjective declension and of the demonstrative pronouns, and in the neuter interrogative pronoun. Elsewhere the instrumental function (usually expressing 'by means of') was expressed by the dative form, as in Latin it was expressed by the ablative.

tion of the vowel of unstressed -*as,* which came also to be written -*es* in Middle English times. New words invariably conform to what survives of the *a*-stem declension — for example *sputnik's, sputniks, sputniks'* — so that we may truly say that it is the only living declension.

Other masculine nouns — the so called *n*-stems — have only four forms, thus *oxa* 'ox':

SINGULAR		PLURAL	
Nom.	oxa	Nom., acc.	oxan
Acc., gen., dat.	oxan	Gen.	oxena
		Dat.	oxum

The Modern English plural *oxen* (from *oxan*) is the only "pure" survival of this declension, which is called the "weak" declension.[24]

A few other masculine nouns must be mentioned here because of the frequency of their occurrence — *fōt* 'foot,' *tōð* 'tooth,' *man(n)* 'man,' and the compound *wīfmann,* whose case endings were affixed to the final consonants of their roots. There are five different forms for each of these, thus:

SINGULAR	
Nom., acc.	fōt, tōð, man(n)
Gen.	fōtes, tōðes, mannes
Dat.	fēt, tēð, men(n)

PLURAL	
Nom., acc.	fēt, tēð, men(n)
Gen.	fōta, tōða, manna
Dat.	fōtum, tōðum, mannum

It will be noted that the dative singular and the nominative-accusative plural forms are identical. This is so because, although in prehistoric Old English the dative singular and the nominative plural forms had the same root vowel as the other forms, each had an *i* in the ending, thus: **fōti, *tōði, *manni.*

Anticipation of the *i*-sound caused mutation of the root vowel — a kind of assimilation, with the vowel of the root moving in its articu-

---

[24] Nouns whose stems had ended in vowels (like the *a*-stems) are traditionally referred to as belonging to "strong" declensions.

lation in the direction of the *i*-sound, but stopping somewhat short of it. English *man–men*,[25] *foot–feet* show the same development as German *Mann–Männer, Fuss–Füsse*, though German has chosen to indicate the mutated vowel in writing by placing a dieresis over the same symbol used for the unmutated vowel, whereas English uses an altogether different letter. The process, which Grimm called *Umlaut*, occurred in different periods and in varying degrees in the various members of the Germanic group, in English beginning probably in the sixth century. The fourth-century Gothic recorded by Bishop Wulfila shows no evidence of it.

Somewhat fewer than a third of all commonly used nouns are feminine, most of them belonging to the so-called *ō*-declension (corresponding to the *ā*-stems, or first declension, of Latin). In the nominative singular, these had *-u* (sometimes *-o*) after a short syllable, as in *lufu* 'love' and no ending at all after a long syllable,[26] as in *lār* 'learning' and *wund.* 'wound.' They were declined as follows:

	SINGULAR		PLURAL
Nom.	lufu	Nom., acc., gen.	lufa
Acc., gen., dat.	lufe	Dat.	lufum

There are a few feminine *n*-stems, most of them with *-e* in the nominative singular (*belle* 'bell,' *eorðe* 'earth') but otherwise precisely the same as the masculine *n*-stems; and there are also a few feminine nouns with mutation in the dative singular and the nominative-accusative plural (sometimes in the genitive singular as well), for example *brōc* 'pants,' *cū* 'cow,' *mūs* 'mouse,' *lūs* 'louse,' and *gōs* 'goose.' The nominative-accusative plural forms of these are respectively *brēc* (whence *breech*, with *breeches* a double plural), *cȳ* (whence *kine*, in which the *n*-stem nominative-accusative plural ending has been added to make yet another double plural), *mȳs, lȳs,* and *gēs*.

About a quarter of the commonly used Old English nouns are neuter. Practically all of these are *a*-stems, differing from the masculine *a*-stems only in the nominative-accusative plural: this ends in *-u* after a short syllable, as in *gatu* 'gate(s),' and has no ending (except for

[25] In *woman–women* the earlier vowel differentiation of the final syllables has been obscured by weakened stress. The modern differentiation between singular and plural depends mainly upon the pronunciation of the first syllable. Mutation has nothing to do with this modern differentiation.

[26] A long syllable is one whose vowel is long or is followed by a sequence of different consonants or a long single consonant (indicated in Old English writing by doubling letters).

an occasional analogical *-u*) after a long one. Under the latter circumstances the most frequently used singular and plural forms, the nominative and the accusative, are identical, for example *word* and *bān*. *Dēor* 'animal(s)' is a neuter *a*-stem which has retained its unchanged plural to this day as *deer*. There are two neuter *n*-stems, declined exactly like the masculine and feminine ones except for their unchanged accusative singular forms: *ēage* 'eye' and *ēare* 'ear.' A very few neuters had nominative-accusative plurals in *-ru:* these include *ǣg* 'egg,' *lamb* 'lamb,' *cealf* 'calf,' and *cild* 'child.' *Cild* frequently has an unchanged nominative-accusative form, but the form with *-r-* has acquired an additional plural ending in *-n* by analogy with the *n*-stems. *Children* is thus a double plural, but the "normal" development *childer* survives in the Northern dialects of English.

Some very frequently used words ending in *-r* and denoting family relationships — *fæder* 'father,' *brōðor* 'brother,' *mōdor* 'mother,' *dohtor* 'daughter,' and *sweostor* 'sister' — exhibit a number of peculiarities; for instance, all occur with uninflected genitive singulars, all have endingless datives, and all save *fæder* occur with unchanged nominative-accusative plurals. The single form *sweostor* was used throughout the singular. Along with the unchanged nominative-accusative plurals, forms in *-ru* (alternating with *-ra* in the three feminine nouns), with loss of the unstressed *o* preceding the *r,* also occur, thus: *brōðru, mōdru, dohtru, sweostru. Mōdor, dohtor,* and *brōðor* had mutated vowels in their dative singular forms, thus: *mēder, dehter, brēðer.*[27] By analogy with the majority of masculine nouns, *fæder* always has a nominative-accusative plural in *-as* and very often a genitive singular in *-es* as well.

Another noun indicating family relationship, *sunu* 'son,' belonged to a minor declension containing not many but rather frequently used words, among them *lagu* 'sea,' *wudu* 'wood,' *medu* 'liquor,' and, with the *-u* lacking after long syllables and after disyllables, *feld* 'field,' *ford* 'ford,' *winter* 'winter,' *sumor* 'summer,' and a few others. These nouns, all masculine, might have only three different forms, thus for *sunu:*

SINGULAR		PLURAL	
Nom., acc.	sunu	Nom., acc., gen.	suna
Gen., dat.	suna	Dat.	sunum

---

[27] The mutated form *brēðer* was later sometimes extended to the nominative-accusative plural and in early Middle English acquired an alternative ending *-en* (the later development of the *-an* of the *n*-stems); hence *brethren*.

The feminine *duru* 'door,' *nosu* 'nose,' *cinn* 'chin,' and *hand* 'hand' were originally treated in exactly the same way. But long-syllabled masculine nouns of this declension (for example *feld*) were for the most part declined like masculine *a*-stems, and long-syllabled feminine ones (for example *hand*) like feminine *ō*-stems.

It will be noted that in all declensions the genitive plural form ends in *-a* and the dative plural in *-m* (usually *-um*). The genitive plural *-a* survived as [ə] (written *-e*) in Middle English in the "genitive of measure" construction and continues to survive in Modern English (with loss of [ə]), in such phrases as *sixty-mile drive* and *six foot tall* (rather than *miles* and *feet*), though *feet* may more often occur in the latter construction; only *foot,* however, is idiomatic in *three-foot board* and *six-foot man.*[28] The dative plural survives in the antiquated form *whilom,* from Old English *hwīlum* 'at times,' and in the analogical *seldom* (earlier *seldan*). The dative singular in *-e* characteristic of the majority of Old English nouns survives in the word *alive,* from Old English *on līfe;* the Old English voiced *f* between vowels, later spelled *v,* is preserved in the Modern English form, though the final vowel is no longer pronounced. These are about the only traces left of the Old English declensional forms of the noun other than the genitive singular and the general plural forms in *-s* (along with a few mutated plurals); there are also a very few relics of Old English feminine genitives without *-s,* for instance *Lady Chapel.*[29]

One other observation before passing on to other matters: Old English had no device for indicating plurality alone — that is, unconnected with the concept of case. It was not until Middle English times that the plural nominative-accusative *-es* (from OE *-as*) drove out the other case forms of the plural (save for the comparatively rare genitive of measure construction discussed in the preceding paragraph). Even in the root consonant stems, the mutated forms were, as we have seen, not exclusively *plural* forms. They occurred also in the dative singular, as in *Beowulf,* lines 2283–85: "Ðā wæs . . . bēne getīðad fēasceaftum men" 'Then was [a] favor granted [the] wretched man.' The *-en* ending (from OE *-an*), surviving in *oxen,* likewise did not indicate plurality

---

[28] It will be remembered that the Old English form *fēt,* becoming Modern English *feet,* occurred in the plural only as the nominative and accusative form; the genitive plural, *fōta,* did not have the mutated vowel.

[29] For other instances of uninflected feminine genitives which survived into early Modern English, see p. 198. The *ō*-declension genitive, it will be remembered, had *-e.* This ending was completely lost in pronunciation by the end of the fourteenth century, along with all other final *e*'s of whatever origin.

alone in earlier periods; in Old English, as a backward glance at the declension of *oxa* will show, the common non-nominative singular form had *-an* and was thus identical with the nominative-accusative plural form, *oxan.*

DEMONSTRATIVE PRONOUNS

Although it is usual to treat adjectives immediately after nouns, we shall here discuss the Old English demonstrative pronouns, on whose occurrence or nonoccurrence depends the use of one or the other Old English adjective declension (that is, the strong or the characteristic Germanic weak declension). There were two such demonstratives. The more frequently used was that which came to correspond in function to our definite article. The singular forms of this demonstrative were as follows:

MASCULINE		NEUTER		FEMININE	
Nom.	sē[30]	Nom., acc.	þæt	Nom.	sēo
Acc.	þone	(otherwise the		Acc.	þā
Gen.	þæs	same as the		Gen., dat.	þǣre
Dat.	þǣm	masculine)			
Ins.	þȳ, þon, þē				

It will be noted that, not including variants of the instrumental, we have here nine different forms, with distinct dative and instrumental forms in the masculine and neuter, though not in the feminine. In the plural there was no distinction of gender:

Nom., acc.	þā
Gen.	þāra
Dat.	þǣm

Because of the analogy of all the other forms, *sĕ* and *sēo* were in late Old English superseded by the variants *þĕ* and *þēo*. The other, less frequently used demonstrative had the nominative singular forms *þes* (masculine), *þis* (neuter, whence ModE *this*), and *þēos* (feminine). Like *sē, þæt, sēo,* it had a distinctive singular instrumental form (*þȳs*) in the masculine and neuter and common gender in the plural. Its nominative-

---

[30] This form had a short *e* when it was used without stress as a definite article.

accusative plural *þās* has developed into *those*. *These* is of Middle English origin.

ADJECTIVES

The adjective in Old English agreed with the noun it modified in gender, case, and number as in Latin; but Germanic, as we have seen, had developed a distinctive adjective declension—the so-called weak declension, used customarily after the two demonstrative pronouns and frequently after possessive pronouns. In this declension *-an* predominates as an ending:

MASCULINE SINGULAR

Nom.	se dola cyning 'the foolish king'
Acc.	þone dolan cyning
Gen.	þæs dolan cyninges
Dat.	þæm dolan cyninge
Ins.	þȳ dolan cyninge

MASCULINE PLURAL

Nom., acc.	þā dolan cyningas
Gen.	þāra dolra (*or* dolena) cyninga
Dat.	þæm dolum cyningum

Modifying neuter nouns, the singular weak adjective forms were the same as the masculine in the genitive, dative, and instrumental, but both the nominative and accusative singular ended in *-e* (*þæt dole bearn* 'the foolish child'). The feminine nominative adjective form likewise ended in *-e*, but the other singular forms were the same as the masculine, with *-an* (*sēo dole ides* 'the foolish woman,' but *þā, þære dolan idese*). As with the pronouns, there was common gender in the plural, with nominative-accusative *-an*, genitive *-ra*, and dative-instrumental *-um*.

The so-called strong declension was used when the adjective was not preceded by a demonstrative or a possessive pronoun, or when it was predicative. Many of the endings are those characteristic of pronouns rather than of nouns, for instance the *-ne* of the masculine accusative singular (as in *hine, þone*), the *-re* of the feminine genitive-dative singular (as in *hire, þære*), the *-m* of the masculine and neuter dative singular (as in *him, þæm*), and the *-ra* of the common-gender genitive plural (as in *hira, þāra*). Paradigms for the singular number, as above modifying appropriate nouns, follow:

MASCULINE

Nom.	dol cyning 'foolish king'
Acc.	dolne cyning
Gen.	doles cyninges
Dat.	dolum cyninge
Ins.	dole cyninge

NEUTER

Nom.	dol bearn 'foolish child'
Acc.	dol bearn
Gen.	doles bearnes
Dat.	dolum bearne
Ins.	dole bearne

FEMININE

Nom.	dolu[31] ides 'foolish woman'
Acc.	dole idese
Gen., dat.	dolre idese

The common-gender genitive and dative plural endings, respectively -*ra* and -*um*, are the same as those of the weak declension. The nominative-accusative plural strong forms are exemplified in *dole cyningas* (masculine), *dolu bearn* (neuter), and *dola idesa* (feminine).

The comparative of adjectives was regularly formed by suffixing -*ra*, as in *heardra* 'harder,' and the superlative by suffixing -*ost*, as in *heardost* 'hardest.' A few adjectives which had mutation by earlier *i* in alternative suffixes -*ira*, -*ist* in the comparative and superlative usually had -*est* in the superlative, for example *eald*, Anglian *ald* 'old'; *yldra*, Anglian *eldra* 'elder'; *yldest*, Anglian *eldest*. A very few others had comparative and superlative forms from a different root from that of the positive, among them *gōd* 'good,' *betra* 'better,' *betst* 'best' and *micel* 'great,' *māra* 'more,' *m$\bar{æ}$st* 'most.'

Certain superlatives were originally formed with an alternative

---

[31] After a long syllable no ending occurs in monosyllabic adjectives, for example *wīs ides* 'wise woman,' *geong ides* 'young woman.' The same is true of the neuter nominative-accusative plural. For what constitutes a long syllable, see n. 26.

suffix *-(u)ma*, for example *forma* (formed from *fore* 'before'). When the ending with *m* ceased to be felt as having superlative force, these words and some others took by analogy the additional ending *-est*. Thus, double superlatives (though not recognized as such) like *formest, midmest, ūtemest,* and *innemest* came into being. The ending appeared to be *-mest* (rather than *-est*), which was even in late Old English times misunderstood as *mǣst*, Anglian *māst* 'most'; hence our Modern English forms *foremost,*[32] *midmost,* and *inmost,* in which the final syllable is and has long been equated with *most,* though it has no historical connection with it. Beginning thus as a blunder, this *-most* has subsequently been affixed to other words, for example *uppermost, furthermost,* and *topmost.*

ADVERBS

Old English adverbs give no particular trouble. Those formed from adjectives — the great majority — added the suffix *-e*, for example *wrāð* 'angry,' *wrāðe* 'angrily.' This *-e* was lost along with all other final *e*'s by the end of the fourteenth century, with the result that many Modern English adjectives and adverbs are identical in form, for instance *loud, deep,* and *slow,* though Modern English idiom sometimes requires adverbial forms with *-ly* ("He plunged deep into the ocean" but "He thought deeply about religious matters"; "Drive slow" but "He proceeded slowly"). Adverbs regularly formed the comparative with *-or* and the superlative with *-ost* or *-est* (*wrāðor* 'more angrily,' *wrāðost* 'most angrily'). In addition, case forms of nouns and adjectives might be used adverbially, notably the genitive[33] and the dative.[34]

[32] Caxton writes (1483) the still common (and tautological) phrase *first and foremost* as *first and formest.*

[33] As in *Beowulf,* lines 2267–69: "Swā giōmormōd . . . unblīðe hwearf dæges ond nihtes" ('So [the one] sad of mind . . . unblithe wandered [by] day and [by] night'). *Dæges* and *nihtes* are genitive singulars. The construction survives in "He worked nights" (labeled "dial[ect] and U.S." by the *OED*), sometimes rendered analytically as "He worked of a night." Nevertheless the usage is, as the *OED* says, "in later use prob[ably] apprehended as a plural," though historically, as we have seen, it is not so. The *-s* of *homewards* (OE *hāmweardes*), *towards* (*tōweardes*), *besides, betimes, needs* (as in *must needs be,* sometimes rendered analytically as *must of necessity be*) is from the genitive singular ending *-es.* The sibilant is merely written differently in *once, twice, thrice, hence,* and *since. Amongst, amidst, against,* and *whilst* have excrescent *t* after the genitive *s,* the same phenomenon occurring in frequent nonstandard pronunciations of *once* and *across.*

[34] As in (sg.) *elne* 'valiantly,' *wihte* 'at all'; (pl.) *hwīlum* 'at times, sometimes,' *þrymmum* 'mightily.'

PERSONAL PRONOUNS

Except for the loss of the dual number and the old second person singular forms, the personal pronouns are almost as complex today as they were in Old English times. *I, me,* and *mine* correspond to the Old English nominative *ic,*[35] accusative-dative *mē,* and genitive *mīn.*

The first person dual forms (meaning 'I, me, or my plus some other person') were *wit* (nominative), *unc* (accusative-dative), and *uncer* (genitive). The second person dual forms (meaning 'singular you or your plus some other person') were *git* (nominative) *inc* (accusative-dative), and *incer* (genitive). Their history has been the same as that of the first person dual forms; they have disappeared completely, though unquestionably their gradual disuse must have been regarded by many as evidence that the English language was going straight to the dogs. *Wit* and *git* took the ordinary plural verb forms.

Old English *wē* (nominative), *ūs* (accusative-dative), and *ūre* (genitive) correspond to the Modern English first person plural forms, *we, us* (allowing for shortening due to lack of stress), and *our.* The Old English second person singular forms *þū* (nominative), *þē* (accusative-dative), and *þīn* correspond to early Modern English *thou, thee,* and *thine,* now archaic.

In the second person plural the forms were *gē* (nominative), *ēow* (accusative-dative), and *ēower* (genitive) corresponding to Modern English *ye, you,* and *your,* with *you* usurping by about 1600 all the nominative functions of *ye,* though this "misuse" began at least two and a half centuries earlier. When used as possessives, the genitives of the first and second persons were declined like the strong adjectives.

Gender appears only in the third person singular forms, exactly as in Modern English. Masculine *hē* (nominative), *him* (dative), and *his* (genitive) correspond to the modern forms which are identical with them in writing (and *him* in sound as well). A fourth form, the accusative *hine,* has survived only in Southwestern dialects of British English as [ən], as in "Didst thee zee un?" that is, "Did you see him?" (*OED,* s.v. *hin, hine*).

For the feminine pronoun, Old English had the following forms: nominative *hēo,* of which *she* is a development; genitive-dative *hi(e)re;* and accusative *hī(e),* which has not survived.

The neuter pronoun likewise had three forms: nominative-accusative *hit,* surviving when stressed, notably at the beginning of a sen-

---

[35] The final consonant was lost in Middle English because of lack of stress (see p. 159). The resultant *i* was restressed as *ī,* which developed into the Modern English sound [aɪ] along with all other long *i*'s.

tence, in some types of nonstandard Modern English;[36] and genitive *his* and dative *him*, which were identical with the masculine forms. *Its* is obviously not a development of the Old English form, but a new analogical form occurring first in Modern English.

The usual common-gender third person plural forms were nominative-accusative *hī(e)*, genitive *hira* (also often *heora*), and dative *him* (also *heom*). Of these only the dative form has survived; it is the regular spoken unstressed objective form in Modern English, with loss of *h-* as in the other *h-* pronouns, for example "I told 'em what to do." The Modern English stressed form, *them*, like *they* and *their*, is of Scandinavian origin.

INTERROGATIVE PRONOUNS

The interrogative pronoun *hwā* 'who' was declined only in the singular and had only masculine and neuter forms. The nominative-accusative neuter *hwæt* is the source of our *what*. The masculine accusative *hwone* did not survive beyond the Middle English period, its functions being taken over by the masculine and neuter dative *hwām* (or *hwǣm*), surviving in *whom*. *Whose* is from the masculine and neuter *hwæs*. The distinctive neuter instrumental *hwȳ* is obviously the source of our *why*. *Hwā*, *hwām*, and *hwæs* were exclusively interrogative in Old English. The particle *þe* was the usual relative in Old English. Since this had only a single form, it is a great pity that we ever lost it; it involved no choice such as that which we must make — in writing, at least — between *who* and *whom*, now that these have come to be used as relatives.

WEAK VERBS

To turn now to the verb, we may note at the outset that the Old English infinitive ended in *-an* or *-ian*, with only a handful of exceptions in which because of contraction the *a* of *-an* was lost, for example *sēon* 'to see' and *dōn* 'to do.' No trace of the Old English ending remains in Modern English.

The great majority of Old English verbs formed their preterits and

[36] The loss of [h-] is due to lack of stress and is paralleled in the other *h-* pronouns when these are unstressed, as, for example "Give her his book," which in the natural speech of all cultural levels would show no trace of an [h]; compare also "rob his bank" and "Robbie's bank," "raise her up," and "razor up," "rub her gloves," and "rubber gloves," "tore his pants," and "Tory's pants." In the neuter, however, the older stressed form has in Standard English been completely lost, even in writing, whereas in the other *h-* pronouns we have two spoken forms but only one written form.

past participles in the characteristically Germanic way,[37] by the addition of a suffix containing *d* or, immediately after voiceless consonants, *t*.[38]

Most of these dental-suffix, or "weak," verbs were derived from nouns, adjectives, or preterits of strong verbs by the addition of an infinitive suffix *-jan,* the *j* effecting mutation of the root vowel. Sometimes they were causative: thus *flȳman,* earlier *flīeman* 'to cause to flee' from the noun *flēam* 'flight,' *fyllan* 'to cause to be full' (to fill) from the adjective *full,* and *settan* 'to cause to sit' (to set) from *sæt,* preterit singular of *sittan* – in pre-mutation form respectively **flēamjan, *fulljan, *sættjan.* A few more examples of Modern English survivals will suffice to illustrate the derivational relationship in both form and meaning: *food–feed, doom–deem, moot* (obsolete noun 'meeting')– *meet, drink–drench* (from **drankjan), fall–fell* 'to cause to fall,' *couth* (obsolete past participle 'known')–*kith* (obsolete 'to make known'), *lust* (in OE 'pleasure')–*list* 'to desire,' *lie–lay.*

A certain number of weak verbs had in the preterit both vowel differentiation and dental suffix. The difference in vowel was not due to anything remotely like the gradation of the "strong" verbs, but to lack of mutation in the preterit. Modern English survivals are *tell–told* (*tellan* 'to count'–*talde*), *sell–sold* (*sellan* 'to give'–*salde*),[39] *seek–sought* (*sēcan–sōhte*), *buy–bought* (*bycgan–bohte*), *think–thought* (*þencan–þōhte*),[40] and *work–wrought* (*wyrcan–worhte*). The real test in all these verbs is not the vowel differentiation, but the presence of the dental suffix in the preterit.

Quite irregular but very frequently used verbs with dental-suffix preterits are *willan* 'to wish, will'–*wolde, dōn* 'to do'–*dyde, habban* 'to have'–*hæfde, libban* 'to live'–*lifde, secgan* 'to say'–*sǣde, hycgan*

---

[37] Though, as Quirk and Wrenn point out (p. 40), many of these occur rather infrequently, whereas the strong verbs occur very frequently.

[38] The same phenomenon occurs in Modern English when the infinitive of this type of verb ends in a voiceless consonant other than *t* (which requires an extra syllable to form its preterit and past participle, for example *heat* [hit], *heated* [hítɪd]). The first of each of the following pairs ends in [-t], the second in [-d]: *tacked–tagged, slapped–slabbed, luffed–loved, lunched–lunged, raced–razed, rushed–rouged, unearthed–bathed.* Old English scribes, who by and large wrote more phonetically than we do, very sensibly used *t* to indicate the voiceless dental when they heard it.

[39] The Old English preterit forms from which *told* and *sold* come are Anglian, with late lengthening of the vowel before *-ld* (see pp. 141–42). The West Saxon forms *tealde, sealde* will be more familiar to students of Old English literature.

[40] *Þencan* 'think' and *þyncan* 'seem' (pret. *þūhte*) were early confused and ultimately fell together. Archaic *methinks* '(it) seems to me' is thus not to be interpreted as 'I think,' but as '[it] seems to me.'

'to think'–*hog(o)de,* and *gān* 'to go'–*ēode,* the preterit form of the last being from an entirely different verb.

STRONG VERBS

Most other Old English verbs – all others, in fact, except for a few very frequently used ones to be discussed later – formed their preterits by a vowel change called gradation (Grimm's *Ablaut*), due to Indo-European variations in pitch and stress. Gradation is by no means confined to these strong verbs,[41] but it is best illustrated by them. Gradation should never be confused with mutation (umlaut), which, as we have seen (pp. 129–30), is the approximation of a vowel in a stressed syllable to another vowel (or semivowel) in a following syllable. Although there are roughly similar phenomena in other languages, the type of mutation we have been concerned with is confined to Germanic languages. Gradation, which is much more ancient, is an Indo-European phenomenon common to all the languages derived from Indo-European.[42] The vowel differences reflected in Modern English *ride–rode–ridden, choose–chose, bind–bound, come–came, eat–ate, shake–shook* are thus an Indo-European inheritance.

Like Germanic, Old English had seven classes of strong verbs. The first of these – the numerical order is merely traditional – had the root vowels *ī, ā, i, i* in the present, the preterit singular first and third persons, the preterit plural, and the past participle, respectively:[43]

     rīdan 'to ride'   rād   ridon   (ge)riden[44]

Had the number distinction in the preterit survived into present-day English, we should be saying *I rode* but *we rid* – the form *rid* being what would survive of *ridon* after loss of final inflectional *-n* and of the unstressed *o,* reduced to [ə] by late Old English times. In the course

---

[41] Simeon Potter, *Modern Linguistics* (London, 1957), pp. 80–81, interestingly demonstrates the gradational relationship of *sit, sat, seat, soot* 'what sits in the chimney,' and *nest. Nest* goes back ultimately to Indo-European **nisdos* 'sitting-down place,' in which the prefix *ni-* (related to *nether*) means 'down' and the *-sd-* corresponds to Germanic *-st-,* the loss of the vowel being due to lack of stress in Indo-European. Compare also *strike, streak, stroke, strick(en).*

[42] There are parallelisms in the Semitic languages, the Finno-Ugric languages, and some of the languages of the Caucasus.

[43] For all strong verbs it is necessary to give four principal parts, that is, forms from which the entire conjugation can be constructed. The singular-plural distinction in the preterit has survived in Modern English only in *was–were.*

[44] Hereafter past participles will be cited without the prefix *ge-,* concerning which see p. 147.

of the development of this particular verb the preterit singular form of the first and third persons[45] has been generalized for both numbers, though not without some wavering until fairly recently, as we shall see in the detailed treatment of Modern English verbs in Chapter VIII. The development of *drīfan* 'to drive,' *wrītan* 'to write,' *smītan* 'to smite,' and *rīsan* 'to rise' has been identical with that of *rīdan*.

Old English strong verbs of Class II had the gradation *ēo (ū), ēa, u, o,* for example:

crēopan 'to creep'	crēap	crupon	cropen
sprūtan 'to sprout'	sprēat	spruton	sproten

Grammatical change (Verner's Law) is responsible for the consonantal shifts in the last two principal parts of *lēosan* 'to lose' (*luron, loren*), *cēosan* 'to choose' (*curon, coren*), *frēosan* 'to freeze' (*fruron, froren*), and *sēoðan* 'to seethe' (*sudon, soden*).

Old English strong verbs of Class III comprise (1) those with root vowel followed by *m* or *n* plus another consonant (or long *m* or *n*, written *mm* and *nn*), with the gradation *i, a, u;* (2) those with root vowel followed by *l* plus a consonant other than *c*, or by long *l* (written *ll*), with the gradation *e, ea, u, o;* and (3) those with *lc* or with *r* or *h* plus another consonant, which differed from those immediately preceding only in having *eo* in the infinitive. An example of each follows:

1. findan 'to find'	fand	fundon	funden
2. helpan 'to help'	healp	hulpon	holpen
3. weorpan 'to throw'	wearp	wurpon	worpen

In two Class III verbs, *byrnan* (*birnan*) 'to burn' and *yrnan* (*irnan*) 'to run,' the older root vowel and *r* have undergone metathesis; consequently the preterit forms are respectively *barn, burnon, burnen* and *arn, urnon, urnen*. Two other verbs of this class had *u* in their infinitives (*murnan* 'to mourn' and *spurnan* 'to spurn'), but otherwise followed the pattern of *weorpan*. A few verbs of Class III had consonants after the root vowel other than those specified. Those which have survived are *bregdan* 'to pull' (whence *braid*), *þerscan* 'to thresh' and *berstan* 'to burst,' the last two of which are methathetic forms of **þrescan* and **brestan;* they have *æ* in their preterit singular forms. In late Old English times originally short vowels followed by the consonant sequences *mb, nd, ld, rd,* and *rð* were lengthened if no third

[45] For the form of the second person, see p. 146.

consonant followed. This lengthening explains the development of the Modern English diphthongs in *find, found* (ME *finden, foūnden*)[46] and the like, in contrast to the simple vowels in *sing, sang, sink, sunk, spin, spun,* and other verbs lacking these sequences.

Class IV comprised a small number of verbs that had single *l, m,* or *r* after the root vowel. Those with *l* and *r* had the gradation *e, æ, ǣ, o,* for example:

teran 'to tear'   tær   tǣron   toren

Niman 'to seize' and *cuman* 'to come' are the only verbs with single *m* following the root vowel, and *cuman,* the only one of these to survive, was irregular even in Old English times, with the preterit forms *cōm, cōmon,* and the past participle *cumen*. *Brecan* 'to break,' as we should expect from the fact that its root vowel is not followed by any of the consonants specified, did not originally belong to Class IV, but formed its past participle as *brocen* (instead of **brecen,* the expected form) by analogy with verbs of Class IV.

Class V, also rather small, comprises verbs whose root vowel is followed by a single consonant other than *m, n, l,* or *r,* with the characteristic gradation *e, æ, ǣ,* for example:

metan 'to mete'   mæt   mǣton   meten

After *g,* the *e* of the infinitive became *ie,* which in turn became late West Saxon *y* or *i,* and *ǣ* in the same situation became *ĕa,* for example:

gyfan (gifan) 'to give'   geaf   gēafon   gifen

The preterit forms of *wesan* 'to be' (indicative *wæs, wǣron;* subjunctive *wǣre, wǣren*) were used, and still are, as the preterit forms of an entirely different verb, *bēon* 'to be.' The *s–r* alternation is due to Verner's Law and is preserved in *was–were*.

Class VI verbs typically have *a* in the infinitive and the past participle, and *ō* in the two preterit forms, for example:

faran 'to go, fare'   fōr   fōron   faren

---

[46] As we have seen (p. 71), *ū* came to be written *ou* in Middle English because of French influence.

Standan 'to stand' has an *n*-infix in its infinitive and its past participle (*standen*), but not in its preterit forms, *stōd* and *stōdon;* hence *stand* and *stood.*

The verbs of Class VII lack the comparative regularity of the other six classes. Called "reduplicating" for reasons inappropriate to go into here, they "present one of the most difficult problems of Germanic grammar," according to an authority whose conclusion regarding them can be taken as representative.[47] It is sufficient here to point out that in the verbs of this class the infinitive forms show considerable variety, though the vowel (or diphthong) of the infinitive is always repeated in the past participle. The preterit vowels, identical in singular and plural, are always either *ē* or *ēo,* for example:

feallan 'to fall'	fēoll	fēollon	feallen
cnāwan 'to know'	cnēow	cnēowon	cnāwen
hātan 'to be called'	hēt	hēton	hāten
slǣpan 'to sleep'	slēp	slēpon	slǣpen
flōwan 'to flow'	flēow	flēowon	flōwen

PRETERIT-PRESENT VERBS

Āgan 'to possess,' *cunnan* 'to know how,' *magan* 'to be able,' *sculan* 'to be obliged,' **mōtan* (the infinitive happens not to be recorded) 'to be allowed,' and a few other verbs had in their present indicative forms the vowels of old strong preterits, but formed their preterits by means of a dental suffix, for example *sceal* 'shall,' *sceolde* 'should,' which are respectively the singular present indicative (first and third persons) and preterit indicative of *sculan.* Verbs of this type, which were and are of very frequent occurrence, are customarily called preterit-present verbs. They survive in modern speech in such forms as the aforementioned *shall–should,* (from *cunnan*) *can–could–(un)couth,*[48] (from *āgan*) *owe–ought* (OE *āhte*), (from *magan*) *may–might* (OE *mæg, mihte*), and (from **mōtan*) archaic *mote–must* (OE *mōt, mōste*).

ANOMALOUS VERBS

It is not really surprising that very commonly used verbs should have developed irregularities. *Bēon* 'to be' was in Old English, as its mod-

[47] E. Prokosch, *A Comparative Germanic Grammar* (Philadelphia, 1939), p. 176.
[48] For the *l* of *could,* see p. 177. *Couth* 'known' is current only in the negative form *uncouth.* It is the past participial form *cūð.* It is obvious from its pronunciation that it got into modern Standard English as a Northern dialect word, inasmuch as Old and Middle English *ū* remained in the North. The mouse and the louse which Robert Burns celebrated in song were to him a "moose" and a "loose."

ern descendant still is, to some extent a badly mixed-up verb, with alternative present indicative forms from several different roots, as follows (with appropriate pronouns):

> ic eom, bēo 'I am'
> þū eart, bist 'thou art'
> hē, hēo, hit is, biŏ 'he, she, it is'
>
> wē sind(on),[49] sint, bēoŏ 'we are'
> gē sind(on), sint, bēoŏ 'you are'
> hī sind(on), sint, bēoŏ 'they are'

The Modern English plural form *are* is an Anglian form. The present subjunctive likewise had alternative forms. The preterit indicative and subjunctive forms were from yet another verb, whose infinitive in Old English was *wesan,* from Class V (see p. 142). Also highly irregular were *dōn* 'to do,' *gān* 'to go,' and *willan* 'to will, want.'

It is notable that *to be* alone has preserved distinctive singular and plural preterit forms (*was, were*) in modern Standard English, though it is highly doubtful that the distinction would have been so preserved if the leveling which is characteristic of all other preterits had been well established in this verb before the beginning of public education. As far as *to be* is concerned, the folk have carried through the tendency which has reduced the preterit forms of all other verbs to a single form, and they get along very nicely with *you was, we was,* and *they was,* which are certainly no more inherently "bad" than *you sang, we sang,* and *they sang*—for *sung* in the plural would be the historically "correct" development of Old English *gē, wē, hī sungon.*

INDICATIVE FORMS OF VERBS

The Old English present indicative singular of verbs typically had the personal endings *-e, -st, -ŏ,* as in *cēpan* 'to keep,' cited here with the appropriate pronouns:

[49] The forms with *s-* are from the same root as *eom* and *is.* In Indo-European the root was **es-. Eom* 'am' is cognate with Sanskrit *as-mi,* Latin *s-um,* and Greek *em-mi* (later *eimi*); all are developments of Indo-European **es-mi.* Similarly *is,* Sanskrit *as-ti,* Latin *es-t,* and Greek *es-ti* are all from an Indo-European form identical with the Greek form *esti* just cited. Old English *s-ind, s-int,* Sanskrit *s-anti,* and Latin *s-unt* are likewise all from Indo-European **s-enti.* The relationship of the forms cited should be apparent even to the nakedest eye. In some (like *sint, sunt*) the vowel before the *s* is missing; in others the *s* itself has disappeared as the result of assimilation to the following *m*—notably in Greek *emmi* and in the Germanic forms (Gothic *im,* OE *eom,* ON *em*). The form with *-r- (eart)* is from another root and the forms with *b-* are from still another, cognate with Latin *fuī.*

> ic cēpe 'I keep'
> þū cēp(e)st 'thou keepest'
> hē, hēo, hit cēp(e)ð 'he, she, it keepeth'

The *-t* of the second person singular is not a part of the original ending; it comes from the frequent use of *þū* as an enclitic, that is, following the verb and spoken without stress as if it were a part of it, for example *beres þū* becoming *beresþu* becoming *berestu*,[50] with later loss of the unstressed *-u*. The *-e-* of the second and third persons singular is usually missing in West Saxon, resulting in various changes of one sort or another when the root ended in *d, s, t, ð,* or *s* (and sometimes in *g*); for example *-dst* becomes *-tst*, *-dð* and *-tð* become *-t(t)*, *-ðst* becomes *-tst* or *-st*, and *sð* becomes *-st*.

All persons of the present indicative plural of practically all verbs ended in *-að*, exceptions being the verbs with infinitives in *-n*, which had *-ð* alone, and for obvious reasons the preterit-present verbs:

> wē, gē, hī cēpað 'we, you (ye), they keep'

Strong verbs had mutation, if their root vowels were capable of it — in general, if they were other than front vowels — in the second and third persons of the present indicative because of their earlier endings *-ist* and *-ið*, for example with *faran* (Class VI) 'to fare, go':

> ic fare 'I fare'
> þū fær(e)st 'thou farest'
> hē, hēo, hit fær(e)ð 'he, she, it fareth'

The first and third persons preterit indicative singular of all weak verbs ended in *e*, the second in *(e)st*, for example with *þancian* 'to thank,' a weak verb of a class which had *-o-* in the preterit:

> ic þancode 'I thanked'
> þū þancodest 'thou thankedest'
> hē, hēo, hit þancode 'he, she, it thanked'

The first and third persons singular preterit indicative of the strong verb were endingless, for example with *singan* (Class III) 'to sing':

> ic sang 'I sang'
> hē, hēo, hit sang 'he, she, it sang'

[50] Cited by A. Campbell, *Old English Grammar* (Oxford, 1959), p. 193.

But the second person singular strong preterit indicative had the same vowel as the preterit plural with the ending *e*, thus *þū sunge*. In addition, if grammatical change had been operative, the shifted consonant also occurred, for example in *cēosan* (Class II) 'to choose' and *snīðan* (Class I) 'to cut':

ic cēas	ic snāð
þū cure	þū snide
hē, hēo, hit cēas	hē, hēo, hit snāð

The preterit plural indicative of all verbs used the single ending *on* for all persons, for example:

(weak) wē, gē, hī þancodon 'we, you (ye), they thanked'
(strong) wē, gē, hī sungon 'we, you (ye), they sang'

SUBJUNCTIVE AND IMPERATIVE FORMS

The subjunctive, used much more extensively than in Modern English, did not indicate person, but only tense and number. The endings were (singular) *-e*, (plural) *-en* in both tenses,[51] the present singular subjunctive form of all verbs thus being identical with the first person forms of the indicative. The preterit subjunctive of strong verbs had in both singular and plural the root of the preterit indicative plural; hence the preterit singular subjunctive form was identical with the second person singular of the preterit indicative. Thus, in *Beowulf*, line 2818, ". . . ǣr hē bǣl cure . . . ," that is, 'ere he chose the pyre.'

The imperative singular of all verbs ended in *-e, -a*, or was endingless, all three types being illustrated in the following passage from *Beowulf*, lines 658–60:

Hafa nū ond geheald hūsa sēlest,
gemyne mǣrþo, mægen-ellen cȳð,
waca wið wrāþum!

Have now and hold (of) houses the best,
remember fame, mighty valor make known,
watch against (the) hostile (one)!

The imperative plural ended in *-(a)ð*.

---

[51] Except for the small group of contracted verbs, which had no *-e* in either their present singular subjunctive or their first person present indicative. In these verbs the present plural subjunctive was identical with the infinitive, for example *fōn* 'to seize,' *flēon* 'to flee,' and *slēan* 'to slay, strike.'

NONFINITE FORMS

The present participle of both weak and strong verbs ended in
-ende (*-nde* in those verbs in which the *-a-* of the infinitive was missing).
The past participle of strong verbs ended, as must have been observed,
in *-en,* which has survived in many strong verbs to the present day.
The prefix *ge-* was fairly general for past participles, but occurs sometimes as a prefix in all forms. It survives in the past participle throughout the Middle English period as *y-* (or *i-*), and is familiar to us in
Milton's archaic use in "L'Allegro": "In heaven ycleped Euphro-
syne . . ." (from OE *geclypod* 'called').

OLD ENGLISH ILLUSTRATED

The following passage in late West Saxon is the beginning of a
sermon by Ælfric, the greatest prose writer of the Old English period,
recounting the martyrdom of a group of Christian soldiers in Asia
Minor. Abbreviations (for instance *þ,* always used for *þæt;* 7, always
used for *and;* and the line over vowels frequently used to indicate a
following *m*) have been expanded. Macrons have been placed over long
vowels. The capitalization and punctuation of the manuscripts are retained — the latter consisting solely of slightly raised points serving to
set off grammatical units and hence indicating pauses in oral delivery.

WĒ	WYLLAÐ	ĒOW[52]	GERECCAN		ÞÆRA	fēowertigra
We	*want*	*[to] you*	*to tell*		*of the*	*forty*

cempena	ðrōwunge·		þæt	ēower	gelēafa	þē	trumre
soldiers	*[the] suffering,*		*that*	*your*	*belief*	*the*	*firmer*

sȳ·	þonne	gē	gehȳrað	hū	þegenlice	hī	þrōwodon
may be,	*when*	*ye*	*hear*	*how*	*thanelike*	*they*	*suffered*

for	crīste·	On	þæs	cāseres	dagum	þe	wæs	gehāten
for	*Christ.*	*In*	*that*	*Caesar's*	*days*	*who*	*was*	*called*

licinius	wearð	āstyred	mycel	ēhtnys		ofer	þā
Licinius	*was*	*stirred up*	*much*	*persecution*		*over*	*the*

crīstenan·	swā	þæt	ælc	crīsten	mann	sceolde	be
Christians,	*so*	*that*	*each*	*Christian*	*man*	*should*[53]	*by*

---

[52] The indirect object of *gereccan* 'to tell'; the direct object is *ðrōwunge* 'suffering.'
[53] That is, 'had to.'

his   āgenum   fēore   þām   hǣlende   wiðsacan   and   tō
his   own   life   the   Saviour   deny   and   to

hǣðenscype   gebūgan·   and   þām   dēofolgyldum   drihtnes
heathenship   bow,   and   to the   idols   [the] Lord's

wurþmynt   gebēodan·   Þā   wæs   geset   sum   wælhrēowa
honor   submit.   Then   was   set   some⁵⁴   bloodthirsty

dēma   agricolaus   gecīged·   on   ānre   byrig   sebastia   gehāten·
judge   Agricolaus   called   in   a   city   Sebastia   called,

on   þām   lande   armenia·   Se   foresǣde   dēma   wæs   swīðe
in   the   land   Armenia.   The   aforesaid   judge   was   very

ārlēas·   crīstenra   manna   ēhtere   and   arod   tō
merciless,   [of] Christian   men   [a] persecutor   and   ready   to

dēofles   willan·   Þā   hēt   se   cwellere   þæs
[the] devil's   will.   Then   ordered   the   murderer   the

cāseres   cempan   ealle   geoffrian·   heora   lāc   þām
Caesar's   soldiers   all   to offer   their   sacrifices   to the

godum·   Þā   wǣron   on   þām   campdōme   cappadonisce
gods.   Then   were   in   the   military service   Cappadocian

cempan·   fēowertig   crīstenra   unforhte   on   mōde·
soldiers,   forty   [of] Christians   unafraid   in   spirit,

ǣwfæstlice   libbende   æfter   godes   lāre·   Þās   gelǣhte   se
devoutly   living   after⁵⁵   God's   lore.   Those   seized   the

dēma   and   gelǣdde   hī   tō   þām   dēofolgyldum·   and
judge⁵⁶   and   led   them   to   the   idols   and

---

⁵⁴ That is, 'a certain.'
⁵⁵ That is, 'according to.'
⁵⁶ In Modern English this must be expressed as "The judge seized those." No ambiguity is involved in the Old English structure, for, although *þās* might be either nominative or accusative, both *se* and *dēma* (a weak, or *n*-stem, noun) are distinctively nominative in form.

cwæð mid ōlecunge· þæt hī æþele cempan wæron·
said with flattery that they noble soldiers were

and on ǣlcum gefeohte fæstrǣde him betwȳnan· and
and in each fight loyal them between,[57] *and*

symle sigefæste on swīþlicum gewinne· ætēowiað nū
ever victorious in violent battle: "Show now

forðī ēowre ānrǣdnysse· and ēow sylfe underþēodað
therefore your loyalty, and yourselves submit to

þǣra cyninga gesetnyssum· and geoffriað þām godum
the kings' decrees, and offer to the gods

ǣr þām þe gē bēon getintregode· Þā cwǣdon þā
ere ye be tortured." Then said the

crīstenan· tō ðām cwellere þus· Oft wē oferswīðdon
Christians to the murderer thus: "Oft we overcame,

swā swā þū sylf wistest ūre wiðerwinnan on
as thou [thy]self knowest, our adversaries in

gehwylcum gewinne· þā þā wē fuhton for ðām dēadlicum
each battle when we fought for the mortal

kynincge· ac ūs gedafenað swȳðor mid geswince tō
king, but us it befits rather with labor to

campigenne· for þām undēadlicum cynincge and þē
do battle for the immortal king and thee

oferswīðan· Þā cwæð se dēma þæt hī ōþer
to overcome." Then said the judge that they other[58]

þǣra dydon·[59] swā hī þām godum
of these should do: either they to the gods

---

[57] That is, 'to one another.' Note this use of *between* (OE *betwȳnan*) for more than two.

[58] That is, 'one of two.'

[59] *Dydon* and the following *geoffrodon*, *hæfdon*, *forsāwon*, and *wurdon* are preterit subjunctives, with *-on* where we would expect *-en*.

geoffrodon   and   ārwurðnysse   hæfdon·   swā   hī
should offer   and   honor   should have,   or   they

ðā   offrunge   forsāwon   and   gescynde   wurdon·
the   offering   might neglect   and   confounded   be:

smēageð   nū   ic   bidde   hwæt   ēow   betst   fremige·   Ða
"Consider   now,   I   bid,   what   you   best   profits."   The

hālgan   andwyrdon   þām   hæðenan   cwellere·   Drihten
saints   answered   the   heathen   murderer,   "[The] Lord

forescēawað·   hwæt   ūs   fremige·
foreshoweth   what   us   profits."

The homily goes on to tell of the bloodcurdling and bone-chilling punishment meted out to the Christian soldiers, who were, among other indignities, shoved into a lake which froze to such an extent that they were completely encased in ice, causing their flesh to break open. The sublinear translation given above furnishes a poor idea indeed of Ælfric's style, which is better indicated by a freer translation of the entire homily included in the most recent edition of "The Forty Soldiers."[60]

THE ENGLISH GOLDEN AGE

It is frequently supposed by those whose knowledge of it is more or less limited to the story of King Alfred and the cakes—and their number includes many otherwise well-educated people—that the Old English period was somehow gray, dull, and crude.[61] Nothing could be further from the truth. England after its conversion to Christianity at

[60] John Thomas Algeo, "Ælfric's 'The Forty Soldiers': An Edition" (unpublished dissertation, University of Florida, 1960), pp. 68–79.

[61] Those who think so are advised to examine the marvelous Sutton Hoo treasure the next time they visit the British Museum. This collection of finely wrought gold jewelry, weapons and armor, and luxurious household furnishings, dating from the seventh century, was discovered in Suffolk in 1939. It is the subject of Chapter 5 of D. Elizabeth Martin-Clarke's *Culture in Early Anglo-Saxon England* (Baltimore, 1947), which contains illustrations. *The Sutton Hoo Ship Burial*, published by the Trustees of the British Museum (London, 1947), has a full description of the finds, with many illustrations. The issue of *Life* for July 16, 1951, pp. 81–85, has some excellent pictures in color. For the benefit of Americans, and doubtless of many Englishmen as well, *Hoo* is a topographical term, from Old English *hōh* 'spur of land.'

the end of the sixth century became a veritable beehive of scholarly activity. The famous monasteries at Canterbury, Glastonbury, Wearmouth, Lindisfarne, Jarrow, and York were great centers of learning where men such as Aldhelm, Benedict Biscop, Bede, and Alcuin pursued their studies. The great scholarly movement to which Bede belonged is largely responsible for the preservation of classical culture for us. It was to the famous cathedral school at York founded by one of Bede's pupils that Charles the Great (Charlemagne) turned for leadership in his Carolingian Renaissance, and especially to the illustrious English scholar Alcuin (Ealhwine), born in the year of Bede's death and educated at York. A Devonshire man, Wynfrith, later known as Boniface, led the band of English missionaries who brought the Christian faith and Christian culture to Germany. Earlier in a brilliant career which ended in his martyrdom by a band of heathen fanatics, Boniface had assisted Willibrord, the English-born and English-educated bishop of Utrecht, in his missionary labors in Frisia (Friesland).

The culture of the North of England in the seventh and eighth centuries was to spread over the entire country, despite the decline which it suffered as a result of the hammering onslaughts of the Danes. Luckily, because of the tremendous energy and ability of Alfred the Great, it was not lost; and Alfred's able successors of the royal house of Wessex down to the time of the second Ethelred consolidated the cultural and political contributions made by their most distinguished ancestor.

With English culture more advanced than any other in western Europe, the Norman Conquest amounted to a crushing defeat of a superior culture by an inferior one, as the Normans themselves were in time to have the good sense to realize—for they, like the Scandinavian invaders who had preceded them, were ultimately to become Englishmen. As for the English language, which is our main concern here, it was certainly one of the most highly developed vernacular tongues in Europe—for French did not become a literary language until well after the period of the Conquest—with a word stock capable of expressing subtleties of thought elsewhere reserved for Latin. This word stock will be dealt with in some detail in a later chapter.

VI

The Middle English
Period (1100–1500)

The dates for the beginning and end of the Middle English period are conventional and more or less arbitrary. By 1100 certain changes, which had begun long before, were sufficiently well established to justify our use of the adjective *middle* to designate the language in what was actually a period of transition from the English of the early Middle Ages—Old English—to that of the earliest printed books, which, despite certain superficial differences, is essentially the same as our own.

The changes which occurred during this transitional, or "middle," period may be noted in every aspect of the language: in its sounds, in its grammatical structure, in the meanings of its words, and in the nature of its word stock, where many Old English words were replaced by French ones. As we proceed, we shall examine these developments in some detail.

THE BACKGROUND OF
THE NORMAN CONQUEST

Almost at the end of the Old English period the great catastrophe of the Norman Conquest befell the English people—a catastrophe more far-reaching in its effects on English culture than the earlier harassment by the Scandinavians who had subsequently become one with them. The Norman Conquest—fortunately for Anglo-American culture and civilization, the last invasion of England—was also carried out by Northmen, who under the leadership of William the Conqueror, the seventh duke of Normandy, defeated the English under the hapless

King Harold II at the battle of Hastings in 1066. Harold was killed by an arrow which pierced his eye, and the English, deprived of his effective leadership and that of his two brothers, who also fell in the battle, were ignominiously defeated.

After the death without issue of Edward the Confessor, the last king in the direct male line of descent from Alfred the Great, Harold, son of the powerful Earl Godwin, was elected to the kingship. Almost immediately his possession of the crown was challenged by Duke William of Normandy, who was distantly related to Edward the Confessor and who felt that he had a better claim to the throne for a number of reasons unnecessary to go into here.

William and the Northmen whose *dux* he was came not immediately from Scandinavia, but from France, a region of whose northern coast their not-very-remote Viking ancestors had invaded and settled as recently as the ninth and tenth centuries, beginning at about the same time that other pagan Vikings were making trouble for Alfred the Great in England. Those Scandinavians who settled in France are commonly designated by an Old French form of *Northmen,* that is, *Normans,* and that section of France which they settled and governed was called Normandy.

The Conqueror was a bastard son of Robert the Devil, who took such pains in the early part of his life to earn his surname—among other things, he was accused, doubtless justly, of poisoning the brother whom he succeeded as duke of Normandy—that he became a figure of legend. So great was his capacity for rascality that he was also called Robert the Magnificent. Ironically, he died in the course of a holy pilgrimage to Jerusalem.

Robert's great-great-grandfather was Rollo (*Hrólfr*), a Danish chieftain who was created first duke of Normandy after coming to terms satisfactory to himself with King Charles the Simple of France. In the five generations intervening between Duke Rollo and Duke William, the Normans had become Frenchmen culturally and linguistically,[1] at least superficially—though we must always remember that in those days the French had no learning, art, or literature comparable to what was flourishing in England, nor had they ever seen anything comparable, as they themselves were willing to admit, to the products of

---

[1] A further instance of the linguistic facility of these erstwhile Norsemen is the fact that, after conquering Sicily (a few years before William conquered England) they learned to speak Arabic, Sicily being in those days part of the Arab world culturally as well as politically.

English artisans and craftsmen: carving, jewelry, tapestry, metalwork, and the like.[2]

THE LINGUISTIC INFLUENCE OF THE CONQUEST

The impact of the Norman Conquest on the English language, like that made by the earlier Norse-speaking invaders, is to a large extent confined to the word stock, though Middle English shows some instances of the influence of French idiom. A huge body of French words were ultimately to become part of the English vocabulary, many of them replacing English words which would have done for us just as well. This older French element (in contrast with newer borrowings like *chef, tête-à-tête,* and *café*) will be discussed in a later chapter dealing specifically with loan-words in English. Suffice it to point out here merely that English acquired, as it were, a new look. Compare the following passages from two different translations of the parable of the prodigal son, the first from the West Saxon Gospels of *ca.* 1000 and the second from John Wyclif's translation in the latter fourteenth century:

Luke xv.12:
Fæder, syle mē mīnne dæl mīnre æhte þe mē tō gebyreþ.
Fadir, ȝyve me a porcioun of þe substance þat falliþ me.[3]

Luke xv.25:
. . . and þā hē þām hūse genēalæhte, hē gehȳrde þone sweg and þæt weryd.
. . . and whanne he cam and was nyȝ þe hous, he herde a symphonie and oþer noise of mynstralcye.[4]

Where the Old English translator renders "uni civium regionis illius" as "ānum burhsittendan men þæs rīces" (that is, '[to] a borough-dwelling man of that kingdom'), Wyclif has "oon of þe citizeins of þat contré." Other correspondences of Old English and French in the two versions of the parable are *gewilnode–coveitide* 'coveted,' *forwurðe–perishe, mildheortnesse–mercy, onfēng–resceyved* 'received,' *hālne*

---

[2] These facts have been frequently pointed out, notably by R. W. Chambers, *On the Continuity of English Prose from Alfred to More and His School* (New York, 1932). See numerous quotations from Chambers and others in Kemp Malone's "Earliest England," *Emory University Quarterly,* 5 (1949), especially 142–46.

[3] The Vulgate, the Latin version of the Bible used by both translators, has "Pater, da mihi portionem substantiae, quae me contingit."

[4] Vulgate: ". . . audivit symphoniam et chorum."

'whole'–*saaf* 'safe,' *biddan–preie* 'to pray,' *bebod–mandement* 'command,' *gǽlsan–lecherie*.

THE RISE OF A LONDON STANDARD

Inasmuch as there is writing in all dialects, it is necessary to take some account of the dialectal diversity of Middle English. The Northern dialect corresponds roughly to Old English Northumbrian, its southernmost eastern boundary being also the Humber. Likewise, the Midland dialects, subdivided into East Midland and West Midland, correspond roughly to Old English Mercian. The Southern dialect, spoken south of the Thames, similarly corresponds roughly to West Saxon, with Kentish a subdivision.

It is not surprising that a type of speech—that of London—essentially East Midlandish in its characteristics, though showing Northern

and to a less extent Southern influences, should in time have become a standard for all of England. London had for centuries been a large (by medieval standards), prosperous, and hence important city.

Until the late fifteenth century, however, authors wrote in the dialect of their native regions — the authors of *Sir Gawain and the Green Knight* and of *Piers Plowman* in the West Midland dialect; the authors of *The Owl and the Nightingale,* of the *Ancrene Riwle,* and of the *Ayenbite of Inwit* in the Southern dialect (including Kentish); the author of the *Bruce* in the Northern dialect; and John Gower and Geoffrey Chaucer in the East Midland dialect, specifically the London variety of East Midland. Modern Standard English — American, however indirectly, as well as British — is a development of the speech of London. To this type of speech people of consequence and those who aspired to be people of consequence or to be the ancestors of people of consequence were endeavoring to conform long before the settlement of America by English-speaking people in the early part of the seventeenth century, though many of those who migrated to the New World obviously retained traces of their regional origins in their pronunciation, their vocabulary, and to a lesser degree in their syntax. Rather than speaking local dialects, most used a type of speech which had been influenced in varying degrees by the London Standard. In effect, their speech was essentially that of London, with regional shadings.

Thus it comes about that the language of Chaucer and of Gower is so much easier for us to comprehend at first sight than, say, the Northern speech (specifically lowland Scots) of their contemporary John Barbour, author of the *Bruce.* In the following lines from Chaucer's *House of Fame,* for instance, an erudite eagle explains to Chaucer what speech really is:

> Soune ys noght but eyre ybroken
> And every spech that ys yspoken,
> Lowde or pryvee, foule or faire,
> In his substaunce ys but aire;
> For as flaumbe ys but lyghted smoke,
> Ryght soo soune ys aire y-broke.
> But this may be in many wyse,
> Of which I wil the twoo devyse:
> Of soune that cometh of pipe or harpe.
> For whan a pipe is blowen sharpe
> The aire ys twyst with violence
> And rent. Loo, thys ys my sentence.
> Eke, whan men harpe strynges smyte,

Whether hyt be moche or lyte,
Loo, with the stroke the ayre to-breketh:
Thus wost thou wel what thinge is speche.[5]

Now compare Chaucer's English, so like our own, with that of the following excerpt from the *Bruce:*

Þan wist he weill þai wald him sla,
And for he wald his lord succour
He put his lif in aventur
And stud intill a busk lurkand
Quhill þat þe hund com at his hand,
And with ane arrow soyn hym slew
And throu the wod syne hym withdrew.[6]

Distinctively Northern forms in this passage are *slā* (corresponding to East Midland *slee*), *wald* (E. Midl. *wolde*[*n*]), *stud* (E. Midl. *sto*[*o*]*d*); *weill*, in which the *i* indicates length of the preceding *e;*[7] *lurkand* (E. Midl. *lurking*), *quhīll* (E. Midl. *whȳl*), *āne* (E. Midl. *ǫn*[8]), *intill* (E. Midl. *intō*), and *syne* (E. Midl. *sith*). *Soyn* 'soon, immediately' is merely a matter of spelling: the *y*, like the *i* in *weill*, merely indicates length in the preceding vowel, and not a pronunciation of the vowel different from that indicated by the usual East Midland spelling *sone*. The nominative form of the third person plural pronoun, *þai* 'they,' was adopted in the North from Scandinavian and gradually spread into the other dialects. The oblique forms *their* and *them* were not used in London English or in the Midland and South generally at this time, though common enough in the North. Chaucer uses *they* for the nominative,

---

[5] Except for modernization of the use of *u* and *v*, this passage is in the spelling of Fairfax MS 16 (Bodleian Library) as reproduced in *A Parallel-Text Edition of Chaucer's Minor Poems*, Part II, ed. Frederick J. Furnivall for the Chaucer Society (London, 1878), pp. 201–202. Inconsistent spellings (for instance *eyre–ayre–aire, is–ys, thinge–thynge, lowde–foule*) did not bother medieval scribes overmuch. The notion that there was one, and only one, "right" way to spell a word was a long time in developing.

[6] Then he knew well they wished to slay him,
And because he wished to succor his lord
He put his life in fortune's hands
And stood lurking in a bush
While the hound came to his hand,
And with one arrow immediately slew him
And through the wood afterward withdrew himself.

[7] This Northern form with long *e* survives in *ne'er-do-weel*, a Northern variant of *ne'er-do-well*. The phrase is of Northern English and Scots origin.

[8] The editorial hook under the *ǫ* indicates the "open o" sound [ɔ]. Likewise, *ę* indicates "open *ē*," that is, [ɛ]. For the development of these sounds, see pp. 160–62.

but retains the native forms *here* (or *hire*) and *hem* as oblique forms. A Northern characteristic not illustrated in the passage cited is the *-es* ending of the third person singular and all plural forms of the present indicative. Also Northern, but not occurring in the passage, is the frequent correspondence of *k* to the *ch* of the other dialects, as in *birk–birch, kirk–chirche, mikel* 'much'*–michel,* and *ilk* 'each'*–ęch.*

THE PRINCIPAL CONSONANTAL CHANGES

Throughout the history of English the consonants have remained relatively stable, as compared with the notable vowel changes which have occurred. The Old English consonant sounds written *b, c* (in both its values in late Old English, [k] and [č]), *d, f* (in both its values [f] and [v]), *ȝ* (in two of its values [g] and [j]), *h* (as [h] and as [x]), *k, l, m, n, p, r, s, t, þ (ð), p,* and *x* (that is, [ks]) remained unchanged in Middle English. Important spelling differences occur, however, most of them due to Anglo-Norman influence. These have been rather fully discussed in Chapter III. In accordance with later Middle English spelling practices, the *ȝ,* the modified form of *ȝ* which was long used in early Middle English for [x] and [ç], will be represented as *gh,* even though such spelling of a few words may not be actually attested. The same symbol will be represented by *y* when it has the value of [j] — also in accord with later Middle English practice. *Th* will hereafter regularly be used for *þ* and the less frequently occurring *ð* in citations of Middle English words.

The more important consonantal changes, other than the part played by *g* in the formations of new diphthongs (see pp. 162–63), may be summarized as follows:[9]

1. The Old English sequences *hl, hn,* and *hr* (as in *hlēapan* 'to leap,' *hnutu* 'nut,' and *hraðor* 'sooner') were simplified to *l, n,* and *r* (as in *lępen, nute,* and *rather*). To some extent *hw,* written *wh* in Middle English, was also frequently so reduced to *w,* at least in the Southern dialect. In the North, however, the *h* in this sequence was not lost. It survives to this day in those types of English derived from the Northern dialect, however indirectly. The sequence was frequently written *qu* and *quh* in Northern texts.

2. The Old English voiced velar fricative *g* after *l* or *r* became *w,* as

---

[9] For a more detailed treatment, see Joseph Wright and Elizabeth Mary Wright, *An Elementary Middle English Grammar,* 2nd ed. (London, 1928), pp. 107–14. Clear examples of some of the phenomena treated are somewhat limited, hence many of the forms cited by the Wrights are used here, as also in other works.

in *halwen* 'to hallow' (OE *halgian*) and *morwe(n)* 'morrow' (OE *morgen*).

3. After consonants, particularly *s* and *t*, and before back vowels, *w* was lost, as in *sǭ* (OE *swā*) and *tō* 'two' (OE *twā*). Since Old English times it had been lost in various negative contractions regardless of what vowel followed, as in Middle English *nil(le)* from *ne wil(le)*, *nǭt* from *ne wǭt*, *nas* from *ne was*, and *niste* from *ne wiste* (in which the *w* was postconsonantal because of elision of the *e* of *ne*). *Nille* survives in *willy-nilly*. A number of spellings with "silent *w*" continue to occur, for example *two*, *sword*, and *answer* (early ME *andswarien*).

4. In unstressed syllables, *-ch* was lost in late Middle English, as in *-ly* (OE *-lic*). The form *ī* for the first person nominative singular pronoun represents a restressing of the *i* which alone remained of *ich* (OE *ic*) after this loss.

5. Before a consonant, though an *e* might intervene, *v* was lost in a few words like *hẹd* (by way of *hẹvd*, *hẹved*, from OE *hēafod*), *lǭrd* (*lǭverd*, OE *hlāford*), *hast*, *hath*, and *had* (OE *hæfst*, *hæfð*, and *hæfde*).

6. The Old English prefix *ge-* became *i- (y-)* as in *iwis* 'certain' (OE *gewiss*) and *ilimpen* 'to happen' (OE *gelimpan*).

7. In the Southern dialect, including Kentish, initial *f*, *s*, and doubtless *þ* as well, were voiced. This characteristic is reflected in spelling in the use of *v* for *f* and *z* for *s*. It was noted as current in some of the Southern counties of England by Joseph Wright in his *English Dialect Grammar* (Oxford, 1905), and is reflected in such Standard English words of Southern provenience as *vixen* 'she-fox' and *vat*.

8. Final inflectional *n* was gradually lost,[10] as was also the final *n* of the unstressed possessive pronouns *mīn* and *þīn* and of the indefinite article before a consonant: compare Old English *mīn fæder* 'my father' with Middle English *mȳ fader* (but *mȳn eye* 'my eye'). This loss of *-n* is indirectly responsible for *a newt* (from *an ewte*) and *a nickname* (from *an ekename* 'an also-name'), where the *n* of the indefinite article has attached itself to the following word. In *umpire* (ME *noumpere*), *adder* (ME *nadder*, compare German *Natter* 'snake'), *auger* (ME *nauger*), and *apron* (ME *napron*, compare *napkin*, *napery*) just the opposite has happened: the *n* of the noun has attached itself to the article.

9. With the introduction of many words from Old French (and much

---

[10] For a detailed study of the loss of final *n*, see David W. Reed, *The History of Inflexional* n *in English Verbs before 1500* (University of California Publications in English, Vol. 74, Berkeley and Los Angeles, 1950).

less frequently from Latin) beginning with [v] (for instance, *veal, virtue, visit*), later with [z] (for instance, *zeal, zodiac*), and with the voicing of initial [θ] in words usually unstressed[11] (for instance *the, this, they*), the voiced fricatives, in Old English allophones of the voiceless ones, achieved phonemic status. With the loss of final -*e* [ə] (below, p. 170), [v], [z], and [ð] came to occur in final position, as in *give, lose, bathe.*[12]

THE MIDDLE ENGLISH VOWELS

The Old English vowels *ē, ī, ō,* and *ū* remained unchanged in Middle English: thus, Old English *fēt* — Middle English *fēt, feet*[13] 'feet'; Old English *rīdan* — Middle English *rīden, rȳden*[14] 'to ride'; Old English *fōda* — Middle English *fo(o)de;* Old English *hūs* — Middle English *hōus*[15] 'house.' Old English *ȳ* was unrounded to [ī] in the Northern and the East Midland areas. It remained unchanged, though written *u* or *ui*, in the greater part of the West Midland and all of the Southwest until the latter years of the fourteenth century, when it was unrounded and hence fell together with the Northern and East Midland development. In Kent and elsewhere in the Southeast the Old English sound became [ē]. Hence Old English *hȳdan* 'to hide' is reflected in Middle English in such dialectal variants as *hīden, hūden,* and *hēden.*

Old English *ā* remained only in the North (*hām* 'home,' *rāp* 'rope,' *stān* 'stone'), becoming [ē], as in *hame, rape,* and *stane,* in Modern Scots; everywhere south of the Humber it became [ɔ],[16] and was spelled *o* or *oo* exactly like the [ō] which remained from Old English, as in *fo(o)de.* One can tell certainly how to pronounce a Middle English word so spelled by referring to its Old English form; thus, if the *o(o)* corresponds to Old English *ā* (*stǫǫn*–OE *stān*), the Middle English sound is [ɔ]; if the Old English word has *ō* (*mōne*–OE *mōna, roote*–OE

[11] See above, p. 59, n. 15, for a complete list of Modern English words beginning with [ð]. It is not long.

[12] For the earlier nonphonemic status of [v], [z], and [ð], see above, p. 125.

[13] Doubling *e* and *o* to indicate length became usual in late Middle English times, though encountered much earlier. Such spelling practices have been discussed above, pp. 70–71. Double *a* and double *i* are much less general, and have not survived. Henceforth double *e* and double *o* forms will sometimes be cited, particularly if they are Chaucerian. They require no macrons.

[14] For the Middle English interchange of *i* and *y*, see p. 72. It is reflected in such variants as American *tire* (for a wheel)–British *tyre*, with the preference reversed in American *gypsy*–British *gipsy*.

[15] This French spelling, alongside *ow*, for [ū] has been discussed on pp. 71–72.

[16] The [ō] of *twō*, cited above in another spelling (that is, without the *w*), as also of *whō* (OE *hwā*), is a special development of early Middle English [ɔ].

rōt), the Middle English sound is unchanged. But there is an easier way for, say, the beginning student of Middle English literature, who may not be familiar with Old English, and it is fairly certain: if the modern sound is [ō], typically spelled *o* with "silent *e*" (as in *roe, rode*) or *oa* (as in *road*), then the Middle English sound is [ɔ̄].[17] If, however, the Modern English sound is [ū], [ʊ], or [ə], spelled *oo*, the Middle English sound is [ō], as in, respectively, Modern English *food, foot,* and *flood,*[18] going back to Middle English [fōdə], [fōt], and [flōd].

West Saxon Old English *ǣ* had two quite distinct sources. It might be either a development of West Germanic **ā* (compare the unchanged vowel of Ger. *Schlāf* 'sleep' with the shifted one of WS *slǣp*), corresponding to non-West Saxon (that is, Kentish, Mercian, and Northumbrian) *ē;* or the result of *i*-mutation of prehistoric Old English *ā,* a development of West Germanic **ai,* as in *dǣl* 'part, deal,' from prehistoric Old English **dāli.*

But in non-West Saxon dialects the first *ǣ* (from W. Gmc **ā*) was raised to *ē* early in the Old English period. On the other hand, the Old English *ǣ* resulting from *i*-mutation remained in the Anglian dialects as well as in West Saxon.[19] It corresponds to [ɛ̄] in the Northern and (what is our principal concern) much of the Midland area. Unfortunately for the novice, both [ē] and [ɛ̄] were written *e* or *ee* in Middle English regardless of their sources, which also include West Germanic *ē* for [ē] and the *e* that was lengthened in open syllables to [ɛ̄] (p. 164) in the early thirteenth century.[20]

In early Modern English times *ea* was adopted as a spelling for most of those words which in the Middle English dialects spoken north of the Thames had [ɛ̄] from whatever source, whereas those words which had in the same dialects [ē] from whatever source usually continued the Middle English *e(e)* spelling (p. 70). This difference in spelling is a great blessing to the beginning student of Chaucer. By reference to

---

[17] Exceptions are *gold* and *Rome,* which had [ō] in Middle English and [ū] in early Modern English. Compare the proper name form *Gould* and early rimes of *Rome* with *doom, room,* and so forth, in the poetry of the early Modern period — for example that of Pope and Dryden. The earlier pronunciation of *Rome* is indicated by Shakespeare's pun in *Julius Caesar* I.ii.156: "Now is it Rome indeed, and room enough . . . ," which he repeats elsewhere. The change back to [rōm] and [gōld] has occurred in fairly recent times.

[18] *Brooch* [brōč] is an exceptional instance of *oo* as a spelling for [ō] from Middle English [ɔ̄]. A spelling pronunciation [brūč] is occasionally heard from naive speakers.

[19] In Kentish it merged with the *ē* that had developed from West Germanic **ā.*

[20] Thus West Saxon Old English *slǣp* and *dǣl* correspond to Northern and Midland Middle English *sleep* [slēp] and *dęęl* [dɛ̄l]; *mētan* 'to meet' and *etan* 'to eat' to *mēten* [mḗtən] and *ęten* [ɛ́tən].

it he may, ascertain that *swete breeth* in the fifth line of the General Prologue to the *Canterbury Tales* is to be read [swḗtə brḗθ]. The Modern English spellings *sweet* and *breath* here, as often, provide the clue to the Middle English pronunciation.

Except for Old English *æ* and *y*, the short vowels of those Old English stressed syllables which remained short were unchanged in most Middle English speech (unless otherwise qualified, *Middle English* will refer to the speech of the East Midland area), for example Old English *wascan* 'to wash' — Middle English *washen, helpan* 'to help' — *helpen, sittan* 'to sit'–*sitten, hoppian* 'to hop'–*hoppen,* and *hungrig* 'hungry'–*hungry* [húŋgrɪ]. Old English short *æ* came to be written *a* in Middle English: Old English *glæd*–Middle English *glad*. In Southwest Midland and in Kentish, however, words which in Old English had short *æ* were written with *e* (for instance *gled*) in early Middle English times — a writing that may have indicated little change from the Old English sound in those areas. In the Northern and East Midland areas Old English *y* was unrounded to *i*, exactly as *ȳ* was unrounded to *ī* in the same areas (see p. 160). In the Southeast it became *e*, but remained as a rounded vowel [y], written *u*, in the West Midland and the Southwest until late Middle English times, when it was unrounded along with [ȳ].

CHANGES IN DIPHTHONGS

The Old English long diphthongs *ēa* and *ēo* were "smoothed," or monophthongized, in late Old English times (eleventh century), occurring in the twelfth century as [ɛ̄] and (in the greater part of England) [ē] respectively, their subsequent Modern English development coinciding with that of [ɛ̄] and [ē] from other origins. Because of this, post-eleventh-century Middle English *lẹẹf* 'leaf' [lɛ̄f] develops out of Old English *lēaf* and *seen* 'to see' [sēn] out of Old English *sēon*. The short diphthongs *ea* and *eo*[21] became by the twelfth century respectively *a* and *e*, as in Middle English *yaf* 'gave' from Old English *geaf, herte* 'heart' from Old English *heorte*.

New diphthongs appear in Middle English, though their development began in late Old English times, from the vocalization of *g* to *i* after front vowels (OE *sægde* 'said'–ME *saide*) and later of *g* (the voiced velar fricative) to *u* after back vowels (OE *boga* 'bow'–ME *bowe*). Before Old English *h,* which other than initially stood for a voiceless fricative, an *i*-glide developed after a front vowel (late

---

[21] Diphthongs according to the traditional view, but see above, p. 123, for another interpretation of these digraphs.

OE *ehta* 'eight'–ME *eighte*) and a *u*-glide after a back vowel (OE *āht* 'aught'–ME *aught*). *W* after a vowel became a *u*-glide, for instance Old English *grōwan* 'to grow'–Middle English *growen,* the *w* continuing to be written. The diphthong [ɔɪ], spelled *oi, oy,* is of French origin, as in *joie* 'joy,' *cloistre* 'cloister,' as is [uɪ], usually also written *oi, oy,* as in *boilen* 'to boil,' *poisen* 'to poison,' and *joinen* 'to join.'[22] The off-glides [ɪ] and [u] merely lengthened *i* and *u* respectively (OE *lige* 'falsehood'– ME *līe;* OE *fugol* 'fowl'–ME *foūl*). It should be noted that diphthongization often involved a new conception of syllabic division, for example Old English *cnāwan* [knã-wan]–Middle English *knowen* [knóu-ən].

Other diphthongal developments are taken up in specialized grammars of Middle English. Before passing on to other matters, it is significant that we note here by way of summarization that as the Old English diphthongs were smoothed into monophthongs, new diphthongs developed in Middle English. These have in turn undergone smoothing in Modern English (for instance, *drawen* [dráuən]–*draw* [drɔ]), new glides have developed (for instance, *rīden* [rídən]–*ride* [raɪd], *hous* [hūs]–*house* [haus]), and others are even now in the course of developing. Some inland Southern American speakers lack off-glides in [aɪ] and [au], so that "My wife is in the house" comes out as something very like [ma waf ɪz ɪn ðə has]; the off-glide may also be lost in *oil, boil,* and the like. Comparatively new *u* and *i* off-glides may occur in *boat, bait,* and the like, which, as we have seen, some phoneticians and most phonemicists nowadays transcribe as diphthongs. As E. E. Wardale aptly puts it, "The constant loss of old and formation of new diphthongs illustrate in a striking manner the life and movement inherent in any spoken language."[23]

THE LENGTHENING AND SHORTENING OF VOWELS

As we have seen (above, pp. 141–42), in late Old English times originally short vowels were lengthened before *mb, nd, ld, rd,* and *rð.* This lengthening frequently failed to maintain itself, and by the end of the Middle English period is to be found only in *i* and *o* before *mb* (*clīmben* 'to climb,' *cọmb* 'comb'); in *i* and *u* before *nd* (*bīnden* 'to bind,' *boūnden* 'bound'); and generally before *ld* (*mīlde* 'mild,' *yēlden* 'to pay, yield,' *ọld* 'old,' *gōld* 'gold'). Reshortening has subsequently occurred, how-

---

[22] Words containing this diphthong have [əɪ] in early Modern English, pronunciations which have survived in nonstandard speech and are reflected in the dialect spellings *bile, pizen,* and *jine.* See p. 187.

[23] *An Introduction to Middle English* (London, 1937), p. 55.

ever, in some words, for instance *wind* (noun), *held, send, friend;* compare *wind* (verb), *field, fiend,* in which the lengthening survives. If another consonant followed any of the sequences mentioned, lengthening did not occur; this fact explains Modern English *child, children* (OE nominative-accusative plural *cildru*).

Considerably later than the lengthenings due to the consonant sequences just discussed, short *a, e,* and *o* were lengthened when they were in open syllables, that is, in syllables in which they were final, for instance *bā-ken* 'to bake' (OE *bacan*). To put it somewhat differently, these vowels were lengthened when followed by a single consonant plus another vowel. In Old English short vowels frequently occurred in such syllables, for example *nama* 'name,' *stelan* 'to steal,' *þrote* 'throat,' which became in Middle English respectively *nāme, stẹlen, thrọte.* This lengthening is interestingly reflected in *staff* (from ME *staf,* going back to OE *stæf*) and its plural *staves* (from ME *stāves,* going back to OE *stafas*). Short *i (y)* and *u* were likewise lengthened in open syllables, beginning in the fourteenth century in the North, but these vowels underwent a qualitative change also: *i (y)* became *ē,* and *u* became *ō,* for example Old English *wicu* 'week,' *yvel* 'evil,' *wudu* 'wood,' which became respectively *wēke, ēvel, wōde.*

This lengthening in open syllables was a new principle in English. Its results are still apparent, as in *staff* and *staves,* though the distinction between open and closed syllables became largely historical with the loss of final unstressed *e,* as a result of which the vowels of, say, *staves, week,* and *throat* now occur in closed syllables ([stēvz], [wīk], [θrōt]). When final unstressed *e* ceased to be pronounced (see below, p. 170), the letter was often used after a consonant to indicate that the preceding vowel was long. This *-e* indicates in Modern English the difference between *win* and *wine* (see above, p. 71), though the vowels of both words appear in closed syllables ([wɪn], [waɪn]); as far as modern practice is concerned, this final *e* serves only as a diacritic — the equivalent of a macron over the preceding vowel. This use of *-e,* beginning in Middle English times, was greatly extended in the sixteenth century.

Conversely, beginning in the Old English period, originally long vowels in closed syllables — that is, followed by consonant sequences, including lengthened (doubled) consonants — were shortened, except when followed by those consonantal sequences which caused lengthening, for example *hidde* 'hid' (OE *hȳdde*), *kepte* 'kept' (OE *cēpte*),[24] *fifty*

---

[24] The alternation of long-voweled infinitives with short-voweled preterits is reflected in Modern English *hide–hid, keep–kept,* and a number of other weak verbs.

(OE *fíftig*), *fiftēne* (OE *fíftỹne*),[25] *twenty* (OE *twēntig*), *wisdom*. It made no difference whether the consonant sequence was in the word originally (as in OE *sōfte*–ME *softe*), was the result of adding an inflectional ending (as in *hidde*), or was the result of compounding (as in OE *wīsdōm* [that is, *wīs* plus *dōm*]–ME *wisdom*). Reduced stress accounts for the shortening of the second syllable of the last cited word – a general tendency which also operated in words which were not normally stressed within the sentence, as in *an,* the indefinite article (OE *ān* 'one'), *but* (OE *būtan*), *not* (OE *nāwiht*). There was considerable wavering in vowel length before the sequence -*st,* as indicated by such Modern English forms as *fist–Christ, lost–ghost, breast–least.* Before two unstressed syllables shortening regularly occurred, as reflected in *wilderness* (*wild*), *Christendom* (*Christ*), and *holiday* (*holy*).

THE LEVELING OF UNSTRESSED VOWELS

As far as the structure of English is concerned, the most significant of all developments in the language occurred with the Middle English falling together of *a, o,* and *u* with *e* in unstressed syllables, all ultimately becoming [ə], for example:

OLD ENGLISH	MIDDLE ENGLISH
lama 'lame'	lāme
faran 'to fare,' faren (past part.)	fāren
stānes 'stone's,' stānas 'stones'	stǫnes
feallað 'falleth'	falleth
nacod 'naked'	nāked
macodon 'made' (pl.)	mākeden
sicor 'sure'	sēker
lengðo 'length'	lengthe
medu 'liquor'	mẹde

This phenomenon has already been alluded to (p. 122), for it began well before the end of the Old English period. The *Beowulf* manuscript (*ca.* A.D. 1000), for instance, has occurrences of -*as* for the genitive singular -*es* ending, -*an* for the preterit plural ending -*on* and the dative plural ending -*um*[26] (and conversely -*on* for the infinitive ending -*an*), -*o* for the genitive plural ending -*a* and for the neuter nominative plural ending -*u,* among a number of such interchanges pointing to identical vowel quality in such syllables.

---

[25] Reflected in Modern English *fifty, fifteen,* contrasted with *five.*
[26] The -*m* in -*um* became *n* late in the Old English period.

THE REDUCTION OF INFLECTIONS

As a result of this merging of unstressed vowels into a single sound, the number of forms in English was drastically reduced. Middle English became a language with few inflectional distinctions, whereas Old English, as we have seen, was relatively highly inflected, though less so than Germanic, which was about as fully inflected as Latin. This reduction of inflections was thus responsible for a structural change of the greatest importance.

In the adjective, for instance, the Old English weak forms — those used after the demonstrative pronouns — ending in -a (masculine nominative) and in -e (neuter nominative-accusative and feminine nominative) fell together in a single form in -e. Thus an indication of gender distinguishing the masculine form was lost. Middle English *the ọlde man* corresponds to Old English *se ealda man,* the ending of the adjective being identical with that used for *the ọlde tāle* (OE feminine *sēo ealde talu*) and *the ọlde sword* (OE neuter *þæt ealde swurd*). The Old English weak adjective endings -an and -um similarly fell together as -en and, with the loss of final -n (see p. 159), these also came to have only -e. The Old English genitive plural forms of the weak adjective in -ena and -ra, after first becoming -ene and -re, were made to conform to the predominant weak adjective form in -e, though there are a very few late survivals of the Old English genitive plural in -ra as Middle English -er, notably in *aller* (OE *ealra*) and related forms. Thus the five singular and plural forms of the Old English weak adjective declension (-a, -e, -an, -ena, and -um) are reduced to a single form ending in -e, with gender as well as number distinctions completely obliterated. For the strong function the endingless form of the Old English nominative singular was used throughout the singular, with a generalized plural form (identical with the plural of the weak adjective declension) in -e: thus (strong singular) *with grẹẹt solempnytee* 'with great solemnity,' (generalized plural) *grẹẹte lordes* 'great lords.'

To describe the situation more simply, Middle English monosyllabic adjectives ending in consonants had a single inflection, -e, used to modify singular nouns in the weak function and all plural nouns. Other adjectives — for example *frē* (or *free*) and all disyllables — were uninflected. This simple grammatical situation can be inferred from many of the manuscripts only with difficulty, because scribes frequently wrote final e's where they did not belong.

Changes resulting from this new identity of vowel in unstressed syllables were considerably more far-reaching than what has been shown in the declension of the adjective. For instance, the older endings -an (infinitives, most of the oblique, or non-nominative, forms of *n*-stem nouns), -*on* (indicative preterit plurals), and -*en* (subjunctive preterit plurals, past participles of strong verbs) all fell together as -*en.* With the later loss of final inflectional -*n* in some of these forms, only -*e* [-ə] was left, and this was in time also to go. This fact accounts for endingless infinitives, preterit plurals, and some past participles of strong verbs in Modern English, for instance:

OLD ENGLISH	MIDDLE ENGLISH	MODERN ENGLISH
findan (inf.)	fīnden	find
fundon (pret. pl.)	fōunde(n)	found
funden (past part.)	fōunde(n)	found

It was similar, as we have seen from the examples cited (p. 165), with the nominative-accusative plural of the most important declension (-*as*) which became a pattern for the plural of most nouns, and the genitive singular of the same declension (-*es*); and with the noun endings -*eð* and -*að* (OE *hæleð* 'fighting-man,' *mōnað* 'month') and the same endings as they occurred in verbs (OE *findeð* 'he, she, it finds,' *findað* 'we, you, they find') — all ending up as Middle English -*eth.*[27] Also similarly, the -*ast* of many Old English weak verbs fell together with the -*est* of strong verbs (and the largest group of weak verbs as well).

THE LOSS OF GRAMMATICAL GENDER

One of the important results of the leveling of unstressed vowels was the loss of grammatical gender. We have seen how this occurred with the adjective. We have also seen that grammatical gender, for psychological reasons rather than phonological ones, had begun to break down in Old English times as far as the choice of pronouns was concerned (see pp. 126–27), as when the English translator of Bede's Latin *Ecclesiastical History* refers to Bertha, the wife of King Ethelbert of Kent as *hēo* 'she' rather than *hit,* though she is in the same sentence designated as *þæt* (neuter demonstrative used as definite article) *wīf* rather than *sēo wīf,* which would still have been impossible.

In Old English, gender was readily distinguishable in most nouns: *a*-stem masculine nominative-accusative plurals, for instance, ended in -*as,* feminines in -*a,* and short-stemmed neuters in -*u.* In Middle English all but a handful of nouns acquired the masculine nominative-accusative plural ending -*es* (OE -*as*). This important development,

---

[27] A present indicative plural form only in the Southern dialect of Middle English.

coupled with the invariable *the* which supplanted the Old English masculine *se,* the neuter *þæt,* and the feminine *sēo* with all their oblique forms (see p. 133), left grammatical gender without a leg to stand on.

THE INFLECTION OF NOUNS

It should be obvious that the structure of English was profoundly affected in all departments by the leveling of unstressed vowels. Among the nouns, to cite some further instances, the Old English distinctive feminine nominative singular form in *-u* fell together with the nominative plural form in *-a,* that is, singular *denu* 'valley' and plural *dena* 'valleys' became for a while Middle English *dęne.* It was similar with the neuter nominative-accusative plurals in *-u* and the genitive plurals in *-a:* all came to have the same *-e* ending. What further happened with *dęne* happened to most other nouns which had not formed their nominative-accusative plurals in *-as* in Old English, and has been alluded to before: namely, the *-es* which was the Middle English reduced form of this ending was made to serve as a general plural ending for such words: thus, singular nongenitive *dęne,* general plural *dęnes.* In like fashion, the genitive singular ending *-es* was extended to nouns which had belonged to declensions lacking this ending; thus the genitive singular and the general plural forms of most nouns fell together, and have remained that way ever since: Old English genitive singular *speres* and nominative plural *speru* become Middle English *spęres,* Modern English *spear's, spears;* Old English genitive singular *tale* and nominative plural *tala* become Middle English *tāles,* Modern English *tale's, tales.*

A few *s*-less genitives — feminine nouns and the family-relationship nouns ending in *-r* — remained throughout the period (as in Chaucer's "In hope to stonden in his lady grace" and "by my fader kyn") and survived into early Modern English, along with a few nouns from the Old English "weak" declension.[28] Sometimes the genitive *-s* was left off a noun which ended in *s*[29] or which was followed by a word beginning with *s.*[30]

---

[28] In this declension the Old English genitive ended in *-an,* which, as we have seen, became Middle English *-en,* then *-e.*

[29] For the same phonological reason that accounts for the occasional modern loss of the genitive *-s* in "Keats' poems, Dickens' novels," assuming that these are not merely matters of writing.

[30] Solely a matter of writing. Compare the occasional modern writing "for pity sake," which indicates the same pronunciation as "for pity's sake."

The few nouns which did not conform to the pattern of forming the plural by suffixing -*es*[31] nevertheless followed the pattern of using the nominative-accusative plural as a general plural form. In Old English the mutated forms *fēt, men, tēð, gēs, lȳs, mȳs* were dative singular as well as nominative-accusative plural forms, whereas the genitive and dative plural forms had unmutated vowels. Mutation in itself thus, as we have seen, was in Old English no sign of the plural, nor did lack of it indicate the singular. From Middle English times onward, however, the mutated vowel in what had been merely the most commonly occurring plural form came to be regarded as a sign of the plural; hence the Modern English plural forms *feet, men, teeth, geese, lice, mice*. This development was precisely parallel to what happened to the Old English nominative-accusative plural -*as* when it became in Middle English simply the plural -*es,* and for that matter to the surviving weak nouns, in which the Old English singular accusative-genitive-dative form in -*n* was made to conform to the nominative without -*n*, whereas the same ending occurring in the nominative-accusative plural was retained as the general plural form; thus -*n* became a sign of the plural. A few long-syllabled words which had been neuters in Old English occurred with unchanged plural forms, especially animal names like *sheep, deer,* and *hors.*

During the Middle English period, then, practically all nouns were reduced to two forms, just as in Modern English — one without -*s* used as a general nongenitive singular form, and one with -*s* used as a genitive singular and general plural form. The English language thus acquired a device for indicating plurality without consideration of case — the -*s* ending, which had been in Old English only one of three plural endings in the strong masculine declension. It also lost all trace of any case distinctions except for the genitive, identical in form with the plural. English had come to depend upon particles — mainly prepositions and conjunctions — and word order to express grammatical relations which had previously been expressed by inflection. No longer could one say, as Ælfric had done, "Þās gelæhte se dēma," (p. 148, n. 56) and expect the sentence to be properly understood as 'The judge seized those.' To say this in Middle English, it is necessary that the subject precede the verb: "The dēme ilaughte thọs."

---

[31] They include those which lack -*s* plurals today, for example *ox, deer, foot.* There were also in Middle English a number of survivals of weak-declension plurals in -*(e)n* which have subsequently disappeared (for example *eyen* 'eyes,' *fọọn* 'foes'). The -*(e)n* was even extended to a few nouns which belonged to the *a*-stem strong declension in Old English, for example *shoon* 'shoes' (OE *scōs*).

THE LOSS OF SCHWA IN FINAL SYLLABLES

The leveled final *e* [ə] was gradually lost[32] in the North in the course of the thirteenth century and in the Midlands and the South somewhat later. Many words, however, continued to be spelled with *-e*, which had earlier been extended by analogy to a number of words in which it was not historical, for example *brīde,* from Old English *brȳd* 'bride.' This inorganic *-e,* as it is called, should not be confused with "scribal *e,*" which was certainly never pronounced. That inorganic *e* was pronounced is indicated in a good many lines of verse, for instance Chaucer's "A bryde shal nat eten in the halle" (*Canterbury Tales,* E 1890).[33]

After the loss of final [ə] of whatever origin, *e* was often suffixed to words ending in a single consonant merely to indicate that the preceding vowel was long. This is the so-called scribal *e* just alluded to (see also above, p. 164). In the fifteenth century, this unetymological final *e* occurs occasionally even after doubled consonants; in such instances it has no significance whatever.

Nonfinal unstressed *e* (written *i, y,* and *u* in some dialects) was ultimately lost in the inflectional ending *-es,* except of course after [s], [z], [š], [č], and [ǰ]. This loss was a comparatively late development, beginning in the North in the early fourteenth century. It did not occur in the Midlands and the South until somewhat later. In the West Saxon and Kentish dialects of Old English the *e* of the ending *-eð* for the third person singular of the present indicative of verbs was usually lost (above, p. 145). It is hence not surprising to find such loss in this ending in the Southern dialect of Middle English and, after long syllables, in the Midland dialects as well, for example *mākth* 'maketh,' *bẹrth* 'beareth,' as also sometimes after short syllables, for example *comth.* Chaucer uses both forms of this ending; sometimes the loss of [ə] is not indicated by the spelling, but is dictated by the meter. The vowel sound was retained in *-ed* until the fifteenth century.[34]

[32] The loss of a final sound is called *apocope.*

[33] For additional examples, see Samuel Moore, *Historical Outlines of English Sounds and Inflections,* rev. Albert H. Marckwardt (Ann Arbor, Mich., 1951), p. 62, which cites *weye* (OE *weg*), *pere* (OF *per*), *bare* (OE *bær*), and *harde* (OE *heard*), all of which appear in the *Canterbury Tales* in lines whose scansion, like that of the line quoted above, requires that the *e* be pronounced. For still further examples, see Joseph Wright and Mary Elizabeth Wright, *An Elementary Middle English Grammar,* p. 71.

[34] It has not yet disappeared in the forms *aged, blessed,* and *learned* when these are used as adjectives. Compare *learnëd man, the blessëd Lord, agëd woman* with "The man learned his lesson," "The Lord blessed the multitude," "The woman aged rapidly." (In "aged whiskey" the form *aged* is used as a past participle — one could not say "very aged whiskey" — in contrast to the adjectival use in *agëd woman.*) There is of course no such loss after *t* or *d.*

PERSONAL PRONOUNS:
LOSS OF THE DUAL NUMBER

As we have noted, simplification occurred in other categories as well. Only the pronouns retained, and for that matter still do retain, a considerable degree of the complexity which characterized them in Old English. These words alone preserved distinctive subject and object case forms, except for the neuter pronouns *(h)it, that, this,* and *what,* which even in Old English had not differentiated the nominative and accusative. With the virtual disappearance of the dual number in Middle English,[35] the objective forms of the personal pronouns surviving from Old English are *mē* (nominative *ich, Ī,* Northern *ik*), *ūs* (nominative *wē*), *thee* (nominative *thōu*), and *yōu* (nominative *yē*). The third person masculine accusative *hine* survived into Middle English only in the South; elsewhere *him* took over. The Old English feminine accusative *hī* likewise survived for a while in the same region, but in the latter thirteenth century was supplanted by the *hir(e)* or *her(e)* current elsewhere.

The feminine pronoun had a variety of subject forms, one of them identical with the corresponding masculine form—certainly a well-nigh intolerable state of affairs, forcing the lovesick author of the lyric "Alysoun" to refer to his sweetheart as *he,*[36] the same form she would have used in referring to him. This and the various other forms (among them *hō, hyō, hyē, hī, chō,* and *shē*) had a fairly well defined dialectal distribution, with *shē* the predominant form in East Midland speech.

The native third person nominative-accusative plural forms in *h-,* which remained current in the Southern dialect, were also varied. In the North and Midlands the Scandinavian-derived nominative forms *they, thei* (or *thay, thai*) prevailed. The Midlands and the South, however, continued to use the native *hem* (or *heom*) as an objective form. This is in perfect accord with Chaucer's usage (see pp. 157–58). Ultimately the Scandinavian objective form *them* (*thaim, thame, theim*) current in the Northern dialect was also to prevail; in the generation following Chaucer it everywhere displaced the English forms save for unstressed *hem.*

The genitive forms of the personal pronouns came in Middle English to be used exclusively as possessives. Such a construction as Old English *nǣnig hira* could be rendered in Middle English only by *of* plus the

---

[35] Such a phrase as *git būtū,* that is 'you two both,' occurring in late Old English, indicates that the form *git* had lost much of its idea of twoness and needed the reinforcement of *būtū* 'both.'

[36] For example, "Bote he me wolle to hire take" means 'Unless she will take me to her.'

objective form *hem,* or *them,* precisely as in Modern English *none of them.* The variant forms of the genitive first and second persons singular—*mīn–mī, thīn–thī*—preceding a noun were in exactly the same type of distribution as the forms *an* and *a,* that is, the *n* was lost before a consonant (see p. 159). Following a noun, the forms with -*n* were invariable (as in the rare construction *baby mine,* as also when the possessives were used as in Modern English "That book is mine," "Mine is that book," and *that book of mine*).[37] The possessive of the neuter third person singular *(h)it* was *his,* the same as the masculine. In the same person the feminine possessive form was *hir(e)* or *her(e).* The first, second, and third person plural possessives were respectively *ōur(e), yōur(e),* and *her(e),* to cite the most usual East Midland spellings. The form *their(e),* Scandinavian like *they* and *them,* was almost exclusively Northern in Middle English times, and *her* for the third person plural possessive survives as an occasional form well into the Modern English period.[38] The personal pronouns in -*r* developed new analogical genitive forms in -*es* rather late in Middle English: *hires, ōures, yōures, heres* (Northern *theires*). These -*es* forms were used precisely like Modern English *hers, ours, yours,* and *theirs*—predicatively, as in "The books on the table are hers (ours, yours, theirs)" and when a word modified by the *s*-less forms was to be inferred, as in "Hers (ours, and so forth) are on the table."

DEMONSTRATIVE PRONOUNS

Old English *se, þæt,* and *sēo,* with their various oblique forms, were ultimately reduced to *the, that,* and plural *thọ;* however, inflected forms derived from the Old English declensions continued to be used in some dialects, though not in East Midland, until the thirteenth century. The *the* which at first replaced only the masculine nominative *se* came to be used as an invariable definite article. *That* and *thọ,* which were used both as articles and as demonstratives in Old English (as *þæt* and *þā*), were thus restricted to the demonstrative function. Another *the,* from the Old English masculine and neuter instrumental *þē* has had continuous adverbial use in English, as in "The sooner the better" and "He did not feel the worse for the experience."

---

[37] By analogy with this unvarying use of the forms in -*n* as pronouns, *hisen, heren, ōuren, yōuren,* and *theiren* arose. From the beginning their status seems to have been much the same as that of their Modern English descendants *hisn, hern, yourn,* and *theirn.*

[38] Otto Jespersen, *A Modern English Grammar on Historical Principles* (Copenhagen, 1949), 7, 306–307, cites three instances in Shakespeare: *Othello* III.iii.66; *1 Henry VI* I.i.83; and *Lucrece,* l. 1588. For the first two of these, modern texts have *their.*

In Old English *þes, þis,* and *þēos,* with their various inflectional forms, were exclusively demonstrative. They remained so in Middle English. By the thirteenth century, when gender distinction and some traces of inflection which had survived up to that time were lost, the singular nominative-accusative neuter *this* was used for all singular functions, and a new plural form, *thise* or *thēse,* the ending *-e* as in the plural of adjectives, appeared. These developments have resulted in Modern English *that–those* and *this–these;* the distinction between the singular forms seems currently in process of breaking down, with "This was right" displacing "That was right."

Thǫ ultimately gave way to *thǫs* (ModE *those*), from Old English *þās,* though the form with *-s* did not begin to become common in the Midlands and the South until the late fifteenth century. Chaucer, for instance, uses only *thǫ·*where we would use *those.* In the North *thās,* the form corresponding to *thǫs* elsewhere, began to appear in writing more than a century earlier.

INTERROGATIVE PRONOUNS

The Old English masculine-feminine interrogative pronoun *hwā* became in Middle English *whō,* and the neuter form *hwæt* became *what.* As with the other pronouns, the dative drove out the accusative (OE *hwone*) of the first of these, the dative *whōm* (OE *hwām, hwǣm*) being used in any objective function. *Hwæt* had the same dative form as *hwā* in Old English, but, as with other neuters, this was given up. The genitive of both *hwā* and *hwæt* was *hwæs;* in Middle English this took by analogy the vowel of *whō* and *whōm:* thus *whōs.*

It should be noted that *whō* was in Middle English customarily used only as an interrogative pronoun or an indefinite relative meaning 'whoever,' as in "Who steals my purse steals trash," a usage that occurs first in the thirteenth century. The simple relative use of *who* was not really widespread until the sixteenth century, though there are occasional instances of it as early as the late thirteenth century. The oblique forms *whōs* and *whōm,* however, were used as relatives in late Middle English, at about the same time that another interrogative pronoun, *which* (OE *hwylc*), also began to be so used, in reference to either persons or things. Sometimes *which* was followed by *that,* as in Chaucer's "Criseyde, which that felt hire thus i-take," that is, 'Criseyde, who felt herself thus taken.'

RELATIVE PRONOUNS

The most frequently used relative pronoun in Middle English is indeclinable *that.* It is of course still so used, though modern literary style limits it to restrictive clauses: "The man that I saw was Jones," but "This man, who never did anyone any real harm, was nevertheless punished severely." A relative particle *þe* usually regarded as a survival of the Old English indeclinable relative-of-all-work occurs in early Middle English side by side with *that* (or *þat*, as it would have been written early in the period).

COMPARATIVE AND SUPERLATIVE FORMS

In the general leveling to *e* of unstressed vowels the Old English comparative ending *-ra* became *-re*, later *-er*, and the superlative suffixes *-ost* and *-est* fell together as *-est*. If the root vowel of an adjective was long, it was shortened before these endings, for example *swēte*, *swetter*, *swettest*, though the analogy of the positive form, as in the example cited, frequently caused the original length to be restored in the comparative and superlative forms; the doublets *latter* and *later* show respectively shortness and length of vowel. As in Old English, *ēvel* (and its Middle English synonym *badde*, of uncertain origin), *gōd*, *muchel* (*mikel*), and *lītel* had comparative and superlative forms unrelated to them etymologically: *werse–werst*, *bettre*, *better–best*, *mọre–mọst*, *lesse*, *lasse–lẹste*. Some of the adjectives which in Old English had mutation in their comparative and superlative forms retained the mutated vowel in Middle English, for instance *long–lengre*, *lenger–lengest*, *ọld–eldre*, *elder–eldest*. The simplification of the Old English adjective declensions has been already discussed in another connection (see above, p. 166).

VERBS

Verbs continued to conform to the Germanic division into strong and weak, as they still do. Although the vowels of endings were leveled, the gradational distinctions expressed in the root vowels of the strong verbs were fully preserved. The tendency to use exclusively one or the other of the preterit vowel grades, however, had begun, though there was little consistency: the vowel of the older plural might be used in the singular, or vice versa. The older distinction (as in *I sang, we sungen*) was more likely to be retained in the Midlands and the South than in the North.[39]

In strong verbs of the first class, the vowel gradation was ī–ọ̄–i–i: *rīde(n)* (infinitive)–*rọ̄d* (preterit singular)–*riden* (preterit plural)–

---

[39] It should be remembered that in Old English the vowel of the first and third person singular of the preterit of strong verbs differed from that of the second person and of all plural forms: thus *ic, hē sang*, but *þū sunge, wē, gē, hī sungon*. See pp. 140 and 146.

(i)ride(n) (past participle), with perfectly regular development from Old English *rīdan–rād–ridon–(ge)riden*. Examples of the other classes follow,[40] which should be compared with the Old English forms (see pp. 140–43):

> II. crēpen–crẹp–crupen–crǫpen[41]
> III. fīnden–fǫnd–foūnden–foūnden
> helpen–halp–hulpen–holpen
> fighten–faught–foughten–foughten
> IV. tẹren–tar–tēren–tǫren
> V. mẹten–mat–mēten–mẹten[42]
> VI. fāren–fōr–fōren–fāren
> VII. fallen–fēl–fēlen–fallen
> hǫten–hēt–hēten–hǫten

By analogy with the considerably larger group of weak verbs, a good many strong verbs in the course of the Middle English period acquired, side by side with their strong forms, dental-suffix preterits and past participles. These include (to take a single example from each class of strong verbs) *glīden* 'to glide,' *crēpen* 'to creep,' *helpen* 'to help,' *shẹren* 'to shear,' *mẹten* 'to mete,' *āken* 'to ache,' and *wēpen* 'to weep.' Ultimately the strong forms were lost altogether in these and other verbs.

THE PERSONAL ENDINGS

When the Old English endings *-ast* and *-að* which were characteristic of the second and third persons of the present indicative of those weak verbs which had infinitives in *-ian* not preceded by *r* (thus *lufian, lufast, lufað*) fell together with the endings *-est* and *-eð* of verbs with infinitives in *-an*, a historical distinction of form which was not worth making in the first place was broken down. When the Old English present indicative plural ending *-að* likewise became *-eth,* the distinction between plural and third person singular was also obliterated:

[40] The forms cited are for the most part those which are the regular developments of the Old English forms. All are attested, but many other "irregular" ones are to be encountered in Middle English writings.

[41] For the sake of consistency, infinitives and past participles will be cited with the *-n* which was ultimately lost in all infinitives, though retained in the past participial forms of some strong verbs. The initial *i* (*y*) of past participles is omitted, though its use in many parts of the country was, as with Old English *ge,* more or less general. See p. 177.

[42] Some verbs belonging originally to the fifth class moved up into the fourth by acquiring participles with *ǭ,* for example *brẹken* (OE *brecan*), *spẹken* (OE *specan*), *wẹven* (OE *wefan*).

Old English *bereð* and *berað* both end up as *bẹreth,* a single form
which continued to do double duty in the South of England. The Midland dialects,[43] however, substituted the *-en* of the plural subjunctive
for the plural *-eth,* and thereby achieved a formal distinction in number
at the expense of one in mood. In the Northumbrian dialect of Old
English *-as* was somewhat more frequent as the present indicative
plural ending, at least in the extant texts.[44] The development of this
ending, *-es* (sometimes spelled *-is*), is characteristic of the Northern
dialect of Middle English: thus *wē, yē, thai bẹres* 'we, you, they bear.'
The same ending is a Northern characteristic in the present indicative
third person singular; this ending was in Modern English times to drive
out the *-eth.* In Middle English times it had spread from the North into
the Midland dialects, which show both *-es* and *-eth* in the third person
and *-es* and *-e(n)* in the plural. Thus with *finden* 'to find' (strong) and
thanken 'to thank' (weak) as models, the indicative forms were as
follows in the Midland dialects:

PRESENT SINGULAR	PRESENT PLURAL (ALL PERSONS)
1. finde, thanke	finde(n)(-s), thanke(n)(-s)
2. findest, thankest	
3. findeth(-es), thanketh(-es)	

PRETERIT SINGULAR	PRETERIT PLURAL (ALL PERSONS)
1. 3. fǫnd, thanked(e)	founde(n), thanked(e)(n)
2. founde, thankedest	

The verbs *been* 'to be' (OE *bēon*), *doon* 'to do' (OE *dōn*), *willen* 'to
want, will' (OE *willan*), and *gǫǫn* 'to go' (OE *gān*) remained highly
irregular in Middle English. Typical Midland indicative forms of *been*
and *willen* follow:

been: PRESENT SINGULAR	PRESENT PLURAL (ALL PERSONS)
1. am	bee(n), beeth, sinden, ār(e)n[45]
2. art, beest	
3. is, beeth	

---

[43] The forms were differentiated in the Southern dialects in those verbs which had *-ien*
(OE *-ian*) in the infinitive: these retained the *i* of Old English *-iað* in the plural: thus
singular *-eth,* plural *-ieth.*
[44] A. Campbell, *Old English Grammar* (Oxford, 1959), p. 302.
[45] This form is comparatively rare in Middle English save in the North and in the
West Midland. Chaucer seldom uses it.

PRETERIT SINGULAR	PRETERIT PLURAL (ALL PERSONS)
1. 3. was 2. wast, wēre	wēre(n)

willen: PRESENT SINGULAR	PRESENT PLURAL (ALL PERSONS)
1. 3. wil(le), wol(le)[46] 2. wilt, wolt	wilen, wol(n)

PRETERIT SINGULAR	PRETERIT PLURAL (ALL PERSONS)
1. 3. wolde 2. woldest	wolde(n)

Developments of the following Middle English forms of the preterit present verbs are still in frequent use: *o(u)ghte* 'owed, was under obligation to,' *can* 'knows how to, is able,' *cōūde* (ModE *could*)[47] 'knew how to, was able,' *shal* 'must,' *mōst(e)* (ModE *must*) 'was able to, must,' *may* 'am able to, may,' *mighte* (preterit of the preceding), *dar* (ModE *dare*), and *durst* (preterit of the preceding).

PARTICIPLES
The ending of the present participle varied from dialect to dialect, with *-and(e)* in the North, *-ende, -ing(e)* in the Midlands, and *-inde, -ing(e)* in the South. The *-ing* ending, which has prevailed in Modern English, is from the old verbal noun ending *-ung,* as in Old English *leornung* 'learning' (that is, knowledge), *bodung* 'preaching' (that is, sermon) from *leornian* 'to learn' and *bodian* 'to announce, preach.' Past participles might or might not have the initial inflection *i- (y-),* from Old English *ge-;* the prefix was lost in many parts of England, including the East Midland, but frequently occurred in the speech of London as this is reflected in the writings of Chaucer.

WORD ORDER
Although all possible variations in the order of subject, verb, and complement occur in extant Middle English literature, as in Old English literature, it must be remembered that much of this is verse, in

---

[46] This late Midland form, with the vowel of the preterit, survives in *won't,* that is, *wol not.*

[47] The preterit of *can* (infinitive *cunnen*), this word later acquired an unetymological *l* by analogy with *would.*

which even today variations (inversions) of what is thought of as "normal" word order may occur. The prose of the Middle English period has much the same word order as Modern English prose.[48] Sometimes a pronoun as object might precede the verb ("Yef þou me zayst, 'How me hit ssel lyerny?' ich hit wyle þe zigge an haste . . . ," that is, word for word, 'If thou [to] me sayest, "How one it shall learn?" I it will [to] thee say in haste . . . ,' or, in Modern English order, 'If thou sayest to me, "How shall one learn it?" I will say it to thee in haste . . .'). In subordinate clauses nouns used as objects might also precede verbs ("And we, þet . . . habbeþ Cristendom underfonge . . . ," that is, 'And we, that have Christian salvation received . . .'). In the frequently occurring impersonal constructions of Middle English the indirect object regularly preceded the verb: *me mette* '(it) to me dreamed,' that is, 'I dreamed'; *me thoughte* '(it) to me seemed.' *If you please* is very likely a survival of this construction,[49] though the *you* is now taken as nominative. Other than these, there are very few inversions that would be inconceivable in Modern English. Strange as parts of the following passage in the Northern dialect may look to modern eyes, it is possible to put it word for word into Modern English:[50]

Twa lyves þar er þat cristen men lyfes: ane es
Two lives there are that Christian men live: one is

called actyve lyfe, for it es mare bodili warke;
called active life, for it is more bodily work;

another, contemplatyve lyfe, for it es in mare swetnes
another, contemplative life, for it is in more sweetness

gastely. Actife lyfe es mykel owteward and in mare
spiritually. Active life is much outward and in more

travel, and in mare peryle for þe temptacions þat
travail, and in more peril for the temptations that

er in þe worlde. Contemplatyfe lyfe es mykel inwarde,
are in the world. Contemplative life is much inward,

[48] According to Charles Carpenter Fries, "almost by 1400 and certainly before 1500 the position following the verb had become the fixed position for the accusative object" (*American English Grammar* [New York, 1940], p. 252). By 1500, more than 98 percent of the instances collected by him and his students showed this order.

[49] Parallel to French *s'il vous plaît* and German *wenn es Ihnen gefällt,* that is, 'if it please(s) you.'

[50] The passage is from *The Form of Living,* by Richard Rolle of Hampole, a gentle mystic and an excellent prose writer, who died in 1349.

and   forþi   it   es   lastandar   and   sykerar,
and   therefore   it   is   more lasting   and   more secure,

restfuller,   delitabiler,   luflyer,   and   mare
more restful,   more delightful,   lovelier,   and   more

medeful,   for   it   hase   joy   in   goddes   lufe   and
full of reward,   for   it   has   joy   in   God's   love   and

savowre   in   þe   lyf   þat   lastes   ay   in   þis   present
savor   in   the   life   that   lasts   forever   in   this   present

tyme   if   it   be   right   ledde.   And   þat   felyng   of   joy
time   if   it   be   rightly   led.   And   that   feeling   of   joy

in   þe   lufe   of   Jhesu   passes   al   other   merites   in
in   the   love   of   Jesus   surpasses   all   other   merits   on

erth,   for   it   es   swa   harde   to   com   to   for   þe   freelte
earth,   for   it   is   so   hard   to   come   to   for   the   frailty

of   oure   flesch   and   þe   many   temptacions   þat   we   er
of   our   flesh   and   the   many   temptations   that   we   are

umsett   with   þat   lettes   us   nyght   and   day.   Al   other
set about   with   that   hinder   us   night   and   day.   All   other

thynges   er   lyght   at   com   to   in   regarde   þarof,   for
things   are   easy   to   come   to   in   regard   thereof,   for

þat   may   na   man   deserve,   bot   anely   it   es   gifen   of
that   may   no   man   deserve,   but   only   it   is   given   of

goddes   godenes   til   þam   þat   verrayli   gifes   þam
God's   goodness   to   them   that   verily   give   them(selves)

to   contemplacion   and   til   quiete   for   cristes   luf.
to   contemplation   and   to   quiet   for   Christ's   love.

THE DECLINE OF FRENCH IN ENGLAND

It should be pointed out in closing that although for a long time after the Norman Conquest French was the language of the governing classes in England, there was never any period during which the majority of the country's population did not speak English. The loss of Normandy in 1204 by King John, a descendant of the Conqueror, removed an important tie with France, and subsequent events were to loosen those which remained. The Hundred Years' War, beginning in 1337, saw England and France bitter enemies in a long-drawn-out conflict — though it actually fell somewhat short of a hundred years — which gave the death blow to the already moribund use of French in England.[51] Those whose ancestors were Normans had come to think of themselves as Englishmen.

[51] For an admirable treatment of this whole state of affairs, see Albert C. Baugh, *A History of the English Language,* 2nd ed. (New York, 1957), Chapter 5, "The Norman Conquest and the Subjection of English, 1066–1200," and Chapter 6, "The Re-establishment of English, 1200–1500."

VII

The Modern English Period to 1800
Sounds and Spellings

The fifteenth century, following the death of Chaucer, marks a turning point in the history of English, for during this period the language underwent greater, more important phonological changes than in any other century before or since. Despite these radical changes in pronunciation, the old spelling was maintained and, as it were, stereotyped. (This has already been pointed out: see p. 70.) William Caxton, who died in 1491, and the printers who followed him based their spelling norm not on the pronunciation current in their day, but on the usage of the medieval manuscripts. Hence, though the quality of every single one of the long vowels had changed, the graphic representation of the newer values remained the same as it had been for the Middle English ones: for instance, though the [ē] of Middle English *feet, see, three,* and so forth had been raised to [ī], all such words went on being written as if no change had taken place.

The influence of printers and that of men of learning—misguided though they frequently were—has been greater than any other on English spelling. The first are responsible for a further normalization of the older scribal practices. While it is true that early printed works exhibit a good many inconsistencies, they are nevertheless quite orderly as compared with the everyday writing of the time.

A SPECIMEN OF ENGLISH IN 1525
The following paragraph is the chapter "Rosemary" from Banckes's *Herball,* a hodgepodge of botanical and medical lore and a good deal of

sheer superstition thrown together and "imprynted by me Richard Banckes, dwellynge in London, a lytel fro y̆ Stockes in y̆ Pultry, y̆ .xxv. day of Marche. The yere of our lorde .M.CCCCC. & xxv." The only known copies of this old black-letter "doctor book" are one in the British Museum and one in the Huntington Library in California. What became of the many other copies of the work, which went through at least fifteen editions, no man can say. It will be noted that *the* is sometimes printed y̆, sometimes *the*. The spelling y̆ is also used three times for the form of the second person singular objective pronoun, *thee,* for which *the* is the usual spelling. The second person plural nominative form, if it occurred, would have been written *ye;* when the *e* was above the line, the *y* was always a makeshift for *þ* (see p. 60), and never to be interpreted as *y*. A line over a vowel (Banckes and a good many other printers actually used a tilde-like diacritic) indicates omission of a following *n* or *m,* as in *thē* for *them* and *thā* for *than*. This device is very ancient. The virgules, or slanting lines, are the equivalents of our commas, used to indicate brief pauses in reading. As was the custom (see p. 62), *v* is used initially (*venymous, vnder*) and *u* elsewhere (*hurte, euyll*), regardless of whether consonant or vowel was to be indicated. Some of the final *e*'s are used for "justifying" lines of type — that is, making even right-hand margins — a most useful expedient before the days of the linotype machine, when type had to be set by hand. The use of the long *s* is explained above, p. 59.

Rofemary.

This herbe is hote and dry/ take the flowres and put them in a lynen clothe/ & fo boyle them in fayre clene water to y̆ halfe & coole it & drynke it/ for it is moche worth agaynft all euylles in the body. Alfo take the flowres & make powder therof and bynde it to the ryght arme in a lynen clothe/ and it fhall make the lyght and mery. Alfo ete the flowres with hony faftynge with fowre breed and there fhall ryfe in the none euyll fwellynges. Alfo take the flowres and put them in a cheft amonge youre clothes or amonge bokes and moughtes [moths] fhall not hurte them. Alfo boyle the flowres in gotes mylke & than let them ftande all a nyght vnder the ayer fayre couered/ after that gyue hym to drynke thereof that hath the tyfyke [phthisic] and it fhall delyuer hym. Alfo boyle the leues in whyte wyne & waffhe thy face therwith/ thy berde & thy browes and there fhall no cornes growe out/ but thou fhall haue a fayre face. Alfo put the leues vnder thy beddes heed/ & thou fhalbe delyuered of all euyll dremes. Alfo breke y̆ leues fmall to powder & laye them on a Canker & it fhall flee it. Alfo take the leues & put thē into a veffel of wyne and it fhall preferue y̆ wyne fro tartneffe & euyl fauour/ and yf thou fell that wyne, thou fhall haue good lucke & fpede [success] in the fale. Alfo yf thou be feble with vnkyndly [unnatural] fwette/ take and boyle the leues in clene water, & whan y̆ water is colde do

[put] therto as moche of whyte wyne/ & than make therin foppes & ete thou well therof/ & thou fhal recouer appetyte. Alfo yf thou haue the flux boyle ẙ leues in ftronge Ayfell [vinegar] & than bynde them in a lynē [c]lothe and bynde it to thy wombe [belly] & anone the flux fhal withdrawe. Alfo yf thy legges be blowen with the goute/ boyle the leues in water/ & than take the leues & bynde them in a lynen clothe aboute thy legges/ & it fhall do ẙ moche good. Alfo take the leues and boyle them in ftronge Ayfell & bynde them in a clothe to thy ftomake/ & it fhall delyuer ẙ of all euylles. Alfo yf thou haue the coughe/ drynke the water of the leues boyled in whyte wyne/ & thou fhalbe hole. Alfo take the rynde of Rofemary & make powder therof and drynke it for the pofe [cold in the head]/ & thou fhalbe delyuered therof. Alfo take the tymbre therof & brūne [burn] it to coles & make powder therof & thā put it into a lynen cloth and rubbe thy tethe therwith/ & yf there be ony wormes therin it fhall flee them & kepe thy tethe from all euyls. Alfo make the a box of the wood and smell to it and it shall preferne[1] thy youthe. Alfo put therof in thy doores or in thy howfe & thou fhalbe without daunger of Adders and other venymous ferpentes. Alfo make the a barell therof & drynke thou of the drynke that ftandeth therin & thou nedes to fere no poyfon that fhall hurte ẙ/ and yf thou fet it in thy garden kepe it honeftly [decently] for it is moche profytable. Alfo yf a mā haue loft his fmellynge of the ayre orelles he maye not drawe his brethe/ make a fyre of the wood & bake his breed therwith & gyue it hym to ete & he fhalbe hole.

THE GREAT VOWEL SHIFT

Comparison of the modern developments in parentheses in the chapter on Old English (p. 123) shows sufficiently clearly what are the modern representatives of the Old English long vowels. As has been pointed out, these changed only slightly in Middle English: [ā], in Old English written *a*, as in *stān*, was rounded except in the Northern dialect to [ɔ], in Middle English written *o(o)*, as in *stoon*. But this was really the only particularly noteworthy change in quality.[2] By the end of what we think of as the Middle English period, or by the beginning of the Modern English period, all these long vowels had shifted: *ē*, as in *sweete* 'sweet,' had already acquired the value [ī] that it currently has,[3] and the others were well on their way to acquiring the values that they have in current English. In phonological terms, Middle English *ē*, *ẹ̄*, *ō*, and *ǭ* were raised in their articulation. Middle

---

[1] The printer has inadvertently turned the *u* that was in his copy, to make an *n*.

[2] There were, as we have seen, important changes in quantity when vowels in open syllables or before certain consonant combinations were lengthened. Two of these involved changes in quality. See p. 164.

[3] As in the preceding chapter, macrons will for the sake of consistency be placed over phonetic symbols for long vowels even when these represent qualitatively distinctive sounds of early Modern and current English. See n. 16.

English *ā*, which comes from Old English short *a* in open syllables (see above, p. 164), was fronted as well. The two highest Middle English front and back vowels, *ī* and *ū* respectively, became sounds traditionally known as diphthongs. These changes in the quality of the long, or tense, vowels constitute what is known as the Great Vowel Shift, which has been alluded to in another connection on p. 70.

Long *ī*, as in Middle English *rīden* 'to ride,' first became a rising diphthong [ɪí],[4] the initial unstressed element of which became [ə] in the course of the fifteenth century. Then, in the course of the following century, the stress shifted to the first element, that is, [əí] became a falling diphthong [ə́ɪ]. This pronunciation survives in certain types of speech, particularly before voiceless consonants. It went on in most types of English to become in the course of the seventeenth century [áɪ], though there are variations in pronunciation.

It was similar with Middle English long *u*, as in *hous* 'house': it became successively the rising diphthongs [ʊú] and [əú], then, with a shift in stress in the course of the sixteenth century, [ə́ʊ]. This [ə́ʊ], surviving in eastern Virginia and in some types of Canadian English, became [áʊ] at about the same time as [ə́ɪ] became [áɪ].

Middle English [ō] as in *ro(o)te* 'root,' became [ū]. Shortening of this [ū] to [ʊ] has occurred in *foot, good, book, look, took,* and other words; in *flood* and *blood* there has been unrounding in addition to shortening, resulting in [ə] in these two words. The chronology of these subsequent shortenings and unroundings is difficult to establish, as is the distribution of the various developments. As Helge Kökeritz points out,[5] Shakespeare's riming of words which had Middle English long close *o* gives no clue to his pronunciation, for he rimes *food* with *good* and *flood, mood* with *blood, reprove* with *love* and *dove*. If these are not merely traditional rimes, we must conclude that the distribution of [ū], [ʊ], and [ə] was not in early Modern English the same as it is in current English, and there is indeed ample evidence that colloquial English did vacillate a good deal. This fact is not particularly surprising when we remember that there is at the present time a certain amount of wavering between [ū] and [ʊ] in such words as *roof, broom, room,* and a few others. Pronunciation of *root* with the shortened vowel is fairly common in some types of American English.

The development of Middle English [ɔ̄] as in *hǭ(ǫ)m* 'home' and *stǭ(ǫ)n* 'stone' presents no special problems. The sound shifted to

---

[4] A rising diphthong is one that is stressed on its second element.
[5] *Shakespeare's Pronunciation* (New Haven, Conn., 1953), p. 236. For a most useful index of Shakespeare's rimes, see Appendix 3 of this work, pp. 399–495.

[ō]. In a few words this [ō] was shortened in early Modern English, for instance *hot,* from Middle English *hǫ(ǫ)t.*

Middle English *ā* as in *name* and *ai* as in *nail* had by the early fifteenth century been leveled as [ā], the low-central vowel current in eastern New England in *ask* and in most types of English as the first element of the diphthongs [aɪ] and [aʊ], subsequently going through the stages [æ], [ɛ̄], [ē]. The resultant homophony of *tale* and *tail* provided Shakespeare and his contemporaries with what seems to have been an almost irresistible temptation for the making of off-color puns.[6] The current pronunciation of such words — that is, with [ē] — became normal in Standard English probably in the early years of the eighteenth century.[7]

Middle English [ɛ̄] as in *hɛ̄ɛth* 'heath' must have been retained by many speakers well into the seventeenth century, as Falstaff's *reason-raisin* pun of 1598, in the passage cited below (pp. 193–94), and many others indicate.[8] But there is also convincing evidence that the present English vowel in *heath,* which is, as we have seen, the Great Vowel Shift reflex of Middle English [ē], existed in such words in early Modern English side by side with [ɛ̄], the continuation of Middle English open *ę̄.* This coexistence presupposes that [ē] occurred in late Middle English times as a variant, perhaps dialectal, of [ɛ̄]. Chaucer very occasionally rimes close *ē* words with words that in his type of English ordinarily had open *ę̄,* indicating his familiarity with a pre-1400 raising of [ɛ̄] to [ē] in some types of English. The present English vowel in such words as *meat* and *heath* is thus obviously, as H. C. Wyld put it, "merely the result of the abandonment of one type of pronunciation and the adoption of another."[9] More recent authorities agree with Wyld's view, for instance Kökeritz[10] and E. J. Dobson.[11]

After about 1600 the polite pronunciation of words that continued Middle English [ɛ̄] had [ē], the vowel that survives to this day in *break, great, steak,* and *yea. Drain* (OE *drēahnian,* unrecorded in ME),

---

[6] See, for instance, *The Two Gentlemen of Verona* II.iii.52ff and *Othello* III.i.6ff.

[7] It should always be borne in mind that all these pronunciations may have existed side by side, just as "retarded" and "advanced" pronunciations may and do exist in current English. Some speakers retain characteristics which, if they are noticed at all, are considered old-fashioned by younger-generation speakers (like *forehead* as [fɑrɪd] in contrast to [fɔ́rhɛ̀d].

[8] For example *abased–a beast, grace–grease–grass.* The fullest treatment of Shakespeare's puns — sometimes childish, but frequently richly obscene — is in Part II of *Shakespeare's Pronunciation.*

[9] *A History of Modern Colloquial English,* 3rd ed. (New York, 1937), p. 211.

[10] *Shakespeare's Pronunciation,* pp. 194–209.

[11] *English Pronunciation: 1500–1700* (Oxford, 1957), II, 606–16.

which is in Standard English pronounced as its current spelling suggests, is yet another example; a variant with [ī] occurs in nonstandard usage. Many rimes from the seventeenth and eighteenth centuries testify to this pronunciation in words that today have only [ī], for instance Swift's "You'd swear that so divine a creature / Felt no necessities of nature" ("Strephon and Chloe"), in which the riming words are to be pronounced [krḗtər] and [nḗtər], and "You spoke a word began with H, / And I know whom you meant to teach" ("The Journal of a Modern Lady"), in which the riming words are [ēč] and [tēč]. A few surnames borne by families with long association with Ireland, like *Yeats* (compare *Keats*), *Re(a)gan,* and *Shea,* have also retained the variant pronunciation with [ē], which also occurs in *Beatty* in American speech.

But, according to what seems to be the best-informed interpretation of the facts, there was no shift in Modern English of this [ē] to [ī]. Middle and early Modern English [ɛ̄], having reached [ē], stopped there, this [ē] surviving in the mere handful of words just cited. Pronunciation of these and all other such words with [ī] had, however, been current all along. As Dobson points out, "throughout the [early] ModE period there was a struggle going on between two ways of pronouncing 'ME ę̄ words' "; ultimately the earlier less polite [ī] pronunciation was to win out, so that only a few words remain as evidence of the sound which prevailed in fashionable circles from about 1600 to the mid-eighteenth century. The process was gradual, involving first one word, then another.

The short vowels have remained relatively stable throughout the history of English. The most obvious changes affect Middle English short *a,* which shifted by way of [a] to [æ], and Middle English short *u,* which was unrounded and shifted to [ə], though the older value survives in a good many words in which the vowel was preceded by a labial consonant, especially if it was followed by *l,* for instance *bull, full, put* (but compare the variant *putt*), *pull,* and *bush.* It is evident that there was an unrounded variant of short *o,* reflected in late sixteenth and in seventeenth-century spellings,[12] and in the most widespread American pronunciation of words which had short [ɔ] in Middle English (*God, stop, clock,* and so forth). This unrounding did not affect the language as a whole, but such doublets as *strop–strap* and *god–gad* remain to testify to its having occurred.[13] Short *e* has not changed,

---

[12] H. C. Wyld, *History of Modern Colloquial English,* pp. 240–41, cites a number of examples of *a* for *o* in spellings, including Queen Elizabeth I's "I pray you stap the mouthes."

[13] The unrounded vowel [ɑ] was later advanced to [æ] in these words.

except occasionally before [ŋ], as in *string* and *wing* from Middle English *streng* and *wenge,* and short *i* remains what it has been since Germanic times.

The first element [ʊ] of a Middle English diphthong written *oi* (for *ui*), as in *poison, join,* and *boil,*[14] and occurring almost exclusively in words of French origin, underwent the shift to [ə] along with other short *u*'s. The diphthong thus fell together with the development of Middle English *ī* as [əɪ], both subsequently becoming [aɪ], so that the verb *boil,* from Old French *boillir* (ultimately Lat. *bullīre*) and the etymologically quite distinct noun meaning 'inflamed, infected sore,' which is of native English origin (OE *bȳl,* occurring in Middle English as *bȳle* or *bīle*), have both become current nonstandard [baɪl]. Many rimes in our older poetry testify to this identity in pronunciation of the reflexes of Middle English *ī* and *ui,* for instance Pope's couplet "While expletives their feeble aid to join;/And ten low words oft creep in one dull line." The current Standard pronunciation of words spelled with *oi* for etymological *ui* is based upon the spelling. The folk, however, preserve the pronunciation with [aɪ].[15] The quite different Middle English diphthong spelled *oi* and pronounced [ɔɪ] is, as we have seen (p. 163), also of French origin, the *o* going back to Latin *au,* as in *joie* (ultimately Lat. *gaudia*) and *cloistre* (Lat. *claustrum*).

Similar Middle English diphthongs written *eu, ew, iu, iw,* and *u* (depending to some extent upon when they were written) merged into [jū], which, as we saw in Chapter II, has tended to be reduced to [ū] in such words as *duty, Tuesday, lute,* and *news.* The [j] has been retained after *b* (*beauty* as distinct from *booty*), *p* (*pew* as distinct from *pooh*), *m* (*mute* as distinct from *moot*), *g* (the second syllable of *argue* as distinct from *goo*), *k* (*c*) (*cute* as distinct from *coot*), *v* (*view* as distinct from the first syllable of *voodoo*), and *f* (*feud* as distinct from *food*). After [z] this [j] gave rise to a new single sound [ž] in *azure, pleasure,* and the like. Similarly the earlier medial and initial [sj] in *pressure, nation, sure,* and the like has become [š], though this was not a new sound, having occurred under other circumstances in Old English (above, p. 124).

The shift of vowels, or in the case of most of the short vowels the lack of any shift, may be indicated thus in tabular and hence somewhat oversimplified form, with the current pronunciations shown being those most widespread in Standard English (the unrounded [ɑ] from

[14] As we have seen (p. 71), *o* was a symbol for *u* in Middle English.
[15] For the distribution of [aɪ] in *oi*-words in the eastern United States, see Hans Kurath and Raven I. McDavid, Jr., *The Pronunciation of English in the Atlantic States* (Ann Arbor, Mich., 1961), pp. 167–68 and maps No. 143–46.

Middle English *o* is not included) and with no indication of such changes as most speakers are not particularly conscious of, for instance the recently developed off-glides in words like *bait* and *boat,* which in early Modern English had simple [ē] and [ō]:

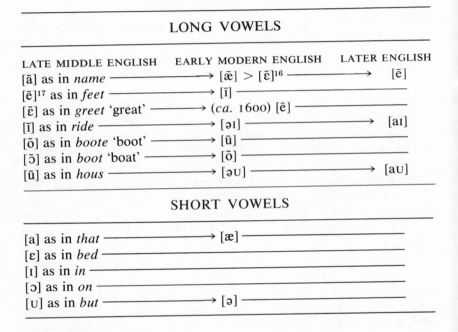

LONG VOWELS

LATE MIDDLE ENGLISH	EARLY MODERN ENGLISH	LATER ENGLISH
[ā] as in *name* ⟶	[ǣ] > [ɛ̄][16] ⟶	[ē]
[ē][17] as in *feet* ⟶	[ī]	
[ɛ̄] as in *greet* 'great' ⟶	(*ca.* 1600) [ē]	
[ī] as in *ride* ⟶	[əɪ] ⟶	[aɪ]
[ō] as in *boote* 'boot' ⟶	[ū]	
[ɔ̄] as in *boot* 'boat' ⟶	[ō]	
[ū] as in *hous* ⟶	[əʊ] ⟶	[aʊ]

SHORT VOWELS

[a] as in *that* ⟶	[æ]	
[ɛ] as in *bed*		
[ɪ] as in *in*		
[ɔ] as in *on*		
[ʊ] as in *but* ⟶	[ə]	

The loss of *e* [-ə] at the end of words is just as widespread a change as the Great Vowel Shift. As we have seen, however, this wholesale apocopation had occurred by the end of the fourteenth century and hence can hardly be regarded as a modern change, though it is frequently so regarded, just as the leveling of all final vowels in inflectional syllables, frequently regarded as a Middle English change, actually began long before the date which is traditionally given for the

[16] Vowel quantity is distinctive in early Modern English only for [æ] and [ɛ]; up to about the middle of the seventeenth century it distinguished such pairs of words as *fate* [fǣt] and *fat* [fæt] and later, when [ǣ] had shifted to [ɛ̄], pairs like *mace* [mɛ̄s] and *mess* [mɛs]. Macrons have, however, been used throughout this table for reasons of history and consistency. The one occurring in the third column is quite unnecessary inasmuch as after about 1700, when the [ɛ̄] from Middle English [ā] advanced to the current sound in *fate, mace,* and the like, all the long vowels were distinguished from the shorts by quality alone (see above, pp. 42–43).
[17] Including the late Middle English close-voweled variant of *ę̄*.

beginning of the Middle English period (see pp. 122 and 165). From early Modern spellings, as well as from poetic meter, this tendency to lose an unstressed -*e* seems also to have affected *the,* as in *th'earth* and the like.

THE EARLY MODERN ENGLISH CONSONANTS

The consonants of English, like the short vowels, have been rather stable, though certain losses have occurred within the Modern English period. The Old English and Middle English voiceless palatal fricative [ç] occurring next to front vowels and still represented in our spelling by *gh* disappeared entirely, as in *bright, sigh,* and *weigh.* The identically written voiceless velar fricative [x] occurring next to back vowels either disappeared, as in *taught, bought,* and *bough,* or became the voiceless labiodental fricative [f], as in *cough, laugh,* and *enough.* These changes occurred as early as the fifteenth century in all England south of the Humber, though there is evidence that as late as the latter part of the sixteenth century old-fashioned speakers and a few pedants retained the sounds[18] or at least thought that they ought to be retained.

In the final sequence -*mb,* the *b* had disappeared in pronunciation before the beginning of the Modern English period, so that it could be added after final *m* where it did not etymologically belong, for instance in *limb.* There was a similar tendency to reduce final -*nd,* as in *lawn,* from Middle English *laund;* confusion seems to have arisen, and a nonetymological -*d* has been added in *sound*[19] and *lend* (ME *soun* and *lene*), though in the latter word the excrescent *d* occurred long before the Modern English period. The *l* of Middle English preconsonantal *al* was lost after first becoming a vowel: thus Middle English *al* and *au* fell together as *au,* ultimately becoming [ɔ] (as in *talk, walk*) except before *f, v,* and *m,* where it became [æ] in such words as *half, salve,* and *psalm.* The *l* retained in the spelling of the cited words and others[20] has led to spelling pronunciations, particularly when it occurs before *m;* many speakers now pronounce the *l* except before *f,* and seem to more traditional speakers to be making a special effort to do so: a certain motor car known as the *Falcon* is everywhere called [fǽlkən], a pronunciation widely current among the pseudoliterate long before the appearance of the car. The spelling has as yet had little if any effect upon the pronunciation of the name of the writer William Faulkner.

[18] Kökeritz, p. 306.
[19] The noun and verb; the adjective is quite another word, from Old English *gesund.*
[20] It has been restored from the Latin etymon in *falcon* (ME *faucon,* from Old French, in which the vocalization to [u] also occurred).

Perhaps if the name had been written *Falconer,* which amounts to the same thing, the spelling pronunciation might in time have come to prevail. The *l* of *ol* was similarly lost before certain consonants by vocalization, as in *folk, yolk, Holmes,* and the like. As we have seen (p. 73), the *l* in *fault* and *vault* has been inserted. The older pronunciation of the first of these words is indicated by Swift's "O, let him not debase your thoughts,/Or name him but to tell his faults" ("Directions for Making a Birth-Day Song").

In French loan-words like *host* and *humble* the *h,* because it is in the spelling, has gradually come to be pronounced in all but a few words (pp. 63–64); it was generally lacking in such words in early Modern English. Renaissance spelling habits are, as we have seen, responsible for the unetymological *h* in *author, throne,* and other words that have been cited (p. 65), but early Modern English continued to use the etymologically correct pronunciation of such words with [t], which gradually was to give way to pronunciation based upon misspelling.

There was an early loss of [r] before sibilants, not to be confused with the much later loss (not really normal before the nineteenth century) before any consonant or before a pause: older *barse* 'fish' by such loss became *bass,* as *arse* became *ass* and *bust, nuss, fust* develop from *burst, nurse, first;* this was not, however, a widespread change. An early loss of [r] before *l* is indicated by such a word as *palsy* (ME *parlesie,* a variant of *paralisie* 'paralysis'). Just as *l* occasionally generates a svarabhakti vowel (above, p. 45), *r* has done likewise in the old form *alarum,* a variant of *alarm.*

The final unstressed syllable *-ure* was pronounced [-ər], with preceding *t, d,* and *s* having the values [t], [d], and [s] or intervocalically [z], for instance in *nature* [-tər], *verdure* [-dər], *censure* [-sər], and *leisure* [-zər], until the nineteenth century, though Noah Webster's use of such pronunciations was considered rustic and old-fashioned by his more elegant contemporaries.[21] The older pronunciation is indicated by many rimes: to mine Dean Swift once more, "If this to clouds and stars will venture,/That creeps as far to reach the centre" ("Verses on Two Celebrated Modern Poets"). Webster was also opposed to [-č-] in *fortune, virtue,* and the like, which he seems to have associated with fast living. He preferred [-t-] in such words. But many of the pronunciations that he prescribed were scorned by the proper Bostonians of his day.

The initial consonant sequences *gn* and *kn,* still represented in our spelling of *gnaw, gnarl, gnat, knave, knead, knee,* and a few other

---

[21] In his *Elementary Spelling Book* of 1843 he gave *gesture* and *jester* as homophones.

words, had lost their first elements by the early seventeenth century. Loss of [k] is evidenced by the Shakespearean puns *knack–neck, knight–night,* and others cited by Kökeritz (p. 305).

Final *ing,* except of course in monosyllables like *sing* and *thing,* had long been practically universally pronounced [-ɪn]. According to H. C. Wyld, "this habit obtains in practically all Regional dialects of the South and South Midlands, and among large sections of speakers of Received Standard English."[22] The velarization of the *n* to [ŋ] began as a hypercorrect pronunciation in the first quarter of the nineteenth century and, still according to Wyld, "has now a vogue among the educated at least as wide as the more conservative one with -*n.*" Long before Wyld wrote these words, which would need some revision for British English today, the [-ɪn] pronunciation had come to be considered substandard in American speech, largely due to the crusade which teachers had conducted against it, though it continues to occur rather widely in unselfconscious speech on all social levels. Many spellings and rimes in our older literature testify to the orthodoxy of what is popularly called "dropping the *g,*"[23] for instance Swift's couplets "See then what mortals place their bliss in!/Next morn betimes the bride was missing" ("Phyllis") and the delicate "His jordan [chamber pot] stood in manner fitting/Between his legs, to spew or spit in" ("Cassinus and Peter"). Inverse spellings such as Shakespeare's *cushings* (*cushions*), *javelings* (*javelins*), and *napking* (*napkin*)[24] tell the same story.

QUANTITATIVE CHANGES

Quantitative changes in the Modern English period have been previously alluded to, such as the lengthening of an originally short vowel before voiceless fricatives (of [æ] as in *staff, glass,* and *path,* the resultant [ǣ] in the late eighteenth century coming to be replaced by [ā] in Standard British English; of [ɔ] as in *soft, lost,* and *cloth*) and before voiced velar stops, as in *dog* and *sag.*[25] The earlier shortening of [ū] to [ʊ] in *hood, good,* and so forth, has already been referred to in connection with the development of [ō] in the Great Vowel Shift. In *mother, brother, other,* and *smother,* all having originally long vowels, the shortening (with eventual modification to [ə]) seems to be due to

---

[22] *History of Modern Colloquial English,* p. 289.
[23] In phonological terms, using the dental [n] instead of the velar [ŋ], for there is of course no [g].
[24] Cited in Kökeritz, p. 314.
[25] Compare *dock* and *sack* with voiceless velar stops, where the lengthening has not occurred.

their disyllabicism, though disyllabic *father* and *rather,* with originally short vowels, have undergone lengthening, for what reason we cannot be sure — quite contrary to the shortening which occurred in *lather* and *gather.*

STRESS

A good many words in early Modern English were stressed otherwise than they are in current speech. *Character, illustrate, concentrate, contemplate* were all stressed on their second syllables, and most polysyllabic words in *-able* and *-ible* had initial stress, frequently with secondary stress on their penultimate syllables, as in " 'Tis sweet and cómmendàble in your Nature Hamlet" (*Hamlet* I.ii.87). *Antique,* like *complete* and other words which now have final stress, had initial stress. But it is not always possible to come to a firm conclusion on the basis of verse, as the many instances of variant stress in Shakespeare's lines indicate.[26] It is likely that most of these variant stressings occurred in actual speech; it would be surprising if they had not, considering the variations which occur in current English.

PRONUNCIATION OF EARLY
MODERN ENGLISH

Our knowledge of early Modern English pronunciation comes from many sources. Fortunately not all gentlefolk knew how to spell in earlier days, which is to say that they did not know what have become in our own day conventional spellings, and were pretty much so even then, thanks to the printers. So they spelled phonetically, according to their lights. What is by modern standards a "misspelling," like *coat* for *court* or *crick* for *creek,* may tell us a good deal about the writer's pronunciation. A good many such writings have come down to us. H. C. Wyld in his *History of Modern Colloquial English* has used many memoirs, letters, diaries, and documents from this period as the basis for his conclusions concerning the pronunciation of early Modern English. Kökeritz relies somewhat more than Wyld on the grammars and spelling books that began to appear around the middle of the sixteenth century, which he considers "our most important sources of information" (p. 17) on the pronunciation of the English of Shakespeare's day — works such as John Hart's *An Orthographie* (1569) and *A Methode or Comfortable Beginning for All Unlearned* (1570), William Bullokar's *Booke at Large* (1580) and *Bref Grammar for*

---

[26] See Kökeritz, Appendix 2, pp. 392–98.

English (1586), Richard Mulcaster's *The First Part of the Elementarie* (1582), and, in the following century, Alexander Gill's *Logonomia Anglica* (1619; 2nd ed., 1621) and Charles Butler's *English Grammar* (1633; 2nd ed., 1634), which has a list of homophones in its "Index of Words Like and Unlike." These same works, with others, provide the basis for E. J. Dobson's two-volume *English Pronunciation: 1500–1700*. There are special studies of these early Modern writers on language by Otto Jespersen (on Hart), Bror Danielsson (Hart), Helge Kökeritz (Hart and Gill), R. E. Zachrisson (Bullokar), along with general studies of early Modern English by Wilhelm Horn (*Historische neuenglische Grammatik*, 1908),[27] Eilert Ekwall (*Historische neuenglische Laut- und Formenlehre*, 3rd ed. [Berlin, 1956]), and Karl Luick (*Historische Grammatik der englischen Sprache* [Leipzig, 1914–40]). The first volume of Jespersen's *Modern English Grammar on Historical Principles* (Copenhagen, 1909) deals with early Modern English phonology and orthography. The use of word-play and rime has already been alluded to a number of times. Kökeritz makes extensive and most effective use of these in *Shakespeare's Pronunciation*, a work which has been cited a number of times heretofore. There is no dearth of evidence, though frequently what we have is difficult of interpretation.

In the passage from Shakespeare's *1 Henry IV* (II.iv.255–66) that follows, the phonetic transcription indicates a somewhat conservative pronunciation that was probably current in the south of England in the late sixteenth and early seventeenth centuries. Vowel length is indicated only in the single word *reason(s)*, in which it was distinctive. Sentence stress and word stress are indicated, but no attempt has been made to show fine gradations. The Prince, Poins, and Falstaff, who has just told a whopping lie, are speaking:

Prin. Why, how could'ſt thou know theſe men in Kendall Greene,
[wəɪ hə́ʊ kúdst ðəʊ nó ðiz mén ɪn kéndəl grín

when it was ſo darke, thou could'ſt not ſee thy Hand? Come,
(h)wɛn ɪt wəz só dǽrk ðəʊ kúdst nɔt sí ðəɪ hǽnd kʊm

tell vs your reaſon: what ſay'ſt thou to this?
tél əs jər rḗzən (h)wæt sést ðəʊ tə ðís

Poin. Come, your reaſon *Iack,* your reaſon.
kúm jər rḗzən jǽk jər rḗzən

[27] Reissued as *Laut und Leben. Englische Lautgeschichte der neueren Zeit (1400–1950)*, rev. and ed. Martin Lehnert, 2 vols. (Berlin, 1954).

Falst. What, vpon compulſion? No: were I at the Strappado, or
(h)wǽt əpón kəmpúlsɪən nó   wɛ́r əɪ æt ðə stræpǽdo   ər

all the Racks in the World, I would not tell you on
ɔ́l ðə rǽks ɪn ðə wúrld əɪ wú(l)d nɔt tél ju   ɔn

compulſion. Giue you a reaſon on compulſion? If Reaſons
kəmpúlsɪən gív   ju ə rɛ́zən ɔn kəmpúlsɪən ɪf rɛ́zənz

were as plentie as Black-berries, I would giue no man a
wɛr əz plɛ́ntɪ əz blǽkbɛ̀rɪz   əɪ wəd   gív nó mæn ə

Reaſon vpon compulſion, I.
rɛ́zən əpón kəmpúlsɪən ɔ́ɪ]

In this transcription it is assumed that Falstaff used an unstressed
form of *would (*[wəd]) in his last sentence, in contrast to the strongly
stressed form [wu(l)d] of his second sentence. It is furthermore assumed that, even though the Prince may have had the sequence [hw] in
his speech, he would not have pronounced the [h] in his opening inter-
jectional *Why,* thus following the usual practice of those present-day
speakers who have [hw] when the word is interrogative, but [w] when
it is an interjection or an expletive.[28]

It is a great pity that there was no tape recorder at the Globe play-
house.

[28] See John S. Kenyon, *American Pronunciation,* 10th ed. (Ann Arbor, Mich., 1961).
p. 159.

VIII

The Modern English
Period to 1800
Forms and Syntax

Inflectional and syntactical developments in early Modern English are important, if somewhat less spectacular than those which occurred in the sound system. As we have seen, by the end of the Middle English period *-es* had been extended to practically all nouns as a genitive singular and caseless plural suffix. The handful of mutated-vowel plurals for the most part resisted the analogical principle, so that *geese, feet, teeth, mice, lice, men,* and *women*[1] have survived to the present and show no tendency to give way to plurals in *-s*. A few plurals in *-n* remained in early Modern English, including *eyen* 'eyes,' *shoon* 'shoes,' *kine* 'cows' (with mutation plus analogical *-n*), *oxen, children,* and *brethren*. Of these, *kine* continues to eke out a precarious existence as an archaic poetic word, and *brethren* has a very limited currency, being confined in serious use to certain religious groups. As with *kine,* the *n* is an accretion in *brethren*[2] and *children,* added by analogy with other plurals in *-n*. The regularly developed *ky* and *childer,* going back respectively to Old English *cȳ* and *cildru,* are current in dialect speech, or were so until fairly recently, in the North of England and in Scotland. *Oxen* is thus the only "pure" survival of the Old English weak declension, which formed its nominative-accu-

---

[1] But see p. 130, n. 25, concerning this word.

[2] The development of this form is too complex to go into here, but it should be pointed out again that the mutated vowel did not occur in the Old English plural (*brōðor* or *brōðru* in the nominative-accusative) any more than did the *n*.

sative plural (as well as all non-nominative forms of the singular) with the suffix *-an* (see p. 129).

Unchanged (or "zero") plurals survive from Old and Middle English times to the present in *deer, sheep, swine, folk,* and *kind.* Analogical *folks* occurred very early in the Modern English period. Despite the precedent of its use by many distinguished writers in "these (those, all) kind of,"[3] *kind* has acquired a new plural in *-s* because of the feeling that the older construction was a "grammatical error." Its synonym *sort,* which is not of Old English origin, acquired as early as the sixteenth century by analogy with *kind* an unchanged plural, as in "these (those, all) sort of,"[4] but this construction also is frowned upon by most writers of school grammars. Doubtless by analogy with singular-plural *deer, sheep,* and the like,[5] the names of other creatures which had *-s* plurals in earlier times came to have unchanged plurals, for example *fish* and *fowl,* particularly when these are regarded as game.[6] The unchanged plural may be extended to the names of quite un-English beasts, like *buffalo* ("a herd of buffalo") and *antelope.*[7]

THE HIS-GENITIVE

The use of *his* (and presumably of *her* as well) as a sign of the genitive began in Old English times, but had its widest currency in the sixteenth and seventeenth centuries, as in Shakespeare's "And art not thou Poines, his Brother?" (*2 Henry IV* II.iv.308) and, in the "Prayer for All Conditions of Men" in the 1662 Book of Common Prayer,

[3] Including Shakespeare, Sidney, Dryden, Swift, Goldsmith, and Jane Austen.
[4] Jespersen (*A Modern English Grammar on Historical Principles* [Copenhagen, 1914], II, 68) cites its occurrence in the writings of Swift, Fielding, Austen, Dickens, Trollope, Meredith, Wells, and others. There are additional examples in the *OED.*
[5] *Horse* retained its historical unchanged plural, as in Chaucer's "His hors were goode . . ." (*Canterbury Tales,* General Prologue, line 74) and Shakespeare's "Come on, then, horse and chariots let us have" (*Titus Andronicus* II.ii.18), surviving until the seventeenth century, though the analogical plural *horses* had begun to occur as early as the thirteenth.
[6] The barnyard creatures take the *-s* (*fowls, ducks, pigs,* and so forth), and Jesus Christ, it will be remembered, distributed to the multitude "a few little *fishes*" (Matt. xv.34). But one shoots (wild) *fowl* and (wild) *duck,* hunts *pig* (that is, wild boars), and catches *fish.*
[7] Jespersen, *Modern English Grammar,* II, 53, quotes from a newspaper dispatch of 1906 as follows: "The gift by the Government of Nepal . . . consists of two *nilgai,* . . . three *sambhar,* two *ogrial,* . . . three *bhurrel,* two *thar.* . . ." *Webster's New World Dictionary of the American Language* (Cleveland, Ohio, 1955) in its entry *plural* has a long list of names of creatures, many of them exotic, which may have unchanged plurals.

"And this we beg for Jesus Christ his sake." The historical genitive ending in *-s* was doubtless regarded by many as having originated in, or as being a corruption of, *his.* H. C. Wyld's explanation of the *his*-genitive as being due to the confusion of the unstressed form of *his* — that is, without [h], as in "He lost 'is hat" — with the *-is, -ys*[8] endings of the genitive in Middle English is very attractive,[9] though one is troubled by the fact that *her* in this construction occurs in writing about a century before *his,* which of course does not necessarily mean that it is of prior origin. The phonetic explanation will not serve for *her* (OE *hire*), though if we assume that *his* did actually occur first in the construction *her* could well be an extension of the *his*-genitive.[10] *Their* in the same construction would seem almost unquestionably to be an extension of *his* and *her,* as in Pepys's reference to "The House of Lords their proceedings in petitioning the King" (*OED* citation). It should be said that *his* (*is, ys*) has been much more common than *her* in this construction, being often used after feminine nouns: Wyld cites "her Grace is requeste" (that is, 'her Grace's request') and "My moder ys sake" ('my mother's sake') among other instances of the feminine use (p. 315). The construction has survived in printed bookplates: "John Smith His Book."

THE GROUP-GENITIVE

The group-genitive construction, as in "King Priam of Troy's son" and "The Wife of Bath's Tale," is a development of the early Modern English period. Though there are sporadic occurrences in Middle English, the usual older idiom is illustrated by Chaucer's "the kyng Priamus sone of Troye" and "The Wyves Tale of Bathe." What has happened is that a word group — usually, as in these examples, two nouns connected by a preposition — has come to be regarded as a unit; the sign of the genitive is thus affixed to the last word of what is in fact a phrase. The construction also occurs with a pronoun plus *else,* as in *everybody else's,* and with nouns connected by a coordinating conjunction, as in "Kenyon and Knott's *Pronouncing Dictionary*" and *an hour or two's time.* There are comparatively few literary examples of clauses so treated, but in everyday speech such constructions as *the little boy that*

---

[8] Northern variants of *-es.*

[9] *A History of Modern Colloquial English,* 3rd ed. (New York, 1937), pp. 314–15. See also Jespersen's *Modern English Grammar,* VI, 301–302.

[10] It is also possible that the sentence from King Alfred's translation of Orosius, cited in the *OED,* is to be regarded as a nonce usage: "Nilus seo ea hire æwielme is neh þæm clife," that is, 'Nile the river her source is near the cliff.'

lives down the street's dog and *the woman I live next door to's husband* are of frequent occurrence.[11]

THE UNINFLECTED GENITIVE

In early Modern English uninflected genitives occur in some nouns which were feminine in Old English, in nouns in *-r* denoting family relationships (see pp. 130–31), and occasionally in nouns ending in [s] or preceding words beginning in [s], for example *for conscience sake* and *for God sake*. A few uninflected genitives, though not generally recognized as such, survive to the present day in reference to the Virgin Mary, for example *Lady Day* (that is, Our Lady's Day 'Feast of the Annunciation'), *Lady Chapel* (Our Lady's Chapel), and *ladybird* (Our Lady's bird).

ADJECTIVES AND ADVERBS

As for the adjective, with general loss of [-ə] in pronunciation, though the letter *e* which symbolized it might be retained in spelling as "silent *e*"[12] and even extended to words which in Middle English did not have it, the distinction between strong and weak adjective forms, already greatly simplified by the Middle English loss of final *n*, was completely lost. The Modern English adjective thus came to be invariable in form regardless of number or of what preceded it.[13]

Adjectives and adverbs continued to form comparatives in *-er* and superlatives in *-est*, along with the analytical formations with *mo(e)* (a semantic equivalent of *more,* though not comparative in form), *more,* and *most* which had occurred as early as Old English times. The present stylistic objection to affixing the endings to polysyllables had somewhat less force in the early Modern English period, when forms like *eminenter, impudentest,* and *beautifullest* are not particularly hard to find, nor, for that matter, are monosyllables with *more* and *most,* like *more near, more fast, most poor,* and *most foul*. As was true in earlier times also, a good many instances of double constructions like *more fitter, more better, more fairer, most worst, most stillest,* and (probably

---

[11] "He is the woman who is the best friend this club has ever had's husband" is an extreme example which I seem to have heard from Gracie Allen; at any rate, it is perfectly in keeping with the lovable birdbrained character which she created professionally.

[12] It should always be borne in mind that, whereas in Middle English *-e* after a single consonant indicated length, with the shifting of all the long vowels in Modern English it came to indicate the quality rather than the quantity of the preceding vowel, as in *mad* and *made*. It may sometimes perform the same function after a consonant sequence, as in *past* and *paste*.

[13] For the situation in Middle English, see p. 166.

the best-known example) *most unkindest* occur in early Modern English.

Many adverbs which now must end in *-ly* did not require the suffix in early Modern English times. The works of Shakespeare furnish many typical examples: *grievous sick, indifferent cold, wondrous strange,* and *passing* ['surpassingly'] *fair.* Note also the use of *sure* in the following citations, which would nowadays be condemned as "bad English" in the schools: "If she come in, shee'l sure speake to my wife" (*Othello* V.ii.96); "And sure deare friends my thankes are too deare a halfe-peny" (*Hamlet* II.ii.282); "Sure the Gods doe this yeere connive at us" (*Winter's Tale* IV.iv.692).

PERSONAL PRONOUNS

Rather important changes are to be noted in the pronouns. In the personal ones the historical forms of the first person remained as *I,*[14] *me,* and *mine* and *my,* with the old distinction between the *n*-less form of the possessive and the older form with *n* being for a long time maintained as it had been in Middle English from the thirteenth century on — that is, *mine* before a vowel or *h,* and *my* before consonants (above, p. 159). This distinction continued to be made down to the eighteenth century, when *my* came to be the only regular first person possessive modifier. The Fool's *nuncle* in *King Lear* is due to his misunderstanding of *mine uncle* as *my nuncle,* and it is likely that *Ned, Nelly,* and *Noll* (a nickname usually associated with Oliver Goldsmith) have the same origin from *mine Edward, mine Eleanor, mine Oliver.* The form with *n* has continued in use as a predicate adjective, in the *of*-possessive construction, and when the word which it modifies is not stated but must be inferred — in other words, precisely as the "double possessives" *hers, ours, yours,* and *theirs* have been used since late Middle English times (see p. 172).

The second person singular forms were nominative *thou,* objective *thee,* and possessive *thine* and *thy.* The situation with the possessive forms was precisely the same as that which has been described for *mine* and *my.* As early as the late thirteenth century, the second person plural forms (*ye, you, your*) began to be used with singular meaning in the so-called polite plural, though it might be better to call the construction a "polite singular."[15] In imitation of the French use of *tu* and

---

[14] Capitalized not through any egotism, but only because lower-case *i* standing alone looks so utterly insignificant.

[15] The distinction is retained in other languages, which may even have a verb meaning 'to use the singular form,' for example French *tutoyer,* Spanish *tutear,* Italian *tuizzare,* German *dutzen.* Late Middle English had *thoute,* with the same meaning.

vous, the English historical plural forms were used in addressing a superior, whether by virtue of social status or age, and in upper-class circles among equals, though high-born lovers might slip into the *th*-forms in situations of intimacy. In losing this distinction English has obviously lost a useful literary device. Even when the two forms were available for choosing, however, the English did not always use them as consistently as the French. There is frequently no apparent reason for their interchange, as in the dialogue between two servants in *The Taming of the Shrew* IV.i.101–104:

> *Cur*[*tis*]   Doe you heare ho? you must meete my maister to
> countenance my mistris.
> *Gru*[*mio*]   Why she hath a face of her owne.
> *Cur*[*tis*]   Who knowes not that?
> *Gru*[*mio*]   Thou it seemes. . . .

Frequently, however, our older writers use the forms with artistic discrimination, as in *Hamlet* III.iv.9–21:

> *Qu*[*een*]   Hamlet, thou hast thy Father much offended.
> *Ham*[*let*]   Mother, you have my Father much offended.
> *Qu*[*een*]   Come, come, you answer with an idle tongue.
>
> .   .   .   .   .
>
> *Qu*[*een*]   What wilt thou do? thou wilt not murther me?

This passage is cited by W. Franz,[16] who points out that the Queen's *thou* in "What wilt thou do?" is an expression of strong emotion. In addition, it might be pointed out that her first "Hamlet, thou hast thy Father much offended" is tender and affectionate. Hamlet's "Mother, you have . . ." is indicative of an attitude of cold dignity; there is even more than a hint of a rebuff in his choice of the more formal pronoun, and the Queen accepts it in effect by her "Come, come, you answer. . . ." It is similar with her passionate "Oh Hamlet, thou hast cleft my heart in twaine" and Hamlet's consistent use of *you* in his response: "Assume a Vertue, if you have it not. . . . Ile blessing begge of you." Elsewhere also Shakespeare chooses the *y*-forms and the *th*-forms with artistic care, though it is sometimes difficult for a present-day reader, unaccustomed to the niceties offered by a choice of forms, to figure him out.

The *th*-forms of the second person singular, which had become quite rare in upper-class speech by the sixteenth century, were completely lost in Standard English in the eighteenth, though they have lingered

---

[16] *Shakespeare-Grammatik,* 2nd ed. (Heidelberg, 1909), p. 256.

on in the dialects.[17] Our familiarity with them is largely due to their occurrence in poetry, in the King James Bible, and in the Book of Common Prayer. When people pray extempore, however, God is usually addressed and referred to by these forms. But for a mere mortal, the *y*-form must be used; grammatically, he must be regarded as if he were two or more mortals. A few elderly Quakers doubtless still use *thee* for both the nominative and the objective functions.

The third person singular masculine pronoun has been relatively stable since late Old English times, when the dative *him* took over all objective functions. The unstressed form of *he* was often written *a,* as in "Now might I doe it, but now a is a-praying, / And now Ile doo't, and so a goes to heaven" from the Second Quarto of *Hamlet* III.iii. 73–74 (the Folio has *he* in both instances). In the feminine, *she* and *her(s)* show no change since Middle English times. In the neuter, however, an important change took place in the latter part of the sixteenth century, when the new possessive form *its* arose. The predominant subject form was the restressed *it,*[18] and, by analogy with other genitives in *'s* the newer form (at first written *it's,* as many unstylish people still write it) began to be used instead of *his,* which nevertheless remained the usual form in the early years of the seventeenth century, as in Shakespeare's *Troilus and Cressida* II.ii.53–54: "But value dwels not in particular will, / It holds his estimate and dignitie. . . ." The *OED* cites an interesting American example from 1634: "Boston is two miles North-east from Roxberry: His situation is very pleasant."

Perhaps because of its ambiguity, *his* was nevertheless to some extent avoided as a neuter possessive even in Middle English times: an uninflected *it* occurs from the fourteenth to the seventeenth century, and to this day in British dialectal usage. The latest citation by the *OED* of its occurrence in Standard English is from 1622: "Each part as faire doth show / In it kind, as white in Snow." *Its* is quite rare in Shakespeare and occurs only twice in Milton's *Paradise Lost;*[19]

---

[17] See William Evans, " 'You' and 'Thou' in Northern England," *South Atlantic Bulletin,* Nov., 1969, pp. 17–21. Evans's conclusions are based on the evidence furnished by the *Survey of English Dialects,* Vol. I, ed. Harold Orton and Wilfred J. Halliday (Leeds, 1962–63), which "gives us the opportunity to make more precise statements about the extent of the survival of *thou* in the twentieth century and about the nature of its use in the areas, like the North [of England], where it seems particularly strong."

[18] That is, older *hit* lost its *h-* when unstressed; then the *h-*less form came to be used in stressed as well as unstressed positions—though, as has already been pointed out, *hit,* the form preferred by Queen Elizabeth I, remains in nonstandard speech as a stressed form.

[19] Jespersen, *Modern English Grammar,* VII, 308.

but by the end of the seventeenth century *its* had become the usual form, completely displacing *his* and the less frequent *it* as a neuter possessive.

Similar to the use of the second person plural form to refer to a single person is the "regal *we*," except that here a sense of one's own importance rather than that of someone else is implied. It is still useful in proclamations by a sovereign, and in earlier times, if we can judge by the older drama, it was even used in conversation. The usage is very ancient. Queen Victoria is said to have been the last monarch in Europe to employ it as a spoken form, as in her famous but doubtless apocryphal reproof to one of her Maids of Honour who had told a mildly improper story: "We are not amused." The "editorial *we*" dates from Old English times. It is sometimes used by one who is a member of a staff of writers who are assumed to share the opinions he is expressing. It may also be used to include one's readers in such phrases as "as we have seen."

In the second person plural, which became singular also, as we have just seen, by the gradual loss of the *th-* singular forms, the old distinction between the nominative *ye* and the objective *you,* though still maintained in the King James Bible,[20] was generally lost during the sixteenth century. Some writers make the distinction, some do not.[21] In time it was the objective form which prevailed to such an extent as to drive *ye* from Standard English. Nonstandard speech distinguishes singular and plural *you* in a number of ways, for example, the analogical *youse* of the "underprivileged" city dweller (also current in Irish English) and the *you-all* and *you-uns* (that is, you ones) which probably stem from Scots English. From the latter seventeenth century and throughout the eighteenth many speakers made a distinction between singular *you was* and plural *you were*. James Boswell uses singular *you was* throughout his *London Journal* (1762–63),[22] and even reports it as coming from the lips of Dr. Johnson: "Indeed, when you was in the irreligious way, I should not have been pleased with

[20] For example: "The Lord deal kindly with you, as ye have dealt with the dead, and with me. The Lord grant you that ye may find rest. . . ." (Ruth i.8–9)

[21] According to Wyld, *History of Modern Colloquial English,* p. 330, the two forms are carefully distinguished by Sir Thomas More and Lord Berners, whereas Bishop Latimer, Ascham, Cavendish, and Lyly (in *Euphues*) "use both forms indifferently for the Nom[inative]," and Queen Elizabeth I seems to have employed only *you* for both functions.

[22] But in the second edition of his *Life of Johnson* he changed over to *you were* for both singular and plural.

you" (July 28, 1763).[23] *You was* was very common in cultivated American usage also: George Philip Krapp cites its use by John Adams in a letter of condolence to a friend whose house had burned down: "You regret your loss; but why? Was you fond of seeing or thinking that others saw and admired so stately a pile?"[24] The construction became unfashionable in the early nineteenth century, but Noah Webster continued to defend it.[25]

In the third person plural the native *h*-forms had become all but archaic by the end of the fifteenth century, in the course of which the *th*-forms current in present English gradually took over. The only *h*-form to survive is that earlier written *hem,* and it survives only as an unstressed form; when it is written at all nowadays, it is written *'em.* The plural possessives in *h-* (*here, her, hir*) occurred only very rarely after the beginning of the sixteenth century (but see p. 172).

RELATIVE AND INTERROGATIVE PRONOUNS

We have noted that the usual Old English relative particle was *þe,* which, since it had only one form, would have continued to do very well. It is rather a pity that it was ever lost. Middle English adapted the neuter demonstrative pronoun *that,* without inflection, for the same relative function, later adding the previously interrogative *which,* sometimes preceded by *the,* and likewise uninflected. It was not until the sixteenth century that the originally interrogative *who* (OE *hwā*), which had already been put to use as an indefinite relative,[26] came to be at all commonly used as a simple relative to refer to persons. The King James Bible, which we should expect to be in its gram-

---

[23] He also reports it from Lord Eglinton and the Honourable Andrew Erskine, who must be presumed to have spoken Standard English. See Esther K. Sheldon, "On Boswell's English in the *London Journal,*" *PMLA,* 71 (1956), 1072, for a review of the status of the construction in Boswell's day; Bishop Lowth (see pp. 17 and 225–26) in his very influential *Short Introduction to English Grammar* (1762) had condemned it in no uncertain terms as "an enormous Solecism," but George Campbell testified in his *Philosophy of Rhetoric* (1776) that "it is ten times oftener heard."

[24] *The English Language in America* (New York, 1925), II, 261.

[25] There were two reasons why Webster should have approved *you was:* it was no longer much used by people of fashion, who merited his hatred by having rejected him as a belligerent though "learned" bumpkin; and it appealed to his sense of logic, order, and reason—for he was essentially a child of the Age of Reason—to have distinctive singular and plural forms.

[26] That is, as the equivalent of present *who(m)ever,* as in Shakespeare's "Who tels me true, though in his Tale lye death,/I heare him as he flatter'd" (*Antony and Cleopatra* I.ii.102–103) and Lord Byron's "Whom the gods love die young" (*Don Juan* IV.12).

mar a little behind the times,[27] has *which* where we should today use *who,* as in "The kingdom of heaven is likened unto a man which sowed good seed in his field" (Matt. xiii.24) and, as everyone knows, in "Our Father which art in heaven." Shakespeare, who with all his daring as a coiner and user of words was essentially conservative in his syntax, also uses *which* in the older fashion to refer to persons and things alike, as in "he which hath your Noble Father slaine" (*Hamlet* IV.vii.4).

THE INFLUENCE OF THE SCHOOLMASTER

In the freewheeling aristocratic usage of earlier days — as in that of the learned and the literary men who looked to a courtly society for their standards — there was not so much concern as now with what are conceived to be "proper" choices of case forms. English had to wait until the latter years of the seventeenth century for the rise of the schoolmaster's attitude towards language which was to become predominant in the eighteenth century and is still so — a relatively new thing, be it noted, which has given us a codified set of rules, some of them based on an arbitrary appeal to logic and "reason," but having very little relevance to older usage. After a coordinating conjunction, for instance, the subjective form tended to occur invariably, as indeed it yet does,[28] whether it is object of verb or preposition or second element of a compound subject. H. C. Wyld cites "with you and I" from a letter by Sir John Suckling, as well as two seventeenth-century occurrences of "between you and I,"[29] to which may be added Shakespeare's "all debts are cleerd betweene you and I" (*Merchant of Venice* III.ii.321). Jespersen cites the usage in question (that is, after *between*) from Congreve, Defoe, and Fielding, along with a few examples from our own day.[30] There is of course no doubt that at the present time the desire to be "correct" causes many speakers who may have been reproved as children for saying "Mary and me went downtown" to use "Mary and I" under all circumstances; but "hypercorrectness" is hardly a satisfactory explanation for the phenomenon as it

[27] It was the work of almost fifty theological scholars designated by James I, and afterwards reviewed by the bishops and other eminent scholars. It is not surprising that these men should have been little given to anything that smacked of innovation.

[28] See the Queen's "for my husband and I" and former President Eisenhower's "for Mrs. Eisenhower and I," below, p. 246, n. 44. The difference between former times and now is that when uttered publicly or printed (as it rarely would be), the construction nowadays invariably gives rise to disapproving comment of the "What is the English language coming to?" variety.

[29] *History of Modern Colloquial English*, p. 332.

[30] *Modern English Grammar*, VII, 273.

occurs in the writings of well-bred people from the sixteenth to the early eighteenth' centuries, a period during which people of consequence talked pretty much as they pleased and others less fortunately placed followed their example. After other prepositions Jespersen cites equally distinguished precedent for *I,* as well as for its use as object, direct or indirect, of a verb. It is not only the first person, however, for which the nominative form occurs after *and* regardless of school grammar; there seems to be a widespread preference for the nominative form of any personal pronoun after this conjunction, though in the nature of things the first person would be most likely to occur.

School grammar requires the nominative form after *as* and *than* in such sentences as "Is she as tall as me?" (*Antony and Cleopatra* III.iii.14). Boswell, who wrote in a period in which men of strong minds and characters were attempting to "regularize" the English language, shows no particular pattern of consistency in this construction. In the entry in his *London Journal* for June 5, 1763, he writes "I was much stronger than her," but elsewhere uses the nominative form in the same construction.[31]

In early Modern English the historical nominative and objective forms of the personal pronouns, particularly of the first person singular, tend to occur more or less indiscriminately after the verb *be.* In *Twelfth Night,* for instance, Sir Andrew Aguecheek, who, though a fool, is yet a gentleman, uses both forms within a few lines: "That's mee I warrant you. . . . I knew 'twas I" (II.v.87–89). The generally inconsistent state of things before the prescriptive grammarians took over is exemplified by Shakespeare's usage elsewhere with other pronouns: "I am not thee" (*Timon of Athens* IV.iii.277); "you are not he" (*Love's Labour's Lost* V.ii.550); "And damn'd be him, that first cries hold, enough"[32] (*Macbeth* V.viii.34); "you are she" (*Twelfth Night* V.i.334). Instances of *her, us,* and *them* in this construction are

[31] As Esther K. Sheldon points out in the article cited above in n. 23, the grammarians of Boswell's day were not in agreement on this particular matter: some demanded the "same case [after *than* and *as*] as before"; others wanted *than* and *as* regarded as prepositions, and would thus require the objective form of the pronoun to be used consistently; still others thought the choice of case form should be determined by expanding the construction, as in "I know him better than she (knows him)"; "I know him better than (I know) her"; "You do not care for him as much as I (care for him)"; "You do not care for him as much as (you care for) me." The last is the rule laid down by present-day prescriptivists.

[32] Pope and other later editors emend this to "damn'd be he." *He* is usual after *be.* Jespersen believes that *damn'd be* is here the equivalent of a single word and governs the same case as *(God)damn* (*Progress in Language, with Special Reference to English,* 2nd ed. [London, 1909], p. 239).

infrequent in early Modern English writings. "Here's them" occurs in *Pericles* II.i.67, but the speaker is a fisherman.

Today also the objective form of personal pronouns continues to occur after *be,* though not without bringing down upon the head of the user the thunder of those who regard themselves as guardians of the language. There are nevertheless a great many speakers of Standard English who do not care and who say "It's me" when there is occasion to do so[33] despite the school doctrine that "the verb *to be* can never take an object." There is little point in labeling the construction colloquial or informal as contrasted with a supposedly formal "It is I," inasmuch as the utterance would not be likely to occur alone in any but a conversational environment. Followed by a relative clause, however, "It is I" is usual, as in "It is I who am responsible," though "it is me" occurs as a rule before relative clauses where the pronoun is the object, as in "It is me that he is hunting." What has been said of *me* after forms of *be* applies also to *us, him, her,* and *them.*

The tendency to use an objective pronominal form after a verb and a subjective form before one is of course due to the structure of Modern English. Every native speaker has a certain "feel" for the subject-verb-complement word order which characterizes most of our statements, the complement usually being an object rather than a so-called predicate nominative. The tendency to frame our utterances in this order is indeed so powerful that when for stylistic reasons we choose to put before the verb a pronoun which is its object — as in "Him I detest" — it goes a little against the grain: despite our consciousness of the principles governing case, we feel a "pull" toward *he* in this position. "Ham I detest" presents no such problem.

The "proper" choice between *who* and *whom,* whether interrogative or relative, frequently involves an intellectual chore that many speakers from about 1500 on have been little concerned with. The interrogative pronoun, coming as it usually does before the verb, tended in early Modern English to be invariably *who,* as it still does in unselfconscious speech. One could cite from the most distinguished writers scores[34] of examples of *who* as the object of a verb or of a preposition (particularly if the preposition is placed last) from the Middle English period on, though because of the emphasis of the schools on the supposed importance of using *whom* in these functions, current printed examples are harder to find than early Modern English

[33] As for the uncontracted form "It is me (I)," frequently cited in handbooks, it is difficult to imagine any circumstances in which it would occur.

[34] Jespersen (*Modern English Grammar,* VII, 241) is probably not exaggerating when he says "hundreds."

ones. Jespersen cites interrogative *who* as object before the verb from
Marlowe, Greene, Ben Jonson, the old *Spectator* of Addison and
Steele, Goldsmith, and Sheridan, with later examples from Thackeray,
Mrs. Humphry Ward, and Shaw. Schmidt's *Shakespeare-Lexicon* furnishes fifteen quotations for interrogative *who* in this construction,
and then adds an *etc.*, though, as Jespersen points out, "Most modern
editors and reprinters add the *-m* everywhere in accordance with the
rules of 'orthodox' grammar."[35]

Relative *who* as object of verb or preposition is hardly less frequent.
For Shakespeare, Schmidt uses the label *etc.* after citing a dozen instances, and Jespersen cites from a few other authors. The *OED*,
along with its statement that *whom* is no longer current in natural
colloquial speech, cites Lord Berners and Edmund Spenser, among
others. It should be noted, however, that there are a good many
instances of *whom* for the nominative, especially where the relative
may be taken as the object of the verb of the principal clause, as in
Matthew xvi.13: "Whom do men say that I the Son of man am?"[36]
Shakespeare's "Whom in constancie you thinke stands so safe"
(*Cymbeline* I.iv.138) and "Yong Ferdinand (whom they suppose is
droun'd)" (*Tempest* III.iii.92) would be condemned by all prescriptive grammarians nowadays; but in Shakespeare's usage, which may in
this respect as in all others be taken as representative of early Modern
English, such constructions stand side by side with "I should do Brutus
wrong, and Cassius wrong:/who (you all know) are Honourable men"
(*Julius Caesar* III.ii.128–29) and others which employ the "approved"
form in the same construction.[37] The fact is, however, that this use
of *whom* (or "misuse," according to one's point of view and one's
teaching) occurs very frequently during the whole Modern English

[35] *Modern English Grammar*, VII, 242. Compare his earlier and somewhat bitter
statement that they show thereby "that they hold in greater awe the schoolmasters of
their own childhood than the poet of all the ages" (*Progress in Language*, p. 216). It is
an amusing irony that *whom*-sleuths, imagining that they are great traditionalists, are
actually adhering to a fairly recent standard as far as the period from the fifteenth century
on is concerned. In view of the facts, such a sentence as "Who are you waiting for?" can
hardly be considered untraditional.

[36] Also in verse 15: "But whom say ye that I am?" Both the Tindale (1526) and the
King James versions have this *whom*. Accusative *hwæne* occurs in the Anglo-Saxon
Gospels. As the *OED* points out, the English construction is sometimes doubtless due
to confusion with the Latin accusative and infinitive construction, as in the Vulgate
"Quem dicunt homines esse Filium hominis?" (13) and "Vos autem quem me esse
dicitis?" (15). The Revised Version (1881) changes to *who* in both verses.

[37] Note the double use of the single form *who* in "the blood o' th' Prince, my Sonne,/
(Who I doe thinke is mine, and love as mine)" (*Winter's Tale* I.ii.330–31).

period. Jespersen, whose *Modern English Grammar* is a storehouse of illustrative material upon which apparently few writers of school grammars have drawn, has many examples ranging from Chaucer to the present day (III, 198–99), and Sir Ernest Gowers cites contemporary instances from E. M. Forster, Lord David Cecil, *The Times,* and Somerset Maugham, all of which might be presumed to be Standard English.[38] What has been said of *who* and *whom* applies also to *who(so)ever* and *whom(so)ever,* as in "The slaves of the lamp . . . render faithful service to whomsoever holds the talisman"[39] and, to give a less eloquent example, "I am beginning to despair of whomever it is that writes the Foreign Secretary's speeches."[40] Examples from early Modern English, as well as two from Middle English, may be found in the *OED.*

VERBS

Throughout the history of English the strong verbs, always a minority, have fought a losing battle, having either joined the ranks of the weak verbs or been lost altogether. Comparatively few which have survived can be said to show what could be called in any way a regular development. A number of factors, which will be dealt with as occasion requires, have brought about such changes that, except for most of the surviving Class I verbs and some from Class III, the orderly arrangement into classes which prevailed in the older periods has now no more than a historical relevance.

Class I remains rather clearly defined. *Write, smite, stride, rise,* and *drive* show in their preterits the regular development from the Old English preterit singular forms with *ā* (*wrāt, smāt,* and so forth). Likewise to be expected from the Old English past participles with short *i* are Modern English *written, smitten,* and so forth. A Northern form, *drave,*[41] sometimes occurs as the preterit of *drive* in early Modern English, for instance "And I delivered you out of the hand of the Egyptians . . . and drave them out from before you . . ." (Judges vi.9). *Bite* and *slide* now have in their preterits the short *i* of the past participle and the old preterit plural, but *bote* and *slode* both occur in literary early Modern English and survive in present British dialectal

---

[38] *Plain Words: Their ABC* (New York, 1954), p. 228.
[39] Sir Winston Churchill, cited in Gowers, pp. 227–28.
[40] "Taper" [Bernard Levin], *Spectator,* May 1, 1959, p. 606.
[41] Old English *ā,* it will be remembered, was not rounded to *ǭ* in the Northern dialect of Middle English. It thus fell together with the Middle English *ā* that resulted from the lengthening of originally short vowels in open syllables and shared its subsequent development.

usage. Until fairly recently there has been wavering in Standard English between *writ* and *wrote, rid*[42] and *rode,* and *ris*[43] and *rose. Dive,* historically a weak verb, has acquired by analogy with Class I verbs a strong preterit *dove,* dialectal in British English but by no means confined to uneducated use in America,[44] where the form seems to be gaining ground rapidly. *Thrive,* of Scandinavian origin, and *strive,* borrowed from Old French (though ultimately Germanic), acquired strong inflection in Middle English times, though *strived* is more common than strong *striven* as a participial form. *Strike* shows the regular preterit development *stroke* (OE *strāc*) until the seventeenth century,[45] when *struck* began to occur, it may be by analogy with *stuck.* The historical participle *stricken* survives in such figurative uses as "stricken in years" and "stricken from the record," but various other forms, including *stroke* and *struck(en),* occurred in early Modern English. In *abide* and *shine* the old preterit singular forms are used as past participles. *Abide* may also have dental-suffix forms ("He abided by the laws"), as may *shine* when used causatively ("He shined his shoes"). *Hide* and *chide,* originally weak verbs, acquired in the early Modern period the participial forms in *-en* characteristic of strong verbs; their preterits with shortened vowels are the normal development of Old English *hȳdde* and *cīdde,* but could quite naturally be felt as analogical with the strong preterits *bit* and *slid.*[46]

Participial forms of verbs of this class frequently occur without *-en* in the seventeenth and eighteenth centuries, for example *rid, writ, bit, smit.* Furthermore, the preterit forms *(a)rose, drove, rode, shone, smote, strove,* and *wrote* were all used as participles and remained current as such in literary English as late as the eighteenth century, for example Boswell's "I imagined that your father had wrote in such a way . . ." (*London Journal,* December 30, 1762).

Other verbs of this class have become weak, for example *glide, gripe, spew,* and *writhe.* Still others have disappeared altogether from the language.

---

[42] The *OED* cites this form from Byron and Thackeray.

[43] Current as a participial form (without *-en*) in eastern New England *ris bread* 'home-made white bread.'

[44] E. Bagby Atwood, *A Survey of Verb Forms in the Eastern United States* (Ann Arbor, Mich., 1953), p. 9. Atwood records *div* and *duv* also, though these were not used by educated speakers. The first is by analogy with *bit* and *slid.*

[45] *Strick, strake,* and *strook* were also current to some extent in earlier times as preterits, as were weak forms *striked* and *stryckt.*

[46] Analogical *chode* also occurs, as in the King James Bible: "And the people chode with Moses . . ." (Num. xx.3).

The verbs of Class II have likewise undergone many changes in the course of their development into their present forms. Some of these could hardly have been predicted, for instance the vowels of *choose* (OE *cēosan*, ME *chēsen*) and *lose* (OE *lēosan*, ME *lēsen*), as contrasted with *creep* (OE *crēopan*, ME *crēpen*). The present English forms are to be explained by a shifting of stress in the Old English diphthong, *céosan* and *léosan* thereby becoming *ceósan* and *leósan*, which would in turn become Middle English *chōsen* and *lōsen* and thus yield the Modern forms with *o(o)*.[47] Alternative forms *che(e)se* and *le(e)se*, however, survived into the fifteenth and seventeenth centuries respectively. *Leese* occurs both in the King James Bible, later printings of which change it to *lose*, and in Shakespeare.[48] Middle English had both strong and weak preterits of *leese*, the weak forms appearing as early as the thirteenth century. Weak forms of *choose, cheese,* and *chuse* also occur as late as the eighteenth century. Both these verbs have lost the *-r-* in their past participles (OE *coren, loren*), the result of Verner's Law with subsequent rhotacization (see above, p. 109). though *loren* survives as an adjective in *lorn* and the compounds *forlorn* and *lovelorn*.

In addition to *choose*, verbs of this class which have retained strong inflection are *fly* (the preterit *flew* is not regularly derived from Old English *flēah*) and *freeze*.[49] E. Bagby Atwood reports from the eastern United States the following variant preterit forms of *freeze: friz, frez, freezen, frozen,* and, with dental suffix, *freezed, frozed,* and *frazed* — all "distinctly older forms [which] are no doubt receding rapidly" (p. 15). *Cleave* is usually weak in Modern English (*cleaved, cleft*[50]), but a strong preterit *clove* is still to some extent current, as is the strong participle in *cloven hoof* (but *cleft palate*). A variant strong preterit form, *clave*, is familiar from the King James Bible, as in "And Abraham rose up early in the morning . . . and clave the wood for the burnt offering" (Gen. xxii.3). The Old English weak verb *cleofian* 'stick' fell together with strong *clēofan* 'split' in Middle English

---

[47] Another form, *chuse*, was common until well into the nineteenth century.

[48] As in Sonnet 5: "But flowers distill'd, though they with winter meet, / Leese but their show, their substance still lives sweet."

[49] Like *choose* and *lose*, this verb in Old English had *-r-* in its past participle. *Frore*, with loss of *-n*, occurs occasionally as an archaism, as in Shelley's "Snow-fed streams now seen athwart frore vapours," which the *OED* suggests is, like other nineteenth-century occurrences of the rhotacized form, a reflection of Milton's "The parching Air Burns frore" (*Paradise Lost* II.594–95).

[50] The vowel differentiation in this preterit form is of course not a matter of gradation, but merely a matter of shortening. The same phenomenon is responsible for the short-voweled preterits of *weep, sleep, sweep, keep,* and a few other verbs.

cle(e)ven, so that it came to acquire the same strong preterit forms. *Clave* thus occurs in the sense 'stuck' also: "Certain men clave to Paul" (Acts xvii.34). Participles of *choose* and *freeze* without *-n* are common in early Modern English, as in Shakespeare's "O what a time have you chose out brave Caius/To weare a Kerchiefe" (*Julius Caesar* II.i.314–15) and "This word (Rebellion) it had froze them up" (*2 Henry IV* I.i.199), as indeed they still are in folk speech. *Flew* occurs as a participle in the seventeenth and eighteenth centuries; it too is still current among those who continue to use the *n*-less participles just cited.

In addition to *lose* and *cleave,* the following surviving verbs of Class II are now weak: *creep, chew, brew, rue, lie* 'prevaricate,' *reek, seethe, flee, bow* 'bend,' *crowd, shove, sprout,* and *suck. Sodden,* the old strong participle (with grammatical change) of *seethe,* is still sometimes used as an adjective. *Crope,* a strong preterit of *creep,* occurs in formal English as late as the eighteenth century and in folk speech to the present day.

Practically all verbs of Class III with nasal consonants which have survived from Old English have retained their strong inflection. Some of those in *-n* (OE *-nn-*), *-m* (OE *-mm-*), *-nk* (OE *-nc-*), or *-ng* preserve in current Standard English the Old English form of the preterit singular, following the pattern *i* (infinitive), *a* (preterit), *u* (past participle), for example *spring, sing, ring, drink, sink, shrink, stink, swim,* and *begin.* But there has been in these verbs since early Modern English times considerable wavering between the historical preterit and participial forms, with *u* for the preterit strongly predominating in the eighteenth century. Preterit *drunk* is still fairly common in New England and the Middle Atlantic states, according to Atwood's survey, and *shrunk* "strongly predominates among all types [cultured and uncultured, old and young] in all areas [of the eastern United States]" (p. 21). Only about half of his cultured New England informants and a third of those in the Middle Atlantic states used the standard combination *drank–drunk* as preterit and past participle respectively. The great majority of those who did not do so used one form or the other for both functions. Participial forms of these verbs, and especially of *drink,* with *a* were by no means uncommon in cultivated usage in earlier days. Jespersen cites *drank* as participle from Scott, Byron, Shelley, Keats, Dickens, Trollope, Kingsley, and, from our own day, Robert Graves.[51] The older participial forms

---

[51] VI, 54. Boswell also uses it in his *London Journal:* ". . . he told me that he had once drank a bottle of sherry . . . (May 11, 1763); "Mr. Johnson and I had formerly drank the health of Sir David Dalrymple" (July 14, 1763).

drunken and *shrunken* occur as adjectives. In *run* (ME *rinnen*) the vowel of the participle was in early Modern English extended into the present tense. An unchanged preterit *run*, coming from early Modern English times, is common in folk speech. The use of *ran* as a participle is equally old.

Other Class III verbs with nasal consonants have in current English the pattern *i, u(o), u(o)*, as in *win, spin, cling, swing, wring, sting,* and *slink*, though these had preterits with *a* also in early Modern English, as in the familiar lines "When Adam dolve and Evë span/ Who was then the gentleman?" A few verbs entering the language after Old English times have conformed to this pattern, for example *fling, sling,* and *string* (from the noun). By the same sort of analogy the weak verb *bring* has acquired in nonstandard speech the strong preterit and participial form *brung*. Though lacking the nasal, *dig* (not of Old English origin) and *stick*, having at first weak inflection, have taken on the same pattern.[52] The preterit *dug* is first recorded in the eighteenth century;[53] as participle the form is much older. Class III verbs in *-nd*, for example *find, bind, grind,* and *wind*, have in their preterits and participles the modern development [aʊ] of the lengthened *u* (spelled *ou*) of the old preterit plural and past participle.

Except for *fight*, the development of whose Modern English preterit and participle presents certain difficulties which we need not go into here,[54] all other surviving verbs of this class have become weak, some in Middle English times: *climb, bark, burn, braid, carve, help, starve, delve,[55] mourn, spurn, yield, yell, yelp, melt, swallow,* and *swell*. The old participial forms *molten* and *swollen* are still used, but only as adjectives. *Holp*, an old strong preterit of *help*, was common until the seventeenth century and survives in current nonstandard usage.[56] The old participial form *holpen* is doubtless familiar to many from its use in the King James Bible, for instance in Luke i.54 ("He hath holpen his servant Israel"), Psalms lxxxvi.17, Isaiah xxxi.3, and Daniel xi.34. Both *holp* and *holpen* have been used by poets as conscious archaisms;

---

[52] *Stack, stake,* and *stoke* also occur in early Modern English as preterits of *stick*.

[53] Note the seventeenth-century and earlier preterit in the King James Bible, for example in the parable of the talents: "But he that had received one went and digged in the earth, and hid his lord's money" (Matt. xxv.18).

[54] The expected form [faʊt] is current in American folk speech, particularly in parts of the South (Atwood, p. 14). *Fit*, presumably analogical with *bit*, is also fairly common, both in British and American folk usage.

[55] But note the older strong form *dolve* in the quotation in the preceding paragraph.

[56] See Atwood, pp. 16–17. Those who use this form pronounce it, and usually *help* as well, without *l*.

the *OED* has citations from Tennyson and Mrs. Browning, among others. The older forms *clum, clam, clim, cloom,* and *clome* survive dialectally as strong preterits of *climb.*[57] The last of these, sometimes written *clomb* or *clombe,* occurs probably as a conscious archaism in Spenser and those other Elizabethan writers who affected old-fashioned forms; it also occurs in the writings of Dryden, Wordsworth, Coleridge, Scott, and Tennyson, doubtless as a reflection of its Elizabethan use. *Burst* has only a single form in current Standard English, though *brast* is common as a preterit in the early Modern period. A weak preterit *bursted* and its variant *busted,* with loss of *r,* frequently occur in nonstandard speech.

The principal surviving verbs of Class IV are *bear, break, shear, steal, tear,* and *come.* All these have remained strong, and all save the last have the inflectional pattern *ea, o, o,* from earlier *ea, a, o* (OE *e, æ, o*). The *o* of the modern preterit is from the past participle. In Middle English times a number of verbs from other classes took over the inflectional system of Class IV: *speak, weave,* and *tread* from Class V; *heave* and *swear* from Class VI; *get,* the Scandinavian word replacing Old English *-gitan,* which, like *tread,* has a short root vowel in all its parts; and the weak verb *wear.*[58] In early Modern English there was considerable variation between preterits in *a* and *o,* for instance *spoke–spake, tore–tare, got–gat, bore–bare, broke–brake.*[59] In time the *o*-preterits came to predominate and ultimately to drive out altogether the forms with *a.* Participial forms of these verbs without *-n* are frequent in the seventeenth and eighteenth centuries; that of *get* has remained in British English, but *gotten* is still very much alive in American English. *Come* frequently occurs as a preterit in early Modern English,[60] as it continues to do in folk speech. *Shear* may have either weak or strong inflection. Analogical *roke* occurs in

[57] For their distribution in eastern American English, see Atwood, pp. 8–9 and Figure 5.

[58] Class V earlier had *e* in the participle and Class VI, *a. Get* conformed to Class V inflection like its Old English cognate *-gitan,* with participle with *e (geten, gete, i-gete)* up to near the end of the sixteenth century. But *gotten,* with root vowel *o* from Class IV participles, occurs as early as the thirteenth century.

[59] The *a*-forms are familiar from their use in the King James Bible, as in "When I was a child, I spake as a child . . ." (1 Cor. xiii.11). Compare also "And when he went forth to land, there met him . . . a certain man, which had devils long time, and ware no clothes . . ." (Luke viii.27); "And when he had taken the five loaves and the two fishes, he looked up to heaven, and blessed, and brake the loaves . . ." (Mark vi.41); "And they brought him unto him; and when he saw him, straightway the spirit tare him . . ." (Mark ix.20).

[60] For example, in Pepys's *Diary:* "Creed come and dined with me . . ." (June 15, 1666) and elsewhere, though Pepys also uses *came.*

the deep South as a past participle (and presumably a preterit as well) of *rake*, as in the common solicitation of itinerant handymen, "Do you want your yard roke?"

Verbs of Class V have all diverged in one way or another from what might be considered regular development. *Speak* and *tread*, as we have just seen, ultimately took on the characteristics of Class IV verbs. For the preterit of *eat*, early Modern English for a while had *at*, but *ate*, with lengthened vowel, and *eat*, pronounced [ɛt], also occur—the last probably by analogy with preterit *read* [rɛd]. The pronunciation today indicated by the spelling *ate* (that is, [et]) is the only one current in educated American speech. The same spelling has, however, long prevailed in British English, though *et* would better indicate the usual pronunciation. The same spoken form [ɛt], written *eat*, was commonly used as a participle in early Modern English and continues to occur as late as the early nineteenth century. Jespersen cites examples from Jane Austen, Lamb, and Shelley (VI, 69). The preterit *(for)bad* is regularly developed from Old English *bæd;* the form *bade*, with lengthened vowel, begins to occur in Middle English times. Since the sixteenth century *bid,* from the participle *bidden,* has also been used as a preterit form. The *i* (instead of *e*) of the participle has been variously explained; it occurs first in Middle English times.[61] The preterit *gave* has predominated since early Modern times, though preterit *give*[62] and participial *gave*[63] also occur fairly frequently. *Sit* had in early Modern English the preterit forms *sat, sate,* and (occasionally) *sit,* the participial forms *sitten, sit, sat,* and *sate. Sit* and *set* were confused as early as the fourteenth century, and continue to be.[64] A nonstandard form *sot* occurs as preterit and participle of both verbs. The confusion of *lie*[65] and *lay* is as old as that of *sit* and *set*. The intransitive use of *lay*, ac-

---

[61] See Eilert Ekwall, *Historische neuenglische Laut- und Formenlehre,* 3rd ed., rev. (Berlin, 1956), pp. 128–29, and H. C. Wyld, *A Short History of English,* 3rd ed. (New York, 1927), p. 276.

[62] As in Pepys's "This day I sent my cozen Roger a tierce of claret, which I give him" (August 21, 1667).

[63] As in Shakespeare's *Venus and Adonis,* line 571: "When he did frown, O, had she then gave over. . . ."

[64] Of the situation in current eastern American English, Atwood states, "In the entire area south of Pa., outside of the larger cities, *sit* is rather uncommon except in cultured speech" (p. 21).

[65] Old English *licgan,* Middle English *liggen.* The expected modern form would be **lidge,* but the infinitive has been re-formed by analogy with the present indicative singular forms. Old English *ligest, ligeþ,* Middle English *lyest, lyeth.* Preterit *lay* and participial *lain* are regular developments of Old English *læg* and *legen. Lien,* or *lyen,* with the vowel of the infinitive, sometimes occurs as a participial form from the fourteenth century on.

cording to the *OED*, "was not app[arently] regarded as a solecism" in the seventeenth and eighteenth centuries. It has been so used by some very important writers, including Francis Bacon. Everyone is familiar with Lord Byron's "There let him lay" in Canto IV of *Childe Harold's Pilgrimage* (line 1620). The brothers H. W. and F. G. Fowler cite with apparently delighted disapproval "I suspected him of having laid in wait for the purpose"[66] from the writing of Richard Grant White, the eminent nineteenth-century American purist—for purists love above all to catch other purists out in some supposed sin against English grammar. Better writers than White have committed the same "error," however: George H. McKnight cites the usage from William Morris, Fiona Macleod, George Moore, Joseph Conrad, and Lytton Strachey.[67] Old English *cweðan* 'say' survives only in *bequeath*, which has weak inflection. *Quod* and *quoth* occur as early Modern English preterits of the simple form. H. C. Wyld suggests that the *o*, which is found also in the participle—the regular development would be **quath*—is due to the analogy of the participles of Class IV.[68] The form *quotha* is for *quoth he* (see p. 201). The preterit *saw* predominates all through the Modern period, though *see,* still common as a preterit in folk speech, also occurs. A weak form *seed* is likewise confined to folk speech, as is *seen,* from the participle. Other surviving Class V verbs have become weak: *mete, knead, reap, scrape, wreak, fret,* and *weigh.*

Some verbs from Class VI show regular development with *a, oo, a,* for example *shake, forsake,* and the Scandinavian *take* which ultimately ousted its Old English synonym *niman* from the language. Early Modern English frequently uses the preterit form of these verbs as participle.[69] *Stand* (and the compound *understand*) has lost its old participle *standen;* the preterit form has served as participle since the sixteenth century, though not exclusively. *Stand* also occurs as participle, as does a weak form *standed.*[70] *Slay* (OE *slēan*) was newly formed in late Middle English from the participle *slayn* (OE *slagen*), though *slea* and *slee*[71] continued in use until the seventeenth century. The preterit

---

[66] *The King's English,* 2nd ed. (Oxford, 1906), p. 40.
[67] *Modern English in the Making* (New York, 1928), p. 534.
[68] *A Short History of English,* p. 279.
[69] As in Shakespeare's "Save what is had or must from you be took" (Sonnet 75), "Have from the forests shook three summers' pride" (Sonnet 104), and "Hath she forsooke so many Noble Matches?" (*Othello* IV.ii.125).
[70] As in "a tongue not understood of the people" in the fourteenth Article of Religion of the Anglican Communion.
[71] See the chapter "Rosemary" from Banckes's *Herball* cited on p. 182: ". . . laye them on a Canker & it shall slee it."

slew supplanted the older form *slow*, apparently by analogy with Class VII preterits like *knew* and *blew;* the same explanation doubtless holds for *drew* (older *drow*). *Quake* is likewise peculiar among Class VI verbs in having *o* rather than *oo* in its preterit; it also has weak inflection. Other surviving verbs of this class have become weak: *fare, gnaw, (en)grave, flay, heave, lade, laugh, shave, step, wade,* and *wash,* though strong participial forms *laden* and *shaven* survive as adjectives, and *heave* has an alternative strong preterit *hove.*

Surviving Class VII verbs which remain strong include *blow, grow, know, fall, hang,* and *hold.* The present and preterit of *beat* have been leveled, but the verb retains its strong participle in *-en. Crow* sometimes has a strong preterit *crew,* but its participle is always *crowed.* The old participle of *hold* survives in the somewhat old-fashioned *beholden. Hang* is frequently weak when used in reference to capital punishment — at least, the books on usage tell us that it ought to be, though no less imposing a personage than a British Lord Chief Justice (Lord Goddard) chose to use the strong form in this connection: "Your lordships can be assured that the only people hung are those guilty of cruel, deliberate murder without mitigation." In reporting this statement, the London *Daily Express* made a point of commenting, "It was noted that the Lord Chief Justice speaks regularly of a man being 'hung.' He does not say 'hanged'" (July 11, 1956, p. 2). In the seventeenth century *fell* was frequent as a participial form, as in Shakespeare's "have with one Winters brush / Fell from their boughes" (*Timon of Athens* IV.iii.264–65). (He also uses *fallen.*) Weak *blowed* and *growed* occur rather often in early Modern English and survive in nonstandard speech.[72]

The following verbs surviving from this group have become weak, the first two acquiring weak preterit forms as early as Old English times: *read* (OE preterit *rǣdde*), *sleep* (OE preterit *slēpte*), *dread, weep, leap, span* 'join,' *mow, hew, fold, sow, flow, walk, wax* 'grow,' and *row.* Strong participial forms *sown, mown,* and *hewn* survive, mainly as adjectives. *Let* is the single form to survive from Old English *lǣtan.*

With the loss of Middle English *-e* as ending for the first person singular present indicative, the endingless form became identical with the infinitive, which had lost first its final *-n* and then its *-e.* The early Modern English second person singular present indicative had *-(e)st,* sometimes *-(e)s,* and the third person varied between *-(e)s* and *-(e)th.* From the beginning of the seventeenth century the *-s* form of the third person was to prevail, though for a while the two forms might be used interchangeably, particularly in verse, for example Shakespeare's "Some-

---

[72] For their distribution in eastern American English, see Atwood, pp. 6 and 15–16.

time she driveth ore a Souldiers necke, & then dreames he of cutting Forraine throats" (*Romeo and Juliet* I.iv.82–83). But *doth* and *hath* went on until well into the eighteenth century. The King James Bible uses only *-th* forms, as does the Book of Common Prayer, but, as H. C. Wyld points out, "Evidently the translators of the Authorized Version of the Bible regarded *-s* as belonging only to familiar speech, but the exclusive use of *-eth* here, and in every edition of the Prayer Book, may be partly due to the tradition set by the earlier Biblical translations and the early editions of the Prayer Book respectively."[73] The *-s* forms of the third person singular present indicative are usually attributed to Northern dialectal influence. In the present indicative plural the endings *-eth* of the Southern dialects and *-en* of the Midland were lost as early as the fourteenth century, resulting in the current endingless forms, though forms in *-eth, -ith* survived into the sixteenth century. Third person plural forms in *-s,* of Northern provenience, occur also, as in "Where lo, two lamps, burnt out, in darkness lies" (*Venus and Adonis,* line 1128) and elsewhere in Shakespeare and other Elizabethan writers; these should not of course be regarded as "ungrammatical" uses of the third person singular for the plural form. Wyld believes that this plural form in *-s* is due to analogy with the singular, however, rather than to Northern influence, inasmuch as to this day "certain sections of the people inflect all Persons of both Sing. and Pl. with *-s* after the pattern of the 3rd Pers. Sing., while others drop the suffix even in the 3rd Sing. and the Pl. of all Persons" (p. 340). The extension of the *-s* to the first and second persons is indeed particularly noticeable in current speech in the usage of naive raconteurs, with their "I says" and "says I," and is the source of the rude expression of disbelief "Sez you!"

The early Modern English preterit had no personal endings save for the second person singular *-(e)st.* This began to be lost in the sixteenth century.

In the verb *to be* the early Modern indicative singular forms were (1) *am,* (2) *art,* (3) *is.* In the plural either *be* or *are* might occur,[74] the first being widely current as late as the seventeenth century. The preterit indicative second person singular was *were* until the sixteenth century, when the forms *wast, werst,* and *wert* began to occur, the last remaining current in literature throughout the eighteenth century. Nineteenth-century poets were also very fond of it ("Bird thou never wert"); it gave a certain archaically spiritual tone to their writing which

---

[73] *History of Modern Colloquial English,* p. 334.
[74] Ekwall cites "The powers that be" as a survival of the *be* form (p. 139).

they presumably considered desirable. *Wast* and *wert* are by analogy with present *art*. In *werst*, the *s* of *wast* has apparently been extended. *Wert* was also used in the second person of the preterit subjunctive. The locution *you was* has been discussed earlier (pp. 202–203).

Of the other highly irregular verbs little need be said. *Could*, the preterit of *can*, acquired its unetymological *l* in the sixteenth century by analogy with *would* and *should*. Early Modern forms which differ from those now current are *durst*, preterit of *dare*, which otherwise had become weak; *mought*, a variant of *might;* and *mowe*, an occasionally occurring present plural form of *may*. *Will* has early Modern forms with *u* and *o*.

Before it was supplanted by *not* (a form of *nought*) in the sixteenth century, *ne* was frequently joined to a following verb if this began with *h* or *w* or with a vowel, for example Old English *nabban* 'not to have,' *neom* 'am not,' *nat* 'know(s) not,' *nyllan* 'be unwilling,' corresponding to Middle English *nave, nam, no(o)t, nille*.[75]

CONTRACTED NEGATIVE FORMS

Most of our current contracted negative forms in *-n't* first occur in writing in the seventeenth century. It is likely that all were actually used long before ever getting written down, for contractions are in their very nature colloquial and thus would have been considered unsuitable for writing, as most people still consider them. *Won't* is from *wol(l) not* (see p. 177, n. 46), and *don't*, the vowel of which presents an annoying problem,[76] may be from either *do* or, in the third person singular, from *does not*, with loss of [-z-]. The *OED* derives third person *don't* from *he* (*she, it*) *do*, and cites a number of instances of *do* in the third person from the sixteenth and seventeenth centuries, including Pepys's "Sir Arthur Haselrigge do not yet appear in the House" (March 2, 1660). Karl W. Dykema, who believes that the most likely explanation of third person *don't* is the principle of morphological analogy—the same tendency which has reduced the various preterit forms of the strong verbs to a single form—has found an occurrence of it in 1697, but none for *doesn't* before 1818, though it is likely, as he admits, that there are some earlier occurrences of the latter form. As far as the evidence goes, however, *doesn't* first occurs one hundred

[75] As in *willy-nilly* 'will I (ye, he), won't I (ye, he).' Not only verbs but other words as well underwent this contraction, for example Old English *nān* (*none*), *nǣnig* 'not any,' *nǣfre* (*never*).

[76] That is, one would expect [dunt] for all forms save the third singular, for which [dənt] would be the expected form. It has been suggested that the [o] of *don't* is analogical with that of *won't* (Jespersen, *Modern English Grammar*, V, 431).

and twenty-one years later than the earliest known occurrence of third person *don't*.[77] Elsewhere Dykema concludes that "Such variants as *don't* and *doesn't* in the third person are considered by speakers of Standard English as the recent innovation and the original contraction respectively, whereas it is probably more nearly the case that *don't* is the older form!"[78]

An't (early ModE [ænt]) for *am* (*are, is*) *not* is apparently of late seventeenth-century origin; the variant *ain't* occurs about a century later. With the eighteenth-century British English shifting of [æ] to [ɑ] as in *ask, path, dance,* and the like, and the loss of preconsonantal *r,* the pronunciation of this word shifted to [ɑnt], and *aren't* was thus a perfectly good spelling for it, suitable alike in *aren't I?* and *aren't you?* This spelling has been grievously misinterpreted by those, including most Americans, who pronounce *r* before a consonant. Of *ain't,* which has fallen victim to a series of schoolteachers' crusades, Dean Alford testified that in his day "It ain't certain" and "I ain't going" were "very frequently used, even by highly educated persons."[79] Frederick James Furnivall (1825–1910), an early editor of the *OED* and founder of the Chaucer Society and the Early English Text Society, is said to have used the form *ain't* habitually.[80] Though he may not have used it himself, the late Monsignor Ronald Arbuthnott Knox, Oxford don and Roman Catholic chaplain at that university, puts it into the mouth of the expensively educated hero of his detective stories.[81]

Contractions of auxiliary verbs occur somewhat earlier, though they must be about equally old. *It's* as a written form is from the seventeenth century, and ultimately drove out *'tis,* in which the pronoun rather than the verb is reduced. There is no current contraction of *it was* to replace older *'twas,* and, in the light of the practical disappearance of the subjunctive, it is not surprising that there is none for *it were.*

---

[77] "An Example of Prescriptive Linguistic Change: 'Don't' to 'Doesn't,'" *English Journal,* 36 (1947), 372.

[78] "How Fast Is Standard English Changing?" *American Speech,* 31 (1956), 90.

[79] *The Queen's English,* 8th ed. (London, 1889), first published 1863, cited in Jespersen, *Modern English Grammar,* V, 434. Henry Alford (1810–71), dean of Canterbury from 1857 until his death, was a Cambridge scholar who edited the New Testament in Greek (a monumental work in four volumes) and was first editor of the *Contemporary Review.* He was the author of a number of well-known hymns.

[80] Jespersen, *Modern English Grammar,* V, 434.

[81] "Yes, but it ain't such plain sailing as all that," *Still Dead* (London, 1952; first published 1934), p. 38, and again on p. 41: ". . . as you justly observe, that ain't much." With a similar disregard for *petit-bourgeois* grammar, the heir to the "Laird of Dorn" in the same novel uses *he don't,* as does the young, charming, and cultured wife of Miles Bredon in these spare-time literary productions of an English gentleman and priest.

It'll has replaced older *'twill; will* similarly is contracted after other pronouns and, in speech, after other words as well. In older times *'ll,* usually written *le* (as in *Ile, youle*), occurred only after vowels and was hence not syllabic, as it must be after consonants. *Would* is contracted as early as the late sixteenth century as *'ld,* later becoming *'d,* which came in the eighteenth century to be used for *had* also. The contraction of *have* written *'ve* likewise seems to have occurred first in the eighteenth century. After a consonant this contraction is identical in pronunciation with unstressed *of,*[82] hence such uneducated spellings as *would of* and *should of,* frequently written in dialogue to indicate that the speaker is unschooled; the point seems to be "This is the way the speaker would write *have* if he had occasion to do so." As indicative of pronunciation the spelling is pointless.[83]

EXPANDED VERB FORMS

Expanded verb forms consisting of a form of *to be* plus a present participle ("I am working"), sometimes called "progressive," occur occasionally in Old English, but do not begin to be used with any frequency until the fifteenth century; even so, they remain relatively infrequent until the seventeenth century. The expanded passive form, the so-called progressive passive, as in "He is being punished," does not occur until the latter part of the eighteenth century. Samuel Pepys, for instance, writes ". . . I met a dead corps of the plague, in the narrow ally just bringing down a little pair of stairs"[84] (August 15, 1665), where we should use the newer construction "being brought down"; and ". . . to Hales's the painter, thinking to have found Harris sitting there for his picture, which is drawing for me" (April 26, 1668), where we should use "is being drawn."

Do is frequently used as a verbal auxiliary in the early Modern period, though it is used somewhat differently from the way it is used

---

[82] Compare "The wood of the tree" and "He would've done it."

[83] This to some extent characterizing device of using distorted spellings which indicate pronunciations not differing from standard ones is called *eye dialect,* in contrast to spellings which actually tell us something of a speaker's regional provenience (like *minny* for *many*) or his cultural status (like *intregal* for *integral* or *nucular* for *nuclear*). Compare also *doncha, cuppa, lotta,* and *wuz,* which indicate the way everyone, educated and uneducated alike, is likely in unselfconscious speech to pronounce *don't you, cup of, lot of,* and unstressed *was.* The old favorites *wimmen* and *likker* merely indicate that the speaker is an ignoramus, a comic, or both. The actual misspellings used are phonetically better representations of the pronunciations of words which all people pronounce alike than are conventional *women* and *liquor.*

[84] "Pair of stairs," "pair of beads" (as in Chaucer's description of the Prioress), and a few other phrases in which *pair* denotes more than two are still current in folk speech.

today, for example "I do wonder, his insolence can brooke to be commanded" (*Coriolanus* I.i.265–266) and "The Serpent that did sting thy Fathers life/ Now weares his Crowne" (*Hamlet* I.v.39–40), where current English would not use it at all. Compare with these instances "A Nun of winters sisterhood kisses not more religiouslie" (*As You Like It* III.iv.17), where we should say *does not kiss*. In such negative expressions, however, the *do*-forms current today were in use in early Modern English side by side with such locutions, now archaic, as *forbid them not* and *I doubt not*.

OTHER VERBAL CONSTRUCTIONS

Impersonal and reflexive constructions are fairly frequent in early Modern English, as they were to a much greater extent in Middle English. Shakespeare has, for instance, "it dislikes [displeases] me," "methinks," "it yearns [grieves] me," "I complain me," "how dost thou feel thyself now?" "I doubt me," "I repent me," and "give me leave to retire myself." Some verbs now intransitive were used transitively, as in "despair [of] thy charm," "give me leave to speak [of] him," and "Smile you [at] my speeches." Verbs of motion frequently have a form of *be* instead of *have* in their expanded perfect forms: "is risen," "are entered in the Roman territories," "were safe arrived."[85]

SHALL AND WILL

In Old and Middle English times *shall* (OE present indicative *sceal,* second person *scealt*) and *will* (OE *wille, wilt*) were sometimes used to express simple futurity, though as a rule they implied respectively obligation and volition. The present prescribed use of these words, the bane of many an American and North British schoolchild, stems ultimately from the seventeenth century, the "rules" having first been drawn up by John Wallis, an eminent professor of geometry at Oxford who wrote in Latin a grammar of the English language.[86] His successors were also men of considerable prestige who have elaborated upon Wallis's prescription and have been to a great extent successful in imposing his idea of a desirable distinction in the use of *shall* and *will* upon a large part of the English-speaking world. Despite the crusade in behalf of the distinction, the rules for making it are not very clear.

Charles Carpenter Fries has pointed out that in the many vigorous discussions concerning *shall* and *will* in recent times, one cannot help

---

[85] Practically all these examples have been cited by Franz, *Shakespeare-Grammatik,* pp. 503–507.

[86] *Grammatica Linguae Anglicanae,* 1653.

"being impressed by the wide diversity of the points of view and the definite conflict of the opinions and conclusions thus brought together."[87] The fact seems to be that, when Fries began to investigate the use of *shall* and *will,* there were "after more than a century of discussion . . . no accepted views of what the actual usage of these two words is, of the meaning and trend of the development of that usage, and of the causes that gave rise to it." In any case, the conventional rules, differing as they do from "authority" to "authority," describe neither pre-eighteenth-century usage nor usage as it was at the time when the eighteenth-century grammars which gave them currency were written. Fries's own investigations indicate that there has been no great change in the use of *shall* and *will* with the first person from the middle of the sixteenth century to the present, *will* greatly predominating; with the second person the situation existing in the sixteenth century, when *shall* predominated, has been completely reversed; similarly with the third person, *will* has come to predominate over *shall.*[88]

THE IMPORTANCE OF PREPOSITIONS

With the Middle English loss of all distinctive inflectional endings in the noun save for the *-s* of the genitive and the plural, prepositions acquired an importance greater than they had ever had in Old English. There was in fact need for more of them in the early Modern period to indicate grammatical relationships that had been indicated by the inflectional endings of earlier times. *During,* apparently first used by Chaucer *ca.* 1385,[89] *concerning, except* (*Piers Plowman, ca.* 1377), and *because,* itself originally a prepositional phrase (*be* being an unstressed form of *by*) all appear first either in the fourteenth or the fifteenth century. Changes in the uses of certain prepositions are illustrated by the practice of Shakespeare, who in this respect as in most others is representative of the early Modern period: "And what delight shall she have to looke on [at] the divell?" (*Othello* II.i.229); "He came of [on] an errand to mee" (*Merry Wives* I.iv.80); "But thou wilt be aveng'd on [for] my misdeeds" (*Richard III* I.iv.70); "'Twas from

---

[87] *American English Grammar* (New York, 1940), p. 151. See also his "The Periphrastic Future with *Shall* and *Will* in Modern English," *PMLA,* 40 (1925), 963–1024, and "The Expression of the Future," *Language,* 3 (1927), 87–95.

[88] *American English Grammar,* pp. 154–55, preceding a discussion of *shall* and *will* in questions, where there has been no shift in usage comparable to that which occurred with the second and third persons in independent-declaritive statements: here *shall* predominated throughout the Modern English period with the first person, *will* with the second and third persons.

[89] According to the *OED,* it is derived from the Latin ablative absolute construction, as in *vita durante* 'while life lasts (or lasted).'

[against] the Cannon [canon]" (*Coriolanus* III.i.90); ". . . we are such stuffe/As dreames are made on [of]" (*Tempest* IV.i.156–57); "Then speake the truth by [of] her" (*Two Gentlemen* II.iv.151); ". . . that our armies joyn not in [on] a hot day" (*2 Henry IV* I.ii.234).

Even in Old English times *on* was sometimes reduced in compound words like *abūtan* (now *about*), a variant of *on būtan* 'on the outside of.' The contracted form was usually written *a*,[90] for instance *aboard, afield, abed, asleep*, and, with verbal nouns in *-ing*, *a-hunting, a-bleeding, a-praying*,[91] and the like. The *a* of "twice a day" and other such expressions[92] has the same origin. *In* was sometimes contracted to *i'*, as in Shakespeare's "i' the head," "i' God's name," and so forth. This particular contraction was much later fondly affected by Robert Browning, who doubtless thought it singularly archaic, for example "would not sink i' the scale" and "This rage was right i' the main" ("Rabbi Ben Ezra," lines 42 and 100).

THE EARLY DICTIONARIES

The first dictionaries appear in the period under discussion. If one had to set up a line of development for these, one would start with the Old and Middle English interlinear glosses in Latin and French texts, then proceed through the bilingual vocabularies produced by schoolmasters and designed for those studying foreign languages, specifically Latin, French, Italian, and Spanish. But the first work designed expressly for listing and defining English words for English-speaking people was the schoolmaster Robert Cawdrey's *A Table Alphabeticall* (1604) ("conteyning and teaching the true writing, and understanding of hard usuall English wordes, borrowed from the Hebrew, Greeke, Latine, or French. &c.") Other dictionaries followed in the same tradition of explicating "hard words," for instance that of J[ohn] B[ullokar], Doctor of Physick, *An English Expositour* (1616), Henry Cockeram's *English Dictionarie* (1623), Thomas Blount's *Glossographia* (1656), Edward Phillips's *New World of English Words* (1658), Edward Cocker's *English Dictionary* (1704),[93] and Nathan Bailey's *Universal*

[90] Less frequently *o'*, which might also be a contraction of *of* (as in *o'clock*).

[91] As in Hamlet's *a-praying*, cited on p. 201.

[92] For a Middle English example, note Chaucer's "ful ofte a day" in the *Knight's Tale*, line 1356.

[93] Cocker died in 1676, but was a person of such importance — not as a lexicographer, but as a teacher of handwriting and arithmetic — that "according to Cocker" became a proverbial phrase, like "according to Hoyle," though Cocker may have had little or nothing to do with the works ascribed to him: only copybooks by him were published during his lifetime, though the eighteenth century regarded him most highly as a mathematician.

Etymological English Dictionary (1721), with a second volume that was really a supplement appearing in 1727. In 1730, Bailey (and others) produced the *Dictionarium Britannicum,* with about 48,000 items (more words than Johnson included), which provided the basis for Johnson's great work. In 1755 appeared both the Scott-Bailey *New Universal Etymological English Dictionary*[94] and Samuel Johnson's two-volume *Dictionary.* For the history of dictionaries up to Johnson's, the best study is that of DeWitt T. Starnes and Gertrude E. Noyes, *The English Dictionary from Cawdrey to Johnson, 1604–1755* (Chapel Hill, N.C., 1946), on which the foregoing summary is based. For Johnson's dictionary, the best study is that of James Sledd and Gwin J. Kolb, *Dr. Johnson's Dictionary: Essays in the Biography of a Book* (Chicago, 1955).

The publication of Johnson's *Dictionary* was certainly the most important linguistic event of the eighteenth century, not to say the entire period under discussion, for it to a large extent "fixed" English spelling and it established a standard for the use of words. Johnson did indeed attempt to exercise a directive function. It would have been strange had he not done so at that time, and we cannot censure him very harshly in view of the fact that most people in our own day expect dictionaries to do so. For most people it is apparently not sufficient even today for the lexicographer simply to record and define the words of the language, and to indicate the way in which they are pronounced by those who use them; he is also supposed to have some God-given power of determining which are "good" words and which are "bad" ones, and to know how they "ought" to be pronounced. But Johnson had the good sense usually to recognize the prior claims of usage over the arbitrary appeals to logic, analogy, Latin grammar, and sheer prejudice so often made by his contemporaries, even if he did at times settle matters by appeals to his own taste, which was fortunately good taste. Though the son of a bookseller in Lichfield, Johnson had a tremendous admiration for those who were his social betters: he was a Tory both by denomination and conviction. Hence, along with his typical eighteenth-century desire to "fix" the language went a great deal of respect for upper-class usage. He can thus be said truly to have consolidated a standard of usage which was not altogether of his own making. His use of illustrative quotations, literally by the thousands, was an innovation; but his own definitions show the most discriminating judgment. The

---

[94] Joseph Nicol Scott, designated as editor (for Bailey died in 1742), was a very big wig at the time. He apparently did little beyond lending the prestige of his name to a volume designed by the booksellers to compete with Johnson's.

quirky definitions, like that for oats — "a grain which in England is generally given to horses, but in Scotland supports the people" — are well-known, so well-known that some people must have got the utterly false impression that there are very many others not so well-known. It is in a way unfortunate that these have been "played up" for their sheer amusement value as much as they have been, for they are actually few in number.

EIGHTEENTH-CENTURY ATTITUDES TOWARD LANGUAGE

The puristic attitude which was predominant in eighteenth-century England was simply the manifestation of an attitude toward language that has been current, as it continues to be in our own day, in all times and in all places. Doubtless there are and have been purists — persons who believe in some sort of absolute and unwavering standard of what they deem to be "correctness" — in even the most undeveloped societies known to man, for purism is a matter of temperament rather than of culture.

Though very dear to American purists — by no means all of them schoolteachers — the "rules" supposed to govern English usage originated not in America, but in the mother country. Those who formulated them were about as ill-informed and as inconsistent as their slightly later American counterparts. Present-day notions of "correctness" are to a large extent based on the notion, prominent in the eighteenth century, that language is of divine origin and hence was perfect in its beginnings but is constantly in danger of corruption and decay unless it is diligently kept in line by wise men who are able to get themselves accepted as authorities, for instance men who write dictionaries and grammars. Latin was regarded as having retained much of its original "perfection." No one seems to have been very much aware that it was the culmination of a long development and had undergone many changes of the sort which were deplored in English. Hence when English grammars came to be written, they were based on Latin grammar, even down to the terminology.

The most influential of the eighteenth-century prescriptive gr? ;marians was Robert Lowth (1710–87), theologian, Hebraist, pro'_ssor of poetry at Oxford from 1741 to 1753, later bishop of Oxford, then of London, and dean of the Chapel Royal, who four years before his death was offered the archbishopric of Canterbury, which he turned down. In the Preface to his *Short Introduction to English Grammar* (1762), Lowth agreed with Dean Swift's charge, made in 1712 in his *Proposal for Correcting, Improving, and Ascertaining* [that is, fixing, making certain] *the English Tongue*,[95] that "our language is extremely imperfect," "that it offends against every part of grammar," and that most of the "best authors of our age" commit "many gross improprieties, which . . . ought to be discarded." Lowth was able to find many of the most egregious blunders in the works of our most eminent writers; his footnotes are filled with them. It apparently never occurred to any of his contemporaries to doubt that so famous and successful a man had inside information about an ideal state of the English language. Perhaps they thought he got it straight from a linguistic Jahveh.

In any case, Lowth set out in all earnestness in the midst of a busy life to do something constructive about the deplorable English written by the masters of English literature. Like most men of his time, he believed in universal grammar—a concept that has been reviewed in our own day by the transformational-generative grammarians (above, p. 26). Consequently he believed that English was "easily reducible to a System of rules." Among many other things, he gave wide currency, probably because of his high position in the Establishment, to those rules for *shall* and *will* as they had been cooked up by John Wallis in his *Grammatica Linguae Anglicanae*.

In actual practice, as we have seen, the "rules," which everybody continues to think are inflexibly right, have been honored more in the breach than in the observance. This is to say that most people, only dimly comprehending their complexities, seem to think that they should observe them more conscientiously than they have actually done. But because of the deference which has been paid to these supposedly omniscient law-givers of the eighteenth century—even though the names of many may have been long forgotten[96]—it is probably safe to say that the most important eighteenth-century development in the English language—as the publication of Johnson's *Dictionary* may be said to have been the most important single event—has been its conscious regulation by those who were not really qualified for the job but who managed to acquire authority as linguistic mahatmas.

Yet it must not be thought that the men who promulgated the rules were contemptible. Bishop Lowth was certainly not and, heaven knows, Dean Swift, one of the glories of English literature, was certainly not. Nor was Joseph Priestley, who, in addition to writing *The*

---

[95] In this, a letter written to the Lord Treasurer, Swift urges the formation of an academy to regulate usage.

[96] Lowth was of course not the only one. For a discussion of the contributions of George Campbell, Joseph Priestley, the Philadelphia-born Lindley Murray, and others, see Sterling A. Leonard, *The Doctrine of Correctness in English Usage, 1700–1800* (Madison, Wis., 1929).

Rudiments of English Grammar (1761), was the discoverer of oxygen, a prominent nonconformist preacher, and a voluminous writer on subjects theological, scientific, political, and philosophical. Like George Campbell, who in his *Philosophy of Rhetoric* (1776) went so far as to call language "purely a species of fashion," Priestley recognized the superior force of usage; he also shared Campbell's belief that there was need for some form of control of language other than that furnished by custom. Being children of the Age of Reason, both would have had recourse to the principle of analogy to settle questions of divided usage, though admitting that it was not always possible to do so. All these men were indeed rather typical of their time, and it was in most respects a good time in which they lived; and they were honest men according to their lights, which in other respects were quite bright indeed. We cannot blame them very harshly for not having information which was not available in their day. And, despite the tremendous advances of linguistic science in the nineteenth and twentieth centuries, attitudes toward language have actually changed very little since Bishop Lowth and Lindley Murray were laying down the law. Their precepts were largely based on what they supposed to be logical and reasonable, for they believed that the laws of language were rooted in the natural order, and this was of course "reasonable." To cite an example, they outlawed, as far as the educated are concerned, the emphatic and still very viable double negative construction on the grounds stated by Lowth that "two Negatives in English destroy one another, or are equivalent to an Affirmative"—in English, that is to say, just as in mathematics, though the analogy implicit in the appeal to logic was quite false. Many very reasonable men before them had spoken and written sentences with two or even more negatives: Chaucer has four in ". . . Forwhy to tellen nas [ne was] nat his entente/ To nevere no man, for whom that he so ferde,"[97] and it certainly never occurred to him that these would cancel out and thus reverse his meaning.

Modern linguistic studies have made very little headway in convincing those who have not made a special study of language that language is a living thing, the possession and the servant of man rather than an ideal toward which we should all fecklessly and hopelessly aspire. Many schoolroom grammars and handbooks of English usage widely used today perpetuate the tradition of Bishop Lowth's *Short Introduction to English Grammar*. Indeed, the very word *grammar* means to

---

[97] *Troilus and Criseyde* I.738–39. There are also four in his description of the Knight in the General Prologue to the *Canterbury Tales:* "He nevere yet no vileynye ne sayde/ In al his lyf unto no maner wight" (lines 70–71).

many highly literate people not the study of language, but merely so simple a thing as making the "proper" choice between *shall* and *will, between* and *among, different from* and *different than, who* and *whom* and the avoidance of terminal prepositions, of *ain't,* and of *it's me.* In the following chapter we shall examine in more detail the later developments of this comparatively recent tradition in England and America.

IX

Recent British and American English

"The American language," despite the distin-
guished precedent of H. L. Mencken's use of the term,[1] is as much of a
misnomer for the English spoken by Americans as would be "the Mexican language" for the Spanish spoken by Mexicans. Though educated
Continental Europeans must certainly be aware of this fact, they are by
and large so overconscious of the differences between it and the way
they as schoolchildren were taught to speak English that one suspects
they regard these differences as somewhat comparable to those which
make Icelandic and Norwegian, or Swedish and Danish, separate
languages.[2]

One suspects indeed that Europeans, including the English themselves,[3] really prefer to think that the speech of Americans is a corrupt
and degraded variety of current Standard British English, which has

---

[1] He was not the first to use it. Noah Webster and others had already done so.

[2] According to an Associated Press item in the Jacksonville *Florida Times-Union*
(October 4, 1957, p. 2), the shortwave broadcast service from West Germany "beams
German language courses to the outside world in French, Spanish, Portuguese, English
and Amerikanisch."

[3] Whoever wrote the blurb on the front flap of the dust cover of the London (1954)
edition of my *Words and Ways of American English* (first pub. New York, 1952) is an
honorable exception. He or she was quite aware of the necessity of informing the pro-
spective English reader, whose name was certainly not Legion, that "the American-
English [*sic*] language . . . has, *after all,* as much claim to the name English as our own
tongue" (italics added). The point of view of Isabel Quigly, the cinema critic for the
Spectator, is much more representative: she writes in a review of *Ben Hur* that the
director had "a cunning idea" regarding the speech of the players, for "Romans speak
English, the rest speak American" (December 18, 1959, p. 909).

presumably remained unchanged, hence "pure," at least since the early years of the seventeenth century, at which time what must have been an inferior brand of Englishmen, unable for one reason or another to make their way in their own land, began to settle the North American continent.

Such notions of course fly in the face of the facts, but they have the virtue, dubious though it is, of fortifying prejudice. It would be just as well if Americans tried to understand this prejudice.

Painful though it is to have to admit it, the course of early American history was not particularly glorious from a cultivated European point of view—despite a spurious sort of admiration for our Old Hickories, our Honest Abes, and our Davy Crocketts. And it is perhaps a bit unreasonable for Americans to expect to be loved—and being loved seems very important to us, to the tune of many millions of dollars—for those aspects of what we are pleased to call the "American way of life" which we take such pride in and insist upon publicizing. There is in fact nothing universally lovable about the dour, hard-working, plain-living, hymn-shouting men and women who supposedly made up the bulk of our early population. Those who must struggle hard all their lives against an uncharitable environment in order merely to survive can have little concern with the blessings of civilization. What is remarkable is that many of these, and their descendants as well, came to prefer the harshness of the simple rustic life to the richness of their European heritage, thus making some sort of virtue—the "American dream" it is sometimes called—out of necessity. It is equally unreasonable to expect others not to perceive the shoddiness and the hypocrisy behind the homespun idealism, the wooden-nutmeg know-how, and the apparently irrelevant concept of "gracious living" upon which we have come to pride ourselves. Yet we must not here oversimplify, for it is certainly true that the European man in the street has avidly adopted many of the least prepossessing features of what Americans are pleased to call their civilization—evangelism, cowboys in form-fitting pants, and cola drinks, for instance.

The fact remains, however, that most cultured Europeans have no great admiration for American speech, regardless of how much they may be awed by the softer aspects of our present "way of life" as this is represented to them by those who write our advertising copy—certainly not great enough for them to have any desire to use it or to substitute it for the British Standard now taught in their schools. British speech continues to have far more prestige, and few Continental Europeans—not to mention the English themselves—have any desire or inclination to speak any other variety. As a German candidate for the doctorate in English once remarked to me in an unusual outburst of frankness, American speech simply lacked *Eleganz*. And when I thought of the speech of some of my countrymen prominent in public life at that time and contrasted them with their English counterparts, I suspect that I got the point of the remark all too well.

For it is true that most American speech does lack this most undemocratic quality of elegance, which still means much to the cultured European. In a classless society — even in one which is only theoretically so — elegance cannot thrive. The very word becomes a smear. In the countries of the Old World, on the other hand, the standard of speech has to a large extent risen out of the usage of a privileged leisure caste, though it has certainly been molded to some extent by men of learning. Americans are proud to suppose that they have no such caste in their society, and that the most horny-handed bumpkin, if he follows the proper precepts, may sit in the seats of the mighty.

Elegance cannot be instilled or inculcated. Even if it were agreed to be a desirable characteristic of speech, who would provide the standards? It is, indeed, a rather casual quality, as such phrases as "well-bred ease" and "careless elegance" would indicate. It is a product of *dolce far niente,* for which democracy has no use. It is quite a different thing from the tortured precision, the "good grammar," which has been our national ideal and which is theoretically within the reach of every man. It must be understood that we are here neither recommending elegance in American speech nor condemning its absence; we are concerned only with a state of things. We are not even attempting to define so intangible a quality, which is as much a matter of an attitude toward life as of articulation and intonation. It is a matter of style, moreover, not an inherent quality of any language or any form of any language: there were certainly tasteless, sloppy speakers of Classical Latin, and one would be very much surprised not to find at least a few elegant speakers of Hottentot. We are here merely pointing out that British English has greater prestige than American English and suggesting a reason for it.

The English have, at least since the latter part of the eighteenth century, cooked up a form of speech based on that of London that kept the darker-skinned "natives" of the Empire in check for a good many years. Even now, when it seems to be losing some of its former political efficacy, it retains its prestige value: English-educated Africans speak it, often with considerable elegance, and doubtless regard American English with a certain scorn, much as Europeans are likely to do. That the British themselves are not uniformly sympathetic toward it is indicated by the following, from the *Spectator:* "Effusive thanks also to

the BBC for the documentary film *Our School,* an absolute cracker
with a dozen moments of sheer delight, including one in which a
(Scottish) English teacher blew his top over his (English) pupils' obsession with 'posh accents' " (May 4, 1962, p. 587). The writer
(Clifford Hanley) goes on to say: "This has always baffled me too. If
we get a United States of Europe, will solemn English codgers have to
teach themselves to identify the Right Type of Frenchman by the way
he pronounces *merde*?" The cream of the jest is that even Americans,
though they may be slightly put off by "posh accents" at times, are impressed by them and hence likely to suppose that Standard British
English is somehow "better" English than what they speak. From a
purely linguistic point of view, this is of course nonsense; but it is a
safe bet that it will long survive any conceivable loss of British influence in world affairs.

Nevertheless, according to three expert British commentators,
although "Standard English as used by the English, spoken with the
accent of RP [that is, "Received Pronunciation," a usual term for the
pronunciation of those who have been educated in the public schools
(in the English sense of public schools) and of many who have not been
to such schools], remains the automatic and obvious choice for most
Europeans and perhaps for the remaining colonies. . . . But even here
we must note the increasing acceptance of American varieties of English, at any rate for adult learners." They go on to say in their following
paragraph that "American forms of English are now accepted, either
side by side with British forms or even in preference to them, in a number of new countries where before 1945 'English' meant 'British
English.' "[4]

THE CONSERVATISM
OF AMERICAN ENGLISH

The fact remains that no form of any language is impugnable by
any objective standards; only those who speak may be so impugned.
Since language undergoes no changes as a result of crossing an ocean,
the first English-speaking colonists in America continued to speak precisely as they had done in England. But people isolated from their
mother country tend always to be conservative, linguistically as well
as in other ways, and the English spoken in America at the present

[4] M. A. K. Halliday, Angus McIntosh, and Peter D. Strevens, *The Linguistic Sciences and Language Teaching* (Bloomington, Ind., 1964), p. 293.

day has retained a good many characteristics of earlier British English which do not survive in present British English, much as Icelandic has retained characteristics of older Scandinavian which have been lost in the other Scandinavian languages.

Thus to regard American English as inferior to British English is to impugn earlier Standard British English as well, for there was doubtless little difference at the time of the Revolution. There is a strong likelihood, for instance, that George III and Lord Cornwallis pronounced *ask, after, path, glass, dance,* and the like exactly the same as did George Washington and John Hancock—that is, as the over-whelming majority of Americans do to this day. It was similar with the treatment of postvocalic *r,* whose loss under certain circumstances did not occur in the speech of the London area until about the time of the Revolution.

Other supposed characteristics of American English are also to be found in pre-Revolutionary British English, and there is very good reason indeed for the conclusion of the eminent Swedish Anglicist Eilert Ekwall that from the time of the Revolution on, "American pronunciation has been on the whole independent of British; the result has been that American pronunciation has not come to share the development undergone later by Standard British, but remains at about the stage it had reached by the time of the Revolution."[5] Ekwall's concern is exclusively with pronunciation, but the principle implied holds good also for many lexical items, some morphological characteristics, and probably to some degree for intonation as well.

American retention of *gotten* is an example of conservatism, though it was of course not consciously preserved. This form, the usual past participle of *get* in older British English, survives in present Standard British English mainly in the phrase "ill-gotten gains"; but it is very much alive in American English, being the usual past participial form of the verb except in the senses 'to have' and 'to be obliged to.'[6] Simi-larly, American English has kept *fall* for the season[7] and *deck* for a pack of cards (though American English also uses *pack*); and it has retained certain phonological characteristics of earlier British English to be discussed later in some detail.

---

[5] *American and British Pronunciation* (Upsala, 1946), pp. 32–33.

[6] For instance, "He hasn't got the nerve to do it" and "He has got to do it." There is, however, a tendency in American English to prefer *got* under all circumstances in writing, which may be due to teaching.

[7] In extant English writing, the earliest use of *autumn* is that of Geoffrey Chaucer (*OED*).

VOCABULARY CHANGES
IN AMERICAN ENGLISH

It works both ways, however; for American English has lost certain features – mostly vocabulary items – which have survived in British English, for example *waistcoat* (the name for a garment which Americans call a *vest,* a word which in England usually means 'undershirt'), *fortnight,* a useful term completely lost to American English, and a number of topographical terms which Americans had no need for – words like *fen, wold, spinney, copse, dell, heath,* and *moor.* Americans, on the other hand, desperately needed terms to designate topographical features different from any known in the Old World. To remedy the deficiency, they used new compounds of English words like *backwoods, watergap,* and *underbrush;* they adapted English words to new uses, like *creek,* in British English 'a small arm of the sea,' which in American English may mean 'any small stream,' and they adopted foreign words like *prairie* (ultimately derived from Fr. *pré* 'field'), *canyon* (Sp. *cañón* 'tube'), and *mesa* (likewise Spanish).

It was similar with the naming of flora and fauna strange to the colonists. When they saw a bird that somewhat resembled the English robin, they simply called it a robin, though it was not the same bird at all. When they saw an animal that was totally unlike anything that they had ever seen before, they might call it by its Indian name, if they could find out what this was, for example *raccoon* and *woodchuck.* It was similar with the names of plants: *catalpa* and its variant *catawba* are of Muskhogean origin; *Johnny-jump-up* was inspired by a crude kind of fancy; *sweet potato* might have originated just as well in England as in America except for the fact that this particular variety of potato did not exist in England.

THE ORIGINS OF AMERICAN ENGLISH

American English is, as we have said, essentially a development of seventeenth-century British English. Except in vocabulary, there are probably few significant characteristics of American English which are not traceable to British English. There are also some American English characteristics which were doubtless dialectal British English in the seventeenth century, for there were certainly dialect speakers among the earliest settlers, though they would seem to have had little influence. A literary standard had arisen in London long before, as we have seen, which had greatly influenced the various regional types of common speech of England – the speech of the majority of those Englishmen to settle permanently in the New World, for these were not illiterate bumpkins but ambitious and industrious members of the upper-lower and lower-middle classes, with a sprinkling of educated men—clergymen, lawyers, and even a few younger sons of the aristocracy. It is likely that there was a cultured nucleus in all of the early American communities. Such facts as these explain why American English resembles present Standard British English more closely than it resembles any other British type of speech.

In American English there are three main regional types—Northern, Midland, and Southern—with a good many different blendings of these as one travels westward (see below, p. 271). There are also a number of subtypes on the Atlantic Coast, such as the speech of the New York and Boston areas in the North and the Charleston-Savannah area in the South. All types of American English have grown out of the regional modifications of the British Standard—with some coloring from the British dialects—as it existed in the seventeenth century, when it was much less rigid than it is today.

Boston failed to maintain its early preeminence as the hub of American culture, such as it was. Otherwise, America might well have had a geographical and ultimately a caste standard based upon the speech of Boston. As things have turned out, an American may use with complete social impunity any of the types of speech to which we have referred or practically any modifications thereof. So long as it is obvious from his bearing and from what he talks about that he is an educated man (in the American sense of the term), his speech will pass muster, that is, be socially acceptable in any part of the country despite occasional references to a "harsh Midwestern *r*" and a "lazy Southern drawl."

It should be stressed at this point that compared with British English, French, Italian, Spanish, German, and other European languages, American speech is quite homogeneous: there are no types of American English that are not readily understood—though regional prejudice may cause an occasional eyebrow to lift—in all parts of the country, with the exception of Gullah, spoken by about 100,000 blacks who live along the coastal region of South Carolina and Georgia, and who have lived there in cultural isolation for many generations.[8] There are other types of speech used by blacks in which, in addition to the factor of intonation, the absence of consonant sounds present in most types of English has created homophones un-

[8] The best treatment of Gullah—actually the only authoritative one—is that of Lorenzo Dow Turner, *Africanisms in the Gullah Dialect* (Chicago, 1949).

familiar to many, like *mask/mass, mind/mine,* and *during/doing.*[9] There is, it must be stressed, nothing distinctively "black" about such consonant loss. Southern and South Midland whites who are far from being "disadvantaged" evince it in their informal (that is, unselfconscious) speech, and sometimes in their formal speech as well. The fact is that many features commonly thought of as characteristic of "black English" occur in the speech of whites on a variety of social and stylistic levels. Still other homophones strange to the Northern city dweller depend upon a treatment of vowels which is by no means confined to black English but which he, unless he happens to be a dialectologist, may attribute to it—for instance, the [ɪ] for his [ɛ] before a nasal, so that *pen* and *pin, meant* and *mint,* and *tent* and *tint* fall together. There is of course nothing un-English or for that matter un-Germanic about this treatment of [ɛ] before nasals (as in the universal pronunciation of the word *English* itself). It occurs in the speech of all social levels, black or white, in the inland South, but apparently it annoys those unaccustomed to it. (I can think of only a single instance in which the inland Southern homophony of *pen* and *pin* baffled me, and the bafflement was only momentary; but for many people momentary bafflement causes annoyance, and annoyance causes willing suspension of any desire to tolerate, let alone understand.) There are also many idioms, presumably confined to black speech—like "came up" for "grew up"—that take some getting used to, if only because they are strange to Northerners of whatever pigmentation.

Leaving aside such more or less exceptional types, which are of especial importance in view of the contemporary American urban situation, the mere use of a regional type of American English is no hindrance to either social acceptance or economic advancement. A Texas oil magnate speaks in one way;[10] a Back Bay Bostonian in a slightly different way; and a landed Virginian in a yet slightly different way. But as long as they all speak like "educated" men, they all speak "good" American English. The Chicagoan is just as proud of pronouncing his *r*'s—provided that he ever gives a thought to the matter—

[9] These examples are taken from Beryl Loftman Bailey, "Some Aspects of the Impact of Linguistics on Language Teaching in Disadvantaged Communities," in *On the Dialects of Children,* ed. A. L. Davis, a publication of the Commission on the English Language of the National Council of Teachers of English (Champaign, Ill., 1968), pp. 15–24.

[10] He may even pronounce *pen* and *pin* identically if it is apparent that he is really a magnate.

as the Charlestonian is of losing them. Neither practice is ordinarily regarded as either superior or inferior; they are merely regarded as somewhat different, and the difference is not always noticed, though it usually is.

A CASE OF MUTUAL INTOLERANCE

Since about 1930 Americans have become increasingly tolerant of British English. Even its most posh variety doubtless offends them less — if indeed it offends them at all — than it does those younger-generation Englishmen who lack it by tradition and have been unable, or in some cases unwilling, to acquire it — the so-called angry young men. For one thing, Americans have become quite familiar with it by way of the radio, the talking films, and television; most now take it pretty much in their stride. But it has not always been so. When Matthew Arnold visited the United States in 1884, he was anything but beloved in Chicago, where it was reported that "he has harsh features, supercilious manners, parts his hair down the middle, wears a single eye-glass and ill-fitting clothes."[11] It is nevertheless likely that even these un-American shortcomings would have been forgiven him had it not been that, according to his American agent, his accent was baffling to his audiences. Other derogatory comments indicate little more than that Arnold spoke the "toniest" type of British English current in his day; he obviously had a posh accent. It should be added that New York seems to have received him a little more graciously. It is impossible to conceive of such comments being made about the speech of Queen Elizabeth II, Sir Winston Churchill, or Lord Avon (best known to Americans as Anthony Eden), not to mention the actor-knights Alec Guinness, John Gielgud, Laurence Olivier, Michael Redgrave, and Ralph Richardson,[12] all of whom have, or have had, a considerable following in the United States.

The English are considerably less tolerant of American speech, which, as has been pointed out, they tend to regard as a corruption of their own rather than as an independent development of earlier British English. When I inadvertently used the term *British English* in conversation with a neighbor in London, she asked in her most fluting upper-class tones (but, in justice it must be said, with some

---

[11] Cited in Allan Nevins, *American Social History* (New York, 1923), p. 501.

[12] Perhaps it is unfair to bring actors into the picture, for American actors of an older school were in fact trained to use a type of artificial stage speech which, though by no means British, had a number of British characteristics.

good-natured amusement), "Why, whatever other kind is there?" The answer, which was easy enough, was not given on this occasion, for feelings about language run so high as to make it a subject unsuitable for social intercourse: there are, of course, in addition to American English, Australian English, Canadian English, South African English, Indian English, among others—all as legitimately English as that form of the language which happens to be spoken in the mother country. Appearing on an American television program, the late Gilbert Harding grumpily pretended misunderstanding a reference to his "English accent." "How could I have an English accent?" he asked; "I *am* English."

Professor Sir Denis Brogan of the University of Cambridge is equally at home in Cambridge, Massachusetts, where he was once a graduate student. He has spent many long periods of time in the United States, has seen more of the country than most Americans ever see, and has written widely on American affairs. In his attitude toward American English, he is, however, a fairly typical cultivated Britisher (one cannot accurately say Englishman, since he is a Scot and rather proud of the fact). Of American speech and writing he has this to say: "Most Americans are very bad linguists [apparently meaning nothing more than that they don't speak British English]. . . . I find when I get to America that it takes some days before I can understand what is being said by people over the telephone and they can understand what I myself am saying." He goes on, "I do not believe it is possible to write a page of English prose (either in the American or the English sense of the words) without betraying on which side of the Atlantic you were brought up."[13] (One would certainly like to see this tested.) In another place Sir Denis tells of his having suggested that "some of the letters and documents that [Bertrand] Lord Russell was supposed to have written must have been tampered with by another hand since he could not possibly have written the horrible American English in which they were couched."[14]

It would be easy to multiply examples from a variety of British commentators. Sir Denis Brogan's *dicta* have been chosen only because he is so well known in America, where he has a host of friends and acquaintances. Recent American slurs on Standard British English, other than those implied in TV comedy caricatures, are quite

---

[13] *Spectator* (London), Jan. 31, 1970, p. 143.
[14] *Spectator*, February 14, 1970, p. 208. Perhaps this was not entirely clairvoyance on Sir Denis' part, since it was well known that Lord Russell in his last years employed an American secretary-companion who is said to have had considerable influence over him.

difficult to come by — perhaps because Americans are, like those "natives," a little overawed by British speech.

AMERICAN INFILTRATION
OF THE BRITISH WORD STOCK

Because in the course of recent history Americans have acquired greater commercial, technical, and perhaps even political prestige than any other English-speaking group, it is perhaps not unnatural that the English and others should take a somewhat high-handed attitude toward American speech. The fact is that the English have done so at least since 1735, when one Francis Moore, describing for English readers the then infant city of Savannah, said, "It stands upon the flat of a Hill; the Bank of the River (which they in barbarous English call a *bluff*) is steep. . . ."[15] Mencken treats the subject of British attitudes toward American speech fully and with characteristic zest in the first chapter of his *American Language* and also in the first supplement to that wonderful work (pp. 1–100).

But the truth is that, as far as vocabulary is concerned — and most people, when they think of language, think of it in terms of vocabulary items — British English has been rather constantly infiltrated by American usage, as the frequent objurgations of English writers indicate. Cyril Ray is particularly vocal on the subject in the "Postscript" which he used to contribute to the London *Spectator;* he makes many disapproving references to "the continuing Americanisation [*sic*] of English usage since the war,"[16] deploring the fact that in a short story by Ian Fleming a "very senior" British official tells the secret-service hero that there will be an "FO pouch" for him. Says Ray, "I have never met *any* Foreign Office official, senior or otherwise, who referred to anything but 'the bag,' which has been English diplomatic usage for generations: 'pouch' is pure American." As a result of the present prominence of America in international affairs, American *top secret* is now being used in England for what used to be merely *secret; high-ranking officer* (an "ugly and otiose American neologism . . . unknown here until the last war . . ."[17]) for what used to be *general, flag, field,*

---

[15] Cited in H. L. Mencken, *The American Language,* 4th ed. (New York, 1936), p. 3, from Moore's *Voyage to Georgia, Begun in the Year 1735* (London, 1744), p. 24.

[16] February 9, 1962, p. 190. It has, as we shall see, been continuing for a much longer time than this.

[17] July 8, 1960, p. 78. It is interesting to note that *The New English Bible: New Testament,* published jointly by the Oxford University Press and the Cambridge University Press (1961) has "high-ranking officers" for the Authorized Version's "chief captains" in Acts xxv.23. One English reviewer has suggested "top brass" as an alternative.

240 Recent British and American English

or, more loosely, *senior officer;* and *career diplomat* (along with the "horrid hybrid" *career diplomatist*) for what used to be *professional diplomatist.* Mr. Ray's own profession of journalism is by no means immune from American corruption, for he alludes to a reference in "a very stylish English newspaper" to the *wire services,* meaning 'news agencies.' Two years earlier, Mr. Ray, whom one can grow very fond of as a writer, asked plaintively why, in some of the new Lyons eating establishments, "we have to call chips — an English form of food — by the longer and inaccurate American name of French Fried?" remarking quite understandably that "it seems stupid to me."[18] Elsewhere this same custodian of the purity of British English deplores the fact that even the august *Times* has taken to calling adolescents *teenagers,* right on its "leader-page" (*Americanice* "editorial page"),[19] and to referring to the American Civil War *centennial,*[20] though "it seems a pity to substitute yet another unnecessary Americanism for the perfectly good English word, 'centenary.' "

Cyril Ray must be having a bad time of it these days if he eats in restaurants of moderate price and elegance in London's West End, where he may find "corn on the cob" (rather than "maize on the ear") on the menu. Without being taken for an American, he may safely ask to have his steak rare if that is the way he likes it, for this use of *rare,* formerly (and wrongly) regarded as an Americanism,[21] has become quite usual for *underdone.*[22] If he prefers a *fillet,* however, he must still

---

[18] March 4, 1960, p. 334. In British English, as can be inferred, *chips* are (or were) what in American English are called *French fries.* What Americans call *potato chips* are *crisps* in England. Thus the famous English "fish and chips" is the same as American "fish and French-fried potatoes." But the distinction in terminology seems to be breaking down, and it is not Americans who are changing over, distressing as the fact may seem to all good Englishmen. The same is true of the old shibboleth distinction between American *can* and British *tin* (both as noun and verb), according to a half-page advertisement in the "posh Sundays" (conservative Sunday newspapers): "So that when your husband returns from his hard day at the office, he finds you waiting like the dedicated wife you are, cool, calm and competent, all ready to open him a can of beer, while a canned steak pie browns in the oven, and canned fruit and cream wait on the sideboard," of which the writer for the *Spectator* comments, "Must have been quite a strong-minded copywriter to resist writing, 'So that when your husband returns canned from his hard day at the office, he finds you waiting like the dedicated wife you are, cool, competent, and canned. . . .' " (December 8, 1961, p. 882).

[19] June 9, 1961, p. 859.

[20] March 17, 1961, p. 382.

[21] "Current in many English dialects . . . and used by English writers in the first half of the 19th c." (*OED*).

[22] The menus of the Lyons chain of restaurants have *underdone,* but the waiters say *rare* to English and American patrons alike.

stress the first syllable of the word and pronounce the final *t*. But, if he still wishes to test the depravity to which his countrymen have sunk, he may ask to have his preprandial drink served "on the rocks" and be immediately understood, though he may get only a single undersized and partially melted "rock." Unless the barman is accustomed to catering to (or catering for, as the English usually say) Americans, he had better not push his luck too far by asking for a *martini,* as in American usage, but for a *martini cocktail;*[23] otherwise he is likely to get nothing but a tot of Martini vermouth.[24] His bitterness over the Americanization of his mother tongue will be only slightly abated when he hears American businessmen using "his" toast "Cheers" instead of "Here's mud in your eye." But, happily, if he wants cream in his after-dinner coffee, he may still—nay, must still—ask for "white coffee."

Americanisms—words and phrases peculiar to the United States, though they may have occurred in earlier English—have indeed made their way into British English in large numbers. The transfer began quite a while ago, long before talking films, radio, and television were ever thought of, let alone World War II, which Mr. Ray considers a main corrupting influence. Sir William Craigie, the eminent editor of the *Dictionary of American English on Historical Principles,*[25] pointed out in 1927[26] that although "for some two centuries . . . the passage of new words or senses across the Atlantic was regularly westwards . . . with the nineteenth century . . . the contrary current begins to set in, bearing with it many a piece of drift-wood to the shores of Britain, there to be picked up and incorporated in the structure of the language," citing such Americanisms in British English as *backwoods,*

[23] It should be some comfort to English linguistic tories that in pubs the martini cocktail is not generally understood. The nearest one can come to getting something vaguely similar is by asking for "gin and French," which is half gin, half dry vermouth. Those who like their mixed drinks sweet ask for "gin and it," the *it* being a clipped form of *Italian.*

[24] *Vermouth* is always pronounced with initial stress in British English, whereas the usual American pronunciation stresses the final syllable. However, in a review of an American musical comedy playing in London, Penelope Houston comments that "connoisseurs of Americanisation may note that it's now possible to rhyme youth and vermouth without stirring a flicker of surprise in an English audience" (*Spectator,* April 7, 1967, p. 401).

[25] This four-volume work was published by the University of Chicago Press (1938–44). For some years unobtainable, it has recently been reissued. It should not be confused with M. M. Mathews' *Dictionary of Americanisms,* published by the same press in 1951.

[26] *The Study of American English,* S. P. E. Tract No. 27 (Oxford), p. 208.

beeline,[27] *blizzard, prairie, swamp, bunkum, caucus, belittle,*[28] *cloud-burst,* and a good many others which have long been completely acclimatized.

Recent years have seen the introduction of many other American-isms into British usage: *cafeteria, electrocute* (both in reference to the distinctively American mode of capital punishment and in the ex-tended sense 'to kill accidentally by electric shock'[29]), *highbrow* (and more recently *egghead*), *lowbrow, cocktail, filling station, fan* 'sports devotee,' and, of course, the ubiquitous *O.K.,* to cite only a handful. American *radio* has superseded British *wireless,* and *TV* has about crowded out the somewhat nurseryish *telly. O.K.* is, if anything, of more frequent occurrence nowadays in England than in the land of its birth, and may occur in quite formal situations such as, for example, on many legal documents to indicate the correctness of details therein.[30] These and other Americanisms have slithered into British English in the most unobtrusive way, so that their American origin is hardly regarded at all save by a few crusted older-generation speakers: since they are used by Englishmen, they are "English," and that is all there is to it. Woe be to the American who tries to convince a run-of-the-mill Englishman to the contrary!

---

[27] Professor Sir Herbert Butterfield, Master of Peterhouse, Cambridge, in an address of welcome to the Jubilee Congress (August, 1968) of the Modern Humanities Re-search Association spoke quite unself-consciously of "scholars making a beeline for Cambridge." He was not "talking down" to the American contingent.

[28] Apparently first used by Thomas Jefferson in his *Notes on the State of Virginia,* written in 1782 and published in 1787, this word brought forth shocked cries from Eng-lish commentators. See Mencken, *American Language,* p. 14, for an amusing example from the *European Magazine and London Review,* ending with the plaintive appeal, "O spare, we beseech you, our mother-tongue."

[29] Thus Edward Marjoribanks in *For the Defence* (New York, 1937), p. 458, first published in London in 1929: "A young collier went ratting with some friends; and, although their dogs passed unscathed through the 'live' wires, when the boy came against it he was electrocuted." The *OED* Supplement of 1933 has British citations with this meaning from 1909 and 1913. Mathews' *Dictionary of Americanisms* does not include this later meaning, in which the connotation of purely accidental death has been added and which may indeed have originated in England, where the word, coined in America to designate a newfangled, ultrascientific way of putting criminals to death, may have lacked some of the immediate horror that it connoted in the United States.

[30] Since the publication of my summarizing account of this most widespread of all Americanisms (in *Words and Ways of American English* [New York, 1952], pp. 158–65), Ralph T. Eubanks in "The Basic Derivation of 'O.K.,' " published in *American Speech* for October 1960 (35, 188–92), cited an occurrence about a month earlier (February 24, 1840) than that hitherto thought to be the earliest, which had been cited by Allen Walker Read from the New York *New Era* of March 23, 1840, in "The

Brian Foster, an Englishman who is anything but run-of-the-mill, has written knowingly of the "enormous impact of American idiom on the standard British usage," though "by a strange paradox few people, even among specialists, are conscious of the extent of its influence, and some . . . virtually deny its existence."[31] Foster cites as firmly established in Standard British English *show business, to build up* (by advertising), *of all time* 'ever,'[32] *star* 'popular performer' (also as verb), *disk jockey* (the more usual British spelling has *disc*), *natural* 'brilliant but untrained performer,'[33] *to put* (something) *over, to get* (something) *across, stooge, double talk,* and *ballyhoo* — all originally from the usage of the world of entertainment, enormously important in modern America, and all, with the possible exception of *of all time,* more or less nonliterary. But the following Americanisms, while they may be offensive in varying degrees to those who, whatever their national ties, have a rarefied and sophisticated sense of style, appear in the formal utterances of V.I.P.'s,[34] as well as in the writings of some quite

---

Evidence on 'O.K.,' " *Saturday Review of Literature,* July 19, 1941, pp. 3–4, 10–11. Read found another occurrence of the word, appearing four days later in the same paper as the slogan of a political club made up of supporters of Martin Van Buren and explained as being from the initials of *Old Kinderhook,* the birthplace of Van Buren. Read is now able to cite a number of earlier occurrences, including Eubanks' find and those set forth by Woodford A. Heflin in " 'O.K.' and Its Incorrect Etymology," *American Speech,* 37 (1962), 243–48. The new material is presented by Read in a series of highly readable and meticulously documented articles in the same journal, as follows: "The First Stage in the History of 'O.K.,' " 38 (1963), 5–27; "The Second Stage in the History of 'O.K.,' " 38 (1963), 83–102; "Could Andrew Jackson Spell?" 38 (1963), 188–95; "The Folklore of 'O.K.,' " 39 (1964), 5–27; "Later Stages in the History of 'O.K.,' " 39 (1964), 83–101; and "Successive Revisions in the Explanation of 'O.K.,' " 39 (1964), 243–67. The word is an acronym of *oll korrect.*

[31] "Recent American Influence on Standard English," *Anglia,* 73 (1956), 328–57. Compare this view with the less realistic one of Eric Partridge, who writes that "the Americanization has, in the main, affected only cant, slang, colloquialisms and catchphrases; indeed, the Americanization of Standard English has been amazingly slight" in *British and American English Since 1900,* in collaboration with John W. Clark (New York, 1951), p. 180.

[32] As in "the greatest film of all time," at first regarded as a "typical example of the American love of grandiloquence."

[33] Later 'something very suitable,' as in the British advertisement for face powder sold in three varieties, cited by Foster: "One of these is a natural for you" (p. 332).

[34] Another Americanism which is now a part of the British vocabulary. It has been used in all seriousness on the floor of the House of Commons, and without any need to define it. Foster, who was puzzled by the term when he first heard it in 1946, reports its use by a clergyman in a B.B.C. religious broadcast as follows: "They [children] are V.I.P.'s to Him" (p. 334). Certainly American taste has never sunk lower.

respectable writers on both sides of the Atlantic:[35] *way of life,*[36] *alibi* 'excuse,' *breakdown* 'analysis,' *blurb* ("now used quite solemnly as an indispensable item in the jargon of literary critics and booklovers"), *quit* (previously regarded as archaic except in a few stock phrases), *maybe,*[37] *crash* 'collide,' *allergy* 'aversion' (and *allergic* 'averse from'), *angle* 'viewpoint,' *sales resistance, to slip up, to stand up to, to go back on, know-how. Fortnight* 'two consecutive weeks,' a stock Briticism to most Americans who know the word at all (as all those who read books do), "seems to appear rarely in the speech of the younger generation," who increasingly are using American *two weeks.*[38] Very valuable also is Foster's book *The Changing English Language* (New York, 1968), particularly for present purposes his first chapter, "The Impact of America." Incidentally, Foster is no professor of English or of linguistics, but is Senior Lecturer in the History of the French Language at Southampton University. Strange as it may seem in the light of his expert knowledge of American English, he has never, up to the time of this writing, visited the United States.

As has been pointed out, words and usages are frequently borrowed from American English quite unconsciously. Where this is not so, the fact that they are of transatlantic provenience is soon forgotten. H. W. Horwill testifies that a good many Americanisms which he

[35] The words to be cited, except for *blurb,* are obviously not of American origin; it is the meanings and in some instances the combinations which have developed in the United States.

[36] In the sentiment-charged phrase "American way of life," denoting freedom, equality, gracious living, super-salesmanship, baseball, and heaven only knows what else, *way of life* shortly petered out to mean nothing more than 'life,' 'living,' or even 'regimen' (as in the statement of a Federal judge in Miami, Florida, in sentencing a vegetarian who evaded the draft on the grounds that his vegetarianism was a religion: "There was . . . evidence that his . . . vegetarianism was regarded by other vegetarians as a philosophy and dietary way of life, rather than a religion" [International News Service item, April 11, 1958]). *Way of life* is listed by the *OED* as occurring in the writings of the Countess of Pomfret in 1741, with subsequent citations from 1777 and 1898. The American use would seem to be of independent origin, though one cannot be absolutely sure. In any case, *British way of life* appears to Foster to stem from the American usage; he first became aware of it in the 1950's.

[37] *Maybe,* labeled archaic and dialectal by the *OED,* has always been common in Northern England, but, as Foster says, "It can hardly be doubted that the revival of this word [in Standard, or Southern, British English] is due to the American example" (p. 336).

[38] Complete loss of this word will blur a distinction previously possible to make in British English, though American English has got on very well without it—that between, to cite Foster's example, "Last year I spent a fortnight at London" and "Last year I spent two weeks (i.e. two separate weeks) at London" (p. 336). (Note British *at* where American English would invariably use *in.*)

wrote down during a residence in the United States between 1900 and 1905 would not have been recognized by him as of American origin in 1935 if he had trusted to his memory alone, for "usages that to-day are peculiar to America are to-morrow adopted by English writers and speakers, frequently without the least suspicion of their transatlantic origin."[39] He cites *cut* in the sense 'reduction' as an Americanism that became widely used in England during the financial crisis of 1931. By 1935 there was no consciousness of its American provenience; it was thoroughly naturalized, though for a time it was written within quotation marks (which Horwill calls by the frequent British variant, *inverted commas*).

The convenient use of noun as verb in *to contact,* meaning 'to see, call, meet, or in any other way to get in touch with,' seems to have originated in America,[40] though it might just as well have done so in England, since there is nothing un-English about such a conversion: scores of other nouns have undergone the same functional shift, as we shall see (pp. 310–11). The fact is that this particular conversion had occurred earlier in British English, but the new verb was confined to technical writing: the *OED* cites "The spark and the gunpowder contacted" from 1834, but calls such use rare. We may thus regard the occurrence in 1929 as to all intents and purposes a new American creation. The verb began to catch on in England around the mid-1940's, though many persons there as well as in the United States objected to it vociferously.[41] No one gets much disturbed over it nowadays. The mandarin attitude of Nigel Strangeways, the aristocratic detective hero of Nicholas Blake (a novel-writing pseudonym of the poet C. Day Lewis), though still faintly persistent on both sides of the Atlantic, is no longer widespread; the speaker is a police inspector who has not had the advantages of Nigel's expensive education: "I've not contacted him yet, sir" (Nigel shuddered inwardly at the word), "but I'm expecting a report. . . ."[42] Crane Brinton, in a review of H. C. Allen's

[39] *A Dictionary of Modern American Usage* (Oxford, 1935), Preface.

[40] Both the *Dictionary of Americanisms* and the *OED* Supplement cite the same American occurrence as the earliest in this sense. Mathews in the former work labels the word as slang, though there is nothing particularly slangy about its use in any of his citations.

[41] To Sir Alan Herbert it was a "loathsome" word, according to Sir Ernest Gowers, *Plain Words: Their ABC* (New York, 1954), p. 53. Ivor Brown, as cited by Gowers, was considerably more tolerant in his judgment that "there is no word which covers approach by telephone, letter and speech, and *contact* is self-explanatory and concise."

[42] *There's Trouble Brewing* (London, 1956), p. 75. The novel was first published some years previous to 1956, when shuddering at the word was more indicative of one's fine-drawn sense of style than it has now come to be.

Great Britain and the United States,[43] cites "Lord North despatched an emissary to contact Benjamin Franklin," written "apparently without a qualm" by the author, an Oxford don. The reviewer concludes that this one word *contact* "carries high symbolic importance. . . . Mr. Mencken was wrong—there will be no American language, for the simple reason that, apart from deviations in ephemeral slang and regional dialects . . . the Queen's English and the President's English grow together.[44]

Actually, though, they were never so far apart as it has been pleasing to American patriotism (which has sometimes manifested itself unpleasingly in a prideful "mucker pose")[45] and British insularity (which has sometimes equally unpleasingly manifested itself in an overweening assumption of superiority) to pretend. "How quaint of the British to call a muffler a silencer!"[46] "How boorish of the Americans to call an egg-whisk an egg beater!" The most striking of such presumably

[43] New York *Herald-Tribune Book Review,* May 1, 1955, p. 3.

[44] It is probably just as well not to take the phrase "President's English" too literally. The President of the United States in 1955 was Dwight David Eisenhower, the most graceless speaker to occupy the White House since Warren Gamaliel Harding. But our concern is primarily with language, not with style, and the then President's English, like that of all native speakers, was certainly basically the same as the Queen's, even to the common, if unorthodox, preference for invariable *I* after *and,* as follows: *Queen* (on returning from her tour of the colonies in 1954): "It is a wonderful moment for my husband and I after nearly six months away to be met and escorted by ships of the Home Fleet" (*Illustrated London News,* May 22, 1954, p. 824). *President* (on returning from Denver, where he suffered an illness): "I am deeply honored that so many of you should have come down to welcome Mrs. Eisenhower and I back to Washington" (*Time,* November 21, 1955, p. 17).

[45] For instance the following, from a review in the *Saturday Review* (May 12, 1962, p. 28): "It [the book] is sometimes too much the author's own, larded with Briticisms as obscure for most of us over here as those uproariously blank jokes in jolly old *Punch* . . . ." One cannot but suspect a trace of inverted snobbery in such a linguistically chauvinistic attitude. If the *Saturday Review* is read in England, the pretense of American provincialism quoted here has done American prestige no good. The English are of course guilty of exactly the same sort of prideful provincialism, as has been indicated by a good many previous citations. As for "jolly old *Punch,*" many Americans—even some who have borne arms in defense of their country—find it quite amusing; the English by and large like the *New Yorker* in a grudging sort of way, and some of them even prefer it to jolly old *Punch.*

[46] The American motoring term is apparently that used by the Swedes when they have occasion to use English. "London Day by Day," a column in the London *Daily Telegraph,* has referred to "the astonishing statement" in a summary of Swedish traffic regulations, printed in English, that "driving without a muffler is forbidden" (September 1, 1956, p. 6). The columnist has chosen to misunderstand *muffler* as a heavy scarf for the neck, a meaning which is also widely current in American English.

amusing differences, however, will not be very important, for they almost inevitably occur on a rather superficial level—in the specialized vocabularies of travel, sports, schools, government, and various trades.

NATIONAL DIFFERENCES IN WORD CHOICE

There are many lists of British and American equivalents,[47] but these must not be taken too seriously. On the American side of the page will be found many locutions perfectly well understood, many of them in use, in Britain[48]—for instance, *automobile,* represented as the American equivalent of *car* or *motor car,* is practically a formal word in America, the ordinary term being the supposedly British *car;* whereas the supposedly American word occurs in the names of two English motoring organizations, the Royal Automobile Club and the Automobile Association. And on the British side will be found many locutions perfectly well known and frequently used in America—for instance *postman* (as in James M. Cain's very American novel *The Postman Always Rings Twice*) and *railway* (as in *Railway Express* and the *Southern Railway*), though it is certain that *mailman* (or *letter carrier*) and *railroad* do occur more frequently in American speech. Similarly, one usually finds *baggage* as the American equivalent of British *luggage,* though *luggage* has come to be very commonly used in American English, perhaps because of its frequent occurrence in "prestige" advertising. Mencken lists *drawers* (men's) as the American equivalent of British *pants.* It is doubtful that this was true even in 1936 (the date of the fourth edition of Mencken's great work), but one can say with confidence that *drawers* has now become archaic for the nether undergarments of either sex—imagine asking to buy a pair in either a men's furnishings or a lingerie shop! The usual American term is *shorts,* which may also designate outer garments; *pants* for the undergarment has become increasingly feminine, though usually in the diminutive form *panties.* British *knickers,* also originally masculine in reference, likewise became feminine, though the term is now quite old-fashioned for ladies' underpants.

[47] For instance, those prepared by Mencken in *The American Language,* pp. 233–37 and in *Supplement I* (New York, 1945), pp. 457–87.

[48] Randolph Quirk, an English observer of American speech, put the matter well in the *New York Times Weekly Review,* International Edition (December 2, 1956, p. 7): "The long and imposing lists of so-called distinctively British and American words and usages are 75 per cent misleading; it turns out either that both the words so neatly separated are used in one or the other country, or that both are found in both countries but are used in slightly different contexts or in different proportions." There is usually no question of influence from one side or the other.

Other hardy perennials of such lists include[49] *mad–angry,* though Americans use *angry* in formal contexts, often under the impression that *mad* as a synonym is "incorrect," and though many speakers of British English use *mad* in the sense 'angry'[50] as it was frequently used in older English, for example in the Authorized (King James) Version of 1611, Acts xxvi.11: ". . . being exceedingly mad against them, I persecuted them even unto strange cities";[51] *sick–ill,* though *sick,* supposed to mean only 'nauseated' in England, is frequently used in the older sense, that which is supposed to be American, in British English: in "A Book for Christmas," a short article printed in *Books of the Month,* an organ of the British Book Centre, Sir Ralph Richardson writes, "I was often sick as a child, and so often lonely, and I remember when I was in hospital a kindly visitor giving me a book. . . ." (November–December 1952, p. 15), in which only the phrase "in hospital" instead of American "in the hospital" indicates the writer's Englishness,[52] except possibly for *visitor* where many Americans, under the impression that the "subject of a gerund" *must* be possessive, would have written *visitor's; mailbox–pillar-box,* though the English use *letter box*[53] for any receptacle for mailing (that is, posting)[54] letters in, other than the actual low pillar with a slit for putting the letters through, which is called a pillar-box because that is precisely what it is; *package–parcel,* though the supposedly British word is perfectly well known to all Americans, who have for a long time sent packages by parcel post (not "package mail"); *stairway–staircase,* though Mary Roberts Rinehart's best seller of the early years of the present century was entitled *The Circular Staircase,* though *stairs* is the usual term in both countries, and though *stairway* is recorded in

[49] The supposedly American term is given first in these pairs.

[50] Note the following striking use of the synonyms in consecutive sentences, from *Speak Justly of the Dead* (Garden City, N.Y., 1953), an English detective story by the highly literate E. C. R. Lorac (a pseudonym of Edith Caroline Rivett, born 1894): "It's no use getting angry, Venner. I know you feel mad with me. . . ." (p. 115). The speaker is a doctor.

[51] The *New English Bible: New Testament* has ". . . my fury rose to such a pitch that I extended my persecution to foreign cities," which does not improve what did not need improvement in the first place.

[52] The new specialized senses 'insane' ("He's a sick man" may mean, depending upon context, "He's a paranoiac, a schizophrenic, or a victim of some other form of 'mental illness' ") and 'morbid, macabre' (as in *sick jokes*) may ultimately come to prevail in all types of English.

[53] Erroneously cited by Mencken in *The American Language* (p. 235) as the American equivalent of *pillar-box.*

[54] The use of *mail* and *post* as verbs is a legitimate difference.

British dictionaries with no notation that it is confined to American usage; and *window shade–blind,* though *blind(s)* is the usual term throughout a thickly populated section of the eastern United States,[55] including the city of Baltimore. There are many other equally weak sisters; these have been chosen almost at random.

This is not to say that there are not many genuine instances of differences in word choice, though most of these would not cause any serious confusion on either side. Testimony is, however, frequently contradictory, because where choice of words is concerned, many other factors — age, social station, and esthetic predilections, to name three — are bound to obtrude themselves. For instance, regarding *filling station,* of American origin but not really synonymous in American English with *garage,* having taken over only part of its semantic content, a then mid-fiftyish titled gentleman wrote me in 1954 as follows: "I deny that this is really used in British English. A few pretentious garages (one in fifty perhaps) may call themselves filling stations, but no motoring Englishman, of whatever age or class, would dream of saying 'Our petrol is low, let's stop at the next filling station.' " Within a few days of my receiving this communication, I heard from a lecturer in an English university, then in his early thirties, as follows: "*Filling station* is obviously ousting *garage* in the specific sense [which is precisely what had already happened in American English], being less ambiguous. An amusing incident here illustrates the importance of 'youth and age' in these matters. A German lady asked the English word for *Tankstelle.* The professor of German replied 'garage' and simultaneously his assistant said 'filling station.' "

No American has ever said *pram* (or the full form *perambulator,* either) for *baby carriage,*[56] *compère* for *M.C.* (or *emcee,* less frequently *master of ceremonies*) in a theatrical or television entertainment, *mental*[57] for *insane, petrol* for *gas(oline), lorry* for *truck, coach* for *bus* (interurban),[58] *treacle* for *molasses, first floor* (or *storey* [*sic*]) for *second floor* (or *story*),[59] or called an *intermission* (between divi-

---

[55] Hans Kurath, *A Word Geography of the Eastern United States* (Ann Arbor, Mich., 1949), pp. 28, 52.

[56] Regional variants are *baby buggy, baby coach,* and the somewhat rare *baby cab.* For their geographical distribution, see Kurath, p. 77 and Fig. 147.

[57] An unaristocratic (non-U) euphemism, according to the Hon. Nancy Mitford, "The English Aristocracy," reprinted from *Encounter* in her *Noblesse Oblige* (London, 1956), pp. 39–61.

[58] The English bus carries passengers from one part of a city or town to another, but motor transportation from, say, London to Brighton is by coach.

[59] In England, as on the Continent, the *first floor* is immediately above the *ground floor* (also used in American English, but as a synonym of *first floor*).

sions of an entertainment) an *interval*,[60] an *orchestra seat* a *seat in the stalls*, a *trillion* a *billion*,[61] or referred to a *raise* (in salary) as a *rise*. But most sophisticated Americans are quite aware of the British equivalents. Unfortunately, America is sometimes judged abroad by small-town magnificos, neatly barbered and bedizened with diamond-encrusted lodge emblems, who make the "grand tour" and who complain loudly of the plumbing and ask in loud tones, when their sightseeing buses pass Trafalgar Square, "Just who in heck was this Nelson?" They are doubtless the salt of the earth, but they are, it is hoped, hardly representative of American culture.

Certainly the average, garden-variety American is not to be unduly censured as if he were some sort of crude hillbilly for not immediately understanding such a sentence as "On one stand, a white-coated mechanic was leaning into the bonnet [American *hood*] of a saloon [American *sedan*] carefully dusting the engine with a piece of rag,"[62] so long as his lack of comprehension has in it no tinge of superiority or of the arrogance that frequently goes hand in hand with provincial ignorance. Nor is there any great sin in not knowing that "an old geyser [if pronounced *geezer*, as it often is] in the bath" refers, not to an eccentric old gentleman in a tub, but to an antiquated gas water-heater in the bathroom. Many educated Americans are, however, quite aware that an English *clerk* is a bookkeeper, unless he happens to be a barrister's (lawyer's) clerk or a parish clerk, whose duties are far less well known. When they read that Charles Lamb was a clerk in the East India House, they do not picture the gentle Elia selling Hindus over the counter of a retail establishment. For many Americans have sufficient acquaintance with, and interest in, the Mother Country to be aware of differences in usage so widely publicized as these, and are likely to feel that their intelligence and sophistication are being traduced when English acquaintances painstakingly and, it is regrettable to have to report, frequently condescendingly "explain" these terms.

The American may equip himself with what are sometimes advertised in his own country as *braces* to hold up the trousers without cuffs (in British English, without turn-ups) that he wears with his tailcoat (if he owns one) or his dinner jacket (not all Americans call it a *tuxedo*,

---

[60] The London Palladium has an intermission instead of an interval.

[61] In British English a billion is a million millions, whereas in American English it is what the British call a *milliard* — a mere thousand millions.

[62] *Spectator*, October 9, 1959, p. 496.

though most probably do),[63] but he never calls them anything but *suspenders*.[64] *Suspenders,* the word for what were earlier intended for the suspension of trousers in British English, came to be used (the first *OED* citation is from 1895) for the device for holding up women's stockings or men's socks.[65] The word is now almost exclusively feminine in British English, as *garters* is in American English, inasmuch as nowadays men's socks frequently have "built-in" elastic tops and hence do not require suspension, though even somewhat before such refinements were available many American men had stopped wearing garters and many Englishmen had stopped wearing sock-suspenders.

There remain valid differences in the use of words other than those which have been mentioned, but, as far as everyday speech is concerned, these are not really very numerous or very significant. The well-known *pitcher–jug* difference continues to hold: what Americans call a pitcher (for cream, milk, cider, and the like) is a jug in England, where a pitcher is something considerably larger, some such receptacle as Rebecca carried to the well; to Americans a jug is ordinarily somewhat larger, with a narrow neck which need have no spout or lip. An English *spool* is for wire, typewriter ribbons, or film; cotton or other thread comes on a *reel.* What Americans call a *trailer* is in England a *caravan,* which may also mean a covered wagon as for gypsies or a house on wheels; a *prep(aratory) school* is a *public school;* a *public school* is a *council school; installment buying* is *hire purchase; chain stores* are usually *multiple stores; sneakers* 'canvas rubber-soled shoes' are *plimsolls* (sometimes capitalized); and, in addition to being a police-

---

[63] In some men's clothing establishments in the United States, only the white coat worn in the summer is called a dinner jacket. The traditional black (or less traditional "midnight blue") garment is the *tuxedo* in such commercial usage. *Tuxedo* is also occasionally used in England to refer to the white coat, thus reversing the American usage.

[64] Rural *galluses* (that is, *gallowses*) is probably obsolete in American English by now, except, according to the Linguistic Atlas records, in rural Tennessee. Brian Foster informs me (in a private communication) that it is still the colloquial term in the county of Durham in northern England, from which region (or from Scotland) it was doubtless brought to America in the beginning — assuming that it was not a general English term at the time. *Suspenders* in the present American sense occurred in nineteenth-century British English (*OED* citations from 1830 and 1841). The fact that the earliest citation of the word is American does not necessarily, or in this case even probably, indicate an American origin; the word is not one which would be expected to occur frequently in the printed works quoted in the *OED.* The earliest citation for *braces* in the same sense is from 1816.

[65] The English limit the meaning of *garter* to the elastic band worn around the leg.

man, a *copper* is a large vat made of copper for boiling clothes in a laundry.[66]

SYNTACTICAL
AND MORPHOLOGICAL DIFFERENCES

Syntactical and morphological differences are quite as trivial as those in word choice. In regard to collective nouns, for instance, the English are much more likely than Americans to use a plural verb form, like "the public are. . . ." I have collected from a single page of the London *Evening News* (July 16, 1956, p. 10) these three specimens of nouns which, because they lack the plural *-s,* would require singular verbs in American usage: "England Await Chance to Mop Up" (a headline, the reference being to England's cricket team, then engaged in a test match with Australia); "Wimbledon Are Fancied for Double" (also a headline); and "Middlesex were in a strong position when they continued their innings at Gloucester. . . ." This usage is not confined to sports pages: witness "The village are livid";[67] "The U.S. Government are believed to favour . . .";[68] "Eton College break up for the summer holidays to-day . . .";[69] "The Savoy [Hotel] have them [that is, lavatories that work straight off the mains]—but the Savoy have their own water supply . . .";[70] and, from a single page of the *Spectator,* "The Government regard . . ." and "Scotland Yard are. . . ."[71]

The following locutions, all from contemporary British writings, would have been phrased as indicated within square brackets by American writers; yet as they stand they would not puzzle an American reader in the least:

Thus Mgr. [Monsignor] Knox is faced by a word, which, if translated by its English equivalent, will give a meaning possibly very different to [from,

[66] The last two terms, along with *Jeyes Fluid* 'an antiseptic and odor-killing liquid' were the only words explained in footnotes by the American editor of Ludovic Kennedy's *Ten Rillington Place* (New York, 1961). The English editor of a work by the present writer needed help with only two words—*campus,* which he thought meant 'playing field,' and *bleachers,* the meaning of which he had no notion of.
[67] "Strix," "Posh Lingo," in *Noblesse Oblige,* ed. Nancy Mitford, p. 59.
[68] London *Star,* September 7, 1956, p. 1.
[69] London *Daily Telegraph and Morning Post,* August 1, 1956, p. 6.
[70] *Spectator,* February 26, 1960, p. 301.
[71] January 27, 1961, p. 103.

than] its sense. (Letter to the editor of the *Spectator* by Quentin de la Bedoyere)[72]

When he found his body on Hampstead Heath, the only handkerchief was a clean one which had certainly not got [certainly did not have] any eucalyptus on it. (Michael Underwood)

She'd got [she had] plenty of reason . . . for supposing that she would count in her father's will. (Ronald Knox)

He hadn't got [didn't have] any relatives . . . except a sister . . . in Canada or somewhere. (Macdonald Hastings)

You don't think . . . that he did confide in any person? – Unlikely. I think he would have done [would have] if Galbraith alone had been involved. (Edmund Crispin [Bruce Montgomery])

I'll tell it you [to you]. (Philip MacDonald)

Are you quite sure you could not give it me [give it to me, give me it] yourself? (Josephine Bell)

In the morning I was woken [waked] up at eight by a housemaid. (Nancy Mitford)

Although the constructions cited are not to be heard in American English, their bracketed equivalents are, or have been in the case of *different than,* common as British variants.

There are certain differences other than *different to* in the choice of prepositions: for instance, the English householder lives *in* a street, the American *on* it; the Englishman gets *in* or *out of* a train when he has occasion to travel, the American *on* or *off* it; still other variations are equally inconsequential. A recent proliferation of redundant prepositions in English may well have received its impetus from American usage, but the tendency is by no means new or native to America. In 1957 Henry George Strauss, first Baron Conesford of Chelsea, attacked American "pretentious illiteracy" in a speech before the Authors' Club of London on these grounds; but the use of prepositions which seem redundant to Lord Conesford really began a long time ago. It is, in fact, a tendency inherent in the Germanic languages, but it does

---

[72] *Different to* is well established in British English, "found in writers of all ages" (*OED*). Even H. W. Fowler approves it (*A Dictionary of Modern English Usage* [Oxford, 1926]), calling the objection to it one of a number of "mere pedantries." He goes on to say, however, that *different from,* far from being wrong, is more usual; "but it is only so owing to the dead set made against *different to* by mistaken critics." (See C. S. Forester's "dead set," below, p. 257, n. 81.) *Different than* has been the target of as much abuse in this country as *different to* in England, but it is equally well established in American usage, as it also was in older British usage; the *OED* cites examples of it from Goldsmith and Cardinal Newman and states that it is also found in Coleridge, Southey, De Quincey, Carlyle, and Thackeray, among others.

seem frequently to have gone haywire in American English, where it is not enough merely to visit someone—one must visit *with* them; or to refer to something, when one can refer *back* to it; or to head, say, a committee, when one can head it *up;* or even to continue, when it sounds so much more impressive to continue *on.* Nowadays we plan *on* doing something or other rather than merely plan doing it; we cancel *out,* when just canceling would be sufficient;[73] and we face *up to* something when it might have been in earlier times considered sufficient merely to face it.

NATIONAL DIFFERENCES IN IDIOM

In general it may be said that, perhaps because America lacks a "caste" dialect comparable to Standard British English, American attitudes toward language lay somewhat greater stress on a more easily acquired "correctness" based on such matters as the supposed "proper" position of *only,* which the English tend to put where it comes more or less naturally to all of us, before the verb.[74] Likewise it becomes a matter of tremendous importance—practically a moral obligation—invariably to use *whom* where what is thought of as good grammar seems

[73] This usage, if it is really of American provenience, has made the Atlantic crossing with the greatest of ease. Note the reference by Gilbert Phelps in the *Spectator* (January 13, 1961, p. 50) to "diffidence that goes a long way to cancelling out the worst of one's first impressions."

[74] As in A. S. C. Ross's "U and Non-U: An Essay in Sociological Linguistics," in *Noblesse Oblige,* ed. Nancy Mitford: "At all events I have only come across one case of it" (p. 33, n. 2). Ross is Professor of English Language in the University of Birmingham (England). It must not be supposed, however, that *only*-snoopers, to use Sir Ernest Gowers's apt term for those who engage in "the sport of pillorying [what they conceive to be] misplaced *onlys*" (*Plain Words,* p. 185), are all American. Gowers was, it must be remembered, writing primarily for English readers. But the English are far more tolerant toward the "illogical" but idiomatic preverbal position of the adverb. Even the frequently crotchety H. W. Fowler was of the very sensible opinion that "when perspicuity is not in danger, it is needless to submit to an inconvenient restriction" as to the position of *only* (*Modern English Usage*). It is yet likely that educated American speakers—more particularly writers, and even more particularly teachers and editors—concern themselves more with the matter than do their English counterparts.

[75] The "Who are you with?" (that is, what newspaper do you work for?) addressed by Queen Elizabeth II to various newspapermen at a reception given for her by the press in Washington (*Time,* October 28, 1957, p. 53) would certainly not pass muster in most educated circles in America.

Compare also the following single specimen from my rather voluminous collection of instances of this "error" from the writings of highly literate writers: "He did not need to look round to know who it came from, but he looked round none the less." The sentence, not in dialogue but in the author's exposition, occurs in Cyril Hare's *With a Bare Bodkin* (London, 1954; first pub. 1946), p. 49. Cyril Hare is the novel-writing pseudonym of

to call for it;[75] to eschew *can* in asking or giving permission[76] and *like* as a conjunction;[77] to choose forms of personal pronouns strictly in accordance with what is conceived to be their proper case;[78] to refer to *everyone, everybody, someone, somebody, no one,* and *nobody* with a personal pronoun singular in form (that is, *he, she,* or any of their

Judge Alfred Alexander Gordon Clark, educated at Rugby and New College, Oxford. George H. McKnight, *Modern English in the Making* (New York, 1928) has citations of objective *who* from Steele, Smollett, Lamb, Jane Austen, Sheila Kaye-Smith, Rose Macaulay, James Stephens, Joseph Conrad, Laurence Housman, George Meredith, Rudyard Kipling, and others (pp. 531–32).

[76] Even small children are frequently corrected when they use the supposedly "ungrammatical" *can* in asking permission: "Mother dear, can I go out to swim?" "Yes, my darling daughter, you *can*—but you *may* not." Compare with this the easygoing "Babs, dear, can I see you for a few moments, please?" from a note written by Sir Richard Cherrington to a young acquaintance in Dilwyn Rees's *The Cambridge Murders* (London, 1952; first pub. 1945), p. 67. Sir Richard Cherrington is Vice-President of "Fisher" College, Cambridge, and Professor of Prehistory in the University. Dilwyn Rees is the pseudonym of Glyn E. Daniel, Fellow and Steward of St. John's College, Cambridge, and a lecturer in archaeology in the university. In view of the similarity in backgrounds, it is probably safe to assume that Sir Richard's grammar is that of his creator. It is doubtful that either Sir Richard or Daniel would pass American College Board Examinations, for Sir Richard also says "prevent him getting back next term" (p. 11) and "Who are you going to shoot?" (p. 15).

[77] This usage, as in Clive Barnes's "These Russians dance like the Italians sing and the Spaniards fight bulls" (*Spectator,* July 1, 1960, p. 21), has been current in self-assured, cultivated English since the early sixteenth century (*OED* s.v. *like, a., adv.* [*conj.*], and *sb.*[2], B6a), but has been banned in more recent times, for purely arbitrary reasons as far as one can determine. The current prejudice is well illustrated by Wolcott Gibbs in a review of a play, *Three by Thurber,* published in the *New Yorker* (March 19, 1955, p. 66), in which he takes to task the adapters of James Thurber's material for "a great deal of text that is far inferior to Thurber's work in wit, style, and even, I'm sorry to say, the simple, correct use of the English language," going on to say, "I have complained too often before of the conjunctional 'like.'"

[78] As in Ben Ray Redman's review (*Saturday Review,* February 22, 1958, p. 19) of *The Conscience of the Rich,* by C. P. (later Lord) Snow—a novelist, a physicist, a literary critic, a Cambridge don, and a life peer, among other distinctions: "... as he has before, Sir Charles does more than his bit towards making misused pronouns one of England's most notable exports." A few examples of this alleged linguistic sin follow: "No one had eyes or thought for anyone but he as he got slowly to his feet...." (Edgar Lustgarten, *Defender's Triumph* [London, 1957], p. 108); "... respectable people like you and I ..." (Sir Winston Churchill, quoted by Sir John Slessor in *The Central Blue;* from the review in *Time,* April 1, 1957, p. 55); "... it would not be right for either you or I to be where we planned to be on D-Day" (King George VI, quoted in Churchill's War Memoirs in *Life,* October 29, 1951, p. 83); "... a good deal older than me" (Somerset Maugham, *The Vagrant Mood,* quoted with a disapproving *sic* by the American reviewer in the New York *Herald Tribune Book Review,* April 5, 1953, p. 5); "... I imagined ... that there was only one 'you' in the world and that was me" (Sarah, heroine of Graham Greene's *The End of the Affair* [New York, 1955], p. 12; first pub. 1951).

oblique forms);[79] and, not to make too long a story of it, to observe the whole set of fairly simple rules and regulations designed for the timorous — prescriptions and proscriptions which those who are secure have never given much thought to.

The examples cited in the footnotes have been chosen almost at random from the many specimens in my "usage" files. American examples, like General Eisenhower's "to welcome Mrs. Eisenhower and I" (p. 236, n. 44), are much harder to find in print. Eisenhower was of course speaking extemporaneously into a microphone. The construction in question would never have occurred in a formal speech, for such speeches by great Americans are nowadays always carefully edited. (Practically all are written in the first place by ghostwriters.) In any event, the use of *I* after *and* in an objective construction, familiar though it is to all of us, brought forth a flurry of letters-to-the-editor of the "what-is-the-English-language-coming-to?" variety from newspaper readers and television viewers all over the country, and there was no doubt some editorial comment as well. In England the "non-U" use of "Mrs. Eisenhower" instead of "my wife" (it will be noted in the parallel citation that the Queen referred to her husband simply and frankly as "my husband") would be more likely to occasion disapproval.

The paucity of American printed examples of such locutions (other than those which occasionally occur in small-town newspapers) may be due to some extent to the greater care given to such details by American editors, which has given rise to a functional variety known as "edited English" — a type of speech which would not necessarily reflect in all details the actual usage of professional writers. Even so, it is likely that most American writers themselves, because of the widespread American concept of a mechanical sort of correctness supposed to be characteristic of cultivated usage, would more or less habitually

---

[79] Note the following, all taken from Standard British English: "Everybody seemed to be particularly on their best front parlour behaviour" (Stephen Potter, as television Guest Critic, London *Evening Standard*, June 5, 1956, p. 6); "No one, when they saw her, could believe . . ." (William Roughead, "To Meet Miss Madeleine Smith," reprinted in *The Pocket Book of True Crime Stories* [New York, 1943], p. 151); "Everyone felt uncomfortable and fidgeted in their chairs" (C. S. Forester, *Plain Murder* [London, 1951], p. 127).

McKnight, *Modern English in the Making,* has specimens of this "solecism" from Jane Austen, James Stephens, Thomas De Quincey, Lord Dunsany, Cardinal Newman, Samuel Butler, and George Moore, along with some older examples (pp. 528–29). Concerning the construction, "established not only by long tradition but by current practice," McKnight concludes: "The awkward necessity, so often met with in American speech of using the double pronoun, 'his or her,' is obviated by the 'misuse' of *their.*"

employ the forms of speech prescribed as standard for American usage, which are certainly not those which have been cited above from English printed works.

BRITISH AND AMERICAN PURISM

It is not to be inferred that the British citations necessarily illustrate constructions which occur most of the time in British English, but only that, despite the feelings of horror which they evince from most educated speakers of American English, they *do* actually occur within the framework of Standard British English.[80] What has already been strongly implied must be strongly stressed at this point, namely, that there are plenty of purists in England, where the "rules" originated. There are plenty everywhere else, for that matter, for the puristic attitude toward language is above all a question of temperament. By no means are all of them teachers, either. Moreover, the English variety are about as ill-informed and as inconsistent as their American counterparts.[81]

It is in fact likely that everyone between the cockney and the peer pays lip-service[82] to the mossy precepts of the eighteenth-century prescriptive grammarians who formulated most of the "rules" which constitute "grammar" in the lay mind. But in actual practice, as we have just seen, English purists — with the possible exception of the late

[80] If a number of my specimens come from "whodunits," it is only because stories of murder and its detection have been in the past a means of escape from a more or less cloistered and hence uneventful life. It will be noted, however, that all the works cited from this *genre*, which has a considerably higher status abroad than in the United States, are highly literate ones, for the most part written by distinguished writers.

[81] For instance, C. S. Forester in *Plain Murder* (London, 1951) writes of a copy writer, characterized as a vulgar fellow, that "split infinitives and 'different to's' meant nothing to him as long as they did not detract from the appeal of advertisement to the class of person to whom it was addressed" (p. 102). But note that Forester frequently offends against schoolroom standards of "correctness," as when he writes "cannot help but" (p. 124) and "why his voice changed was because he was not at all sure that it [his decision] was a wise one" (p. 151), whereas prescriptive grammar calls for *that* instead of *because*. His use of *everyone . . . their* has already been cited in another connection (above, n. 79). Purists, who should not be expected to be scholars also, are frequently "pure" only in regard to a few stigmatized constructions of which they happen to be especially aware (terminal prepositions and split infinitives are favorite bugaboos with them), and quite unconscious of others which have been just as arbitrarily stigmatized.

[82] For instance, C. Day Lewis (using the pseudonym Nicholas Blake) in *There's Trouble Brewing* (London, 1956; first pub. 1937), has a doctor, an old Oxonian, apologize for his natural speech as follows: "Besides, if the remains were not Bunnett, yet are dressed up to make us believe that they are him — I'm getting ungrammatical — the deduction would be that it was Bunnett who did the murder" (p. 62).

H. W. Fowler, whose pleasantly magisterial *Dictionary of Modern English Usage* enjoys considerable prestige in England as in America, perhaps because it makes such beguiling reading — have not been accorded the deference enjoyed by the American variety.[83] Standard British English is still essentially the speech of those who are expected to speak Standard British English. With the new distinction acquired by a good many "angry young men" from the "red-brick universities" north of the Thames, like the unbrushed young D. H. Lawrence of a generation or so ago — young men who have had little or no acquaintance with the "language of well-bred ease" — all this may change. Many of these new men have an emotional bias against Southern, that is, Standard British, pronunciation which is somewhat like the ambivalent attitude of many Americans toward it. So long as they remain angry, they will doubtless retain this bias, tinged though it is with envy. But success and prosperity go a long way in mollifying ire, and it may well be that they will want their sons and daughters to acquire the speech as well as the social deportment of the Establishment which they now affect to despise. For there is no snob like a self-made man — a statement which is not in the least irrelevant when we are considering linguistic usages. It will be most interesting to observe developments in Standard British English a generation hence.

Katharine Whitehorn, an English journalistic writer who is quite familiar with America, has put the matter very well: "In America, where it is grammar, not accent, that places you, anyone can learn the grammar; maybe Bostonians don't accept it, but Bostonians only impress other Bostonians."[84] The "American way" in language has been to make gentility accessible to all not by laying the stress on anything so subtle, let alone aristocratic, as "accent," but by basing "good usage" wholly upon certain morphological and syntactical shibboleths — the avoidance of *ain't, he don't, it's me,* terminal prepositions, split infinitives, dangling participles, and the like. These are rather easy for all to learn, even though not all bother to do so. Those who do not conform to the supposedly inflexible rules are thought to speak "bad English," even though they may be persons of considerable consequence in the national life; it is as simple as all that.

---

[83] Enjoyed, it should be said in all justice, for a very good reason: in the absence of a type of speech stemming from an aristocratic society, they have kept in circulation a set of easy precepts, the conscientious observance of which enables, or is supposed to enable, any man to speak as well as any other man. Most of these precepts are based on logically and analogically sound principles, and some of them have even been drawn from the actual observation of usage.

[84] "What Makyth Manners?" *Spectator,* March 9, 1962, p. 317.

By *accent* Miss Whitehorn means, or certainly ought to mean, those intonational characteristics — risings and fallings in pitch — plus to an unrealized extent timbre of voice which distinguish British English from American English far more than pronunciations of individual words, for, as we shall see, there is actually only a handful of words for which all speakers of Standard British English use pronunciations which are not current in any part of America. Voice quality in this connection has not been much investigated, and most statements about it are impressionistic; but there can be little doubt of its significance. Even if he were to learn British intonation, the American (say, a Bostonian) whose treatment of *r* and of the vowel of *ask, path,* and the like agreed with that of Standard British English would never in the world pass among English people for an Englishman. Almost before he could finish saying "A packet of Players, please," he would be spotted as a "Yank" by practically any tobacconist in the British Isles. Precision in the description of nationally characteristic voice qualities must, however, be left for future investigators.

In regard to intonation, the differences are most noticeable in questions and requests. Contrast the intonational patterns of the following sentences, very roughly indicated as they are, as they would customarily be spoken in Standard British English and American English:[85]

SBE: Where are you going to be?

AE: Where are you going to be?

SBE: Are you sure?

AE: Are you sure?

SBE: Let me know where you're going to be.

AE: Let me know where you're going to be.

SBE: Don't tell me that you're sure.

AE: Don't tell me that you're sure.

---

[85] Standard works on British English intonation are those of Harold E. Palmer, *English Intonation* (Cambridge, Eng., 1922), and Lilias E. Armstrong and Ida C. Ward, *A Handbook of English Intonation,* 2nd ed. (Cambridge, Eng., 1931). The most thorough study of American intonation is that of Kenneth L. Pike, *The Intonation of American English* (Ann Arbor, Mich., 1945).

It should be noted that it is usually difficult or impossible to tell whether a singer is English or American, for the intonational patterns in singing are those of the composer.

It is most unlikely that tempo plays any part in the identification of a British or an American "accent." To Americans unaccustomed to hearing it, British speech frequently seems to be running on at a great rate, but this impression of speed is doubtless also experienced by those English people who have not come into contact with American television shows, movies, and tourists, if there be any such remaining, in regard to American English. Some people speak slowly, some rapidly, regardless of nationality; moreover, the same individual is likely to speak more rapidly when he knows what he is talking about than when he must "make conversation."

NATIONAL DIFFERENCES IN PRONUNCIATION

As for the pronunciation of individual words, much the same situation holds true as for word choices: the differences are really inconsequential. The pronunciation of a given word which is most widely current in American English may occur in Standard British English as a less frequently used variant; for instance, for *either* and *neither* an overwhelming majority of Americans have [i] in the stressed syllable, though some—largely from the Atlantic coastal cities—quite naturally acquired [aɪ] when they were learning to talk, and others all over the country have doubtless affected this pronunciation because they have supposed it to have social prestige. In any case, the [aɪ] pronunciation cannot be said to be exclusively British; and it may come as a surprise to some Americans to learn that the [i] pronunciation occurs in Standard British English, probably much more frequently than the [aɪ] pronunciation occurs in American English. Pronunciation with [i] is in fact listed first in the *OED*, which notes, however, that the pronunciation [áɪðə] "is in London somewhat more prevalent in educated speech" than [íðə].[86] All dictionaries of British English, in fact, list the supposedly "American" pronunciation as a variant.

The prevalent Standard British English pronunciation of each of the following words differs from the usual or only pronunciation in American English: *ate* [ɛt], *been* [bin], *evolution* [ìvəlúšən], *fragile* [frǽǰaɪl], *medicine* [mɛ́dsɪn], *nephew* [nɛ́vju], *process* [prósɛs], *trait* [tre], *tryst* [traɪst], *valet* [vǽlɪt], *zenith* [zɛ́nɪθ]. But it is a fact that the

---

[86] It should be remembered that the *E–Every* section of the *OED* was published in 1891. For *neither* also the [i] pronunciation is given first (1906).

prevalent American pronunciation of each (allowing for an interchange of [ɔ] and [ɑ] in *process*) occurs also in Standard British English, thus, *ate* [et], *been* [bɪn], *evolution* [ɛvəlúšən], *fragile* [frǽjɪl], *medicine* [médɪsɪn], *nephew* [néfju], *process* [prɔ́sɛs], *trait* [tret], *tryst* [trɪst], *valet* [vǽle],[87] *zenith* [zínɪθ]. The pronunciation [ɛt] for *ate* occurs in American speech but is regarded as substandard. For *nephew*, [névju] is current in America according to Hans Kurath and Raven I. Mc-David, Jr., "both in folk speech and in cultivated speech, in Eastern New England, in Chesapeake Bay, and especially in South Carolina, rarely elsewhere."[88]

The prevalent American pronunciations of the following words do not occur in Standard British English: *figure* [fígjər], *leisure* [lížər], *quinine* [kwáɪnaɪn], *squirrel* [skwɔ́rəl] (also *syrup* and *stirrup* with the same stressed vowel), *tomato* [təméto], *vase* [ves].[89] But the prevalent British pronunciations of all of them are current, though indeed not widespread, in American English, that is, [fígə(r)], [léžə(r)], [kwɪnín], [skwírəl], [təmɑ́to], [vɑz], though the first of these, for *figure*, is regarded as substandard. (The British have [-j-] in *figurative, figuration, figurant,* and *figurine*.)

The British English pronunciation of *lieutenant* as [lɛfténənt] when it refers to the army subaltern is now never heard in American English, though it was usual until [luténənt] was recommended for Americans by Noah Webster in his *American Dictionary of the English Language* (1828). As we have seen in another connection (see p. 66), Webster also recommended *schedule* with [sk-].[90] It is likely, however, that the historical pronunciation with [s-] was that most widely used in both England and America in 1828.

Other pronunciations which are nationally distinctive include (with the American pronunciation given first) [šəgrín]/[šǽgrɪn] for *chagrin*, [kɔ́rəlɪrɪ]/[kərɔ́lərɪ] for *corollary*, [dáɪnəstɪ]/[dínəstɪ] for *dynasty*, [prɪmír]/[prémjə] for *premier*, [klərk]/[klɑk] for *clerk*, [mísəlènɪ]/

---

[87] It is not unusual in American English to stress the final syllable of this and other French words (for example *café, ballet, Calais*), or even words thought to be French.

[88] *The Pronunciation of English in the Atlantic States* (Ann Arbor, Mich., 1961), p. 176.

[89] For the American distribution of some of these, see Kurath and McDavid, p. 127 (*squirrel, syrup, stirrup*), p. 151 (*tomato*), p. 166 (*quinine*), and p. 177 (*vase*).

[90] Webster's choice was not unknown in England in the eighteenth century and earlier, being favored on theoretical grounds by a number of the orthoëpists, though John Walker in his *Critical Pronouncing Dictionary,* 2nd ed. (1797) says that "entirely sinking the *ch* in *sedule* seems to be the prevailing mode, and too firmly fixed by custom to be altered." He seems not to have heard the pronunciation now current in British English with [š-].

[mɪsélənɪ] for *miscellany,* [frəntír]/[frɔ́ntjə] for *frontier,* and [læbrətɔ̀rɪ]/
[ləbɔ́rət(ə)rɪ] or [lǽbrət(ə)rɪ] for *laboratory.*[91] American *carburetor*
[kárbərètər] and British *carburettor* [kábjʊrètə] are, in addition to
being pronounced differently, variant written forms, as are *alúminum*
(again, old Noah Webster's choice) and *àlumínium.* The American pronunciation of *carburetor,* in which one would expect [-ìtər], is apparently due to the analogy of the many nouns of agency in *-ator.*

A few more items might be added to the differentiae cited above, but
actually not very many. As for more sweeping differences, what strikes
most American ears most strongly (for the differences in intonation
and voice quality are rather too subtle for ready identification) is the
modern Standard British shift of an older [æ], which survives in American English except before *r* (as in *far*), *lm* (as in *calm*), and in *father*
(and to some extent in *rather*), to [ɑ] in a number of very frequently
used words.[92] Up to the very end of the eighteenth century [ɑ] in these
and the other words affected was considered vulgar. This shift cannot,
however, be regarded as exclusively British, inasmuch as its effect is
evident in the speech of eastern New England and to some extent in the
tidewater South. Present American usage in regard to such words is by
no means consistent: a Bostonian may, for instance, have [ɑ] in *half*
(and then perhaps only some of the time), but not in *can't,* or vice versa.
An intermediate [a] is sometimes heard in America as a variant of this
[ɑ]. According to the late John S. Kenyon, "The pronunciation of '*ask*'
words with [a] or [ɑ] has been a favorite field for schoolmastering and
elocutionary quackery."[93] (Bracketed symbols replace his boldface
ones.) One cannot but agree when one hears American actresses
(mainly actresses, but quite a few actors also) pronounce [a] in words
like *hat, and, happy,* and others spelled with *a* which were not affected
by the aforementioned shift.[94]

The use of [ɑ] in what Kenyon calls the "*ask*" words, supposed by
some naive American speakers to have higher social standing than [æ],

[91] The difference between the less usual British English pronunciation (cited second)
and the American is due to American retention of secondary stress on the penultimate
syllable of polysyllables in *-ary, -ery,* and *-ory,* to be discussed below. But the British
pronunciation of the word in question with stress on the first syllable seems to be dying
out; it is seldom if ever heard from younger-generation speakers.

[92] This has been alluded to, pp. 41, 191, and 233.

[93] *American Pronunciation,* 10th ed. (Ann Arbor, Mich., 1961), p. 183.

[94] Jayne Crane Harder has dealt effectively with "elocutionary quackery" in "The
Influence of the Teaching of Elocution on Modern English Pronunciation" (unpublished
dissertation, University of Florida, 1956). See also the same writer (under the name
Jayne Crane), "Quest for a Standard: A Study of Stage Diction," *Southern Speech
Journal,* 15 (1950), 280–85.

is fraught with danger. With speakers of Standard British English, who use it naturally, in the sense that they acquired it when as children they were learning to talk, it never occurs in a great many words in which it might be expected if one were going only by analogy; thus, *bass, crass, mass,*[95] and *lass* have [æ], in contrast to the [ɑ] of *grass, class, glass,* and *pass;*[96] *gastric* has [æ], but *plaster* has [ɑ]; *ample* has [æ], but *sample* and *example* have [ɑ]; *romance* and *fancy* have [æ], but *dance, glance,* and *chance* have [ɑ]; *can't* 'cannot' has [ɑ], but *cant* 'hypocritical talk' has [æ]; *mascot, massacre,* and *pastel* have [æ]; *master, basket,* and *nasty* have [ɑ]; and *bastard, mastiff,* and *masquerade* may have either [æ] or [ɑ]. It is obvious that few status-seekers could master such complexities, even if there were any real point in so doing. There is none, actually, for no one really worth fooling would be really fooled by such a shallow display of linguistic virtuosity.

Somewhat less noticeable, perhaps because it is more widespread in American English than the use of [ɑ] or [a] in the *ask* words, is the Standard British English loss of [r] before a consonant or in final position in an utterance (that is, before a pause) heretofore alluded to (pp. 35–36), though the American treatment of this sound is as a rule somewhat less consistent and hence more complicated to describe than the British. In American English it may, for instance—to some extent depending upon the speech area—be retained preconsonantally in stressed syllables but lost in final position, particularly in final unstressed syllables (in *further* [fə́rðə], for instance); or it may be lost under the same conditions as in Standard British English; or it may even, as in parts of the deep South, be lost before a vowel, as in *Carolina* and *far away.* Postvocalic [r] is lost, in one way or another, in eastern New England, in New York City, and in most of the coastal South.[97] Away from the Atlantic Coast, it is retained in all positions. There are other less striking phonological differences, like the British slightly rounded "short *o*" in contrast to the unrounded [ɑ] in *got, stop, collar,* and the like heard in American English except for western Pennsylvania and eastern New England (pp. 47, n. 40 and 186).

Though there are signs of its return, British English long ago lost its secondary stress on the penultimate syllables of polysyllables in *-ary, -ery,* and *-ory* (for example *military, millinery, obligatory*). This subordinate stress is regularly retained in American English. Many Ameri-

---

[95] Similarly with *Mass,* the sacrament, though this may sometimes occur with [ɑ].
[96] But *classic, classical, classicism, classify, passage, passenger,* and *passive* all have [æ]. *Ass* may have either [æ] or [ɑ].
[97] Kurath and McDavid, pp. 170–72.

cans, it is true, are fond of [díkšən(ə)rı] as a pronunciation of *dictionary* — presumably it gives a certain social "tone" to the word — but few if any who use this pronunciation pronounce other such words in any save the usual American and older British fashion, that is, as *sécretàry, mónastèry, térritòry,* and the like. In my native usage (that of the area dominated by Baltimore), *stationery* 'writing paper' was by many speakers distinguished from *stationary* 'fixed' by omission of the secondary stress. Such stress was also frequently lacking in *primary, confectionery, cemetery,* and *library* (sometimes reduced to disyllabic [láɪbrɪ]), but it regularly occurred as in all types of American English in all other such words. A restoration of the secondary stress in British English, at least in some words, is more likely due to spelling-consciousness than to any transatlantic influence. I have noted it from well-educated younger-generation British speakers in *secretary* and, for the first time about twenty years ago, in *extraordinary* (as [ɪkstrɔ́dɪnèrɪ]). Brian Foster, in "Recent American Influence on Standard English," says that "it is increasingly common" for *secretary,* in which secondary stress "is now to be heard from some excellent British speakers" (p. 356).

The fact seems to be that, if we leave the very important matter of intonation, a handful of word choices, and the as yet unascertained question of voice quality out of consideration, the remaining distinctive features of British and American English are comprised in the pronunciation of a smallish number of words, some of them rather infrequently used words. It is nonetheless true that British speech is likely to be unclear to some Americans according to their own testimony, though it is doubtful that there are many such nowadays. It must be remembered, however, that unsophisticated people are very provincial in their reaction to any type of speech which differs from their own, and may even take a certain pride in their provincialism. Nationalistic prejudice, evincing itself frequently in a kind of obstinate refusal to tolerate differences, however slight they may be, has something to do with this reaction. It is not, however, wholly a matter of nationalism, for the Georgia "cracker" is likely to be almost as vexed — and because of this vexation perhaps indisposed to listen carefully — by the speech of an older-generation Boston Brahmin as by that of an Oxford professor of classical literature. And, be it said in all justice, the Oxonian, from whom we should expect a more enlightened linguistic attitude, is not at all unlikely to be equally intolerant of American speech — or, for that matter, of the folk speech of his own countrymen.

The type of American speech that one nowadays hears most frequently in nationally televised "commercials" is highly standardized and essentially synthetic. Spoken by trained speakers who, with the possible exception of the evangelical ministry in those parts of the country which Mencken called the Bible Belt, are probably as influential a group of persuaders as any in the United States, this speech evinces few if any regional or individual characteristics discernible to the untrained ears of those who listen glazed-eyed to it. In it the usage of the majority of Americans is reflected in the following respects: (1) *r* is carefully articulated in all positions; (2) medial *t* is voiced,[98] so that *matter* and *madder* are homophones, or practically so, and the naked ear has difficulty distinguishing "Atoms for Peace" from "Adams for Peace"; and (3) [hw-] occurs in the *wh*-words (see pp. 67–68).[99] Unstressed syllables are frequently given somewhat more attention than natural, traditional speech gives them; for instance [ɛ] is often preferred to [ə] in the unstressed final syllable of *president,* [o] to [ə] in the unstressed initial syllables of *obey, o'clock,* and the like, and [i] to [ɪ] or [ə] in the unstressed initial syllables of *effect(ive), efficient,* and the like. The plural of *process* is quite likely to end in [-iz]. The names of the days of the week end in [-de] rather than in [-dɪ].[100]

Those who are professionally concerned with public speaking, either as teachers or as performers, sometimes attempt to justify such distortions of what is still the natural usage of cultivated speakers on the grounds that they make for greater clarity. Actually, they seldom if ever do so. In "Cultural Levels and Functional Varieties of English,"[101] John S. Kenyon quotes the statement of the great English phonetician Henry Sweet that "we cannot make words more distinct by disguising them," in reference to the use of full vowels in unstressed syllables where Standard speech, British or American, has reduced [ə] or [ɪ]. Kenyon reports the following momentarily confusing utterance from a radio announcer: "This program will be heard again tomorrow from one two three." No one could possibly be confused by "one [tə] three." Other instances of such "overpronunciation" cited in Kenyon's article are (to use his respellings for them) *ay man* ("a man"), *cahnsider, too-*

---

[98] The sound is called a "voiced flap consonant" by Edward Artin, pronunciation editor of *Webster's Third New International Dictionary* (Springfield, Mass., 1961), who uses a special symbol in transcribing it (p. 41a).
[99] Occasionally [hw-] occurs by overcorrection in *w*-words as well, for instance *water.*
[100] The pronunciation with [-de] has become usual for younger-generation speakers. Many, if not most, older-generation speakers, however, continue to use the alternative pronunciation indicated by such seventeenth-century spellings as *Mundy* and *Fridy.* It is doubtful that the new analysis of such previously closely welded compounds is altogether or even partially attributable to the overcareful pronunciation of the auditory mass media. It is recorded long before the advent of the media.
[101] *College English,* 10 (1948), 31–36.

day, too go ("to go"), and *Coalumbia;* "Sunday will be Mother's Day" with the full vowel in -*day* was misheard as "Some day will be Mother's Day."

The glamour girls and the efficient, wholesome-looking women who on televison extol the glories of cosmetics, shampoos, "washday products" (for *soap* has become practically a dirty word in such rarefied circles), refrigerators, and cleansers for the "food preparation area" (kitchen) and what is discreetly referred to as the "bathroom bowl" follow much the same patterns as their male counterparts. In addition, they are quite likely, when they think of it, to substitute [a] for Standard [æ] in, say, *dishpan hands.*

The extent of the influence and prestige of those who speak the commercials may be gauged by the astronomical sums spent on such advertising. Who can say that their standardized form of speech, based to a large extent upon writing, may not in time become the basis for, or for that matter may itself become, a nationwide caste dialect?

BRITISH AND AMERICAN SPELLING

Finally, there is the matter of spelling, which looms larger in the consciousness of those who are concerned with national differences than it deserves to do. Somewhat exotic to American eyes, though by no means unfamilar to those of the educated, are *gaol, kerb* (of a street), *pyjamas, tyre* (around a wheel), *cyder, cypher, syren, cheque* (for drawing money from bank), and *shew.* But *jail, curb, pajamas, tire, cider, cipher, siren, check,* and *show* are also current in England in varying degrees. *Shew,* prevalent in the eighteenth century, was in fact called "obs[olete] exc[ept] in legal documents" by the *OED* (then the *NED*) in 1914. H. C. Wyld's *Universal Dictionary of the English Language* (London, 1932) states that it is archaic. But it is nevertheless still current, if very rare.[102] The spelling, like that of *sew,* indicates a pronunciation no longer current.

Noah Webster, whom many regard as a sort of linguistic mahatma, is responsible for excising the *u* from a group of words spelled in his day prevailingly in -*our: armour, behaviour, colour, favour, flavour, harbour, labour, neighbour,* and the like. The resultant American -*or* spellings are today far more obnoxious to the English than the alternative forms with -*our* are to Americans, who, in addition to reading a great many books printed in England, are quite accustomed to seeing *Saviour* and *glamour* (widely current in America in the phrase *glamour*

---

[102] It is, for instance, consistently used in the Randolph Quirk and C. L. Wrenn *Old English Grammar* (London, 1955), occurring on pp. 6, 9, and elsewhere.

girl) in books printed in their own country. All these words have been current in earlier British English without the *u*, though most Englishmen today are probably unaware of the fact; Webster was making no radical change in English spelling habits. Furthermore, the English had themselves struck the *u* from a great many words earlier spelled *-our*, alternating with *-or: author, doctor, emperor, error, governor, horror, mirror*, and *senator*, among others. Perhaps they might also have shortened the remaining *-our* words if the self-righteous and nationalistic-minded Webster had not put their backs up by doing so first. As it is, they are so offended by what they regard as American misspellings of those words in which they retain the *u* that American books are sometimes reset before their publication in England, even though money might be saved by using the American plates.

Webster is also responsible for the American practice of using *-er* instead of the customary British *-re* in a number of words, for instance *calibre, centre, litre, manoeuvre, metre* (of poetry or of the unit of length in the metric system),[103] *sepulchre*, and *theatre*. The last of these spellings has nowadays probably a wider currency in American English than has *theater;* it is consistently used, for instance, in the announcement of course offerings of the Department of Speech in the University of Florida ("Theatre Appreciation," "History of the Theatre," and "Aesthetics of the Theatre"), and the yellow classified section of my telephone directory lists only "Theatres." Except for *litre*, which did not come into English until the nineteenth century, all these words occur in earlier British English with *-er*.

The fact that *c* before *e* indicates [s] must have irritated Webster. At one time he wanted to have *acre* spelled *aker*, but he was still left with *lucre* and *mediocre*, in the case of which he seems to have given up fighting the good fight. There was also *ogre*, about which little could be done; **oger* would have suggested [ójər].

The American use of *-se* in *defense, offense*, and *pretense*, in which the English usually have *-ce*, is also attributable to the precept and practice of Webster, though he did not recommend *fense* for *fence*, which is simply an aphetic form of *defense* (or *defence*). Spellings with *-se* have occurred in earlier British English for all these words, including *fence*. *Suspense* is now usually so spelled in British English.

Webster proposed dropping final *k* in such words as *almanack, musick, physick, publick*, and *traffick*, bringing about a change which

---

[103] The homophone meaning an instrument for measuring is of different origin and is written *meter* in British as well as American English: thus *gas meter, barometer, thermometer*. Here the *-er* is the familiar English suffix of nouns of agency.

has occurred, in British English as well, though not because old Noah recommended it. The single word with older *ck* after *o* in which he neglected to drop the *k* is *havock*, everywhere spelled without it nowadays. His *burdoc, cassoc,* and *hassoc* seem to have got nowhere.[104]

Though he was not the first to recommend doing so, Webster is doubtless to be credited with the American spelling practice of not doubling final *l* when adding a suffix except in words stressed on their final syllables, for example *gróvel, groveled, groveler, groveling,* but *propél, propelled, propeller, propelling, propellant.* Modern British spelling usually doubles *l* before a suffix regardless of the position of the stress, thus *grovelled, groveller,* and so forth.

The English use of *ae* and *oe* (or *æ* and *œ*) looks strange to Americans in *anaemic, paediatrician, gynaecology, haemorrhage, oesophagus, homoeopathy, manoeuvre,* and *diarrhoeia,* but not in *encyclopaedia* and *aesthetic,* which are fairly common in American usage. Some words earlier written with one or the other of these digraphs long ago underwent simplification, for example *phaenomenon, poenology,* and *oeconomy.* Others are in process of simplification: *hemorrhage, hemorrhoids,* and *medieval* are frequent British variants of the forms with *ae,* but *haemophilia, haematic, haemostatic,* and *haemoglobin* seem not to have lost the *a* as yet.

Most English writers use *-ise* for the verbal suffix written *-ize* (ultimately Greek *-izein*) in America in such words as *organize, baptize,* and *sympathize;* however, the *Times* of London, the *OED,* H. C. Wyld's *Universal Dictionary* (London, 1932), and Daniel Jones's *English Pronouncing Dictionary,* 13th ed. (London, 1967), and a number of other publications of considerable intellectual prestige prefer the spelling with *z,* which, in the words of the *OED,* is "at once etymological and phonetic." The *ct* of *connection* and *inflection* is due to the influence of *connect* and *inflect;* the etymologically sounder spellings *connexion* and *inflexion,* reflecting their sources in Latin *connexiōn(em)* and *inflexiōn(em),* are used by most writers, or at any rate by most printers, in England.

THE STUDY OF AMERICAN ENGLISH

Interest in American English has been very lively and scholarship very productive in recent years. In 1889, however, long before the

---

[104] Webster, who loved tinkering with all aspects of language, had contemplated far flashier spelling reforms, for instance, lopping off the final *e* of *-ive, -ine,* and *-ite* in final syllables (thus *fugitiv, medicin, definit*), using *oo* for *ou* in *group* and *soup,* writing *tung* for *tongue,* and deleting the *a* in *bread, feather,* and the like, but in time gave them up.

publication of the revered H. L. Mencken's *The American Language,* the American Dialect Society was formed at Harvard for "the investigation of the English dialects in America with regard to pronunciation, grammar, vocabulary, phraseology, and geographical distribution,"[105] as the result of a suggestion made by Charles Hall Grandgent, then a young instructor, later to become a distinguished professor of Romance languages at Harvard.[106] One of the aims of the Society has been the preparation of a great American dialect dictionary. Although much preliminary work has been done toward this end, the completion and publication of such a work still lies in the future.

According to the authoritative historical sketch of the American Dialect Society by Louise Pound,[107] who was its president from 1938 to 1941, the "leading spirits" behind its foundation were Sheldon, Grandgent, and Francis James Child, the great editor of *English and Scottish Popular Ballads* (1883–98), who was the first president. George Lyman Kittredge, then on his way to an assistant professorship at Harvard,[108] the poet James Russell Lowell, and John Matthews Manly, later of the University of Chicago, were among the earliest members.

The publication of the Society was *Dialect Notes,* which ran from 1890 to 1939. There was no publication during the war period 1939–44. The successor to *Dialect Notes* is called simply the *Publication of the American Dialect Society* or, more usually, *PADS.* It is issued twice yearly, some of its issues being full-length monographs, including Frederic G. Cassidy's *A Method for Collecting Dialect* (1953), Sumner Ives's *The Phonology of the Uncle Remus Stories* (1954), David W. Maurer's *Whiz Mob: A Correlation of the Technical Argot of Pickpockets with Their Behavior Pattern* (1955), Einar Haugen's *Bilingualism in the Americas* (1956), and Dwight L. Bolinger's *Interrogative Structures of American English* (1957). The titles give some notion of the scope of interests of the Society. Under its sponsorship is what, when completed, will be a scholarly work of considerable magnitude, the *Dictionary of American Regional English,* usually referred to by scholars in acronymic fashion (see below, pp. 299–301) as *DARE.* The director of this project, with headquarters at the University of Wisconsin, is Frederic G. Cassidy, a former president of the Society.

H. L. Mencken testifies that it was "a chance encounter" with *Dia-*

---

[105] As set forth by Edward S. Sheldon, then an assistant professor, later professor of Romance philology at Harvard. Sheldon became the first secretary of the Society.
[106] Grandgent was the Society's first treasurer.
[107] *Publication of the American Dialect Society,* No. 17 (April, 1952), pp. 3–28.
[108] He was president of the Society in 1897, succeeding Sheldon and Grandgent in that office.

lect Notes around 1905 which urged him to a systematic study of American English, and says "I was a steady customer of *Dialect Notes* after my discovery of its riches."[109] The first edition of his own zestful and stimulating book appeared in 1919; revised editions appeared in 1921 and 1923; then, in 1936, the great fourth edition, "corrected, enlarged, and rewritten." This was followed, in 1945 and 1948, by two fat supplements — in all a total of more than 2500 pages. An abridgment, with revisions, has been prepared by Raven I. McDavid, Jr. (New York, 1963), with the chapter on slang, cant, and argot under the charge of David W. Maurer.

The year 1925 saw the publication of George Philip Krapp's *The English Language in America* and the first issue of *American Speech.* Krapp's two-volume work is still indispensable; in addition to its learning, it is written with style and grace. *American Speech,* now published by the Columbia University Press, is, like the various publications of the American Dialect Society, both lively and learned. It was founded by H. L. Mencken, Kemp Malone, Louise Pound,[110] and Arthur Garfield Kennedy, who, though not many years Miss Pound's junior, had been her student at the University of Nebraska. According to Malone, "the idea was Mencken's."[111] As it was planned, it was not to be "so academic as to attract only the austerest scholars as contributors and subscribers" (L. Pound, *loc. cit.*); and to this day, though it has always maintained the highest scholarly standards, it continues to demonstrate that sound scholarship need not be dull.

One of the most monumental scholarly undertakings of the present century is the Linguistic Atlas of the United States and Canada, begun under the direction of Hans Kurath, with the aid of a large staff of highly trained helpers. Work on this huge project began in 1931. An outgrowth of the interest in dialect geography which had begun in Europe, it has successfully carried through a study of the language — its phonology, morphology, syntax, and vocabulary — in a great number of communities in each region of the country, communities which have been carefully selected on the basis of their economic, social, and cultural history. Settlement history is obviously very important.

In each of these communities at least two informants have been interviewed by means of a questionnaire which is carefully and expertly devised to elicit characteristic locutions in response. According to

---

[109] *The American Language: Supplement I,* Preface, p. ix.

[110] According to Mencken, her "early work put the study of American English on its legs" (*Supplement I,* vi). Miss Pound died, full of years and honors, in 1958.

[111] The story of the beginnings of the journal is told by the four founders in "*American Speech,* 1925–1945: The Founders Look Back," *American Speech,* 20 (1945), 241–46.

Raven I. McDavid, Jr., in charge of the project for the Middle and South Atlantic States,[112] an interview takes from four to seven hours under favorable circumstances. One informant is ideally an elderly native of the community whose speech has been relatively uncontaminated by schooling and can thus be presumed to represent old-fashioned usage; the other one middle-aged, with, say, a high school education. In addition, in many communities, particularly in those cities which are centers of culture and fashion, cultured informants have been interviewed.

Thus far, only the New England materials have been published, in the huge *Linguistic Atlas of New England,* with an accompanying *Handbook of the Linguistic Geography of New England* by Kurath and others (Washington, D.C., 1939; 2nd printing, New York, 1954). Pending the publication of the complete materials for regions other than New England, three important works based upon the materials for the Atlantic States have appeared as "Studies in American English" published by the University of Michigan Press: Kurath's *A Word Geography of the Eastern United States,* which demonstrates that there is a well-defined American Midland type of speech, the Midland area on the Atlantic coast lying between the traditionally recognized North and South;[113] E. Bagby Atwood's *A Survey of Verb Forms in the Eastern United States* (1953); and the work which has been previously cited a number of times, Kurath and McDavid's *The Pronunciation of English in the Atlantic States* (1961). Readable brief treatments of American dialects are McDavid's in Chapter 9 of W. Nelson Francis' *The Structure of American English* (1958), Carroll E. Reed's *Dialects of American English* (1967), and Roger W. Shuy's *Discovering American Dialects* (1967).

Two other monumental works, the four-volume *Dictionary of American English,* edited by Sir William Craigie and James R. Hul-

---

[112] Other regional surveys are or have been in charge of Harold B. Allen (the Upper Midwest), Albert H. Marckwardt and McDavid (the North-Central States), the late E. Bagby Atwood and Rudolph C. Troike (Texas), the late Marjorie Kimmerle (Colorado), David W. Reed (California and Nevada), and H. Rex Wilson (Nova Scotia). Announced as forthcoming is *The Linguistic Atlas of the Upper Midwest,* edited by Allen.

[113] The Midland extends on the coast only from southern New Jersey to midway through Delaware, but its boundaries widen considerably as one goes westward; the southern boundary, for instance, goes through northern Maryland, then turns sharply southwestward and runs along the crest of the Blue Ridge in Virginia through North Carolina and upper South Carolina; the northern boundary swings northwestward and goes along the northern part of Pennsylvania. These boundaries were first shown in the map which is Figure 3 in Kurath's book.

WORD GEOGRAPHY OF THE EASTERN STATES

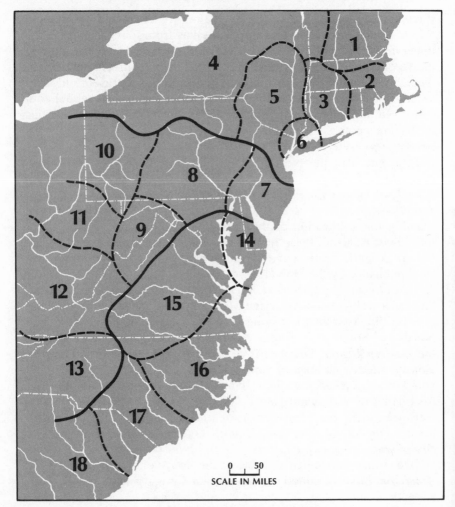

THE SPEECH AREAS OF THE EASTERN STATES

The North	The Midland	The South
1. N.E. New England	7. Delaware Valley	14. Delamarvia (E. shore of
2. S.E. New England	8. Susquehanna Valley	Maryland and Virginia,
3. S.W. New England	9. Upper Potomac and	and S. Delaware)
4. Upstate New York	Shenandoah Valleys	15. Virginia Piedmont
and W. Vermont	10. Upper Ohio Valley	16. N.E. No. Carolina (Albemarle
5. Hudson Valley	11. N. West Virginia	Sound and Neuse Valley)
6. Metropolitan	12. S. West Virginia	17. Cape Fear and Peedee Valleys
New York	13. W. No. and W. So. Carolina	18. So. Carolina

Reproduced from *Aspects of Language* by Dwight Bolinger (Adapted from Hans Kurath, *A Word Geography of the Eastern United States,* University of Michigan Press, 1949), © 1968 by Harcourt Brace Jovanovich, Inc.

bert, and the originally two-volume *Dictionary of Americanisms* of
M. M. Mathews, both published by the University of Chicago Press,
have already been alluded to a number of times. Both works were
prepared according to the historical principles laid down by the
OED, of which Craigie was also an editor.

Although interest in the study of the living spoken language in
Great Britain antedates that in America, British scholarship has
lagged somewhat behind in the years under discussion. Linguistic
atlases of England and Scotland are, however, now well under way;
the first two volumes of the *Survey of English Dialects* by Harold
Orton and Wilfred J. Halliday were published in Leeds in 1962. The
Introduction to a Survey of Scottish Dialects (Edinburgh, 1952) by
Angus McIntosh is a noteworthy sign of things to come. Since American English is a development of British English, it is inevitable that
such investigations will enhance our knowledge of American English,
for, as Kurath has pointed out, in the Preface to *The Pronunciation
of English in the Atlantic States,* while some of the divergencies
between present-day American English and British English reflect
"unsettled usage in Standard English during our Colonial period,"
others unquestionably stem from English dialect speech. We shall
never, alas, have any tape recordings of either the British Standard or
the folk speech of the seventeenth and eighteenth centuries, but the
scientific study of modern folk speech, conservative as such speech
always is in comparison with Standard, cannot fail to throw light on
certain features of American English.

THE ESSENTIAL ONENESS OF ALL ENGLISH

We have now come to an end of our comparative survey of the
present state of British and American English. He who looks for
differences is sure to find them. We can only hope that he does not
choose to magnify them. All too often treatments of the subject have
been of what Robert A. Hall, Jr., has somewhere called the "Old
Curiosity Shop" variety—even Mencken is in some measure guilty of
this—playing up isolated differences in a wholly misleading way. What
should have emerged from the present treatment is a conception of
the essential unity of the English language in all its national, regional,
and local manifestations. What, then, it may be asked, *is* the English
language? Is it the speech of London, of Boston, of New York, of
south Georgia, of Melbourne, of Montreal, of Calcutta? A possible
answer might be, none of these, but rather the sum of them all, along
with all other blendings and developments which have taken place
wherever what is thought of as the English language is spoken by those

who learned it as their mother tongue.[114] The most important of these happen to be Standard British English and the English spoken by Americans — and it should be clear by now that their importance is due, not to any inherent virtues which they may possess, but wholly to the present importance in the affairs of the English-speaking world — some might go so far as to say of western European civilization — of those who speak them.

[114] The fears of Sir David Eccles, former British Minister of Education, as reported in *Time* (June 22, 1962, p. 33), that English may split up into a number of mutually unintelligible dialects, as Latin did in a quite different sort of world from that in which we live, have often been voiced before, and are quite unjustified by the facts. As Philip B. Gove, editor-in-chief of the Merriam-Webster dictionaries, pointed out in an Associated Press interview inspired by Sir David's contention that "we must get down to the job of preserving meanings [those in his own type of English?] and standards of purity [to be decided by whom?] for the English language," an American says "gasoline" and a Briton says "petrol," but "that doesn't mean they don't know each other's tank is empty." Air travel, intermarriage, exchange of radio and television programs, and the printed word, Gove went on to say, have brought American English and British English closer together than ever before. And, as we have seen, they were never really very far apart.

X

New Words from Old
Coinages and Adaptations

In the present state of our knowledge, there is, as we have seen, little point in speculating about the ultimate origins of words. But we can know with varying degrees of certainty a good deal about the making of words in historical times, and our principal concern in this chapter will be an examination of the various processes involved in the making.

ROOT CREATIONS

It is unlikely that very many words have come into being during the historical period which have not been suggested in one way or another by previously existing words.[1] An oft-cited example of a word completely without associations with any existing word or words is *Kodak,* which made its first appearance in print in the *U.S. Patent Office Gazette* in 1888[2] and was, according to George Eastman, who invented the word as well as the device which it names, "a purely arbitrary combination of letters, not derived in whole or in part from any exist-

---

[1] A good many given names, encountered primarily in the American Deep South and the Southwest, but of a type current all over the United States, are doubtless pure root creations, for example *Lugen, Zedro* (suggested by *Pedro?*), *Velpo, Phalla, Morta* (*Marta?*), and *Venrean.* I have cited these and scores of others in "Onomastic Individualism in Oklahoma," *American Speech,* 22 (1947), 257–64, and in "Bible Belt Onomastics, or Some Curiosities of Anti-Pedobaptist Nomenclature," *Names,* 7 (1959), 84–100.

[2] M. M. Mathews, *A Dictionary of Americanisms on Historical Principles* (Chicago, 1951).

ing word,"[3] though according to his biographer a very slight association was in fact involved in his use of the letter *k*, for his mother's family name began with that letter. *Nylon, Dacron,* and *Orlon* are similarly etymologyless words.

TRADE NAMES

Most trade names, however, are clearly suggested by already existing words. *Vaseline,* for instance, was made from German *Wasser* 'water' plus Greek *elaion* 'oil';[4] *Kleenex* by *clean* and *Cutex* by *cuticle* plus a rather widely used but quite meaningless pseudoscientific suffix *-ex; Socony* by the initial letters of *Standard Oil Company of New York;* and *Uneeda* by "you need a," a process now rather old-fashioned in the naming of products.[5]

ECHOIC WORDS

Sound alone is the basis of a limited number of words, called echoic or onomatopoeic, like *bang, burp, splash, tinkle, ping, bobwhite,* and *cuckoo.* Leonard Bloomfield distinguishes between words which are actually imitative of sound, like *meow, moo,* and *bow-wow*—though as we have seen these differ from language to language—and those which he appropriately calls symbolic ("somehow illustrating the meaning more immediately than do ordinary speech-forms. . . . To the speaker it seems as if the sounds were especially suited to the meaning"), like *bump* and *flick,* but the distinction between these need not really concern us here.[6] Such words frequently show doubling, sometimes with slight variation, as in *bow-wow, choo-choo,* and *pe(e)wee,* the last of which by its sound is merely suggestive of tininess—a quality that could hardly be imitated in sound save by a reduction in volume—and is hence symbolic, though as the name of a bird it is, like its variant *peewit* (or *pewit*), actually a fair imitation of the bird's cry.

[3] From a letter written by Eastman to the late John Matthews Manly in 1906, quoted from Carl W. Ackerman's *George Eastman* (New York, 1930) by H. L. Mencken, *The American Language: Supplement I* (New York, 1945), p. 342, n. 1.

[4] H. L. Mencken, *The American Language,* 4th ed. (New York, 1936), p. 172, n. 3.

[5] Louise Pound, "Word-Coinage and Modern Trade-Names," *Dialect Notes,* 4 (1913), 29–41, discusses various processes. Though many of the proprietary names cited designate products no longer existing, Miss Pound's conclusion still holds good: ". . . the present day reveals a fluctuating and bewildering variety of commercial terms without apparent limits of kind or quantity."

[6] *Language* (New York, 1933), p. 156.

EJACULATIONS

Sounds supposedly imitative of more or less instinctive vocal responses to emotional situations have frequently become words in their own right. One of these, *ouch,* is something of a mystery: it does not appear in British writing except as an Americanism. The *OED* derives it from German *autsch,* an exclamation presumably imitative of what a German exclaims at fairly mild pain, such as stubbing a toe or hitting a thumb with a tack hammer—hardly anything more severe, for when one is suffering really rigorous pain one is not likely to have the presence of mind to remember to say "Ouch!" The vocal reaction, if any, is likely to be a shriek, a scream, or a long-drawn-out [o] or [ɔ], followed sometimes by something like [č], in any event difficult to represent in writing. But regardless of the origin of *ouch,* it may be regarded in American English as a conventional representation of the sounds supposedly, if not indeed actually, made when one is in pain. The interesting thing is that the written form has become so familiar, so completely conventionalized, that Americans (and Germans) do actually say "Ouch!" when they have hurt themselves so slightly as to be able to remember what they *ought* to say under the circumstances.

Other such written representations, all of them highly conventionalized, of what are thought to be "natural utterances" have also become actual words, for instance *ha-ha,* with the variant *ho-ho* for Santa Claus and other jolly fat men, and the girlish *tehee* which the naughty but nonetheless delectable Alison gives utterance to in Chaucer's *Miller's Tale,* in what is perhaps the most indecorously funny line in English poetry. Now, it is likely that, if Alison were a real-life girl (rather than better-than-life, as she is by virtue of being the creation of the male wishful thinking of a superb artist), upon receipt of the misdirected kiss she might have tittered, twittered, giggled, or gurgled under the decidedly improper circumstances in which she had placed herself. But how to write a titter, a twitter, a giggle, or a gurgle? Chaucer was confronted with the problem of representing by alphabetical symbols whatever the appropriate vocal response might have been, and *tehee,* which was doubtless more or less conventional in his day, was certainly as good a choice as he could have made. The form with which he chose to represent girlish glee has remained conventional. When we encounter it in reading, we think —and, if reading aloud, we actually say—[tihí],[7] and the effect seems perfectly realistic to us. But it is highly doubtful that anyone ever

---

[7] It was presumably [tehé] in Alison's pre-vowel-shift pronunciation.

uttered *tehee,* or *ha–ha,* or *ho–ho,* except as a reflection of the written form. Laughter, like pain, is too paroxysmal in nature, too varying from individual to individual, and too unspeechlike to be represented accurately by symbols which are not even altogether adequate for the representation of speech sounds.

It is somewhat different with a vocal manifestation of disgust, contempt, or annoyance which might be represented phonetically (but only approximately) as [č]. This was as early as the mid-fifteenth century represented as *tush,* and somewhat later less realistically as *twish.* *Twish* became archaic as a written form, but [təš] survives as a spoken interpretation of *tush.* As in the instances cited, and in others to be cited, sounds came first; then the graphic representation, always somewhat inadequate; then finally a new word in the language based on an interpretation of the graphic representation of what was in the beginning not a word at all, but—to use a modern term in describing it— merely something in the nature of a sound effect.

Pish and *pshaw* likewise represent "natural" emotional utterances of disdain, contempt, impatience, irritation, and the like, and have become so conventionalized as to have been used as verbs.[8] Both began as something like [pš]. W. S. Gilbert combined two such utterances to form the name of a "noble lord," Pish-Tush, in *The Mikado,* with two similarly expressive ones, Pooh-Bah, for the overweeningly aristocratic "Lord High Everything Else."[9]

Pugh is imitative of the disdainful sniff with which many persons react to a bad smell, resembling a vigorously articulated [p]. But, as with the examples previously cited, this has been conventionalized because of the written form into an actual word pronounced [pju] or prolongedly as [píjú]. *Pooh* (sometimes with reduplication as *pooh-pooh*) is a variant, with somewhat milder implications. The reduplicated form may be used as a verb, as in "He pooh-poohed my suggestion." *Fie,* used for much the same purposes as *pugh,* is now archaic; it likewise represents an attempt at imitation. *Faugh* is probably a variant of *fie;* so, doubtless, is *phew. Ugh,* in its purest form a tensing of the stomach muscles followed by a glottal stop (p. 30, n. 1), has not been conventionalized to quite the same extent when used as

---

[8] See the citation in *Webster's Third New International Dictionary* (Springfield, Mass., 1961), which combines both, s.v. *pish* (". . . pished and pshawed a little at what had happened").

[9] Yum-Yum, the name of the delightful heroine of the same opera, is similarly a conventionalized representation of sounds supposedly made as a sign of pleasure in eating. These have given us a new adjective, *yummy,* as yet more or less confined to juvenile use—but give it time.

an exclamation of disgust or horror. As a grunt supposedly made by a comedy Indian it is, one hopes only facetiously, pronounced [əg].

The palatal click, articulated by placing the tongue against the palate and then withdrawing it by sucking in the breath, is an expression of impatience or contempt. It is also sometimes used, or at least used to be, in reduplicated form (there may in fact be three or more such clicks) in scolding children, as if to express shock and regret at some anti-social act. Its best-known written form nowadays is *tut(-tut)*, which has become a word in its own right, pronounced not as a click but according to the spelling. However, *tsk-tsk*, which apparently is intended to represent the same click, is gaining ground, though as yet unlisted in dictionaries. Teen-agers read it in the comic strips as [tísktísk]. Older written forms are *tchick* and *tck* (with or without reduplication). *Tut(-tut)* has long been used as a verb, as in Bulwer-Lytton's "pishing and tutting" (1849) and Hall Caine's "He laughed and tut-tutted" (1894), both cited by the *OED*.

A sound which we frequently make to signify agreement may be represented approximately as [m̀hm̀]. This is written as *uh-huh,* and the written form is altogether responsible for the pronunciation [əhə́]. The *p* of *yep* and *nope* was probably intended to represent the glottal stop frequently heard in the pronunciation of *yes* (without -*s*) and *no,* but one also frequently hears [yɛp] and [nop], which may be pronunciations based on the written forms.

There is, so far as I know, no written representation of the so-called Bronx cheer. Eric Partridge has suggested, however, that Hamlet's "Buz, buz!" (II.ii.396), spoken impatiently to Polonius, is intended to represent the vulgar noise also known as "the raspberry."[10]

THE USE OF PREFIXES AND SUFFIXES

New words are, however, much more commonly acquired by other processes, the most common of these being the use of prefixes and suffixes. Many of these affixes were at one time independent words, like the insignificant-seeming -*ly* of many adjectives, such as *manly, godly,* and *homely,* which has developed from Old English *līc*[11] 'body,'

[10] *Shakespeare's Bawdy* (New York, 1948), pp. 12, 83. Julian Franklin in his *Dictionary of Rhyming Slang* (London, 1960) plausibly states that *raspberry* in this sense comes from the Cockney "rhyming slang" phrase *raspberry tart* for *fart.*

[11] Surviving in *lich gate,* the roofed gateway of a churchyard where the body of the deceased is set down to await the clergyman. Though the Old English word might be applied to either a living or a dead body, in later times the meaning 'dead body' came to prevail, as in the aforementioned *lich gate* and in *lich owl,* another name for the screech owl, whose cry was supposed to be an omen of death.

and the *a-* of *aside, alive, aboard,* and *a-hunting,* which was earlier *on,* with the usual old loss of *-n* in this word when unstressed and followed by a consonant (see p. 223). When unstressed, as it inevitably came to be when used so frequently as a suffix,[12] the vowel of *līc* was shortened. Old English, as we have seen (p. 136), regularly added *-e* to adjectives to make adverbs of them, thus *riht* 'right,' *rihte* 'rightly'; and adjectives formed with *-lic* acquired adverbial forms in exactly the same way, thus *cræftlic* 'skillful,' *cræftlice* 'skillfully.' With the late Middle English loss of both final *-e* and final unstressed *-ch,* earlier Middle English *-lich* and *liche* fell together as *-li* (*-ly*). Because of these losses, we do not ordinarily associate Modern English *-ly* with *like,* the Northern dialect form which ultimately was to prevail in all dialects of English, and which stands in the same relationship to non-Northern *līch* as *dike* to *ditch.* The full form has more recently been used again as a suffix—history thus repeating itself—as in *gentlemanlike* and *godlike,* which are quite distinct creations from *gentlemanly* and *godly.*[13]

Other affixes surviving from Old English times include *be-,* the unstressed form of *by* (OE *bī*), as in *believe, beneath, beyond, behalf, between; for-,* either intensifying, as in *forlorn,* or negating, as in *forbid, forswear; -y* (OE *-ig*), as in *thirsty, greedy, bloody;*[14] *-ness,* which may be affixed to practically any adjective (or participle) to form an abstract noun, as in *manliness, dedicatedness, obligingness; un-,* for an opposite or negative meaning, as in *undress, unafraid, un-English; -dom* (OE *-dōm,* earlier an independent word which has developed into *doom,* in Old English meaning 'judgment, statute,' that is, 'what is set,' and related to *do*), as in *freedom, filmdom, gangsterdom;*[15]

---

[12] When so used, it originally meant something like 'having the body or appearance of': thus the literal meaning of, say, *manly* is 'having the body or form of a man.'

[13] The earliest instances of this new use of *like* cited in the *OED* are from the latter part of the fifteenth century.

[14] The diminutive *-y* (or *-ie*) of *Kitty, Jackie, baby,* and *hippie* (or *hippy*) is from another source and occurs first in Middle English times. The *-y* occurring in loan-words of Greek (*phlebotomy*), Latin (*century*), and French (*contrary*) origin may represent Greek *-ia* (*hysteria*), Latin *-ius, -ium, -ia* (*radius, medium, militia*), or French *-ie* (*perjury*), *-ee* (*army*). This *-y* is not a living suffix. Diminutive *-y* is living; that is, it is still available for forming new diminutives, like *Esky,* the name of the bulbous-eyed, girl-watching old gentleman who is a sort of mascot for the magazine *Esquire.* Similarly, we continue to form adjectives with the *-y* from Old English *-ig,* for example *jazzy, loony, tubby.*

[15] This has been called a "dead" suffix; but, as the last two examples indicate, it is by no means so. See Harold Wentworth, "The Allegedly Dead Suffix *-dom* in Modern English," *PMLA,* 56 (1941), 280–306.

-ing, to form verbal nouns;[16] *-ful,* to form adjectives, as in *baleful, sinful, wonderful,* and, with secondary stress, to form nouns as well, as in *handful, mouthful, spoonful; -less* (OE *-lēas* 'free from,' also used independently and cognate with *loose*), as in *wordless, reckless, hopeless; -ship* (OE *-scipe*), to form abstract nouns, as in *lordship, fellowship, worship* (that is, 'worth-ship'); *-ed,* to form adjectives from nouns, as in *storied, crabbed, bowlegged; -en,* also for adjectives, as in *golden, oaken, leaden;* and *-er* (OE *-ere*), to form nouns of agency, as in *singer, baby-sitter, do-gooder,* a suffix which, when it occurs in loan-words, for instance *butler* (from Anglo-French *butuiller* 'bottler, manservant having to do with wines and liquors') and *butcher* (from Old French, literally 'dealer in flesh of billy-goats'), goes back to Latin *-ārius,* but which is nevertheless cognate with the English ending.

Still other affixes which go back at least to Old English times are *-ster* (OE *-estre*), originally feminine, as in *spinster* 'female spinner' and *webster* 'female weaver,' but later losing all sexual connotation, as in *gangster* and *speedster; -hood* (OE *-hād*), as in *manhood* and *priesthood,* earlier an independent word meaning 'condition, quality'; *-ish* (OE *-isc*), to form adjectives, as in *English* and *womanish; -some* (OE *-sum*), likewise adjective-forming, as in *lonesome, wholesome, winsome* (OE *wynn* 'joy' plus *sum*); *under-,* as in *understand, undertake, underworld; up-,* as in *upright, upheaval, upkeep; out-* (OE *ūt-*) as in *outside, outfield, outgo; after-,* as in *aftermath, aftereffect, afternoon; -ward,* as in *homeward, toward, outward; mis-,* as in *misdeed, misalign, mispronounce; with-* 'against,' as in *withhold, withstand, withdraw;* and *-th,* for abstract nouns, as in *health, depth, sloth.*

Many of these affixes are still living, in that they may be used for the creation of new words. Most have been, and many can still be, affixed to non-native words, as in some of the examples cited, for instance *obligingness, mispronounce;* also *Czardom, Romish, orderly (-liness), sugary (-ish), pocketful, coffeeless.* A number of others very common in Old English times either have not survived at all or survive only as fossils, like *ge-* in *enough* (OE *genōg, genōh*), *afford* (OE *geforðian*), *aware* (OE *gewær*), *handiwork* (OE *handgeweorc*), and *either* (OE *ǣgðer,* a contracted form of *ǣg[e]hwæðer*). *And-* 'against, toward,' the English cognate of Latin *anti-,* survives only in *answer* (OE *andswaru,* literally 'a swearing against') and, in unstressed form with loss of both *n* and *d,* in *along* (OE *andlang*).

---

[16] Quite distinct from the archaic *-ing* used to indicate derivation from, as in *king* (OE *cyning,* literally 'son, or ideal representative, of the race, or kin'), *atheling,* and *lording,* and frequent in Old English patronymics, as in *Æðelwulfing* 'son of Æðelwulf.'

Those languages with which English has had the closest cultural contacts—Latin, Greek, and French—have furnished a number of freely used affixes for English words. The assimilation of native and foreign began quite early and has never ceased, though in earlier times it was the English suffix which was joined to the borrowed word rather than the other way round, as in Old English *grammatisc* 'grammatish,' later supplanted by *grammatical.*[17] Since English has a lexicon culled from many sources, it is not surprising that one finds a good many hybrid creations, like Greek-French *autocade* (the *auto-* of *automobile* plus the *-cade* of *cavalcade*).[18] It should likewise be noted that the *auto* of *automobile*, taken from French, in which it was also a hybrid creation, has itself become a new combining element, as in *autocar, autotruck, autobus, autocamp,*[19] quite distinct in signification from the *auto-* 'self' of *autointoxication, autoerotic,* and *automat,* which have no suggestion of automotiveness. The second element of *automobile* also, it should be noted, has acquired a suffixal function, as in *bookmobile* 'library on wheels' and *bloodmobile* 'blood bank on wheels.'

One of the most commonly used prefixes of non-native origin is Greek *anti-* 'against,' which, in addition to its occurrence in long-established learned words like *antipathy, antidote,* and *anticlimax,* has been rather freely used since the seventeenth century for new, mostly American, creations, for instance *anti-Federalist, anti-Catholic, antitobacco, antislavery, antisaloon, antiallergent,* and *antiaircraft. Pro-* 'for' has been somewhat less productive.

Other foreign forms which have been affixed to English words (whatever their ultimate origin) include the *-(i)an* of *Nebraskan, Miltonian* (Lat. *-[i]ānus*), used to form adjectives from nouns, and the neuter plural *-(i)āna* of the same Latin ending, as in *Americana, Menckeniana* —limited though the use of the latter ending might be nowadays; Latin *-orium,* as in the late Robert Ripley's *Odditorium* 'place where oddities are on display' (with a pun on *auditorium*), *pastorium* 'Baptist parsonage,' and *washatorium* 'self-service laundry'; and *-or,* as in

---

[17] For other examples, see A. Campbell, *Old English Grammar* (Oxford, 1959), pp. 206–207. Albert C. Baugh, *A History of the English Language,* 2nd ed. (New York, 1957), pp. 215–16, has an excellent brief discussion of this type of derivation—loanword plus native suffix—in Middle English times.

[18] It is likely that the *-cade* combinations were at first thought of as blends—the fusing, or telescoping, as it were—of two different words (see pp. 298–99). But *-cade* seems now to have lost its earlier association with *cavalcade* and to have become a free compounding element, at least in the world of entertainment, with the meaning 'spectacular display,' as in *aquacade, musicade, motorcade.*

[19] As also in German *Autobahn.*

chiropractor and *realtor,* words which were never known to the ancients, who were probably just as happy without them. The *-ician* of *beautician* and *mortician* is Latin, from *-ic* plus *-ian.* While these must be regarded as mere linguistic bijouteries, they at least indicate the viability of the suffixes. Still others are the *-ese* of *Federalese, Johnsonese,* and *journalese,* coming to us directly from Old French but ultimately going back to Latin *-ēnsis;* the verb-making *-ize* of *pasteurize, criticize,* and *harmonize,* along with a host of other more recent flowerings, of which we shall have more to say later; and *ante-, de-, dis-, ex-, inter-, multi-, non-, neo-, post-, pre-, pseudo-, re-, semi-, sub-, ultra-, -able, -al, -ette, -mania, -oid, -phile (-philia),* and *-phobe (-phobia),* all more or less freely adaptable. *Super-,* as in *Superman, supermarket,* and *superhighway,* has even become an independent adjective in childish and familiar usage, as in "Our new car's super"; there is also a reduplicated form *superduper* 'very super.' The independent use of *super* as a noun dates from the mid-nineteenth century; it is a clipping of *supernumerary (actor),* though in New York City it may be used for the superintendent of an apartment house.

NEW AFFIXES AND NEW USES OF OLD ONES

As has doubtless always been true, linguistically naive misunderstanding has created new suffixes in our day. In German *Hamburger* 'pertaining to, or associated with, Hamburg,' for instance, the *-er* is affixed to the name of the city. This adjectival suffix may be joined to any place name in German, for example *Kassler Rippenspeer* 'Kassel spareribs,' *Münchner Bier* 'Munich beer,' *Braunschweiger Wurst* 'Brunswick sausage,' *Wiener Schnitzel* 'Vienna cutlet,' and the like. In English, however, the *-burg-,* and, to a lesser extent the *-furt-* of *Frankfurter* 'pertaining to Frankfurt,' have been taken as suffixal elements: witness the scores of *-burger* combinations which have appeared within the past thirty years or so—most of them probably ephemeral, though *cheeseburger* has certainly acquired a permanent place in the American culinary vocabulary (*O tempora, O mores!*).[20] The same misunderstanding of *Frankfurter* is indicated by *shrimpfurter* and a few other such gaucheries. *Burger* is entered independently as a noun in *Webster's Third New International Dictionary,* denoting a sandwich containing a patty of meat or some other food (*any* other food, in fact) capable of being made into a patty. **Furter*

[20] Many of these were recorded in the pages of *American Speech* between 1939 and 1944.

has not as yet made the grade; it is doubtless dying even as a suffix. Purists will not lament its demise.

Whereas the proliferating of *-burger* is limited only by the number of edibles and near-edibles which can be patted into cakes, that of *-copter,* which is also due to a misunderstanding, is more or less limited to aviation enthusiasts. In *helicopter,* the source of the various new combinations, the *-o-* is the combining element between Greek *helix* 'spiral' and *pter(on)* 'wing,' but the word has been blunderingly analyzed as *heli-copter* rather than as *helico-pter*[21] and, in addition to the independent *copter,* such combinations as *gyrocopter* and *hoppicopter* have come into being.[22]

Though no man can say why—fashion would seem to be the principal determinant—certain affixes have been particularly popular during certain periods. For instance, *-wise* affixed to nouns and adjectives to form adverbs was practically archaic until, approximately, the 1940's, occurring only in a comparatively few well-established words, such as *likewise, lengthwise, otherwise,* and *crosswise.* The *OED* cites a few examples of its free use in modern times, for instance *Cardinalwise* (1677), *festoon-wise* (1743), and *Timothy* or *Titus-wise* (1876). But around 1940 began a mighty proliferation of words in *-wise,* for instance *budgetwise, saleswise, weatherwise, healthwise,* and literally scores of others which can hardly be written off as ephemeral. Because of its economy in circumventing such phrases as *in respect of* and *in the manner of,* many such new coinages are likely to become permanent additions to the language, despite all the objurgations of older-generation speakers, who of course get along well enough without them, just as they always have done. The sudden resuscitation of this suffix—an independent word so used even in Old English times, as in *rihtwīs* 'rightwise,' developing into Modern English *righteous*—is incapable of explanation. There are no inhibitions whatever on its free employment in either American or British English,[23] as in the winning coinage of Mrs. Lyndon B. (Lady Bird) Johnson: "Fabric-wise, I like this room best."[24]

---

[21] An etymologically correct **pter* would of course present certain difficulties in pronunciation.

[22] These facts are pointed out by Svante Stubelius in his *Balloon, Flying-Machine, Helicopter,* Gothenburg Studies in English, No. 9 (Göteborg, 1961), pp. 268–70.

[23] For example, "The balletgoers see lively, leaping girls and boys whirling over the stage American-wise . . ." in the London *Tatler,* November 11, 1960, p. 39; "Alex Comfort's *Come Out to Play* may not be the most accomplished of books, construction-wise, but . . ." in the London *Spectator,* November 10, 1961, p. 675.

[24] Quoted in *Time,* November 17, 1961, p. 34.

Type has enjoyed a similar vogue, and is well on its way to being a freely used suffix, though previously it was restricted to such words as *electrotype* and *prototype*. With it, adjectives may be formed from nouns, as in "Both Methodists and Episcopalians have Catholic-type bishops with considerable authority"[25] and ". . . undraped girls, in a 'Las Vegas-type revue.' "[26] Like *-wise, -type* is also economical, enabling us to short-cut such locutions as *bishops of the Catholic type* and *a revue of the Las Vegas type.*

The suffix *-ize* has been heretofore alluded to. Ultimately from Greek *-izein*, it has had a centuries-old life as a means of making verbs from nouns and adjectives — not only in English, but in other languages as well, for instance French *-iser,* Italian *-izare,* Spanish *-izar,* and German *-isieren.* Many English words with this suffix are borrowings from French, for instance (with *z* for French *s*) *authorize, moralize, naturalize;* others are English formations (though some of them may have parallel formations in French), for instance *concertize, patronize, fertilize;* still others are formed from proper names, for instance *Bowdlerize, mesmerize, Americanize.*

This suffix became very productive around 1950, and dozens of new creations have come into being: *moisturize, sanitize, glamorize, personalize* 'to mark with name, initials, or monogram,'[27] *tenderize,* and a good many others. The most widely discussed of all these creations, however, must surely be *finalize,* which descended to general usage from the celestial mists of bureaucracy, business, and industry, where nothing is merely ended, finished, or concluded. It is a great favorite of administrators of all kinds and sizes — including the academic, for one comes upon it in the "directives" of university presidents, deans, and department heads. The verb would seem to be of American origin,[28] though certainly not regarded as alien corn by the English, who by and large prefer spelling it and other such words with the French-derived

---

[25] Jacksonville *Florida Times-Union,* December 5, 1960, p. 1.

[26] *Time,* December 29, 1961, p. 13.

[27] In other senses, for example 'personify,' this word is considerably older, but is almost certainly a new creation in the sense specified.

[28] Kelsie B. Harder, in *American Speech,* 36 (1961), 239, cites an early use (1943) in a letter written by an officer of the Royal Australian Naval Volunteer Reserve to Lieutenant (later President) John F. Kennedy. H. L. Mencken in *The American Language: Supplement I* (New York, 1945), p. 402, n. 12, states that a New South Wales correspondent of *John o' London's Weekly* reported in 1936 that the word was used in Australia at the end of World War I. Harder admits the possibility, which seems to be also an extreme probability, that the term is nevertheless in its present manifestation an independent American coinage.

-ise.[29] Dwight D. Eisenhower gave it his imprimatur in a State of the Union Message, so that it automatically became "President's English" and retained this exalted status in the usage of his immediate successor, John F. Kennedy. Though there are no records of its occurrence in the public addresses of Lyndon B. Johnson and Richard M. Nixon, there is no reason to believe that the word would have been in the least offensive to men of such world-shattering consequence. Doubtless it does not occur in their public utterances only because their ghost-writers have been well aware of the puristic whoop-de-do over it. When *Webster's Third* quite properly listed the word, bellows of anger and groans of outraged propriety issued from editorial writers (notably in the *New York Times* and in *Life*), who seem with a few honorable exceptions to regard themselves as custodians of the English language.[30]

Greek formed nouns of action from verbs in *-izein* by modifying the ending to *-ismos* or *-isma,* as reflected in many pairs of loan-words in English, such as *ostracize–ostracism* and *criticize–criticism.* The suffix *-ism* may be used as an independent word, as in *creeds and isms.* Such use of suffixes must be rather rare, though *-ology* has also been so used to mean 'science,' as in "Chemistry, Geology, Philology, and a hundred other ologies."[31] Prefixes have fared somewhat better; *anti, pro, con,* and *ex* are all used as nouns.

De-, a prefix of Latin origin with privative force, is still much alive. Though many words beginning with it are from Latin or French, it has for centuries been used for the formation of new words. *Demoralize* was claimed by Noah Webster as his only coinage, and it is a fact that he was the first to use it in English; but it could just as well be from French *démoraliser.* The prefix is used before words of whatever origin, as in *defrost, dewax,* and *debunk.* Gowers cites, from a collection of "septic verbs" made by Sir Alan Herbert, such poisonous speci-

[29] It is listed by Sir Ernest Gowers, along with *casualise, civilianise, editorialise,* and *publicise* (the last two of which will not seem in the least strange to Americans except in their spelling), as one of the darlings of British bureaucratese, in his *Plain Words: Their ABC* (New York, 1954), p. 54.

[30] Apparently they were unaware that the word had also been entered in *Webster's New International Dictionary,* 2nd ed. (Springfield, Mass., 1934), in the *American College Dictionary* (New York, 1947), in *Webster's New World Dictionary of the American Language* (Cleveland, Ohio, 1953), and the *Funk and Wagnalls Standard Dictionary,* International Edition (New York, 1958).

[31] Cited from 1811 in *OED,* whose latest citation is from 1884. As we have seen, *burger,* which is commonly regarded as a suffix, has a vigorous independent existence. *Bus,* it should be noted, is part of the suffix of *omnibus.*

mens as *debureaucratise, dewater, deinsectize,* and *deratizate* 'get rid of rats,'[32] reporting *defeathered geese* from a directive issued by the British Ministry of Food. Two other *de-* words from Herbert's Index seem considerably less septic nowadays than they must have done when the list was made—*decontaminate* and *dehumidify,* which we have learned to take in our stride, though what point there was in coining them in the first place is difficult to see; they seem to be merely pompous ways of saying 'purify' and 'dry out.' The *Chamber of Horrors* (London, 1952) of "Vigilans," a glossary "of official jargon both English and American," with an introduction by Eric Partridge, lists *dehydrofreezing* (called an "American term," like most of those which the English disapprove of), *derequisition,* and *derestricted,* among others. *Dis-,* likewise from Latin, is freely used in the same privative function, particularly in officialese, as in *disincentive* 'deterrent,' *disassemble* 'take apart,' and *dissaver* 'one who does not save his money.' Other voguish affixes are *non-,* from Latin, used according to Gowers "to turn any word upside-down," as in *nonsick* 'healthy,' presumably,[33] and *nonavailability* 'lack'; *-ee,* from French, as in *draftee, trainee, donee,* and *escapee* 'escaper'; and *re-,* from Latin, as in *redecontaminate* 'purify again,' *recivilianize* 'return to civilian life,' and *recondition* 'repair, restore.'

The very popular *cafeteria* is characterized by a Swiss observer of American life as a place for "grasping food from a counter, swallowing it in record time, and rushing back to work," which has "not merely ruined the health of millions of Americans, but has also affected their mentality, humour and outlook on life." According to this jaded commentator, the American, "with his power and ingenuity for shortening life's pleasures in order to gain time for remunerative occupation and toil, has invented mass-feeding."[34] The word is of Mexican Spanish origin and originally designated an establishment for coffee-drinking rather than for food-eating. It has provided us with a suffix *-teria,* which used to carry implications of self-service and hence speed, as in *washateria, bookateria, shaveteria,* and *sodateria,* though it need no longer do so, being used frequently in the names of mere retail business establishments, like *hatateria* 'hat shop' and *snacketeria* 'snack shop or counter.'

[32] *Plain Words: Their ABC,* p. 55.
[33] Gowers cites "Institutions for the care of the non-sick" (p. 57).
[34] J. Henry Wild, *Glimpses of the American Language and Civilization* (Bern, 1945), pp. 44–45.

The -*teria* suffix began in the 1950's to be rivaled in popularity by -*rama*, from Greek *horama* 'view.' John Lotz suggests that the widespread use of this suffix stems from *Cinerama*, the wide-screen motion picture which was first shown in New York in 1952, and there is every reason to believe that he is right.[35] Lotz points out that *Cinerama* "was obviously coined on the analogy of *panorama* and the less frequent *cyclorama*." The first of its offshoots was doubtless *liquorama*, the name given to his window display by the dealer in spirits whose shop was next door to the theater where Cinerama made its debut.

Panorama, diorama, and *cyclorama,* which first appeared, according to the *OED*, in 1796, 1823, and 1840 respectively, are of course made up of Greek *pan-* 'all,' *di-* 'though,' and *kyklos* 'circle' plus *horama;* hence the -*o*- is correctly retained in these words, as it is not in *Cinerama* and other recent creations such as *beautyrama* 'beauty shop,' *bowlerama* 'bowling alley,' *icecreamerama*,[36] *Bridge-A-Rama* 'a large bridge party, the project of a University Women's Club to raise money for a fund to aid co-eds,' and, to cite a British example, *sexerama.*[37]

In the early examples cited by Lotz, the implication of -*rama* is 'spectacular display,' but more recent creations do not necessarily sustain the idea of a view; they may imply either largeness or nothing at all.[38] Ryan cites uses of the suffix to designate a process (*Slenderama*, a reducing method) or merely a product (*Coolerama*, pajamas; *Taperama*, Scotch tape).

As we have seen, many affixes can be shown to have been at one time independent words. Such words become affixes when they can no longer stand alone, that is, when they are no longer regarded as independent words. An Old English adjective in -*līc* thus may be regarded as a compound until the ending has gone through the various phonetic changes which reduced it to -*ly*. It is likely that the first of these

---

[35] "The Suffix '-Rama,'" *American Speech,* 29 (1954), 156–58. *Futurama,* the name of the General Motors exhibit during the New York World's Fair of 1939–40, as Lotz points out, seems not to have created the vogue.

[36] The most nauseating specimen cited by William M. Ryan in his aptly titled "A Plethorama," *American Speech,* 36 (1961), 230–33. It presumably designates a party of some sort with ice cream as the *pièce de résistance.*

[37] "*Accatone* [an Italian motion picture] has the breath of life in it and deserves a better fate than to be billed as just another sexerama..." (*Spectator,* November 3, 1961, p. 627).

[38] The only "Beautyrama" with which I am personally acquainted is situated in a notably rundown neighborhood and is considerably smaller and, viewed from without, less pretentious than most establishments dedicated to the beautification of the American homemaker.

changes, the shortening of the vowel because of lack of stress, was insufficient to disguise the origin of the suffix, and that analysis of such compounds was still possible and even usual, just as we still analyze *postman* as *post* plus *man* although for the second element of this compound we no longer say [mæn]; instead, the vowel is reduced to schwa, thus [pós(t)mən].

COMPOUNDS

Putting two or more words together to make a new word with a meaning in some way different, if only in being more specific, from that of its separate elements in juxtaposition—for instance, a *blackboard* is not the same thing as a *black board*[39]—has been very common in English, as in the other Germanic languages as well, from earliest times. Old English has *blīðheort* 'blithe-heart(ed),' *eaxlgestella* 'shoulder-companion, that is, comrade,' *brēostnet* 'breast-net, that is, corslet,' *leornungcniht* 'learning retainer (knight), that is, disciple,' *wǣrloga* 'oath-breaker, devil (warlock),' *woroldcyning* 'world-, that is, earthly-king,' *fullfyllan* 'to fulfill,' and many other such compound words.

The compounding process has gone on continuously. In the early 1960's, for instance, the American people heard over their radio and television sets of a *manshoot*, that is, the propelling of an astronaut into outer space. The creation did not seem particularly strange—shocking as it may have been to some from a purely humane point of view—but merely new. *Manshoot* has not lasted, but *splashdown*, in origin roughly contemporaneous with it, is still with us.

As far as writing is concerned—and we are not overmuch concerned with it at the moment—compound adjectives are usually hyphenated, like *one-horse, loose-jointed,* and *front-page,* though some which are particularly well established, like *outgoing, overgrown, underbred,* and *forthcoming,* are written solid. It is similar with compound verbs, like *overdo, broadcast, sidestep,* beside *double-date, baby-sit,* and *goose-step,* though these sometimes occur as two words. With the writing of compound nouns the situation is likewise somewhat inconsistent: we write *ice cream, Boy Scout, real estate, post office, high school* as two words; we hyphenate *sit-in, go-between, fire-eater, higher-up;* we

[39] The fact is that nowadays many blackboards are green, or some other color. A blackboard may thus be defined as a slab of slate or similar material fixed to a wall or mounted in a standing frame for writing upon with chalk. They are sometimes referred to in Educationese as *chalkboards.*

write solid *firearm, icebox, postmaster, highball.* But hyphenation varies to some extent with the dictionary one consults, the style books of editors and publishers, and individual whim, among other things — including chronology, for the preference in recent years has been to write compounds solid: the *high-brow* of *Webster's New Collegiate Dictionary* (Springfield, Mass., 1949) has become *highbrow* in *Webster's Seventh New Collegiate* (Springfield, Mass., 1963); *egghead,* a new creation, was so written from the beginning. Compound prepositions like *upon, throughout, into,* and *within* are always written solid, as are compound adverbs like *nevertheless, moreover,* and *henceforth,* and compound pronouns like *whoever* and *myself.*[40]

A more significant and interesting characteristic of compounds — one that tells us whether we are dealing with two or more words used independently or as a unit — is their tendency to be more strongly stressed on one or the other of their elements, in contrast to the more or less even stresses characteristic of phrases. A *man-eating shrimp* would be a quite alarming marine phenomenon; nevertheless, the sharply contrasting primary and secondary stresses of *man* and *eat* (symbolized in writing by the hyphen) make it perfectly clear that we are here concerned with a hitherto unheard-of anthropophagous decapod. There is, however, nothing in the least alarming about a *man eating shrimp,* with approximately even stresses on *man* and *eat.*

Without this type of stress in compounds, the close connection between the constituents that gives them their special meanings would not be readily apparent. In effect, it welds together the elements and thus makes the difference between *hótbèd* 'heated bed of earth for growing plants' and *hot bed* 'midsummer sleeping place'; between *híghbròw* 'intellectual' and *high brow* 'result of receding hair'; between *bláckbàll* 'vote against' and *black ball* 'ball colored black'; between *gréenhòuse* 'heated structure for growing plants' and *green house* 'house painted green'; between *mákeùp* 'cosmetics' and *make up* 'reconcile'; between *hándòut* 'gift to beggar' and *hand out* 'driver's turning signal'; between *héadhùnter* 'savage' and *head hunter* 'top man on safari'; between *lóudspèaker* 'sound amplifier' and *loud speaker* 'noisy talker'; between *báby-sìts* 'takes care of infant(s) while parents go to movies or party' and *baby sits* 'infant rests weight on buttocks' — but one could go on and on with this sort of thing. In compound nouns it is usually the first element which gets the primary stress, as in all the

---

[40] For a very careful study of the writing of compounds, see *Webster's Third New International Dictionary,* pp. 30a–31a.

examples of compound nouns given above, and in adverbs and prepositions the last (*nèvertheléss, withóut*). For verbs and pronouns it is impossible to generalize (*bróadcàst, fulfíll; sómebody* [or *sómebòdy*], *whoéver*). The important thing is the unifying function of contrasting stress in the formation of compounds of whatever sort.[41]

It is a general principle that when complete loss of secondary stress occurs, phonetic change occurs as well. For instance, *Énglish mán*, having in the course of compounding become *Énglish-màn*, proceeded to become *Énglishman* [-mən]. The same vowel reduction has occurred in *highwayman* 'robber,'[42] but not in *businessman;* in *gentleman* and *horseman* (as also in the previously mentioned *postman*), but not in *milkman* and *iceman*.[43] It is similar with the [-lənd] of *Maryland, Iceland, woodland*, and *highland* as contrasted with the secondarily stressed final syllables of such newer compounds as *wonderland, movieland*, and *Disneyland;* with the *-folk* of *Norfolk* and *Suffolk* (there is a common American pronunciation of the former with [-fòk] and, by assimilation, with [-fɔ̀rk]); and with the *-mouth* of *Portsmouth*, the *-combe* of *Wyecombe*, the *-burgh* of *Edinburgh* (usually [-brə]), and the *-stone* of *Folkestone*. Even more drastic changes occur in the final syllables of *coxswain* [káksən], *Keswick*

---

[41] In *Boy Scout* and *ice cream* the primary stress may be on either element. Frequently these particular compounds may have approximately level stress. Under such circumstances, according to Leonard Bloomfield, we are dealing with a phrase rather than a compound, "although there is no denotative difference of meaning" (*Language*, p. 228). From a historical point of view, however, we may follow Otto Jespersen, who in turn is following Henry Sweet (*A New English Grammar, Logical & Historical* [Oxford, 1900] I, 286–90). Jespersen considers such combinations as representative of "a new type of compounds" which "has sprung up in ModE, in which each part is more independent," and in which level stress is approximated or even completely achieved, citing as examples, among others, *lead pencil, plum pudding, toothbrush, ground floor, downhearted*, and *old-fashioned*. But, as Jespersen says, "individual pronunciations vary not a little," and "very often instead of the fully [or approximately] equal stress of the theory we have either fore-stress or end-stress" (*A Modern English Grammar on Historical Principles* [Copenhagen, 1909] I, 154–55). The plain fact is that in every one of these compounds there usually occurs what Jespersen calls unity-stress, and it seems likely that the unity-stress principle will prevail.

[42] Though, as John S. Kenyon and Thomas A. Knott point out in their *Pronouncing Dictionary of American English* (Springfield, Mass., 1951), the secondary stress is retained when the word is used to mean 'one who oversees the building and upkeep of roads.'

[43] Pronunciation with [-mən] is recorded for this word by Kenyon and Knott, which saves it from the ignominy of having become practically archaic before it ever had a chance of attaining to what might be regarded as the final stage of *man* as part of a compound.

[kézɪk], and *Durham* [dɔ́rəm] (though in *Birmingham,* as the name of a city in Alabama, the *-ham* is pronounced as the spelling suggests it "should" be), and in both syllables of *boatswain* [bósən], *forecastle* [fóksəl], *breakfast, Christmas* (that is, Christ's mass), *cupboard,* and *Greenwich,*[44] to cite only a few of many examples. Perhaps it is lack of familiarity with the word—just as the landlubber might pronounce *boatswain* as [bótswèn]—which has given rise to an analytical pronunciation of *clapboard,* traditionally [klǽbə(r)d], on the part of younger-generation speakers (see above, p. 76). *Grindstone* and *wristband* used to be respectively [grínstən] and [rízbənd]. Not many people have much occasion to use either word nowadays; consequently, the older tradition has been lost, and the words now have secondary stress and full vowels instead of [ə] in their last elements. The same thing has happened to *waistcoat,* now usually [wéstkòt]; even among those who use the word at all, that is, the English, the traditional [wéskət] has become old-fashioned. Lack of familiarity can hardly explain the phenomenon in this instance, nor will it do for the new analysis of *forehead* (see p. 75). Perhaps a consciousness of the spelling of the word on the part of those who distrust cultural tradition is responsible. It is ironical that literacy has engendered this distrust.

Such phonetic changes as we have been considering have the effect of welding the elements of certain compounds so closely together that, judging from sound (and frequently also from their appearances when written), one would sometimes not suspect that they were indeed compounds. In *daisy,* for instance, phonetic reduction of the final element has caused that element to be identical with a suffix. Geoffrey Chaucer, without benefit of either the *OED* or scientific training in historical linguistics, guessed better than he could have known for certain when he referred to "The dayesyë, or elles the yë (eye) of day" in the Prologue to *The Legend of Good Women,* for the word is really and truly from the Old English compound *dægesēage* 'day's eye.' The *-y* of *daisy* is thus not an affix like the diminutive *-y* of *Katy* or the *-y* from Old English *-ig* of *hazy;* instead, the word is from a historical point of view a compound.

Such closely welded compounds have been called "amalgamated" by Arthur G. Kennedy,[45] who lists, among a good many others, *as* (OE *al* 'all' plus *swā* 'so'), *garlic* (OE *gār* 'spear' plus *lēac* 'leek'), *hussy* (OE

---

[44] Except for Greenwich Village in New York and Greenwich, Connecticut, this is as an American place name usually pronounced as spelled, rather than as [grénɪč] or [grénɪǰ]. The usual English pronunciation is [grínɪǰ].

[45] *Current English* (Boston, 1935), p. 350.

hūs 'house' plus *wīf* 'wife'),[46] *lord* (OE *hlāf* 'loaf' plus *weard* 'ward'), *marshal* (OE *mearh* 'horse' plus *scealc* 'servant'), *nostril* (OE *nosu* 'nose' plus *þyrel* 'hole'), and *sheriff* (OE *scīr* 'shire' plus *(ge)rēfa* 'reeve').

Many proper names are such amalgamated compounds, for instance, among place names, *Boston* ('Botulf's stone'), *Sussex* (OE *sūð* 'south' plus *Seaxe* 'Saxons'; compare *Essex* and *Middlesex*), *Norwich*[47] (OE *norð* 'north' plus *wīc* 'village'), and *Bewley* (Fr. *beau* 'beautiful' plus *lieu* 'place'). The reader will find plenty of other interesting examples in Eilert Ekwall's *Concise Oxford Dictionary of English Place-Names*, 4th ed. (Oxford, 1960). It is similar with surnames (which are of course sometimes place names as well), for instance *Durward* (OE *duru* 'door' plus *weard* 'keeper'), *Purdue* (Fr. *pour* 'for' plus *Dieu* 'God'), and *Thurston* ('Thor's stone,' ultimately Scandinavian); and with a good many given names as well, for instance *Ethelbert* (OE *æðel* 'noble' plus *beorht* 'bright'), *Alfred* (OE *ælf* 'elf' plus *rēd* 'counsel'), and *Mildred* (OE *milde* 'mild' plus *þryð* 'strength').

The making of a compound is inhibited by few considerations other than those dictated by meaning. A compound may be used in any grammatical function: as noun (*wishbone*), adjective (*foolproof*), adverb (*overhead*), verb (*gainsay*), or preposition (*without*). It may be made up of two nouns (*baseball, mudguard, manhole*);[48] of an adjective followed by a noun (*bluegrass, madman, first-rate*); of a noun followed by an adjective or a participle (*bloodthirsty, trigger-happy, homemade, heart-breaking, time-honored*); of a verb followed by an adverb (*pinup, breakdown, setback, cookout, sit-in*); of an adverb followed by a verb form (*upset, downcast, forerun*); of a verb followed by a noun which is its object (*daredevil, blowgun, touch-me-not*); of a noun followed by a verb (*hemstitch, pan-fry, typeset*); of an adverb followed by an adjective or a participle (*overanxious, oncoming, well-known, uptight*); of a preposition followed by its object (*overland, indoors*); and of a participle followed by an adverb (*washed-up, carryings-on, worn-out*). There are in addition a number of phrases which have become welded into compounds, for example *will-o'-the-wisp, happy-go-lucky, hop-o'-my-thumb, mother-in-law, tongue-in-cheek, hand-to-mouth, lighter-than-air, love-in-a-mist*. Many compounds are made up of adjective

---

[46] A beautiful example of pejoration. The two words following illustrate the opposite semantic development, melioration.

[47] Traditionally pronounced to rime with *porridge*, as in the old nursery jingle about the man from Norwich who ate some porridge. The name of the city in Connecticut is, however, pronounced as the spelling seems to indicate.

[48] The first noun is in a few traditional compounds the genitive form, for example *bird's-eye, marksman*, and *daisy*.

plus noun plus the ending *-ed,* for example *bald-headed, dimwitted, hairy-chested,* and some of noun plus noun plus *-ed,* for example *pig-headed* and *snow-capped.*

CLIPPED FORMS

An abbreviation, or clipped form, must be regarded as a new word, particularly when, as it frequently does, it supplants the longer form altogether. Thus, *mob* can be said to have supplanted *mobile vulgus* 'movable, or fickle, common people,' and *omnibus,* literally 'for all,' is in the sense 'motor vehicle for paying passengers' almost as archaic as *mobile vulgus,* having been strangely clipped to *bus*—strangely only because *bus* is no root, but merely part of an ending *-ibus* occurring in the dative (and ablative) plural forms of all Latin nouns of the third declension, that to which *omnis* 'all' belongs. But there is really no reason why English usage should reflect, or even particularly respect, the grammatical features of other languages from which it has borrowed words. Certainly it has not done so here, nor with *burger* and *copter* (pp. 283–84). *Periwig,* like the form *peruke* (Fr. *perruque*) of which it is a modification, is completely gone; only the abbreviated *wig* survives, and those who use it are not likely to be even slightly aware of the full form. *Taxicab* has so completely superseded *taximeter cabriolet* that no one associates it with the longer forms, if indeed they are known at all, and has supplied us with two new words, *taxi* and *cab.*[49] *Pantaloons* seems quite archaic.[50] The clipped form *pants* may be said to have won the day completely. The singular form *pant,* previously occurring mainly in *pant-leg,* is coming to be more and more used, at least in advertising directed to women, in reference to what is called a *pantsuit.* Advertisements in the *New York Times* during 1970 featured such fine flowerings of *haute couture* as a "top-stitched pant-coat," a "jumper-and-pant set," and a "marvelous tunic and pant idea"—all presumably conducive to "pantdressing in a softer vein." The diminutive form of the singular is, it should be noted, long established in *pantywaist* and *panty girdle.*

Bra seems similarly to be pushing out *brassière,* which in French means a shoulder-strap (it is a derivative of *bras* 'arm') or a bodice

---

[49] As a shortening of *cabriolet, cab* is almost a century older than *taxicab.*

[50] I can, however, remember hearing it used in all seriousness by my maternal grandfather (1857–1924), who considered *trousers* non-U ("Let the tailors call 'em that") and *pants* inexpressibly low. He was a very conservative man in almost every respect.

fitted with such straps.[51] British English *perm,* from *permanent wave,* has found little favor with the American homemaker and those who have dedicated their lives to her beautification. No drinker nowadays imbibes *geneva* as the principal ingredient of his martinis; the clipped *gin,* first noted by Bernard Mandeville in 1714 in his *Fable of the Bees,* has driven out the full form, which, incidentally, has nothing to do with the Swiss city in which John Calvin flourished, but which has come to us by way of Dutch (p. 334). *Whisk(e)y* and *brandy* are similarly clippings of *whiskybae* and *brandywine.*

Other abbreviated forms more commonly used than the longer ones include *phone, zoo, extra, flu, auto,* and *ad. Zoo* is of course from *zoological garden* with the sound-change from [zoə-] to [zu-] because of the spelling. *Extra,* which is probably a clipping from *extraordinary,* has become a separate word. *Auto,* like the full form *automobile,* is rapidly losing ground to *car,* an abbreviated form of *motorcar.* In time *auto* may become archaic. *Advertisement* has become *ad* in American English, but was clipped less drastically to *advert* in British English, though *ad* is rapidly gaining ground in England. *Razz,* a clipped form of *raspberry* 'Bronx cheer' (see above, p. 279), is doubtless more frequently used, since it may be either noun or verb, than the full form.

Clipped forms occur in practically all, if not indeed in all, walks of life, for instance the collegian's *lab, exam, lit, math, Bus Ad* (for *Business Administration,* a fully developed course of study in American universities, the pronunciation varying, depending upon the school, as [bəs ǽd] and [bìz ǽd]); the housewife's *perk* (*percolate*), *vac* (*vacuum cleaner,* also 'to clean with a vacuum cleaner'), *fridge* (*refrigerator,* pretty much confined to British use); the oil-field worker's *reefer*[52] (*refrigerator car*), *toolie* (*tool dresser*), *forams* (*foraminifera*);[53] the criminal drug addict's *Chino*[54] (*Chinese*), *benny* (*benzedrine*), *Harry* (*heroin*);[55] and the cowboy's *tarp* (*tarpaulin*), *wrango* (*wrangler*), *bronc*

[51] The woman's garment worn for uplifting, exaggerating the proportions, or otherwise modifying the contour of the breasts is in French called a *soutien-gorge.*

[52] To the drug addict this word means 'marijuana cigarette.'

[53] Lalia Phipps Boone, *The Petroleum Dictionary* (Norman, Okla., 1952).

[54] The *o*-suffix is of fairly frequent occurrence in unconventional English, for instance *righto, kiddo, cheerio, daddy-o, ammo, blinko, stinko, blotto, combo, billy-o, bingo, weirdo,* and a good many others. Eric Partridge, *Dictionary of Slang and Unconventional English,* 3rd ed. (New York, 1950), records *like Jimmy-o* as a variant of *like Billy-o, dekko* 'look,' *blindo* 'drunk' (hence synonymous with *stinko* and *blotto*), among a number of others.

[55] From "A Glossary of Terms Commonly Used by Underworld Addicts," in Chapter 10 of David W. Maurer and Victor H. Vogel, *Narcotics and Narcotic Addiction* (Springfield, Ill., 1954).

(*bronco*).[56] Many of the clipped forms recognizable as such which have been hitherto mentioned are by no means characteristic of informal speech. They occur in all varieties; this is to say, there are practically no situations in life so exalted that one would not say *car* (for *motorcar*), *phone, zoo, cab,* and *flu.* As for *mob, bus, wig,* and the names of the alcoholic drinks which have been cited, these are the only terms extant; between them and their full forms no choice is possible.

A special type of abbreviation consists of what is left over after an initial unstressed syllable has been lost, as in childish "'Scuse me" and "I did it 'cause I wanted to." Frequently this phenomenon has resulted in two different words, for instance *fender, fence, cute, squire,* and *sport,* which are simply aphetic forms of *defender, defense, acute, esquire,* and *disport.* Sometimes, however, an aphetic form may occur simply as a variant of the longer form, for instance *possum* (from *opossum*) and *coon* (from *raccoon*). Early Modern English *pothecary* and *spittle* (or *spital*) are aphetic forms of *apothecary* and *hospital.* The meanings of *etiquette* and the aphetic form *ticket* have become rather sharply differentiated; the primary meaning of French *étiquette* is preserved in the English shortening.

BACK FORMATIONS

Back formation—the making of a word from a word which is mistakenly assumed to be a derivative of it, as in *to burgle* from *burglar,* the final *ar* of which suggests that the word is a noun of agency and hence *ought* to mean 'one who burgles'[57]—has been the source of a smallish number of new words. In origin the final consonant [-z] of *pease* is not, as it seems to the ear to be, the English plural suffix -*s;* it is in fact not a suffix at all. But by the seventeenth century *pease* was mistaken for a plural, and a new singular, *pea,* was derived from a word which was itself singular,[58] precisely as if we were to derive a form **chee* from *cheese* under the impression that *cheese* was plural; then we should have *one chee, two chees,* just as we now have *one pea, two peas. Cherry* has been derived by an identical process from Old English *ciris,* a Latin loan-word (compare Fr. *cerise*), the final *s* having been assumed to be the plural suffix. Similarly, *sherry wine* was once

---

[56] Ramon F. Adams, *Western Words* (Norman, Okla., 1944). The first known occurrence of *tarp* in print is from 1906 and comes from Los Angeles (M. M. Mathews, *A Dictionary of Americanisms* [Chicago, 1951]). The clipped form is by now as familiar to campers and to truck drivers as to cowboys. The *DA*'s second citation is from an issue of the magazine *Outing* for 1920 and refers to camping.

[57] Similarly with facetious *to ush* from *usher* and *to buttle* from *butler.*

[58] It had an unchanged plural.

sherris wine, to cite one of the English spellings for Xeres[59] (now Jerez), the city in Spain where the wine was originally made. The wonderful one-hoss *shay* of Holmes's poem was so called because of the notion that *chaise* was what it sounds like, a plural form, and the heathen *Chinee* of Bret Harte's poem is similarly explained.[60]

The adverb *darkling* 'in the darkness' (*dark* plus adverbial *-ling*, a suffix which in Old English denoted direction, extent, or something of the sort) has been misunderstood as a present participial form, giving rise to a new verb *darkle,* as in Lord Byron's "Her cheek began to flush, her eyes to sparkle,/And her proud brow's blue veins to swell and darkle" (*Don Juan* VI.101), in which *darkle* is construed to mean 'to grow dark.' A few years previously, in his "Ode to a Nightingale," John Keats had used *darkling* in "Darkling I listen; and, for many a time,/I have been half in love with easeful Death," where it presumably has the historical adverbial sense. It is not here implied that Byron misunderstood Keats's line; the examples merely show how easily the verb might have developed as a back formation from the adverb.[61] *Grovel,* first used by Shakespeare (*OED*), comes to us by way of a similar misconception of *groveling* (*grufe* 'face down' plus *-ling*), and *sidle* is likewise from *sideling* 'sidelong.'[62]

---

[59] In Spanish *x* formerly had the value [š], so that the English spelling was perfectly sound phonetically.

[60] Other nouns in the singular which look like plural forms are *alms* (OE *ælmysse,* from Lat. *eleēmosyna*), *riches* (ME *richesse* 'wealth'), and *molasses.* The first two are in fact now construed as plurals. Nonstandard *those molasses* assumes the existence of a singular *that *molass,* though such a form is not indeed heard. A story is told of a Southern "colonel" who, in the course of reproving his small black servitor for spilling a jug of molasses, said, "You git down theah, suh, and lick them every one up," but it is doubtless apocryphal. I am informed, however, on unimpeachable feminine authority, that those who sell women's hose sometimes refer to a single stocking, or perhaps to a pair collectively, as a "very nice hoe."

License, pulse, and *appendix* sound like plurals. I have heard the back formation **licent* a good many times from unsophisticated speakers, usually in the phrase "licent tag," and the fact that *pulse* and *appendix* in nonstandard use frequently take plural verbs indicates the existence, somewhere in the tortuous maze of the *psyche linguistica* of the common man, of assumed singular forms **pult* and **appendick,* even though these may never be heard.

[61] The earliest citation of the newer verb in the *OED* is from the year 1800, when it occurs in Tom Moore's "Ode to Anacreon." Could Byron, who first used the word in 1819, have picked it up from his friend Moore?

[62] Compare the now forgotten back formation *to quisle* 'to act as a traitor,' from Vidkun Quisling, the Norwegian traitor, executed in 1945. An intentional humorous assumption of *-ing* as a participial ending occurs in J. K. Stephen's immortal "When the Rudyards cease from Kipling,/And the Haggards ride no more."

There is another species of back formation, in which the secondary form could just as well have been the primary one, and in which no misunderstanding is involved. *Typewriter,* of American origin, came before the verb *typewrite;* nevertheless, the ending *-er* of *typewriter* is actually the noun-of-agency ending, so that the verb could just as well have come first, only it didn't. It is similar with *housekeep* from *housekeeper* (or *housekeeping*) and *baby-sit* from *baby sitter.* The adjective *housebroken* 'excretorily adapted to the indoors' is older than the verb *housebreak;* but, since *housebroken* is actually a compounding of *house* and the past participle *broken,* the process might just as well have been the other way around — the usual way — except that it wasn't.

BLENDS

The blending of two existing words to make a new word was doubtless an unconscious process in the oldest periods of our language. The *haþel* 'nobleman' in line 1138 of the late fourteenth-century masterpiece *Sir Gawain and the Green Knight* is apparently a blend of *aþel* (OE *æðele* 'noble') and *haleþ* (OE *hæleð* 'man'). Other early examples[63] are *flush* (*flash* plus *gush;* the *Random House Dictionary* says "in some senses, further blended with *blush*") [1548]; *twirl* (*twist* plus *whirl*) [1598]; *dumfound* (apparently *dumb* plus *confound*) [1653]; and *flurry* (*flutter* plus *hurry*) [1698].

Lewis Carroll (Charles Lutwidge Dodgson[64]) made a great thing of such blends, which he called "portmanteau words," particularly in his "Jabberwocky" poem. Two of his creations, *chortle* (*chuckle* plus *snort*) and, to a lesser degree, *galumph* (*gallop* plus *triumph*), have become established in the language. His *snark,* a blend of *snake* and *shark,* though widely known, failed to find a place because there was no need for it.

Recent years have seen a mighty proliferation of conscious blendings. Perhaps the most successful of these — certainly the most well established — are *smog* (*smoke* plus *fog*) and *motel* (*motor* plus *hotel*).[65] *Urinalysis* (*urine* plus *analysis*), of American origin also, first appeared in 1889 and has since attained to scientific respectability,[66] as has the

[63] The dates of earliest occurrence are those given in the *OED.*

[64] His endearing passion for "fooling around" with language is indicated by his pen name: *Carolus* is the Latin equivalent of *Charles,* and *Lutwidge* must have suggested to him German *Ludwig* (on phonological grounds, Latin *Ludovicus* seems less likely), the equivalent of English *Lewis. Charles Lutwidge* thus became (in reverse) *Lewis Carroll.*

[65] There are also, at least in Florida, *botels* for those who arrive in boats.

[66] That the English are perfectly well able to do this sort of thing is indicated by *breathalyser* and *bloodalyser* (*breath, blood* plus *analyser*) 'apparatus used by British police for testing whether one has been drinking' (*Spectator,* January 22, 1961, p. 920).

much more recent *quasar* (*quasi* plus *stellar*). *Cafetorium* (*cafeteria* plus *auditorium*) has made a great deal of headway in the American public school systems, and would seem to be a useful term for a large room planned for the double purpose indicated by it. Boy Scouts frequently have *camporees* (*camp* plus *jamboree*[67]). A number of eating establishments now feature *broasted* (*broiled* plus *roasted*) chicken, which a nonepicurean — say, a growing boy — might conceivably order for *brunch* (*breakfast* plus *lunch*).

The news magazine *Time* has originated a number of blends, of varying degrees of ingenuity. Some of these are widely known, but they cannot be said to be really current in speech. *Cinemactor* (*cinema* plus *actor*) is probably the one which comes first to mind, but it is not likely ever to be taken very seriously. Walter Winchell in his column made great use of the blend as a stylistic device. His most successful creation, and the one most worthy to survive, though it doubtless will not do so, is *to infanticipate* 'to be expecting a baby' (*infant* plus *anticipate*); but even this, though amusing and very widely known, cannot really be said to be in current use.

The number of examples which have been cited might be multiplied without any citations of trade names, in the making of which blending has in recent times played an important part; but there is no point in doing so. Blends are easy to create, which is doubtless why there are so very many of them, and they are at the moment very popular. It would have been very surprising if John Fitzgerald Kennedy's program of medical care for the elderly had not become *Medicare*.

ACRONYMS

The use of the initial letters of the words in phrases (*O.K.*, *Y.M.C.A.*), sometimes of syllables (*TB, TV, PJs* 'pajamas'), as if these were words has long been common. Usually the motive for this is either brevity or catchiness, though sometimes euphemism may be involved, as with *B.O., B.M.,* and *VD* — all listed in *Webster's Third New International*. Perhaps *TB* also was euphemistic in the beginning, when the disease was a much direr threat to life than it now is and its very name was uttered in hushed tones. A few forms so abbreviated have undergone expansion for some special reason, such as aural clarity; for instance A.M. and P.M., which are to the British railway signalman *ack emma* and *pip emma*. These expansions were also used in the British military services as early as World War I.

[67] According to the *Random House Dictionary* (New York, 1966), this word is itself "apparently" a blend of *jabber* and *shivaree*, with the *m* from *jam* 'crowd.'

The "New Deal" of Franklin Delano Roosevelt, the first of our chief executives to be known by his initials only, dealt out among its other blessings a good many alphabetically named government agencies: *NRA, HOLC, OPA, WPA,* and others, the whole business being summarized in a famous *bon mot* by Al Smith—"alphabet soup." Such lavish use of initials in circles so exalted was bound to confer dignity and status upon what had hitherto been regarded as a more or less informal sort of abbreviation like, to cite a few earlier examples, *P.D.Q., I.W.W., G.O.P.,* and *O.K.*

It is inevitable that it should have dawned upon some waggish genius that the initial letters of words in certain combinations frequently spelled other words, or at least made pronounceable sequences of letters: thus, though C.O.D. has never actually been so treated, it might have been pronounced like *cod.* This is in fact what children sometimes do with the initial letters of their names if they are lucky enough to have a vowel in the middle. There had to be a learned word to designate such a process, and *acronym* was coined from Greek *akros* 'tip' and *onyma* 'name,' by analogy with *homonym.* The British seem to have beaten us to the discovery of the joys of making acronyms, even though the impressively learned word to designate what is essentially a letters game was probably born in America. In any case, as early as World War I days the *D*efence [*sic,* in British spelling] *of* the *R*ealm *A*ct had come to be called *Dora* and a member of the *Wo*men's *R*oyal *N*aval *S*ervice had come to be called (with the insertion of a vowel) a *Wren. Wren* furnished the pattern in World War II for *Wac* (*W*omen's *A*rmy *C*orps) and a number of others—our happiest being *Spar* 'girl Coast Guard,' from the motto of the U.S. Coast Guard, *S*emper *Par*atus. The euphemistic *fu* words—the most widely known are *snafu, tarfu,* and *fubar*—are also among the acronymic progeny of World War II. The process has in some instances been reversed, for example. *Wave,* which resembles a genuine acronym, but which one would suspect preceded the phony-sounding supposed source, *W*omen *A*ccepted for *V*olunteer *E*mergency *S*ervice. The much more recent *Yippie* is probably best regarded as a reverse acronym. The *yip* is explained by the Yippies themselves as from *Y*outh *I*nternational *P*arty, but it seems very likely that *hippie* (*hip* 'aware' plus diminutive ending, and thus not an acronym) furnished the pattern. It is highly likely and in most instances certain that the following are also reverse acronyms: *CORE* (*C*ongress *o*f *R*acial *E*quality), *NEGRO* (*N*ational *E*conomic *G*rowth and *R*econstruction *O*rganization), *JOBS* (*J*ob *O*pportunities in the *B*usiness *S*ector), *NOW* (*N*ational *O*rganization of *W*omen), and *WITCH* (*W*omen's *I*nternational *T*errorist *C*onspiracy from *H*ell). The last, which has appeared frequently in the public prints, is probably not to be taken seriously.

The business of shooting people through space, into orbit, and ultimately to the moon and other planets has been organized by NASA, pronounced [nǽsə] or [nɑ́sə], from *N*ational *A*eronautics and *S*pace *A*dministration. It may well be that in time acronyms will be as common as coinage from Greek roots in the naming of scientific developments. The best-known scientific acronym is *radar,* from *ra*dio *d*etecting *a*nd *r*anging, but there are a good many others less widely current, like the more recent *laser* (*l*ight *a*mplification by *s*timulated *e*mission of *r*adiation). *Laser* was obviously suggested by an earlier acronym *maser* (*m*icrowave *a*mplification by *s*timulated *e*mission of *r*adiation).

The use of acronyms for trade names is well understood and has been established for a long time. Louise Pound said of them in 1913 — she did not of course use the word *acronym* to designate them, for the very good reason that it had not yet been coined — that "there are probably many terms so built; but they are not always easy to recognize, especially by those unfamiliar with the inventor's or the manufacturer's name, or with the story of the naming," and cites *Reo* (automobile, made by the *R. E. O*lds Company), *Sebco* (extension drill, made by the *S*tar *E*xpansion and *B*olt *Co*mpany), and *Pebeco* (tooth powder, made by *P. Be*iersdorf and *Co*mpany, Hamburg, Germany).[68]

FOLK ETYMOLOGY

Folk etymology — the naive misunderstanding of a more or less esoteric word which renders it into something more familiar and hence seems to furnish it with a new etymology, false as it may be — has been a minor source of new words. Spanish *cucaracha* 'wood louse' has thus been modified to *cockroach,* though the justly unpopular creature so named is neither a cock nor a roach in the earlier sense of the word (that is, a freshwater fish). Notions of verbal delicacy have largely done away with what looks like the first element of an English compound (but which, as we have just seen, really isn't anything of the sort), with the consequence that *roach* has come to mean what *cucaracha* originally meant.

A very neat example of how the folk-etymological process works is furnished by the experience of a German teacher of ballet who attended classes in modern dance at an American university in order to observe American teaching techniques. During one of these classes, she heard a student describe a certain ballet jump which he referred to as a "soda box." Genuinely mystified, she inquired about the term. The student who had used it and other members of the class averred that it was precisely what they always said and that it was spelled as they pronounced it — *soda box*. What they had of course misheard from their instructor was the practically universal ballet term *saut de basque* 'Basque leap.' One cannot but wonder how widespread the folk-etymologized term is in American schools of the dance.[69]

All of us sometimes hear a new word imperfectly, and frequently when among friends we ask, "How do you spell it?" — as if such knowledge were necessarily a sure clue to either its standard pronunciation or its meaning. But often we think that we have understood and go on thinking so, perhaps for years, like the woman who told me with considerable amusement at her own naiveté that it was only after her marriage that she realized that the name of a certain piece of furniture which she thought of as a *Chester drawers* was really a *chest of drawers*.[70] Sometimes our misunderstanding is aided by sheer and amazing coincidence. As a child too young to read, I misheard *artificial snow* as *Archie Fisher snow*, a plausible enough boner for one who lived in a town in which a prominent merchant was named Archie Fisher. In any case, Mr. Fisher displayed the stuff in his window, and for all an innocent child knew he might even have invented it.

When this sort of misunderstanding of a word becomes widespread, we have acquired a new item in the English lexicon — one which usually completely displaces the old one and frequently seems far more appropriate than the displaced word. Thus *isinglass,* which, though not really glass, is at least glasslike in that one can see through it after a fashion, makes far more sense to English-speaking people than obsolete Dutch *hysenblas* 'sturgeon bladder.'[71] Similarly, *crayfish* seems more fitting than would the normal modern phonetic development of its source, Middle English *crevice,* taken from Old French,[72] which language in turn took it from Old High German *krebiz* 'crab' (Modern *Krebs*). And *taffrail,* since it actually came to designate a rail around the stern of a ship, made better sense to seafaring men than Dutch

<hr>

[69] For this example, which is fresh as far as I know, I am indebted to my former colleague, Ernest H. Cox, who got it from the American husband of the baffled *Ballettmeisterin.*

[70] I am indebted to Virginia Glenn McDavid and William Card for the information that *Chester draws* is a frequent written form in student themes.

[71] The Dutch now say *vislijm,* that is, 'fish-lime (glue).'

[72] The Modern French form is *écrevisse.*

tafereel 'picture' (in reference to the carvings once decorating the stern).

Other examples of folk etymology follow, many of them well known and often cited in other works.[73]

ACORN: Middle English *akern*, Old English *æcern* 'oak or beech mast' — nothing to do with *corn;*

BELFRY: Middle English *berfrey* 'tower' — nothing to do with *bell;*

BRIDEGROOM: Middle English *bridegome*, Old English *brȳd* 'bride' plus *guma* 'man' — nothing to do with *groom;*

CARRYALL: French *cariole* — nothing to do with *carry* or *all;*

COLDSLAW: Dutch *koolsla*, compound of *kool* 'cabbage' plus *sla* 'salad' — nothing to do with *cold;*

CONTREDANSE, CONTRADANCE: French mistranslation of English *country dance*, reborrowed by English — nothing to do with French *contre* 'counter';

CURTAIL: older *curtal*, from French *courtault* 'shortened' — nothing to do with *tail;*

CUTLASS: French *coutelas*, ultimately Latin *cultellus* 'little knife' — nothing to do with either *cut* or *lass;*

CUTLET: French *côtelette* 'little rib,' ultimately Latin *costa* 'rib' — nothing to do with *cut;*

FEMALE: Old French *femelle* 'little woman' — nothing to do with *male;*

GREYHOUND: Scandinavian *grey* 'dog, bitch' plus *hound* — nothing to do with *grey* 'color';

HANGNAIL: earlier *angnail*, from Old English *ange* 'painful' plus *nægl* 'nail' — nothing to do with *hanging;*

HELPMATE: *help* plus *meet* 'fitting,' misunderstood as a compound in two occurrences in Genesis ii as "an help meet for him," subsequently influenced by *mate*, with which it has nothing to do;

HICCOUGH: variant spelling of imitative *hiccup* showing influence of *cough;*

HUMBLE PIE: pie made of *umbles* 'inferior parts of deer,' formerly fed to menials;

JERUSALEM ARTICHOKE: from Italian *girasole* 'sunflower' — nothing to do with Jerusalem;

MANDRAKE: from the herb *mandragora* — nothing to do with *man* or *drake;*

---

[73] Particularly George H. McKnight, *English Words and Their Background* (New York, 1923), Chapter 13, and James Bradstreet Greenough and George Lyman Kittredge, *Words and Their Ways in English Speech* (New York, 1901), Chapter 23.

-MOST (as in *foremost, utmost,* and so forth): Old English *-mest,* for
which see pp. 135–36;

MUSKRAT: Algonquian *musquash*—nothing to do with either *musk* or
rat;

PENTHOUSE: Middle English *pentis,* aphetic form of Old French
apentis, connected with *pend* 'hang'—nothing to do with either
pent 'confined' or *house;*

PICKAX: Middle English *picois,* from Old French—nothing to do with
ax;

REINDEER: Scandinavian *hreinn,* the name of the animal, plus *deer*
'animal'—nothing to do with *rein;*

SALTCELLAR: Middle English *saltsaler,* the second element from Old
French *saliere* 'pertaining to salt,' ultimately Latin *salārium,*
whose specific meaning 'money paid to soldiers for purchase of
salt' accounts for *salary*—nothing to do with *cellar* 'basement';

SHAMEFACED: earlier *shamefast,* Old English *sceamfæst,* that is,
'bound by shame';

SIRLOIN: French *sur* 'above' plus *loin*—nothing to do with *sir;*

TITMOUSE: Middle English *titmose*—nothing to do with *mouse;*

TUBEROSE: Latin *tūberōsa* 'tuberous,' misinterpreted as *tube* plus *rose;*

WELSH RAREBIT: what solemn people have done with humorous *Welsh
rabbit;*

WOODCHUCK: Algonquian *otchek*—nothing to do with either *wood* or
chucking; and

WORMWOOD: Old English *wermōd*[74] 'absinthe'—nothing to do with
worm or *wood.*

Note that all of the forms which have just been cited, with the possible exception of *coldslaw,* are standard, even though they are the
results of what were once blunders. A classical example of folk etymology, *sparrowgrass* (from *asparagus*) is no longer widely current, but
was once apparently standard usage, judging by its occurrence in the
writings of older periods. The last citation of the *OED* (from 1865) is
interesting: "I have heard the word sparrowgrass from the lips of a
real Lady—but then she was in her seventies." The word was country
usage in western Maryland, and doubtless elsewhere, as recently as
the 1930's; it may still be. Hucksters frequently shortened it to *grass.*
Chaise lounge for *chaise longue* 'long chair' is not yet standard in that
it is not used by the really cultivated. Judging by the fact that it is listed

---

[74] The name of what is, after the olive, the most expendable ingredient of the martini
cocktail is a French borrowing, as *vermout(h),* of the German form of this word,
Wermut.

as a variant in *Webster's Third,* it seems to be on the way to social respectability. A dealer informs me that the prevailing pronunciation, both of those who buy and of those who sell, is either [šɛz laʊnǰ] or [čes laʊnǰ], the first of these in some circles being considered somewhat elite, not to say snobbish, in that it indicates that the user has "had" French. In any case, as far as speakers of English are concerned, the boner is remarkably apt, as indeed are many of the folk-etymologized forms which have been cited. And there can be little doubt that the aptness of the blunder has much to do with its ultimate acceptance.

COMMON WORDS FROM PROPER NAMES

A large number of words have come to us from proper names — enough to have made up a dictionary of 476 pages with an average of between four and five entries to the page, with 165 additional pages of "border-liners and potential candidates."[75] From names of persons, to begin with, the three best-known examples are probably *lynch* (by way of *Lynch's law,* from the Virginian Captain William Lynch [1742–1820], who led a campaign of "corporeal punishment" against those "unlawful and abandoned wretches" who were harassing the good people of Pittsylvania County, such as "to us shall seem adequate to the crime committed or the damage sustained"),[76] *boycott* (from another captain, Charles Cunningham Boycott [1832–97], who, because as a land agent he refused to accept rents at figures fixed by the tenants, was the best-known victim of the policy of ostracization of the Irish Land League agitators), and *sandwich* (from the fourth Earl of Sandwich [1718–92], said to have spent twenty-four hours at the gaming table with no other refreshment than slices of meat between slices of bread). The following words are also the unchanged names of actual people: *ampere, bloomer,*[77] *bowie* (knife), *brougham, burke,*[78] *cardi-*

[75] Eric Partridge, *Name into Word* (New York, 1950).

[76] From the compact drawn up by Captain Lynch and his neighbors, cited by Mathews, *Dictionary of Americanisms,* s.v. *lynch law.*

[77] Usually in the plural, from Mrs. Amelia Jenks Bloomer (1818–94), who publicized the most unbecoming female garb ever known to man. One could devise no more appropriate name for voluminous drawers for women than the surname of the lady's unfortunate husband, though since he had nothing to do with their design or with advocating their adoption it would be more just to call them *jenkses.* But the innocent must suffer with the guilty.

[78] Meaning 'to hush up, stifle' and now rather rare in American English, though listed in all American dictionaries. The word is from William Burke, a notorious murderer (hanged, 1829) who, doubtless thinking to advance the study of anatomy and line his own pockets at the same time, smothered besotted derelicts lured from the streets and the public houses and sold their bodies to the medical school of the University of Edinburgh.

gan, chesterfield (overcoat or sofa), *davenport, derby, derrick,*[79]
derringer, gage (plum),[80] *graham* (flour), *guy, hansom, jaeger* (under-
clothes), *lavaliere, macintosh,*[81] *maudlin,*[82] *maverick, ohm, pinchbeck*
(alloy or sham jewelry), *pompadour, pullman, shrapnel, solon* (legis-
lator), *timothy* (grass), *titian* (color), *valentine, vandyke* (beard or
collar), *watt, zeppelin.* Comparatively slight spelling modifications
occur in *dunce* (from John Duns[83] Scotus [d. *ca.* 1308], who was in
reality anything but a dunce – to his admirers he was *Doctor Subtilis*)
and *praline* (from Maréchal Duplessis-Praslin [d. 1675]). *Tawdry* is a
clipped form of *Saint Audrey,* and first referred to the lace bought at
St. Audrey's Fair in Ely. *Epicure* is an anglicized form of *Epicurus.*

Kaiser and *czar* are from *Caesar,* and *faro,* the name of a card game,
is simply a spelling for *Pharaoh,* though what the connection is would
be difficult to say. *Volt* is a clipped form of the surname of Count
Alessandro Volta (d. 1827), and *farad* is derived likewise from the
name of Michael Faraday (d. 1867). The name of an early American
politician, Elbridge Gerry, is blended with *salamander* in the coinage
gerrymander. Slumber Jay, the name of an electric logging device used
in oil fields, is the result of folk etymologizing; it is from the name of
the German inventor, Schlumberger, whose name acquired a French
pronunciation when his invention was sold to a Frenchman.[84] The
following are derivatives of personal names: *begonia, bougainvillea,*
bowdlerize, camellia, chauvinism, comstockery, dahlia, jeremiad,
lewisite, lobelia, masochism, mercerize, mesmerism, nicotine, onanism,
pasteurize, platonic, poinsettia, sadism, spoonerism, wisteria, zinnia.
Bobby 'British policeman' is from the pet form of the name of Sir
Robert Peel, who made certain reforms in the London police system.
It has almost driven out the synonymous *peeler. Pantaloon,* in the
plural the old-fashioned name (see p. 294) for what used to be the most
distinctive masculine garment, is only a slight modification of French
pantalon, which in turn is from Italian *Pantalone,* the name of a silly

[79] The name of a famous hangman who operated at Tyburn in the early seventeenth
century.

[80] Usually preceded by *green-,* from Sir William Gage, who introduced the fruit into
England.

[81] Mostly British, frequently clipped to *mac.*

[82] Long an English spelling for Old French *Madelaine,* ultimately from Latin *Mag-*
dalen, that is, Mary Magdalene, who was frequently represented as lachrymose by
painters.

[83] Like many personal names, this is from a place name – Duns, Scotland, the birthplace of John, whose full style means 'John of Duns the Scotsman.'

[84] Boone, *Petroleum Dictionary.*

senile Venetian of early Italian comedy who wore such close-fitting nether coverings. *Pantalone,* in Italian meaning 'Venetian' and then 'buffoon,' is from *San Pantaleone,* the name of the patron saint of Venetians. Derivatives of the names of two writers — *Machiavellian* and *Rabelaisian* — are of such wide application that capitalizing them hardly seems necessary, any more than *platonic.*

The names of the following persons in literature and mythology (if gods, goddesses, and muses may be considered persons) are used unchanged: *atlas, babbitt, calliope, galatea, gamp* (mostly British), *hector, hermaphrodite, mentor, mercury, nemesis, pander, psyche,*[85] *trilby* (mostly British), *volcano.*[86] *Benedick,* the name of Shakespeare's bachelor *par excellence* who finally succumbed to the charms of Beatrice, has undergone only very slight modification in *benedict* '(newly) married man.' *Don Juan, Lothario, Lady Bountiful, Mrs. Grundy, man Friday,* and *Pollyanna* (which even has a derivative, *Pollyannaism*), though written with initial capitals, probably belong here also.

The following are derivatives of personal names from literature and mythology: *aphrodisiac, bacchanal, herculean, jovial, malapropism, morphine, odyssey, panic, quixotic,*[87] *saturnine, simony, stentorian, tantalize, terpsichorean, venereal, vulcanize.* Despite their capitals, *Gargantuan* and *Pickwickian* should doubtless be included here also.

Names may be used generically or because of some supposed appropriateness, like *billy* (in *billycock, hillbilly, silly billy,* and alone as the name of a policeman's club), *tom(my)* (in *tomcat, tomtit, tomboy, tommyrot, tomfool*), *john* 'toilet' (compare older *jakes*), *johnny* (in *stagedoor johnny, johnny-on-the-spot,* and perhaps *johnnycake,* though this may come from American Indian *jonikin* 'type of griddlecake' plus *cake*), *jack* (in *jackass, cheapjack, steeplejack, lumberjack, jack-in-the-box, jack-of-all-trades,* and alone as the name of a small metal piece used in a children's game known as *jacks*), *rube* (from *Reuben*), *hick* (from *Richard*), and *toby* 'jug' (from *Tobias*).

Place names have also furnished a good many common words. The following, the last of which exists only in the mind, are unchanged in form: *arras, babel, bourbon, billingsgate, blarney, buncombe* (see p. 309), *champagne, cheddar, cheviot, china, cologne, grubstreet, guinea,*

---

[85] With a good many derivatives and compoundings, for example *psychology, psychiatric, psychosomatic, psychometric, psychotherapy, psychopathy,* and the quite recent *psycholinguistics.*

[86] The Italian form of *Vulcan,* Latin *Volcānus.*

[87] In view of the prevailing fashion for a pseudo-Spanish pronunciation of the don's name, one wonders how long it will be before this adjectival derivative of it will be pronounced [kihótɪk].

homburg, japan, java 'coffee,' *limerick,*[88] *lisle, mackinaw, madeira, madras, magnesia, meander, morocco, oxford* (shoe or basket-weave cotton shirting), *panama, sauterne, shanghai, shantung, suède* (French name of Sweden), *tabasco, turkey, tuxedo, ulster, utopia.*

The following are either derivatives of place names or place names which have different forms from those which are known to us today: *bayonet, bedlam, bock, brummagem, calico, canter, cashmere, copper, damascene, damask, damson, frankfurter, gamboge, gauze, hamburger, hock, italic, jeans* (pants), *laconic, lawn* (fabric), *limousine, mayonnaise, milliner, roman* (type), *romance, sardonic, sherry* (see pp. 296–97), *sodomy, spaniel, spartan, stogy, stygian, wiener, worsted. Damascene, damask,* and *damson* all three come from *Damascus. Canter* is a clipping of *Canterbury (gallop),* the easy-going pace of pilgrims to the tomb of St. Thomas Becket in Canterbury, the most famous and certainly the "realest" of whom are a group of people who never lived at all save in the poetic imagination of Geoffrey Chaucer and everlastingly in the hearts and minds of those who know his *Canterbury Tales. Bock* and *hock* are likewise abbreviated forms, the first from *Eimbocker* in Prussia and the second from *hockamore,* which shows what the English did to *Hochheimer (Wein).*

VERNACULAR, SLANG, AND ARGOT

The specialized languages of games, trades, criminal activities, and the like have contributed a number of new words and phrases, or at least new uses of old ones, like *roughneck, roustabout, wildcatter, logrolling, crestfallen, to tilt at, to fence, fair play, to cross swords, to ante up, knockout, below the belt, mark* 'dupe,' *to bowl over, in the chips, on the lam, to take the rap,* and many others. The line between these and slang would be difficult to draw. In any case, slang has been for a long time one of the most productive forms of language. Among its more recent contributions to more or less general language are *hip* (formerly *hep*); *far out* 'eccentric, extreme'; *split* 'leave'; *cool* 'superior, sophisticated'; *straight* (formerly 'heterosexual,' but now extended to include many of the "Establishment" connotations of older *square*); the reduplicated *no-no* 'something taboo, as in "That's a no-no" '; a number of verb-adverb combinations such as *cop out* (used as verb and noun, with differentiating stress) and *hang-up* 'inconvenience, inhibition' (also used as a verb, as in "I was hung up"). Less recent are metaphorical *pad* 'lodgings,' *eye* 'detective,' *take a powder* 'run away,'

---

[88] A newer stanzaic form for humorous verse is called the *clerihew,* from the middle name of its originator, Edward Clerihew Bentley.

and the compounds *soap opera* and *whirlybird.* There are a limited number of what are doubtless pure root creations, for example *snide, bazooka* (which may owe something to both *bazoo* and *kazoo*), and the reduplicated *heebie-jeebies.*

A good many slang terms are merely clipped forms, like the aforementioned once slangy *mob,* which was reprehended, along with a number of other such abbreviations, by Jonathan Swift in a famous paper printed in the *Tatler* of September 28, 1710.[89] *Bunk* is an abbreviation of *Buncombe,* the name of a county in North Carolina, whose representative in Congress in the early 1800's once remarked in the course of a particularly dull and windy speech that he was "only talking for Buncombe." *Kook* 'eccentric person' is a shortening of *cuckoo,* which with the same meaning or used as an adjective meaning 'crazy' is also slang.[90]

LITERARY COINAGES

At what would seem to be another extreme, but is not necessarily so, literary men have also coined new terms, like Gelett Burgess' *blurb,* Will Irwin's *highbrow,* and H. L. Mencken's *Bible Belt* and the less viable *booboisie* and *ecdysiast.* Henry Bradley in his still valuable *The Making of English* (New York, 1924; first published 1904) points

[89] He did not call such terms *slang,* however; the word appeared first in print in 1756, according to the *OED.*

[90] There are many books dealing with slang. The seven-volume *Dictionary of Slang and Its Analogues* (London, 1890–1904) by John S. Farmer and William Ernest Henley —the "Invictus" poet—is practically a classical work. It is now available in a one-volume reprint. Partridge's *Dictionary of Slang and Unconventional English* is a valuable collection; so, for American slang, are *The American Thesaurus of Slang,* 2nd ed. (New York, 1953), by Lester V. Berrey and Melvin Van den Bark, and the *Dictionary of American Slang* (New York, 1960), edited by Harold Wentworth and Stuart Berg Flexner. Partridge has also written *Slang Today and Yesterday* (London, 1933). H. L. Mencken's *The American Language,* 4th ed. (New York, 1936) has an excellent discussion in Chapter 9, which is amplified in *Supplement II* (New York, 1948). References to earlier works will be found in some of these more recent ones. A very prolific American writer on argot is David W. Maurer. His *Whiz Mob: A Correlation of the Technical Argot of Pickpockets with Their Behavioral Pattern* was published by the American Dialect Society in 1955, and his *The Argot of the Racetrack* by the same Society in 1951. There are a good many word lists and articles on argot and specialized vernaculars in other publications of the American Dialect Society and in *American Speech.* Eric Partridge has a *Dictionary of the Underworld* (London, 1949), and there is a *Dictionary of American Underworld Lingo* (New York, 1950), edited by Hyman E. Goldin, Frank O'Leary, and Morris Lipsius, described in the Introduction to the work as "two long-term convicts and a prison chaplain," who were assisted by more than a score of "expert advisers whose qualifications were born of years of criminal activity and years of imprisonment alike."

out that "it is a truth often overlooked, but not unimportant, that every addition to the resources of a language must in the first instance have been due to an act (though not necessarily to a voluntary or conscious act) of some one person," and devotes an entire chapter (pp. 215–40) entitled "Some Makers of English" to illustrating this truth. He cites among others *lovingkindness* (Coverdale), *peacemaker* (Tindale), *braggadocio* and *derring-do*[91] 'chivalry' (Spenser), *lonely, dwindle,* and *orb* 'globe' (Shakespeare), *pandemonium, irresponsible,* and *impassive* (Milton), and *raid, gruesome, uncanny,* and *glamour* (Scott).[92] To these Stuart Robertson and Frederic G. Cassidy add a good many more recent examples.[93] I. Willis Russell, as chairman of the New Words Committee of the American Dialect Society, has made extensive collections of new words. These have been published in the *Encyclopædia Britannica Yearbook* and in *American Speech.*

ONE PART OF SPEECH TO ANOTHER

A very prolific source of new words from old is the happy facility of Modern English, because of its paucity of inflection, for converting words from one grammatical function to another with no change in form. Thus, the name of practically every part of the body has been converted to use as a verb—one may *head* a committee, *shoulder* or *elbow* one's way through a crowd, *hand* in one's papers, *finger* one's tie, *thumb* a ride, *back* one's car, *leg* it along, *shin* up a tree, *foot* a bill, *toe* a mark, and *tiptoe* through the tulips—without any modification of form such as would be necessary in other languages, for instance German, in which the suffix *-(e)n* is a necessary part of all infinitives. It would not have been possible to do this in Old English times either, when infinitives ended in *-(a)n* or *-ian*. But Modern English does it with the greatest ease; to cite a few nonanatomical examples, *to contact, to chair* (a meeting), *to telephone, to date, to park, to proposition,* and *to M.C.* (or *emcee*). Verbs may also be used as nouns. One may, for instance, take a *walk*, a *run*, a *drive*, a *spin*, a *cut*, a *stand*, a *break,* a *turn,* or a *look.* Nouns are just as freely used as adjectives, or practically so as attributives (*head bookkeeper, handlebar mustache, stone wall*), and adjectives and participles are used as nouns, for instance *commercial* 'sales spiel on a television or radio show,' *formals* 'evening

---

[91] This stemmed from Spenser's misunderstanding of Middle English *durrying* (*dorryng*) *don* 'daring to do,' as in Chaucer's *Troilus and Criseyde* V.837: "In durrvng don that longeth to a knyght" ('In daring to do what appertains to a knight').

[92] Bradley makes it clear that the first *known* occurrences are in the works of the authors named; there may have been earlier ones.

[93] *The Development of Modern English,* 2nd ed. (New York, 1954), pp. 215–31.

clothes,' *clericals* 'clergyman's street costume,' *devotional* 'short prayer service subsidiary to some other activity,' *private* 'noncommissioned soldier,' *elder, painting,* and *earnings.*

Adjectives may also be converted into verbs, as with *better, round, tame,* and *rough.* In advertising "literature" we have been urged to "pleasure up" our smoking with a particular brand of cigarette, though some would doubtless have preferred a rival brand which "gentles the smoke and makes it mild." One wonders why it would not *mild* it as well as gentle it; it could perfectly well do so in English. Even adverbs and conjunctions are capable of conversion, as in "the *whys* and the *wherefores,*" "*but* me no *buts*" (in which *but* is first used as a verb, then as a pluralized noun), and *"ins* and *outs."*[94] Transitive verbs may be made from older intransitive ones, as has happened fairly recently to *to shop* ("Shop Our Fabulous Sale Now in Progress"; "It's smart for all / To shop Duvall") and *to sleep* ("Her [a cruising yacht's] designer has claimed that she can sleep six"[95]).

VERB-ADVERB COMBINATIONS

There are a good many combinations of verbs and adverbs which are used primarily as verbs, for instance *slow down, check up, fill in* 'furnish with a background sketch,' *break down* 'analyze,' and *set up,* but which are easily convertible into nouns, though usually with shifted stress, as in *to check úp* contrasted with *a chéckup.* Some such combinations are also used as adjectives, for instance *sit-down strike, sit-in demonstration,* and *drive-in theater.*

As with the verb-adverb combinations, change of form is sometimes involved when verbs, adjectives, and nouns shift functions, the functional shift being often indicated by a shift of stress: compare *upsét* (verb) and *úpset* (noun), *prodúce* (verb) and *próduce* (noun), *pérfect* (adjective) and *perféct* (verb).[96] Not all speakers make the functional stress distinction in *ally* and *address,* but many do.

---

[94] The attributive use of *in* and *out,* as in *inpatient* and *outpatient,* is quite old, as is the usage as nouns in the citation. The adjectival use of *in* meaning 'fashionable' or 'influential,' as in "the in thing" and "the in group" is, however, recent. Compare the adjectival use of the adverb *now* meaning 'of the present time' (as in "the now king"), dating from the fifteenth century; the meaning 'modern, and hence fashionable,' as in "the now thing" is a product of our own times.

[95] Let this not be supposed an instance of peculiarly American linguistic depravity; the citation is from the London *Daily Telegraph and Morning Post* of August 13, 1956 (p. 3).

[96] Jespersen, *Modern English Grammar,* I, 173–84, cites the varying stress according to grammatical function in *affix, absent, compact, conduct, content, insult, minute, object, perfume, progress, rebel, record, subject,* along with a good many others.

In this chapter we have surveyed in some detail how English has used its own resources for enriching its vocabulary. Some of the newer forms cited will probably not be approved by all, though it should be noted that they differ from forms universally accepted only in being of more recent coinage or adaptation, not in the process by which they have come into being. In the following chapter we shall examine another important process, borrowing, by which the English language has enriched itself—a process which has already been referred to many times.

XI

Foreign Elements in the English Word Stock

Thus far we have dealt only incidentally with the non-English elements in the English lexicon. In the present chapter we shall make a rapid survey of these, along with some examination of the various circumstances – cultural, religious, military, and political – surrounding their adoption.

LATIN LOAN-WORDS IN GERMANIC

Long before Anglo-Frisian began its separate existence, while it was merely a regional type of Germanic, those who spoke it had acquired, along with the other Germanic tribes, a number of Latin words – loan-words which are common to several or to all of the Germanic languages to this day. Unlike a good many later borrowings, they are for the most part concerned with military affairs, commerce, agriculture, or with refinements of living which the Germanic peoples had acquired through a fairly close contact with the Romans since at least the beginning of the Christian era. *Wine* (OE *wīn,* Lat. *vīnum*), for instance, denotes an appurtenance of the good life which the Germanic peoples learned about from the Romans. It is to be found in one form or another in all the Germanic languages – the same form as the Old English in Old Frisian and Old Saxon, *Wein* in Modern German, *wijn* in Modern Dutch, *vin* in Danish and Swedish.[1] It was brought to Britain by the Germanic warrior-adventurers who in the mid-fifth century, as we have seen, became the first English people. Their not-so-remote ancestors had known malt drinks very well – *beer* and *ale* are both

---

[1] The Balto-Slavic and Celtic peoples also acquired the same word from Latin.

Germanic words, and mead was known to the Indo-Europeans. Apparently the principle of fermentation of fruit juices was a specialty of the Mediterranean peoples, for the word for the juice of the vine after it has passed through this benevolent, civilizing, and eupeptic process comes from the Romans. Roman merchants had penetrated into the Germania of these early centuries, Roman farmers had settled in the Rhineland and the valley of the Moselle, and Germanic soldiers had marched with the Roman legions.[2]

There are about 175 such words, most of them indicating special spheres in which the Romans excelled, or were thought to do so by the Germanic peoples.[3] Many of these words have survived into Modern English. They include *ancor* 'anchor' (Lat. *ancora*), *butere* 'butter' (Lat. *būtyrum*), *cealc* 'chalk' (Lat. *calc-*), *cēap*[4] 'marketplace, wares, price' (Lat. *caupō* 'tradesman,' more specifically 'wineseller'), *cēse* 'cheese' (Lat. *cāseus*), *disc* 'dish' (Lat. *discus*), *cetel* 'kettle' (Lat. *catillus* 'little pot'), *cycene* 'kitchen' (Lat. *coquīna*), *mīl* 'mile' (Lat. *mīlia [passuum]* 'a thousand [paces]'), *mynet* 'coin, coinage, Modern English *mint*' (Lat. *monēta*), *mangere* '-monger, trader' (Lat. *mangō*), *piper, -or* 'pepper' (Lat. *piper*), *pund* 'pound' (Lat. *pondō* 'measure of weight'), *sacc* 'sack' (Lat. *saccus*), *sicol* 'sickle' (Lat. *secula*), *strǣt* 'paved road, street' (Lat. *[via] strāta* '[road] paved'),[5] and *weall* 'wall' (Lat. *vallum*).

Since all these are popular loan-words, resting upon a purely oral

---

[2] See Robert Priebsch and W. E. Collinson, *The German Language,* 4th ed., rev. (London, 1958), pp. 264–65

[3] For a detailed classification, see Mary S. Serjeantson, *A History of Foreign Words in English* (London, 1935), Appendix A, pp. 271–77

[4] Obsolete as a noun except in proper names such as *Chapman, Cheapside* (once simply *Cheap,* then *Westcheap*), *Eastcheap, Chepstow, Wincheap* (the name of a street in Canterbury, the first element of which Eilert Ekwall in his *Street-Names of the City of London* [Oxford, 1954], p. 182 n., tentatively derives from Old English *wægn* 'wain,' hence 'a market where goods were sold in wagons'). The adjectival and adverbial use of *cheap* is of early Modern English origin and is, according to the *OED,* a shortening of *good cheap* 'what can be purchased on advantageous terms.' *To cheapen* is likewise of early Modern English origin and used to mean 'to bargain for, ask the price of,' as when Defoe's *Moll Flanders* went out to "cheapen some laces."

[5] The earlier meaning survives in *Watling Street,* the name of what was a Roman road from London past St. Alban's to Wroxeter, near Shrewsbury. Edgware Road in London is part of the old Watling Street. Old English *strǣt* survives in a good many place names, for example *Stratford* 'ford by which a paved Roman road crossed a river,' *Stratton* 'a tūn (enclosure) on a Roman road,' *Streatley, Streatham, Stradbroke, Stradishall* (OE *Strǣt-gesell* 'place on a Roman road'), and a good many others listed in Eilert Ekwall's *Concise Oxford Dictionary of English Place-Names,* 4th ed. (Oxford, 1960), s.v. *strǣt, strēt.* Other old highways were Ermine Street and Icknield Street.

tradition, they have gone through all phonological developments which occurred subsequently to their adoption in the various Germanic languages. *Chalk, dish,* and *kitchen,* for instance, show respectively in their initial, final, and medial consonants the Old English palatization of *k;* in addition, the last-cited word in its Old English form *cycene* shows mutation of Vulgar Latin *u* in the vowel of its stressed syllable. German *Küche* and *Münze* (corresponding to OE *mynet*) show the same mutation. An earlier *a* has been mutated by *i* in a following syllable in *cetel* (compare Ger. *Kessel*). It is similar with the German development of the same words. All have undergone the High German sound shift (see below, p. 111), the *d* of Latin *discus* occurring as *t* in *Tisch,* the medial *t* of *monēta* and *strāta* as *z* [ts] and *ss* in German *Münze* and *Strasse,* the *p* of Latin *pondō* and *piper* as *pf* and *ff* in German *Pfund* and *Pfeffer,* and the postvocalic *k* of Latin *secula* as *ch* in German *Sichel.* The fact that none of these early loan-words has been affected by the First Sound Shift (see pp. 105–108) indicates that they were borrowed after this shift had completed itself.

POPULAR AND LEARNED LOAN-WORDS

It is important at this point to make a distinction between popular and learned loan-words, one which was first made a good many years ago by Alois Pogatscher.[6] Popular loan-words, as has been pointed out, are of oral transmission and are part of the vocabulary of every-day communication, like those words which have been cited. For the most part they are not felt to be in any way different from English words; in fact, those who use them are seldom aware that they are of foreign origin. Learned words, on the other hand, owe their adoption to more or less cultural influences. The principal influence in Old English times was, as we should expect, the church.[7]

Such words were as a rule taken over in their Latin written forms, in contrast to the early orally transmitted loans. Latin inflectional endings were, however, usually lost; the words in question were made to conform to the Old English inflectional system. The directly transcribed

---

[6] *Zur Lautlehre der griechischen, lateinischen und romanischen Lehnworte im Altenglischen* (Strassburg, 1888).

[7] The word *church* (OE *cir(i)ce*) itself is, however, the English development of a West Germanic word ultimately from Greek *kyriakon* 'of the Lord.' The pagan Germanic peoples were perfectly familiar, if only through their pillagings of churches in Roman provinces, with a number of words pertaining to Christianity. *Devil* (OE *dēofol*) is such a word, and may even be directly from Greek *diabolos,* according to A. Campbell (*Old English Grammar* [Oxford, 1959], p. 199). *God* is, on the other hand, a native Germanic word.

vowel symbols in Latin stressed syllables were pronounced according to the English system, as is inevitable when words go over from the phonetic system of one language into that of another. Such pronunciation would have approximated that of the literary Latin of the educated classes on the Continent much more closely then than now. In the interpretation of consonant symbols the medieval school tradition usually prevailed — not surprisingly in view of the fact that learned loan-words were, in the beginning at least, the more or less exclusive possession of learned men.[8]

Learned words may in time become part of the living vocabulary, even though their use may be confined to a certain class or group; or they may, as with *clerk* (OE *cleric, clerc* from Lat. *clēricus*), pass into the usage of the common people. *Cleric* was once more taken from Latin as a learned word to denote a clergyman, since *clerk* had acquired other meanings, including 'scholar,' 'scribe,' 'one in charge of records and accounts in an organization,' and 'bookkeeper.' It was later to acquire yet another meaning, 'one who waits upon customers in a retail establishment,' in American English, the equivalent of the British 'shop assistant.' The earliest English meaning has survived in legal usage, in which a priest of the Church of England is described as a "clerk in holy orders."

LATIN WORDS
IN OLD ENGLISH

The approximate time at which a word was borrowed is often indicated by its form: thus, as Serjeantson points out,[9] Old English *scōl* 'school' (Lat. *schola,* ultimately Greek) is obviously a later borrowing than *scrīn* 'shrine' (Lat. *scrīnium*), which must have been adopted before the Old English change of [sk-] to [š-] in order for it to have acquired the later sound. At the time when *scōl* was borrowed, this sound change was no longer operative. Had the word been borrowed earlier, it would have developed into Modern English **shool.* The medial consonant of Old English *fefer* 'fever'[10] (Lat. *febris*), on the other hand, reflects a late Latin change. *Febrile,* a learned loan, came into English centuries later — specifically in the seventeenth century.

Among the early English loan-words from Latin, some of which

---

[8] I have discussed these matters more fully in "The Pronunciation of Latin Learned Loan Words and Foreign Words in Old English," *PMLA,* 58 (1943), 891–910.

[9] *History of Foreign Words in English,* p. 13.

[10] It should be remembered that Old English *f* between vowels stood for [v].

were acquired from the British Celts, are *tæfl* 'gaming board' (Lat. *tabula*), *candel* 'candle' (Lat. *candēla*), *sealtian* 'to dance' (Lat. *saltāre*), *sealm*[11] (Lat. *psalmus*, taken from Greek), *leahtric* 'lettuce' (Lat. *lactūca*), *eced* 'vinegar' (Lat. *acētum*), *Læden* 'Latin' (Lat. *Latīna*), *mægester* 'master' (Lat. *magister*), *cest* 'chest' Lat. *cista*, later *cesta*), *peru* 'pear' (Lat. *pirum*), *senop* 'mustard' (Lat. *sināpi*), *regol* 'rule' (Lat. *rēgula*), *port* 'harbor' (Lat. *portus*), *mynster* 'monastery' (Lat. *monastērium*), *earc* 'ark' (Lat. *arca*), *tīgle* 'tile' (Lat. *tēgula*), *sicor* 'secure' (Lat. *sēcūrus*), *stær* 'history' (Lat. *historia*, with aphesis and an unusual vowel development),[12] *crisp* 'curly' (Lat. *crispus*), *segn* 'mark, banner' (Lat. *signum*), and *ceaster* 'city' (Lat. *castra* 'camp').[13]

Somewhat later, after approximately A.D. 650, and hence not showing English sound changes, such learned loan-words as the following occur: *plaster*[14] (medical) (Lat. *emplastrum*), *alter* 'altar' (Lat. *altar*), *magister* 'master,' *martir* 'martyr' (Lat. *martyr*), *templ* 'temple' (Lat. *templum*), *(a)postol* 'apostle' (Lat. *apostolus*), *dēmon* (Lat. *daemon*), *mæsse, messe* (Lat. *missa*, later *messa*), *circul* 'circle' (Lat. *circulus*), *paper* (Lat. *papȳrus*), *cālend* 'month's beginning' (Lat. *calendae* 'calends'), *comēta* 'comet,' *balsam* (Lat. *balsamum*), *sōn* 'musical sound' (Lat. *sonus*), *fers* 'verse' (Lat. *versus*), and *cristalla* 'crystal' (Lat. *crystallum*). Since Latin borrowed freely from Greek, it is not surprising that some of the loans cited are of Greek origin, for example (to cite their Modern English forms), *apostle, demon, paper, comet, balsam,* and *crystal.* This is of course the merest sampling of Latin loan-words in Old English. Somewhat more than five hundred in all occur in the entire Old English period up to the Conquest. This is not actually a large number as compared with the Latin borrowings in later times. Serjeantson lists, aside from the words from the Continental period, 111 from the period from approximately A.D. 450 to 650, and 242 from approximately A.D. 650 to the time of the Norman Conquest.[15]

---

[11] The learned form *psalm* is of course a later borrowing.

[12] Sound changes in the early Latin loan-words are treated in detail by Campbell, *Old English Grammar*, Chapter 10.

[13] This survives in *Chester, Castor, Caister,* and as an element in the names of a good many English places, many of which were once in fact Roman stations, for instance *Manchester, Gloucester, Worcester, Casterton, Chesterfield, Lancaster,* and *Exeter* (earlier *Execestre*). The differences in form are mostly dialectal.

[14] Where only a single form is cited, as here, it is unchanged in Modern English, and where no Latin form is given, it is to be assumed that it is the same as the Old English form.

[15] Appendix A, pp. 277–88 .

Many of these words, particularly those from the later period, were certainly never widely used, or even known. Some occur only a single time, or in only a single manuscript. Many were subsequently lost, some to be reborrowed, often with changes of meaning, at a later period from French or from Classical Latin. For instance, our words *sign* and *giant* are obviously not from Old English *segn* and *gīgant*, but are later borrowings from Old French *signe* and *geant*. In addition, it should be mentioned that a learned and a popular form of the same word might coexist in Old English, for instance *Latin* and *Laeden*, the second of which might also mean 'any foreign language.'

These loan-words, the later learned ones as well as the earlier popular ones, were usually made to conform to Old English declensional patterns, though occasionally, in translations from Latin into Old English, Latin case forms, particularly of proper names, may be retained, for example "fram Agustō þām cāsere" from the translation of Bede's account of the departure of the Romans from Britain: 'from Augustus the emperor,' with the Latin ending -*ō* in close apposition with the Old English dative endings in -*m* and -*e*. As with earlier borrowings, there came into being a good many hybrid formations: that is, native endings were affixed to foreign words, for example -*isc* in *mechanisc* 'mechanical,' -*dōm* in *pāpdōm* 'papacy,' and -*ere* in *grammaticere* 'grammarian,' and hybrid compounds such as *sealmscop* (Lat. *psalma* and OE *scop* 'singer, bard'). Infinitives took the Old English ending -*ian*, for example the grammatical term *declīnian* 'to decline.'

LATIN WORDS BORROWED
IN MIDDLE ENGLISH TIMES

Many borrowings from Latin occurred during the Middle English period. Frequently it is impossible to tell whether a word is from French or from Latin, for instance *complex, miserable, nature, relation, register, rubric,* and *social,* which might be from either language, judging by form alone. Depending upon its meaning, the single form *port* may come from Latin *portus* 'harbor,' French *porter* 'to carry,' Latin *porta* 'gate,' or Portuguese *Oporto* (that is, *o porto* 'the port,' the city where "port" wine came from originally) — not to mention the nautical use of the word for one side of a ship, the origin of which is uncertain.

In the period between the Norman Conquest and 1500, many Latin words having to do with religion appeared in English, among them *collect*[16] 'short prayer,' *dirge, mediator,* and *Redeemer* (first used with reference to Christ: the synonymous *redemptor* occurs earlier). To these, legal terms might be added, for instance *client, subpoena,* and *conviction,* as well as words having to do with scholastic activities, for instance *simile, index, library,* and *scribe,* and with science,[17] for instance *dissolve, equal, essence, medicine, mercury, opaque, orbit, quadrant,* and *recipe.* These are only a few out of hundreds of Latin words which were adopted before 1500: a longer list would include verbs (for example *admit, commit, discuss, interest, mediate, seclude*) and adjectives (for example *legitimate, obdurate, populous, imaginary, instant, complete*).

LATIN WORDS BORROWED IN MODERN ENGLISH TIMES

The great period of borrowings from Latin and from Greek by way of Latin is the Modern English period. The century or so after 1500 saw the introduction of, among many others, the words *area, abdomen, compensate, composite, data, decorum, delirium, denominate, digress, edition, education, fictitious, folio, fortitude, gradual, horrid, imitate, janitor, jocose, lapse, medium, modern, notorious, orb, pacific, penetrate, querulous, resuscitate, sinecure, series, splendid, strict, superintendent, transition, ultimate, urban, urge,* and *vindicate.*[18]

GREEK LOAN-WORDS

Even before the Conquest a number of Greek words had entered English by way of Latin, in addition to those very early loans discussed above (p. 315, n. 7) which may have come into Germanic directly from Greek, such as *church.* Latin and French are the immediate

[16] Stressed on the first syllable. The word was in Middle English also used as a noun in other senses, now obsolete. The verb, with stress on the second syllable, occurs considerably later, in the sixteenth century. The prayer was presumably so called in the Gallican liturgies because it was a sort of summarization (Lat. *collectus,* past participle of *colligere* 'to gather together'). The *Catholic Dictionary,* 3rd ed., ed. Donald Attwater (New York, 1958), derives the word from *oratio ad collectam* 'prayer at the gathering,' that is, a prayer said at one of the appointed stations where the people gathered in order to proceed together to the Mass. The *OED* states that there was apparently no connection originally between the Roman and the earlier Gallican uses.

[17] The word *science* itself is from Old French, and originally had a much broader meaning than it has at present. In the Middle Ages "the seven sciences" was often synonymous with "the seven liberal arts," that is, grammar, logic, rhetoric, arithmetic, music, geometry, and astronomy (*OED*).

[18] Some of these words are derived from French by the *OED*.

sources of most loan-words ultimately Greek from the Middle English period on, for instance (from Latin) *allegory, anemia, anesthesia,*[19] *aristocracy, barbarous, chaos, comedy, cycle, dilemma, drama, electric, epoch, enthusiasm, epithet, history, homonym, metaphor, mystery, paradox, pharynx, phenomenon,*[20] *rhapsody, rhythm, theory, zone;* (from French) *center, chronicle, character, democracy, diet, dragon, ecstasy, fantasy, harmony, lyre, machine, nymph, pause, rheum, tyrant.* Straight from Greek (though some are combinations unknown in classical times) come *acronym, agnostic, anthropoid, autocracy, chlorine, idiosyncrasy, kudos, oligarchy, pathos, phone, telegram,* and *xylophone,* among many others.

The richest foreign sources of our present English word stock are Latin, French, and Greek (including those words of Greek origin which have come to us by way of Latin and French). Many of the Latin and Greek words which have been cited were in the beginning confined to the language of erudition, and some of them still are; others have passed into the stock of more or less everyday speech. It must be remembered in this connection that in earlier periods Latin was to the English the language of literature, science, and religion. Although Greek had tremendous prestige as a classical language, there was comparatively little first-hand knowledge of it in western Europe until the advent of refugee Greek scholars from Constantinople. Hence, most of the Greek words which appear first in early Modern English occurred, as far as the English were concerned, in Latin works, though their Greek provenience would usually have been recognized. Latin was, in fact, in every respect a living language among the learned all over Europe throughout the medieval and early modern periods. Petrarch, it will be remembered in this connection, translated Boccaccio's story of the patient Griselda into Latin to insure that such a highly moral tale should have a wider circulation than it would have had in Boccaccio's Italian, and it was this Latin translation that Chaucer used as the source of his *Clerk's Tale.* More, Bacon, and Milton all wrote in Latin, just as Bede and other learned men had done centuries earlier.

---

[19] In its usual modern sense 'drug-induced insensibility,' this word was first used in 1846 by Oliver Wendell Holmes, who was a physician as well as a poet.

[20] A few words in *-on* from Greek, though in other respects completely naturalized, retain Greek plurals in *-a,* for example *phenomena, criteria, automata.* There is a tendency among the half-educated to use these plurals as if they were singulars. Singular *phenomena* occurs as early as the sixteenth century, and a new plural *phenomenas* in the seventeenth. The blundering *phenominae* is recorded from the eighteenth century.

AFFIXES FROM LATIN AND GREEK

Not only entire words such as have been cited were taken from Latin and Greek (including Greek by way of Latin and Latin by way of French), but many affixes commonly used in English as well. These were originally for the most part adverbs and prepositions. They have become completely naturalized, as has been shown (pp. 282–83).

EARLY CELTIC LOAN-WORDS

It is likely that even before the beginning of Latin borrowing in England, the English must have acquired some words from the Celts. As has been pointed out, some of the Latin loans of the period up to approximately A.D. 650 were acquired by the English indirectly through the Celts. It is likely that *ceaster* and *-coln,* as in *Lincoln*[21] (Lat. *colōnia*), were so acquired. Phonology is not much help to us as far as such words are concerned, since they underwent the same prehistoric Old English sound-changes as the words which the English brought with them from the Continent.

There are, however, a number of genuinely Celtic words acquired during the early years of the English settlement. We should not expect to find many, for the British Celts were a subject people, and a conquering people are unlikely to adopt many words from those obviously inferior people whom they have conquered. The very insignificant number of words from American Indian languages which have found a permanent place in American English strikingly illustrates this fact. The Normans are exceptional in that they ultimately gave up their own language altogether and became Englishmen, in a way in which the English never became Celts. Probably no more than a dozen or so Celtic words other than place names were adopted by the English up to the time of the Conquest.[22] These include *bratt* 'cloak,' *cumb* 'combe, valley,' *brocc* 'badger,' *torr* 'peak,' and *bannuc* 'a bit.' Just as many American place names are of Indian origin, so many English place names are of Celtic provenience: *Cornwall, Devon, Avon, Usk, Dover, London, Carlisle,* and scores more.

More recent times have seen the introduction of a few more Celtic words into English: from Irish Gaelic in the seventeenth century

---

[21] *Lindon colōnia.* The first word is connected with British *llyn* 'lake.'

[22] There were, however, doubtless some Celtic loan-words in Germanic and also in Latin: Old English *rīce* as a noun meaning 'kingdom' and as an adjective 'rich, powerful' (cf. Ger. *Reich*) is almost certainly of Celtic origin, borrowed before the settlement of the English in Britain. The Celtic origin of a few others (for example OE *ambeht* 'servant,' *dūn* 'hill, down') has been seriously questioned.

shamrock, brogue, leprechaun, tory, galore, and subsequently *banshee, shillelagh, blarney, colleen;* from Scots Gaelic, in addition to *loch, clan,* and a few rarely used words which entered English in late Middle English times, *bog, plaid, slogan, cairn, whiskey,* and some others less familiar; from Welsh, *crag,* occurring first in Middle English, is the best known; others of more recent introduction include *cromlech* and *eisteddfod.*

SCANDINAVIAN LOAN-WORDS IN OLD AND MIDDLE ENGLISH

Most of the Scandinavian words in Old English do not actually occur in written records until the Middle English period, though there can of course be no doubt of their currency long before the beginning of this period. Practically all of the extant documents of the late Old English period come from the south of England, specifically from Wessex. It is likely that Scandinavian words were recorded in nonextant documents written in that part of the country to which Alfred the Great by force of arms and diplomacy had persuaded the Scandinavians to confine themselves – the Danelaw, comprising all of Northumbria and East Anglia and half of Mercia.

In the latter part of the eleventh century the Scandinavians became gradually assimilated to English ways, though Scandinavian words had been in the meanwhile introduced into English. As we have seen, many Scandinavian words closely resembled their English cognates; sometimes, indeed, they were so nearly identical that it would be impossible to tell whether a given word was Scandinavian or English. Sometimes, however, if the meanings of obviously related words differed, semantic contamination might result, as when Old English *drēam* 'joy' acquired the meaning of the related Scandinavian *draumr* 'vision in sleep.' Jespersen cites also *brēad* 'fragment,'[23] *blōma* 'lump of metal,' and poetic *eorl* 'warrior, noble' (ModE *bread, bloom* 'flower,' *earl*). The last of these words acquired the meaning of the related Scandinavian *jarl* 'underking, governor.' Similarly, the later meanings of *dwell* (OE *dwellan, dwelian*), *plow* (OE *plōh*), and *holm* 'islet' (same form in Old English) coincide precisely with the Scandinavian meanings, though in Old English these words meant respectively 'to lead astray, hinder,' 'measure of land,' and 'ocean.'[24]

[23] The usual Old English word for the food made from flour or meal was *hlāf*, as in "Ūrne gedæghwāmlīcan hlāf syle ūs tō dæg" 'Our daily bread give us today.'
[24] Otto Jespersen, *Growth and Structure of the English Language*, 9th ed. (Oxford, 1954), pp. 64–65.

Late Old English and early Middle English loans from Scandinavian were made to conform wholly or in part with the English sound and inflectional system. These include (in modern form) *by* 'town, homestead,'[25] *carl* 'man' (cognate with OE *ceorl*, the source of *churl*), *fellow*, *hit* (first 'meet with,' later 'strike'), *law*, *rag*, *riding* 'administrative division of Yorkshire,'[26] *sly, swain, take* (completely displacing *nim*, from OE *niman*), *thrall*, and *want*. The Scandinavian provenience of *sister* has already been alluded to (p. 119).

A good many words with [sk] are of Scandinavian origin, for, as we have seen, early Old English [sk], written *sc*, came to be pronounced [š]. Such words as *scathe, scorch, score, scowl, scot* 'tax' (as in *scot-free* and *scot and lot*), *scrape, scrub, skill, skin, skirt* (compare native *shirt*), and *sky* thus show by their initial consonant sequence that they entered the language after this change had ceased to be operative. All have been taken from Scandinavian.

Similarly the [g] and [k] before front vowels in *gear, geld, gill* (of a fish), *kick, kilt*, and *kindle* point to Scandinavian origins for these words, since the velar stops became in Old English under such circumstances [j] and [č] respectively. The very common verbs *get* and *give* come to us not from Old English *gitan* and *gifan*, which began with [j], but instead from cognate Scandinavian forms in which the palatalization of [g] in the neighborhood of front vowels did not occur.[27]

As a rule the Scandinavian loans involve little more than the substitution of one word for another (such as *window*, from *vindauga*, literally 'wind-eye,' replacing *eyethurl*, literally 'eye-hole,' from OE *ēagþyrl*), the acquisition of new words for new concepts (such as certain Scandinavian legal terms) or new things (such as words for various kinds of warships with which the Scandinavians made the English acquainted), or the more or less sporadic and invariably slight modification in the form of an English word due to Scandinavian influence (like *sister*). More important and more fundamental is what happened to the Old English pronominal forms of the third person

[25] As in *bylaw* 'town ordinance.' The word also occurs in place names, for instance *Derby, Grimsby*, and *Rigsby*.

[26] Yorkshire was divided by the Scandinavians into three districts, each appropriately called a *þriðjungr* 'third part,' adapted in late Old English as *þriðing* or *þriding*. In East Riding and West Riding the initial *þ* has been assimilated to the final *t* of *east* and *west*, the resultant *East Triding* and *West Triding* being subsequently simplified. In *North Riding* the earlier initial consonant has been absorbed by the identical final consonant of *north*.

[27] Native forms of these verbs with [j-] occur throughout the Middle English period side by side with the Scandinavian forms with [g-] which were ultimately to supplant them. Chaucer consistently used *yive, yeve*, and preterit *yaf*.

plural: all the *th*- forms, as we have seen (pp. 157 and 171), are of Scandinavian origin. Of the native forms in *h*- (p. 138), only *'em* (ME *hem;* OE *him*) survives, and it is commonly but mistakenly thought of as a reduced form of *them.*

SCANDINAVIAN LOAN-WORDS IN MODERN ENGLISH

A number of Scandinavian words have entered English during the modern period. The best known of them are *scud, rug, muggy,* and *ski,* the last of these dating from the latter years of the nineteenth century. *Skoal* (Danish *skaal*) has had a recent alcoholic vogue. It comes as a surprise to learn that it first appears in English as early as 1600, though its early use seems to have been confined to Scotland. The *OED* reasonably suggests that it may have been introduced through the visit of James VI of Scotland (afterwards James I of England) to Denmark, whither he journeyed in 1589 to meet his bride. *Geyser* (1763; for a heater for bath water, 1871), *rune* (1685),[28] *saga* (1709), and *skald* (ca. 1763) are all from Icelandic. *Smörgåsbord* entered English from Swedish around the mid-1920's. It is usually written in English without the Swedish diacritics. Swedish *ombudsman* 'official, as in Sweden and New Zealand, who looks into citizens' complaints against government bureaus and against other officials' has as yet only limited currency, though it is entered in recent dictionaries.

FRENCH LOAN-WORDS IN MIDDLE ENGLISH

No loan-words unquestionably of French origin occur in English earlier than 1066. Leaving out of the question doubtful cases, some of the earliest loans which are unquestionably French are (to cite their Modern English forms) *service, juggler, prison,* and *castle.*[29] *Capon* could be French but was most likely taken directly from Latin.

The Norman Conquest made French the language of the official class in England. Hence it is not surprising that many words having to do with government and administration, lay and spiritual, are of French origin: the word *government* itself, along with Middle English *amynistre,* later replaced by the Latin-derived *administer* with its derivative *administration.* Others include *attorney, chancellor, country, court, crime* (replacing English *sin,* which thereafter came to designate

---

[28] Old English had the cognate *rūn* 'secret, whisper,' which became Modern English *roun.* The last citation in the *OED* is from 1567.

[29] Campbell, *Old English Grammar,* p. 221: "Even after 1066 French words flow into the literary language more slowly than Norse ones, and they do not occur frequently until the last hand of the *OE Chron[icle]* begins," that is, in 1132.

the proper business of the Church, though the State has from time to time tried to take it over), *(e)state*,[30] *judge, jury, noble, royal;* in the religious sphere, *abbot, clergy, preach, sacrament, vestment,* among a good many others. Words designating English titles of nobility except for *king, queen, earl, lord,* and *lady* — namely, *prince, duke, marquess, viscount, baron,* and their feminine equivalents — date from the period when England was in the hands of a Norman French ruling class. Even so, the earl's wife is a *countess,* and the peer immediately below him in rank is a *viscount* (that is, 'vice-count'), indicating that the earl corresponds in rank with the Continental count. In military usage, *army, captain, corporal, lieutenant* (literally 'place-holding'), *sergeant* (originally a serving-man or attendant), and *soldier* are all of French origin.[31]

French names were given not only to various animals when served up as food at Norman tables — *beef, pork, veal,* and *mutton,* for instance — but also to the culinary processes by which the English cow, pig, calf, and sheep were prepared for human consumption, for instance *boil, broil, fry, stew,* and *roast.* English *seethe* is now used mostly metaphorically,[32] as in *to seethe with rage* and *sodden in drink;* another Old English culinary verb, *brǣdan,* with a rather general meaning, survived into early Modern English as *brede;* the last citation in the *OED* is from 1509. Other French loans from the Middle English period, chosen more or less at random, are *dignity, enamor, feign, fool, fruit, horrible, letter, literature, magic, male, marvel, mirror, oppose, question, regard, remember, sacrifice, safe, salary, search, second* (replacing OE *ōðer*), *secret, seize, sentence, single, sober,* and *solace.*

Borrowing from French has gone on ever since, though never on so large a scale. It is interesting to note that the same French word may be borrowed at various periods in the history of English, like *gentle, genteel,* and *jaunty,*[33] all from French *gentil* — the last two of seventeenth-century introduction, as one might suppose from their

---

[30] *State* is an aphetic form. Both it and the full form *estate* were obviously borrowed before French loss of *s* before *t* (Mod. Fr. *état*).

[31] *Colonel* does not occur in English until the sixteenth century (as *coronnel,* whence the pronunciation). French *brigade* and its derivative *brigadier* were introduced in the seventeenth century. *Major* is Latin, occurring first (as an adjective) in *sergeant major* in the latter years of the sixteenth century; the nonmilitary adjectival use in English is somewhat earlier. The French equivalent has occurred in English since the end of the thirteenth century, its Modern English form being *mayor.*

[32] It was occasionally so used in Old English, as in *Beowulf,* lines 190 and 1993 (in the preterit singular form *sēað*).

[33] *Gentile* was taken straight from Latin *gentīlis,* meaning 'foreign' in post-Classical Latin.

pronunciations. It is similar with *chief*, first occurring in English in the fourteenth century, and *chef*, in the nineteenth — the doublets show by their pronunciation the approximate time of their adoption: the Old French affricate [č] survives in *chief*, in which the vowel has undergone the expected shift from [ē] to [ī]; *chef* shows the Modern French shift of the affricate to the fricative [š].[34]

Carriage, courage, language, savage, village, and *viage* (later modernized as *voyage*) came into English in Middle English times and have come to have initial stress in accordance with English patterns. Chaucer and his contemporaries could have it both ways in their poetry — for instance either *couráge* or *cóurage*, as also with other French loans, for instance *colour, figure, honour, pitee, vertu, valour.* This practice is still evidenced by such doublets as *dívers* and *divérse* (showing influence of Lat. *dīversus*). The position of the stress is frequently evidence of the period of borrowing: compare, for instance, older *válour* with newer *velóur, cárriage* with *garáge*,[35] or *véstige* with *prestíge.*

French words might come into English from two dialects of French, the Norman spoken in England (Anglo-Norman) and the Central French (that of Paris, later Standard French). Just as the pronunciation of *ch* and in most instances the position of the stress in words of French origin indicate their relative age as English words, so we may frequently tell by the form of a word whether it is of Norman or of Central French provenience. For instance, Latin *c* [k] before *a* developed into *ch* [č] in Central French, but remained in the Norman dialect; hence *chapter*, from Middle English *chapitre* (from Old French), ultimately going back to Latin *capitulum* 'little head,' a diminutive of *caput*. Compare also the doublets *chattel* and *cattle*, from Central French and Norman respectively, both going back to

[34] In words of French origin spelled with *ch*, the pronunciation is usually indicative of the time of adoption: thus *chase, chamber, chance, chant, change, champion, charge, chattel, chaste, check, choice* were borrowed in Middle English times, whereas *chauffeur, chamois, chevron, chic, chiffon, chignon, douche,* and *machine* have been taken over in Modern English times. Since *chivalry* was widely current in Middle English, one would expect it to begin in Modern English with [č]; the word has, as it were, been re-Frenchified, perhaps because with the decay of the institution it became more of an eye-word than an ear-word. Daniel Jones's *English Pronouncing Dictionary*, 13th ed., rev. A. C. Gimson (London, 1967), records [č] as current, but labels such pronunciation old-fashioned.

[35] This word has primary stress on its first syllable in British English, as [gǽràž] or [-ràǰ]. A completely Anglicized pronunciation, with reduction of the [ɑ] of the second syllable — hence riming with *carriage* — is also current in British use, though it would be regarded as eccentric, not to say substandard, in America.

Latin *capitāle* 'possession, stock,' *capital* in this sense being a Latin loan. Old French *w* was retained in Norman French, but elsewhere became [gw] and then [g]: this development is shown in such doublets as the frequently cited *wage–gage* and *warranty–guarantee.* There are a good many other phonological criteria.

The century and a half between 1250 and the death of Chaucer was a period during which the rate of adoption of French loan-words was greater than it had ever been before or has ever been since. According to Jespersen, nearly half (42.7 percent) of the French borrowings in English to *ca.* 1900 belong to this period.[36] His estimate is based on the dates of earliest occurrence in writing as supplied by the *OED,* and he is quite aware that these may be somewhat later, by as much as fifty years, than the actual first use of the more popular words; nevertheless it is likely that he is not far out of the way, as subsequent studies based on the completed *OED* have shown.

Let us pause to examine the opening lines of the *Canterbury Tales,* written toward the end of this period. The italicized words are of French origin:

Whan that Aprille with hise shoures soote
The droghte of *March* hath *perced* to the roote
And bathed every *veyne* in swich *licour*
Of which *vertu engendred* is the *flour;*
Whan Zephirus eek with his swete breeth   5
Inspired hath in every holt and heeth
The *tendre* croppes, and the yonge sonne
Hath in the Ram his half[e] *cours* yronne,
And smale foweles maken *melodye,*
That slepen al the nyght with open eye —   10
So priketh hem *nature* in hir *corages* —
Thanne longen folk to goon on *pilgrimage[s],*
And *Palmeres* for to seken *straunge* strondes,
To ferne halwes kowthe in sondry londes
And *specially* from every shires ende   15
Of Engelond to Caunturbury they wende
The hooly blisful martir for to seke
That hem hath holpen whan þat they were seeke.
Bifil that in that *seson* on a day,
In Southwerk at the *Tabard* as I lay   20
Redy to wenden on my *pilgrymage*

---

[36] *Growth and Structure,* pp. 86–87.

To Caunterbury with ful *devout corage,*
At nyght were come in to that *hostelrye*
Wel nyne and twenty in a *compaignye*
Of sondry folk by *aventure* y-falle   25
In felaweshipe, and *pilgrimes* were they alle
That toward Caunterbury wolden ryde.[37]

In these twenty-seven lines there are 189 words. Counting *pilgrimage* and *corage* only once, twenty-four[38] of these words come from French. Such a percentage is doubtless also fairly typical of cultivated London usage in Chaucer's time.[39] It will be noted, as has been pointed out before, that the indispensable, often used, everyday words — auxiliary verbs, pronouns, and particles — are of native origin. To the fourteenth century, as Serjeantson points out (p. 136), we owe most of the large number of still current abstract terms from French ending in *-ance, -ence, -ant, -ent, -tion, -ity, -ment* and those beginning in *con-, de-, dis-, ex-, pre-,* and the like, though some of these do not actually show up in writing for another century or so.

LATER FRENCH LOAN-WORDS

Loans from French since the late seventeenth century are, as we should expect, less completely naturalized by and large than most of the older loans which have been cited, though some, like *cigarette, picnic, police,* and *soup,* seem commonplace enough. These later loans[40] also include *aide-de-camp, amateur, ballet, baton, beau, bouillon, boulevard, brochure, brunette,*[41] *bureau, café, camouflage,*

---

[37] From the Ellesmere MS (now in the Huntington Library, California), as given in *A Six-Text Print of Chaucer's Canterbury Tales,* Part I, ed. Frederick J. Furnivall for the Chaucer Society (London, 1868), p. 1. As in other citations from old texts, except for the two extended passages quoted in Chapter VII, *v* has been used for older *u* with consonantal value. A necessary *-e* has been added in the eighth line and an obvious omission of *-s* rectified in the twelfth. Note the scribe's inconsistent use of *th* and *þ* in the eighteenth line; other manuscripts of the *Canterbury Tales* use *þ* much more than does the Ellesmere.

[38] *Aprille* is from Latin, but the French form with *v* for Latin *p* was also widely current in Chaucer's day, occurring (as *Averylle*) in one of the better MSS of the *Canterbury Tales.* Regardless of the written form, the word is to be stressed on the first syllable and the final *e* is not to be pronounced.

[39] According to Serjeantson, "the proportion of French words used by Chaucer varies, sometimes being ten or eleven per cent, and sometimes rising as high as fifteen per cent" (p. 151).

[40] In the forms cited, the French accents and other diacritics have been used, though many of the words cited with such markings are now printed without them in English.

[41] Its antonym *blond(e)* occurs as early as the late fifteenth century.

chaise longue (see p. 304), *champagne, chaperon* (in French, a hood or cap formerly worn by women),[42] *chemisette,*[43] *chi-chi* 'chic gone haywire,' *chiffonier* (in France, a rag-picker), *chute, cliché, commandant, communiqué, connoisseur, coupé* ('cut off,' past participle of *couper,* used of a closed car with short body and practically always pronounced [kup] in American English), *coupon, crêpe, crochet, débris, début(ante), de luxe, dénouement, détour, élite, embonpoint,*[44] *encore, ensemble, entrée, envoy, etiquette, fiancé(e), flair, foyer* (British [fwáje] or [fɔ́ɪje]; American [fɔ́ɪər]), *fuselage, genre, glacier, grippe, hangar, hors d'oeuvre, impasse, invalid, laissez-faire, liaison, limousine, lingerie, massage, matinée,*[45] *mêlée, ménage, menu, morale, morgue, naïve, négligé* (as *negligee*), *nuance, passé, penchant, plateau, première, protégé, rapport, ration,*[46] *ravine, repartee, repertoire, reservoir, restaurant, reveille* (British [rɪvéli]; American [révəli]), *revue, risqué, roué, rouge, saloon* (and its less thoroughly Anglicized variant *salon*), *savant, savoir faire, souvenir, suède, surveillance, svelte, tête-à-tête, vignette,* and *vis-à-vis.* There are also a fairish number of loan translations from French, for example *trial balloon* (*ballon d'essai*), *marriage of convenience* (*mariage de convenance*), and *that goes without saying* (*ça va sans dire*).[47] The suffix -*ville* in the names of so many American towns is of course of French origin; of the American love for it, Matthew Arnold declared, with some justice: "The mere nomenclature of the country acts upon a cultivated person like the incessant pricking of pins. What people in whom the sense of beauty and fitness was quick could have invented, or could tolerate, the hideous names ending in *ville,* the Briggsvilles, Higginsvilles, Jacksonvilles, rife from Maine to Florida; the jumble of unnatural and inappropriate names

---

[42] The English meaning is explained, doubtless correctly, as deriving from the notion that a married woman shields the younger girl as a hood shields the face. (See *OED,* s.v. *chaperon* 3, quotation for 1864.)

[43] *Chemise* is of Middle English introduction, though pronounced as if modern. *Shimmy,* both for the undergarment and the wiggling dance of the 1920's, is a back formation from it, like *shay* from *chaise,* which because of the final sibilant was mistakenly regarded as a plural.

[44] Compare the loan translation *in good point,* which occurs much earlier, for example, in Chaucer's description of the Monk in line 200 of the General Prologue of the *Canterbury Tales:* "He was a lord ful fat and in good poynt."

[45] Earlier, as its derivation from *matin* implies, a morning performance.

[46] The traditional pronunciation, riming with *fashion,* indicates the French origin of this word meaning originally 'portion of food given to a soldier.' It has acquired within the past thirty years or so a pronunciation based on the analogy of *nation* and *station,* which came into English during the medieval period.

[47] The last two examples are cited by Winfred P. Lehmann, *Historical Linguistics* (New York, 1962), pp. 215–16.

everywhere?"[48] *Chowder, depot* 'railway station,' *gopher, levee* 'embankment,' *picayune, prairie, praline, shivaree* (*charivari*), and *voyageur* are Americanisms of French origin.

LOAN-WORDS FROM SPANISH

English has taken words from various other European languages as well, as we should expect in the light of the external history of the language, involving as this does the contact of English-speaking people with Continental Europeans as a result of cultural exchanges of one sort or another, of trade, of exploration, and of colonization. Moreover, a good many non-European words entered English by way of Spanish, and to a smaller extent by way of Portuguese, mostly from the sixteenth century on. Spanish words and words of Spanish transmission, many coming from the New World, include *alligator* (*el lagarto* 'the lizard'), *anchovy, armada, armadillo* (literally 'little armed one'), *avocado* (ultimately Nahuatl *ahuacatl*, confused with Sp. *abogado* 'advocate, lawyer'), *barbecue, barracuda, bolero, cannibal* (*Caribal* 'Caribbean'), *cargo, cask* (*casque*), *castanet, chocolate* (ultimately Nahuatl), *cigar, cocoa, cockroach* (see p. 301), *cordovan* (leather; an older form, *cordwain*, comes through French), *cork,*[49] *corral, desperado, domino* 'cloak or mask,' *embargo, flotilla, galleon, guitar, junta, key* 'reef' (*cayo*), *maize* (ultimately Arawak), *mescal* (ultimately Nahuatl), *mantilla, mosquito* 'little fly,' *mulatto, negro, palmetto, peccadillo, plaza,*[50] *potato* (ultimately Haitian), *punctilio, sherry* (see pp. 296–97), *silo, sombrero, tango, tomato* (ultimately Nahuatl), *tornado,*[51] *tortilla,* and *vanilla* — many of these, for instance *barbecue, barracuda,* and *tortilla,* being more familiar to Americans than to the English, though they may have occurred first in British sources. A good many words were adopted from Spanish in the nineteenth century by Americans: *adobe, bonanza, bronco, buckaroo* (*vaquero*), *calaboose* (*calabozo*), *canyon, chaparral* 'scrub oak' (whence *chaps,* or *shaps,* 'leather pants worn by cowboys as protection against such vegetation'),

[48] *Civilization in the United States* (Boston, 1888), reprinted in *American Social History as Recorded by British Travellers,* ed. Allan Nevins (New York, 1923), p. 509. Pylesville, in Harford County, Maryland, would really have set the pins to pricking in Arnold's soul. Fortunately, he seems not to have encountered this seat of American culture and fashion.

[49] Occurring somewhat earlier than the other words cited, this is an apheetic form of *alcorque* 'cork shoe,' taken into Spanish from Arabic but ultimately going back to Latin *quercus* 'oak.'

[50] From Latin *platēa,* also the ultimate source of the English loan-word *place,* which occurs in Old English times, and of the Italian loan-word *piazza.*

[51] A blend of *tronada* 'thunderstorm' and *tornar* 'to turn.'

cinch, frijoles, hacienda, hoosegow (*juzgado,* in Mexican Spanish 'jail'), *lariat* (*la reata* 'the rope'), *lasso, mesa, mustang, patio, pinto, poncho, pueblo, ranch, rodeo, sierra, siesta, stampede* (*estampida*), *stevedore* (*estivador* 'packer'), *vamoose* (*vamos* 'let's go'). *Tamale, mescal,* and *mesquite* are ultimately Nahuatl, entering American English before the nineteenth century, like similar loans in British English, by way of Spanish. *Chili,* also of Nahuatl origin, entered British English in the seventeenth century, but it is likely, as M. M. Mathews points out, that its occurrence in American English in the nineteenth century — "at the time we began to make first hand acquaintance with the Spanish speakers on our Southwestern border" — is not a continuation of the British tradition, but represents an independent borrowing of a word for which Americans had had till that time very little if any use.[52]

No words came into English direct from Portuguese until the modern period; those which have been adopted include *albino, flamingo, madeira* (from the place), *molasses, pagoda, palaver,* and *pickaninny* (*pequenino* 'very small'). There are a few others considerably less familiar.

LOAN-WORDS FROM ITALIAN

From yet another Romance language, Italian, English has acquired a good many words, including much of our musical terminology. As early as the sixteenth century *duo, fugue, madrigal, violin,* and *viola da gamba* 'viol for the leg' appear in English; in the seventeenth century, *allegro, largo, opera, piano*[53] 'soft,' *presto, recitative, solo,* and *sonata;*[54] in the eighteenth, when interest in Italian music reached its apogee in England, *adagio, andante, aria, cantata, concerto, contralto, crescendo, diminuendo, duet, falsetto, finale, forte*[55] 'loud,' *libretto, maestro, obbligato, oratorio, rondo,*[56] *soprano, staccato, tempo, trio, trombone, viola,* and *violoncello;*[57] and in the nineteenth, *alto, cadenza,*

---

[52] *Some Sources of Southernisms* (University, Ala., 1948), p. 18.

[53] As the name of the instrument, a clipped form of eighteenth-century *pianoforte,* the earliest occurrence cited by the *OED* is in 1803.

[54] In regard to this word the *OED* manages to antedate itself by eleven years. Its first citation is from 1694, though elsewhere (s.v. *piano* 'soft') there is a citation of Purcell's *Sonnatas* [sic] *in Three Parts,* the date of which is 1683.

[55] The identically written word pronounced with final *e* silent and meaning 'strong point' is from French.

[56] The literary terms *rondeau* and *rondel* are from French. Though their English meanings differ, they are simply variant forms, *rondeau* being the later development. *Rondeau* was taken into Italian from French and written *rondo,* entering English in this form as a musical term.

[57] The clipped form *cello* does not occur until the late nineteenth century.

diva, legato, piccolo, pizzicato, prima donna, and *vibrato*. Other loan-words from Italian include *artichoke, balcony, balloon, bandit, bravo, broccoli, cameo, canto, carnival, casino, cupola, dilettante,*[58] *firm* 'business association,' *fresco, ghetto, gondola, grotto, incognito, inferno, influenza, lagoon, lava, malaria (mala aria* 'bad air'), *maraschino, miniature, motto, pergola, piazza, portico, regatta, replica, scope, stanza, stiletto, studio, torso, umbrella, vendetta,* and *volcano,* not to mention those words of ultimate Italian origin, like *cartoon, citron, corridor, gazette,* and *porcelain,* which have entered English by way of French. *Macaroni* (Mod. It. *maccheroni*) came into English in the sixteenth century,[59] *vermicelli* in the seventeenth, and *spaghetti* and *gorgonzola* (from the town) in the nineteenth. *Ravioli* (as *rafiol*) occurs in English in the fifteenth century, and later as *raviol* in the seventeenth century. Both forms are labeled obsolete and rare; it is indeed likely that the single occurrence of each form cited by the *OED* is the only one. The modern form thus can hardly be considered as continuing an older tradition, but is instead a reborrowing, perhaps by way of American English in the twentieth century. *Lasagna* and *pizza* are also doubtless of twentieth-century introduction into English—probably in America, where Italian cooking is more popular than in England, despite the excellent Italian restaurants in Soho.

LOAN-WORDS FROM HIGH GERMAN

High German has made comparatively little impact upon English. Much of the vernacular of geology and mineralogy is of German origin, for instance *cobalt, feldspar* (a half-translation of *Feldspath*), *gneiss, kleinite* (from Karl Klein, mineralogist), *lawine* 'avalanche,' *loess, meerschaum, nickel* (originally *Kupfernickel,* perhaps 'copper demon,' partially translated as *kopparnickel* by the Swedish mineralogist Von Cronstedt, from whose writings the abbreviated form entered English in 1755), *quartz, seltzer* (ultimately a derivative of Selters, near Wiesbaden), and *zinc. Carouse* occurs in English as early as the sixteenth century, from the German *gar aus* 'all out,' meaning the same as *bottoms up.* Originally adverbial, it almost immediately came to be used as a verb, and shortly afterwards as a noun. Other words taken from German include such culinary terms as *sauerkraut* (occurring first in British English, but the English never cared particularly for the dish,

---

[58] Frequently pronounced as if French, by analogy with *debutante*.

[59] Its doublet *macaroon,* though designating quite a different food, entered English by way of French in the seventeenth century. *Maccaroni* was the plural of *maccarone;* the singular form was taken into French and adapted as *macaron,* whence the English form *macaroon*.

and the word may to all intents and purposes be considered an Americanism, independently reborrowed), *noodle* (*Nudel*), *delicatessen, wienerwurst, braunschweiger, schnitzel, pretzel, zwieback,* and *pumpernickel. Liederkranz, knackwurst,* and *sauerbraten* are fairly well known, but can hardly be considered completely naturalized. *Liverwurst* is a half-translation of *Leberwurst. Hamburger* and *frankfurter* have been discussed in another connection (pp. 283–84). The vernacular of drinking includes *lager, bock* (from *Eimbocker Bier* 'beer of Eimbock,' shortened in German to *Bockbier*), *schnapps, kirsch(wasser),* and *katzenjammer* 'hangover' (though more widely known from *The Katzenjammer Kids*). Other words from German include *drill* 'fabric,' *plunder* (*plündern*), *hamster, waltz, landau* (from the place of that name), and the dog names *dachshund, Doberman(n) pinscher, poodle* (*Pudel*), and *spitz. Alpenstock, edelweiss, ersatz, hinterland, leitmotiv, poltergeist, rucksack, schottische, yodel* (*jodeln*), and the not yet thoroughly naturalized *Gestalt, Weltanschauung,* and *Weltansicht. Ablaut, umlaut,* and *schwa* (ultimately Hebrew) have been frequently used as technical terms in this book. *Blitz(krieg)* and *Luftwaffe* had an infamous success in 1940 and 1941, but they have since receded.

Seminar and *semester* are of course ultimately Latin, but they entered American English by way of German—*seminar,* as M. M. Mathews says, probably "independent of the British borrowing of about the same date,"[60] that is, the late nineteenth century, when many American and English scholars went to Germany in pursuit of their doctorates. *Semester* is known in England, but the English have little use for it save in reference to foreign universities. *Academic freedom* is a loan translation of *akademische Freiheit. Bummeln* is used by German students to mean 'to loiter, waste time,' and may be the source of American English *to bum* and the noun in the sense 'loafer,' though this need not be an academic importation.

On a less elevated level, American English uses such expressions as *gesundheit* (when someone has sneezed) and *nix* (*nichts*), and German-Americans have doubtless been responsible for adapting the German suffix *-fest,* as in *Sängerfest,* to English uses, as in *songfest* and *gabfest. Biergarten* has undergone translation in *beer garden; kindergarten* is frequently pronounced as though the last element were English *garden.* Yiddish (that is, *Jüdisch* 'Jewish') has been responsible for the introduction of a number of German words and minced forms of German words, some of them having special meanings in Yiddish: *kibitzer, phooey, schlemiel, schmaltz, schnozzle, shmo, shnook, shtick,* and

---

[60] *A Dictionary of Americanisms on Historical Principles* (Chicago, 1951).

others less widely known to non-Jews. By way of the Germans from the Palatinate who settled in southern Pennsylvania in the early part of the eighteenth century come a number of terms of German origin little known in other parts of the United States, such as *sots* 'yeast,' *snits* 'fruit cut for drying,' and *smearcase* 'cottage cheese' (*Schmierkäse*). *Kriss Kingle* or *Kriss Kringle* (*Christkindl* 'Christ child') and *to dunk* have become nationally known.

LOAN-WORDS FROM LOW GERMAN

Dutch and other forms of Low German have contributed a number of words to English, to a large extent by way of the commercial relationships existing between the English and the Dutch and Flemish-speaking peoples from the Middle Ages on. Even before the beginning of the Modern English period the words *boor* (*boer*), *booze, brake, hop* 'twining plant,' *kit, luck, pickle, spool,* and *snap* occur, among others less well known; later, *brandywine, cambric, duffel* (from the name of a place), *easel, frolic* (*vrolijk* 'joyful,' cognate with Ger. *fröhlich*), *gimp, gin* (short for *genever,* borrowed by the Dutch from Old French, ultimately Lat. *juniperus* 'juniper'; *genever* was confused in English with *Geneva*), *isinglass* (a folk-etymologized form of *hysenblas,* see p. 302), *landscape, mahlstick, rant, skate, split, wagon* (the related OE *wægn* gives modern *wain*), and *wiseacre* (Middle Dutch *wijsseggher* 'soothsayer'). It is not surprising in view of their eminence in seafaring activities that the Dutch should have contributed a number of nautical terms, as the Scandinavians had done earlier, though these latter have not survived. From Dutch nautical usage come *buoy, cruise, deck* (Dutch *dec* 'roof,' then in English 'roof of a ship,' a meaning which later got into Dutch), *luff, marline* (the name of the fish, *marlin,* is short for *marlinespike*), *pea jacket, scow; skipper* (*schipper* 'shipper, that is, master of a ship'), *sloop, taffrail* (see p. 302), *yacht,* and *yawl. Trek, commandeer, commando, outspan,* and *apartheid* have come to English from South African Dutch (Afrikaans). Americanisms of Dutch origin include *boss* (in the beginning a democratic euphemism to avoid having to refer to one's master as one's master), *bowery, coleslaw* (*koolsla* 'cabbage salad'), *cooky, dope, pit* 'fruit stone,' *Santa Claus* (*Sante Klaas,* from *Sant Nikolaas* 'Saint Nicholas'), *sleigh, snoop, spook,* and *waffle.*

LOAN-WORDS FROM THE EAST

As early as Old English times words from the East doubtless trickled into the language, then always by way of other languages. *Mancus* 'coin' and *ealfara* 'pack horse' have been cited as commercial loans from Arabic. Neither word has survived, and the second occurs only once in the Old English writings which have come down to us.[61] A number of words ultimately Arabic, most of them having to do in one way or another with science or with commerce, came in during the Middle English period, usually by way of French or Latin. These include *amber, camphor, cipher,*[62] *cotton, lute, mattress, orange, saffron, sugar, syrup,* and *zenith.* The Arabic definite article *al* is retained in one form or another in *almanac, alchemy, alembic, algorism, alkali, azimuth* (as [for *al*] plus *sumūt* 'the ways'), *elixir* (*el* [for *al*] plus *iksīr* 'the philosopher's stone'), and *hazard* (*az* [for *al*] plus *zahr* 'the die'). In *admiral,* occurring first in Middle English, the Arabic article occurs in the final syllable: the word is an abbreviation of some such phrase as *amīr-al-baḥr* 'commander (of) the sea.' Through confusion with Latin *admīrābilis* 'admirable,' the word has acquired a *d; d*-less forms occur, however, as late as the sixteenth century, though ultimately the blunder with *d,* which occurs in the first known recording of the word — in Layamon's *Brut,* written around the end of the twelfth century — was to prevail. *Alcohol* (*al-kuḥl* 'the kohl, that is, powder of antimony for staining the eyelids'),[63] *alcove,* and *algebra,* all beginning with the article, were introduced in early Modern times, along with a good many words without the article, for instance *apricot, assassin* (originally 'hashish-eater'), *caliber, candy, carat, caraway, fakir, giraffe, garble, harem, hashish, henna, jinn* (plural of *jinnī*), *lemon, magazine* (ultimately an Arabic plural form meaning 'storehouses'), *minaret, mohair, sherbet,* and *tariff.* Some of these were transmitted through Italian, others through French; some were taken directly from Arabic. *Coffee,* ultimately Arabic, was taken into English by way of Turkish. Other Semitic languages have contributed little directly, though a number of words ultimately Hebrew have come to us by way of French. Regardless of the method of their transmission, most of us must be aware of the ultimate or immediate Hebrew origin of *amen, behemoth, cabbala, cherub, hallelujah, jubilee, rabbi, Sabbath, seraph, shekel,* and *shibboleth.* Both *Jehovah* (*Jahveh*) and *Satan* are Hebrew. Yiddish uses a very large number of Hebrew words and seems to have been the me-

[61] Serjeantson, p. 214.
[62] From Arabic *ṣifr* by way of Medieval Latin. The Italians modified the same Arabic word as *zero,* by way of **zefiro* (*OED*). This Italian form entered English in the early Modern period.
[63] The modern meaning, which occurred in the European languages borrowing the word, has come about in a rather complicated way. Its development from a specific powder to any powder to essence (or "spirit," as in obsolete *alcohol of wine*) to the spirituous element in beverages is traced in the *OED* for anyone who wishes to follow it.

dium of transmission for *kosher, tokus* 'backside,' *mazuma, matzo* (plural *matzoth*), and *goy.*

Persian and Sanskrit are not exotic in the same sense as Arabic, for both are Indo-European; yet the regions in which they were spoken were far removed from England, and they were to all intents and purposes highly exotic. Consequently, such words as Persian *caravan* (in the nineteenth century clipped to *van*) and *bazaar* must have seemed as exotic to the English in the sixteenth century, when they first became current, as Chinese *kumquat* and Japanese *sukiyaki* seem to most people past middle age today. *Tiger, paradise, satrap, scarlet, azure, taffeta,* and *musk* occur, among others, in the Middle English period. None of these are direct loans, coming directly from Latin or Old French; later, from the same two direct sources, come *naphtha, tiara,* and a few Persian words borrowed through Turkish, such as *giaour.* In addition, some Persian words were borrowed in India: *cummerbund* 'loin-band,' which first appears (as *combarband*) in the early seventeenth century, to reappear within the last forty years or so as a name for an article of men's semiformal evening dress frequently replacing the low-cut waistcoat. The word in this sense obviously returned to English by way of Englishmen posted for one reason or another in India, for the last citation in the *OED* is from 1869 and defines it in effect as a belt worn to protect one from the onslaught of cholera; it is similar with *seersucker,* an Indian modification of Persian *shīr o shakkar* 'milk and sugar,' the name of a fabric which came into vogue in America less than half a century ago, and with *khaki* 'dusty,' recorded in English first in 1857 but not widely known in America until much later, when it was at first pronounced in the traditional fashion [kákɪ], though [kǽkɪ] seems to prevail nowadays. Direct from Persian, in addition to *caravan* and *bazaar,* come *baksheesh, dervish, mogul, shah,* and *shawl.* *Chess* comes directly from Old French; it is an aphetic form of *esches,* but the word is ultimately Persian, as is *check* (in all its senses), from the variant Old French form *eschecs.* The words go back to Persian *shāh* 'king,' which was taken into Arabic in the specific sense 'the king in the game of chess,' whence *shāh māt* 'the king is dead,' the source of *checkmate.* The derivative *exchequer* (OF *eschequier* 'chess board') came about through the fact that accounts used to be reckoned on a table marked with squares like a chess (or *checker,* in British English usually *chequer*) board. *Rook* 'chess piece' is also ultimately derived from Persian *rukhkh* 'castle.'

From Sanskrit come, along with a few others, *avatar, mahatma, swastika,* and *yoga* ('union,' akin to English *yoke*). *Swastika* denotes in English a symbol of the Nazi party in Germany, but is actually little known in that country, where the name of the figure is usually *Haken-kreuz* 'hook-cross'; the word occurs in English first in the latter half of the nineteenth century. Sanskrit *dvandva, sandhi,* and *svarabhakti* are pretty much confined to the vernacular of linguistics; nonlinguists get along without them very well indeed. *Ginger,* which occurs in Old English (*gingifere*), is ultimately Prakrit. From Hindustani come *bandanna, bungalow, chintz, cot, dinghy, dungaree, gunny* 'sacking,' *juggernaut, jungle, loot, maharaja* (and *maharani*), *nabob, pajamas, pundit, sahib, sari, shampoo,* and *thug,* along with a number of other words which are much better known in England than in America (for instance *pukka, durbar, babu,* and *bangle* 'claspless ringlike bracelet'). *Pal* is from Romany, or Gypsy, which as we have seen (p. 97) is an Indic dialect. A good many Indic words have achieved general currency in English because of their use by literary men; the name of Kipling comes first to mind, though he had distinguished predecessors, including Scott, Byron, and Thackeray.

The non-Indo-European languages, called Dravidian, spoken in southern India have contributed a few fairly well-known words, for instance *copra, curry, mango, pariah,* and *teak.* Of these, *curry* and *pariah,* from Tamil, are direct loans; the others have come to us by way of Portuguese, *mango* from Portuguese by way of Malay.

Other English words from languages spoken in the Orient are comparatively few in number, but some are quite well known. *Silk* may be ultimately from Chinese, although there is no known etymon in that language; as *seoloc* or *sioloc* the word came into English in Old English times from Baltic or Slavic. Serjeantson cites *tea, catchup (ketchup)*,[64] and *japan* 'varnish' (from the Chinese name of the country, called *Nippon* by the Japanese), along with the names of some varieties of tea (*pekoe, oolong, bohea, souchong*) (p. 237). *Ginseng, kowtow, litchi,* and *pongee* have come direct from Chinese, along with the Americanisms of Chinese origin *chow, chow mein, chop suey,* and *tong* 'secret society.' From Japanese have come *banzai, geisha, hara-kiri, (jin)ricksha, kimono, sake* 'liquor,' *samurai,* and *soy(a),* along with the ultimately Chinese *tycoon, judo,* and *ju-jitsu. Kamikaze* had a certain vogue during World War II. The word, designating so-called suicide pilots, literally means 'divine wind.'

From the languages spoken in the islands of the Pacific come *bamboo, gingham, launch,* and *mangrove,* and others mostly adopted before the beginning of the nineteenth century by way of French, Portuguese, Spanish, or Dutch. *Rattan* (as *rattoon*), direct from Malay,

---

[64] The variant *catsup* has given rise to a pronunciation based on its spelling.

appears first in Pepys's *Diary,* where it designates, not the wood, but a cane made of it: "Mr. Hawley did give me a little black rattoon, painted and gilt" (September 13, 1660). Polynesian *taboo* and *tattoo*[65] 'decorative permanent skin marking,' along with a few other words from the same source, appear in English around the time of Captain James Cook's voyages (1768–79); they occur first in his journals. *Ukulele* is Polynesian, entering American English by way of Hawaii around 1900; *luau,* also Polynesian, came in fairly recently. Captain Cook also first recorded Australian *kangaroo; boomerang* (as *wo-mur-rāng*), from the same source, occurs first somewhat later. *Budgerigar,* also Australian and designating a kind of parrot, is well known in England, where it is frequently clipped to *budgie* by those who fancy the birds, usually known as *parakeets* in America.

LOAN-WORDS FROM
THE AFRICAN LANGUAGES

A few words from those languages spoken by blacks on the west coast of Africa have entered English by way of Portuguese and Spanish, notably *banana* and *yam,* both appearing toward the end of the sixteenth century. It is likely, as M. M. Mathews points out, that *yam* entered the vocabulary of American English independently. In the South, where it is used more frequently than elsewhere, it designates not just any kind of sweet potato, as in other parts, but a red sweet potato, which is precisely the meaning it has in the Gullah form *yambi.* Hence Mathews thinks, very plausibly, that this word was introduced into Southern American English direct from Africa, even though there is no question of its Portuguese transmission in earlier English: "Our word came to us directly from headquarters, that is from Africa" he declares, pointing out that "we had in our midst the very people who gave the word to the Portuguese" (pp. 111–12). *Voodoo,* with its variant *hoodoo,* is likewise of African origin and was introduced by way of American English. *Gorilla* is apparently African: it first occurs in English in the *Boston Journal of Natural History* in 1847, according to Mathews' *Dictionary of Americanisms,* though a plural form *gorillae* occurs in 1799 in British English. *Juke* (more correctly *jook*) and *jazz* are Americanisms of African origin. Both were more or less disreputable when first introduced, but have in course of time lost most of their earlier sexual connotations. Other African words transmitted into American English are *banjo, buckra, cooter* 'turtle,' the synonymous

---

[65] Not the same as *tattoo* 'drum or bugle signal, (later) military entertainment' which is from Dutch *tap toe* 'the tap (is) to,' that is, 'the taproom is closed.'

goober and *pinder* 'peanut,' *gumbo, jigger* 'sand flea,' recorded in the dictionaries as *chigoe,* and *zombi. Samba* and *rumba* are ultimately African, coming to English by way of Brazilian Portuguese and Cuban Spanish respectively. There can no longer be much doubt that *tote* is of African origin; the evidence presented by Lorenzo Dow Turner[66] seems fairly conclusive.

OTHER SOURCES:
SLAVIC, HUNGARIAN, TURKISH,
AND AMERICAN INDIAN

Very minor sources of the English vocabulary are Slavic, Hungarian, Turkish, and American Indian, with few words from these sources used in English contexts without reference to the countries from which they have been borrowed. Most of these have been borrowed during the Modern period, since 1500, and practically all by way of other languages. Thus Slavic *sable* comes to us in Middle English times not direct but by way of French. Later we acquired, also indirectly, *polka. Astrakhan* and *mammoth* are direct from Russian. Other Russian words which are known but hardly thoroughly naturalized are *bolshevik, borzoi, czar* (ultimately Lat. *Caesar*), *intelligentsia* (ultimately Latin), *kopeck, muzhik, pogrom, ruble, samovar, soviet, steppe, tovarisch, troika, tundra, ukase, vodka,* and the fairly recent *sputnik.* Serjeantson cites *hussar* and *coach* as Hungarian loans (p. 211); the first of these is ultimately from Italian *corsaro* 'corsair,'[67] but the second is apparently a direct loan from *kocsi. Goulash* and *paprika* are also direct loans; both are too recent to be entered in the *OED* proper, though they are in the 1933 Supplement from 1900 and 1898 respectively. *Jackal,* ultimately Persian, comes to English by way of Turkish; *khan* occurs as a direct loan quite early. Other Turkish words used in English include *fez, horde,* and *tulip,* from *tulipa(nt),* a variant of *tülbend* (taken by Turkish from Persian *dulband*), coming into English in modified form as *turban(d),* and the fairly recent *shish kebab.* The flower was so called because it was thought to look like the Turkish headgear. *Coffee,* as has been pointed out, is ultimately Arabic, but comes to us direct from Turkish; the same is true of *kismet.* American Indian words do not loom large, even in American English, though many have occurred in American English writings. Most of the 132 words borrowed from Algonquian dialects compiled by Alexander F.

---

[66] *Africanisms in the Gullah Dialect* (Chicago, 1949), p. 203.
[67] *Corsair* comes into English by way of French.

Chamberlain in 1902[68] have now gone out of use or are but dimly known, for instance *sagamore, squantum,* and *peag.* Many place names are of course taken from Indian languages.

ENGLISH REMAINS ENGLISH

Enough has been written to indicate the cosmopolitanism of the present English vocabulary. Yet English remains English in every essential respect: the words that all of us use over and over again, the grammatical structures in which we couch our observations upon practically everything under the sun remain as distinctively English as they were in the days of Alfred the Great. What has been acquired from other languages has not always been particularly worth gaining: no one could prove by any set of objective standards that *army* is a "better" word than *dright* or *here,* which it displaced, or that *advice* is any better than the similarly displaced *rede,* or that *to contend* is any better than *to flite.* The fact that we have taken words from many sources is indicative of a cosmopolitan attitude which is the very opposite of the lexical provincialism of, say, Icelandic and to a lesser extent German. Those who think that *manual* is a better, or more beautiful, or more intellectual word than English *handbook* are of course entitled to their opinion. But such esthetic preferences are purely matters of style and have nothing to do with the subtle patternings which make one language different from another. For, as has been demonstrated time and again in this book, language is nothing so simple as words. The words we choose are nonetheless of tremendous interest in themselves, and they throw a good deal of light upon our cultural history.

But with all its manifold new words from other tongues, English could never have become anything but English. And as such it has given to the world, among many other things, some of the best books the world has ever known. It is not unlikely, in the light of writings by Englishmen in earlier times, that this would have been so even if we had never taken any words from outside the word hoard which has come down to us from those times. That what we have borrowed has

---

[68] Many of these are cited by H. L. Mencken in *The American Language, Supplement I* (New York, 1945), pp. 167–71. Those which have survived are, thanks to the European vogue of James Fenimore Cooper, about as well known transatlantically as in America: they include *moccasin, papoose, squaw, tomahawk,* and *toboggan.* Others with perhaps fewer literary associations are *opossum, skunk, moose, terrapin, pecan,* and *woodchuck.* Muskhogean words are more or less confined to the southern American states, for instance *bayou, catalpa,* and a good many proper names like *Tallahassee, Tuscaloosa,* and *Tombigbee.* Loans from Nahuatl, almost invariably of Spanish transmission, have been included as if Spanish (see pp. 330–31).

given greater wealth to our word stock no man can gainsay, but the true Englishness of our mother tongue has in no way been lessened by such loans, as those who speak and write it lovingly can never forget.

It is highly unlikely that many readers will have noted that the preceding paragraph contains not a single word of foreign origin. It was perhaps not worth the slight effort involved to write it so; it does show, however, that English would not be quite so impoverished as some commentators suppose it would be without its many accretions from other languages.

XII

Words and Meanings

In considering meaning, we cannot here be concerned with those larger philosophical aspects of language which have increasingly in recent years engaged the attention of scholars like Rudolf Carnap, Charles W. Morris, I. A. Richards, Ernst Cassirer, and Susanne K. Langer, nor with the "general semantics" of Alfred Korzybski, whose disciples with evangelical zeal unwittingly made *semantic* a vogue word meaning little more than 'verbal.' These approaches are certainly of great interest and value, but are not directly connected with such changes in meaning in the course of the development of the English language as we shall examine in this chapter.

DEVICES FOR SIGNALING MEANING

The educated man or woman is by long tradition expected to possess what is frequently referred to as "a good command of language." Actually, as has been pointed out in our introductory chapter, a child of five or so already has a "good command," in the sense that he uses without effort practically all the devices by which meaning is signaled vocally, sometimes with the aid of gestures. No normal child of even tenderer years would fail to understand, and to make an appropriate response to, such an utterance as "Is your mother busy?" or to distinguish it from the utterances "Your mother is busy" and "Your mother is busy?" It will be noted that the words in these utterances are identical in form and in meaning. What, then, are the linguistic devices by which the child distinguishes any one of these utterances from the others? Word order and intonation do the trick; in "Your mother is busy?" intonation alone (the rising tone beginning on the first syllable of *busy*) does it.

After we have mastered the use of such devices—we did so more or less unconsciously, of course, long before we could make any analysis of what we do or how we do it—about all that we acquire, except for a few more or less sophisticated "literary" constructions, are vocabulary items. Though we should as educated persons be able to analyze the linguistic devices by which we communicate with one another, we actually acquire these devices without formal instruction. But in the process we acquire only the most useful, everyday words—usually words which have been a part of the English language from the earliest times (*mother, moon, busy, ready, good, run, have, to, and*), along with some words of foreign origin which have been a part of it for a very long time (*giant, chase, catch*) or which for some other reason have been thoroughly naturalized—more or less homely words which continue for all our lives to provide our basic word hoard. But such equipment, common to all speakers of a language, does not comprise what is meant by "a good command of language."

WHY STUDY WORDS?

The fact is that, if we are going to be able to talk about anything very far beyond our day-to-day, bread-and-butter living, if we are going to associate in an easy manner with cultivated people, if we are going to read books which such people have found to be important and significant, then we must have at our command a great many words that the man in the street and the man with the hoe have little occasion to use. This is not to imply that the common man has only a rudimentary vocabulary. He certainly has the words he needs and he knows, via the mass media if not via the classroom, a good many more that he has no particular need for. Differences in vocabulary cannot be glibly summed up.

To begin the study of language with an examination of its word stock is, however, to put the cart before the horse, for words come later to us in our linguistic development than sentences—even the child's first meaningful utterances are sentences, though many of them may consist of only a single word each. But the fact remains that most people find the study of words and their meanings interesting and colorful. Witness in newspapers and magazines the numbers of "letters to the editor," usually sadly misinformed, which are devoted to the uses and misuses of words. These are frequently etymological in nature, like the old and oft-recurring wheeze that sirloin is so called because King Henry VIII (or James I or Charles II) liked a loin of beef so well that he knighted one, saying "Arise, Sir Loin" at the conferring of the accolade.

WHY MEANING VARIES

The attribution of some sort of meaning to combinations of distinctive speech sounds and in a few instances to single sounds is, in addition to being a natural process, a matter of social custom, and like other customs may vary in time, place, and situation: thus *tonic* may mean 'soft drink made with charged water' in parts of eastern New England, though elsewhere it usually means 'liquid medicinal preparation to invigorate the system' or in the phrase *gin and tonic* 'quinine water'; in the usage of musicians the same word may also mean the first tone of a musical scale. It is also true that many words in frequent use, like *nice, God,* and *democracy,* have among speakers and writers of the same intellectual and social level meanings which are more or less subjective, and hence loose. All meanings of what is thought of as the same word have, however, certain elements in common—elements which may be said to operate within a certain field of meaning. If this were not true, there would be no communication.[1] But this is quite different from assuming the existence of "fixed," or "real," meanings.

Even though words do not have such inflexible meanings as we might prefer them to have, but only a field of meaning in which they operate and which may be extended in any direction or narrowed likewise, it is possible to be irritated at what we may consider a too-loose use of words. For instance, after relating that he had seen a well-dressed man take the arm of a blind and ragged beggar and escort him across a crowded thoroughfare, a rather sentimental man remarked, "That was true democracy." It was, of course, only ordinary human decency, as likely to occur in a monarchy as in a democracy, and by no means impossible under a totalitarian form of government like, say, that of Oliver Cromwell or Adolf Hitler. The semantic element of the word *democracy* which was in the speaker's mind was kindness to those less fortunate than oneself. He approved of such kindness, as indeed we all do; it was "good," and "democracy" was also "good." Hence, as soft-minded people are quite prone to do, he equated "democracy" with goodness.

We are defeating the purpose of accurate communication when we use words thus loosely. It is true that some words are by general consent used with a very loose meaning, and it is very likely that we could not get along without a certain number of such words—*nice,* for instance, as in "She's a nice girl" (meaning that she has been well brought

---

[1] It is neither appropriate nor necessary here to go into the vexed philosophical question of what constitutes meaning—the "meaning" of *meaning*—which belongs in the realm of general semantics.

up, is kind, gracious, and generally well-mannered, or, with the word stressed, merely that she is chaste), in contrast to "That's a nice state of affairs" (meaning that it is a perfectly awful state of affairs). There is certainly nothing wrong with expressing pleasure and appreciation to a hostess by a heartfelt "I've had a very nice time," or even "I've had an awfully nice time." To seek for a more "accurate" word, one of more limited meaning, would be self-conscious and affected.

A large number of educated speakers and writers, for whatever reason, refuse to use *disinterested* in the sense 'uninterested, unconcerned,' a sense which it previously had and lost for a while, and reserve the word for the meaning 'impartial, unprejudiced.' The reprehended use has nevertheless gained ground at a terrific rate, and it is possible that before long it will completely drive out the other one. There will have been no great loss to language *qua* communication. We shall merely have lost a synonym for *impartial* and acquired on all levels another way of saying 'uninterested' or 'unconcerned.' Educated readers of the future will be no more annoyed by the change than they are by similar changes that have given some of the words used in, say, the plays of Shakespeare and in the King James Bible different meanings for us from those which they had in early Modern English. Uneducated readers will be baffled and misled, to be sure; but simple people today frequently misinterpret the King James Bible (the only literature in early Modern English which they are likely ever to read) with complete satisfaction to themselves. It is hardly feasible to expect language to stand still for the sake of ignorant people, who as a matter of fact manage quite well enough, as do the rest of us so long as our less informed fellows are restrained from forcibly imposing their interpretations of what they read, whether sacred or profane, upon us. How long they can be so restrained in a democracy, where numbers are all-important, is a very important question, but it is outside the scope of the present discussion.

ETYMOLOGY AND MEANING

There is a widespread belief, held even by some quite learned people, that the way to find out what a word means is to find out what it previously meant — or, preferably, if it were possible to do so, what it originally meant — a notion similar to the Greek belief in the etymon. Such is the frequent method of dealing with borrowed words, the mistaken idea being that the meaning of the word in current English and the meaning of the non-English word from which the English word is derived must be, or at any rate ought to be, one and the same. As a matter of fact, such an appeal to etymology to determine present meaning is as unreliable as would be an appeal to spelling to determine modern pronunciation. Change of meaning—semantic change, as it is called—may, and frequently does, alter the so-called etymological sense, which may have become altogether obsolete. (The etymological sense is only the earliest sense we can *discover,* not necessarily the very earliest.) The study of etymologies is of course richly rewarding. It may, for instance, throw a great deal of light on present meanings, and it frequently tells us something of the workings of the human mind in dealing with the phenomenon of meaning, but it is of very limited help in determining for us what a word "actually" means.

Certain popular writers, overeager to display their learning, have asserted that words are misused when they depart from their etymological meanings. Thus Ambrose Bierce once declared that *dilapidated,* because of its ultimate derivation from Latin *lapis* 'stone,' could appropriately be used only of a stone structure.[2] Such a notion if true would commit us to the parallel assertion that only what actually had roots could properly be eradicated, since *eradicate* is ultimately derived from Latin *rādix* 'root,' that *calculation* be restricted to counting pebbles (Lat. *calx* 'stone'), that *sinister* be applied only to leftists, and *dexterous* to rightists. By the same token we should have to insist that we could *admire* only what we could wonder at, inasmuch as the English word comes from Latin *ad* 'at' plus *mīrāri* 'to wonder';[3] or that *giddy* persons must be divinely inspired, inasmuch as *gid* is a derivative of *god;*[4] or that only men may be virtuous, because *virtue* is derived from Latin *virtus* 'manliness,' itself a derivative of *vir* 'man.' Now, alas for the wicked times in which we live, *virtue* is applied exclusively to women. *Virile,* also a derivative of *vir,* has retained all of its earlier meaning, and has even added to it.

From these few examples, it must be obvious that we cannot ascribe anything like "fixed" meanings to words. What we actually encounter much of the time are meanings that are variable, and that may have wandered from what their etymologies suggest. To suppose that invariable meanings exist, quite apart from context, is to be guilty of a type of naiveté which may vitiate all our thinking.

[2] In his *Write It Right* (New York, 1928), cited in Stuart Robertson, *The Development of Modern English,* 2nd ed., rev. Frederic G. Cassidy (New York, 1954), p. 234.

[3] Compare Hamlet's use of *admiration* in the sense 'wonderment, amazement' in "Season your admiration for a while/With an attent eare" (I.ii.192–93).

[4] Compare *dizzy,* which may in very early times have had the same meaning. See Henry Bradley, *The Making of English* (New York, 1904), pp. 198–200. *Enthusiastic,* from the Greek, also had this meaning.

HOW MEANING CHANGES

Change of meaning — a phenomenon common to all languages — while frequently unpredictable, is not wholly chaotic. Rather, it follows certain paths which we might do well to familiarize ourselves with. Much, probably most, of the illustrative matter which is to follow, like that which precedes, has come from many books read over a long period of years. Some of the examples are by now more or less stock ones, but they make their point better than less familiar ones would do, and hence are used without apology, but with gratitude to whoever first dug them out. It is likely that many of them will be found in James Bradstreet Greenough and George Lyman Kittredge's old, but still good, *Words and Their Ways in English Speech* (New York, 1901).

GENERALIZATION AND SPECIALIZATION

An obvious classification of meaning is that based on scope. This is to say, meaning may be generalized (extended, widened) or it may be specialized (restricted, narrowed). When we increase the scope of a word, we reduce the elements of its contents. For instance, *tail* (from OE *tægl*) in earlier times seems to have meant "hairy caudal appendage, as of a horse.' When we eliminated the hairiness (or the horsiness) from the meaning, we increased its scope, so that in modern English the word means simply 'caudal appendage.' The same thing has happened to Danish *hale,* earlier 'tail of a cow.' In course of time the cow was eliminated, and in present-day Danish the word means simply 'tail,' having undergone a semantic generalization precisely like that of the English word cited; the closely related Icelandic *hali* still keeps the cow in the picture. Similarly, a *mill* was earlier a place for making things by the process of grinding, that is, for making meal. The words *meal* and *mill* are themselves related, as one might guess from their similarity. A mill is now simply a place for making things: the grinding has been eliminated, so that we may speak of a woolen mill, a steel mill, or even a gin mill. The word *corn* earlier meant 'grain' and is in fact related to the word *grain*. It is still used in this general sense in England, as in the "Corn Laws," but specifically it may mean either oats (for animals) or wheat (for human beings). In American usage *corn* denotes maize, which is of course not at all what Keats meant in his "Ode to a Nightingale" when he described Ruth as standing "in tears amid the alien corn." The building in which corn, regardless of its meaning, is stored is called a barn. *Barn* earlier denoted a storehouse for barley; the word is in fact a compound of two Old English words, *bere* 'barley' and *ærn* 'house.' By elimination of a part of its earlier content, the scope of this word has been extended to mean a store-house for any kind of grain. American English has still further general-ized by eliminating the grain, so that *barn* may mean also a place for housing livestock.

The opposite of generalization is specialization, a process in which, by adding to the elements of meaning, the semantic content of a word is reduced. *Deer,* for instance, used to mean simply 'animal' (OE *dēor*) as its German cognate *Tier* still does. Shakespeare writes of "Mice, and Rats, and such small Deare" (*King Lear* III.iv.144). By adding something particular (the family *Cervidae*) to the content, the scope of the word has been reduced, and it has come to mean a specific kind of animal. Similarly *hound* used to mean 'dog,' as does its German cognate *Hund.* To this earlier meaning we have in the course of time added the idea of hunting, and thereby restricted the scope of the word, which to us means a special sort of dog, a hunting dog. To the earlier content of *liquor* 'fluid' (compare *liquid*) we have added 'alco-holic.' But generalization, the opposite tendency, has occurred in the case of the word *rum,* the name of a specific alcoholic drink, which in the usage of those who disapprove of all alcoholic beverages long ago came to mean strong drink in general, even though other liquors are much more copiously imbibed today. The word has even been per-sonified in *Demon Rum.*

Meat once meant simply 'food,' a meaning which it retains in *sweet-meat* and throughout the King James Bible ("meat for the belly," "meat and drink"), though it acquired the meaning 'flesh' much earlier and had for a while both the general and the specialized meaning. *Starve* (OE *steorfan*) used to mean simply 'to die,' as its German cognate *sterben* still does.[5] Chaucer writes, for instance, "But as hire man I wol ay lyve and sterve" (*Troilus and Criseyde* I.427). A specific way of dying had to be expressed by a following phrase, for example "of hunger, for cold." The *OED* cites "starving with the cold," pre-sumably dialectal, as late as 1867. The word came somehow to be primarily associated with death by hunger, and for a while there existed a compound verb *hunger-starve.* Usually nowadays we put the stress altogether on the added idea of hunger and lose the older mean-ing altogether. Although the usual meaning of *to starve* now is 'to die of hunger,' we also use the phrase "starve to death," which in earlier times would have been tautological. An additional, toned-down mean-ing grows out of hyperbole, so that "I'm starving" may mean only 'I'm very hungry.' The word is of course used figuratively, as in "starv-

[5] An even earlier meaning may have been 'to grow stiff.'

ing for love," which, as we have seen, once meant 'dying for love.' This word furnishes a striking example of specialization and proliferation of meaning.

PEJORATION AND AMELIORATION

Change in meaning is frequently due to ethical, or moral, considerations. A word may, as it were, go downhill, or it may rise in the world; there is no way of predicting what its career may be. *Politician* has had a downhill development in American English; in British English it is still not entirely without honor. *Knave* (OE *cnafa*), which used to mean simply 'boy'—it is cognate with German *Knabe,* which retains the earlier meaning—is another example of pejorative (from Lat. *pējor* 'worse') development; it came to mean successively 'serving boy'[6] (specialization), like that well-known knave of hearts[7] who was given to stealing tarts, and ultimately 'bad human being,' so that we may now speak of an old knave, or conceivably even of a knavish woman. On its journey downhill this word has thus undergone both specialization and generalization. *Boor,* once meaning 'peasant,'[8] has had a similar pejorative development, as has *lewd,* earlier 'lay, as opposed to clerical,' and thereafter 'ignorant,' 'base,' and finally 'obscene,' which is the only meaning to survive.[9] The same fate has befallen the Latin loanword *vulgar,* ultimately from *vulgus* 'the common people'; the earlier meaning is retained in *Vulgar Latin,* the Latin that was spoken by the people up to the time of the early Middle Ages and was to develop into the various Romance languages. *Censure* earlier meant 'opinion.' In the course of time it has come to mean 'bad opinion'; *criticism* is well on its way to the same pejorative goal, ordinarily meaning nowadays 'adverse judgment.' The verbs *to censure* and *to criticize* have undergone a similar development. *Deserts* (as in *just deserts*) likewise started out indifferently to mean simply what one deserved, whether good or bad, but has come to mean 'punishment.' A few more examples of this tendency must suffice. *Silly* (OE *sǣlig*), earlier 'timely,' came to mean 'happy, blessed,' and subsequently 'innocent, simple'; then the

[6] Cf. French *garçon* 'boy,' which in a similarly specialized use means 'waiter.'
[7] Actually a further specialization: the jacks in card games are called the knaves in upper-class British usage.
[8] Its cognate *Bauer* is the usual equivalent of *jack* or *knave* in German card-playing, whence English *bower* (as in *right bower* and *left bower*) in certain card games such as euchre and five hundred.
[9] The development of *nice,* going back to Latin *nescius* 'ignorant,' has been just the opposite. The Old French form used in English meant 'simple,' a meaning retained in Modern French *niais*. In the course of its career in English it has had the meanings 'foolishly particular' and then merely 'particular' (as in *a nice distinction*), among others.

simplicity, a desirable quality under most circumstances, was misunderstood (note the present ambiguity of *a simple man*), and the word took on its present meaning. Its German cognate *selig* progressed only to the second stage, though the word may be used facetiously to mean 'tipsy.'

Like *censure* and *criticize, praise* started out indifferently; it is simply *appraise* 'put a value on' with loss of its initial unstressed syllable (aphesis). But *praise* has come to mean 'value highly.' Here what has been added has ameliorated, or elevated, the semantic content of the word. Amelioration, the opposite of pejoration, is well illustrated by *knight,* which used to mean 'servant,' as its German relative *Knecht* still does.[10] This particular word has obviously moved far from its earlier meaning, denoting as it usually now does a very special and exalted man who has been signally honored by his sovereign and who is entitled to prefix *Sir* to his name. *Earl* (OE *eorl*) once meant simply 'man,' though in ancient Germanic times it was specially applied to a warrior, who was almost invariably a man of good birth, in contrast to a *ceorl* (*churl*), or ordinary freeman. When under the Norman kings French titles were adopted in England, *earl* failed to be displaced, but remained as the equivalent of the Continental *count.*

CHANGES DUE TO SOCIAL CLASS

The meaning of a word may vary even with the group in which it is used. For all speakers *smart* has the meaning 'intelligent,' but there is a specialized class usage in which it means 'fashionable.' The meaning of *a smart woman* may thus vary with the social level of the speaker; it may, indeed, have to be inferred from the context. The earliest meaning of this word seems to have been 'sharp,' as in *a smart blow.* It is interesting to note that *sharp* has also been used in the sense 'up-to-date, fashionable,' as in *a sharp dresser,* by certain groups of speakers who admire this particular type of "sharpness."

Similarly, a word's meaning may vary according to the circumstances under which it is used. *Hall* (OE *heall*), for instance, once meant a very large roofed place, like the splendid royal dwelling place Heorot in which Beowulf fought Grendel. Such buildings were usually without smaller attached rooms, though Heorot had a "bower"[11] (*būr*),

[10] It must not be supposed that, because German cognates have frequently been cited as still having meanings which have become archaic in English, German words are necessarily less susceptible to semantic change than English ones. With different choices of examples it is possible that a contrary impression might be given.

[11] Note that this word survives only in the sense 'arbor, enclosure formed by vegetation.'

earlier a separate cottage, but in *Beowulf* a bedroom to which the king and queen retired. For retainers the hall served as meeting room, feasting room, and sleeping room. Later *hall* came to mean the largest room in a great house, used for large gatherings such as receptions and feasts, though the use of the word for the entire structure survives in the names of a number of manor houses such as Little Wenham Hall and Speke Hall in England. There are a number of other meanings, all connoting size and some degree of splendor, and all a far cry from the modern American use of *hall* as a narrow passageway leading to rooms.[12] The meaning of *hall* must be determined by the context in which it occurs.

Akin to what we have been considering is modification of meaning as the result of a shift in point of view. *Crescent,* from the present participial form of Latin *cresco,* used to mean simply 'growing, increasing,' as in Pompey's "My powers are Cressent, and my Auguring hope/Sayes it will come to'th'full" (*Antony and Cleopatra* II.i.10–11). The new, or growing, moon was thus called the crescent moon. There has been, however, a shift in the dominant element of meaning, the emphasis coming to be put entirely on shape, specifically on a particular shape of the moon, rather than upon growth. *Crescent* has thus come to mean 'new-moon-shaped.' Similarly, in *veteran* (Lat. *veterānus,* a derivative of *vetus* 'old'), the emphasis has shifted from age to military service, though not necessarily long service: a veteran need not have grown old in service, and we may in fact speak of a *young veteran.* The fact that etymologically the phrase is self-contradictory is of no significance as far as present usage is concerned. The word is of course extended to other areas, for instance *veteran politician;* in its extended meanings it continues to connote long experience and usually mature years as well.

THE VOGUE FOR WORDS OF LEARNED ORIGIN

When learned words acquire popular currency, they almost inevitably acquire at the same time new, less exact, meanings, or at least new shades of meaning. *Philosophy,* for instance, earlier 'love of wisdom,' has now a popular sense 'practical opinion or body of opinions,' as in "the philosophy of salesmanship," "the philosophy of Will Rogers," and "homespun philosophy." An error in translation from a foreign language may result in a useful new meaning, for example

---

[12] In British English the reduced meaning of *hall* refers to the vestibule or entrance passage immediately inside the front door of a small house.

psychological moment, now 'most opportune time,' rather than 'psychological momentum,' which is the proper translation of German *psychologisches Moment,* the ultimate source of the phrase. The popular misunderstanding of *inferiority complex,* first used to designate an unconscious sense of inferiority manifesting itself in assertive behavior, has given us a synonym for *diffidence, shyness.* It is similar with *guilt complex,* now used to denote nothing more psychopathic than a feeling of guilt. The term *complex* as first used by psychoanalysts more than half a century ago designated a type of aberration resulting from the unconscious suppression of more or less related attitudes. The word soon passed into voguish and subsequently into general use to designate an obsession of any kind — a bee in the bonnet, as it were. Among its progeny are *Oedipus complex, herd complex,* and *sex complex.* The odds on its increasing fecundity would seem to be rather high.

Other fashionable terms from psychoanalysis and psychology, with which our times are so intensely preoccupied, are *subliminal,* which has been widely used in reference to a very sneaky kind of advertising technique; *behavior pattern,* meaning simply 'behavior'; *neurotic,* with a wide range of meaning, including 'nervous, highstrung, artistic by temperament, eccentric, or given to worrying'; *compulsive* 'habitual,' as in *compulsive drinker* and *compulsive criminal;* and *schizophrenia* 'practically any mental or emotional disorder.'

It is not surprising that the newer, popular meanings of what were once more or less technical terms should generally show a considerable extension of the earlier, technical meanings. Thus, *sadism* has come to mean simply 'cruelty' and *exhibitionism* merely 'showing off,' without any of the earlier connotations of sexual perversion, as in fact the word *psychology* itself may mean nothing more than 'mental processes' in a vague sort of way. An intense preoccupation in the mid-twentieth century with what is fashionably and doubtless humanely referred to as *mental illness* — a less enlightened age than ours called it *insanity,* and people afflicted with it were said to be *crazy* — must to a large extent be responsible for the use of such terms as have been cited. Also notable is the specialization of *sick* to refer to mental imbalance.

The greatest darling among the loosely used pseudoscientific vogue words of recent years is unquestionably *image* in the sense 'impression that others subconsciously have of someone.' A jaundiced observer of modern life might well suppose that what one actually is is not nearly so important as the image of oneself that one is able — to use another vogue word — to project. If the "image" is phony, what difference does it make? Everyone must get along; all must be allowed to have what the political orators refer to as human dignity, whatever the phrase means.

From an interview with two eminent psychiatrists syndicated by the Women's News Service,[13] one may learn that Governor Nelson Rockefeller's campaign headquarters before the political conventions of 1960 "had an 'image division,' set up to help project a favorable impression." One of the sages being interviewed declared, after consulting his badly clouded crystal ball: "There is no doubt that Mr. [John F.] Kennedy appeals to women. He is the image of their little boy. . . . But they will not vote for him because they do not want a boy in the White House. Women want a father image as president—especially if they have weak husbands." "Many psychologists have said," according to the same gentleman, "that President Eisenhower's great personal hold on the public is due to the fact that he creates a strong father image" and moreover "has nurtured this image by never taking a single act not compatible with the subconscious concept of the ideal father." Images do not necessarily have to be those of persons, for a quarterly report of the Standard Oil Company of New Jersey states that "a current advertising campaign featuring the skillful, courteous service available at Esso stations is proving remarkably effective not only at building a favorable dealer service image in the public mind but also at encouraging and stimulating dealers and service station attendants to measure up to this image."[14]

The awesome prestige of science and technology in our day is indicated by the diversion of terms previously associated with them to humbler activities. A Reading *Clinic*, for instance, is a department of a college or university for the "diagnosis" and correction of the reading difficulties of students (why not "patients"?) who have not hitherto learned to read—at least, not without moving their lips. A Retail Hardware Salesmanship *Clinic* is, as far as the layman is able to determine, nothing more than a conference of hardware salesmen. An Auto *Clinic* is a hospital for ailing cars. The exact nature of the "second annual Evangelism Clinic at the Pine Grove [Florida] Baptist Church,"[15] with the pleasantly alcoholically named Rev. Tom Collins as "principal inspirational speaker," is difficult to determine. A Writing *Laboratory* (or *Lab*) is a classroom with chairs, tables, and dictionaries where students of what used to be unassumingly called Freshman English write themes under the supervision of graduate assistants, who in due

---

[13] Published in the Jacksonville *Florida Times-Union*, February 9, 1960, p. 10.
[14] Quoted in the *New Yorker*, December 3, 1960, p. 100.
[15] Gainesville, Florida, *Sun*, February 10, 1960, p. 14.

time will probably wish to be regarded as "lab assistants." Similarly, an *intern* may nowadays just as well be a beginning teacher in a public school as an M.D. serving in a hospital. By a sort of inverted snobbery, *workshop,* sharing much the same range of meaning as *laboratory,* has become quite voguish, for instance *Writers' Workshop.*

Among the more impressive vogue words of the late 1960's and the early 1970's are *establishment* 'group of people, usually thought of as heartless, wicked, and ultraconservative, with power to control policies in government, education, religion, and other fields of activity,' *confrontation* 'meeting between those demanding reform or redress and an establishment of the appropriate sort,'[16] *extrapolate* 'infer' (taken from mathematics, where it has a technical meaning), *empathy* 'sympathy' (though this was not its meaning for psychologists), *dialogue* 'argument, usually ill-mannered, practically the same as *confrontation,*' *identify* used intransitively (as in "Those whites who go to black schools identify with the goals of the blacks"), and *relevant* 'of supposed immediate importance.' The last cited word has, in university circles at least, practically ousted the older vogue words *significant* and *meaningful.* We shall doubtless hear and read these much more for some years to come, until they are supplanted by other vogue words.

Less mouth-filling than the preceding examples but of considerable emotional appeal is *ghetto* 'slums,' which no longer has anything to do with that section of a city, not necessarily impoverished, in which in former times Jews were required to live or even, as in more recent times, a predominantly Jewish section of a large city. It is likely that many if not most members of the rising generation are quite unaware of the older meanings, which have come to be largely historical in a period in which one reads and hears of "black ghettos" and "Puerto Rican ghettos"—though not as yet of "white hillbilly ghettos" and "Indian ghettos." The inhabitants of modern ghettos are said to be "disadvantaged" (see below, p. 360). It is altogether meet and right that no such verbal humanitarianism should be extended to their landlords, who remain "slum landlords" or "slumlords," not "ghetto landlords." A ghetto in this newest sense is sometimes referred to as an "inner

---

[16] The *American Heritage Dictionary* (Boston, 1969), which quite properly includes those monosyllables known to everyone over eight years old and having to do with anatomy, sexuality, and excretion—though it has overlooked a few of these—needlessly justifies the inclusion on the grounds that such words are part of the "language of confrontation." It takes care, however, to label them all *vulgar* or *vulgar slang,* just in case the unsuspecting reader might not know.

city," but this term has come to seem coldly sociological; it somehow lacks the emotional impact of *ghetto.*

TRANSFER OF MEANING (SPECIAL TYPES)

There are a good many special types of transfer of meaning. *Long* and *short,* for instance, are on occasion transferred from the spatial concepts to which they ordinarily refer and made to refer to temporal concepts, as in *a long time, a short while;* similarly with such nouns as *length* and *space.* Metaphor is involved when we extend the word *foot* 'lowest extremity of an animal' to all sorts of things, as in *foot of a mountain, tree,* and so forth. The meaning of the same word is specialized or restricted when we add to its original content something like 'approximate length of the lowest extremity of the male human animal,' thereby making the word mean a unit of measure; we do much the same thing to *hand* when we use it as a unit of measure for the height of horses.

Meaning may be transferred from one sensory faculty to another (synesthesia), as when we apply *clear,* with principal reference to sight, to hearing, as in *clear-sounding. Loud* is transferred from hearing to sight when we speak of *loud colors. Sweet,* with primary reference to taste, may be extended to hearing (*sweet music*), smell ("The rose smells sweet"), and to all senses at once (*a sweet girl*). *Sharp* may be transferred from feeling to taste, and so may *smooth. Warm* may shift its usual reference from feeling to sight, as in *warm colors,* and along with *cold* may refer in a general way to all senses, as in *a warm* (*cold*) *welcome.*

Abstract meanings may evolve from more concrete ones. Latin *cantus* 'the act of singing' came to acquire the more abstract meaning 'song.' The compound *understand,* as Leonard Bloomfield points out, must in prehistoric Old English times have meant 'to stand among, that is, close to' — *under* presumably having had the meaning 'among,' like its German and Latin cognates *unter* and *inter.*[17] But this literal, concrete meaning gave way to the more abstract meaning which the word has today. Bloomfield cites parallel shifts from concrete to abstract in German *verstehen* ('to stand before'), Greek *epistamai* ('I stand upon'), Latin *comprehendere* ('to take hold of'), and Italian *capire,* based on Latin *capere* 'to grasp,' among others.

The first person to use *grasp* in an abstract sense, as in "He has a good grasp of his subject," was coining an interesting metaphor. But

---

[17] *Language* (New York, 1933), pp. 425, 429–30.

the shift from concrete to abstract, or from physical to mental, has been so complete that we no longer think of this usage as metaphorical: *grasp* has come to be synonymous with *comprehension* in such a context as that cited, though the word has of course retained its physical reference. It was similar with *glad,* earlier 'smooth,' though this word has completely lost the earlier meaning (except in the proper name *Gladstone,* if surnames may be thought of nowadays as having meaning) and may refer only to a mental state. Likewise, meaning may shift from subjective to objective, as when *pitiful,* earlier 'full of pity, compassionate,' came to mean 'deserving of pity'; or the shift may be the other way round, as when *fear,* earlier 'danger,' something objective, came to mean 'terror,' a state of mind.

ASSOCIATION OF IDEAS

Interchange of meaning may be due simply to association of ideas. Latin *penna,* for instance, originally meant 'feather,' but came to be used to indicate an instrument for writing, whether made of a feather or not, because of the association of the quill with writing. Our word *pen* is ultimately derived from the Latin word, though it comes to us by way of Old French. Similarly, *paper* is from *papyrus,* a kind of plant, and the two were once invariably associated in people's minds, though paper is nowadays made from rags, wood, straw, and other fibrous materials, and this association has been completely lost. Sensational magazines used to be printed on paper of inferior quality made from wood pulp; these were referred to by writers, somewhat derisively, as wood-pulp magazines, or simply as the *pulps,* in contrast to the *slicks,* those printed on paper of better quality. Such "literature" has come up in the world, at least as far as its physical production is concerned, and many magazines whose reading matter is considered by serious-minded people to be of low quality are actually printed on paper with no pulp content. These are nevertheless still referred to as "the pulps," and a writer who keeps the wolf from his door by supplying them with stories and articles is known as a "pulp writer." Thus, because of an earlier association the name of a physical product, wood pulp, has been applied to a type of periodical with reference to the literary quality of its contents. *Silver* has come to be used for eating utensils made of silver — an instance of specialization — and sometimes, by association, for the same articles even when not made of silver, so that we may even speak of ten-cent-store silver. The product derived from latex and earlier known as *caoutchouc* soon acquired a less difficult name, *rubber,* from association with one of its earliest uses, making erasures on paper by rubbing. *China* 'earthenware' originally designated porcelain of a type first manufactured in the country for which it is called, and the name of a native American bird, the *turkey,* derives from the fact that our ancestors somehow got the notion that it was of Turkish origin.[18] These names, like others which might be cited, arose out of associations which have long since been lost.

THE EFFECT OF LATIN MEANINGS

In olden times, when every educated person knew Latin, Latin semantics might affect English word meanings. *Thing,* for example, meant in Old English 'assembly, sometimes for legal purposes,' a meaning which it had in the other Germanic languages and has retained in Icelandic, as in *Alþingi* 'all-assembly,' the name of the Icelandic parliament. English *thing* thus acquired from Latin *rēs,* which was used in much the same sense and was translated by *thing,* 'case at law' as one of its meanings. This meaning was subsequently lost, but because of the association, originally at one small point, the English word came to acquire every meaning that Latin *rēs* could have, which is to say, practically every other meaning of *thing* in present English. German *Ding* has had, quite independently, the same sense-history.

SOUND ASSOCIATIONS

Similarity or identity of sound may likewise influence meaning. *Fay,* from the Old French *fae* 'fairy' has influenced *fey,* from Old English *fǣge* 'fated, doomed to die' to such an extent that *fey* is practically always used nowadays in the sense 'spritely, fairy-like,' as in "It may sound an odd criticism to make of a creature who is first cousin to a fairy, but Miss [Leslie] Caron's Ondine was at the start of the evening rather too fey."[19] Here there is an association of meaning at one small point: fairies are mysterious; so is being fated to die, even though we all are so fated.

TABOO AND EUPHEMISM

It will by now be apparent that many factors must be taken into account in any discussion of change in meaning. It is not surprising that superstition should play a part, as when *sinister,* the Latin word for 'left' (the unlucky side) acquired its present baleful significance. The verb *die,* of Germanic origin, is not once recorded in Old English. This does not necessarily mean that it was not a part of the Old English word stock; however, in the writings that have come down to us,

---

[18] In French the same creature is called *dinde,* that is, "d'Inde." The French of course thought that America was India at the time when the name was conferred.

[19] London *Spectator,* January 20, 1961, p. 76.

roundabout, toning-down expressions such as "go on a journey" are used instead, perhaps because of superstitions connected with the word itself—superstitions which survive into our own day, when people (at least those whom we know personally) "pass away," "go to sleep," or "go to their Great Reward." Louise Pound collected an imposing and—to the irreverent—amusing list of words and phrases used in referring to death in her article "American Euphemisms for Dying, Death, and Burial."[20] She concludes that "one of mankind's gravest problems is to avoid a straightforward mention of dying or burial."

Name-shifting is especially frequent, and probably always has been, when we must come face to face with the less happy facts of our existence, for life holds even for the most fortunate of men experiences which are inartistic, violent, and hence shocking to contemplate in the full light of day—for instance, the first and last facts of human existence, birth and death, despite the sentimentality with which we have surrounded them. And it is certainly true that the sting of the latter is somewhat alleviated—for the survivors, anyway—by calling it by some other name, such as "the Great Adventure," "the flight to glory," and "the final sleep," which are among the many terms cited by Pound in the article just alluded to. *Mortician* is a much flossier word than *undertaker* (which is itself a euphemism with the earlier meanings 'helper,' 'contractor,' 'publisher,' and 'baptismal sponsor,' among others), but the *loved one* whom he prepares for public view and subsequent interment in a *casket* (earlier a jewel-box, as in *The Merchant of Venice*) is just as dead as a *corpse* in a *coffin*. But such verbal subterfuges are apparently thought to rob the grave of some of its victory; the notion of death is made more tolerable to the human consciousness than it would otherwise be. Birth is much more plainly alluded to nowadays than it used to be, particularly by young married people, who seem to be strangely fascinated by the unpleasant clinical details attendant upon it. The free use of *pregnant* is not much older than World War II. A woman *with child, going to have a baby,* or *enceinte* used to terminate her condition by her *confinement,* or, if one wanted to be really fancy about it, her *accouchement.*

Ideas of decency likewise profoundly affect language. All during the Victorian era, ladies and gentlemen were very sensitive about using the word *leg, limb* being almost invariably substituted, sometimes even if only the legs of a piano were being referred to. In the very year

[20] *American Speech,* 11 (1936), 195–202. Reprinted in *Selected Writings of Louise Pound* (Lincoln, Nebr., 1949), pp. 139–47.

which marks the beginning of Queen Victoria's long reign, Captain Frederick Marryat noted in his *Diary in America* (1837) the American taboo on this word, when, having asked a young American lady who had taken a spill whether she had hurt her leg, she turned from him, "evidently much shocked, or much offended," later explaining to him that in America the word *leg* was never used in the presence of ladies. Later, the captain visited a school for young ladies where he saw, according to his own testimony, "a square pianoforte with four limbs," all dressed in little frilled pantalettes. For reasons which it would be difficult to analyze, a similar taboo was placed upon *belly, stomach* being usually substituted for it, along with such nursery terms as *tummy* and *breadbasket* and the advertising copy writer's *midriff*. *Toilet*, a diminutive of French *toile* 'cloth,' in its earliest English uses meant a piece of cloth in which to wrap clothes, subsequently coming to be used for a cloth cover for a dressing table, and then the table itself, as when Lydia Languish in Sheridan's *The Rivals* says, "Here, my dear Lucy, hide these books. Quick, quick! Fling *Peregrine Pickle* under the toilet—throw *Roderick Random* into the closet. . . ."[21] There are other related meanings. The word came to be used in America as a euphemism for *privy*—itself in turn a euphemism, as are *latrine* (ultimately derived from Lat. *lavāre* 'to wash') and *lavatory* (note the euphemistic phrase "to wash one's hands"). But *toilet* is now frequently replaced by *rest room, comfort station, powder room,* or the intolerably coy *little boys'* (or *girls'*) *room,* and younger-generation speakers minding their manners invariably use *bathroom,* even though there may be no tub and no occasion for taking a bath. One may even hear of a dog's "going to the bathroom" in the living room. It is safe to predict that these evasions will in their turn come to be regarded as indecorous, and other expressions substituted for them.

Euphemism is likewise resorted to in reference to certain diseases. Like that which attempts to prettify, or at least to mollify birth, death, and excretion, this type of verbal subterfuge is doubtless deeply rooted in fear and superstition. An ailment of almost any sort, for instance, is nowadays often referred to as a *condition* (*heart condition, kidney condition, malignant condition,* and so forth), so that *condition,* hitherto a more or less neutral word, has thus had a pejorative development, coming to mean 'bad condition.'[22] *Leprosy* is no longer used by the Ameri-

---

[21] It should be pointed out that about fifty years ago the direction for the disposal of *Roderick Random* would have been as risible as that for *Peregrine Pickle,* when *closet* was frequently used for *water closet,* now practically obsolete.

[22] Note that, although *to have a condition* means 'to be in bad health,' *to be in condition* continues, confusingly enough, to mean 'to be in good health.'

can Medical Association because of its repulsive connotations; it is nowadays replaced by the colorless *Hansen's disease. Cancer* may be openly referred to, though it is notable that in the syndicated horoscopes of Carroll Righter, a well-known Hollywood astrologer, the term is no longer used as a sign of the zodiac; those born under Cancer are now designated "Moon Children." The taboo has been removed from reference to the various specific venereal diseases, formerly *blood diseases* or *social diseases.*

Old age and its attendant decay have probably been made more bearable for many elderly and decrepit people by calling them *senior citizens.* A similar verbal humanitarianism is responsible for *underprivileged* 'poor,' now largely supplanted by *disadvantaged;* the previously mentioned *sick* 'insane'; *exceptional child* 'a pupil of subnormal mentality';[23] and a good many other voguish euphemisms, some of which have been cited in another connection. In the last cited example, pejoration has also operated—unless it can be conceived generally that being below par intellectually is a desirable thing, as the schools would seem to have supposed. One wonders whether to the next generation an "exceptional man" will be thought of as a dull and stupid man, that is, an exceptional child grown to maturity, and whether the "exceptional bargains" offered by the stores had not better be passed up in favor of merely average ones. Sentimental equalitarianism has led us to attempt to dignify humble occupations by giving them high-sounding titles: thus a *janitor* (originally a doorkeeper, from *Janus,* the doorkeeper of heaven in Roman mythology) has in many parts of America become a *custodian* and there are many engineers who would not know the difference between a slide rule and a cantilever. H. L. Mencken cites, among a good many others, *demolition engineer* 'house-wrecker,' *sanitary engineer* 'garbage man,' and *extermination engineer* 'rat-catcher.'[24] The meaning of *profession* has been generalized to such an extent that it may include practically any trade or vocation. The writer of a letter to the editor of *Life* comments as follows on the publication of a picture of a plumber in a previous issue: "I think you have done an injustice to the plumbing profession" (August 6, 1951); and a regional chairman of the Wage Stabilization Board informed a waitress who complained of the smallness of her tips, according to an Associated Press item of June 19, 1952, that "if tipping were viewed by your profession as a true incentive for better,

---

[23] Note that the child who exceeds expectations has been stigmatized by the schools as an *over-achiever.*

[24] *The American Language,* 4th ed. (New York, 1936), pp. 289–91.

faster and more agreeable service, this might go a long way toward relieving the situation." Long ago James Fenimore Cooper in *The American Democrat* (1838) denounced such democratic subterfuges as *boss* for *master* and *help* for *servant,* but these seem very mild nowadays. One of the great concerns of the democratic and progressive age in which we live would seem to be to ensure that nobody's feelings shall ever be hurt—at least, not by words.

It is characteristic of the human mind, in varying degrees of course, to identify words with objects, persons, and ideas—to think much of the time not in terms of the actual situations of flesh-and-blood life, but in relation to words, like that oft-quoted little girl who, upon first seeing a pig, remarked that it was certainly rightly named, for it was a very dirty animal. But a pig by any other name—even if it were called a rose—would smell as bad. What one happens to call it—*Schwein, lechón, porco,* or *pig*—makes no difference in the nature of the creature, nor is one name any more appropriate than another. To suppose that our term is superior—that a pig really *is* a pig and hence that we who speak English are more perceptive than foreigners in calling it by its "right" name—is so naive that no one would own to such a belief. Yet it is certainly true that in their everyday lives people frequently act as though they thought words were identical with what they designate.

During World War II the name of a widely known and highly satisfactory pencil was changed from Mikado to Mirado—a hardly noticeable change, involving a single letter. Yet it is doubtful that the manufacturer would have gone to such trouble and expense as must have been involved in making that little change had he not been convinced that, with Japan as our enemy, many patriots would refuse to buy a pencil named for its emperor, although no one in his right mind could imagine that the pencil was a whit superior because of the change of name.

THE FATE OF INTENSIFYING WORDS

Intensives constantly stand in need of replacement, being so frequently used that their intensifying force is worn down. As an adverb of degree, *very* has only an intensifying function; it has altogether lost its independent meaning 'truly,' though as an adjective it survives with older meanings in such phrases as "the very man for the job" and "this very afternoon." Chaucer does not use *very* as an intensive adverb; the usage was doubtless beginning to be current in his day, though the *OED* has no contemporary citations. As everyone must be aware, the *verray* in the well-known line "He was a verray, parfit gentil knyght" is an adjective modifying *knyght:* the meaning is approximately 'He was a fully accomplished gentle knight in the widest sense of the term.'

For Chaucer and his contemporaries *full* seems to have been the usual intensive adverb, though Old English *swīðe* (the adverbial form of *swīð* 'strong') retained its intensifying function until the middle of the fifteenth century, with independent meanings 'rapidly' and 'instantly' surviving much longer. *Right* was also widely used as an intensive in Middle English times, as in Chaucer's description of the Clerk of Oxenford: "he nas [that is, *ne was*] nat right fat," which is to say 'He wasn't very fat.' This usage survives formally in *Right Reverend,* the title of a bishop;[25] in *Right Honourable,* that of members of the Privy Council and a few other dignitaries; and in *Right Worshipful,* that of most lord mayors; as also in the more or less informal usages *right smart, right well, right away, right there,* and the like.

Sore, as in *sore afraid,* was similarly long used as an intensive modifier of adjectives and adverbs; its use to modify verbs is even older. Its cognate *sehr* is still the usual intensive in German, in which language it has completely lost its independent use.

In view of the very understandable tendency of such intensifying words to become dulled, it is not surprising that we should cast about for other words to replace them when we really want to be emphatic. "It's been a very pleasant evening" seems quite inadequate under certain circumstances, and we may instead say, "It's been an *awfully* pleasant evening"; *very nice* may likewise become *"terribly* nice." In negative utterances, *too* is coming to be widely used as an intensive: "Newberry's not too far from here"; "Juvenile-court law practice is not too lucrative."

Prodigiously was for a while a voguish substitute for *very,* so that a Regency "blood" like Thackeray's Jos Sedley might speak admiringly of a shapely woman as "a prodigiously fine gel" or even a "monstrous fine" one. The first of these now-forgotten intensifiers dates approximately from the second half of the seventeenth century; the second is about a century earlier. An anonymous contributor to the periodical *The World* in 1756 deplored the "pomp of utterance of our present women of fashion; which, though it may tend to spoil many a pretty mouth, can never recommend an indifferent one," citing in support

---

[25] The dean's title *Very Reverend* has exactly the same meaning, but is, naturally, less exalted in its connotations.

of his statement the feminine overuse of *vastly, horridly, abominably, immensely,* and *excessively* as intensives.[26]

SEMANTIC CHANGE IS INEVITABLE

It is a great pity that language cannot be the exact, finely attuned instrument that deep thinkers wish it to be. But the facts are, as we have seen, that the meaning of practically any word is susceptible to change of one sort or another, and some words have so many individual meanings that we cannot really hope to be absolutely certain of the sum of these meanings. But it is probably quite safe to predict that the members of the human race, *homines sapientes* more or less, will go on making absurd noises with their mouths at one another in what idealists among them will go on considering a deplorably sloppy and inadequate manner, and yet manage to understand one another well enough for their own purposes.

The idealists may, if they wish, settle upon Esperanto, Ido, Ro, Volapük, or any other of the excellent scientific languages which have been laboriously constructed. The game of constructing such languages is still going on. It is naively supposed by some that, should one of these ever become generally used, there would be an end to misunderstanding, followed by an age of universal brotherhood — an assumption being that we always agree with and love those whom we understand, though the fact is that we frequently disagree violently with those whom we understand very well. (Cain doubtless understood Abel well enough.)

But be that as it may, it should be obvious that, if such an artificial language were by some miracle ever to be accepted and generally used, it would be susceptible to precisely the kind of changes in meaning that have been our concern in this closing chapter as well as to such changes in structure as have been our concern throughout — the kind of changes undergone by those natural languages that have evolved over the eons. And most of the manifold phenomena of life — hatred, disease, famine, birth, death, sex, war, atoms, isms, and people, to name only a few — would remain as messy and hence as unsatisfactory to those unwilling to accept them as they have always been, no matter what words we use in referring to them.

[26] Reprinted in Susie I. Tucker's useful little collection, *English Examined: Two Centuries of Comment on the Mother Tongue* (Cambridge, Eng., 1961), p. 96.

Selected Bibliography

The books and periodicals listed below, the former ranging from the semipopular to the scholarly abstruse, should prove useful in one way or another to the student of linguistics. Not all are cited in the text. Specialized studies of technical problems have not been included. A few items deal with general linguistic theory.

AARSLEFF, HANS. *The Study of Language in England, 1780–1860*. Princeton, N.J., 1967.

ABBOTT, E. A. *A Shakespearian Grammar*. London, 1897.

ABERCROMBIE, DAVID. *Studies in Phonetics and Linguistics*. London, 1965.

ADAMS, RAMON F. *Western Words: A Dictionary of the Range, Cow Camp, and Trail*. Norman, Okla., 1944.

ALEXANDER, HENRY. *The Story of Our Language*. Rev. ed. New York, 1962.

ALLEN, HAROLD B. *Linguistics and English Linguistics*. New York, 1966. (Goldentree Bibliographies.)

———, ed. *Readings in Applied English Linguistics*. 2nd ed. New York, 1964.

The American Heritage Dictionary of the English Language. Boston, 1969.

American Speech: A Quarterly of Linguistic Usage. 1925–date.

ARMSTRONG, LILIAS E., and IDA C. WARD. *A Handbook of English Intonation*. 2nd ed. Cambridge, Eng., 1931.

ATWOOD, E. BAGBY. *The Regional Vocabulary of Texas*. Austin, Tex., 1962.

———. *A Survey of Verb Forms in the Eastern United States*. Ann Arbor, Mich., 1953.

BACH, EMMON. *An Introduction to Transformational Grammars*. New York, 1964.

BARBER, CHARLES. *Linguistic Change in Present-Day English*. University, Ala., 1966.

BARTLETT, JOHN RUSSELL. *Dictionary of Americanisms: A Glossary of Words and Phrases Usually Regarded as Peculiar to the United States*. 2nd ed. Boston, 1859.

BAUGH, ALBERT C. *A History of the English Language.* 2nd ed. New York, 1957.

BENDER, HAROLD H. *The Home of the Indo-Europeans.* Princeton, N.J., 1932.

BENSE, J. F. *A Dictionary of the Low-Dutch Element in the English Vocabulary,* pts. I–V. London, 1926–39.

BERREY, LESTER V., and MELVIN VAN DEN BARK. *The American Thesaurus of Slang.* 2nd ed. New York, 1953.

BLAIR, PETER HUNTER. *An Introduction to Anglo-Saxon England.* Cambridge, Eng., 1956.

BLOCH, BERNARD, and GEORGE L. TRAGER. *Outline of Linguistic Analysis.* Special Publications of the Linguistic Society of America. Baltimore, 1942.

BLOOMFIELD, LEONARD. *Language.* New York, 1933.

BLOOMFIELD, MORTON W., and LEONARD NEWMARK. *A Linguistic Introduction to the History of English.* New York, 1963.

BOLINGER, DWIGHT. *Aspects of Language.* New York, 1968.

BOONE, LALIA PHIPPS. *The Petroleum Dictionary.* Norman, Okla., 1952.

BRADLEY, HENRY. *The Making of English.* New York, 1904.

BRÉAL, MICHEL. *Semantics: Studies in the Science of Meaning,* trans. Mrs. Henry Cust. New York, 1964. (Originally pub. 1900.)

BRIGHT, WILLIAM, ed. *Sociolinguistics.* The Hague, 1966.

BROOK, G. L. *English Dialects.* London, 1963.

––––––. *A History of the English Language.* London, 1958.

––––––. *An Introduction to Old English.* Manchester, Eng., 1955.

BRUNNER, KARL. *Altenglische Grammatik (Nach der angelsächsischen von Eduard Sievers).* Tübingen, 1965.

––––––. *An Outline of Middle English Grammar,* trans. G. K. W. Johnston, from the 5th ed. of *Abriss der mittelenglischen Grammatik* (1962). Oxford, 1963.

BRYANT, MARGARET. *Current American Usage.* New York, 1962.

––––––. *Modern English and Its Heritage.* 2nd ed. New York, 1962.

BÜLBRING, KARL. *Altenglisches Elementarbuch. I. Teil: Lautlehre.* Heidelberg, 1902.

CAMPBELL, A. *Old English Grammar.* Oxford, 1959.

CARROLL, JOHN B. *The Study of Language: A Survey of Linguistics and Related Disciplines in America.* Cambridge, Mass., 1953.

CATFORD, J. C. *A Linguistic Theory of Translation.* London, 1965.

CHOMSKY, NOAM. *Aspects of the Theory of Syntax.* Cambridge, Mass., 1965.

––––––. *Language and Mind.* New York, 1968.

––––––. *Syntactic Structures.* The Hague, 1957.

––––––, and MORRIS HALLE. *The Sound Pattern of English.* New York, 1968.

CLARK, JOHN W. *Early English.* New York, 1964. (Originally publ. Oxford, 1957.)

COTTLE, BASIL. *The Penguin Dictionary of Surnames.* Baltimore, 1967.

CRAIGIE, W. A. *English Spelling: Its Rules and Reasons.* New York, 1927.

CRAIGIE, W. A., and JAMES ROOT HULBERT, eds. *A Dictionary of American English on Historical Principles.* 4 vols. Chicago, 1938–44.

CURME, GEORGE O. *A Grammar of the English Language,* Vols. II and III. Boston, 1931, 1935.

———. *Principles and Practice of English Grammar.* New York, 1947.

DARMESTETER, ARSÈNE. *La Vie des Mots.* Paris, 1887.

DAVIES, CONSTANCE. *English Pronunciation from the Fifteenth to the Eighteenth Century.* London, 1934.

Dialect Notes. Publication of the American Dialect Society. Vols. I–VI (1890–1939).

DINNEEN, FRANCIS P. *An Introduction to General Linguistics.* New York, 1967.

DIRINGER, DAVID. *Writing.* London, 1962.

DOBSON, E. J. *English Pronunciation, 1500–1700.* 2 vols. Oxford, 1957.

EKWALL, EILERT. *American and British Pronunciation.* Essays and Studies on American Language and Literature, II. Upsala, 1946.

———. *The Concise Oxford Dictionary of English Place-Names.* 4th ed. Oxford, 1960.

———. *Historische neuenglische Laut- Und Formenlehre.* 3rd ed., rev. Berlin, 1956.

EMERSON, OLIVER FARRAR. *A Middle English Reader.* New and rev. ed. New York, 1948.

ENTWISTLE, WILLIAM J. *Aspects of Language.* London, 1953.

EVANS, BERGEN, and CORNELIA EVANS. *A Dictionary of Contemporary American Usage.* New York, 1957.

FARMER, JOHN S., and WILLIAM ERNEST HENLEY. *Dictionary of Slang and Its Analogues.* 7 vols. New York, 1890–1904. (Repr. in 1 vol., New York, 1970.)

FIRTH, J. R. *Papers in Linguistics, 1934–1951.* London, 1957.

———. *The Tongues of Men and Speech.* London, 1964.

FISIAK, JACEK. *Morphemic Structure of Chaucer's English.* University, Ala., 1965.

FOSTER, BRIAN. *The Changing English Language.* New York, 1968.

FOWLER, H. W. *A Dictionary of Modern English Usage.* 2nd ed., rev. Sir Ernest Gowers. Oxford, 1965. (1st ed. 1926.)

———, and F. G. FOWLER. *The King's English.* 2nd ed. Oxford, 1906.

FRANCIS, W. NELSON. *The English Language: An Introduction.* New York, 1963.

———. *The Structure of American English.* With a chapter on American English dialects by Raven I. McDavid, Jr. New York, 1958.

FRANKLYN, JULIAN. *A Dictionary of Rhyming Slang.* London, 1960.

FRANZ, W. *Shakespeare-Grammatik.* 2nd ed. Heidelberg, 1909.

FRIEND, JOSEPH H. *The Development of American Lexicography, 1798–1864.* The Hague, 1967.

———. *An Introduction to English Linguistics.* Cleveland, Ohio, 1967.

FRIES, CHARLES CARPENTER. *American English Grammar.* New York, 1940.

————. *The Structure of English.* New York, 1952.

Funk and Wagnalls New Standard Dictionary of the English Language. New York, 1925.

Funk and Wagnalls Standard College Dictionary. New York, 1963.

GALINSKY, HANS. *Die Sprache des Amerikaners: Eine Einführung in die Hauptunterschiede zwischen amerikanischem und britischem English der Gegenwart.* 2 vols. Heidelberg, 1951, 1952.

GELB, I. J. *A Study of Writing: The Foundations of Grammatology.* 2nd ed. Chicago, 1969.

GIMSON, A. C. *An Introduction to the Pronunciation of English.* London, 1962.

GLEASON, H. A., JR. *An Introduction to Descriptive Linguistics.* Rev. ed. New York, 1961.

————. *Linguistics and English Grammar.* New York, 1965.

GOLDIN, HYMAN E., FRANK O'LEARY, and MORRIS LIPSIUS, eds. *Dictionary of American Underworld Lingo.* New York, 1950.

GOWERS, SIR ERNEST. *Plain Words: Their ABC.* New York, 1954.

GRAFF, WILLEM L. *Language and Languages.* New York, 1932.

GRAY, LOUIS H. *Foundations of Language.* New York, 1939.

GREENOUGH, JAMES BRADSTREET, and GEORGE LYMAN KITTREDGE. *Words and Their Ways in English Speech.* New York, 1901.

GREET, W. CABELL. *World Words: Recommended Pronunciations.* New York, 1944.

HALL, JOHN R. CLARK. *A Concise Anglo-Saxon Dictionary.* 4th ed., with a supplement by Herbert D. Meritt. Cambridge, Eng., 1960.

HALL, ROBERT A., JR. *Hands Off Pidgin English!* Sydney, Australia, 1955.

————. *Introductory Linguistics.* Philadelphia, 1964.

————. *Linguistics and Your Language.* New York, 1960. (Originally pub. as *Leave Your Language Alone!* [Ithaca, N.Y., 1950].)

————. *Sound and Spelling in English.* Philadelphia, 1961.

HALLIDAY, M. A. K., ANGUS MCINTOSH, and P. D. STREVENS. *The Linguistic Sciences and Language Teaching.* Bloomington, Ind., 1964.

HAMP, ERIC P. *A Glossary of American Technical Linguistic Usage, 1925–1950.* Utrecht/Antwerp, 1963. (Originally pub. 1957.)

HARRIS, ZELLIG S. *Structural Linguistics.* Chicago, 1960. (Originally pub. as *Methods in Structural Linguistics* [1951].)

HILL, ARCHIBALD A. *Introduction to Linguistic Structures.* New York, 1958.

————, ed. *Linguistics Today.* New York and London, 1969. (Also issued by Voice of America Forum Lectures, 1969, under the title *Linguistics.*)

HOCKETT, CHARLES F. *A Course in Modern Linguistics.* New York, 1958.

————. *The State of the Art.* The Hague, 1968.

HOIJER, HARRY, ed. *Language History.* New York, 1965. (A reprint of Chapters 17–27 of Leonard Bloomfield's *Language* [1933].)

HOLTHAUSEN, FERDINAND. *Altenglisches etymologisches Wörterbuch.* 2nd ed. Heidelberg, 1963.

HORN, WILHELM. *Laut und Leben. Englische Lautgeschichte der neuren*

Zeit (1400–1950). Rev. and ed. Martin Lehnert. 2 vols. Berlin, 1954.

HORWILL, H. W. *An Anglo-American Interpreter: A Vocabulary and Phrase Book*. Oxford, 1939.

———. *A Dictionary of Modern American Usage*. Oxford, 1935.

HUBBELL, ALLAN F. *The Pronunciation of English in New York City: Consonants and Vowels*. New York, 1950.

HUGHES, JOHN P. *The Science of Language*. New York, 1962.

HULBERT, JAMES ROOT. *Dictionaries: British and American*. London, 1955.

HULME, HILDA M. *Explorations in Shakespeare's Language: Some Problems of Lexical Meaning in the Dramatic Text*. London, 1962.

JACOBS, RODERICK A., and PETER S. ROSENBAUM. *English Transformational Grammar*. Waltham, Mass., 1968.

JAKOBSON, ROMAN, and MORRIS HALLE. *Fundamentals of Language*. The Hague, 1956.

JESPERSEN, OTTO. *Efficiency in Linguistic Change*. Copenhagen, 1941.

———. *Essentials of English Grammar*. New York, 1933.

———. *Growth and Structure of the English Language*. 9th ed. Oxford, 1954. (Originally pub. 1905.)

———. *Language: Its Nature, Development and Origin*. New York, 1922.

———. *A Modern English Grammar on Historical Principles*. 7 vols. Copenhagen, 1909–49.

———. *Negation in English and Other Languages*. Copenhagen, 1917.

———. *The Philosophy of Grammar*. New York, 1965. (Originally pub. 1924.)

———. *Progress in Language, with Special Reference to English*. 2nd ed. London, 1909.

———. *Selected Writings*. London, 1962.

JONES, DANIEL. *An English Pronouncing Dictionary*. 13th ed., rev. A. C. Gimson. London, 1967.

———. *The Pronunciation of English*. 4th ed. Cambridge, Eng., 1958.

JOOS, MARTIN. *The English Verb: Form and Meanings*. Madison, Wis., 1968.

———. *The Five Clocks*. New York, 1967.

JORDAN, RICHARD. *Handbuch der mittelenglischen Grammatik,* pt. I. 2nd ed. Heidelberg, 1934.

Journal of English Linguistics. 1967–date.

KATZ, JERROLD J., and PAUL A. POSTAL. *An Integrated Theory of Linguistic Descriptions*. Cambridge, Mass., 1964.

KENNEDY, ARTHUR G. *A Bibliography of Writings on the English Language from the Beginning of Printing to the End of 1922*. Cambridge, Mass., and New Haven, Conn., 1927.

———. *Current English*. Boston, 1935.

———. *English Usage: A Study in Policy and Procedure*. New York, 1942.

KENT, ROLAND G. *Language and Philology*. New York, 1932.

———. *The Sounds of Latin: A Descriptive and Historical Phonology*. Special Publications of the Linguistic Society of America. 3rd ed. Baltimore, 1945.

KENYON, JOHN S. *American Pronunciation*. 10th ed. Ann Arbor, Mich., 1961.

————, and THOMAS ALBERT KNOTT. *A Pronouncing Dictionary of American English.* Springfield, Mass., 1951.

KING, ROBERT D. *Historical Linguistics and Generative Grammar.* Englewood Cliffs, N.J., 1969.

KLUGE, FRIEDRICH. *Etymologisches Wörterbuch der deutschen Sprache.* 10th ed. Berlin and Leipzig, 1924.

————, and F. LUTZ. *English Etymology.* Strassburg, 1898.

KÖKERITZ, HELGE. *A Guide to Chaucer's Pronunciation.* New York, 1962.

————. *Shakespeare's Pronunciation.* New Haven, Conn., 1953.

KOUTSOUDAS, A. *Writing Transformational Grammars: An Introduction.* New York, 1966.

KOZIOL, HERBERT, and FELIX HÜTTENBRENNER. *Grammatik der englischen Sprache.* Heidelberg, 1956.

KRAPP, GEORGE PHILIP. *The English Language in America.* 2 vols. New York, 1925.

————. *Modern English: Its Growth and Present Use,* rev. Albert H. Marckwardt. New York, 1969. (Originally pub. 1909.)

————. *The Pronunciation of Standard English in America.* New York, 1919.

KRUISINGA, E. *A Handbook of Present-Day English.* Pt. I, 4th ed. Utrecht, 1925; pt. II, 5th ed. Groningen, 1931, 1932.

————. *An Introduction to the Study of English Sounds.* 12th ed., rev. C. Hedeman and J. J. Westerbeek. Groningen, 1960. (Originally pub. 1914.)

KURATH, HANS. *A Phonology and Prosody of Modern English.* Ann Arbor, Mich., 1964.

————. *A Word Geography of the Eastern United States.* Ann Arbor, Mich., 1949.

————, et al. *Handbook of the Linguistic Geography of New England.* Providence, R.I., 1939.

————, et al. *Linguistic Atlas of New England.* 3 vols. in 6. Providence, R.I., 1939–43.

————, and RAVEN I. McDAVID, JR. *The Pronunciation of English in the Atlantic States.* University of Michigan Studies in American English, No. 3. Ann Arbor, Mich., 1961.

————, and SHERMAN M. KUHN, eds. *Middle English Dictionary.* Ann Arbor, Mich., 1954– (in progress).

LABOV, WILLIAM. *The Social Stratification of English in New York City.* Washington, D.C., 1966.

LAIRD, CHARLTON. *The Miracle of Language.* New York, 1957.

LAMB, SYDNEY M. *Outline of Stratificational Grammar.* Washington, D.C., 1966.

LANDAR, HERBERT. *Language and Culture.* Oxford, 1966.

LANGACKER, RONALD W. *Language and Its Structure: Some Fundamental Linguistic Concepts.* New York, 1967.

LANGENDOEN, D. TERENCE. *Essentials of English Grammar.* New York, 1970.

Language: Journal of the Linguistic Society of America. 1925–date.

LARSEN, THORLEIF, and FRANCIS C. WALKER. *Pronunciation: A Practical Guide to American Standards.* London, 1930.

LASS, ROGER, ed. *Approaches to English Historical Linguistics.* New York, 1969.

LEE, DONALD W. *Functional Change in Early English.* Menasha, Wis., 1948.

LEHMANN, WINFRED P. *Historical Linguistics: An Introduction.* New York, 1962.

LEHNERT, MARTIN. *Altenglisches Elementarbuch.* 4th ed., rev. Berlin, 1959.

LEONARD, STERLING A. *Current English Usage.* NCTE Monograph, No. 1. Chicago, 1932.

_____. *The Doctrine of Correctness in English Usage, 1700–1800.* University of Wisconsin Studies in Language and Literature, No. 25. Madison, Wis., 1929.

Linguistics. 1945–date.

LLOYD, RICHARD J. *Northern English.* 2nd ed. Leipzig and Berlin, 1908.

LONG, RALPH B. *The Sentence and Its Parts.* Chicago, 1961.

LUICK, KARL. *Historische Grammatik der englischen Sprache.* Leipzig, 1914–40.

LYONS, JOHN. *Introduction to Theoretical Linguistics.* Cambridge, Eng., 1968.

MARCKWARDT, ALBERT H. *American English.* New York, 1958.

_____. *Introduction to the English Language.* New York, 1942.

_____. *Linguistics and the Teaching of English.* Bloomington, Ind., 1966.

_____, and FRED C. WALCOTT. *Facts About Current English Usage.* New York, 1938.

_____, and RANDOLPH QUIRK. *A Common Language: British and American English.* London, 1964. (Radio series broadcast by BBC and Voice of America.)

MARTINET, ANDRÉ. *Elements of General Linguistics,* trans. Elizabeth Palmer. London, 1964.

MATHEWS, M. M. *The Beginnings of American English.* Chicago, 1931.

_____. *Some Sources of Southernisms.* University, Ala., 1948.

_____, ed. *A Dictionary of Americanisms on Historical Principles.* 2 vols. Chicago, 1951.

MATTHEWS, C. M. *English Surnames.* New York, 1967.

MAURER, DAVID W. *The Argot of the Racetrack.* Publication of the American Dialect Society, No. 16. Greensboro, N.C., 1951.

_____. *Whiz Mob: A Correlation of the Technical Argot of Pickpockets with Their Behavior Pattern.* Publication of the American Dialect Society, No. 24. Gainesville, Fla., 1955.

MAYHEW, A. L., and WALTER W. SKEAT. *A Concise Dictionary of Middle English from A.D. 1150 to 1580.* Oxford, 1888.

MCINTOSH, ANGUS. *An Introduction to a Survey of Scottish Dialects.* Edinburgh, 1952.

MCKERROW, RONALD B. *An Introduction to Bibliography.* Oxford, 1928.

MCKNIGHT, GEORGE H. *English Words and Their Background.* New York, 1923.

_____. *Modern English in the Making.* New York, 1928.

McLaughlin, John C. *Aspects of the History of English.* New York, 1970.

Mencken, H. L. *The American Language.* 4th ed. New York, 1936. (Originally pub. 1919.)

_____. *The American Language: The Fourth Edition and the Two Supplements,* abridged and ed. Raven I. McDavid, Jr. New York, 1963.

_____. *The American Language, Supplement I.* New York, 1945.

_____. *The American Language, Supplement II.* New York, 1948.

Mitchell, Bruce. *A Guide to Old English.* Oxford, 1965.

Moore, Samuel. *Historical Outlines of English Sounds and Inflections,* rev. Albert H. Marckwardt. Ann Arbor, Mich., 1951.

_____, and Thomas Albert Knott. *The Elements of Old English.* 10th ed., rev. James Root Hulbert. Ann Arbor, Mich., 1955.

Moorhouse, A. C. *Writing and the Alphabet.* London, 1946.

Mossé, Fernand. *Esquisse d'une Histoire de la Langue Anglaise.* Lyon, 1947.

_____. *A Handbook of Middle English,* trans. James A. Walker. Baltimore, 1952.

_____. *Manuel de L'Anglais du Moyen Age des Origines au XIVe Siècle.* Pt. I, *Vieil-Anglais.* 2 vols. Paris, 1950.

Mustanoja, Tauno F. *A Middle English Syntax, Part I: Parts of Speech.* Helsinki, 1960.

Myers, L. M. *The Roots of Modern English.* Boston, 1966.

Names: Journal of the American Name Society. 1953–date.

Nicholson, Margaret. *A Dictionary of American-English Usage.* New York, 1957.

Nist, John. *A Structural History of English.* New York, 1966.

Onions, C. T. *An Advanced English Syntax.* London, 1965. (Originally pub. 1904.)

_____, ed. *The Oxford Dictionary of English Etymology.* Oxford, 1966.

_____. *A Shakespeare Glossary.* 2nd ed. Oxford, 1919.

Orton, Harold, and Wilfred J. Halliday. *Survey of English Dialects,* Vols. I and II. Leeds, 1962–63.

The Oxford English Dictionary. 13 vols. Oxford, 1933. (Originally pub. 1884–1928 as *A New English Dictionary on Historical Principles,* reissued with Supplement in 1933.)

Palmer, Harold E. *English Intonation.* Cambridge, Eng., 1922.

_____. *The Principles of Language-Study.* London, 1964. (Originally pub. 1921.)

Partridge, Eric. *A Dictionary of Slang and Unconventional English.* 3rd ed. New York, 1950.

_____. *Dictionary of the Underworld.* London, 1949.

_____. *Name into Word.* New York, 1950.

_____. *Shakespeare's Bawdy: A Literary and Psychological Essay and a Comprehensive Glossary.* New York, 1948.

_____. *Slang Today and Yesterday.* London, 1933.

PARTRIDGE, ERIC, and JOHN W. CLARK. *British and American English Since 1900.* New York, 1951.

PEDERSEN, HOLGER. *The Discovery of Language,* trans. John Webster Spargo. Bloomington, Ind., 1962. (Originally pub. as *Linguistic Science in the Nineteenth Century* [Cambridge, Mass., 1931].)

PEDERSON, LEE A. *The Pronunciation of English in Metropolitan Chicago.* Publication of the American Dialect Society, No. 44. University, Ala., 1965.

PETERS, ROBERT A. *A Linguistic History of English.* Boston, 1968.

PIKE, KENNETH L. *The Intonation of American English.* Ann Arbor, Mich., 1945.

POGATSCHER, ALOIS. *Zur Lautlehre der griechischen, lateinischen, und romanischen Lehnworte im Altenglischen.* Strassburg, 1888.

POKORNY, JULIUS. *Indogermanisches Etymologisches Wörterbuch.* Bern, 1959.

POOLEY, ROBERT C. *Teaching English Grammar.* New York, 1957.

――――. *Teaching English Usage.* New York, 1946.

POTTER, SIMEON. *Language in the Modern World.* Baltimore, 1960.

――――. *Modern Linguistics.* London, 1957.

――――. *Our Language.* London, 1950.

POUTSMA, H. *A Grammar of Late Modern English.* 4 vols. Groningen, 1904–26. (Pt. I, 2nd ed. in 2 sections, 1928, 1929.)

PRICE, H. T. *Foreign Influences on Middle English.* Ann Arbor, Mich., 1947.

PRIEBSCH, R., and W. E. COLLINSON. *The German Language.* 4th ed., rev. London, 1958.

PROKOSCH, E. *A Comparative Germanic Grammar.* Special Publications of the Linguistic Society of America. Philadelphia, 1939.

Publication of the American Dialect Society. 1944–date.

PYLES, THOMAS. *The English Language: A Brief History.* New York, 1968.

――――. *Words and Ways of American English.* New York, 1952; London, 1954.

――――, and JOHN ALGEO. *English: An Introduction to Language.* New York, 1970.

QUIRK, RANDOLPH. *Essays on the English Language: Medieval and Modern.* Bloomington, Ind. and London, 1968.

――――. *The Uses of English.* With supplements by A. C. Gimson and Jeremy Warburg. New York, 1962.

――――, and JAN SVARTVIK. *Investigating Linguistic Acceptability.* The Hague, 1966.

――――, and C. L. WRENN. *An Old English Grammar.* London, 1955.

The Random House Dictionary of the English Language. New York, 1966.

RAO, G. SUBBA. *Indian Words in English.* Oxford, 1954.

REANEY, P. H. *A Dictionary of British Surnames.* London, 1958.

――――. *The Origin of English Place-Names.* London, 1960.

REED, CARROLL E. *Dialects of American English.* Cleveland, Ohio, 1967.

RIPMAN, WALTER. *The Sounds of Spoken English.* Rev. ed. New York, 1930.

ROBERTS, A. HOOD. *A Statistical Linguistic Analysis of American English.* The Hague, 1965.

ROBERTS, PAUL. *English Syntax.* Alternate ed. New York, 1964.

———. *Understanding English.* New York, 1958.

———. *Understanding Grammar.* New York, 1954.

ROBERTSON, STUART. *The Development of Modern English.* 2nd ed., rev. Frederic G. Cassidy. New York, 1954.

ROBINS, R. H. *Ancient and Mediaeval Grammatical Theory in Europe.* London, 1951.

———. *A Short History of Linguistics.* London, 1967.

ROSS, ALAN S. C. *Etymology.* London, 1958.

SALUS, PETER H., ed. *On Language: Plato to Von Humboldt.* New York, 1969.

SAPIR, EDWARD. *Language: An Introduction to the Study of Speech.* New York, 1921.

SAUSSURE, FERDINAND DE. *Course in General Linguistics,* ed. Charles Bally and Albert Sechehaye in collaboration with Albert Reidlinger, trans. Wade Baskin. New York, 1959.

SCHLAUCH, MARGARET. *The English Language in Modern Times (Since 1400).* Warsaw, 1959.

———. *The Gift of Language.* New York, 1955. (Originally pub. as *The Gift of Tongues* [New York, 1942].)

SCHMIDT, A. *Shakespeare-Lexicon.* 4th ed. 2 vols. Berlin and Leipzig, 1923.

SCOTT, CHARLES T., and JON L. ERICKSON, eds. *Readings for the History of the English Language.* Boston, 1968.

SERJEANTSON, MARY S. *A History of Foreign Words in English.* London, 1935.

SHEARD, J. A. *The Words We Use.* New York, 1954.

SHUY, ROGER W. *Discovering American Dialects.* Champaign, Ill., 1967.

———, ed. *Social Dialects and Language Learning.* Champaign, Ill., 1965.

SKEAT, WALTER W. *English Dialects from the Eighth Century to the Present Day.* Cambridge, Eng., 1911.

———. *An Etymological Dictionary of the English Language.* 4th ed. Oxford, 1910.

———. *Notes on English Etymology.* Oxford, 1901.

SLEDD, JAMES. *A Short Introduction to English Grammar.* Chicago, 1959.

———, and GWIN J. KOLB. *Dr. Johnson's Dictionary: Essays in the Biography of a Book.* Chicago, 1955.

———, and WILMA R. EBBITT, eds. *Dictionaries and That Dictionary: A Casebook on the Aims of Lexicographers and the Targets of Reviewers.* Chicago, 1962.

SMITH, HENRY LEE, JR. *Linguistic Science and the Teaching of English.* Cambridge, Mass., 1956.

STARNES, DEWITT T., and GERTRUDE E. NOYES. *The English Dictionary from Cawdrey to Johnson, 1604–1755.* Chapel Hill, N.C., 1946.

STERN, GUSTAV. *Meaning and Change of Meaning, with Special Reference to the English Language*. Bloomington, Ind., 1963. (Originally pub. 1931 [Göteborg].)

STEVICK, ROBERT D. *English and Its History: The Evolution of a Language*. Boston, 1968.

STRANG, BARBARA M. H. *Modern English Structure*. New York, 1962.

STRATMANN, FRANCIS HENRY. *A Middle-English Dictionary*, rev. Henry Bradley. Oxford, 1891.

STURTEVANT, E. H. *An Introduction to Linguistic Science*. New Haven, Conn., 1947.

———. *The Pronunciation of Greek and Latin*. 2nd ed. Special Publications of the Linguistic Society of America. Philadelphia, 1940.

SWEET, HENRY. *A New English Grammar, Logical and Historical*. 2 vols. Oxford, 1900, 1903.

———. *The Practical Study of Languages*. London, 1964. (Originally pub. 1899.)

TEN BRINK, BERNHARD. *The Language and Metre of Chaucer*. 2nd ed., rev. Friedrich Kluge, trans. M. Bentinck Smith. London, 1901.

THIEME, PAUL. *Die Heimat der indogermanischen Gemeinsprache*. Wiesbaden, 1954.

THOMAS, CHARLES KENNETH. *An Introduction to the Phonetics of American English*. 2nd ed. New York, 1958.

THOMAS, OWEN. *Transformational Grammar and the Teaching of English*. New York, 1965.

TOLLER, T. N. *An Anglo-Saxon Dictionary Based on the Manuscript Collections of the Late Joseph Bosworth*. Oxford, 1882–98. Supplements, 1908–20.

TRAGER, GEORGE L., and HENRY LEE SMITH, JR. *An Outline of English Structure*. Studies in Linguistics: Occasional Papers, 3. Norman, Okla., 1951.

TUCKER, SUSIE I., ed. *English Examined: Two Centuries of Comment on the Mother-Tongue*. Cambridge, Eng., 1961.

———. *Protean Shape: A Study in Eighteenth-Century Vocabulary and Usage*. London, 1967.

TURNER, LORENZO DOW. *Africanisms in the Gullah Dialect*. Chicago, 1949.

ULLMAN, B. L. *Ancient Writing and Its Influence*. New York, 1932.

"Vigilans." *Chamber of Horrors*. Introduction by Eric Partridge. London, 1952.

VISSER, F. TH. *An Historical Syntax of the English Language*. 3 vols. Leiden, 1963, 1966, 1969.

WALKER, JOHN. *A Critical Pronouncing Dictionary, and Expositor of the English Language*. . . . London, 1791.

WARDALE, E. E. *An Introduction to Middle English*. London, 1937.

———. *An Old English Grammar*. London, 1964. (Originally pub. 1922.)

WATERMAN, JOHN T. *Perspectives in Linguistics*. Chicago, 1963.

Webster's New World Dictionary of the American Language. Cleveland, Ohio, 1955.

Webster's Third New International Dictionary. Springfield, Mass., 1961.

WENTWORTH, HAROLD, ed. *American Dialect Dictionary.* New York, 1944.

——, and STUART BERG FLEXNER, eds. *Dictionary of American Slang.* New York, 1960.

WHATMOUGH, JOSHUA. *Language: A Modern Synthesis.* New York, 1956.

WHITEHALL, HAROLD. *Structural Essentials of English.* New York, 1956.

WIJK, AXEL. *Rules of Pronunciation for the English Language.* London, 1966.

WILLIAMS, EDNA REES. *The Conflict of Homonyms in English.* New Haven, Conn., 1944.

WILLIAMSON, JUANITA VIRGINIA. *A Phonological and Morphological Study of the Speech of the Negro of Memphis, Tennessee.* Publication of the American Dialect Society, No. 50. University, Ala., 1968.

WITHYCOMBE, E. G. *The Oxford Dictionary of English Christian Names.* New York and London, 1947.

Word: Journal of the Linguistic Circle of New York. 1945–date.

WRENN, C. L. *The English Language.* London, 1952.

——. *Word and Symbol: Studies in English Language.* London, 1967.

WRIGHT, JOSEPH. *The English Dialect Grammar.* Oxford, 1905.

WRIGHT, JOSEPH, and ELIZABETH MARY WRIGHT. *An Elementary Historical New English Grammar.* London, 1924.

——. *An Elementary Middle English Grammar.* 2nd ed. London, 1928.

——. *Old English Grammar.* 3rd ed. London, 1925.

WYLD, HENRY CECIL. *A History of Modern Colloquial English.* 3rd ed. New York, 1937.

——. *A Short History of English.* 3rd ed. New York, 1927.

——, ed. *The Universal Dictionary of the English Language.* London. 1932.

ZANDVOORT, R. W. *A Handbook of English Grammar.* 5th ed. London, 1957.

ZACHRISSON, R. E. *The English Pronunciation at Shakespeare's Time as Taught by William Bullokar.* Upsala, 1927.

——. *Pronunciation of English Vowels, 1400–1700.* Göteborg, 1913.

Index of Modern English
Words, Affixes, and Phrases

a, 22
abactinal, 76
abased, 185 n.
abbot, 325
abdomen, 319
abed, 223
abhominable, 63
abide, 209
-able, 192
aboard, 223, 280
abominably, 363
about, 48, 223
abrus, 76
absent, 311 n.
academic freedom, 333
acaulose, 76
accretion, 43
acid, 38
ack emma, 299
acorn, 303
acre, 267
acronym, 320
actor, 45
ad, 295
adagio, 38, 331
add, 37
adder, 3, 159
address, 311
administer, 324
administration, 324
admire, 346
admit, 319
adobe, 330
advert, 295
advertisement, 295
advice, 340
Aeneas, 43
aerial, 43
aeronaut, 44
Aeschylus, 45

Aesop, 43
aesthetic, 44, 268
affix, 311 n.
afford, 281
afield, 223
after-, 281
aftereffect, 281
again, 44
age, 61
aged, 170 n.
aghast, 37
agnostic, 320
ah, 47
a-hunting, 280
aide-de-camp, 328
ain't, 28, 219, 258
air, 44, 91
aisle, 48
alarm, 45, 190
alarum, 45, 190
albino, 331
alchemy, 335
alcohol, 335
alcoholic, 6
ale, 313
alembic, 335
aleph, 51, 52
alert, 48
alert patrol, 48
Alfred, 293
algorism, 335
alibi, 244
alive, 132, 280
alkali, 335
all, 46
allegro, 331
allergy, 244, 320
alligator, 330
ally, 311
almanac, 335

almanack, 267
alms, 47 n., 297 n.
alone, 45
alpenstock, 333
alpha, 51–52
alto, 331
Altrincham, 39
aluminium, 262
aluminum, 262
amateur, 328
amber, 335
amen, 335
America, 35
Americana, 282
Americanize, 285
amoeba, 57
ammo, 295 n.
ampere, 305
-ana, 282
anæmia, 57
anaemic, 268
anchovy, 330
and, 262, 343
andante, 331
anemia, 58, 320
anesthesia, 320
angle, 244
angry, 248
answer, 38, 281
an't, 219
ante-, 283
antelope, 196
ante up, 308
anthem, 65
Anthony, 65
anthropoid, 320
anti-, 281, 282
anti-Federalist, 282
antipathy, 282
antique, 192

antislavery, 282
antitobacco, 282
any, 29
apartheid, 334
ape, 44
aphrodisiac, 307
apostle, 317
apothecary, 65
appendix, 297
apple, 37
appraise, 350
apricot, 335
apron, 159
aquacade, 282 n.
are, 47, 144
area, 43, 319
aren't, 36
aren't I, 219
'arf, 36
aria, 331
aristocracy, 320
Arkansas, 47
armada, 330
armadillo, 330
armour, 266
army, 325, 340
arras, 307
arrow, 45 n.
arse, 190
art, 47
arthritis, 45
Arthur, 65
artichoke, 332
as, 292
aside, 280
ask, 41, 42, 219, 232, 259, 262
asleep, 223
asparagus, 304
ass, 190
assassin, 335
as tall as I, 205
astrakhan, 339
at, 44
ate, 44, 140, 214, 260, 261
athlete, 45
atlas, 307
attorney, 324
auger, 159
aught, 47
aunt, 41, 47
author, 65, 190, 267
authority, 45
authorize, 285
auto, 47, 295
auto-, 282
autocracy, 320
autocratic, 282
autointoxication, 282
automat, 282
automata, 320 n.

automobile, 247, 282
Automobile Association, 247
avatar, 336
avocado, 330
avoir, 54
avoirdupois, 45
awe, 22, 46
awfully, 362
axle, 92
ay, 22, 48
aye, 48
azimuth, 335
azure, 38, 187, 336

baa, 44
Baal, 44
babbit, 307
babel, 307
babu, 337
baby, 280 n.
baby carriage, 249
baby mine, 172
baby-sit, 289, 290, 298
baby-sitter, 281, 298
baccarat, 47
bacchanal, 307
back, 42, 310
backwoods, 234, 241
bacon, 35, 37
bad, 42
bag, 42
baggage, 247
bait, 41, 42
baksheesh, 336
balcony, 332
bald-headed, 294
baleful, 281
ballet, 44, 328
balloon, 332
ballyhoo, 243
balm, 42, 47 n.
balsam, 317
bamboo, 337
banana, 338
bandanna, 337
bandit, 332
bang, 276
bangle, 337
banjo, 338
banshee, 322
banzai, 337
baptize, 268
barbarous, 320
barbecue, 330
bare, 3, 39, 44
bark, 212
barn, 347
barometer, 267 n.
barracuda, 330
barren, 39
baseball, 293

basin, 44
basket, 263
bass, 190, 263
bastard, 263
bat, 42
bate, 41
bath, 41
bathe, 37, 160
bathroom, 359
baton, 328
bayonet, 308
bayou, 340 n.
bazaar, 336
bazooka, 309
bdellium, 37
be, 10, 206
be-, 280
bear, 3, 89, 93, 213
beard, 45
beat, 29, 42
Beatty, 186
beau, 46, 328
Beauchamp, 43
Beaulieu, 44
beautician, 283
beautifullest, 198
beauty, 46, 189
beautyrama, 288
because, 222
bedlam, 308
beech, 58 n.
beef, 325
beekeeper, 124
beeline, 242
been, 43, 260, 261
beer, 313
beer garden, 333
beet, 42
begonia, 306
behalf, 280
behavior, 266
behavior pattern, 352
behemoth, 335
beholden, 216
belfry, 303
believe, 280
belittle, 242
belly, 359
below the belt, 308
beneath, 280
Benedick, 307
benny, 295
bet, 44
beta, 51
beth, 51
better, 311
better-best, 174
Betty, 44 n.
between, 280
between you and I, 204
Bewley, 293
beyond, 280
bheesty, 37

bias, 45
bib, 37
Bible Belt, 309
bid, 214
bidden, 214
Biergarten, 333
bifurcate, 45
billingsgate, 307
billion, 250
billy, 307
billycock, 307
billy-o, 295 n.
bind, 212
bind-bound, 103, 140
bingo, 295 n.
bird, 44
bird's-eye, 293 n.
Birmingham, 292
biscuit, 44
bit, 12, 29, 42
bite, 71, 208
bited, 12
biter, 71
bitter, 71
bizarre, 39
blackball, 290
blackboard, 289
blackguard, 37
blancmange, 45
blarney, 307 n., 322
blessed, 170 n.
blew, 216
blind, 249
blinko, 295 n.
Blitz(krieg),333
blizzard, 242
blonde, 328 n.
blood, 44, 184
bloodalyser, 298 n.
blood diseases, 360
bloodmobile, 282
bloodthirsty, 293
bloody, 280
bloomer, 305
blotto, 295 n.
blow, 216
blowgun, 293
bluff, 239
blurb, 244
blush, 41 n.
B.M., 299
B.O., 299
boarder, 46 n.
boat, 42, 71
boatswain, 292
bobby, 306
bobwhite, 276
bock, 308, 333
body, 37, 44
Boer, 46
bog, 47, 322
bohea, 337
Bohun, 46

boil, 187, 325
bolero, 330
bolshevik, 339
bomb, 42
bonanza, 330
bone, 79
bonnet, 250
bonus, 45
booboisie, 309
book, 58 n., 184
bookateria, 287
bookkeeper, 124
bookmobile, 282
boomerang, 338
boor, 334, 349
booty, 37, 187
booze, 334
border, 46 n.
borzoi, 339
borough, 45
boss, 334, 361
Boston, 293
bottoms up, 332
bougainvillea, 306
bough, 12, 48, 189
bought, 189
boulevard, 46, 328
bouillon, 39, 46, 80, 328
Boulogne, 48
bourbon, 307
bourse, 45
bow, 12, 211
Bowdlerize, 285, 306
bowery, 334
bowie knife, 305
bowlegged, 281
bowlerama, 288
bowl over, 308
bow-wow, 9, 276
boy, 36, 48
boycott, 305
Boy Scout, 289, 291 n.
bra, 294
braces, 250
braggadocio, 310
braid, 212
brake, 334
brandy, 295
brandywine, 334
brassière, 294
brast, 213
braunschweiger, 333
bravo, 332
breadbasket, 359
break, 70, 117, 185, 213, 310
break down, 311
breakdown, 244, 293
breakfast, 75, 292
breast, 165
breathalyzer, 298 n.
brethren, 131 n., 195
brew, 211

bride, 37
bridegroom, 303
Bridge-A-Rama, 288
brigade, 325 n.
brigadier, 325 n.
bright, 189
bring, 103
Britannia, 58
broad, 46, 110
broadcast, 289, 291
broasted, 299
broccoli, 332
brochure, 328
brogue, 322
broil, 325
broke-brake, 213
bronc, 295 n.
bronco, 330
brooch, 46, 161 n.
broom, 184
brother, 191
brougham, 46, 305
brummagem, 308
brunch, 299
brunette, 328
brung, 212
bub, 43 n.
buckaroo, 330
bucket, 44
buckra, 6, 338
bud, 43 n.
budgerigar, 338
budget, 39
budgie, 338
buffalo, 196
Buhl, 46
build, 43
build up, 243
bulb, 43 n.
bull, 186
bullion, 39
bum, 333
bump, 276
buncombe, 307, 309
bungalow, 337
bunk, 309
bunkum, 242
buoy, 48, 334
burdoc, 268
bureau, 45, 46, 328
bureaucracy, 47
burger, 283, 294, 296
-burger, 283
burglar, 296
burke, 305
Burleigh, 44
burn, 212
burp, 276
burred, 43 n.
bursar, 45
burst, 190, 213
bus, 249, 294
bush, 41 n., 186

businessman, 291
bust, 190
busted, 213
busy, 43, 343
but, 44, 165
butcher, 39
but me no buts, 311
butt, 37
butter, 45
buy, 48, 103
buy-bought, 139
bylaw, 323 n.

cab, 294
cabbala, 335
caballo, 80
cache, 38
cachet, 44
cadenza, 331
Caedmon, 44
Caesar, 57, 306
café, 44, 328
cafeteria, 242, 287
cafetorium, 299
cairn, 45, 322
Caius, 43, 76 n.
calaboose, 330
Calais, 44
calculation, 346
caliber, 335
calibre, 267
calico, 308
call, 29
caller, 47
calliope, 307
calm, 29, 34, 47, 262
cambric, 334
camellia, 43, 306
cameo, 332
camouflage, 328
camphor, 335
camporees, 299
can (n.), 42, 240 n.
can (v.), 42, 119, 218, 255
candy, 335
cannibal, 330
cañon, 39
cant, 263
can't, 262, 263
cantaloupe, 46
cantata, 331
canter, 308
canyon, 39, 234, 330
capercailzie, 39
capital, 327
captain, 325
car, 37, 247, 296
carat, 335
caravan, 251, 336
caraway, 335
carburetor, 262

carburettor, 262
cardigan, 306
Cardinal-wise, 284
career diplomat, 240
Carew, 44
cargo, 330
carnival, 332
Carolina, 263
carouse, 332
carriage, 326, 326 n.
carryall, 303
carryings-on, 293
cartoon, 332
carve, 212
case, 71
cashmere, 38, 308
casino, 332
cask, 330
cassoc, 268
castanet, 330
castle, 324
Castlereagh, 44
cat, 29, 57
catalpa, 234, 340 n.
catarrh, 39
catawba, 234
catch, 44, 66, 343
catchup, 337
cate, 29
Catherine, 65
cattle, 326
caucus, 242
cause, 46
'cause, 296
cawf, 12
cede, 43
ceiling, 43
cello, 39, 331 n.
cemetery, 264
censure, 190, 349
centennial, 240
center, 320
centre, 267
cereal, 38
ceremony, 43 n.
certain, 68
chagrin, 261
chain stores, 251
chair, 310
chaise, 296
chaise longue, 329
chaise lounge, 304
chalk, 315
challis, 44
chamber, 326 n.
chamois, 38, 44, 326 n.
champagne, 44, 307, 329
champion, 326 n.
chance, 263, 326 n.
chancellor, 324
change, 326 n.
chant, 326 n.
chaos, 320

chaparral, 330
chaperon, 329
chaps, 330
chapter, 326
charabanc, 39
character, 192, 320
charge, 326 n.
chase, 326 n., 343
chasm, 37
chaste, 326 n.
Chatham, 66
chattel, 326
chauffeur, 46, 326 n.
chauvinism, 306
cheapen, 314 n.
cheapjack, 307
check, 326 n., 336
checker board, 336
check up, 311
checkup, 311
cheddar, 307
cheerio, 295 n.
cheese, 69, 210, 296
cheeseburger, 283
chef, 326
chef (d'oeuvre), 44
Chekhov, 13, 37
chemise, 329 n.
chemisette, 329
cheque, 266
cherry, 296
cherub, 335
chess, 336
chesterfield, 306
chest of drawers, 302
chew, 46, 211
cheviot, 307
chevron, 326 n.
chic, 326 n.
chi-chi, 329
chide, 209
chief, 326
chiffon, 326 n.
chiffonier, 329
chignon, 39, 326 n.
child, 66, 164
children, 131, 164, 195
china, 307, 356
Chinee, 297
Chino, 295
chintz, 337
chips, 240 n.
chiropractor, 283
Chisholm, 45
chlorine, 320
chocolate, 330
choice, 326 n.
choir, 48
choo-choo, 276
choose, 210
chop suey, 337
chortle, 298
chorus, 66

chose, 140
chosen, 210
chow, 337
chowder, 330
chow mein, 337
Christ, 165
Christian, 39
Christendom, 165
Christmas, 292
chronicle, 320
chthonian, 38
chukker, 37
church, 39, 315 n., 319
chute, 329
cigar, 330, 339
cigarette, 37, 328
cinch, 330
Cincinnati, 45
cinemactor, 299
Cinerama, 288
cipher, 335
Cirencester, 76
citron, 332
clam, 213, 322
clamor, 39
clapboard, 76, 292
Clapham, 37
class, 263
clear, 355
clear-sounding, 355
cleave, 210, 211
cleft palate, 210
clergy, 325
clericals, 310
clerk, 250, 261, 316
cliché, 329
client, 319
clim, 213
climb, 5, 212, 213
cling, 212
clinic, 353
clock, 47 n., 186
clog, 47
clome, 213
cloom, 213
Cloris, 47
cloth, 191
clothes, 38
cloudburst, 242
cloven hoof, 210
clum, 213
coach, 249, 339
coat, 192
cobalt, 332
cocoa, 46, 330
cockroach, 301, 330
cocktail, 241, 242
C.O.D., 300
coelacanth, 57
coelostat, 57
coelum, 57
cœnobite, 57
coffee, 44, 335, 339

coffeeless, 281
coffin, 358
cog, 47
coldslaw, 303, 304
coleslaw, 334
cologne, 46, 307
collar, 47, 47 n., 263
colleen, 322
college, 44
colonel, 325 n.
colour, 266, 326
comb, 39
combo, 295 n.
come, 119, 140
comedy, 320
comet, 317
comfort station, 359
command, 41
commandant, 329
commandeer, 334
commando, 334
commercial, 310
commit, 319
communiqué, 329
compact, 311 n.
compensate, 319
compère, 249
complete, 192, 319
complex, 318, 352
composite, 319
comprehension, 356
comptroller, 72
compulsive, 352
compulsive drinker, 352
Comstockery, 306
concentrate, 192
concerning, 222
concertize, 285
concerto, 331
condition, 359
confectionery, 264
confinement, 358
confrontation, 354
congratulate, 39
connection, 268
connexion, 268
conoisseur, 329
contact, 28, 245, 246, 310
contend, 340
content, 311 n.
contralto, 331
contredanse, 303
controller, 72
conviction, 319
cookout, 293
cooky, 334
cool, 308
coon, 296
coot, 187
cooter, 338
cop out, 308
copper, 252, 308
copra, 337

copse, 234
copter, 284, 294
cordovan, 330
cordwain, 330
CORE, 300
cork, 330
corn, 347
corollary, 261
corporal, 325
corpse, 358
corral, 330
corridor, 332
corsair, 339, 339 n.
cot, 337
cotton, 335
cough, 189, 303
could, 46, 218
council school, 251
count, 350
countess, 325
country, 324
coupé, 329
coupon, 329
courage, 44 n., 326
court, 192, 324
courthouse, 65
coward, 45
Cowper, 46
coxswain, 291
crabbed, 281
crag, 322
Cranford, 45
crash, 244
crass, 263
crayfish, 302
crazy, 352
creek, 192, 234
creep, 123, 210, 211
crêpe, 329
crescendo, 38, 331
crescent, 351
crestfallen, 308
crick, 192
crime, 324
crisps, 240 n.
criteria, 320 n.
critic, 68
criticize, 283, 349
critique, 68
crocket, 329
cromlech, 322
crope, 211
crosswise, 284
cross swords, 308
crow, 216
crowd, 211
cruise, 334
crystal, 317
Cuba, 45
cuckoo, 276, 309
cue, 46
cummerbund, 336
cupboard, 37, 45

cupola, 332
cured, 45
curry, 337
curtail, 303
curtain, 68
custodian, 360
cut, 41 n., 310
cute, 187, 296
Cutex, 276
cutlass, 303
cutlet, 303
cycle, 320
cyclorama, 288
cyder, 266
cypher, 266
czar, 38, 306
Czardom, 281
Czech, 39

dachshund, 333
Dacron, 276
dactyl, 44
daddy-o, 295 n.
dahlia, 306
daisy, 292
damascene, 308
damask, 308
damson, 308
dance, 41, 111, 233, 263
daredevil, 293
darkle, 297
darkling, 296
data, 319
date, 11, 310
davenport, 306
Daventry, 76
de-, 283, 286
deaf, 70
death, 70
débris, 329
debt, 37, 72
debunk, 286
debureaucratise, 287
débutante, 329, 332 n.
deck, 233, 334
decontaminate, 287
decorum, 319
deem, 139
deer, 131, 169, 196, 348
defense, 267
defrost, 286
dehydrofreezing, 287
dekko, 295 n.
delicatessen, 333
delirium, 319
dell, 234
delusion, 38
de luxe, 329
delve, 212
democracy, 320, 344
demolition engineer, 360
demon, 317

Demon Rum, 348
demoralize, 286
denominate, 319
dénouement, 329
depot, 330
depth, 281
deratizate, 287
derby, 306
derequisition, 287
derestricted, 287
derrick, 306
derring-do, 310
derringer, 306
dervish, 336
descent, 38
deserts, 349
desperado, 330
détour, 329
Devereux, 46
devil, 315 n.
devotional, 310
dew, 46
dewater, 286
dewax, 286
dexterous, 346
dhoti, 37
dialogue, 354
diarrhoeia, 268
dictionary, 264
die, 357
diet, 320
different from, 228
different than, 228, 253
different to, 253
diffidence, 352
dig, 212
dignity, 325
digress, 319
dilapidated, 346
dilemma, 320
dilettante, 332
diminuendo, 331
dimwitted, 294
dine, 39
diner, 71
dinghy, 337
dinner, 39, 71
dinner jacket, 251 n.
diorama, 288
dirge, 319
dis-, 283
disadvantaged, 360
disassemble, 287
discuss, 319
dish, 315
disincentive, 287
disk jockey, 243
Disneyland, 291
dissaver, 287
dissolve, 319
ditch, 280
diva, 332
do, 220

Doberman(n) pinscher,
    333
dock, 191 n.
doctor, 267
does, 44
dog, 6, 47, 191
do-gooder, 281
-dom, 280
domino, 330
donee, 287
Don Juan, 307
do not, 5
Don Quixote, 38
don't, 5, 218, 219
doom, 139
door, 46 n., 47
dope, 334
Doris, 47
Dorothy, 47, 65
double-date, 289
double talk, 243
doubt, 72
douche, 326 n.
dout, 72
dove, 184, 209
Dover, 71
dower, 71
downcast, 293
downhearted, 291 n.
draftee, 287
dragon, 320
drain, 185
drama, 320
drank, 211
draught, 44
drave, 208
drawers, 247
dread, 216
drench, 139
drew, 35
drill, 333
drink, 110, 211
drive, 110, 208, 310
driven (driuen), 63
drive-in theater, 311
drunk, 211
drunken, 212
duck, 6
dud, 37
duet, 331
duffel, 334
dug, 212
duke, 325
dumb, 5
dumbfound, 298
dunce, 306
dungaree, 337
dunk, 334
duo, 331
durbar, 337
Durham, 45, 293
during, 222, 236
durst, 218

Durward, 293
duty, 46, 187
dvandva, 337
dwindle, 310
dye, 48
dynasty, 261

ear, 45
earl, 325, 350
earn, 44
earnings, 310
easel, 334
eat, 43, 140, 214
ebb, 37
ecdysiast, 309
ecstasy, 320
-ed, 281, 294
edelweiss, 333
Edinburgh, 45
edition, 319
educate, 39
education, 319
-ee, 287
eel, 43
Eeyore, 36
effect(ive), 265
efficient, 265
egg, 37
egg beater, 246
egghead, 242, 290
egg-whisk, 246
eh, 44
eisteddfod, 37, 322
either, 37, 80, 260, 281
elbow, 103 n., 310
elder, 174, 310
eldest, 135, 174
electric, 320
electrocute, 242
electrotype, 285
elephant, 37
élite, 329
elixir, 335
Elizabeth, 65
Ellen, 64
elm, 45
elope, 45
else, 197
elude, 43
'em, 324
emanate, 48
embargo, 330
embonpoint, 329
emcee, 249
eminenter, 198
emir, 44
empathy, 354
emperor, 267
-en, 281
enamor, 325
encore, 329

encyclopædia, 57, 268
encyclopedia, 58
English, 43
Englishman, 291
ennui, 47
enough, 189, 281
ensemble, 329
enthusiasm, 320
entrée, 329
envoy, 329
Ephraim, 43
epicure, 306
epithet, 320
epoch, 320
equal, 319
equation, 38
-er, 198, 281
eradicate, 346
erg, 44
err, 39
error, 267
ersatz, 333
-es, 195
escapee, 287
-ese, 283
essence, 319
Essex, 293
-est, 198
establishment, 354
estate, 325
Esther, 65
eth, 37
Ethelbert, 293
ether, 38
etiquette, 296, 329
Europe, 46
evanesce, 38
ever (euer), 62
everybody, 255
everybody else's, 197
everyone, 255
everyone . . . their, 257 n.
evil, 43
evolution, 260, 261
ewe, 46
ewt, 3
exaggerate, 39
exam, 295
example, 41, 263
except, 222
exceptional child, 360
excessively, 363
exchequer, 336
exercise, 109
exert, 109
exhibitionism, 352
exist, 109
extermination engineer,
    360
extra, 295
extraordinary, 264
extrapolate, 354
eye, 10, 48, 308

façade, 38
face, 125
faint, 44
fair play, 308
fakir, 335
falcon, 189, 189 n.
fall, 139, 216, 233
false, 73
falsetto, 331
famous, 45
fan, 242
fancy, 263
fantasy, 320
far, 45, 262
farad, 306
far away, 263
fare, 216
farm, 45, 47
faro, 306
far out, 308
fart, 279 n.
fashion, 38
fate, 69 n.
father, 41, 47, 104, 109 n.,
    192, 262
faugh, 278
Faulkner, 47, 189
fault, 73
favour, 266
fay, 357
fear, 356
feast, 29
febrile, 316
Federalese, 282
feed, 139
feel, 125
feet, 169, 181
feign, 325
feldspar, 332
fell, 39, 139
fellow, 39
fellowship, 281
felon, 39
female, 303
femur, 45
fen, 234
fence, 267, 296, 308
fender, 296
fertilize, 285
-fest, 333
fete, 44, 69
feud, 46
fever, 316
few, 46
fey, 44, 357
fez, 38, 339
fiancée, 329
fictitious, 319
fie, 278
field, 164
fiend, 164
fife, 37
figurative, 261

figure, 261, 326
fillet, 240
fill in, 311
filling station, 242, 249
film, 45
filmdom, 280
finale, 331
finalize, 28, 285
find, 142, 212
finger, 39, 310
firearm, 290
fire-eater, 289
firm, 332
first, 190
first and foremost, 136 n.
first floor, 249
first-rate, 293
fist, 29, 165
fizzle, 38
flair, 329
flamingo, 331
flavour, 266
flay, 216
flee, 211
flew, 210
flick, 276
fling, 212
flow, 216
flood, 161, 184
floor, 46
florid, 47
Florida, 47
flotilla, 330
flu, 295
fog, 47
fold, 216
folio, 319
folk, 46, 119, 190, 196
-folk, 291
Folkestone, 291
food, 139, 161
fool, 325
foolproof, 293
foot, 91, 161, 184
for, 45
for-, 280
forams, 295
(for)bad, 214
forbid, 280
forbid them not to, 221
force, 45
for conscience sake, 198
forecastle, 292
forehead, 75, 185 n., 292
foreign, 45
forerun, 293
forfeit, 44
for God sake, 198
forlorn, 210, 280
form, 45, 49
formals, 310
forsake, 215
forswear, 280

forte, 331
forthcoming, 289
fortitude, 319
fortnight, 234, 244
fortune, 190
found, 142
four, 45, 46, 46 n.
fowl, 110
fox, 63
foyer, 44, 329
fragile, 260, 261
frankfurter, 283, 308, 333
freedom, 280
freeze, 69, 210
French fries, 240 n.
fresco, 332
fret, 215
fridge, 295
friend, 44
frijoles, 331
frolic, 334
frontier, 262
front-page, 289
froth, 38
frozed, 210
fruit, 46, 325
fry, 325
fubar, 300
fuchsia, 38
fuel, 46
fugue, 331
-ful, 281
fulfill, 291
full, 41 n., 186, 362
further, 263
fuselage, 329
fust, 190
fuzz, 29, 38

garbardine, 45
gabfest, 333
gad, 186
gag, 37
gage, 306, 327
gainsay, 293
galatea, 307
galleon, 330
galluses, 251
galore, 322
galumph, 298
gamboge, 308
gamp, 307
Gandhi, 37
gangster, 281
gangsterdom, 280
gaol, 44, 266
garage, 249
garble, 335
Gargantuan, 307
garlic, 292
garters, 251
gas meter, 267 n.

gas(oline), 249
gat, 213
gather, 192
gauge, 44
gauze, 308
gave, 214
gazette, 332
ge-, 281
gear, 323
geese, 169, 195
geezer, 250
Geiger, 48
geisha, 337
geld, 323
gem, 39, 61
generate, 61
genre, 38, 329
genteel, 325
gentile, 325 n.
gentle, 61, 325
gentlemanlike, 280
George, 39
gerrymander, 306
Gestalt, 333
gesture, 56
gesundheit, 333
get, 213, 233, 323
get (something) across, 243
gewgaw, 46
geyser, 43, 324
ghastly, 56
ghazi, 67
Ghent, 56, 67
gherkin, 67
ghetto, 332, 354
ghost, 37, 56, 67, 165
ghoul, 67
giant, 318, 343
giaour, 336
gibe, 56
giddy, 346
gila, 38
gill, 323
gimp, 334
gin, 295, 334
gin and tonic, 344
ginger, 337
gingham, 337
ginseng, 337
giraffe, 335
give, 34, 160, 323
glacier, 329
glad, 356
Gladstone, 356
glamorize, 285
glamour, 45, 266, 310
glance, 263
glass, 79, 191, 233, 263
Gloucester, 47
gnaf-gnaf, 10
gnarl, 190
gnaw, 39, 190, 216

gneiss, 332
go, 46
go back on, 244
go-between, 289
God, 186, 315 n., 344
god, 186, 346
Goddamn, 205 n.
godlike, 280
Goethe, 45
going to have a baby, 358
gold, 161 n.
gondola, 332
gone, 34, 46
goo, 46
goober, 339
good, 46, 184, 191, 343
goose-step, 289
G.O.P., 300
gopher, 330
gorgonzola, 332
gorilla, 338
got, 47 n., 213, 263
Gotham, 65
Gothic, 110 n.
gotten, 233
goulash, 339
Gould, 161 n.
government, 39, 324
governor, 267
goy, 336
grace, 185 n.
Grade A, 3
gradual, 319
graham, 306
grain, 347
grammatical, 282
grandeur, 39
grasp, 355, 356
grass, 41, 185 n., 263
gray, 44
gray day, 3
grease, 185 n.
great, 44, 70, 185
greedy, 280
Greenwich, 292
greyhound, 303
grievous sick, 199
grill, 41 n.
grind, 212
grindstone, 292
grippe, 37, 329
grotto, 332
ground floor, 249 n.,
    291 n.
groveled, 268
groveling, 297
grow, 216
grubstreet, 307
gruesome, 310
guarantee, 327
guess, 37
guile, 48
guilt complex, 352

guinea, 44, 307
guitar, 330
gules, 46
gumbo, 339
gunny, 337
guy, 306
gynaecology, 268

ha, 38
haberdasher, 45
habit, 63
habundance, 63
hacienda, 331
had drank, 211 n.
haemophilia, 268
haemorrhage, 268
ha-ha, 277
Haigh, 37
hairy-chested, 294
hale, 347
half, 41, 42, 189, 262
halfpenny, 44
hall, 350
hallelujah, 39, 335
halve, 42
-ham, 65, 292
hamburger, 308, 333
hamster, 333
hand, 132, 310, 355
handbook, 340
handkerchief, 39
handiwork, 281
handlebar moustache,
    310
hand-to-mouth, 293
hang, 216
hangar, 329
hangnail, 303
hang-up, 308
Hansen's disease, 360
hansom, 306
happy, 262
happy-go-lucky, 293
hara-kiri, 337
harbour, 266
harem, 335
harmonize, 283
harmony, 320
Harry (heroin), 295
hashish, 335
hassoc, 268
hatateria, 287
have, 42, 343
havoc, 268
head, 70, 91, 310
head bookkeeper, 310
health, 281
hear, 119
heart, 47, 91
heart-breaking, 293
heart condition, 359
heath, 185, 234

heave, 216
hector, 307
he don't, 258
heebie-jeebies, 309
heifer, 44
height, 48
heir, 64
held, 164
Helen, 64
helicopter, 284
help, 212, 361
helpmate, 303
hemorrhage, 39, 269
hemorrhoids, 268
hemstitch, 293
henna, 335
Henry, 45
hep, 308
herbage, 63
herculean, 307
herd complex, 352
hermaphrodite, 307
heroin, 295
hers, 172, 199
hew, 46, 216
hiccough, 37, 303
hick, 307
hide, 209
hie, 48
high, 36
highball, 290
highbrow, 242
high-brow, 290
higher-up, 289
highland, 291
high school, 289
highwayman, 291
hillbilly, 307
hinterland, 333
hip, 308
hippie, 280 n., 300
hire purchase, 251
history, 320
hit, 201 n.
hoar, 4
hoarse, 46 n.
hock, 308
HOLC, 300
hold, 110, 216
hole, 4
holiday, 61 n., 165
Holmes, 190
holp, 212
holy, 124
holy day, 61 n.
homburg, 308
home, 79
Home, 46
homemade, 293
Homer, 64
homeward, 281
homoeopathy, 268
homonym, 320

honest, 64
honey, 44, 71
honor, 39, 64
honour, 326
hood, 191, 250
-hood, 281
hoosegow, 331
hop, 334
hopeless, 281
hop-o'-my-thumb, 293
hopped, 37
horde, 339
horrible, 325
horrid, 319
horridly, 363
horror, 267
hors d'oeuvre, 329
horse, 6, 46 n.
host, 190
hot, 262
hotbed, 290
hot tamale, 124
hound, 348
hour, 64
hour or two's time, an, 197
house, 48, 119
housebroken, 298
housekeeper, 298
hove, 216
how, 48
huarache, 39
hue, 46
Hulme, 46
human, 46
humble, 64, 190
humble pie, 303
hund-, 91
hundred, 96 n.
hunger-starve, 348
hurry, 44 n.
hussar, 339
hussy, 292
hysteric, 43

I, 48
iambic, 62
-ible, 192
-ic, 68
icebox, 290
ice cream, 289, 291 n.
icecreamerama, 288
Ida, 11
identify, 354
idiosyncrasy, 320
I doubt not, 221
if, 37
Ifor, 37
i' God's name, 223
ill, 248
illume, 43
illustrate, 192

image, 352
imaginary, 319
imitate, 319
immensely, 363
impasse, 329
impassive, 310
impatient, 311
importunity, 45
impudentest, 198
in (on), 253
incense, 3.
incognito, 332
index, 61, 319
indict, 37, 72
indifferent cold, 199
indoors, 293
infanticipate, 299
inferiority complex, 352
inferno, 332
inflection, 268
influenza, 332
-ing, 281 n.
in good point, 329 n.
in group, 311 n.
inn, 39
ins and outs, 311
insane, 249
insanity, 352
installment buying, 251
instant, 319
insult, 311 n.
intelligentsia, 339
interest, 319
intermission, 249
intern, 354
interval, 250
in the chips, 308
in thing, 311 n.
invalid, 329
Iowa, 44
ire, 45
irresponsible, 310
is, 10
-ise, 268
-ish, 281
isinglass, 301, 334
isle, 48
-ism, 286
Israel, 43
isthmus, 38
it, 43
italic, 308
itch, 39
it'll, 220
its, 202
it's, 219
it's me, 28, 206, 228, 258
I.W.W., 300
-ize, 268, 283, 285

Jack (Iack), 62
jack, 307

jackal, 339
jackass, 307
jack-in-the-box, 307
jack-of-all-trades, 307
jacks, 307
jaeger, 39, 306
jail, 266
jakes, 307
jamb, 62
jamboree, 299
jangle, 62
janitor, 319, 360
japan, 308, 337
jaunty, 325
java, 308
jazz, 338
jazzy, 280 n.
jeans, 308
Jehovah, 335
jeremiad, 306
Jerusalem artichoke, 303
jigger, 339
jinn, 335
(jin)riksha, 337
JOBS, 300
jocose, 319
john, 307
johnny, 307
johnnycake, 307
Johnny-jump-up, 234
johnny-on-the-spot, 307
join, 187
Jolla (La), 39
journal, 44
journalese, 283
jovial, 307
Juan, 39
jubilee, 335
judge, 39, 61, 325
judicial, 61
judo, 337
jug, 251
juggle, 61
juggler, 324
ju-jitsu, 337
juke, 338
junk, 38
junta, 38, 330
jury, 46, 325

kaiser, 48, 57, 306
kamikaze, 337
kangaroo, 338
Kate, 65
Katherine (Kathleen), 35
katzenjammer, 333
keep, 210 n.
Kenny, 60 n.
Kenzie, 60 n.
kerb, 266
Keswick, 291
ketchup, 337

Kew, 46
key, 43, 330
khaki, 37, 336
khan, 339
kibitzer, 333
kick, 323
kiddo, 295 n.
kidney condition, 359
kiln, 39
kilt, 323
kimono, 337
kin, 34, 55
kind, 196
kindergarten, 333
kindle, 323
kine, 130, 195
king, 325
kirsch(wasser), 333
kismet, 339
kit, 37, 65, 334
kitchen, 315
Kitty, 280 n.
Kleenex, 276
kleinite, 332
knackwurst, 333
knave, 190, 349
knead, 190, 215
knee, 190
knew, 216
knickers, 247
knight, 350
knockout, 308
knotty, 47
know, 39, 216
know-how, 244
Kodak, 275
kook, 309
kopek, 339
kosher, 336
kowtow, 337
kraal, 47
Kriss Kringle, 334
kudos, 320
kumquat, 336

lab, 42, 295
laboratory, 262, 354
labour, 266
laconic, 308
lade, 216
laden, 216
lady, 325
ladybird, 198
Lady Bountiful, 307
Lady Chapel, 132, 198
Lady Day, 198
lag, 214 n., 215
lager, 37, 333
laggard, 37
lagoon, 332
laissez-faire, 329
lamb, 5, 131

-land, 291
landau, 333
landscape, 334
language, 326
languish, 39
lap, 42
lapel, 39
Lapp, 37
lapse, 319
largo, 331
lariat, 331
lasagna, 332
laser, 301
lass, 263
lasso, 331
last, 41
later, 174
lather, 192
latrine, 359
latter, 174
laugh, 41, 42, 189, 216
launch, 337
lava, 332
lavaliere, 306
lavatory, 359
law, 46
law[r] enforcement, 36
lawine, 332
lawn, 189, 309
lax, 93
leaden, 281
lead pencil, 291 n.
leaf, 125
leak, 29
leap, 216
learned, 170 n.
least, 165
leave, 125
lecher, 39
lee, 43
leeward, 46
leg, 310, 358
legato, 332
legitimate, 319
Leigh, 43
leisure, 38, 190, 261
leitmotiv, 333
lemon, 335
lend, 189
length, 355
lengthwise, 284
leopard, 44
leprechaun, 322
leprosy, 359
-less, 281
letter, 325
letter box, 248
letter carrier, 247
lettuce, 44
levee, 330
Leveson, 46
lewd, 46, 349
Lewisham, 66 n.

lewisite, 306
liaison, 329
library, 264, 319
libretto, 331
lice, 169, 195
license, 297 n.
lich gate, 279 n.
lick, 29
lie, 211, 215
liederkranz, 333
lief, 43
lien, 45
lieutenant, 37, 46, 261,
   325
lighter-than-air, 293
like, 255
likewise, 284
limb, 358
limerick, 308
limousine, 45, 308, 329
Lincoln, 45
linger, 125
lingerie, 329
liquid, 348
liquor, 220 n., 348
lisle, 308
litchi, 337
literature, 325
litre, 267
little boy that lives down
   the street's dog, the,
   197–98
little boys' (or girls')
   room, 359
live (liue), 62
liverwurst, 333
Lloyd, 39
lobelia, 306
loch, 322
loess, 332
log, 47
log-rolling, 308
lonely, 310
lonesome, 281
long, 355
look, 184, 310
loony, 280 n.
loose-jointed, 289
lord, 293, 325
lordship, 281
lorry, 249
lose, 160, 210, 211
lost, 165, 191
Lothario, 307
loud, 355
loudspeaker, 290
love, 184
loved, 139
loved one, 358
love-in-a-mist, 293
lovelorn, 210
lovingkindness, 310
lowbrow, 242

lox, 93 n.
luau, 338
luck, 334
lucre, 267
luff, 334
luffed, 139
Luftwaffe, 333
luggage, 247
lumberjack, 307
lunched, 139
lung, 91
lunged, 139
luscious, 38
lute, 46, 187, 335
-ly, 199, 288–89
lynch, 305
lyre, 320
lyric, 43

ma'am, 44
macaroni, 332
macaroon, 332 n.
Macaulay, 44
Machiavellian, 307
machination, 37, 67
machine, 38, 69, 320,
    326 n.
macintosh, 306
mackerel, 37
Mackinac, 47
mackinaw, 308
Macleod, 48
mad, 248
madder, 265
madeira, 308, 331
Madelaine, 76 n.
madras, 308
madrigal, 331
maelstrom, 44
maestro, 48, 331
magazine, 335
Magdalen(e), 47, 76
magic, 325
magnesia, 308
mahatma, 336
maharaja, 91
mahlstick, 334
mailbox, 248
mailman, 247
maize, 330
major, 39, 325
malady, 45
malapropism, 307
malaria, 332
male, 325
Mall, 44
mamma, 41
mammoth, 339
mammy, 41
man (men), 56, 119
mandrake, 303
man Friday, 307

mango, 337
mangrove, 337
manhole, 293
manhood, 281
manliness, 280
manly, 279
manoeuvre, 267, 268
mans, 12
manshoot, 289
mantilla, 330
manual, 340
many, 44
maraschino, 332
Marchbanks, 39
Marjoribanks, 39
mark, 308
marksman, 293 n.
Marlborough, 47
marlin, 334
marline, 334
marlinespike, 334
marquess, 325
marriage, 44
marriage of convenience,
    329
marry, 61 n.
marshal, 38, 293
martial, 38
martin, 45
martini, 241
marvel, 325
mascot, 263
maser, 301
mask, 236
masochism, 306
masquerade, 263
mass, 38, 236, 263
massacre, 263
massage, 329
masseur, 44
master, 17, 263, 361
master of ceremonies,
    249
mastiff, 263
matinee, 329
matter, 35, 37, 265
mattress, 335
matzo, 336
maudlin, 76, 306
Maugham, 47
maverick, 306
maximum, 43 n.
may, 255 n.
maybe, 244
mayonnaise, 308
mayor, 325 n.
mazuma, 336
mbakara, 5
M.C., 249, 310
me, 10
mead, 91, 92
meal, 347
meander, 308

meaning, 344 n.
meaningful, 354
mediate, 319
mediator, 319
Medicare, 299
medicine, 260, 261, 319
medieval, 268
mediocre, 267
medium, 319
measure, 61
meat, 7, 110, 185, 348
meerschaum, 332
meet, 139
mêlée, 44, 329
melody, 45
melon, 45
melt, 212
men, 12, 169
Menckeniana, 282
mental, 249
mental illness, 352
mentor, 307
Menzies, 60 n.
ménage, 329
menu, 329
meow, 276
mercerize, 306
mercury, 307, 319
mere, 43
meringue, 44
mesa, 44, 234, 331
mescal, 330, 331
mesmerism, 306
mesmerize, 285
mesquite, 331
metaphor, 320
mete, 69, 71, 215
meter, 43
methinks, 139 n.
metre, 267
mew, 46
mezzo, 38 n.
Miami, 45
mice, 169, 195 n.
midriff, 359
Middlesex, 293
Mildred, 293
military, 263
milkman, 291
mill, 347
milliner, 308
millinery, 263
million, 79
Miln(e), 39
minaret, 335
mind, 236
mine, 69, 119, 199, 236
mine uncle, 199
miniature, 332
minute, 44, 311 n.
mirage, 69
mirror, 43, 267, 325
mis-, 281

misalign, 281
misdeed, 281
miserable, 318
miscellany, 262
mischief, 44
misled, 75
mispronounce, 281
Missouri, 45
mnemonic, 39
mob, 294, 309
moccasin, 340 n.
modern, 319
mohair, 335
Mohawk, 38
Mojave, 38
molasses, 45, 249, 297 n.,
    331
molten, 212
monastery, 264
monk, 71
Montaigne, 44
moo, 46, 276
mood, 184
moon, 91, 343
moor, 234
moose, 340 n.
moot, 46, 139
moral, 47
morale, 329
more, 198
more better, 198
more fast, 198
more near, 198
morgue, 329
morn, 46 n.
morocco, 308
morphine, 307
mortgage, 37
mortician, 283, 358
mosquito, 330
Mossadegh, 13
most, 198
-most, 304
most foul, 198
most poor, 198
most unkindest, 199
most worst, 198
motel, 298
mother, 109 n., 119, 191,
    343
mother-in-law, 293
motorcade, 282 n.
motor car, 247, 295
motto, 332
mourn, 46 n., 212
mouth, 125
mow, 216
Mozart, 38 n.
Mrs. Grundy, 307
muddle, 37
mudguard, 293
muffler, 246 n.
muggy, 324

mulatto, 330
multiple stores, 251
mum, 39
musk, 336
music, 37, 46, 68
musick, 267
muskrat, 304
mustang, 331
mutton, 325
muzhik, 339
my, 48
myrrh, 44
mystery, 320

nadder, 3
nadir, 45
nail, 185
naïve, 329
naked, 37
name, 185
naphtha, 336
napkin, 191
narrow, 45 n.
NASA, 301
nasty, 263
nation, 78, 187, 329 n.
natural, 243
nature, 39, 190, 318
naughty, 47
nausea, 38
Nausicaa, 43
near, 43
Ned, 199
negligee, 329
negro, 330
NEGRO, 300
neighbour, 266
neither, 260
Nelly, 199
nemesis, 307
neo-, 283
nephew, 260, 261
-ness, 280
neurotic, 352
neutral, 46
news, 46, 187
newt, 3
nice, 344, 349 n.
niche, 39
nickel, 332
nicotine, 306
night, 48, 75, 91
night rate, 3
nite, 61
nitrate, 3
Noah, 45
noble, 325
Noll, 199
non-, 283, 287
nonavailability, 287
no-no, 308
nonsick, 287

noodle, 333
nope, 279
Norfolk, 291
Norwich, 293
nostril, 293
not, 165
notorious, 319
nought, 218
NOW, 300
NRA, 300
nuance, 329
nuclear, 46
null, 29
nun, 39
nuncle, 199
nurse, 190
nuss, 190
nylon, 276
nymph, 320

-o, 295 n.
oaken, 281
oar, 46
Oaxaca, 39
obbligato, 331
obdurate, 319
obey, 265
object, 311 n.
obligatory, 263
obligingness, 281
ocean, 38
o'clock, 265
Odditorium, 282
odyssey, 307
oeconomy, 268
Oedipus, 43
Oedipus complex, 352
oesophagus, 268
of all time, 243
off, 37
offense, 267
often, 74
ogre, 267
oh, 46
ohm, 306
oil, 48
O.K., 242, 243 n., 299,
    300
old-fashioned, 291 n.
oligarchy, 320
Omaha, 47
Omar, 64
ombudsman, 324
omicron, 53
omnibus, 294
onanism, 306
once, 68
oncoming, 293
one, 68, 92
one-horse, 289
on the lam, 308
oolong, 337

ooze, 38, 46
OPA, 300
opaque, 319
open, 35
opera, 331
opossum, 340 n.
oppose, 325
or, 46
-or, 282, 283
oral, 47
orange, 335
oratorio, 331
orb, 310, 319
orbit, 319
orchestra seat, 250
orderliness, 281
ore, 46
organize, 268
-orium, 282
Orlon, 276
orphan, 74
Osbourne, 45
ostracize, 286
other, 44, 191
Otto, 47
ouch, 277
ought, 47, 73
ouija, 39
our, 45
ours, 172, 199
out-, 281
outfield, 281
outgoing, 289
outside, 281
outspan, 334
outward, 281
over, 37, 119
overanxious, 293
overdo, 289
overgrown, 289
overhead, 293
overland, 293
owe, 22, 46
oxen, 129, 132, 195
oxford, 308

pacific, 319
pack, 233
package, 248
pad, 308
paediatrician, 268
pagoda, 331
Pago Pago, 39
painting, 310
pal, 337
palace, 44
palaver, 331
Pall Mall, 44
palm, 47 n.
palmetto, 330
palsy, 190
panama, 308

pandemonium, 310
pander, 307
pandit, 44
pan-fry, 293
panic, 307
panorama, 288
pans, 12
pantaloon, 306
panties, 247
pant-leg, 294
pants, 247, 294
pantsuit, 294
panty girdle, 294
pantywaist, 294
papa, 41
paper, 317, 356
papoose, 340 n.
pappy, 41
paprika, 339
papyrus, 356
paradigm, 39
paradise, 336
paradox, 320
parakeet, 338
parcel, 248
pariah, 337
park, 310
parliament, 73
pass, 263
passé, 329
passing fair, 199
passion, 38, 78
passive, 38
pastel, 263
pasteurize, 283, 306
path, 17, 42, 79, 191, 233, 259
pathos, 320
patio, 331
patronize, 285
pause, 320
P.D.Q., 300
pea, 296
peacemaker, 310
peag, 340
pea jacket, 334
Pebeco, 301
pecan, 340 n.
peccadillo, 330
peeler, 306
peer, 43
peewit, 276
pekoe, 337
pen, 356
penchant, 329
penetrate, 319
penthouse, 304
people, 20, 43
pepper, 111
perfect, 311
perfume, 311 n.
pergola, 332
periwig, 294

perk, 295
perm, 295
persons, 20
pert, 41
pervade, 45
pervasive, 38
petrol, 249
pew, 46, 187
phaenomenon, 268
phantom, 37
Pharaoh, 46, 306
pharynx, 320
phase, 38, 125
phenomena, 320 n.
phenomenon, 320
-phile, 283
philosophy, 351
phlegm, 44
-phobe, 283
phone, 295, 296, 320
phooey, 333
phthalein, 38
phthisic, 37
physic, 68
physick, 267
physique, 37, 68
pi, 48
piano, 45, 331
piazza, 332
picayune, 330
piccolo, 332
pick, 37
pickaninny, 331
pickax, 304
pickle, 334
Pickwickian, 307
picnic, 328
picot, 46
pier, 43
pig, 361
pigheaded, 294
pilgrimage, 328
pillar-box, 248 n.
pin, 55
pinchbeck, 306
pinder, 339
ping, 276
pinto, 331
pinup, 293
pip emma, 299
piquet, 37
pish, 278
pit, 36, 334
pitcher, 251
pitiful, 356
pizza, 332
pizzicato, 332
PJs, 299
plaid, 44, 322
plateau, 329
platonic, 306, 307
plaza, 330
pleasure, 187

plimsolls, 251
plow, 36
plumber, 39
plum pudding, 291 n.
plunder, 333
pneumonia, 39
pocketful, 281
poenology, 268
pogrom, 339
poi, 48
poinsettia, 306
poison, 187
police, 41, 43, 328
politician, 349
polka, 339
Pollyanna, 307
poltergeist, 333
pompadour, 306
poncho, 331
pone, 30
pongee, 337
poodle, 333
pooh, 46, 187, 278
pooh-pooh, 278
populous, 319
porcelain, 332
pork, 325
porridge, 293 n.
port, 318
portent, 40
portico, 332
portrait, 44
Portsmouth, 291
possum, 296
postman, 247, 291
postmaster, 290
potato, 330
potato chips, 240 n.
potent, 40
pouch, 239
powder room, 359
prairie, 242, 330
praise, 350
praline, 306, 330
pram, 249
prayer, 44
preach, 325
precious, 38
preëminent, 56
pregnant, 358
premier, 261
première, 329
prep(aratory) school, 251
president, 265
pressure, 187
prestige, 326
presto, 331
pretense, 267
pretzel, 333
priesthood, 281
prima donna, 332
primary, 264
prince, 325

prison, 324
private, 311
privy, 359
pro-, 282
process, 260, 261, 265
prodigiously, 362
produce, 311
professional diplomatist,
    240
programme, 39
progress, 311 n.
propelled, 268
propeller, 268
proposition, 310
protégé, 329
prototype, 285
provost, 46
psalm, 47 n., 189, 317 n.
pshaw, 278
psyche, 307
psychological moment,
    352
psychology, 38, 307 n.,
    352
psychometric, 307 n.
psychopathy, 307 n.
psychosomatic, 307 n.
psychotherapy, 307 n.
ptomaine, 37
publick, 267
public school, 251
pueblo, 331
pugh, 278
pukka, 337
pull, 186
pullman, 306
pulps, 356
pulse, 297 n.
pumpernickel, 333
punctilio, 330
pundit, 337
pup, 37
Purdue, 293
pure, 45, 46
pursue, 45
put, 36, 41 n., 46, 186
put (something) over, 243
putt, 41, 186
pyjamas, 266

quadrant, 319
quake, 216
quality, 3
quartz, 332
quasar, 299
quay, 43
queen, 69, 325
queer, 37
quellen, 69
querulous, 319
question, 39, 325
queue, 37, 46

Quincy (Mass.), 38
quinine, 261
quisle, 297 n.
quit, 244
quixotic, 307
quotha, 215

rabbi, 335
rabble, 37
Rabelaisian, 307
raccoon, 234, 296
raced, 139 n.
radar, 301
radio, 242
raffle, 37
rage, 69
ragout, 46
raid, 71, 310
railway, 247
rain, 110
raise, 250
raj, 39
rajah, 38
rake, 214
Ralegh, 44
Ralph, 37, 44, 66
-rama, 288
ran, 212
ranch, 331
rang, 12
ranking officer, 239
rant, 334
rapport, 329
rare, 240
raspberry, 38 295
raspberry tart, 279 n.
rate, 37
rather, 192, 262
ration, 78, 329
rattan, 337
ravine, 329
ravioli, 332
Rayburn, 45
razed, 139 n.
razz, 295
re-, 287
read, 214
ready, 343
Reagan, 186
real estate, 289
realtor, 283
reap, 215
rear, 39
reason, 193
rebel, 311 n.
receipt, 37
recipe, 44, 319, 331
recivilianize, 287
reckless, 281
recondition, 287
record, 311 n.
redecontaminate, 287

Redeemer, 319
reefer, 295
reek, 211
reel, 251
regard, 325
regatta, 332
regiment, 39
region, 39
register, 318
reign, 44
rein, 44
reindeer, 304
relation, 318
relevant, 354
remedy, 45
remember, 325
Renaissance, 45
rendevous, 46
renege, 43
Reo, 301
repartee, 329
repertoire, 329
replica, 332
reprove, 184
reservoir, 47, 329
restaurant, 39, 329
rest room, 359
resume, 46
resuscitate, 319
retch, 43
Reuters, 48
rev (revved), 103 n.
reveille, 329
revue, 329
Reynolds, 44
rhapsody, 320
rhetoric, 39
rheum, 320
rheumatic, 46
rhythm, 320
rid, 209
ride, 48, 119, 140
riding, 323
right, 42, 362
right away, 362
righteous, 284
Right Honourable, 362
righto, 295 n.
right smart, 362
Right Reverend, 362
right there, 362
right well, 362
Right Worshipful, 362
ring, 211
ringer, 125
ripe, 37
ripple, 35
ris, 209
ris bread, 209
rise, 208, 250
risqué, 329
roach, 301
road, 71

roast, 325
rode, 46, 70, 209
rodeo, 331
roke, 214
roll, 41
roman, 308
romance, 263, 308
Roman numerals, 61
Romany rye, 97 n.
Rome, 161 n.
Romish, 281
rondel, 331 n.
rondeau, 331 n.
rondo, 331
rood, 70
roof, 46, 184
room, 46, 184
rose, 209
rote, 71
rotten, 35
roué, 329
rouge, 38, 61, 329
rough, 12, 37, 310
roughneck, 308
round, 311
roustabout, 308
rout, 42
row, 216
rowed, 12
royal, 325
Royal Automobile Club,
    247
rube, 307
rubber, 356
ruble, 339
rubric, 318
ruby, 37
rucksack, 333
rude, 46, 70
rue, 46, 211
ruf, 12
rug, 324
rule, 41
rum, 348
rumba, 339
ruminate, 45
run, 212, 310, 343
rune, 58, 324

Sabbath, 335
sable, 339
sack, 191 n.
sacrament, 325
sacrifice, 325
sadism, 306, 352
safe, 325
saffron, 335
sag, 191
saga, 324
sagamore, 340
sahib, 337
sake, 337

salamander, 306
salary, 325
sales resistance, 244
saleswise, 284
Sally, 35
salmon, 44
salon, 329
saloon, 329
saltcellar, 304
salve, 189
samba, 339
sample, 263
samovar, 339
samurai, 337
sandhi, 337
sandwich, 305
sang, 144, 174
sängerfest, 333
sanitary engineer, 360
Santa Claus, 334
saque, 37
Sarah, 35
sardonic, 308
sari, 337
sat, 214
Satan, 335
sate, 214
satrap, 336
saturnine, 307
sauerbraten, 333
sauerkraut, 48, 332
sauterne, 308
savage, 326
savant, 329
Saviour, 266
savoir faire, 329
saw, 215
says, 44
scandal, 67
scarlet, 336
scathe, 323
scene, 67
scent, 67
schedule, 66, 72
schism, 38
schizophrenia, 38 n., 352
schlemiel, 333
schmaltz, 333
schnapps, 333
schnitzel, 333
schnozzle, 333
school, 37, 316
schottische, 333
schwa, 37, 333
science, 67
scion, 38, 67
scope, 332
scorch, 323
scorpion, 67
scot, 323
scoured, 45
scow, 334
scowl, 323

scrape, 215, 323
scribe, 319
scripture, 67
scrub, 323
scud, 324
sculpture, 67
scythe, 67
sea, 43
seal, 125
search, 325
seat, 29
Sebco, 301
seclude, 319
second, 325
secret, 325
secretary, 264
sedan, 250
see, 11, 119, 181
seek, 139
seen, 162
seersucker, 336
seethe, 211, 325
seethed, 37
seize, 325
seldom, 132
sell, 139
seltzer, 332
semantic, 342
semester, 333
seminar, 333
senator, 267
senior citizens, 360
senior officer, 240
sentence, 325
sepulchre, 267
seraph, 335
sergeant, 47, 325
sergeant major, 325 n.
series, 319
servant, 361
service, 324
setback, 293
set up, 311
sew, 46, 91, 266
sewer, 3, 46
sexerama, 288
shah, 336
shake, 140, 215
shall, 67, 221, 228
shamefaced, 304
shampoo, 337
shamrock, 322
shanghai, 308
shantung, 308
sharp, 350, 355
sharp dresser, 350
shave, 216
shaveateria, 287
shaven, 216
shawl, 336
shay, 297, 329 n.
Shea, 186
shear, 213

sheep, 169, 196
shekel, 335
shepherd, 45
sherbet, 335
sheriff, 293
sherry, 296, 308, 330
shew, 266
shibboleth, 335
shillelagh, 322
shimmy, 329 n.
shin, 310
shine, 209
-ship, 281
shirt, 323
shish kebab, 339
shivaree, 330
shmo, 333
shnook, 333
shoe, 46
short, 355
shorts, 247
should, 218
shoulder, 310
should of, 220
shove, 211
show business, 243
shrapnel, 306
Shrewsbury, 76
shrimpfurter, 283
shrink, 211
shrunk, 211
shrunken, 212
shtick, 333
shush, 38
shyness, 352
sick, 248, 352, 360
sidestep, 289
sidle, 297
sierra, 331
siesta, 331
sieve, 43
sigh, 189
sign, 39, 318
significant, 354
silk, 337
silly, 31, 349
silly billy, 307
silo, 330
silver, 356
simile, 319
simony, 307
sin, 324
sinecure, 319
sinful, 281
sing, 39, 142, 191, 211
single, 325
sink, 39, 142, 211
Sioux, 46
Sir, 350
sirloin, 304, 343
sis, 38
sister, 119
sit, 29, 214

sit-down strike, 311
sit-in, 289, 293, 311
sitting, 124
six-foot man, 132
six foot tall, 132
sixty-mile drive, 132
skald, 324
skate, 334
ski, 324
skill, 323
skin, 55, 323
skipper, 334
skirt, 323
skoal, 324
skull, 67
skunk, 340 n.
slabbed, 139 n.
slapped, 139 n.
Slav, 37
slay, 215
sleep, 210 n., 311
sleigh, 334
slicks, 356
slide, 208
sling, 212
slip up, 244
slogan, 322
sloop, 334
sloth, 281
slow down, 311
Slumber Jay, 306
smart, 350
smart blow, 350
smart woman, 350
smearcase, 334
smit, 209
smite, 208
smitten, 208
smog, 298
smooth, 355
smörgåsbord, 324
smother, 191
Smyrna, 45
snackateria, 287
snafu, 300
snap, 334
snark, 298
sneakers, 251
snide, 309
snits, 334
snoop, 334
snow, 19, 91
snowcapped, 294
soap opera, 309
sober, 325
social, 318
social diseases, 360
Socony, 276
soda box, 301
sodateria, 287
sodden in drink, 325
sodomy, 308
sofa, 41, 48

soft, 191
soften, 37
soiree, 47
solace, 325
sold, 139
solder, 47
soldier, 39, 325
solemn, 39
solo, 331
solon, 306
sombrero, 330
-some, 281
somebody, 255
someone, 255
sonata, 331
songfest, 333
soprano, 331
sore, 362
sore afraid, 362
sorority, 47
sots, 334
souchong, 337
sought, 139
soul, 46
sound, 3, 29, 189
sound quality, 3
soup, 328
souvenir, 329
soviet, 339
sow, 216
soy(a), 337
space, 355
spaghetti, 332
spake, 213
span, 216
spaniel, 308
sparrow grass, 304
spartan, 308
speak, 213, 214
spear's, 168
specie, 44
speedster, 281
sphinx, 37
spin, 55, 142, 212, 310
spinach, 39
spinney, 234
spinster, 281
spitz, 333
splash, 276
splashdown, 289
splendid, 319
split, 308, 334
Spokane, 44
spoke, 213
spook, 334
spool, 251, 334
spoonerism, 306
sport, 296
spring, 211
sprout, 211
spurn, 212
sputnik, 129, 339
squantum, 340

square, 308
squaw, 340 n.
squire, 296
squirrel, 261
staccato, 331
staff, 17, 41, 79, 191
stagedoor johnny, 307
stairway (staircase), 248
stale, 4
stalls, 250
stampede, 331
stand, 215, 310
standed, 215
stand up to, 244
stang, 12
stanza, 332
star, 91
starve, 212, 348
state, 325, 325 n.
station, 329 n.
stationary, 264
stationery, 264
staves, 164
steak, 70, 185
steal, 4, 213
steeplejack, 307
stentorian, 307
step, 103, 216
Stephen, 37
steppe, 339
-ster, 281
stevedore, 331
stew, 325
stick, 212
stile, 48
stiletto, 332
sting, 55, 212
stink, 211
stinko, 295 n.
stirred, 43 n.
stirrup, 261
stogy, 308
stomach, 37, 359
stone, 30, 79
stone wall, 310
stooge, 243
stop, 47, 47 n., 186, 263
storied, 281
story (storey), 249
Strachan, 47
straight, 308
strap, 186
strict, 319
stride, 208
string, 212
strike, 209
strive, 209
strop, 186
struck, 209
stuck, 209
stud, 43 n.
studio, 332
stupid, 37

stung, 12
stygian, 308
style, 48
subject, 311 n.
subliminal, 352
subpoena, 319
subtle, 37, 72
suck, 211
sue, 46
suède, 308, 329
sugar, 335
sugary(-ish), 281
sukiyaki, 336
summer, 39, 119
sun, 91
super-, 283
superduper, 283
superhighway, 283
superintendent, 319
supernumerary, 283
sure, 38, 187, 199
surgeon, 39
surveillance, 329
suspenders, 251
suspense, 267
Sussex, 293
sustain, 45
svarabhakti, 45, 337
svelte, 329
swallow, 212
swamp, 47, 242
swan, 47
swastika, 336
sweep, 210 n.
sweet, 355
sweetmeat, 348
sweet potato, 234
swell, 212
swim, 211
swing, 212
swollen, 212
sword, 38
symbol, 43
sympathize, 268
syren, 266
syrup, 261, 335
syrupy, 45

tabasco, 308
taboo, 338
tacked, 139 n.
taffeta, 336
taffrail, 302, 334
tagged, 139 n.
tail, 4, 185, 347
Taj (Mahal), 38
take, 37, 215
take a powder, 308
take the rap, 308
tale, 4, 185
talk, 46, 189
tamale, 331

tame, 311
tango, 330
tantalize, 307
Taperama, 288
tarfu, 300
tariff, 335
tarp, 295
tattoo, 338
taught, 189
tawdry, 306
taxi, 44, 44 n., 294
taxicab, 294
TB, 299
tchick, 279
tea, 337
teak, 337
tear, 213
teat, 43
tehee, 277
teenagers, 240
teeth, 169, 195
telegram, 320
telephone, 43 n., 310
tell, 139
telly, 242
tempo, 331
tenderize, 285
tension, 38
-teria, 287
terpsichorean, 307
terrapin, 340 n.
terribly, 362
terrify, 43 n.
territory, 264
tête-à-tête, 329
Teuton, 46
-th, 281
Thames, 65
than, 59 n.
that, 59 n., 173, 203
that book of mine, 172
that goes without saying,
   329
the, 59 n.
theater, 267
theatre, 267
thee, 59 n., 199
their, 44, 45
theirs, 59 n., 172, 199
them, 59 n., 171, 172,
   324
then, 37, 59 n.
thence, 59 n.
Theobald, 77
theory, 320
there, 59 n.
Theresa, 65
thermometer, 267 n.
these, 59 n., 173
theta, 31
thew, 46
the which, 203
they, 59 n., 171, 172

thigh, 29, 125
thin, 38, 59
thine, 59, 119, 199
thing, 119, 191, 357
think, 103, 119, 139
thirsty, 280
this, 59 n., 173
thither, 59 n.
tho, 12, 61
Thomas, 37, 65
thorough, 44 n.
those, 173
thou, 59 n., 199, 201 n.
though, 12, 46, 59 n.
thought, 73
threat, 44
three, 181
three-foot board, 132
threw, 12, 35
thrive, 209
throat, 164
throne, 65, 72, 190
through, 12, 46, 75
throwed, 12
thru, 12, 61
thug, 337
thumb (a ride), 310
Thurston, 293
thus, 59 n.
thy, 29, 59 n., 199
thyme, 59
tiara, 336
Tibbald, 77
ticket, 296
tiger, 336
tilt at, 308
time, 39
time-honored, 293
timothy, 306
tin, 55, 240
tinkle, 276
tiptoe, 310
tired, 45
'tis, 219
titian, 306
titmouse, 304
Titus-wise, 284
to, 46, 343
toboggan, 340 n.
toby, 307
toe, 46, 310
toilet, 359
tokus, 336
told, 139
tomahawk, 340 n.
tom(my), 307
tomato, 261, 330
tomb, 5, 46
tomboy, 307
tomcat, 307
tomfool, 307
tommyrot, 307
tomtit, 307

tone, 30
tongue, 39, 71
tongue-in-cheek, 293
tonic, 344
tony, 337
Tony, 65
too, 46, 362
took, 184
toolie, 295
toot, 37
toothbrush, 291 n.
topic, 43
top secret, 239
tornado, 330
torso, 332
tortilla, 330
tortoise, 44
tory, 322
tote, 339
touch-me-not, 293
toughen, 37
tour, 45
Tourneur, 45
tovarisch, 339
tow, 46
toward, 281
traffick, 267
trailer, 251
trainee, 287
trait, 260, 261
transition, 319
treacle, 249
tread, 213, 214
trek, 37, 334
tremble, 5
trial balloon, 329
tribe, 37
trigger-happy, 293
trilby, 307
trillion, 250
trio, 43, 331
troika, 339
trombone, 331
truck, 249
true, 35
tryst, 260, 261
tubby, 280 n.
tuberose, 304
Tucson, 38
Tuesday, 187
tulip, 339
tummy, 359
tundra, 339
tune, 46
turban, 339
turkey, 308, 357
turn, 310
tush, 278
tut(-tut), 279
tuxedo, 250, 308
TV, 242, 299
'twas, 219
'twill, 220

twish, 278
twopence, 44
two weeks, 244
tycoon, 51, 337
-type, 285
typeset, 293
typewriter, 298
tyrant, 320
tyre, 266
Tyrwhitt, 44

ugh, 44, 278
uh, 44
uh-huh, 279
ukase, 339
ukulele, 338
ulcer, 62
ulster, 308
ultimate, 319
umbrella, 332
umlaut, 333
umpire, 159
un-, 280
uncanny, 310
undiminished vigor, 48
under, 62 (vnder), 119
under-, 281
underbred, 289
underbrush, 234
underdone, 240
underprivileged, 360
understand, 215, 281, 355
undertake, 281
undertaker, 358
undress, 280
Uneeda, 276
unzoned, 62
up-, 281
upkeep, 281
upright, 281
upset, 293, 311
uptight, 293
urban, 319
urge, 44, 319
urinalysis, 298
use, 46
usury (vsury), 62
Utah, 47
utopia, 308

vac, 295
vague, 37
valentine, 306
valet, 260, 261
value, 79
valve, 37
vamoose, 331
van, 336
vandyke, 306
Van Eyck, 48

vanilla, 330
vary, 42
vase, 261
Vaseline, 276
vastly, 363
vat, 159
VD, 299
veal, 125, 160, 325
veldt, 37
vendetta, 332
venereal, 307
venereal diseases, 360
verdure, 190
vermicelli, 332
vermouth, 241 n., 304
very, 35, 42, 62, 63, 361
very nice, 362
Very Reverend, 362 n.
vest, 234
vestige, 326
vestment, 325
veteran, 351
vibrato, 332
vice, 38
victual(s), 37, 72
vignette, 329
village, 326
-ville, 329
vindicate, 319
viola, 331
viola da gamba, 331
violin, 331
violoncello, 331
V.I.P., 243
virile, 346
virtue, 160, 190, 346
visage, 38
viscount, 325
vis-à-vis, 329
vise, 38
visitor, 248
vixen, 63, 159
vizier, 62
vocable, 62
vocal, 63
vodka, 339
voice, 63
volcano, 307, 332
volt, 306
volume, 79
voodoo, 187, 338
voyage, 326
voyageur, 330
vulcanize, 307
vulgar, 63, 349

Wacs, 300
wade, 216
waffle, 334
wage, 327
wagon, 334
waif, 66

wail, 67
wain, 334
waistcoat, 234, 292
walk, 189, 216, 310
Waltham, 65
waltz, 333
war, 46
-ward, 281
warm, 355
warranty, 327
was, 29, 44
wash, 36, 47, 216
washateria, 287
washatorium, 282
washed-up, 293
Washington, 36
was not, 5
wasn't, 5
wast, 217
watch, 44, 47
water, 111
watergap, 234
Watling Street, 314 n.
watt, 306
wau-wau, 10
Waves, 300
wax, 216
way of life, 244
we, 202
weak, 3
weatherwise, 284
weave, 91, 213
webster, 281
week, 3, 164
weep, 210 n., 216
weigh, 44, 189, 215
weird, 43
weirdo, 295 n.
well-known, 293
Welsh rarebit, 304
wen, 68
were, 217
wert, 217
Weltanschauung, 333
Weltansicht, 333
whale, 67
wheel, 92
when, 67
wherefores, 311
which, 39, 68, 203, 204
whilom, 132
whirlybird, 309
whisk(e)y, 295, 322
who, 38, 68, 138, 173, 204, 206, 228
whole, 4, 68
whom, 68, 138, 173, 206, 207, 228
who(so)ever, 208
whom(so)ever, 208
whore, 4, 68
whose, 68
wiener, 308

wienerwurst, 333
wife, 110, 119
wig, 294
wildcatter, 308
wilderness, 165
will, 119, 218, 221, 228
William, 79
will-o'-the-wisp, 293
willy-nilly, 218 n.
win, 164, 212
wind, 91, 164, 212
window, 45, 323
window shade, 249
wine, 164, 313
Winston, 76
winter, 119
wireless, 242
wire services, 240
wisdom, 165
-wise, 284
wiseacre, 334
wishbone, 293
wisteria, 306
witch, 68
WITCH, 300
with-, 281
with child, 358
withhold, 281
without, 293
withstand, 281
Wodehouse, 46
wold, 234
wolf, 46, 93
woman (women), 43,
   130 n., 220 n.
woman I live next door
   to's husband, the, 198
womanish, 281
won, 39

wonder, 71
wonderful, 281
wondrous strange, 199
woodchuck, 234, 304,
   340 n.
woodland, 291
word, 44, 131
wordless, 281
work, 139
workshop, 354
wormwood, 304
worn-out, 293
worries, 6
worry, 35, 44 n.
worship, 281
worsted, 46, 308
would, 218, 220
would not, 5
wouldn't, 5
would of, 220
WPA, 300
wrango, 295
wreak, 215
Wrens, 300
wring, 212
wringer, 39
wristband, 292
writ, 209
write, 39, 58 n., 208
Writers' Workshop, 354
written, 208
wrote, 209
wrought, 139
wung-wung, 10
Wycombe, 291

xylophone, 38, 320

-y, 280
yacht, 334
yam, 338
yawl, 334
ye, 199, 202, y^e, 37, 60
yea, 185
Yeats, 186
yell, 212
yelp, 212
ye olde, 60
yeoman, 46
yep, 279
yet, 39
yield, 212
yippee, 300
Y.M.C.A., 299
yodel, 333
yoga, 336
yoke, 91, 92
yolk, 190
you, 46, 54, 199, 202
you-all, 202
young, 44
your(s), 172, 199
youse, 202
you-uns, 202
you was, 218
y^t, 60

zeal, 125
zenith, 260, 261, 335
zeppelin, 306
zero, 335 n.
zinc, 332
zinnia, 306
zone, 320
zoo, 38, 295, 296
zwieback, 333

Subject Index

A in Greek alphabet, 52
Abbreviations and clipped forms, 294–95
Ablaut (gradation), 140
Ackerman, Carl W., 276 n.
Acronyms, 299–301
Adams, John, 203
Adams, Ramon F., 296 n.
Addison, Joseph, 207
Adjectives
  in Modern English, 198–99
  in Old English, 134–36
  as verbs, 311
Adverbs
  in Modern English, 198–99
  in Old English, 136
ae digraph, 57
  simplification to *e* of, 268
Ælfric, 147
Affixes
  from Latin and Greek, 321
  new or revived, 283–89
Affricate, 31, 34, 39
African languages, 5, 83, 338–39
Afrikaans, 334
Age of Reason, usage in, 227
Agglutinative languages, 81
Ainu, 83–84
Albanian language, 98
Alcuin, 151
Aleut language, 84
Alford, Henry, 219
Alfred the Great, 11, 78, 115–16, 118–19, 150, 153, 197, 340
Algeo, John, 27, 27 n., 150 n.
Allen, Gracie, 198 n.
Allen, Harold B., 271 n.
Allophone, 30
  Old English, 160
Alphabet
  derivation of word, 52
  Roman, 29

Alveolar, 31
Alveolar ridge, 32
Alveolar stop, 34
Ambiguity, in ordinary speech, 3–4
American Dialect Society, 21, 269, 309 n.
American Dictionary of the English Language (Webster), 261
American Democrat, The (Cooper), 361
American English, 41
  attitudes of speakers toward British speech, 237
  British attitudes toward, 237–39
  conservatism of, 232–33
  infiltration into British word stock, 239–47
  intonation patterns in, 259
  national differences in idiom in, 254–57
  national differences in pronunciation in, 260–66
  origins of, 234–37
  precision in, 257–60
  regional types in, 235, 270–71
  vs. Standard British English, 47, 239–47
  study of, 268–73
  syntactical and morphological characteristics of, 252–54
  vocabulary changes in, 234
American English Grammar (Fries), 178 n.
American Heritage Dictionary, 28, 92 n., 354 n.
American history, European culture and, 230
American idiom, in British usage, 243
American Indian languages, 19, 21 n.
  ideographic writing of, 50
  loan-words from, 339–40
American Language, The (Mencken), 239, 269, 309 n.

American Medical Association, 359–60
American pronunciation, 260–66
   see also Pronunciation
American Pronunciation (Kenyon), 47
American speech
   "elegance" lacking in, 231
   pre-Revolutionary, 233
   see also Speech
American Speech, 270
American spelling, vs. British, 266–68
Anaptyxis, 46
Ancrene Riwle, 156
Angles, 114
Anglian dialects, 120
Anglo-Frisian language, 111
Anglo-Saxons, 114–17
Animals, communication of, 8–10
Anomalous verbs, in Old English, 143–44
Antony and Cleopatra (Shakespeare), 205, 351
Aphetic forms, 296, 325 n., 336
Arabic language, 82, 153 n.
Aramaic language, 82
Argot, contribution of, 308–09
Armenian language, 98
Armstrong, Lilias E., 259 n.
Arnold, Matthew, 237, 329
Artin, Edward, 265 n.
-ary, polysyllables in, 263
Ascham, Roger, 202
Ascher, Robert, 1 n., 2 n., 9
"ash" ligature, 57
As You Like It (Shakespeare), 221
Attwater, Donald, 319 n.
Atwood, E. Bagby, 209 n., 210, 212 n., 216 n., 271
Augustine, St., 114, 116
Austen, Jane, 196, 214, 255 n., 256 n.
Avestan language, 96–97
Avon, Lord (Anthony Eden), 237
Ayenbite of Inwit, 156

b
   articulation of, 34
   in Greek alphabet, 52
Back formations, 296–98
Back vowels, 46
Bacon, Francis, 215, 320
Bailey, Beryl Loftman, 236 n.
Bailey, Nathan, 223–24
Baker, George, 73
Balto-Slavic languages, 10, 98–99
Banckes, Richard, 59, 181–83, 215 n.
Barbour, John, 156
Barnes, Clive, 255 n.
Barritt, C. W., 123 n.
Basque language, 84
Battle of Maldon, The, 118
Baugh, Albert C., 112 n., 121 n., 180 n., 282 n.
Be, objective pronoun following, 206

Becket, St. Thomas, 308
Bede, Venerable, 114, 117, 151, 167, 320
Behaviorist psychology, 22
Bell, Josephine, 253
Bengal Asiatic Society, 86
Bengali language, 97
Bentley, Edward Clerihew, 308 n.
Beowulf, 14, 112 n., 115 n., 118, 132, 136 n., 146, 165, 325, 351
Berners, Lord, 202 n., 207
Berrey, Lester V., 309 n.
Bible
   King James, *see* King James Bible
   Revised Version, 207
   Vulgate, 207
Bible Belt, 265
Bidialectalism, 23 n.
Bierce, Ambrose, 346
Birds, communication of, 8–9
Black English, 235–36
Blair, Peter Hunter, 117 n.
Blake, Nicholas, 245, 257 n.
Blends, 298–99
Bloomer, Amelia Jenks, 305 n.
Bloomfield, Leonard, 13 n., 19–22, 24, 42, 276, 291 n., 355
Blount, Thomas, 223
Bodily parts, words for, 91
Bolinger, Dwight L., 22 n., 31 n., 269, 272
Boniface, St., 151
Book of Common Prayer, 201, 217
Boone, Lalia Phipps, 295 n.
Bopp, Franz, 28, 87
Boston speech, 235, 258
Boswell, James, 202, 203 n., 205, 209, 211 n.
Boustrophedon writing, 52
Boycott, Capt. Charles Cunningham, 305
Bradley, Henry, 309, 310 n., 346 n.
Brando, Marlon, 17
Breton language, 101
Brinton, Crane, 245
Britannia, 112–13
British Celtic language, 113, 119
British English
   American English and, 234–39
   American infiltration of, 239–47
   mutual intolerance and, 237–39
   national differences in idiom in, 254–57
   recent, 229–74
   syntactical and morphological differences from American English in, 252–54
   see also Standard British English
British pronunciations, 37, 260–64
British spelling, 266–68
Brogan, Sir Denis, 238
Bronx cheer, 279
Browning, Elizabeth Barrett, 213

Browning, Robert, 44 n., 223
Bruce (Barbour), 156–57
Bullokar, John, 223
Bullokar, William, 192–93
Bulwer-Lytton, Lord, 279
Burgess, Gelett, 309
Burgundy, Duchess of, 18
Burke, William, 305 n.
Burns, Robert, 11 n., 71
Butler, Samuel, 256 n.
Butterfield, Sir Herbert, 242 n.
Byrhtnoth, 118
Byron, Lord, 203 n., 209 n., 215, 297, 337

c
  in Roman alphabet, 53
  sounds symbolized by, 68
Caccia, Sir Harold, 36
Caesar, Julius, 113
Caine, Hall, 279
Calvin, John, 295
Campbell, A., 145 n., 176 n., 282 n., 315 n.
Campbell, George, 203 n., 226 n., 227, 324 n.
Canterbury Tales (Chaucer), 170, 227 n., 327–28
Card, William, 302 n.
Carini, Louis, 1 n.
Carlyle, Thomas, 253 n.
Carnap, Rudolf, 342
Carroll, Lewis (Charles Lutwidge Dodgson), 298
Cassidy, Frederic G., 269, 310
Cassirer, Ernst, 342
Catholic Dictionary, The (Attwater), 319 n.
Cavendish, George, 202 n.
Cawdrey, Robert, 223
Caxton, William, 18, 136 n., 181
Cecil, Lord David, 208
Cedilla, 56
Celtic languages, 100–01
  loan words from, 321–22
Celts, 113
Centum languages, 96
ch
  as digraph, 66
  sounds symbolized by, 326 n.
Chamberlain, Alexander F., 339–40
Chambers, R. W., 154 n.
Changing English Language, The (Foster), 244
Chapin, Miriam, 19 n.
Charles the Simple, 153
Chaucer, Geoffrey, 60, 64, 70, 78, 156–57, 161–62, 170, 173, 176 n., 177, 197, 222, 227, 233 n., 277, 292, 308, 310 n., 320, 323 n., 327, 329 n., 348, 361–62
Chaucer Society, 219

Chekov, Anton, variant spellings of, 13
Chi, 53
Child, Francis James, 269
Childe Harold's Pilgrimage (Byron), 215
Chimpanzees, "speech" of, 8
Chinese language, 80–81
  loan words from, 337
Chippewa language, 19
Chomsky, Noam, 8, 23–26
Churchill, Sir Winston, 208 n., 237, 255 n.
Clark, Alfred Alexander Gordon, 255 n.
Clark, John W., 243 n.
Claudius, Emperor, 113
Clipped forms, 294–96
Cnut (Canute), 118
Cocker, Edward, 223
Cockeram, Henry, 223
Cockney rhyming slang, 279 n.
Cognate words, in Indo-European languages, 91–93
Coinages and adaptations, 275–312
Coleridge, Samuel Taylor, 213, 253 n.
Collective nouns, plural verb with, 252
Collinson, W. E., 110 n., 314 n.
Colloquialisms, 17 n.
Comfort, Alex, 284 n.
Communication, voice in, 4
Comparative forms, 135, 174
Compounds
  hypenation and, 289–90
  as new words, 289–94
Conesford of Chelsea, Lord (Henry George Strauss), 253
Congreve, William, 204
Conrad, Joseph, 215, 255 n.
Consonantal changes in Middle English, 158
Consonants
  classification, 30–36
  in Greek alphabet, 53
  spelling of, 36–43
Convention, language systems as, 9–11
Cook, Capt. James, 338
Cooper, James Fenimore, 340 n., 361
Coptic language, 83
Coriolanus (Shakespeare), 221, 223
Cornwallis, Lord, 233
Course in Modern Linguistics, A (Hockett), 23
Coverdale, Myles, 310
Cox, Ernest H., 302 n.
Craigie, Sir William, 241
Cymbeline (Shakespeare), 207
Cyrillic alphabet, 57
Czech language, 55–56

d
  articulation of, 34
  in Roman alphabet, 53
Daleth, 53

Danes, invasion by, 117–19
Daniel, Glyn E., 255 n.
Danielsson, Bror, 193
Daunt, Marjorie, 123 n.
Davis, A. L., 236 n.
Deep structure, 25–26
Defoe, Daniel, 204, 314 n.
Delta, 53
Demonstrative pronouns
    in Middle English, 172–73
    in Old English, 133–34
Demotike, 99
De Quincey, Thomas, 253 n., 256 n.
Deutsche Grammatik (J. Grimm), 87
Dg digraph, 69
Diacritical markings, 55–56
Dialect Notes, 269–70
Dickens, Charles, 64, 196 n., 211
Dictionaries, early, 223–25
Dictionaries and That Dictionary
    (Sledd & Ebbitt), 21
Dictionarium Britannicum (Bailey), 224
Dictionary (Johnson), 224–25
*Dictionary of American English on
    Historical Principles* (Craigie &
    Hulbert), 241, 271–73
Dictionary of Americanisms (Mathews),
    273, 333 n., 338
Dictionary of American Regional English
    (DARE), 269
Dictionary of Modern English Usage
    (Fowler), 258
Dictionary of Slang and Its Analogues
    (Farmer & Henley), 309 n.
*Dictionary of Slang and Unconventional
    English* (Partridge), 309 n.
Dieresis, 56
Digamma, 53, 54
Digraphs, 56–57, 66–69
Diphthongs, 42
    in Middle English, 152–63, 187
    in Old English, 123
Dobson, E. J., 185–86, 193
Double letters, 70–71
Double negative, 227
Dravidian languages, 83, 337
Dryden, John, 196 n., 213
Duke William of Normandy, *see* William
    the Conqueror
Dunsany, Lord, 256 n.
Duplessis-Praslin, Maréchal, 306
Dutch language, 102, 334
Dykema, Karl W., 218

e
    in Greek alphabet, 52
    in Roman alphabet, 54
ea-spellings, 70, 161
Early English Text Society, 219
East, the, loan words from, 334–38
East Anglia, 115, 119, 322

Eastern United States, speech areas of,
    272
Eastman, George, 275, 276 n.
East Midland dialect, 155
Ebbitt, Wilma R., 21
Eccles, Sir David, 274 n.
Ecclesiastical History (Bede), 167
Echoic words, 2, 9, 276
Eden, Anthony (Lord Avon), 237
Edward the Confessor, 118, 153
Edward III, 11
Efik language, 5
Egbert, 115
Egyptian language, 83
ei-spellings, 70
Eisenhower, Dwight D., 204 n., 246 n.,
    256, 286
Ejaculations, 277–79
Ekwall, Eilert, 193, 214 n., 217 n., 233,
    293, 314 n.
Elizabeth I, 201 n., 202 n.
Elizabeth II, 237, 254 n.
Elphinston, James, 73
Encyclopædia Britannica, 58 n.
English accent, 238
English Dialect Grammar (Wright), 159
English Dictionarie (Cockeram), 223
English Dictionary (Cocker), 223
English Golden Age, 150–51
English language
    American vs. British, 35–37, 239–68
    backgrounds of, 78–112
    conservative spelling system of, 12
    consonants of, 32–39
    defined, 273–74
    as "difficult" language, 11
    Early Modern, 181–228
    essential oneness of, 273–74
    French loan words in, 61, 190, 320,
        324–28
    genitive inflection in, 15
    "good," 18
    grammar of, 7, 19
    London Standard, rise of, 155–58
    modern, *see* Modern English
    new words and adaptations in, 275–
        312
    old, *see* Old English
    "pure," 16
    sounds and spellings of, 5, 29–49
    Standard British, 35–36 (*see also*
        Standard British English)
    transition from Germanic, 111–12
    usage "rules" in, 225
    vowels of, 39–48
    writing of, 12, 58–59
    see also American English; British
        English
English Language in America, The
    (Krapp), 270
English nation, rise of, 114–17
English Pronouncing Dictionary (Jones),
    268, 326 n.

English usage, "rules" of, 225
English word stock, foreign elements (loan-words) in, 313–41
English writing, early, 12, 58–59
Epenthesis, 46
Epiglottis, 32
Epsilon, 54
Erse (Scots Gaelic), 101
-*er* endings, 267
-*ery*, polysyllables in, 263
-*es* endings, 195
Eskimo language, 19, 84
Esophagus, 32
Esperanto, 363
Essex, 115
Eta, 53
Eth (ð), 59–60
Ethelbert of Kent, King, 115–16, 167
Ethelred I, 117
Ethelred II, 118
Etruscan language, 84
Etymology, meaning and, 345–46
Eubanks, Ralph T., 242 n.
Euphemisms, 357–61
Euphues (Lyly), 202 n.
Evans, William, 201

Faraday, Michael, 306
Farmer, John S., 309 n.
Faulkner, William, 189
Feminine pronoun in Middle English, 171
Fielding, Henry, 196 n., 204
Fifteenth century as turning point, 181
Final schwa, loss of, 188
Finno-Ugric languages, 84
First Folio, Shakespeare, 62
First Sound Shift (Grimm's Law), 108–09
Firth, J. R., 27 n.
Fleming, Ian, 239
Folk etymology, 301–05
Forester, C. S., 253 n., 256 n., 257 n.
Forster, E. M., 208
Foster, Brian, 243–44, 264
Fowler, H. W., 215, 253 n., 254, 258
Francis, W. Nelson, 23, 271
Franklin, Benjamin, 246
Franklyn, Julian, 279 n.
Franz, W., 200, 221 n.
French accent marks, 56
French dialects, 99–100
French language
  decline of in England, 179–80
  early glosses in, 223
  Norman Conquest and, 154–55
  Standard, 100
French loan words, 38, 47, 61, 190, 320, 324–28
French nouns, plural and possessive in, 7
Fricative, 31, 34, 37–38

Fries, Charles Carpenter, 15, 22, 178 n., 221
Frisian language, 111
Function words, 15
Furnivall, Frederick J., 157 n., 219, 328 n.
Futhorc, 58 n.

g, articulation of, 34
Gallic (Gaulish) language, 100
Gamma, 53
Geez language, 83
Gelb, I. J., 50 n., 52 n., 53 n.
Gender, grammatical and natural, 126–27
General Dictionary of the English Language (Sheridan), 73
Generalization, vs. specialization, 347–49
Genetic classification of languages, 81
Genitive case, loss in Romance languages, 15
Geology, vernacular of, 332
George III, 233
George VI, 255 n.
Georgia "cracker," 264
Germanic languages, 101–02
  change from Indo-European, 102–11
  compared with Indo-European, 104–07
  Latin loan-words in, 313–15
  transition to English, 111–12
  words lacking known Indo-European cognates, 110
Germanic runes, 58
Germanic sea raiders, 114
German language
  dialects of, 102
  loan-words from, 332–34
Gerry, Elbridge, 306
Gestures, speech and, 4
Gh digraph, 67
Ghetto areas, language of, 23
Ghostwriters, 256
Gibbs, Wolcott, 255 n.
Gielgud, Sir John, 17, 237
Gilbert, W. S., 66 n., 73 n., 74, 278
Gill, Alexander, 193
Gimel, 53
Gimson, A. C., 326 n.
Gleason, H. A., Jr., 23, 27
Glossographia (Blount), 223
Gn- sequence, 190–91
Golden, Hyman E., 309 n.
Goldsmith, Oliver, 196 n., 207, 253 n.
Gothic language, 110–11
  verb endings in, 90
Gove, Philip B., 274 n.
Gowers, Sir Ernest, 208, 245, 254 n., 286, 287 n.
Gradation (*Ablaut*), as Indo-European phenomenon, 140

Graff, Willem L., 84 n.
Grammar
  behaviorist psychology and, 22
  English, 6–7, 19, 22–28
  Latin, 7
  structural, 22
  theories of, 22–27
  transformational-generative, 23–26
  word position as device in, 7
Grammatical change. *See* Verner's Law
Grammatical gender, loss of in Middle
  English, 167–68
Grandgent, Charles Hall, 269
Graves, Robert, 211
Gray, Louis H., 85
Great Vowel Shift, 183–89, 191
Greek alphabet, 51–52
  Roman adoption of, 53–55
Greek language
  affixes from, 321
  classical compared with modern, 14,
    30, 99
  consonant symbols in, 53
  loan-words from, 319–20
  vowel symbols in, 52–53
Green, John Richard, 119, 207
Greene, Graham, 255 n.
Greenough, James Bradstreet, 303 n.,
  347
Grimm, Jacob, 28, 87, 130, 140
Grimm, Wilhelm, 87 n.
Grimm's Law, 87, 105–09
Grisons canton, dialects of, 99
Group-genitive, 197–98
Gu digraph, 56, 69
Guinness, Sir Alec, 237
Gullahs, speech of, 5, 235, 338
Guthrum, King, 117
Gypsy language, 97

h
  after *t*, 65–66
  pronunciation in French loan-words,
    63–64
Halfdan, 117
Hall, Robert A., Jr., 7 n., 273
Halle, Morris, 26
Halliday, M. A. K., 27 n., 232 n.
Halliday, Wilfred, J., 201 n., 273
Hamitic languages, 82
Hamito-Semitic, 82
Hamlet (Shakespeare), 15, 199, 201,
  204, 221
Hancock, John, 233
Hanley, Clifford, 232
Harder, Jayne Crane, 262 n.
Harder, Kelsie B., 285 n.
Harding, Warren G., 246 n.
Hare, Cyril, 254 n.
Harold II, 153
Hart, John, 192–93
Harte, Bret, 297

Harthacnut, 118
Harris, Zellig S., 23
Hastings, battle of, 153
Hastings, Macdonald, 253
Haugen, Einar, 269
Hebrew language, 82–83
  loan-words from, 335
Heflin, Woodford A., 243 n.
Hengest, 115
Henley, William Ernest, 309 n.
Henry IV (Shakespeare), 59, 193, 196,
  223
Henry VI (Shakespeare), 172 n.
Henry VIII, 343
Herball (Banckes), 59, 181, 215 n.
Herbert, Sir Alan, 245 n., 286
High German, 102
  consonant shift in, 111
  loan-words from, 332–34
Hill, Archibald A., 2 n., 23
Hindustani, 97
His-genitive, 196–97
History of Modern Colloquial English
  (Wyld), 192
Hittite language, 88
H.M.S. Pinafore (Gilbert & Sullivan),
  66 n.
Hockett, Charles F., 1 n., 2 n., 9, 23, 26
Hoijer, Harry, 2 n.
Holmes, Oliver Wendell, 320 n.
Homograph, defined, 4 n.
Homophones, 4 n., 193
Homonyms, 4
Homo sapiens, 1
Horsa, 115
Horwill, H. W., 244–45
House of Fame (Chaucer), 156
Housman, Laurence, 255 n.
Houston, Penelope, 241 n.
Hundred Years' War, 179
Hungarian language, 81, 84
Hyphenation and compounding, 289–90

i
  interchange with *y*, 72, 160 n.
  in Roman and Greek alphabets, 54
Ibibio language, 5
Icelandic language, 89
Ideographic writing, 50–51
Ideas, association of as factor in
  semantic change, 356–57
Ido, 363
ie spellings, 70
Illyrian language, 93
Incorporative languages, 81
Indicative forms, in Old English, 144–
  46
Indic dialects, 97
Indo-Chinese language, 83
Indo-European culture, 92–93
Indo-European homeland, 93

Indo-European languages, 10, 21 n., 80–82
  cases in, 15, 127
  cognate words in, 91–92
  early studies of, 85–88
  gender in, 126–27
  inflection in, 88–91
  main divisions of, 93–102
Indo-Germanic, 81 n.
Indo-Iranian languages, 82 n., 96–98
Infixes, 81
Inflections, reduction of in Middle English, 166–67
-ing, pronunciation of, 191
Insular hand, 58
Intensifying words, fate of, 361–63
International Phonetic Alphabet, 38 n.
International Phonetic Association, 39 n., 106 n.
Interrogative pronouns
  in Middle English, 173
  in Old English, 138
Intonation, 2, 17
  contrast in British and American, 259–60
  meaning in, 342
Introduction to Descriptive Linguistics (Gleason), 23
Introduction to Linguistic Structures, An (Hill), 23
Intrusive *r,* 36
Inverse spellings, 191
Ionic alphabet, 53
Iota, 54
Irish Gaelic, 58, 101
  loan-words from, 321–22
-ise and *-ize* endings, 268, 283, 285
Italian, loan-words from, 331–32
Italic languages, 99–100
Ivar the Boneless, 117
Ives, Sumner, 269

j, use of, 61–62
"Jabberwocky" (Carroll), 298
James I, 324
Japanese, loan-words from, 337
Jefferson, Thomas, 242 n.
Jespersen, Otto, 2 n., 18, 21, 28, 38 n., 60 n., 71 n., 74 n., 87, 119, 172 n., 193, 196 n., 197 n., 201 n., 204–05, 206 n., 207–08, 211, 214, 218 n., 219 n., 291 n., 311 n., 322 n.
John, King, 179
Johnson, Lyndon B., 47, 286
Johnson, Mrs. Lyndon B., 284
Johnson, Samuel, 7, 62, 73, 86, 202, 224, 226
Jones, Daniel, 76 n., 268, 326 n.
Jones, Sir William, 86
Jonson, Ben, 207

Julius Caesar (Shakespeare), 161, 207, 211
Jutes, 114–15

k
  articulation of, 34
  dropping of letter after *c,* 267–68
  loss of sound before *n,* 191
Kappa, 54
Katz, Jerrold J., 25 n.
Kaye-Smith, Sheila, 255 n.
Keats, John, 186, 211, 297, 347
Kemal Atatürk (Mustapha Kemal Pasha), 14
Kennedy, Arthur Garfield, 270, 292 n.
Kennedy, John F., 285 n., 286, 299, 353
Kent, 115
Kentish dialect, 155, 162
Kenyon, John S., 47, 194 n., 197, 262, 265, 291 n.
Kimmerle, Marjorie, 271 n.
King James Bible, 62, 201–03, 207, 209 n., 210, 212, 213 n., 217, 345, 348
King Lear (Shakespeare), 199, 348
King, Robert D., 79 n.
Kingsley, Charles, 211
Kipling, Rudyard, 255 n.
Kittredge, George Lyman, 269, 303 n., 347
Klein, Karl, 332
Knott, Thomas A., 197, 291 n.
Knox, Msgr. Ronald A., 219, 252
Koht, Paul, 10 n.
Koine, 99
Kökeritz, Helge, 184–85, 189 n., 191, 193
Kolb, Gwin J., 224
Koppa, 54
Korzybski, Alfred, 342
Krapp, George Philip, 203 n., 270
Kruisinga, E., 21
Kuhn, Sherman M., 123 n.
Kurath, Hans, 23 n., 44 n., 47, 187 n., 249 n., 261, 263 n., 270–71, 273

l
  British doubling of with suffixes, 268
  insertion of, 73
Labial, 31
Labov, William, 23 n.
Lamb, Charles, 214, 250, 255 n.
Lamb, Sydney, 27
Lambda, 54
Langer, Susanne K., 342
Language
  acquisition of, 7–8
  American Indian, 19, 21 n., 339–40
  antiquity of, 2

Language (cont.)
  deep structure of, 25
  defined, 5
  different systems, 6–8
  change in, 78–80
  echoic, 2
  eighteenth-century attitudes toward, 225–28
  ejaculatory, 2
  "good command" of, 342–43
  nationality and, 18
  as "natural," 10
  origin of, 1–2
  scholarly study of, 21–28
  secondary response to, 20
  "soul" and, 18
  structural theory of, 22–23
  surface structure of, 25
  tertiary response to, 20
  transformational-generative theory of, 23–26
  writing and speech, 2–5, 11–14
Language (Bloomfield), 21, 42
Language: An Introduction to the Study of Speech (Sapir), 21
Language families, 80–82
Language systems, as conventions, 9–11
Larynx, 32
Last Puritan, The (Santayana), 16
Latimer, Bishop Hugh, 202 n.
Latin
  affixes from, 321
  classical, 7, 14
  as dead language, 80
  early glosses in, 223
  effect of meanings in, 357
  French and, 100
  genitive in, 15
  in Germanic, 313–15
  influence on spelling of French and English, 63
  as living language in Middle Ages, 320
  loan-words from, 313–19
  in Middle English, 318–19
  in Modern English, 319
  in Old English, 316–18
  "perfection" of, 225
  pronunciation of, 69
  Romance languages as developments of, 99
  Vulgar, 14, 99, 349
  word-endings in, 7
Lawrence, D. H., 258
Learned origins, vogue for words of, 351–55
Lehmann, Winifred P., 329 n.
Lehnert, Martin, 193 n.
Leonard, Sterling A., 226 n.
Levin, Bernard, 208 n.
Lewis, C. Day, 245, 257 n.
Ligatures, 57
Linguistic Atlas of New England (Kurath), 271

Linguistic Atlas of the United States and Canada, 270
Linguistic "corruption," 14–17
Linguistic families, 80
Linguistic Science in the Nineteenth Century (Pedersen), 88
Lipsius, Morris, 309 n.
Liquids, 35, 39
Literary coinages, 309–10
Lithuanian language, 56
Loan-words, 61, 69, 93 n., 105 n., 122
  from African languages, 338–39
  American Indian, 339–40
  Celtic, 321
  Chinese, 337
  French, 190, 324–30
  Dravidian, 337
  Dutch, 334
  from East, 334–38
  Greek, 319–20
  Hebrew, 335
  from High and Low German, 332–34
  Hungarian, 339–40
  Italian, 331–32
  Japanese, 337
  Latin, 313–19
  Persian, 336
  Polynesian, 338
  popular and learned, 315–16
  Russian, 339
  Sanskrit, 336
  Scandinavian, 322–24
  Slavic, 339
  Spanish, 330–31
  Turkish, 339–40
  Yiddish, 333–34
London Journal (Boswell), 202, 205, 209, 211
London standard, 155–56
Lorac, E. C. R., 248 n.
Lothbrok, Ragnar, 117
Lotz, John, 288
Love's Labour's Lost (Shakespeare), 64, 205
Lowell, James Russell, 269
Low German, 102, 111, 334
Lowth, Bishop Robert, 17–18, 203 n., 225–27
Luick, Karl, 21, 193
Lustgarten, Edgar, 255 n.
-*ly* adverbs, 199, 280, 288
Lyly, John, 202 n.
Lynch, Capt. William, 305

Macaulay, Rose, 255 n.
Macbeth (Shakespeare), 205
McDavid, Raven I., Jr., 25 n., 44 n., 68 n., 187 n., 261, 263 n., 270–71
McDavid, Virginia Glenn, 68 n., 302 n.
MacDonald, Philip, 253
Macedonian language, 93
McIntosh, Angus, 232 n., 273

McKnight, George H., 215, 256 n., 303 n.
Macleod, Fiona, 215
Macron, 122 n.
Making of English, The (Bradley), 309
Malay-Polynesian language, 84
Malone, Kemp, 42, 112, 154 n., 270
Mandeville, Bernard, 295
Manly, John Matthews, 269
Marckwardt, Albert H., 170 n., 271 n.
Marjoribanks, Edward, 242 n.
Marlowe, Christopher, 207
Marryat, Capt. Frederick, 16, 359
Martin-Clarke, D. Elizabeth, 150
Mathews, M. M., 24 n., 242 n., 273, 275 n., 331, 333, 338
Matres lectionis, 51
Maugham, Somerset, 208, 255 n.
Maurer, David W., 269–70, 295 n., 309 n.
-*mb* sequence, 5–6, 189
Meaning
    change of, 346–47
    devices for signaling of, 342–43
    etymology and, 345–46
    intonation and, 342
    pejoration and amelioration in, 349–50
    reasons for variations in, 344–45
    social class and, 350–51
    transfer of, 355–56
    words and, 342–63
Melanesian Pidgin English, 7
Mencken, H. L., 229, 239, 242 n., 246–48, 265, 269–70, 273, 276 n., 285 n., 309, 340 n., 360
Mental structure, language and, 24–25
Merchant of Venice, The (Shakespeare), 204, 358
Mercia, 115, 322
Mercian dialect, 155, 161
Meredith, George, 196 n., 255 n.
Merry Wives of Windsor, The (Shakespeare), 222
Metaphor, 355
Methods in Structural Linguistics (Harris), 23
Middle English, 48, 63–64, 68, 70–72, 74, 85, 152–80
    comparative and superlative forms in, 174
    consonantal changes in, 158–60
    demonstrative pronouns in, 172–73
    diphthong changes in, 162–63
    dual number in, 171
    French influence in, 142 n., 154, 324
    Latin words in, 318–19
    loss of grammatical gender in, 167–68
    neuter demonstrative pronouns in, 203
    noun inflection in, 168–69
    participles in, 177
    personal endings in, 175–77
    personal pronouns in, 171–72

reduction of inflections in, 166–67, 222
relative pronouns in, 173–74
schwa loss in, 170
verbs in, 174–75
vowels in, 160–65, 183, 188
word order in, 177–78
Mikado, The (Gilbert & Sullivan), 278
Milton, John, 147, 201, 210 n., 310, 320
Mitford, Nancy, 249 n., 252 n., 253
Modern English, 181–228
    adjectives and adverbs in, 198–99
    consonants in early period, 189–91
    contracted negative forms in, 218–20
    early consonants in, 189–91
    early pronunciation in, 192–94
    to 1800, 195–228
    expanded verb forms in, 220–21
    forms and syntax in, 195–228
    gender in, 137
    group genitive in, 197–98
    his-genitive in, 196–97
    Latin words in, 319–21
    Old English and, 126–33
    personal pronouns in, 199–203
    possessive and plural forms in, 128, 169
    prepositions in, 222–23
    quantitative changes in, 191
    relative and interrogative pronouns in, 203–04
    Roman alphabet and, 29
    schoolmasters' influence on, 204–08
    sounds and spellings in, 29–49, 181–94
    specimen of (1525), 181–83
    stress in early period, 192
    transition to, 85
    uninflected genitive in, 198
    verbs in early period, 208–18
    vowels in early period, 183–89
Modern English Grammar (Jespersen), 207 n., 208
Montgomery, Bruce, 253
Moore, Francis, 239
Moore, George, 215, 256 n.
Moore, Samuel, 170 n.
Moore, Tom, 297 n.
More, Sir Thomas, 202 n., 320
Morphemes, 22
Morris, Charles W., 342
Morris, William, 215
Mu, 54
Mulcaster, Richard, 193
Murray, Lindley, 226 n., 227
Musical terminology from Italian, 331
Mutation (*Umlaut*), 129–30

Nares, Robert, 73
Nasal cavity, 32
Nasals, 35, 39
Nation, language and, 18–19

Negative, double, 227
Negative forms, contracted, 218–20
Nevins, Allan, 237 n., 330 n.
New Deal acronyms, 300
New England speech, 35, 42
New English Bible, 248 n.
New English Dictionary on Historical Principles, A, 21, 28, 75 n.
Newman, John Cardinal, 253 n., 256 n.
New Testament, 110
   see also King James Bible
New Universal Etymological English Dictionary (Scott & Bailey), 224
New words, 275–312
   acronyms as, 299–301
   affixes in, 283–89
   back formations as, 296–98
   blends as, 298–99
   clipped forms as, 294–96
   compounds as, 289–94
   conversions as, 310–11
   folk etymologies as, 301–03
   prefixes and suffixes in, 279–83
   from proper names, 305–08
   root creations as, 275–76
New World of English Words (Phillips), 223
Nixon, Richard M., 286
Noah, sons of, 82
Non-Indo-European languages, 82–85
   loan-words from, 337
Norman Conquest, 58, 61, 151, 153, 179, 318, 324
   background of, 152–54
   French, decline of in England, 179
   linguistic influence of, 154–55
North, Lord, 246
Northern dialect, ME, 155
Northumbria, 115–17
Northumbrian dialect, 161
Nouns, 6
   in early Modern English, 195–98
   in Middle English, 168–69
   in Old English, 128–33
   as verbs, 310–11
Noyes, Gertrude E., 224
Nu, 54
Numbers, cognate in Indo-European languages, 92

o, in Greek alphabet, 53
o and *ou* spellings, 71–72
Objective form of pronoun after be, 205–06
ō-declension, 130
æ ligature, 57
Off-glides, 36, 42, 163
O.K., derivation of, 243 n.
Old English, 48, 63, 68, 72, 78, 85, 111–51
   anomalous verbs in, 143–44

adjectives in, 134–36
adverbs in, 136
consonantal sounds in, 158
demonstrative pronouns in, 133–34
dialects of, 120–21
diphthongs in, 123
gender in, 137
illustrated, 147–50
indicative forms of verbs in, 144–46
interrogative pronouns in, 138, 173
Latin words in, 316–18
Modern English and, 126–28
nonfinite verb forms in, 147
nouns in, 128–33
Old Norse and, 119
personal pronouns in, 137–38
preterit-present verbs in, 143
pronunciation of, 121–26
"reduplicating" verbs in, 143
strong verbs in, 140–43
subjunctive and imperative forms in, 146
vowel symbols in, 122
weak verbs in, 138–40
word order in, 127
Old High German, 112
Old Kinderhook (O.K.), 243 n.
Old Norse, Old English and, 119
Old Saxon, 112
O'Leary, Frank, 309 n.
Olivier, Laurence, 237
Omega, 53
Omicron, 53
Onomatopoeic words, 2, 276
oo spellings, 46, 70
Open syllables, lengthening in, 164
Oral cavity, 32
Orton, Harold, 201 n., 273
-ory, polysyllables in, 263
Oscan dialect, 99
Othello (Shakespeare), 172 n., 199, 215 n., 222
-our spellings, British, 266–67
Outline of English Structure, An (Trager & Smith), 22, 42
Owen, Robert L., 13
Oxford English Dictionary, 21 n., 75, 201, 207, 209 n., 213, 218, 219, 242 n., 244 n., 245, 251, 253, 255 n., 266, 268, 277, 279, 284, 288, 292, 297, 304, 309 n., 319 n., 324, 327, 329 n., 331 n., 332, 335 n., 336, 339, 348, 361

Palatal click, 279
Pali, religious language, 97
Palmer, Harold E., 259 n.
Panini, 97
Paradise Lost (Milton), 15, 201
Paralanguage, 5

Participles, in Middle English, 177
Partridge, Eric, 243 n., 279, 287, 295 n., 305 n., 309 n.
Pedersen, Holger, 50 n., 53 n., 88
Pederson, Lee A., 23 n.
Peel, Sir Robert, 306
Pejoration and amelioration, 349–50
Pepys, Samuel, 197, 213 n., 214 n., 218, 220, 338
Pericles (Shakespeare), 206
Perrin, Noel, 10 n.
Persian language, 98
  loan-words from, 336
Personal pronouns
  in Middle English, 171–72
  in early Modern English, 199–203
  in Old English, 137–38
Ph digraph, 66
Pharynx, 32
Phelps, Gilbert, 254 n.
Phi, 53
Phillips, Edward, 223
Philosophy of Rhetoric (Campbell), 227
Phoenician syllabary, 51
Phoneme, 22, 30–31
  defined, 30
  in Old English, 125
Phonemic transcription, 42
Phonogram, 51
Phrase-structure rules, 24
Phrygian language, 93
Pi, 53–54
Pictish, 101
Pidgin English, 7
Piers Plowman, 156, 222
Pike, Kenneth L., 27 n., 259 n.
Pinafore, H.M.S., see H.M.S. Pinafore
Pirates of Penzance (Gilbert & Sullivan), 74
Place names, new words from, 307–08
Plosives, 34
Plural forms
  in Middle English, 169
  in Modern English, 169
  in Old English, 132
Pogatscher, Alois, 315
Polish diacritical markings, 55
"Polite" singular and plural, 199–201
Polynesian languages, loan-words from, 338
Pope, Alexander, 205 n.
Portmanteau words, 298
Portuguese language, 63 n., 99
  loan-words from, 330
Possessive *s*, 6, 128–29
Potter, Simeon, 140 n.
Potter, Stephen, 256 n.
Pound, Louise, 269–70, 276, 301, 358
Poutsma, H., 21
Prakrits, 97
Prepositions, 15, 222–23
  redundant, 253
Preterit tense, 103 n.

Preterit-present verbs, in Old English, 143
Priebsch, Robert, 110 n., 314 n.
Priestley, Joseph, 226–27
Printers, influence of, 181
Prokosch, E., 143 n.
Pronunciation
  American and British differences in, 260–66
  in Shakespeare's day, 192
  spelling and, 74–77
Proper names, new words from, 305–08
Psi, 53
Puns, 4, 185
Purcell, Henry, 331 n.
Purism, British and American, 257–60
Pyles, Thomas, 27 n.

Q, in Roman alphabet, 54
Qu sequence, 69
Quigly, Isabel, 229 n.
Quirk, Randolph, 121 n., 123 n., 128 n., 139 n., 247 n., 266 n.
Quisling, Vidkun, 297 n.

r
  final or preconsonantal [r], 44–45, 79, 233
  intrusive, 36
  linking, 36
  "Midwestern," 235
  postvocalic, 233
  r-less speech, 43 n., 44, 45
  retroflex, 35, 126
  in television commercials, 265
  as trill in Old English, 126
Random House Dictionary, 298, 299 n.
Rape of Lucrece, The (Shakespeare), 122 n.
Rask, Rasmus, 28, 87
Ray, Cyril, 239–41
Read, Allen Walker, 242 n.
Received Pronunciation, 232
Received Standard English, 191
  see also Standard British English
Redgrave, Sir Michael, 237
Redman, Ben Ray, 255 n.
Redundant prepositions, 253
Reduplicating verbs, in Old English, 143
Reed, David W., 159 n., 271 n.
-re spellings, British, 267
Rees, Dilwyn, 255 n.
"Regal *we*," 202
Regional speech, 47, 269, 270–72
Relative pronouns
  in early Modern English, 203–204
  in Middle English, 173–74
  in Old English, 138
Renaissance respellings, 72–73
Rho, 54

Rhotacism (rhotacization), 108 n., 109, 210
Richard III (Shakespeare), 222
Richards, I. A., 342
Richardson, Sir Ralph, 237, 248
Righter, Carroll, 360
Rimes and riming in early Modern English, 184, 185, 186
Ro, 363
Robertson, Stuart, 310, 346 n.
Robert the Devil, 153
Rockefeller, Nelson, 353
Rolle, Richard, 178 n.
Rollo (Hrólfr), 153
Roman alphabet, 29, 53–55
Romance languages, loss of genitive in, 15
Roman Empire, 113
Romany (Gypsy) language, 97
Romeo and Juliet (Shakespeare), 217
Roosevelt, Franklin Delano, 300
Root creations, 275–76
"Rosemary" specimen, 181–83
Ross, A. S. C., 254 n.
Roughead, William, 256 n.
Rounded vowels, 41
Rounding, 79
Rudiments of English Grammar, The (Priestley), 227
Rules of usage, changed attitude toward, 225–28
Runes, Germanic, 58
Russell, Lord (Bertrand Russell), 238
Russell, I. Willis, 310
Russian language, 10
loan-words from, 339
Ryan, William M., 288 n.

-*s*, in Modern English possessive and plural 127–28
s and *z* spellings, 68–69
Sanskrit, 86, 96
loan-words from, 336
Vedic, 96
Santayana, George, 16–17
Sapir, Edward, 21
Satem languages, 96
Saxons, 113
Scandinavian (North Germanic) languages, 102; loan-words from, 322–24
Sc digraph, 67
Schmidt, A., 207
Schoolcraft, Henry R., 50 n.
Schoolmaster, influence of, 204–08
Schwa [ə], 44
intrusive, 45–46
loss of in Middle English, 170
Scots English, 202
Scots Gaelic language, 101
loan-words from, 322
Scott, Joseph Nicol, 224
Scott, Sir Walter, 211, 213, 310, 337
Scottish dialect studies, 273

Scotus, John Duns, 306
Scythian language, 93
Second language, acquisition of, 8, 12
Semantic change, 346–63
Semitic languages, 82–83, 140 n.
Semitic syllabary, 51–53
Semivowels, 36, 39, 61
Sentence, subject-verb-complement order in, 6
Serjeantson, Mary S., 314 n., 328 n., 339
Shakespeare, William, 4, 17, 62, 64, 72, 172 n., 184–85, 193, 196, 199, 203 n., 204–05, 207, 210–11, 215 n., 216, 221, 223, 297, 307, 345, 348
Shakespeare-Grammatik (W. Franz), 200
Shakespeare-Lexicon (A. Schmidt), 207
Shall and *will* rules, 221–22, 226, 228
Shaw, George Bernard, 36 n., 207
Sh digraph, 67
Sheldon, Edward S., 269 n.
Sheldon, Esther K., 203 n., 205 n.
Shelley, Percy Bysshe, 210 n., 211, 214
Sheridan, Richard Brinsley, 73, 207, 359
Sheridan, Thomas, 73
Short Introduction to English Grammar, A (Lowth), 17, 225, 227
Short Introduction to English Grammar, A (Sledd), 43 n.
Short-*o* words, 47 n.
Shuy, Roger, 23 n.
Sidney, Sir Philip, 196 n.
Sigma, 53, 54, 55
Singing, intonational patterns in, 260
Sir Gawain and the Green Knight, 14–15, 156, 298
Skeat, Walter W., 76
Skinner, B. F., 8 n.
Slang, 308–09
Slashes (virgules), use of, 31
Slavic languages, 98–99
Sledd, James, 21, 23 n., 43 n., 224
s-less genitives, in Middle English, 168
Slessor, Sir John, 255 n.
Smith, Alfred E., 300
Smith, Henry Lee, Jr., 5 n., 22, 42, 48
Smollett, Tobias, 255 n.
Sneer, in speech, 4
Snow, Lord (C. P. Snow), 255 n.
Social class, changed meanings and, 350–51
Sociolinguistics, 23
Sound associations, 357
Sound Pattern of English, The (Chomsky & Halle), 26
Sounds and spelling, 29–49
Sound Shift, First, 105–09
see also Grimm's Law
Southern dialect, ME, 155
Southey, Robert, 253 n.
Southwestern American speech, 47
Spanish language
double-*l* spellings in, 63 n.

loan-words from, 330–31
Standard, 100
Spargo, John Webster, 88 n.
Specialization, vs. generalization, 347–49
Speech
 elegance in, 231
 gestures and, 4
 organs of, 31–32
 transitions in, 2–3
 voice tones in, 4
Spelling
 British vs. American, 266–68
 sounds and, 29–49
Spelling pronunciations, 74–77
Spenser, Edmund, 207, 213, 310
Spirant (fricative), 34
Split infinitive, 257 n., 258
Standard British English, 35–36, 41, 46 n., 47, 78, 233
 American idiom in, 243
 intonation in, 259
 purism in, 257–58
Standard English, 185–86, 201–02
Starnes, DeWitt T., 244
Steele, Sir Richard, 207
Stephen, J. K., 297 n.
Stephens, James, 255 n., 256 n.
Stockwell, R. P., 123 n.
Stop(s), 31, 34
Stoppage, consonants and, 34
Strachey, Lytton, 215
Strauss, Henry George (Lord Conesford of Chelsea), 253
Stress, 2, 48
 in early Modern English, 192
Strevens, Peter D., 232 n.
Strong declension, in Old English adjectives, 134–35
Strong verbs, 140–43, 208–09
Structure of American English, The (Francis), 23
Structure of English, The (Fries), 15, 22
Stubelius, Svante, 284 n.
Sturtevant, E. H., 50 n., 88 n.
Subject-verb complement, 6
Subjunctive mood, 16, 146
Suckling, Sir John, 204
Suffixes, new words and, 279–83
Sullivan, Sir Arthur, 74
Superlative forms, 135, 174
Surface structures, 25–27
Survey of English Dialects (Orton & Halliday), 273
Sussex, 115
Sutton Hoo ship burial, 150 n.
Svarabhakti vowel, 45, 190
Svein Forkbeard, 118
Sweet, Henry, 21, 42, 291 n.
Swift, Jonathan, 186, 190–91, 225–26, 309
Syllabary, Semitic, 51
Syllabic writing, 50–51

Syllables
 lengthening in, 164–65
 unstressed, 48
Symbolization, 22
Syntactic Structures (Chomsky), 23–24, 26–27

t
 medial, voicing of, 265
 sound of, 34
Table Alphabeticall, A (Cawdrey), 223
Taboo words, 91
 euphemisms and, 357–61
Tacitus, Cornelius, 112 n.
Tagmeme, 27 n.
Taming of the Shrew, The (Shakespeare), 200
Tau, 53–54
Television commercials, speech in, 265
Tempest, The (Shakespeare), 207, 223
Tennyson, Alfred, Lord, 213
-teria suffix, 288
Teutonic languages, 101 n.
 see also Germanic languages
Texas speech, 236
Thackeray, William Makepeace, 207, 209 n., 253 n., 337, 362
Theta, 30, 55, 59
Thieme, Paul, 86 n.
Thomas, C. K., 47 n.
Thorn (þ), 57, 59–60, 90, 158
th sounds and forms, 59, 65, 158, 202–03
Thurber, James, 255 n.
Time, 8, 299
Timon of Athens (Shakespeare), 205, 216
Tindale Bible, 207 n., 310
t-like sounds, 30
Tocharian language, 88, 96
Tongue position, vowels and, 40
Trachea, 32
Trade names, 276
Trager, George L., 2 n., 5 n., 42, 48
Transformational-generative theory, 24, 26, 48, 79
Transitions, speech and, 3
Transliteration, variations in, 13–14
Troike, Rudolph C., 271 n.
Troilus and Cressida (Shakespeare), 201
Troilus and Criseyde (Chaucer), 14, 227 n., 310 n., 348
Trollope, Anthony, 196 n., 211
-tr- sounds, 35
Tryggvason, Olaf, 118
Tucker, Susie I., 363 n.
Turkish language, 14, 81, 85, 98
Turner, Lorenzo Dow, 235 n., 339
Twaddell, W. F., 108 n.
Twelfth Night (Shakespeare), 205

Two Gentlemen of Verona (Shakespeare), 223

u
spellings, 71
use of, 62
Umbrian language, 99
Umlaut (mutation), 129–30
Underwood, Michael, 253
Uninflected genitive, 198
United States, speech areas of, 272
see also American English
Universal Dictionary (Wyld), 268
Universal Etymological English Dictionary (Bailey), 223–24
Unstressed syllables, 48
Unstressed vowels, 165
Upsilon, 53, 55
Ural-Altaic language, 84
-ure endings, 190
Urdu language, 97
Usage, 17–18
"rules" of, 225
Uto-Aztecan languages, 84
uu or *w*, 59

v, use of, 62
Van Buren, Martin, 243
Van den Bark, Melvin, 309 n.
Vater, consonant sound in, 63 n.
Velar, 31
Velar fricative, 106 n.
Velar stops, 34
Venus and Adonis (Shakespeare), 217
Verb-adverb combinations, 311–12
Verbs
Class I strong verbs, 140–41, 174–75, 208
Class II strong verbs, 141, 175, 208
Class III strong verbs, 141–42, 175, 212
Class IV strong verbs, 142, 175, 213
Class V strong verbs, 142, 175, 213
Class VI strong verbs, 142, 175, 213, 215
Class VII strong verbs, 143, 175, 216
expanded forms of, 220
in Middle English, 174–75
in Modern English, 208–18
as nouns, 310–11
weak, 103, 138–40, 174–75, 208–18 *passim*
Vernacular, 308–09
Verner, Karl, 108–09
Verner's Law, 108–11, 141, 210
Victoria, Queen, 202
Victorian speech, 358–59
Viking conquests, 117–19
Virgules, 31
Vocal cords, 32
Vogel, Victor H., 295 n.

Voiced fricatives as phonemes in Middle English, 160
Voice tones, in speech, 4–5
Volapük, 363
Volta, Alessandro, 306
Vowels
chart of, 40
back, 41, 46–48
central, 41, 44–46
front, 41, 43–44
lengthening and shortening of, in Middle English, 163–65
in Middle English, 160–62
rounded, 41
shift of in Modern English, 183–89
spelling, 43–48
symbols for, 29, 40, 43–48, 69–70
see also Diphthongs
"Vulgar" words, 354 n.

Walker, John, 73, 261 n.
Wallis, John, 221, 226
Ward, Mrs. Humphry, 207
Ward, Ida C., 259 n.
Wardale, E. E., 163
Washington, George, 233
Waterman, John T., 88 n.
Watkins, Calvert, 92 n.
waw, Semitic, 53, 54
Weak adjective declension, 104, 134
Webster, Noah, 19 n., 82 n., 190, 203, 229 n., 261, 266–68, 286
Webster's New Collegiate Dictionary (1949), 290
Webster's Seventh New Collegiate Dictionary (1963), 290
Webster's Third New International Dictionary, 20, 278 n., 283, 286, 290 n., 299, 305
Wells, H. G., 74 n., 196 n.
Welsh language, 101
Wentworth, Harold, 309 n.
Wessex, 115
West Midland dialect, 155
West Saxon dialect, 120–21
specimen of, 147–50
Whatmough, Joshua, 2 n.
White, Richard Grant, 215
Whitehorn, Katharine, 258–59
Whom, as subject, 207–08
Wh- words, 39 n., 67–68
Wild, J. Henry, 287 n.
William the Conqueror, 112, 152–53
Williamson, Juanita Virginia, 23 n.
Wilson, H. Rex, 271 n.
Wilson, R. A., 36 n.
Winchell, Walter, 299
Winter's Tale, The (Shakespeare), 199
Woden, 119
Word choice, British and American differences in, 247–52

Word order
  grammatical function of, 7, 15
  in Middle English, 177–78
  in Old English, 127
Words
  "fixed" meanings, 346
  meanings and, 342–63
  pejoration and amelioration in, 349–50
  reason for studying, 343
Words and Their Ways in English Speech
  (Greenough & Kittredge), 347
Wordsworth, William, 213
Wrenn, C. L., 121 n., 128 n., 139 n.,
  266 n.
Wright, Joseph, 158 n., 159, 170 n.
Wright, Mary Elizabeth, 158 n., 170 n.
Writing
  conventions and choice in, 5
  history of, 50–77
  ideographic and syllabic, 50–51
  vs. language, 11–14
  pronunciation and, 74–77
Wulfila (Ulfilas), 110, 130

Wyld, H. C., 21, 38 n., 185, 186 n., 191–
  92, 197, 202 n., 204, 214 n., 217,
  266, 268
Wynn (Þ), 57, 59

y
  in Old and Middle English, 72
  Old English value of, 39 n., 72, 122–
    23
  for *thorn*, 60
Yiddish, 83 n., 102 n.
  loan-words from, 333
Yogh (ʒ) symbol, 60–61
Yorkshire, Scandinavians in, 323 n.

z and *s* spellings, 68–69
Zachrisson, R. E., 193
Zend language, 97
Zeta, 55

39137